KNIGHTS
AT
COURT

Published with the cooperation of the
CENTER FOR MEDIEVAL AND RENAISSANCE STUDIES
University of California, Los Angeles

KNIGHTS
AT
COURT

Courtliness, Chivalry, & Courtesy

From Ottonian Germany To

The Italian Renaissance

ALDO SCAGLIONE

UNIVERSITY OF CALIFORNIA PRESS
Berkeley • Los Angeles • Oxford

University of California Press
Berkeley and Los Angeles, California

University of California Press
Oxford, England

Copyright © 1991 by The Regents of the University of California

Library of Congress Cataloging-in-Publication Data

Scaglione, Aldo D.
  Knights at court : courtliness, chivalry, and courtesy from
Ottonian Germany to the Italian Renaissance / Aldo Scaglione.
      p.   cm.
  Includes bibliographical references and index.
  ISBN 0-520-07270-7 (cloth)
    1. Courts and courtiers.   2. Civilization, Medieval.   3. Courts
and courtiers in literature.   4. Chivalry.   5. Knights and
knighthood.   6. Literature, Medieval—History and criticism.
7. Humanism.   I. Title.
GT3520.S34 1991
940.1—dc20   91-6703
                                                              CIP

Printed in the United States of America

1 2 3 4 5 6 7 8 9

Contents

Illustrations

Preface and Acknowledgments

The following can neither be an exhaustive treatment of what is a forbidding amount of material, nor a comprehensive survey, which would only result in surface generalizations. The method of presentation will be one of sampling a number of relevant cases, although a degree of "connective tissue" in the form of secondary episodes, texts, and authors will be supplied, especially for the Italian part, both as background to the major texts and as documentation of the evolution of ideas and attitudes. Since the literature I shall examine belongs mostly to Germany, France, and Italy, the sociohistorical material will also be limited to these areas. The documents I shall sample range mostly between the establishment of Otto I's court around 950 and the publication of the *Astrée* (1607–1628).

For encouragement as well as advice on form and content I am grateful to several colleagues and friends, among whom I must single out Allen Mandelbaum, Teodolinda Barolini, and Ronald G. Witt, in addition to the expert readers and editors of the University of California Press. Whatever stylistic felicity may be found here is likely to be due to the editorial virtues of Marie M. Burns, an elegant writer and scrupulous reader.

Introduction

"Thou wert the kindest man that ever struck with sword." [1]
"Manners makyth the man." [2]

On the wall of a dark cell in the Martelet dungeon of Loches where the once powerful duke of Milan, Ludovico il Moro, was a prisoner until his death, the visitor can still see a sensitive graffito, presumably a self-portrait in the garb of a condottiero. [3] We may wonder why this victim of his own ruses would have chosen to see himself as a knight in shining armor at the head of a professional army. In his ambitious career of diplomatic guile there had been no direct exercise of knightly or military arts beyond the memory of his father Francesco Sforza—the only condottiero to rise from humble origins to a dukedom. The self-image that Ludovico was contemplating was only wishful thinking—in line with the well-known equestrian statue Leonardo had projected for him. In the privacy of his cell, in the authenticity of a dialogue with himself alone, he was probably indulging in an "ideological" act, a homage to a governing ideology of which he had been protagonist, witness, and victim all in one. Much better known is Titian's equestrian portrait (1548) of the Emperor Charles V at the battle of Mühlberg (1547). Although throughout his eventful career Charles V was indeed inspired by knightly ideals (even to the extent of challenging Francis I of France to personal combat in 1536), he was hardly in a position to go to battle with the lance he symbolically carries in the portrait. Yet he, too, wanted to see himself as a fighting knight.

In the course of my survey we shall observe other characters typically looking at themselves, at their self-fashioned mental portraits, and eagerly, willfully seeking identities. Literary knights and courtiers from

1

Chrétien's *Yvain* to Castiglione's *Courtier* will ask themselves: "Who am I?"[4] The answer could only come from the surfacing to the level of individual consciousness of a socially bound criterion, since it derived from belonging to a group. Medieval and Renaissance man and woman could acquire an identity either by statute (as by the feudal, chivalric notion of nobility through blood and inheritance) or by education (as in the sociocultural making of the Renaissance courtier), but actions were always to be judged on the basis of membership in a specific social group. Michel Foucault has postulated that the modern alliance between criminal law and psychiatry has shifted from a criterion of sanctioning only deeds, as in Cesare Beccaria, to a need to associate action to individual character. The modern justice system is baffled by a criminal who admits everything but offers no reason, motive, or cause. In a way, the situations we shall observe are the obverse of this predicament: virtues and crimes were, officially, neither objective facts nor consequences of psychological motives, but projections of the doer's social position. It was *not* a crime for a knight to kill a commoner, nor to kill another knight in a fair encounter. It *was* a crime for a commoner to hurt a knight for whatever reason, or for a king to injure a knight by denying him his statutory rights.[5]

Admittedly, we have come a long way from the New Critics' view of literary "well-wrought urns" as self-contained artifacts speaking for themselves through their structure and texture, synchronically and without necessary ties to a historic ambiance. Even Austin Warren and René Wellek's focus (in 1948) on "intrinsic" versus "extrinsic" approaches as the most appropriate way of understanding literary products may now sound rather remote.[6] On the premise that works of art are only very special results of social and cultural conditions, the search for "literariness" no longer seems to preclude "total historicization." All existential experience is seen as the stuff of which literary works are textured. More important than the literary work's discrete "content" is the semiotic realization that, like any other message, it also obeys the principle that "a message signifies only insofar as it is interpreted from the point of view of a given situation, a psychological as well as a historical, social and anthropological one."[7] The well-wrought urn is no longer isolated either from the "producer" or from the "consumer." Conversely, we have been witnessing the intensive application of "literary" criteria to cultural works of all types, including the Bible.[8]

Inadequate as New Criticism may appear to us in this respect, it is nevertheless far from dead: some critics have analyzed American decon-

structionism as an extreme phase of it.[9] In the sense of a radical subjec-
tivization of texts and readers as essentially deprived of hard objective
rapport with an outside reality, the deconstructionist's point is that the
text's referential quality is inherently ambiguous and inward-looking.
The following study assumes, instead, that the text has a meaningful
mode of existence by outward referentiality both at the point of origin
(in the author's intention to express and represent) and at the point of
communication (in the reader's response by recognition of interpreted
reality).

Literary historians have long agreed that social questions are central
to the Arthurian texts, since these texts ostensibly frame individual des-
tinies within social bonds and duties.[10] Dealing with Occitan literature,
even the results of formal criticism (by, say, Robert Guiette, Roger Dragonetti, and Paul Zumthor) have turned out to accord with the analysis
of social and moral thematic content as practiced by a Pierre Bec or an
Erich Köhler.[11] To relate literature to society is productive for both literary history and social history because, just as social structures condition literature, so literature can condition social behavior. This is particularly true of chivalry and courtliness. In response to the deacon of
Toledo's claim that knights errant were but figments of the imagination,
Don Quixote reeled off a list of fully documentable historic characters
fitting the description (*Don Quixote* part 1, chap. 47). Early romances
had conspired with historical institutions to create patterns of conduct
that affected many a daily life well into the seventeenth century and
beyond.[12]

The daily life and rituals of dominant social groups constitute the
backdrop of my inquiry into literature's significant role.[13] The method
of critical literary history I shall exemplify and test sees this discipline
as "a body of signifieds to which literary signifiers must be attached, or
re-attached by the scholar after time has eroded the connections,"[14] for,
contrary to the "isolating" view (like that of New Critics and later seekers of a pure "literariness" inherently transcending history), literature
"also creates the culture by which it is created, shapes the fantasies by
which it is shaped, begets that by which it is begotten,"[15] in a constant
symbiosis that requires both terms, the cultural and the poetic, the ideological or even the material and the imaginary, for true understanding.
Literature is not merely an epiphenomenon arising out of social reality:
it is part of the cultural forces that both reflect and motivate real behavior. This type of hermeneutics is shared by the New Historicists, who
for some years have been reexamining our image of the past in terms of

correspondences between material situations ("motives") and seemingly free constructs of the artistic imagination. Cultural forms are seen to mirror social structures, although they do so through interpretation and imaginative reaction.[16] My threefold theme is an exemplary ground for sociological analysis because it ideally shows the bidirectional movement from reality to imagination and vice versa, each pole being necessary and functional for a fuller understanding of the other. The sociological perspective will therefore see society both as the point of genesis of the work of art and as its point of destination. Literary history thus becomes at the same time history of authors and history of readers, history of the input and impact of social groups and situations on the production of literary works, and history of their collective reception in society. As Köhler states, this approach to literature should be called sociological literary history or sociohistorical literary criticism.[17] Sociology of literature as such is, instead, mostly concerned with the impact of literature on society—which will be only subsidiary and occasional here, and is not centrally an aesthetic question. Rather than the history of social realities, my aim shall be the history of the cultural models that affected behavior and conditioned literary production, and which hold for us a key to a fuller understanding of literature in its historical context.

Sociological criticism relates imaginative ideals to material interests. The demystification effected by the discovery of material interests does not rewrite but rather enhances the enduring work of idealization that poetic imagination performed on those motives, thus creating noble causes by which to live, dream, and even die. This is the peculiarity of the human condition: no matter how lowly the material motives that the historian is able to discover and analyze, every society is invested by its culture with something that heartens and inspires. Conscious motives overlie material interests through a rhetoric that verbalizes powerful ideals—an efficient rhetoric of "impure persuasion," to use Kenneth Burke's felicitous phrase. But there are two sides to the dialectical coin of artistic representation, for poets and literati are the conscience of their society. Even while they join and serve the ruling power game by expressing it as a noble ideology, they also look at it critically and show its inner tensions and contradictions. Tristan, Lancelot, and Siegfried are superior to the system of their social group even while they mirror it and serve it. At the same time they are proud and humble, at the same time they serve and rule, operating as both victims and conquerors. Thus do their poets see them and present them to us.

Much literary sociology has been under the flag of a more or less explicit Marxism, but the serious problem of this orientation—so serious as to appear disqualifying—has been the tendency to reduce literary production to the instances of "commissioning" (by actual or potential patrons and "masters") and "consumption" (by the intended or actual users/readers). These two instances have a recognizably determining role only in the cases of commercialized, aesthetically inadequate production. Within this frame of reference such a masterwork as the *Divine Comedy* would remain an unexplainable outsider, since it had neither a commissioner nor a specific audience. Although Marxist critics have been aware of this contradiction, their mental conditioning has continued to lead them to this same impasse since, if the structure is paramount, the superstructure must be not only dependent, hence secondary, but ultimately irrelevant or at least dispensable.

An offshoot of this orientation is the school of Frankfurt, whose main exponents, Walter Benjamin, Theodor Adorno, and Max Horckheimer, have developed a view of avant-garde art and literature that can encompass much of the chivalric dream by insisting on art as negation of the world and affirmation of a utopia, a statement of faith in the individual in the face of the infamy of the existent. In particular, Benjamin's view of art as the "unceasing expectation of a miracle" clearly fits the dream of knight-errantry, with Perceval as its ultimate religious-metaphysical stage. The distance of poetry from mere existence is seen as a salutary indictment of what is evil and rotten in the latter. Asocial art (as the lyric is) thus becomes a saving social act, while all art is essentially wishful thinking. Given the apparent shortcomings of this school, with its projection of the present (and its perceived problems of modern alienation) into the past, this sophisticated type of sociological criticism is perhaps destined to remain a self-contained exercise.[18]

We may recall Erich Auerbach's seminal judgments concerning the abstract and "absolute" quality of the Arthurian world as represented in the romances.[19] Yet it can be shown that Arthurian courtesy (*courtoisie*) lived in a dynamic symbiosis with a conscious social and moral commitment which contrasted with that world from within, and ultimately dissolved it. All this occurred while courtesy, an ethos that pursued its own social and literary development, conspired with "chivalry" and "courtliness" to form a triad of value systems that operated both inside and outside the world of chivalry. All the sundry possibilities came to fruition. The chivalry of the Perceval story entailed a metaphysical, mystical, and theological level of *courtois* refinement in an effort to attain a supreme level of personal perfection. The courtliness of a Tristan, instead, involved personal survival in the real world of hostile social forces. Yvain, in turn, worked both inside and outside the Arthurian court to achieve a purposefulness that would satisfy the image of the whole man.

An impressive body of medieval literature is deeply pervaded by a sense of courtliness, chivalry, and courtesy. Much ink has been spilled on the presumed essence or unity of these ideals and, especially among German scholars, on the ethic of chivalry (*ritterliches Tugendsystem*). But, rather than a unitary ethical system, an ideal nomenclature, a philosophy, or an educational pattern, the common ground of all this literature is an underlying social reality which linked heterogeneous groups through a somewhat vague yet powerful ideology. The ideology existed in the form of a common mentality even without a unitary verbal expression for it—a realization which should help us to dispose of such lingering polemics as, for instance, whether courtly love was only Gaston Paris's invention.

Beyond the literary forms that in shifting ways partook of the common themes, there were three types of "chivalry." There was, first, a Christian knighthood, centered in northern France and reaching its consciousness in 1050–1100. This was followed by a courtly knighthood and, finally, a culture of courtly love. The latter two matured in southern France between 1100 and 1150, then quickly extended to northern France and beyond by 1150–1180. The three phenomena are distinct and partly antagonistic. Nonetheless, they converged and thrived side by side, leaving their imprints on ways of life and ways of thinking, feeling, speaking, writing, and reading for several centuries.

The identification of these three currents is similar to Carl Erdmann's 1935 thesis (*Die Entstehung des Kreuzzugsgedankens*, The Rise of the Crusade Idea), apparently endorsed by E. R. Curtius (*European Literature* 536), which explains Christian knighthood as arising out of the contrast between pagan Germanic warlike attitudes and the Church's sense of Christian meekness. French epics expressed this evolving knightly ethos in the two distinct forms of Christian transcendence and struggling baronial fealty, while Germanic epics incorporated the growing elements of courtesy over the substratum of a pagan military ethos. The courts of Provence and then Champagne and Flanders harbored a different knightly spirit that fed on the assimilation of service to the lord and service to the lady, thus combining chivalry and love. Similar mental states developed in other regions even before direct French influence.

Curtius (537) reminds us that Islam evolved both a knightly ideal and a theory of courtly love which showed "striking coincidences" with the West, Spain being a possible intermediary between the two continental cultures.

Taking his cue from the German sociologist Norbert Elias, the Germanist C. Stephen Jaeger has recently tendered a set of political, philosophical, and didactic documents that compel reconsideration of the development of "courtliness" and "courtesy," including the two historical poles of Cicero's *De officiis* and Castiglione's *Cortegiano*.[20] Drawing upon some elements of Jaeger's thesis, the research of Elias, the Romanist Erich Köhler, the social historian Georges Duby, the historians Maurice Keen and Lauro Martines, and others, I propose to explore the continuous vitality of curial and courtly traditions through the Middle Ages and the Renaissance, and the way these traditions affected the development of three separate yet coexistent codes: (1) the courtly, (2) the chivalric/heroic, and (3) the chivalric/*courtois*. The third code combined the other two, adding to them the element of love, represented by a courtly-mannered knight who was motivated by both heroism and love in a state of harmonious symbiosis. The three codes belong to both social and literary spheres, and they often conspired in a tense, unstable mixture within various literary genres. Without ever coinciding with any of them, the codes govern the genres of (1) epic tales, (2) lyric poetry together with the romance, and (3) treatises on conduct and manners or etiquette. The cultural and literary contents of curiality or courtliness, chivalry or knighthood, and courtesy intersect with literary genres and constantly overlap them. To use H.-R. Jauss's schema, we are dealing with "dominants" which surfaced as constants in different literary forms, both shaping and threatening them from within.[21] In a way, the codes were more "real" than the literary genres through which they operated: they constantly spilled over from genre to genre.

As we shall see, the inner tensions of the literature, reflecting the paradoxes of the social reality and its accompanying ideology, were rooted in the dual nature of both knighthood and courtliness: the denizens of the court were inherently torn between their servile status toward the lord and their exalted status as part of the power structure. They thought, felt, and operated as both free and unfree agents: free in their privileges vis-à-vis subjects and commoners, unfree vis-à-vis the masters. Even as servants they worked both to enact a superior will and for their own preferment, to become "lords" on their own. In their way, Arthur's knights share this duality with the courtiers of Castiglione.

Social background and ethical principles closely connect the culture of courtliness to the literature of courtesy. In fact, English usage merges—or confuses—the two when it refers to "courtly love" and "courtly literature." For clarity's sake I shall use the terms as follows. Courtly and courtliness will refer to the social and cultural environment of princely courts, with the more special terms of curial and curiality (corresponding to Med. Lat. *curialis, curialitas*) reserved for imperial chapels and episcopal courts. Knightly and knighthood will refer to the trained, horse-mounted warriors who formed a varied yet ideologically homogeneous group either within the titled and dubbed nobility or aspiring to become such—all these individuals operating mostly in courtly environments. Chivalry will be used for the ethico-ideological frame of mind that extended from knights to other classes and that informed patterns of behavior regarded as "noble." Even though, English usage notwithstanding, courtliness and *courtoisie* are not the same thing, I shall use the formula "courtly love" for whatever cultural attitudes or products bear the stamp of the doctrine of sublimated and ennobling love which originated among the troubadours and in the Arthurian romances: the formula has currency and should cause no confusion. Courteous and courtesy (occasionally, for greater clarity, Fr. *courtois, courtoisie*) will refer to the results of the civilizing process (connected with both courtliness and chivalry) whereby respect for others' feelings and interests was expected as acceptable behavior and a sign of noble nature. The literature of manners which is part of this study, and which translated the ideals of courtesy into specific norms, shared all the ideological features just mentioned.

Three levels of reality will confront us: (1) the social structures; (2) the ethical framework invoked by rulers, diplomats, statesmen, and their close associates; (3) the behavioral ideology affecting such diverse yet closely associated personages as chaplains, bishops, courtiers, chancery functionaries, knights, and court poets. The texts will show convergences and divergences between these levels of reality, as well as styles of life, thought, and writing. Our readings will focus on the relationship between poetics and historical meta-ethics, understanding the latter as analysis of the language of ethics. For this purpose I shall pursue the surfacing of moral concepts in certain literary forms, and the way such texts incorporated the supporting moral judgments that suited their societies' expectations. I shall attempt to interpret events, ideas, and stylistic forms that most directly pertain to the life and thoughts of medieval and Renaissance courts and their denizens, mainly the upper and lower nobility with the surrounding functionaries. These patterns of behavior will be shown to have acted as models for other social layers, principally in the burgher townships.

The literature that concerns us grew in social spheres of varying kinds at different times and places, but it was always affected by the presence of clergy and aristocracy as producers or consumers, authors or audiences. Feudal nobility does differ from Renaissance and post-Renaissance aristocracy, and this is reflected in the culture, art, and literature, but social settings must be kept in mind in order to understand the specific import of themes and motifs that may occasionally sound as timeless rhetorical topoi. For even the latter owe their vitality and endurance to their responsiveness to concrete expressive needs, although the eminent investigator of the durability of topoi, E. R. Curtius, did not focus on this vital relationship. Lack of detailed evidence on producers and publics notwithstanding, we can assume that most producers were the intelligentsia of the day, chiefly the clerics and then, progressively, a mix of clerics and noblemen or their direct clients.

This is not to deny the presence of a popular layer in the production of medieval and Renaissance literature. Historians who stress orality of production and transmission, typically Paul Zumthor and, in an independent way, Mikhail Bakhtin, appear to assign a considerable role to commoners as active public, viewing them rather as the German Romantics used to view the *Volk*. What I shall try to do here, above all, is to recapture medieval meanings, whereas Zumthor, in whose discourse meaning plays no appreciable role, chiefly strives to hear medieval voices.[22] More specifically, Zumthor suggests a reading of all medieval poetry according to a sharp opposition between a written literature (*stricto sensu* the only "literature"), which began around Chrétien de Troyes, no earlier than 1160, and all that other poetry which until at least the end of the fifteenth century continued to be orally produced and orally transmitted.[23] All of this would oppose a largely "popular" public of producers and consumers of oral literature to a distinct élite public of written literature.

Another way to discover the popular inspiration in medieval or Renaissance literature is to join Mikhail Bakhtin's search for what he called comic realism. Such a register is of limited interest to the present discourse since, except for stressing the joie de vivre that was typical of some Renaissance literature—especially Rabelais—Bakhtin's "popular comic" is not a special response to historical and social circumstances: it is beyond time, hence it cannot help our effort to historicize. Bakhtin sees Rabelais's laughter as essentially unconnected with the dominant ideas of contemporaneous aristocracy, clergy, or bourgeoisie. Like Zumthor's common man of the street, Bakhtin's "people" enact in carnival festivities a nonchalant realism that is absolutely egalitarian, whereas official literature stages the triumph of the ruling social hierarchy. Nevertheless, both elements are relevant to a proper reading of our literature since the two mix in the jongleur, and this mixture demands interpretation in order to explain some apparent contradictions or exceptions that do not derive from the inherent contrast between the "official" codes. The utopic element of the carnival can be related to the utopic element of the Arthurian world and the knightly (even Quixotic) ideals as a way to turn the world of official values upside down. Bakhtin has recalled how the egalitarian aspect of absolutism resulted in an alliance with the popular spirit of the carnival in a way that affected everyday life as well as literary expression in such attacks on feudal aristocratic privileges as Peter the Great's symbolic cutting of the boyars' beards, or Ivan the Terrible's establishment of the personal royal demesne under a special personal police and bodyguard (*oprichnina*).[24] We shall see direct analogies in Louis XIV's method of taming the French nobility, and we shall see how this general process directly affected the literature that concerns us.

The discrete codes of the clergy, the feudal nobility, the knights, and the courtiers coexisted by juxtaposing inherited ancient standards and Christian ideology, in a dynamic tension that produced a certain degree of contradiction in the literature but also lent it much of its mysterious fascination—part of its poetic appeal even at this chronological remove. This dynamism of ideas and forms makes up the contextual message through its linguistic surface and literary style. The dialectical game played by the coming together of ancient naturalism and Christian spirituality contributed to produce a style of antitheses and oxymora as well as a psychology of instability and conflict—the supreme example being Francesco Petrarca as originator of the centuries-long tradition of "Petrarchism."

The major literary genres to be explored as hosts of chivalric ideals are the epic, the romance, and the lyric. Speaking of the epic in 1948, E. R. Curtius recalled Max Scheler's identification of the five basic anthropological/ethical values (the holy, the intellectual, the noble, the useful, and the pleasant) corresponding to five "personal value types" (the saint, the genius, the hero, the leader, and the artist). He then observed that "a comparative phenomenology of heroism, heroic poetry, and the heroic ideal is yet to be given us."[25] Forty years of research may not have brought us much closer to fulfilling this desideratum. The following is a comparative and interdisciplinary discussion of textual data relating to the sense of nobility, heroism, and models of civilized behavior, toward a reconstruction of the ideology of medieval and Renaissance ruling classes. Some hesitation might be caused by the historians' insistence that the terms of nobility, knighthood, chivalry, and courtliness can be used meaningfully only with careful qualifications as to regional and chronological varieties.[26] It is difficult to define at any given time and place who exactly was a nobleman, a knight, or a courtier, and what this status precisely meant legally, institutionally, and in practical consequences. Yet all specialists are aware that, aside from local predicaments, the mental structures that operated on the level of perception, feeling, and practical behavior enjoyed a surprising pervasiveness and endurance. These structures were as much the function of material conditions as of imaginative roles created and promulgated by a massive literary tradition. A sensible degree of generalization seems, therefore, legitimate and even necessary if we are to understand the common factors in a host of complex cultural phenomena. The most problematic relationship may be between medieval and Renaissance courtiers. Even there, however, it is to be hoped that the following exposition will show significant elements of real continuity without prejudice to all the intervening historical changes.

In its broadest form, my theme is the literary and cultural role of the European nobility in the sense of a convergence of two distinct, occasionally opposite functions: the warrior ethic versus the ethic of courtliness and courtesy. In the sixteenth and seventeenth centuries the centripetal forces of the absolutist state forced the nobility to give up its belligerence in favor of a sharper concentration on its role as model of *politesse*, high culture, and social refinement. But in the Middle Ages the culture of courtliness and courtesy had managed to combine the two ethics: the knight was both a brave warrior and an artistic lover. Chrétien de Troyes's *Erec et Enide* and *Yvain* confronted the problem inherent in this uneasy association from the two opposite ends: the ideal noble knight must be a great fighter to be a worthy lover, but can hardly be both at the same time. Erec forgot his knightly duty for too much dallying with Enide, whereas, conversely, Yvain forgot his wife while pursuing his knightly adventures. The paradox was evident and dramatic: we must fight to qualify for love, yet we cannot love while we fight. By the very nature of the genre, lyricists chose to concentrate on loving, always subsuming the fighting qualities. I could summarily show the multiple oppositions by saying that for the people around the *Nibelungenlied*'s King Gunther, love is only a marginal source of warfare: they fight much more than they love. For King Arthur's people, instead, valorous fighting is propaedeutic to worthy love. But for most troubadours, fighting is a rather accidental and unwelcome interruption to lovemaking. We thus have an opposition between epic and lyric, with the romance standing in between and trying to harmonize the two in a difficult, problematic, and precarious balance.

A significant element in literary history is the growth and refinement of the psychological content. In its most impressive outcomes it has become a trademark of French literature, from Chrétien de Troyes to Marcel Proust and beyond. This exquisite psychologism is in good part the result of a social condition, the centrality of the court in the life of the French nation: sheer survival demanded close observation of the behavioral traits of one's peers, allies or rivals as they might be, yet not as individuals, as we might be tempted to surmise, but rather "as human beings in relation to others, as individuals in a social situation."[27]

The study of literature gains by balancing our concern for singularity and uniqueness with the collective semantic context that made the individual works intelligible and meaningful. Both traditional historians and literary critics tend to emphasize uniqueness, hence to isolate practical deeds and literary works in their individual peculiarities. Elias objects that our interest in individuals is really conditioned by their having played a part in social entities of one kind or another,[28] and Georges Duby agrees.[29] Similarly, we attribute importance to certain works of literature because they play a role in specific cultural patterns which they represent, and from which they cannot be abstracted without loss of meaning and relevance.

A sociologist with a many-faceted background of medical, psychological, and, as a student of Edmund Husserl, philosophical studies, Elias proposes a reading of cultural phenomena on the basis of sociological "figurations" that explain not only the historical roles of individuals and groups but also the deep meanings of their self-images as expressed in cultural products. By contrast, he criticizes traditional historians for a failure to understand that unique historical situations, events, and personalities can become the object of scientific analysis only if seen in their relationship to the collective consciousness of social groups.

Elias describes changes in human sensibility as part of a civilizing process that required the taming of emotions and resulted from the development of self-consciousness: the acceptance of a social code of behavior went hand in hand with learning to discipline the emotions. Civilization as self-control overcame, through a growing aptitude for introspection, the more primitive and barbarous self-expressive spontaneity of feudal society, as individuals eventually attained a realization of self-identity qua members of a civilized society. Social institutions changed together with the collective mentalities.

What Elias calls "the court society" came to maturity under Louis XIV. His study of aristocracies and courts discloses interests and tensions that explain how the particular themes that emerged in such societies took specific expressive forms. We can then understand how such cultural ideologies as courtliness, chivalry, and courtesy in the Middle Ages, the courtliness of the Renaissance signories and principalities (most typically, the kind envisaged by Castiglione), the strict codification of the aristocratic/bourgeois courts of the French kings from Henry IV to Louis XIV down to the Revolution, and finally the model of the despotic Prussian court of the eighteenth and nineteenth centuries, all have something in common even while they are unique in their precise social and cultural makeup. The reasons for such apparently unrelated phenomena as the confrontation of the Weimar Republic by National Socialism and then the latter's method of governing in a way that seemed chaotic and self-contradictory are explained by certain habits of public and psychological behavior. The period that concerns us was characterized by the coexistence, in a state of constant competition, of forms of feudal aristocracy, monarchic centralization, and relative democracy. It is therefore relevant to keep in mind how some recent societies failed in their struggle to survive the challenge of representative government and yielded to the apparent peacefulness of princely management of public affairs where the inner conflicts were handled behind the scenes of closed aristocratic courts. In the Prussian state, for one,

> state affairs were carried on essentially at the princely court. The rivalries, differences of opinion, and conflicts . . . were confined to the inner circle. They were often conducted behind closed doors. At any rate, up to 1870 and in some cases up to 1918, the mass of the German people had little opportunity to participate in such arguments with a sense of shared responsibility.

The personality structure of many citizens was adjusted to this way. . . . Many Germans felt distinctly uncomfortable when, after 1918, the arguments about the management of state affairs . . . now took place far more in public view, and when they themselves were required to take part in these discussions." [30]

We can easily see that Elias's approach demonstrates how knowledge of the past is the best way to understand some essential aspects of the present, for, in final analysis, the past *is* present.

PART ONE

Material Conditions and Social Background

CHAPTER ONE

Noblemen at Court

NOBILITY AND KNIGHTHOOD

Courtliness and knightly mentality originated in the courts—busy centers where several strata of society interacted in multiple functions. *Ministeriales* carried out basic administrative duties, the clergy provided not only religious guidance but administrative support and political advice, certain ladies performed as political and administrative agents, and members of the high nobility served as chief ministers. A special group of social and economic dependents variably integrated with the others and living in and around the feudal lord's castle was that of the knights or *milites* (soldiers), useful in warfare and as police agents.[1] The court was also the favorite and more or less permanent habitat of those first professional men and women of letters we know as minstrels, though many of them were vagrants, showing up especially at events like dubbings, weddings, crownings, and popular festivals and carnivals.[2] At a time when, writing and reading being rare, most cultural and literary communication was oral, minstrels were the principal carriers of the literature with which we are concerned, and often its authors.

Knighthood was a rather late development of the feudal system, which, although its immediate origins can be traced to the eighth century, reached its peak in the twelfth—the time of the flowering of "chivalry" or knightly ethos. The *milites* were recognized since A.D. 980 as a separate secular "class" or *ordo*, distinct from the *rustici* and immediately below the *nobiles*, until they eventually became part of the nobility.

Feudal power and privilege were the prerogatives of a class of noblemen whose rights and status soon became hereditary. So was the status of knight once this too became a recognized order. Nobility and knighthood must nevertheless be kept distinct even after they started to undergo a broad though partial process of merging around 1150. Since, as Frederick II's chancellor, Peter de Vineis, summarily stated, nobility was basically hereditary, it was a matter of blood, lineage, or birth—what the Germans call *Geburtstand*. In contrast, knighthood or chivalry was a *Berufstand*, a professional estate tied to actual exercise of the military arts and to official recognition by ritual dubbing.[3] True enough, in the thirteenth century descendants of knights generally started to inherit the title, yet they were not considered full knights unless formally dubbed. The ceremonial dubbing of knights, widely practiced from early in the twelfth century, was more than a ritual: it picturesquely symbolized a set of mental attitudes which related to the practical functions of knighthood, and it also marked the official recognition of a special status for these mounted soldiers.[4]

Such symbolic acts were an extension of the ritual sequence constituting the investiture or enfeofment of the feudal lord, which usually began with a man declaring himself liege or vassal of the lord by kneeling in front of him and placing his hands in the lord's hands.[5] This expressed feudal homage, subjection, and request for protection. After receiving the oath of fidelity the lord gave his liege some token of what was to be the fief, a grant of land in exchange for a formal promise of military and other aid. In later times grants could take the alternative form of moneys (tenure, indenture), so that the lord would not divest himself of land ownership and the vassal would not be tied to a territory.[6]

The specific ceremony of the granting of knighthood culminated in the girding or belting with the sword and tapping with the lord's sword on the shoulder or "dubbing." The custom of an all-night vigil before the investiture confirmed the sacramental nature of the procedure, which appears to have become ritualized around 1160–1180.[7] Since the tenth and eleventh centuries the terminology relating to the ceremony of girding included such common phrases as *cingulo decoratus*, "distinguished with a belt," *miles factus*, "made into a knight," *gladio, ense, cingulo accinctus*, "girded with a sword, a belt," *consecratio ensis*, "dedication of the sword," and *benedictio novi militis*, "benediction of the new knight." In its heyday, the ritual was predicated upon so much training and such steep expenses that many a prospective knight had to forego investiture. They thus forfeited the title they had inherited and settled for that of "esquire" or "squire" (Fr. *damoiseau*, Prov. *donzel*, G. *Edelknecht*, Sp. *hidalgo*).[8] Indeed, the young nobleman's economic predicament was not without stress: whereas he was barred from working for a living, he nevertheless needed to keep up with the standards of the rich princes who replaced the petty local lords. Prodigal display was a distinguishing trait of the chivalric class all along, but financial irresponsibility took its toll and many an indebted knight had to sell his land to the hated parvenu villains or give it back to the prince, perhaps in return for a place at court.[9]

As with the granting of nobility, a fief could also be granted to a knight on condition of performing service to the lord, usually for a set period of, say, forty days per year, and in the form of warfare, expeditions of a routine police nature (Fr. *chevauchée*), and garrison duty at the castle. The second was the literal background of adventure-seeking errantry, the third of court service as "courtiers." Starting in the twelfth century, unfit sons of knights could retain their rights by substituting direct service with payment in money (Eng. scutage) when fighting could be performed by mercenaries. Normally, landed knights had received both the nobleman's investiture and the chivalric girding in distinct rituals, although the two ceremonies could occasionally be conflated into one.

Medieval society lacked a planned, generalized configuration of the kind we are accustomed to in modern times. Largely local and personal, social relationships were governed by custom rather than by clear and precise laws, and only minimally regulated by impersonal state-directed institutions. France was less uniform than Germany and more fragmented into multilayered feudal vassalage. It was not uncommon in France to owe homage to several lords, while in Germany it tended to be reserved to one lord only, since it involved dependence and carried the stigma of servitude. Accordingly, the German higher nobility recognized only, if at all, the emperor, while counts and margraves could rely on all their subjects to remain collectively loyal to them.

Léopold Génicot's exemplary 1960 study of noble families in the county of Namur reminds us of the difficulty of generalizing about the noble estate.[10] It contains valuable data on the complex social situation and genealogical history of the class, though the cases are not typical, since the free state (*ingenuitas*) seemed to be particularly infrequent in that region. Around 1150 the county had twenty noble families (*nobiles*), some with *familiae* or courts, which included *milites* or knights. The latter increased in number and power within the next one hundred years, even while the number of *nobiles* decreased by more than half, partly through lack of surviving offspring. By the end of the thirteenth century the knights were free and equal in rank to the older nobility; by 1420 the two types of nobility had become indistinguishable.[11] As in Germany and elsewhere, the considerable rights and privileges of noble status were hereditary around Namur, too, but knights could retain them only if their titles were sanctioned by ceremonial dubbing after the actual exercise of arms. For failure to exercise this right and duty, many sons of knights had to give up their status, although enforcement had so many exceptions that a majority among later nobles descended from knights retained their status even without any military practice.

Like the title of nobility, the dignity of knighthood was incompatible with the practice of mechanical arts, especially farming. A nobleman must not be confused with a peasant. The thirteenth-century statutes of Fréjus issued by the count of Provence threatened the loss of the *ban*, or fiscal exemption, for knights' sons who were guilty of humble pursuits or who had not been dubbed by the age of thirty.[12] True enough, this French prejudice against commercial involvement was not generally shared along the Mediterranean. Italian noblemen eagerly joined the merchants within the free communes both practically and formally by becoming members of the guilds—a juridical requirement in Florence for any nobleman aspiring to a political career after Giano della Bella's 1282 Ordinances of Justice. In Siena the largest bank of the time, the Gran Tavola, was founded and run by the prominent landed gentry of the Bonsignori family, reaching a peak of prosperity around 1260. In Catalonia even the fiscal officialdom of the count-kings included members of the knightly class.[13]

While much of medieval literature was produced at court, it also flowered in the cities, which, as centers of merchants, manufacturers, hired labor, and craftsmen, were often outside the basic feudal structures. The type of free commune that became typical of northern and central Italy and of the regions of the Hanseatic League in northeastern Germany and western Norway was, however, uncommon in the rest of Europe. Most cities were under the protection of monarchs or feudal lords, who could ensure for them the same kind of safety the guilds sought for themselves in the independent communes, and often with greater effectiveness and coordination over large territories. The rise of mercantile cities demanded safety in the countryside, and merchants depended on local protection in moving their wares by land, sea, or waterways.

The rise of the merchants also had an impact on life at court when merchants began to compete with noble courtiers for administrative positions. The intrusion of this alien social element into the ministerial ranks introduced new ethical factors which were at variance with the mental attitudes of clergy and warriors (*oratores* and *bellatores*). This bourgeois invasion was to have a significant impact on the relationship between the sexes. In the mid-twelfth century, at the same time that matrimony became a sacrament, the mercantile view of marriage as a contract freely entered upon by mutual consent, like a mercantile contract, started to infiltrate and eventually, though slowly, to overrun the heroic view of marriage as possession of the woman by right of conquest, even by force.[14] We shall see how this encounter of competing ideologies may also have affected the literary representation of the knight.

GERMANY

The story of courtliness begins with Otto I the Great (king of Germany from 936, emperor 962–973) and his brother Brun (summoned to court around 939, bishop of Cologne from 953), when they started placing in important episcopal seats those former royal chaplains who had proven aptitudes for courtly and public service.[15] It was a first step in what would become the long-drawn-out investiture struggle, and it lay the foundation for the modern ethic of the high public servant. A number of cathedral schools became centers for a new type of education that shifted the emphasis from turning out teachers of the Bible to producing religious leaders and public administrators. More than a dozen major cathedral schools arose in Germany alone within a mere sixty years, starting in 952 at Würzburg and including Magdeburg, Cologne, Hildesheim, Trier, Bremen, Mainz, Worms, Liège, Speyer, Bamberg, Regensburg, and Paderborn. These schools remained the most important educational centers until the rise of the universities in the early thirteenth century. They must be placed alongside their counterparts in Italy (e.g., the well-endowed cathedral schools of Milan and Verona), England (York, eighth century), and France, where after Orléans, Auxerre (ninth century), and Paris (tenth century), the Aquitanian Gerbert of Aurillac's famous school at Reims (972–982) emerged to produce such luminaries as Richer of Saint-Rémi, Atto of Fleury, Adalbero of Laon, and especially Chartres's celebrated teacher Fulbert (bishop 1006–1028), not to mention the future King Robert, son of Hugh Capet.[16]

The idea of *curialitas* or courtliness appears to have originated among the *curiales* (from *curia*, "court"), the secular clergy trained in the royal chapels, which supplied the bulk of high civil servants and royal counselors. Josef Fleckenstein (1956) mapped out the flowering of the newly revived cathedral schools of the tenth century under the aegis of a new policy of imperial patronage, and argued that the direction of these new schools changed purposely from the Carolingian emphasis on the training of preachers and teachers of Scripture to the formation of statesmen and administrators.[17] Jaeger agrees:

> The goal was not knowledge for its own sake or knowledge for the glory and worship of God, but rather knowledge to be applied in the practical duties of running the empire. Brun of Cologne as imperial chancellor is known for transforming the royal chapel into a sort of academy of philosophy and school for imperial bishops. The instruction that turned gifted young men into trained administrators and loyal supporters of the emperor originated at court, in the chapel. But it was so valuable that it spilled over the borders of that tiny, elite institution, and sought accommodation elsewhere. This gave cathedral schools their new role. . . . Cathedral school education becomes identical with preparation for service at court, be it secular or episcopal.[18]

Thus, following Roman models, Otto I and Brun created an institutional basis for the teaching of courtly manners while trying to take care of the actual needs of effective and orderly government. The courtier bishops and the cathedral schools they controlled became the centers for the education of clerics in courtly manners.

This vigorous educational program went hand in hand with the Saxon emperors' will to restore the empire and revive the ancient cultural splendor. A telling episode illustrates the new enthusiasm. The Saxon emperor Otto II's interest in things Greek had been aided by his wedding to the Byzantine princess Theophanes. Otto was so impressed by Gerbert of Aurillac's knowledge that he made him abbot of Bobbio (983) and invited him to join his court as tutor to his son, the future Otto III (983–1002). "Remove from us our Saxon uncouthness and allow the Greek refinement to grow in us. . . . A spark of the Greek spirit will then be found in us. . . . Arouse in us the lively genius of the Greeks." In his enthusiasm for his exalted protectors Gerbert would later assert that "something divine manifests itself when a man of Greek origin and with Roman power in his person requests almost by hereditary right the treasures of Greek and Roman wisdom."[19] Otto III made Gerbert archbishop of Reims (991), archbishop of Ravenna (998), and finally pope with the name of Sylvester II (999). Like a later "civic humanist," Gerbert would take pride in being deeply involved in political affairs, "rei publicae permixtus."[20]

This marriage between ruler and cleric naturally led to a struggle between state and Church for control of investiture. The Concordat of Worms (1122) attempted to settle the dispute by favoring papal appointment of bishops. Nevertheless, the succeeding Hohenstaufens continued the broader struggle for imperial supremacy. In the spirit of rebuilding the glory and honor of the ancient Roman emperors, as his Ottonian predecessors had done, Frederick I Barbarossa (crowned emperor in 1155) vigorously attempted the enforcement of lawful "regalian rights" by cajoling and coaxing the Italian communes. The Lombard League managed to frustrate his efforts even after he had destroyed Milan in 1162. The battle of Legnano (1176) ended in his defeat, and in 1183 the Peace of Constance sealed the communes' triumph, sanctioning their de facto independence despite formal assurances of allegiance to the sovereign.[21] Still the struggle went on, especially under the unyielding Frederic II (d. 1250).

Indeed, in and outside German territories the Concordat of Worms did not close the matter, and high ecclesiastics retained an important role within the political order and in their relationship with secular authorities.[22] The closeness of the Church hierarchy to the centers of power remained an open issue, just as Gallicanism remained permanently operative in the French Church. When Luther started his revolt against Rome, his case was still resting in part on the popular desire for independence from Rome. His reliance on the princes to decide even the religious affiliation of their subjects carried on, in its way, the joining of temporal and spiritual authority that dated from the early Ottos. German Protestantism became an instrument of princely, and later monarchic, absolutism until the kaiser and the regional princes were dethroned in 1918. The precedent set by Otto the Great in appointing his brother Brun as bishop was followed by later monarchs and princes who formally acted as bishops of the Protestant churches within their lands. The Hohenzollern kings remained the titular heads of the Prussian Church.

This dependence of Church authority on state authority has been likened to the situation prevailing within Orthodox Slavic states, especially czarist Russia.

> Bishops and pastors, with few exceptions, stood solidly behind the sovereign, the Junkers and the army, and during the nineteenth century they opposed the rising liberal and democratic movements. Even the Weimar republic . . . was anathema to most Protestant pastors, as it had been to Niemöller, not only because it had deposed the kings and princes, to which they owed allegiance, but because it drew its main support from the Catholics, the Socialists, and the Trade Unions.[23]

This also explains, in part, the ease with which in modern times Adolf Hitler crushed the organized Protestant resistance by citing the right of the state to appoint and direct high Church authorities. Hitler was following a tradition that preceded the Concordat of Worms.[24]

In the course of the twelfth century, courtly culture completed its shift from cathedral schools and episcopal courts to secular courts. In comparing twelfth-century Germany with France, as I shall do shortly, we must be aware that the social makeup of the German courts, where knights were markedly more dependent on their lords, differed from the French. The German lower nobility was divided into a hereditary nobility of lineage and a new nobility made up of active or former *ministeriales* (G. *Ministerialen*), that is, administrators and functionaries of bourgeois origin, bureaucrats *avant-la-lettre* in both secular and episcopal courts.[25] From the end of the eleventh century, legal documents formally refer to both hereditary and ministerial noblemen as *milites*, "knights" (G. *Ritter*). The studies of J. Bumke (1964), J. Johrendt (1971), and H. J. Reuter (1971) have shown that between 1050 and 1250 the Latin term *miles* or the German term *Ritter* applied in Germany to any horse-mounted soldier of whatever class and origin, without designating a special social group (*ritterlich* meant "knightly"). Closely associated with the category of *ministeriales* from which it often derived, the profession of knighthood was not restricted to a specific social layer and even included individuals who did not enjoy a free state, hence it did not by itself grant the legal status of nobleman. In turn, a *ministerialis*, himself in a servile status, could have a large number of knights at his service, as was the case of Frederic Barbarossa's *ministerialis* Werner von Bolanden who, according to the chronicler Gislebert of Mons (*Chronicon Hanoniense*), at the end of the twelfth century had eleven hundred *milites* as his vassals.[26]

Great princes could behave with considerable independence toward their only superior, the emperor. They could even openly oppose him, as happened in the struggle over investiture and the consequent civil war. Directly below the princes came the free lesser nobility, the *Edelfreie*, flanked by the servant-knights (*Edelknecht*) or *ministeriales*, who, owing to their lords both their personal power and inalienable feudal estates, could not leave their service. Together, these aristocratic ranks made up the hierarchy of the military nobility (*Heerschild*). Being a soldier, however, even on horseback, did not automatically mean being a knight, since this implied, beyond the formal dubbing and the special status this conferred, the adoption of a mentality which was largely based on literary-ideological sources of French origin (after 1150). Hence "knighthood did not originate from cavalry soldiers,"[27] since, once again, far from being a homogeneous social class, the motley category of mounted soldiers (all *milites*) included considerable numbers of peasants selected and hired for their soldierly dispositions as well as professional mercenaries who never, either in the Middle Ages or in the Renaissance, acquired noble status through the mere exercise of their profession. Both armed peasants and mercenaries comprised de facto the bulk of the princes' armies. They were kept around the court for prompter and more reliable employment than the armies that could be raised by calling on vassals' feudal services.[28]

Technological advances in military equipment reduced the knights' value in warfare after 1200. The foot soldier armed with an *arbalète* threatened the strongest horse-mounted and sword-armed fighter, and any peasant with a good knife could kill a knight who, having fallen off his horse, lay immobilized by his heavy armor.[29] Shortly before 1206 Guiot de Provins complained that an *arbalétrier* was becoming more valuable, hence more expensive, than a knight.[30] Cervantes would later note that a coward with a gun could kill the bravest knight. Within the ministerial ranks the high administrators, now glorified bureaucrats (with an enhanced sense of their worth and value, as possibly illustrated, according to some interpreters, in Hartmann's epics), started turning to law as educational background for their business.

FRANCE

Courtesy was born at court, first perhaps among clerical chaplains, then among the lesser nobility. The fact that courtly literature was born in southern France is related to the crucial function of princely courts in that area. The weakened central authority in the wake of the dissolution of monarchic power in France after Charlemagne's immediate successors made the feudal lords effective centers of regional power, but the weakness of central government was also reflected in the heightened independence of the lower vassals. Even such great counts as those of Poitiers and Toulouse had great difficulties in restraining their vassals. Hence the comital courts had to be turned into attractive centers of noble living so that the counts could cultivate the loyalty of their vassals by keeping them at close quarters.[31]

The vacancy of a legitimate central temporal power prompted the Church to fill the vacuum and arrogate to itself some basic duties of government. The Church started preaching the Peace of God (*Pax Dei*) in the hope of preserving peace and justice from the anarchic, bellicose counts emboldened by the lack of effective checks from above. The Church was thus taking a stand as protector of the weak and poor—a role attributed to the monarchy by the Carolingian capitularies and edicts. This movement started in southern France, where it remained particularly operative; it was less defensible in Germany as long as the bishops were controlled by the emperor and loyal to him. Dominated by the bishops and the great abbots, the councils assembled for the first stage of the Peace of God (roughly 990–1040) opposed the armed *nobiles* and *milites*, as aggressors, to the potential victims of their rapacious violence, namely unarmed *rustici/villani*, clerics (with all Church property in its various forms), and women of the nobility. For some historians the Peace of God movement was responsible for triggering powerful forces among the populace.[32]

Amounting to both a Christianization of militarism and a militarization of Christianity, the *Pax Dei* bears the seeds of chivalry, since the knightly class responded to the complex situation created by the Peace of God.[33] The original intent was to restrain the destructively barbarous forms of military activity prevailing among feudal bands. In a second stage, during the second quarter of the eleventh century, the Church went farther by proclaiming the "Truce of God" (*Treuga Dei*), which declared private warfare a sinful pleasure to be restrained. During specified periods of "abstinence" the penitent knights were urged to put down their armor and swords and join the *inermes*, the unarmed under the spiritual protection of the Church. It was a further progression toward chivalric deeds.

As early as the 930s, Odo of Cluny, founder of the Cluniac order, had recognized the ethical utility of military life.[34] This idea finally came to fruition in the alliance between *militia saecularis* and *militia spiritualis* brought about by the Cluniac reform, which, in particular, exercised a strong influence on the Norman nobility. Military knightly orders, like the Templars, the Hospitallers, and the Teutonic Knights ("Deutscher Orden"), arose in the wake of the preaching of the Crusades, which marked the third phase of the Peace of God, and the new spirituality erupted in the enthusiasm for crusading in Europe and in the Orient. The knight's ethic thus became ambivalent, entailing a denial or limitation of his right and duty to do battle except for Christ. The principle was clearly stated at the Council of Narbonne in 1054 and made universal at the Council of Clermont in 1095.

The *militia* was given a chance to become what Pope Gregory VII and St. Bernard of Clairvaux (1090/91–1153) would then call a *nova militia*, the *militia Dei* or *Christi*, if it abided by its purported divine calling to be a providential arm for justice, peace, and social order.[35] Such a role was far less urgent in Germany, as the bishop of Cambrai had affirmed as early as 1025, since there the sovereign had sufficient power to keep the peace.[36] Knightly status generally rose in prestige as a result of the ecclesiastical reform movements which moralized and spiritualized the social function of knighthood, and this rise in prestige fostered the assimilation of the two orders of *nobiles* and *milites*, which, for the same reason of lesser urgency, did not take place in Germany.

The active alliance between religious and secular knighthood exhausted itself when the crusading spirit failed. Hence, the Church's rejection of warlike attitudes forced a new justification of chivalry, with a displacement of values that could take one of two directions: (1) a willful acceptance of military action (even outright brigandage) for economic and political reasons of a purely secular nature, or (2) a shift in emphasis from the military aspect of chivalry to the nonmilitary, that is, to a noble code of loving (the ideology of courtly love) and behaving at court (the ideology of manners).

Georges Duby has proposed to view the poor nobility as both creator and direct audience of the literature of *courtoisie*. The *curiales* or curial clerics and the knights, most commonly poor nobles, shared economic interests and social background, both often being noble cadets who could neither inherit their fathers' domains nor aspire to independent sources of livelihood. They could enter a monastery or seek ecclesiastical careers as court clerics, or they could turn to the knightly profession. Starting in the tenth or eleventh century the members of the landless lower nobility who turned to knightly status gravitated around the seigniorial courts as their natural habitat, since, deprived of permanent residences and personal holdings in the form of fiefs, they depended on the liberal hospitality of a lord and mistress. In return for hospitality these "marginal men" served according to a regular contract that specified the duty to perform *chevauchées* through the countryside. The purpose of such errands, which became the practical model of the knight errant's idealized adventure trips, was not to find portentous encounters with ogres, dragons, or magic villains, but to ensure the orderly collection of levies and taxes and strike terror in the hearts of the peasants. The knights were the lord's militia, police, and law enforcers.[37]

In southern France more than elsewhere, the knights came to constitute a sort of state within the state, taking right and justice into their own hands for largely uncensurable and uncontrollable purposes.[38] Their livelihood could be supplemented from acts of violence at the expense of various property owners. "Le milieu économique que représente, dans la société de ce temps, le groupe des chevaliers est, par vocation professionnelle, celui de la rapine."[39] Indeed, it was not always easy to distinguish between knights and bandits, since even the most fearsome bandits might display the same chivalrous and courtly conduct toward ladies and the downtrodden. When his superiors decided a knight's behavior was no longer acceptable or manageable, he would be declared an outlaw, which occasionally turned him into a popular hero (vide the various Robin Hoods of British and continental history).[40]

Duby's picture of the social predicament confirms Erich Köhler's interpretations of troubadour lyrics. Yet we must be careful to give each factor its due.[41] Typically for most historians, Duby tends to explain all sociohistorical phenomena, including the rise of chivalry, on the basis of political, social, and economic forces. Even while he vigorously advocates the joining of material causes to the study of mental attitudes, he only occasionally refers to purely cultural factors as expressed and, in part, created by literature.[42] Yet a balanced reconstruction of behavioral patterns requires a full realization of the enduring impact of purely mental attitudes, often induced by literary models even when the material conditions have made them obsolete. The prestige of chivalry long continued to produce among the leading classes a "reproduction fidèle du discours romanesque et courtois," a general mimesis of Arthurian and Carolingian heroes through a need to see life as a work of art.[43] Chivalry remained a live cultural model even when, after Crécy (1346) and Agincourt (1415), it was out of tune not only with the new military techniques but with the moral perception of the practical irrelevance and visible "frivolity" of the knight in shining armor. Typically, like paladins from the old epics, Louis of Orléans, Philip the Good of Burgundy, and even the emperor Charles V could still respectively call to personal combat Henry IV of England (challenged by Louis), Duke Humphrey of Gloucester (challenged by Philip in 1425), and Francis I (twice engaged in challenges with Charles V, in 1528 and 1536), ostensibly "to avoid shedding the blood of their Christian subjects."[44] True enough, these carefully staged and widely advertised challenges never came to execution, thus looking rather like self-seeking rhetorical displays for purposes of propaganda, but it is remarkable that they would be taken seriously by the public, starting with the chroniclers.

The public of courtly lyrics and chivalric romances appears to have comprised mainly *milites* and *ministeriales*—*ministeriales* being the majority of court denizens in Germany, the *milites* in southern France.[45] The composite group making up the court was often referred to as *maisnada* in southern France (Fr. *maisnie* or *compagnie*, It. *masnada*). The equivalent Latin term was, significantly, *familia*, commonly used throughout Europe, including Germany: the court was defined as the prince's "family" well into the Renaissance. In addition to poor knights (Prov. *paubres chavaliers*) and court functionaries, the *maisnada* comprised lower domestics (*sirvens, doncels*), *soudadiers*, troubadours, and *joglars* or minstrels. Though low on the social scale, the *ministeriales* could be the most influential. The *soudadiers* (Fr. *soudoiers*) were the mercenary soldiers (Bertran de Born, e.g., addresses them by that name). The members of all these diverse groups of the lord's "family" referred to one another as *companhos*, "comrades," as does, for instance, Marcabru (1129–1150), a troubadour of lowly origin, when he speaks of his peers and, in the same breath, the *soudadiers*.[46] The death of Henry the Young (*el rei joven* of Bertran de Born's and Dante's memory), son of Henry II of England, was said to have saddened, left *doloros*, all the "brave and young," *pretz e joven*, especially "li cortes soudadiers / e'l trobador e.lh joglar avinen."[47]

The terminology was similar in the French *chansons de geste*. In the *Chanson d'Aspremont* Charlemagne distributes presents to his *maisnie* according to rank, distinguishing the *riches hommes de riche lin* from the *pauvres chevaliers*; a third group is made up of *bacheliers légers, damoiseaux* (pages), and *vaillans soldoiers*. A similar phraseology is in other epic songs, like *Girart de Roussillon*.[48] All these terms, together with *écuyers* (squires), collectively comprise the *bacheliers*, that is, "the young." This term, indicating not years of age but social state, can be defined as "between the knighting and having become a father."[49] Provençal *damoisial, damizel, donzel*, and the French *damoiseau* or *écuyer*,

corresponding to Latin *domicellus*, used in the south of France, and
armiger, used in the north, before 1100 generally referred to men-at-
arms educated and trained at court as future knights, and after 1200 to
noblemen's sons not yet knighted. The German terminology was equally
rich: *gesellen* "companions," *reitgesellen* "mounted fellows," *knechte*
"servants," *swertgenôze* "fellows of the sword," *swertdegen* "sword-
warriors," *schiltgesellen* "fellows of the shield," *knappen* "squires,"
kint "young men." [50]

Duby's picturesque description of the psychological climate of the
maisnada points to some of the constant motifs of troubadour poetry:
"La joie règne dans ces bandes. Le chef dépense sans compter, aime le
luxe, le jeu, les mimes, les chevaux, les chiens. Les moeurs y sont fort
libres. La grande affaire est cependant de combattre, 'en tournoiements
et en guerre.' " [51] The poets transformed this theme of constant gaiety
and *joi* into a sublime criterion of self-satisfaction, along with the cult
of feasts, games, tourneys, and hunting parties, all in lavish display of
"liberality" and wealth. The very common term *jove* (Fr. *jeune*) applied
to all the members of the group and was used constantly with a positive
connotation, referring to all that is good and excluding all that is undesirable and harmful. [52] The remarkable educational value of courtesy
can be easily grasped when we realize that these were the same sort of
people who made up the notorious mercenary armies of Italian and
other *condottieri* through the Renaissance and then served as the lords'
private armies in the baroque age (remember Manzoni's *bravi*), spreading terror wherever they went through their reckless plundering, raping,
and, often, through the sheer glee they derived from destruction. [53] The
literature made some of them see themselves as romantic heroes and, at
least occasionally, behave as noble characters.

Sections of "companies" often lived away from court as knights errant. Unlike the adventure seekers of the romances, knights seldom traveled alone. At the very least they traveled with a squire, like Don Quixote, but more often they went out as a troop led by a more experienced
"young" knight assigned by the lord as mentor to his own errant sons,
and were followed by a train of domestics and harlots. Their approach
could not have been welcomed by the poor "villeins," the merchants,
and other lords with the enthusiastic, hospitable favor that the romances usually portray. Despite the element of turbulence and violence
and despite the danger (violent death prevented many from returning),
such sallies suited both the ideal of knighthood and the interests of the
lords, since the latter welcomed the opportunity of ridding themselves

of cadet sons who might rival the firstborn for the patrimony. It was true, however, that the eldest son also was expected to undergo the experience of militant knighthood.

A noble father hoped as well that the game of errantry would produce happy and profitable encounters with widows of high social standing to be carried off to the altar. For his own benefit, the father tended to postpone his children's marriages as long as possible, since weddings entailed some division of patrimony and the new offspring might be in competition with older heirs. This reluctance to *caser* ("marry off") the children, male and female, held even for the firstborn male, since he could then claim his patrimonial rights immediately.[54]

In an anthropological sense, one could also read into knightly behavior some patterns of what Mikhail Bakhtin has called popular comic culture, grotesque realism, and the carnival spirit. The Russian critic reminded us of the terracotta figurine in the Hermitage, the laughing pregnant old woman of Kertch allegedly expressing the joyous coupling of imminent death with the birth of new life, a symbol of fertility in the readiness for death. Bakhtin saw in this spirit of cosmic renewal the enactment of the perpetual youth of the world of nature. The apparently irrational joie de vivre of a Guillaume of Poitier, the first troubadour; the *laetitia spiritualis* of St. Francis praising God through communion with all the creatures of the world; the chaotic, irrepressible, even destructive "joy" of the companies of roaming knights constantly exalting in their boastful "youth"; and the contradictory thrusts of the knights of the Round Table—all these disparate yet related manifestations contain in a Bakhtinian sense elements of the need for survival in a *renovatio*, a rebirth that had deep biological and cultural roots. In the sense of Bakhtin's "lowering" (*snizenie*), the disorderly impetuosity of the youthful knights was a folkloric counterpart of the medieval and Renaissance crusading spirit.[55]

The prestige of the knightly state was such that as early as the middle of the twelfth century, French juridical documents used the title to cover all layers of the nobility, the great aristocrats taking pride in being associated with what in other parts of the empire continued to be a lower status.[56] A significant document of the nobility of blood deciding to join the knights by adopting their title is Lambert of Ardres's *Historia comitum Ghisnensium* (ca. 1195), which records how the powerful counts of Guines had themselves formally knighted.[57] An eloquent example of this phenomenon concerns the early career of Henry of Anjou, who in 1149, when only sixteen, persuaded David I, King of the Scots, to knight him. Having become king as Henry II of England, he returned the favor in 1159 by knighting David's grandson, the seventeen-year-old Malcolm King of Scots, who had been eager to receive the honor. In France, between 1180 and 1230 a juridical quasi-fusion took place between the *domini castellani*, feudal lords possessing castles and subject only to the sovereign, hence the true, hereditary nobility of blood (*nobiles* in the official documents), and the knights (*milites*) who were their dependents, living in their castles as part of their *familia* and originally subjected to them, hence juridically not free.[58]

Gradually, the knights began to appropriate the title and authority of *domini*—French *sires, messires*. It is typical of more bourgeois Italy that there the title *ser*, of analogous etymology, indicated not nobility but the notarial status, although, as in France starting in the last third of the twelfth century, it could also indicate the status of ordained priest.[59] The knights' ascendancy through the eleventh century accompanied the weakening of the *domini*'s power because of the strengthening of the central authority of the knights' natural allies, namely the sovereign, dukes, and princes. The greater lords had an interest in favoring the fragmentation of the *castellani*'s power into more local administrative units around the houses of simple knights. The Peace of God and the Crusades also contributed to the respective weakening and strengthening of the two *ordines* of *domini* and *milites*. Knights who owned large farms began to rebuild them in imitation of castles, with moats, strong outer walls, and towers—the *domus fortes*, French *maisons fortes*.[60] Around 1200 they started to acquire true freedom and noble status by arrogating to themselves the noble rights previously reserved for the *domini*, which consisted of exemption from taxation (*ban*) and the authority to judge and punish the "villeins." They also started to marry women from the higher rank and to adopt primogeniture for their succession, in order to preserve the inviolability and indivisibility of their fiefs. The contemporaneous use of heraldic shields symbolically sealed their entrance into the higher order.[61]

If on the one hand the knights could be seen as a means to reduce the power of the lords, the closeness between nobility and knights could on the other hand unite them in the king's distrust when he was trying to restrain the lords' and their knights' anarchic, destructive, and criminal rampages against neighbors and subjects. Suger of St. Denis showed this side of the coin when, in his *Life of Louis VI* (before 1145), he exposed feudatories and knights as unruly outlaws to be restrained and punished by the good king.[62]

After A.D. 1000 the growth of cities as centers of manufacturing, trade, and crafts was a negative development for the nobility. Wresting their civic freedoms from the lords, the burghers escaped the constraints of the feudal system. As the cities became important centers of productivity and culture, regional lords and knights remained more and more tied to the agricultural world of the countryside, outside the new monetary and mercantile economy. The burghers could increase their independence from the lesser feudatories by keeping ties with the greater lords, especially the sovereign. Bourgeois bankers helped in the raising of mercenary armies to be paid with currency: this bypassed the more cumbersome feudal fealties and rendered the knightly order dispensable.

In southern France courts and town merchants lived in much better harmony than in the north. Both there and in Italy the towns gave themselves republican statutes reflecting the new monetary economy that had freed them from feudal controls. The lords in control of the countryside tolerated the heretical sects of Albigensians and Valdensians that flourished within the towns, at times even sympathizing with them. Hence in the south the ideological opposition between *cortesia* and *vilania* did not involve the merchants, as it did in the north, but only the lowly peasants.[63] We shall see this clearly reflected in the literature.

ITALY

In Italy, too, through the tenth and eleventh centuries the German emperors pursued a steady policy of transferring authority from local secular feudatories to the bishops, so that by 1050 most leading bishops in northern Italy enjoyed the judicial powers of the former counts.[64] The emperors' attempts to control the bishops, however, met with particularly fierce resistance from the rising Italian townships. When Conrad II (1024–1039) tried to depose the proud and powerful archbishop of Milan, Ariberto d'Intimiano, Ariberto, supported by the local nobility and the burghers, refused to give up. The imprisonment of the bishops of Cremona, Vercelli, and Piacenza by order of the same emperor provoked enmity in those cities, too. On the other hand, most Tuscan, Emilian, and Lombard bishops remained loyal to Henry IV even during his struggle against the pope, whereas the populace grew increasingly sympathetic to papal authority, which appeared as the natural champion of territorial independence.[65]

Italy's social makeup was unique in that it had a comparatively weak feudal nobility facing a predominant merchant class who operated from extraordinarily vibrant bases of teeming communes. We must not, however, underestimate the ideological power of the nobility. Not only did the burghers of the communes adopt many of the cultural ideals of the knightly caste, as would be the case throughout European society for centuries to come, but even in practical terms the nobility dominated the communes through the end of the twelfth century. Although cities were not enfeoffed and had no lords within the feudal order, it was not until the end of the thirteenth century that the *popolo*, to wit, the organized class of wealthy merchants and entrepreneurs, managed to take control of most communes. Even so, the *popolo*'s almost complete triumph in such city-states as Florence and Bologna was exceptional. In most of the towns, the *popolo* could not wrest from the hands of the nobility and the knights more than one third or at best one half of the voting rights and public offices, and in one of the largest communes, Milan, the popular faction succumbed to a strong counterattack from its traditional enemy. This occurred in 1277, when Archbishop Ottone Visconti reentered the city at the head of a victorious army of noblemen and quickly proceeded to turn back to the knighted class all the most prized dignities, including cathedral canonries.[66]

Even in Florence, though less so than in most communes, the presence of noblemen was real and conspicuous, with the difference that they were highly urbanized, hence closely tied to business activities.[67] They did keep their landed bases, but joined the merchants within the cities. As for Venice, recent research has underlined how the patriciate of that hardy republic consistently behaved according to patterns of both feudal and mercantile self-interest, despite the rhetoric of the official "myth of unanimity."[68] One of the most authoritative politico-historical analyses of Venetian society in the Cinquecento, Donato Giannotti's *Libro della Repubblica de Vinitiani* (1526–1530), objected to the established view that Venetians were divided into two classes only, *popolari* and *gentil'huomini*, and insisted on a threefold articulation entailing a further distinction of *popolari* into *popolari* proper, engaged in servile or "mechanical" tasks, and *cittadini*, wealthy tradesmen and merchants dedicated to "arti più honorate."[69] The established view was represented, for instance, by the equally respectable analyst of the Venetian constitution, Gasparo Contarini, who in his *De Magistratibus et Republica Venetorum* (1523–1531 or later)[70] praised the wisdom of the city fathers for having ordered the citizenry along a rigidly dual system. All "mercenari e artigiani" had to be considered servile populace, servants of the commonwealth, deprived of the dignity of true citizens. Power in the republic had to remain in the hands of free men, the only true citizens: "il cittadino è huomo libero." Reflecting the spirit of the time, even a Sienese observer of the quality of Alessandro Piccolomini, Professor of Philosophy at Padua, praised the Venetian constitution for recognizing that long noble heritage was a prerequisite to good and stable city governance (*Della institution di tutta la vita dell'huomo nato nobile e in città libera*, 1542).[71] No matter how one looked at the social structure of the Serenissima, a unique brand of aristocratic ideology played a crucial role in its government.

Starting in Germany in the tenth century, the clerical circles at court developed an ideology that contrasted with that of the warrior class. The opposition between the mores of warriors and those of court clerics is somewhat similar to the opposition between the *consorterie* of nobles or *magnati* that controlled the Italian communes in the eleventh and twelfth centuries and the new merchant guilds that emerged at the end of the twelfth century.[72] Merchants were naturally more disposed than nobles to adopt the literati's ideology of *gentilezza* (i.e., courtesy and good manners) as a sign of true superiority and inner nobility. The theme had enjoyed great popularity among the troubadours, and in its abstract form as rhetorical topos it had an ancient history going back to Juvenal. Even though the burghers' guilds first asserted themselves by imitating the aggressiveness and bellicosity of the armed *magnati*, they soon recognized that their interests were best served through the peaceful means of influence and control. Where money is power, the merchant prevails over the soldier. In fact, peaceloving merchants often did prevail, sometimes to the extent that they compelled the nobles to give up their warlike ways and accept the powerfully symbolic razing of their forbidding high towers within city walls. Just the same, the established methods of governance remained for the most part unruly, grasping, and violent: to ensure the safety of their own money, the burghers had little choice but to imitate their opponents and do their best to grab power for themselves. Daily life in the communes thus remained one of constant dissent and strife, always verging on civil war and war with neighbors. Within the walls of the Italian communes the more civilized side of courtliness and courtesy could be felt more as an idea (the literati's protests in favor of the nobility of heart, mind, and manners) than in fact. All in all, the grabbing of lucrative positions as well as the exercise of political and fiscal rights remained more a matter of organized power than of merit- and law-based apportionment.

When knights were ousted from their positions of control, they could find a substitute form of employment in the mercenary armies which spread throughout Italy in the thirteenth and fourteenth centuries. It was an occupation and social function somewhat similar to that of the impoverished knights who attached themselves to the twelfth-century courts. We must remember that Castiglione's court of Urbino belonged to a lordly dynasty of captains commanding richly rewarding mercenary armies generation after generation, beginning with Guido da Montefeltro of Dantesque memory. Yet even the Montefeltro's power was originally based on landed wealth. Their ability to draw authority from feudal land ownership and power from the armed men at their disposal was typical. As early as 1216 the Montefeltro could put three hundred men into the field. Similarly, Salinguerra Torelli took control of Ferrara before 1220 through the help of a force of eight hundred horsemen, holding it until the Estensi ejected his family in 1240. Manfredi Lancia attempted to establish tyranny in Milan by making use of his thousand-man mercenary cavalry in 1252.[73] Even the popular communes had to use noblemen on the battlefield. The Genoese chronicler Caffaro (ca. 1080–1166) reports that in 1163 the consuls created more than a hundred knights from within Genoa and outside. The same commune of Genoa dubbed two hundred knights to serve against the Malaspina in 1211. Giovanni Villani tells us that in 1285 there were three hundred dubbed knights in Florence, and that when Florence moved against Arezzo in 1288, the Guelf force of allies that took the field included 250 cavalrymen assembled by "the Guelf Counts Guidi, Mainardo da Susignana, Jacopo da Fano, Filippuccio di Iesi, the Marquis Malaspina, the Judge of Gallura, the Counts Alberti, and other minor Tuscan barons."[74] In 1294, at a great court of peers he held in Ferrara, Azzo VIII of Este was dubbed a knight by the lord of Treviso, Gherardo da Camino, and then proceeded to dub fifty-two new knights with his own hand.

War had been and remained the business of noblemen, and the popular communes often entrusted themselves to noble leaders to ensure their defense, as they did with the Della Torre in Milan and the Della Scala in Verona. The middle class preferred to tend to business and leave warfare to others, thus becoming the best clients for the mercenary army leaders, often men of noble origin. Dino Compagni (*Cronica* 1.20: 27) gives a picturesque differential portrait of the Cerchi and the Donati, the two leading families of the Florentine White and Black Guelfs, the former being very rich members of the mercantile estate, the latter less rich but of more ancient blood: "Those who knew said: 'They [the Cerchi and other Whites] are only merchants, hence they are naturally cowardly, while their enemies [the Donati and other Blacks] are proud, valorous men, expert in warfare.'"

As far as the rural population was concerned, it is hard to tell whether in medieval and Renaissance Italy the peasants fared better under the burghers than under feudal lords: bourgeois landowners had the same contempt and condescension for their tenants as the lords had in France, even though rustics were "free" in Italy.

Some historians describe Italian city-states of the thirteenth century as often made up of two contiguous and competing communes.[75] The *comune del podestà*, clustered within the walls of the old town, like the Florence of Dante's Cacciaguida, represented the interests of noblemen and prelates; the *comune del popolo*, under the leadership of the *capitano del popolo*, represented the interests of the high burghers. This second commune had its own courts, notarial agencies, armed citizen companies, trade guilds, and even electoral structures.

The institution of *podestà* became common shortly before 1200, replacing the consuls whose appearance around 1100 must be taken as a sign of a commune coming into being.[76] Interestingly enough, the troubadour Folquet de Romans saw in the north-Italian institution of the *podestà* a triumph of personal merit over the stasis of feudal order. In Provence privilege no longer followed valor: "I wish we had a lord with enough power and authority to take away riches and lands from the ignoble who do not deserve them, and give them to those who are deemed brave" ("a tal que fos pros et presatz"—which, he thought, was the way nobility began in the world); "and he should not regard lineage but change the status of the ignobly rich, as the Lombards do with their *podestà*"—"e no.i gardes linhatge, / e mudes hom los rics malvatz, / cum fan Lombart las poestatz."[77] Folquet seems to call for revolution from above, asserting that the "popular" structures of northern and central Italy were a triumph of meritocracy, which, the troubadours hoped, could give the troubadours their due within the feudal system.

The transition through each stage of the commune, from the consular and then the podestarial form, both dominated by the noblemen, to the popular form, dominated by the merchant guilds, and finally to the *signorie*, which around the end of the thirteenth century usually returned the power to an aristocratic family of ancient or recent blood, varies from region to region but shows common patterns, with occasional alliances between aristocratic and high ecclesiastical interests.[78]

In Milan the Della Torre were followed by the Visconti bishops; in Verona and Mantua the new *signori* got their power riding on the shoulders of the local guilds and the *popolo*, but soon, as was usual everywhere, they proceeded to divest the popular institutions of their influence and to ground the new government on the support of the signori's natural allies, the local aristocracy. In Ferrara the new lord Obizzo d'Este suppressed the guilds outright in 1287. There, as in Mantua, large scale patronage sealed the victory of despotism by turning over to the new lord's allies and acolytes all sorts of confiscated rural properties. In November 1283 Treviso witnessed a tense *coup-d'état* whereby Gherardo, head of the White (Guelf) party and of the influential noble family Da Camino, was popularly elected captain of the city and district and given absolute power to interpret the communal statutes according to his will. He immediately banned the rival Castelli feudal clan, leaders of the Red (Ghibelline) party, and confiscated their property. In Orvieto the long struggle between the *popolo* and the nobility ended in 1334, when the council of the *popolo* voted to suspend many constitutional clauses and handed full power over to Ormanno Monaldeschi, leader of the principal noble family, as "Gonfalonier of the Popolo and of Justice" for life.[79]

Starting early in the thirteenth century, the education of the ruling classes, which had passed from the hands of chaplains on to the cathedral schools and then to the courts, was shared, especially in Italy, by rhetoricians and masters of *ars dictandi*. The later humanists would inherit this role, since humanists were often lawyers and notaries who pursued their philological interests alongside their bureaucratic and administrative careers.[80] An early example of a militant notary is the famous Bologna professor of *ars notaria* Rolandino dei Passeggeri of Padua, who in 1274 captained the armed companies that drove the Ghibelline nobility from the city of Bologna. Rolandino had his counterparts in Brunetto in Florence, Ptolemy of Lucca in Lucca, and later Marsilius of Padua at the imperial court.[81]

In Italy, too, the cult of knighthood survived the loss of the military functionality of court knights, and chivalric models remained operative for centuries in everyday life. Huizinga's *The Waning of the Middle Ages* (1927) described the impassioned ritualization of chivalry at the court of Burgundy in the fifteenth century, but that court was only extreme, not unique: similar patterns of thinking and behaving were widespread, and Renaissance Italy was no exception. For anecdotal but typical examples, Martín de Riquer tells the stories of several of the

Aragonese knights who found the Italian courts a logical setting for bloody duels fought under extremely elaborate rules of chivalry. In 1432 the Marquis Niccolò d'Este summoned to Ferrara the Valencian knights Joan Tolsà and Joan Marrades for the armed encounter for which they had been desperately trying to find a worthy setting, with noble judges and witnesses. In 1457 Sigismondo Malatesta, signor of Rimini, agreed to convoke Pere Sarriera and Genís Miquel of Gerona to Rimini for a duel to the death, but realizing that the demanded conditions amounted to cruel suicide, he managed to arrange a solemn diplomatic reconciliation on the field of battle, resulting in great rejoicing of the whole court, and ending in the public dubbing of Miquel and of Sarriera's son. Splendid festivities followed, with dancing attended by Sigismondo's famous mistress, Isotta degli Atti. In 1465 the Duke of Milan, Francesco Sforza, agreed to sit as judge at the duel between the Portuguese João de Almada, Count of Abranches, and the prominent Navarrese knight Juan de Beaumont, to be held in Mantua.[82] We shall see that even in the sixteenth century and later, Italy remained a fertile ground for private challenges and spectacular duels of this sort.

The generation of Castiglione, Machiavelli, Ariosto, Guicciardini, and Bembo experienced what Guicciardini termed "the horrendous calamities" of the Italian wars, which brought out all the weaknesses of Italian social and political structures. It was difficult enough for regional powers to resist the onslaught of national foreign neighbors, but perhaps more decisive were the inner tensions of nobility versus high bourgeoisie, with the lower *popolo* being unwilling to display loyalty to systems that kept it outside any decision-making mechanism and oppressed it economically and fiscally. Spain and France could count on armies of citizens that felt much more united under their kings than was the case for any Italian populace. In the meantime, the disoriented and stunned ruling castes emulated the court aristocracy (made up of old nobility, high clergy, and ennobled high bourgeoisie) with a feeling of idealized cultural self-satisfaction that made them cling ever more tightly to their egotistical privileges, while their economic productivity had become disrupted and depressed by political and military vicissitudes.

The world of the courtiers was also the world of Italian diplomacy, which has been recognized as influential in shaping the typology of this varied profession for centuries.[83] To offset the Italian states' political, social, and military disadvantages, their diplomats had been hoping to "make the foxes masters of the lions": cunning should have had the best of sheer military force by using those behavioral principles of dis-simulation, calculation of interests and passions, oratorical persuasive-ness, and compromise which they had inherited from their "curial" medieval predecessors. The cleric and the courtier hoped to domi-nate knight and soldier and bend them to their interests. In vain, we now know.

In any event, in Italy and elsewhere court life changed and yet con-tinued to show certain similarities of patterns between A.D. 950 and the French Revolution. European courts gradually evolved from the feudal and then chivalric type to the monarchic centralism of Louis XIV, where both noblemen and high bourgeois administrators became dependent subjects of the king to a degree that had not yet been seen. Francis I marked the point of transition, when France saw the birth of aristo-cratic society. Some large fiefs still remained, but the king's law courts, staffed by the bourgeois personnel of the *parlements,*

> increasingly displaced the feudal administration and jurisdiction. . . . At the
> same time Francis I built up, beside the landowning nobility with its hierar-
> chy of fiefs, a new titular nobility extending from the simple noblemen to the
> princes and peers of France. . . . As early as the second half of the sixteenth
> century almost all the names of the aristocracy are new names.

What the king rewarded in this manner was military service. "As before, therefore, the nobility was a military estate."[84] Hence one thing re-mained constant in the midst of these social upheavals: the *homines novi,* like the old feudal lords, were warriors, and their mentality con-tinued to hinge on certain moral principles that we see reflected, with the necessary adaptations, in the literary genres that concern us.

It seems fair to assimilate the changes in Italian society to this grand pattern of evolution. The secular courts of Castiglione or the ecclesias-tical ones of Paolo Cortesi were, in their mixture of new aristocrats of the sword, bourgeois mercantile tycoons, and high bureaucrats, analo-gous to the French court and different from the displaced medieval feu-dal nobility. At the same time they harbored cultural and moral images which were an adapted inheritance from medieval chivalry.[85]

Should we choose to look further, we would find French society growing stronger from the sixteenth century on, just as Italian society declined with the waning strength of its independent entrepreneurial merchant class after 1500. The French bourgeoisie continued to play a vital role through the nobility of the robe centered in the *parlements,* for which there was no equivalent in Italy after 1500. The relative cultural lag of Italy versus France after 1600 had its superficial manifestations in the literature of the two countries, but our subject here is the themes and forms of chivalry and courtliness, which is one part of that broader story.

FURTHER SUGGESTIONS

Despite its extended ideological impact, the feudal regime enjoyed a relatively short life in western Europe, achieving its full maturity in the twelfth century. But besides the vertical ramifications that, as we shall see, extend feudalism up and down a long chronological span even to our own time, our theme can also have horizontal ramifications that overlap its European geographic boundaries. Indeed, the study of the triangular relationship among feudal structures, chivalric ideology, and literature should gain by being extended beyond Europe. To illustrate the avenues that would open up to a comparative exploration of feudalism's cultural dimensions it should suffice to extract some elements that parallel the ones I am about to retrace in western Europe.

Knights and clerics were cosmopolitan classes in the Middle Ages, and good travelers, too. The Norman horsemen about whom we shall hear a good deal were active from Norway to northern France, Sicily, and Anatolia in the tenth and eleventh centuries. They operated by the thousands as mercenary soldiers in the Byzantine empire.[86] Like the West, only with more dire consequences, the Byzantine empire witnessed in those centuries a fierce struggle between the military party and the court bureaucrats, vying with each other for supremacy even while the Turks were waiting at the borders, ready to invade Anatolia under propitious circumstances. The generals were large provincial landowners with long military experience through many generations. Not unlike the western ministerials, the bureaucrats, mostly around the court of Constantinople, were clerics, intellectuals (like Psellos, intimate of Michael VII Ducas, emperor since 1071), and functionaries, some with landed property to back up their influence and power. The dissension between the two parties prompted both to seek support outside the regular army, in mercenary armies of foreigners like Normans, Slavs, and even Turks, with the result that foreign armed groups managed, as they had once done within the Roman empire, to take advantage of their entry into the state system until they could openly go to the attack and eventually overrun the whole region.[87] A consequence of these changes was the decline of the free peasantry, forced to give up their land to the generals and high clergy. Since these latter acquired progressive exemptions from the taxes that the free peasants had been paying, the state was deprived of precious tax moneys. The peasants, now disenchanted and less productive, became serfs (*paroicoi*) of the secular and church magnates. It was the conclusion of a process that, "for want of a better word, must be described as 'feudalization.'" [88]

The most extensive experiments in feudal organization probably took place in eastern Asia, and I shall summarize them in a way that demonstrates some of the analogies with European phenomena treated in the forthcoming analysis. In its centuries-long variations, the Confucian doctrine which dominated Chinese life generally emphasized loyalty (*chu* in Japan), moral reform, reason as distinct from (alternatively opposed to or cooperating with) instinct or desire (the basis of violence and warfare), subordination of private to public good, and the cult of family (*ko* in Japan) and ancestors. These were some of the more elementary teachings of Confucius (551–479 B.C.), a scholar of court ritual and music who later turned to moral philosophy and the teaching of government and social ethics. It is easy to see the analogy of such principles with those of western curiality and courtliness which shall be described presently. The Confucian cult of ancestors displaced the Chinese aristocratic tradition of regarding ancestors as the divine source of power and privilege. Believing that the individual is responsible for his own actions, that only the virtuous and capable are entitled to govern, and that ability and character are developed by education through formal schooling, Confucius taught that those in power must be able to choose capable ministers (like the western courtiers and ministerials) to whom to delegate all administrative authority.

His most influential successor, Mencius (late fourth century B.C.), was an itinerant philosopher going from court to court to teach compassion and virtue as a more successful way of governing than self-seeking guile or force. Belief in the inherent goodness of human nature was the humanistic foundation of this moral philosophy. The Orthodox Neo-Confucianism of Chu Hsi (1130–1200) became the official state doctrine in China from his time to the end of the empire in 1911, with a relative revival after the conservative victory of Chang Kai-shek in 1926.

Confucianism had a powerful influence in Japan, where a characteristic form of feudalism embodied in the class of *daimyo* ("great names") ruled from the late twelfth century until 1869, when the new Meiji regime forced the daimyo to turn their lands over to the emperor. Not unlike the high courtiers and great knights we are about to meet, these feudal barons were dedicated warriors as well as educated practitioners of the arts, which they also patronized at their courts. Above them sat the shoguns, who derived their authority directly from the emperor at Kyoto. The samurai or professional warriors, developing into a class since the tenth century, ranked immediately below the daimyo. Like the emperor and the shoguns, the daimyo held court at their towns of residence, at the center of the territory they owned hereditarily and governed as military leaders, provincial magistrates, legislators, and judges. Their court culture included the aptitude to administer according to the learned ways of the imperial court, and consisted of a combination, developed under Chinese influence, of the arts of war (*bu*) with the arts of peace (*bun*), the latter serving as a way to legitimize the former. This is in close parallel with the combination of knightly militarism and the civilizing arts of courtesy and humaneness that we shall observe in the West.

The regime of the daimyo, which superseded the previous system of public domain, fragmented the country into a set of personal power centers subjected to the nominal authority of the shoguns. The four-teenth- and fifteenth-century *shugo daimyo* were appointed by the Ashi-kaga shoguns, a dynasty of hereditary military warlords, and in turn they appointed their own vassals to rule over minor fiefs. After 1467 a period of chronic civil war set in, with *sengoku daimyo* ruling independently together with their vassals and waging war against their neighboring rivals. In 1603 Tokugawa Ieyasu (d. 1616) was recognized as leader of the daimyo and started the long, peaceful period of the Tokugawa shogunate that lasted until 1867. By administrative and juridical measures Ieyasu managed to constrain the daimyo as well as the imperial court nobles, the clerics, and his own vassals. To ensure his succession, in 1605 he made his son Hidetada supreme shogun or generalissimo. Hidetada managed to force the daimyo to build a huge new palace at Edo (present-day Tokyo) at their expense and with their labor; by 1614 Edo had become the Versailles of Japan, with the daimyo living in nearby mansions as court nobles and practically as hostages. The analogy with Versailles is striking. The daimyo, who toward the end of the period became a parasitic aristocratic class, were classified by their relationship to the ruling shogun, that is, as kinsmen, hereditary vassals (*fudai*), or allies. Their spiritual and martial education took place mainly in the temples and focused on writing, reading, philosophy, religion, literature, and the fine arts. Neo-Confucianism, originally

propagated by Zen Buddhist masters, was the guiding principle of the
Tokugawa regime all along, and was characterized by mind-to-mind
instruction from master to disciple rather than reliance on scripture and
set doctrine—similar to the method of the imperial and episcopal chapels to be described in my next chapter.[89]

It would be rewarding to interpret the courtly and knightly elements
in the literatures of China and Japan by comparing them systematically
to their analogous manifestations in the West. Court novels and diaries
reached an unparalleled degree of sophistication in Japan around the
year 1000, the period of such masterpieces as Lady Murasaki Shikibu's
(ca. 978 to ca. 1031) *Genji monogatari* ("The Tale of Genji," ca.
1001–1008) and Sei Shonagon's (ca. 966 to after 1013) *Makura-no-
soshi* ("The Pillow Book," ca. 1000–1015). One wonders about the
analogies that might result from an investigation of the cultural and
literary constants emerging from the literature of such disparate yet inherently similar feudal societies.

PART TWO

The Ethical Codes

CHAPTER TWO

The Origins of Courtliness

CURIALES AND COURTIER BISHOPS

Although the evidence is limited, it seems clear that at least since Carolingian times a court was conceived as a formative milieu. In his highly descriptive household book *De ordine palatii* (A.D. 882), Archbishop Hincmar of Reims, a good authority on courts, defined the formative function of the court by calling it a school, *scola*, not in the sense of an institution of formal teachers (*scolastici*), but of a group of leaders who by discipline and constraint, *disciplina id est correctio*, affect their peers' and juniors' "behavior, bearing, speech, deeds, and the general restraints of a good life."[1] Hincmar also defined the head chaplain (*archicapellanus*) as the grand chancellor in charge of secretarial and archival functions as well as of the palatine school proper. It is amply documented that from at least as early as the tenth through the thirteenth and fourteenth centuries and beyond, the courts acted as centers of social education by developing a continuous ethos of curial/courtly values.

In Germany and France the period 950–1150 saw the emergence of remarkable teachers in royal courts (*curiae*) as well as in cathedral schools largely influenced by the royal courts. They were "curial" teachers insofar as they issued from courtly environments, and the substance of their teaching can be called "curiality" (*curialitas*) since it first aimed at the formation of good candidates for positions at court. True enough, we get little hard evidence about "government" being the Ottonian courtiers' original concern, nor do historians tell us much about this.[2] But the scarcity of direct documents before 1150 is a result of the "Socratic" attitude of these teachers, who left practically nothing to writing because they acted through personal and oral communication. Their numerous extant biographies share the rhetorical image of educators whose effectiveness rested on eloquence and example, even in the absence of original or substantive content. Jaeger does not hesitate to call their ideas and methods "humanistic."[3] Pupils worshiped their masters to the point of feeling that they could acquire excellence, virtue, and personal greatness by imitating their noble and dignified bearing. Adelman, for one, praised Fulbert's student Hildegar for having taken over his master's "facial expression, tone of voice, and manners": "magistrum referebat vultu, voce, moribus."[4]

As Fleckenstein has emphasized, Otto the Great found a new use for scholars. No longer merely teachers, as at Charlemagne's court, nor simply erudite men of God, as the monastic schools conceived them, they became the building blocks of a solid administrative foundation for the empire. Acting through the various diocesan centers, this "royal priesthood," *regale sacerdotium*, their wisdom gleaned from literary scholarship, assisted the king in matters of state: "[ut] rem publicam fide et viribus tuerentur," "to preserve the state by their faith and strength."[5]

As to the content of their teaching, the apparent connection with later humanism is a Platonic emphasis on ethics as the core of education and learning: even physics, cosmology, and astronomy could be conceived as proof of the divine order of the universe, which man must imitate in his moral and aesthetic behavior. Jaeger (1987: 580–591) sees this as the true reason for the popularity of Plato's *Timaeus* in the eleventh and twelfth centuries in both Germany and France. Typically those teachers, down to the masters of Chartres, emphasized the coupling of letters and virtue, *litterae et mores*, aiming at character formation rather than mere instruction or Christian doctrine.[6] According to the biographer of Abbot Angelran of St. Riquier, Fulbert of Chartres taught Angelran letters as much as virtue and manners: "hic ei monitor, hic tam morum quam litterarum fuit institutor."[7] John of Salisbury saw a harmonious coupling of morals and aesthetics as the goal for a true rhetoric when he declared *ethica* the source of *gratia decoris*, the gracefulness of a beautiful deportment, and Onulf of Speyer professed a study of rhetoric as the source of *morum elegantia*.[8] Despite the dangers of uncritical superficiality, subjective cult of personality and fashion, and insensitivity to substance, such attitudes remind us of the most illustrious heir of this cultural approach, Francesco Petrarca. He not only managed to turn himself into the object of a Europe-wide personality cult even before his writings had become widely accessible, but also professed the clear superiority of eloquence (or rhetoric) to philosophy by extolling the power of moral improvement inherent in poetic texts such as Virgil's, in contrast to Aristotle's pragmatic aridity, even when dealing with virtue in the *Nicomachean Ethics*.[9]

Teachers of this sort were influential members of their societies and became cultural models for generations to come: "A career followed by many of the most distinguished imperial bishops since Ottonian times led from student to schoolmaster to court chaplain to bishop, with perhaps stations in between as provost or chancellor" (Jaeger 1987: 589). The masters of *curialitas*, future imperial bishops, had typically been, first, *magistri scholarum* or headmasters, namely the practical teachers subordinated to the *scholasticus* (Fr. *écolastre*), administrator of all religious schools in the diocese starting with the cathedral school. If the *magister*'s main concern was *boni* or *nobiles mores*, that is, the moral content of indoctrination, he had to reach it through the propaedeutic curriculum of the liberal arts, more specifically the arts of the Trivium which were centered on the reading of literary *auctores*. The substance of the curriculum was a combination of *litterae* and *mores* in varying degrees. This formula remained the staple of courtly education even as late as Castiglione, for whom "good masters teach children not only letters, but also good and seemly manners in eating, drinking, speaking and walking, with appropriate gestures."[10]

By the twelfth century, cathedral schools like the one at Chartres had overtaken imperial chapels and episcopal courts as the primary centers of education for statesmen and bureaucrats through the instillation of the curial ideology. The nomenclature consistently employed in all these centers can rightly be regarded as humanistic, and contained clear echoes of the "Carolingian Renaissance": in Alcuin's *Dialogus de rhetorica et virtutibus*, for example, the coupling, even in the title, of rhetoric and ethic, in the best Aristotelian, Ciceronian, and Quintilianean tradition, contrasted with the dialectically-grounded reduction of rhetoric to style and ornament at the hands of the later Scholastics. Alcuin typically addressed himself to those who aimed at civil manners, "civiles cupiat cognoscere mores," and at inner and outer moral beauty, gesture and manners included: "disce, precor, juvenis, motus moresque venustos" (*Patrologia Latina*, hereafter *PL*, 101: 919, 950).

The considerable number of surviving biographies of bishops document the standards of morality and social conduct for court-appointed bishops and high prelates. Episcopal *vitae* and related tracts predicated a mixture of Christian virtues overlaid on a range of somewhat heterogeneous Ciceronian/Stoic ones. We could list them as: *formositas* (beauty), *eruditio* (education or learning), *virtus* (encompassing eloquence as *eloquentia* or *facundia*), *mansuetudo*, *discretio* or *reticentia*, *amabilitas*, and *mensura* (Jaeger: 30–48). *Mansuetudo*, surely an unheroic quality, included patience in the face of offense: the *Roman de la rose* 1.39: 1236–1237 said of the allegorical figure Cortoisie: "donc ne fut hom par li deditz, / ne ne porta autrui rancune," "never spoke ill of anyone, nor did she bear rancor toward anyone." Discretion or reticence was meant as calculated underplaying of talents, somewhat analogous to Castiglione's *sprezzatura*. *Mensura*—also *moderamen* or *moderatio*, originally the Aristotelian *mesotes*, balance between opposite extremes—also included a sort of diplomacy that allowed the subject to survive under the most trying circumstances without taking a dangerous stand on matters of principle. The whole was made effective by a cultivated personal charm of the type that we would now call charisma (Jaeger 1987: 595).

A more articulate portrait of the courtly type included, within the ethical framework of *elegantia morum: disciplina* (self-restraint), *urbanitas* (entailing eloquence), *kalokagathia* (harmony of inner and outer man), and, under the rubric of behavioral patterns, *decorum, facetia, hilaritas/jocunditas*, and *curialitas*, a comprehensive term.[11] We are about to see how this schema also subsumed an aptitude for connivance and a taste for intrigue. These two qualities were seldom mentioned explicitly yet they were clearly represented in the literature; they were also part of the needed self-restraint in the face of the warrior/ knight's tendency to act boldly on first impulse and without regard to consequences.[12] All these courtly qualities would contrast directly with the image of the chivalrous gentleman and knight as frank, straightforward, and naively loyal.

Kalokagathia, rooted in the classical notion of symbiosis of the beautiful and the good, and deeply embedded in the Greek paideia ever since Isocrates, could be defined as perfect rectitude united with urbanity and good breeding. It implied qualities clearly at work in the images of the Ottonian and Salian royal bishops. Capellanus seemed to have such a distinction in mind when he coupled *curialitas* (as the outer refinement that, together with *liberalitas*, makes the lover socially attractive) with *probitas* (the inner virtue that makes the lover truly lovable).[13] This aestheticizing of manners and conduct as part of an ideal education remained operative through Castiglione and beyond.[14]

When, in the 1589 letter to Raleigh that became a preface to his *Faerie Queene*, Edmund Spenser declared his intent "to fashion a gentleman or noble person in vertuous and gentle discipline," this key word "discipline" was the equivalent of a medieval semantic coinage that originated in Germany both in Latin and in the vernacular.[15] Classical Latin *disciplina* had meant only learning and art, as in "the school disciplines." Medieval Latin added the connotation of monastic rule and/or chastisement. But in eleventh- and twelfth-century Germany, *curiales disciplinae* (*hövesche zühte*), like the singular *elegans et urbana disciplina* (*schöne und hövesche zuht*), became common terms, all hovering around the clerical intellectual circles of towns and courts (especially about the court chapels). They signified the kind of elegant self-control that distinguishes the moral makeup and outward behavior of the sophisticated courtier.[16]

Somewhat paradoxically, the resolution of the investiture conflict in favor of the Church did not strengthen but, rather, scaled down the once lofty moral and cultural status of the bishops. The Bamberg schoolmaster Hugo of Trimberg eloquently lamented the decline of the episcopate toward the end of the thirteenth century, nostalgically evoking the imposing personalities of the past. Their likes were no longer thinkable because the Church, now free to place its own candidates, had no more reason to select strong personalities with the impressive courtly qualities once at home at the imperial court:

> Sant Otten, sant Annen, sant Gothart
> Und sant Thomas von Kandelberc
> Brâhte ir zuht und reiniu werc
> Ze hofe an hôhe wirdikeit.
> (*Renner* 782–785; Jaeger 255)

(St. Otto of Bamberg, St. Anno of Cologne, St. Godehard of Hildesheim, and St. Thomas Becket of Canterbury attained high honor at court by their courtesy and their good works.)

These were, indeed, some of the great figures whose *vitae* allow us to reconstruct the court ambiance from which courtly behavior had issued. At the same time that this decay in high ecclesiastical offices was taking place, the literary romances lost their roots in social reality, among both the clergy and the laity. The thirteenth century is one of imitation and

pessimism: King Arthur is "dead," and the compilations of the great
cycles tell of the dissolution of his once great court.[17]

A CICERONIAN CONNECTION

With its largely Stoic philosophical content, Cicero's *De officiis* was a
major source of ethical speculation in the Middle Ages, its impact being
enhanced by the important intermediary of St. Ambrose's version of it.
The term *officia* appeared in the titles of numerous derivations from
St. Ambrose, starting with St. Isidore, whose *De ecclesiasticis officiis*
turned the focus further toward Christian cult, down to the two treatises *De divinis officiis* by Rupert of Deutz (twelfth century) and Durand
de Mende (thirteenth). It has been noted that Cicero's *officia*, which can
be rendered as "civic duty," was somewhat of a mistranslation of his
Stoic model, Panaitios's *Perì tou kathékontos*, where *kathékon* meant
"what is becoming" to social function, individual condition, and the
status of citizen. Cicero developed his theme in a somewhat meandering
way by embroidering around the cardinal virtues of justice, fortitude,
temperance, and prudence, insisting repeatedly on the centrality, particularly for the public servant, of what he called *honestum*, a term
which, in turn, can be rendered as "the moral good" or "the morally
beautiful," corresponding closely to Greek *tò kalón*. In book 3 Cicero
argued at length that *honestum* and *utile* cannot be in conflict: when
properly understood they practically coincide. Speaking of the apt use
of speech (2.48), he pointed to the power of "comitas affabilitasque
sermonis" in winning friendship and influence, with an interesting coupling of courtesy and affability as aspects of effective speech.[18]

The qualities analyzed in *De officiis* (especially 1.93–1.113) that
bear more directly on the new curial ideal were those of urbanity (*urbanitas*), modesty, moderation, restraint, considerateness (*verecundia*),
and self-control in the sense of subjection of passion to reason, all subsumed under the rubric of *temperantia*, the fourth cardinal virtue, like
the other major quality of *decorum*, which also includes *reverentia* or
reverence toward deserving men (116 f.). All these qualities, together
with *affabilitas* and *iocunditas* or *hilaritas*, affability and good disposition, win friendship, and act both through decorous speech, which
includes *facetia*, *iocus*, and *urbanitas* (Gr. *eiróneia*), and decorous bearing, which includes a beautiful appearance (*formositas*), grace (*ornatus*), and cleanliness in dress (*munditia*). Once again, we can think
ahead to the German terms *schöne sîte* and *schöne zuht* as well as to

Castiglione's *grazia*. Cicero ascribed this type of behavior particularly to the statesman, whose public service it aids and enhances, thus making him a more valuable member of society and a more heroic citizen than the warrior with his military prowess (115 f.).

Let us look at some key passages (1.27.93–94, 98, 107):

> We must next speak of the one remaining part of *honestas*, wherein we find reverence (*verecundia*) and a certain ornament of life, temperance, modesty, and all restraint of the perturbations of the soul, together with a sense of measure in all things. Here is contained what Latins call *decorum*, the Greeks *prepon*. The force of this quality is such that it cannot be separated from honesty: indeed, what is becoming is honest, and what is honest is becoming. . . . Similar is the nature of fortitude. For what is done with a manly and great soul appears worthy of a man and dignified, whereas whatever is contrary to this is morally ugly, hence unbecoming.

> Hence poets will see what is becoming in the great variety of their characters, even the vicious ones; as to ourselves, whatever nature has given us in the form of constancy, moderation, temperance, and reverence, and since nature teaches us not to overlook the manner in which we act toward others, it is clear how wide the realm of dignified behavior (*decorum*) is, to wit what is part and parcel of honesty as a whole, as well as what pertains to every single kind of virtue.

> We all partake of reason and of that quality by which we are above the beasts, from which we derive all honesty and dignity (*honestum decorumque*) as well as the method of finding out what duty is.[19]

Note this gathering of key concepts: *verecundia, ornatus, temperantia, modestia, decorum, fortitudo, animus magnus, constantia, honestum, ratio*, and also the closeness of *decorum* (or its synonym *decor*) and *honestum*, yielding an insight into their ethical and social connotations. These terms constitute an important segment of the broad semantic field of Latin *decorum/decor/decus*. The term "decoration," still applied today to a social status or dignity that is added for its display value as "an ornament of life," is etymologically and semantically derived from *decor* and *decus*. It first appeared in this acceptation in medieval French *décorement*, with its allied adjective *aournez*.

Besides the *De officiis*, Cicero's *Disputationes Tusculanae* was the source of ethical teaching for a number of didactic tracts from Germany and, later, France between 1000 and 1150. Acclaimed by Meinhard of Bamberg as the foremost work of philosophy from ancient Rome, it was a suitable source for teachers of state administrators, inculcating the twofold message that we must make ready for the trials of public life and be able to find ascetic consolation in the contemplation of higher wisdom and philosophical truths in case of serious upsets.[20] There the medieval moralist could find pagan confirmation for an Augustinian attitude toward the state, respecting authority as worthy of service and obedience while being prepared for the worst excesses of tyrants and perverts in power. Furthermore, in that work Cicero assessed the originality of Roman practical ethics in terms that suited the great moral teachers of curiality in the eleventh century, since teaching by doing and by example kept both early Romans and medieval masters too busy to write philosophical speculations. Thus Cicero's recipe for a successful public career accorded with another characteristic of eleventh/twelfth-century thinking and speaking on the primacy of the practical versus the merely intellectual, and the moral versus the merely cognitive. It did so by stressing, as the medieval literature of curiality repeatedly did, the coupling of virtue and beauty, the moral and the aesthetic, inner and outer behavior. The life of the wise public man was perceived as beautiful in itself and successful precisely by virtue of its aesthetically attractive and persuasive qualities. Likewise, Heraclius of Liège (d. 971), his mid-twelfth-century biographer tells us, was equal to the greatest philosophers not only for his mastery of human and divine learning, but especially because "his splendid manners gilded his physical beauty," "presertim cum venustatem corporis mores etiam inaurarant splendidi."[21] He was a forerunner of the mentality that students of fifteenth-century Italian humanism have labeled "civic humanism" ever since the studies of Hans Baron and Eugenio Garin, a mentality that harmonized with Cicero's emphasis on the life of the public servant as morally beautiful if based on *honestum, decorum*, and *tò kalón*.[22]

Admittedly, the tenor of the *De officiis* is rather remote from the specific context of the courtier's behavior: a comparative reading of pertinent works bears out the originality of the literature of courtliness and courtesy. The more concrete traits of the courtier bishop could hardly be derived from the rather non-specific, relatively vague compilatory lucubrations of the great orator and influential moralist. Yet, the impact of Cicero's ethical framework on later developments concerning civil service is clear and widespread.[23] More generally, we must be aware that all established educational methods, the ancient, the medieval, and those of the Renaissance (as well as the ancient Chinese and Japanese, as examples of non-Western ones), have traditionally aimed at producing civic leaders, orators, and bureaucratic officials rather than, say, creative writers. This explains how, even while a liberal education was traditionally centered on the extensive reading of the classical literary heritage, the curricula favored works with a moral and civic content, thus emphasizing oratory and historiography and slanting the reading of poetic or narrative texts by interpreting them for their presumed ethical content. The Homeric cycles and Virgil, for example, were annotated as allegories of civic wisdom and social leadership. What we perceive as original, individual poetic qualities were downplayed or ignored.

In essence, the medieval civic ethos derived, through Cicero and other authorities, from the classical (mostly Stoic) system of the cardinal virtues of prudence, fortitude, justice, and temperance as reinterpreted by the Christian fathers. This civic ethos would later be extended from the formation of the curial courtier to that of the knight. In the process, in both courtly and chivalric ethics, prudence was commonly defined as knowing what is fitting and acting accordingly; temperance as moderation from excess and pride; fortitude as valor and bravery; and justice as service to the weak and the needy, especially if they were victims of injustice. Prudence came to include cunning in courtliness while fortitude became daring adventurousness in chivalry, as a means to prove one's true worth. Of course, the classical, traditional sense was betrayed here, since the typical excesses of the knights' adventurousness defied prudence and also contravened the attendant virtue of moderation or measure. Nevertheless, the knight who exceeded (i.e., when the story explicitly presented his behavior as excessive) was punished with failure. Moderation, in turn, was a standard virtue in the Middle Ages. One explicit example is John of Hauteville's *Architrenius*, a moral allegory of 1184–1190 dedicated to John of Coutances, bishop of Lincoln, and dealing with Architrenius's search for Nature to overcome the evils of the world. After visiting, in vain, the Palace of Venus, the University of Paris, the Mount of Ambition, the Hill of Presumption, and even "Ultima Thule," Architrenius manages to find Nature, who happily ends his quest by giving him Moderation as wife.

EVOLUTION OF THE CURIAL ETHOS

From the late tenth century on, a pattern of behavior appropriate to a successful life at court was a prerequisite for the pursuit of an episcopal seat.[24] Despite the traditional inclination not to go further back than twelfth-century French and Provençal vernacular literature, the origins of courtliness are Latin rather than vernacular: it suffices to take a look at Du Cange and the indices to the *Scriptores* Series in the *Monumenta Germaniae Historica.*[25] The symbiosis of outer and inner honesty is reflected in a persistent terminology of *elegantia morum, venustas morum, gratia morum,* and *pulchritudo morum,* which moves alongside the allied perception of *decor* and *disciplina.* Another term, *humanitas,* also occurs early in contexts that betray their Ciceronian heritage with a ring of later humanistic perceptions. In the mid-eleventh century Meinhard of Bamberg spoke of *lepor humanitatis:* "Est enim vir ille omni genere virtutis instructus, omni lepore humanitatis mirifice conditus."[26] Hugh of St. Victor (ca. 1096–1141) spoke of *disciplina* as an inner habit that keeps instincts and passions in check and as an outer form which confers a convenient dignity on appearance, gesture, speech, and behavior in public, specifically at the table.[27] Hugh saw *gestus, habitus, gressus, incessus, motus corporis, locutio, cibus,* and *potus,* namely gesture, comportment, gait, way of walking, movements of the body, speech, and ways of eating and drinking, as signs of inner virtue (*De institutione novitiorum*). These were not mere rhetorical topoi conventionally repeated, since they occur within specific pragmatic contexts.

This emphasis on the aesthetic aspects of virtue and on the importance of outer signs of inner dispositions was clearly part of the political dimension of the special ethos for public administrators and social leaders. The idea was powerful enough to affect the sensibilities of contemporaries in other social and intellectual spheres. Performing exegesis upon the line "The Lord desireth your beauty" in Psalm 92, St. Bernard of Clairvaux (d. 1153) wondered: "What is beauty of soul (*decor*)? Is it perhaps what we call moral beauty (*honestum*)? But whenever the luminosity (*claritas*) of this beauty fills the heart's inner depths, it must needs overflow and surge outward, . . . and then the beauty of the soul will become outwardly visible."[28] We are struck by the precise echoes of Cicero, and we also note the artistic-sounding and sensuous term *claritas,* destined to become a key term in Thomas Aquinas's aesthetic.

In his *Dialogus de vita Sancti Ottonis episcopi Babenbergensis,* Herbord of Michelsberg (1159) attributed to Otto of Bamberg a *composicio,* or harmonization, between the inner man and his outward behavior—*elegans et urbana disciplina*—where we can note the aestheticizing notion of the beauty of manners as a distinguishing trait of the élite, to be admired, imitated, and respected. Similarly, in a letter of Guido de Basochis (cleric of St. Stephen of Châlons, d. 1203) to Archbishop Henry of Reims, two qualities are singled out as pertinent "to

the elegant bearing of a person of high status," "ad elegantiorem personae dignioris ornatum," that is, "high birth and a shining appearance
of manners," "imperiosa generis dignitas . . . et lucidior morum venustas."[29] Such notions would play a role in courtly societies to come.

In consequence of these advertised prerequisites, the courtier became
"the master of his every word and act, of his diction and gestures. . . .
The mask and the disguise became major psychic vestments of the
courtier" (Jaeger: 7). The courtly code is an assurance of the courtier's
aptitude or fitness (*idoneitas*) for the fulfillment of his political function.
The *amabilitas* of the Ottonian chaplain, hence of the courtier bishop,
included the attitude of affability, which in Castiglione aimed at winning and maintaining the favor of the prince—the *cortegiano*'s raison
d'être according to the conclusive fourth book (Jaeger: 43).

Courtoisie, hövescheit, and *cortesia* are the vernacular code words
for a type of conduct that the medieval cleric/courtier had fashioned for
himself on the basis of ancient ideals of the Greek *asteîos anér* (= urban, hence urbane < *ástu* "town") and the Roman *urbanus*, endowed
with *urbanitas*, as opposed to the *rusticus* (Gr. *agroîcos*).[30] The concept
of urbanity as synonym for civilized behavior extended with greater
force of logic to the culture of the burgher towns, while its etymological
counterpart of rusticity was reflected in that scorn for the peasant which
pervades medieval lyrics and chivalric romances and which is implied
in the frequent references to the *rusticus* (Fr. *vilain*, G. *dörperlich*). We
are dealing here with a shifting code for the ruling classes. The Greek
city states had set off the ideal of the *asteîos anér* against the mores of
the subjected countryside. In the Middle Ages clerical commoners protested their inner nobility and nobility of manners against the privileges
of the aristocracy. In the Renaissance, this *elegantia morum* became the
distinguishing trait of a new, non-feudal court nobility.

The perception of the courtier's role is a chapter in the history of the
ancient, medieval, and Renaissance debate on the relative merits of *vita
activa* and *vita contemplativa*. A relevant text is a small treatise from
the 1220s in the genre of education of princes, to wit Johannes of Limoges's *Morale somnium Pharaonis*. When Joseph fears that entering
the king's service will cause envy and lead to worldly distractions, Pharaoh admonishes him: "Is it not worse for you to fear the loss of life
than to fear the extinction of justice and fairness in the kingdom? Is it
not more glorious to die in the active struggle for justice than to wait
passively for sickness and old age to produce the same effect?" (*Epistolae* 8, 8 ff.).[31] This was a positive view of the active duties of rulers

and counselors, who must leave contemplation and prayer to those who
do not carry the burden of government. This ethic of worldly service
developed by court clerics eventually contributed to the civilizing of the
nobility and the formulation of the type of knight and lover that we find
in the courtly lyric and the chivalric romance; it is still detectable as
background to the model Renaissance courtier.

MONASTIC REACTIONS

Orthodox ascetic monasticism took a critical stance of varying sharp-
ness against the worldliness of these attitudes, with Peter Damian (Petrus Damiani) as the foremost among such early critics (*Contra clericos
aulicos*, ca. 1072).[32] Reformers' tracts turned the virtues of *aulici* and
curiales on their heads and treated them as canonical vices, seeing modesty as false submissiveness, affability as obsequiousness, and zeal as
downright ambition, leading to intrigue. All along, clerics had been exerting their civilizing influence by functioning as court educators, so
that when chivalry was adopted by the nobles, it was also a sublime
ideal resulting from intellectual education and character formation.
But with typical sarcasm, Peter of Blois would charge that the courtly
clerics' pretense of aiming at "the alleged correction and instruction
of kings" ("ad correctionem et instructionem regum, inquiunt, missi
sunt") was nothing but a cover for their true motive: ambition.

The canonical literature of court criticism was part of the large motif
of the topsy-turvy world that in the seventeenth century would become
a major topic of baroque literature. One must, however, keep in mind
that this distaste for courtly ways did not affect the reformers' attitudes
toward secular authority's divinely-sanctioned role, which the Church
viewed as an essential part of the social order. Peter Damian, for one,
displayed full respect for the role of *milites saeculares*, including the
need for *bellatores* as *defensores* of Church people, and he regretted
that, in the absence of adequate defense from the weak secular authorities, clerics were forced into the distasteful task of defending themselves
by bearing arms.[33]

A most prolific center of court criticism was the court of Henry II of
England (1154–1189), with such authorities as Gerald of Wales (Gir-
aldus Cambrensis, *De principis instructione*), Nigel Wireker (*Tractatus
contra curiales et officiales clericos*),[34] Herbert of Bosham, Walter Map
(ca. 1140—ca. 1210: *De nugis curialium*),[35] and especially John of Salisbury (1115/20–1180)[36] and his disciple, Peter of Blois. To this im-

pressive list we must add, as court critic in deed rather than word, the unfortunate Thomas Becket, Henry II's chancellor and archbishop of Canterbury (d. 1170). After a lively and contrasted career as a courtier, Peter of Blois spoke of envy and avarice as the scourges of courts, and of himself as their victim. It was he who coined the phrase *miseriae curialium*, later borrowed by Aeneas Silvius Piccolomini as title for his own anticourt tract, the *De curialium miseriis epistola*.[37]

The orthodox ascetic milieus had always held to an austere view of moral life that took issue with one distinct feature of courtliness: *hilaritas* or *iocunditas*. Whereas praiseworthy courtiers, bishops, and rulers were regularly described as always ready to show good humor and jolly temperament, St. Bernard of Clairvaux sternly reminded his monks of Ecclesiastes 7.5: "Cor stultorum, ubi laetitia," "gaiety dwells in the heart of the fool," even associating *laetitia* with the most heinous sin, pride: "Proprium est superborum, laeta semper appetere et tristia devitare."[38] This was part of his general condemnation of the world of chivalry as a synthesis of all worldly vices: "they spout abominable mimes, magic and fabulous tales, obscene songs, and idle spectacles, like vanities and lying insanities."[39] We shall see how within the rigoristic monastic circles this distrust of courtly ways accompanied an underlying suspicion of chivalry that had a powerful political motivation: that is, the strong alliance that tied some leading monasteries and cathedrals to centralizing, antifeudal monarchic policies. Cluny, Chartres, and Saint-Denis (this latter under the formidable leadership of the great Abbot Suger) were firmly collaborating with monarchy.[40]

FROM *CURIALES* TO COURTIERS

Interestingly enough, the strong reaction in courtly circles to his Epistle 14 soon compelled Peter of Blois to recant in his Epistle 150 (*PL 207*: 439–442): "Indeed, I acknowledge the sanctity of assisting our royal lord." He went on quoting Horace: "Having pleased our leaders is not the last of merits," adding, for good measure: "I deem it to be worthy of not simply praise but glory to be of help to a royal lord and to the state, to be unconcerned about one's own self, and to belong completely to all people."[41] The last phrase was a recurrent topos of the literature on the courtly cleric, ultimately derived from Paul's *omnia omnibus factus sum*, "a man for all seasons."

I have mentioned that the courtier's aptitude for calculation and intrigue was conspicuous in the literature though seldom defined as a spe-

cific psychological quality. The *Facetus de moribus et vita*, a mid-
twelfth century versified manual of behavior which established a minor
genre of didactic poems known by the same title, can boast a sort of
priority in setting a canon of prudent dissimulation in public behavior
for the sake of avoiding unnecessary offense.[42] It admonishes us to use
restraint and be considerate of others by lying at the proper time, for to
speak the truth at all time is counterproductive: "Esto verecundus, falsum quandoque loquaris, / Nam semper verum dicere crede nephas."[43]
Once again, we are bound to think ahead to Castiglione's advice concerning a prudent dissimulation as an essential part of the art of surviving and thriving at court.

Even more intriguing is that the *Facetus* conceived of both humanity
and the civilized state as products of human "art," art being innate in
man as a *potentia*, which it is up to the individual to bring forth into
actuality: "Ars hominem format" (86), and "habet omnis homo quo se
possit fabricare."[44] A remarkable thought indeed, with a clear "pre-
humanistic" sound. Jaeger (168) may be overstressing it when he speaks
of an "aesthetic of ethics," attributing to the author a "measure of humanity" in this degree of "aestheticization." The "art" of which the
author speaks is not necessarily aesthetic, though it includes the aesthetic moment of human activity: it is rather the broad concept of "human activity," *homo faber*, common to antiquity and the Middle Ages
as well.

At the hands of the Ottonian and Salian clerics, courtliness was
clearly not "art" but, precisely, "civilization": culture was at the service
of society, not, as it became in some extreme forms of Romanticism, a
tool to subvert society and reject its given order. In this Germany made
an original early contribution, and it may well have been "next to Christian ideals, the most powerful civilizing force in the West since ancient
Rome" (Jaeger: 261) if, as Jaeger postulates, the "curial" ethos of state
service spread from Germany to France and England and was eventually accepted by the knightly class, probably first in France. But before
we accept this genetic process, further investigation is in order to supply
some missing links (more on this later). The current state of our knowledge allows us to proceed on the assumption that further developments
were entirely possible on the basis of the natural evolution of regional
situations. Between courtier clerics and knights at court Jaeger sees a
community of interests, which urged both to discipline themselves and
to "behave" for success, while he wonders (264–265) why the free high
nobility would have felt any need to tame their warrior ways. He suggests, in one word, fashion, with a strong role for literature in it. For

the time being, it appears reasonable to assume that the chivalric code which ripened in France spread to Germany by inserting itself into the rich underlying structure of the native ethical and social traditions. It was thus that the literary superimposed itself upon the practical.

German scholarship has experienced "agony" over the genesis of German chivalry (Jaeger: 174 f.). The ensuing polemic between Gustav Ehrismann and Ernst R. Curtius, as reflected in the miscellany *Ritterliches Tugendsystem* (1970), focused on the unnecessary postulate of Wernher von Elmendorf's translation (ca. 1170–1180) of the *Moralium dogma philosophorum* (perhaps wrongly attributed to Guillaume de Conches) as the intermediary between a creative, original French system of *courtoisie* and German adaptations.[45] But both "Guillaume" and Elmendorf were "compilers, not innovators," and even the Ciceronian content of Elmendorf's tract was not a necessary importation, since it corresponded to the preexisting German substratum derived from court practices. These widely circulating compilations showed that a summary presentation of ethical wisdom tended to encompass Stoic criteria: John Holmberg's valuable edition of the *Moralium dogma* and its vernacular versions (1929) showed 165 quotations from Cicero's *De officiis*, along with 92 from Seneca, 104 from Horace, 40 from Juvenal, and so on. Jodocus Clichtoveus, publisher of the 1511 Paris edition, remarked that it "collected, among others, copious sentences on the four sources of the moral duties (*officia*) according to the Stoic division that is called the four cardinal virtues."[46] In any event, a close critical analysis of the *Moralium dogma* shows that it has no direct bearing on courtly/chivalric ethos.[47]

The fact remains that the tradition of courtesy and courtly love spread throughout the western lands under the impact of twelfth-century French literature, through the reinforcement and reinterpretation that came about with Dante and, even more, with Petrarca and then with Ficino's Platonism. Jaeger thus does not appear to succeed in his attempt to displace the origins of this phenomenon from France to Germany. But he does succeed brilliantly in locating an important background element of that literary phenomenon in the earlier curial ethos of imperial Germany.

THE GERMAN/FRENCH CONNECTION

Jaeger has proposed to read the historical documents of medieval *curialitas* as evidence that the German imperial chapels were the fountainheads of later developments of courtliness, courtesy, and to some extent, chivalry. Questions arise from the fact that he isolates the German world from that of other monarchical courts, like the English (he does mention the court of Henry II), the Italian, and most important, the Frankish ones. True enough, France was under German influence in the tenth century, and the Saxon emperors controlled Alsace and Lorraine as well as parts of Flanders. They had strong allies among bishops who were close to the Carolingian center of power, like Archbishop Adalbero of Reims, a Lorrainer by birth. German reaction to attempts by the late Carolingians to interfere in Lorraine has been regarded as one of the causes for the fall of that house. When the young Louis V died unexpectedly, German interests were strong enough to place Hugh Capet on the throne, in opposition to Duke Charles of Brabant, the last Carolingian descendant. Hugh was consecrated in Reims by the man who had played a major role in the selection, namely Adalbero (July 987). In the eleventh century the house of Saxony, though weakened, still could manage to succeed to the "kingdom" of Burgundy, vacant in 1032, thus acquiring the Romance area of Switzerland, the Franche-Comté, the region of Lyon, and that part of the southeast that came to be called the kingdom of Arles. But the trickling in from Germany of administrative and educational standards of *curialitas* through these or other channels remains to be proved.

Jaeger does not investigate whether the portraits of bishops outside Germany were really essentially different from the German ones. If records are silent in other areas in the form of episcopal *vitae*, the thriving contemporary Latin tradition of praise of kings and abbots should be contrasted with the Ottonian texts in order to assess the relative originality of the latter. In the tenth century St. Odo of Cluny's *Vita Geraldi* (Life of St. Gerard of Aurillac, 1.15, 24, 30, etc.) similarly attributes to his subject affability, *facetia*, and good temper in adversity. What did such praiseworthy qualities mean in Ottonian Germany that they could not also mean in the Frankish-descended entourages of Flanders, Anjou, and Aquitaine? How exactly did personal virtues become social prerequisites? One area of intense chivalric activity in early periods that Jaeger does not cover in detail is that of the Flemish provinces of Hennegau (Hainaut), Brabant, and Flanders; a host of political and literary historians have pointed out their influence on Germany in addition to the impact of Burgundian mores on the Hohenstaufen rulers.[48] Before one can argue for imperial origins, one has to take a close look at such French texts as Odo of St. Maur, Galbert of Bruges, and Flemish genealogies.

If the German episcopate was a training ground for manners, we are not told what happened to it after the civil wars of the late eleventh century. Yet, there is no lack of evidence for episcopal prosopography, and to idealize the German imperial court outside Germany after 1100 would presumably have struck a note of novelty. What I find most persuasive in the documentation brought forward by Jaeger is, rather, the suggestion that, without necessarily deriving from German sources, the ways of curiality combined (independently and spontaneously in various regions) with those of courtliness and chivalry in a dynamic interplay of far-reaching consequences.[49]

Most important for the literary historian, Jaeger fails to do justice to the uniquely creative power of the Provençal and French poets of love lyric and romance, who need to be seen together for their fashioning, in strikingly different ways, of the ideal of the amorous courtly knight. This historical reality introduced decisive secular elements that could be, and undoubtedly were, conditioned by clerical elements but had little to do directly with episcopal models. One text that he neglects would have corrected his emphasis on the ecclesiastical and shown the coexistence of the secular and the religious, of the courtier-knight as a contemporary of the courtier-bishop: the *Ruodlieb*. A Latin poem written before 1070 (but variously dated even as early as 1030–1050), probably by a Bavarian monk who was close to the court of Henry III and who showed political and secular concerns, it focuses on a noble lord rather than a bishop.[50]

The standards of education for civilized and noble behavior lived on in other than the ecclesiastical spheres as their principal source and nurturing agent: just as the centers of this new pedagogy had first shifted from imperial chapel and episcopal courts to the cathedral schools in the eleventh century, so the second half of the twelfth century witnessed a new shift from the latter to the secular and high ecclesiastical courts. In France the influence of the cathedral schools was diminished by the so called "Battle of the Seven Arts," in which the army of dialecticians and scholastic logicians carried the day. The triumph of Paris was the undoing of Chartres and Orléans, but Petrarca would once again resume the battle, and for even higher and more systematic goals. In the meantime, his future message was foreshadowed in Alan of Lille's (d. Cîteaux 1203) *Anticlaudianus*. Alan presented the allegory of a New Man who was to be read as a model man of court, guided in his progress by Copia (Bounteousness), Favor, Fame, Youth, Laughter (we are reminded of liberality, the currying of social success, the troubadours'

joven, and *facetia*), Chastity, and then Modesty and Constancy, who
together discipline his behavior according to the principle of *moderamen* (the golden mean) in his action, speech, gestures, and general external bearing; finally come Reason and *Honestas*. Most significantly,
Reason teaches the New Man not purely intellectual pursuits but the
practical ones that befit the public figure and the administrator, that
is, the eminent domain of ethical and practical philosophy. These are
not the virtues of monks or contemplators but of men of the world, and
they are such as to have an outer, visible beauty, "down to dress, personal grooming, and table manners."[51]

Later texts offering full portraits of a suitable courtier also testify to
the continuity of the ethical framework. As Jaeger (108) tells us,

> In an English *Fürstenspiegel* from 1445, one of many that went under the
> title of *Secretum Secretorum*,[52] we find the following list of requirements for
> a "truw counseiler or servaunt" of the king: (1) "perfeccion of lymmes"
> [limbs]; (2) "godness of lernyng and wille to understonde"; (3) a good
> memory; (4) a clear and level head in difficult situations; (5) "courtly, faire
> spekyng, of swete tonge, . . . sped in eloquence"; (6) learned; (7) "of good
> manners and complexion, softe, meke and tretable" (here follows a list of
> vices to be avoided in a counselor); (14) composed and moderate in his man-
> ners, "yevying himself curiously to men benyngly tretyng." Many tracts on
> the counselor, the legate and ambassador from the Renaissance, could be
> cited here, but this passage gives us a concise and remarkably comprehensive
> list of the chief characteristics of our type. The Latin vocabulary for most of
> these is readily at hand: *moderamen, eloquentia*, and *lineamentorum gratia*.
> "Softe, meke and tretable" are the counterpart of *mansuetus, mitis et trac-
> tabilis*; "men benyngly tretyng" is *benignitas* and *affabilitas*. The tract pre-
> dates Castiglione by more than half a century.

THE TERMINOLOGY

The term *curia* for the royal court had disappeared since Charlemagne,
replaced by *palatium* and *aula*. It came back into use under Emperor
Henry III. *Curialis* first appears in Lanfranc of Bec circa 1063, and *curialitas*, "courtliness," still used in a negative sense, in a text of 1080 by
a chronicler of the church of Hildesheim: Azelinus, former chaplain of
Henry III who nominated him bishop of Hildesheim (1044–1054), decided to increase the amenities of monastic life and allowed an ambitious courtliness (*curialitas*) to creep into the monasteries, with the consequent relaxation of discipline.[53] Referring to chaplains at court, Peter
Damian (*Contra clericos aulicos*, ca. 1072) used the (derogatory) adjec-

tive *curialis*: "qui de clerico efficitur curialis." *Curialitas* became positive by the mid-twelfth century. Associated with the clearly moral term
of (inner) *probitas*, it signified the social qualities of the good chaplain
and bishop, and by extension the good lay courtier. Thomas Becket, for
example, was said to have received the king's son in his care in order to
instruct him in manners and courtly ways, *mores et curialitates*.[54]

The terms *curia*, *curialis* and their vernacular cognates underwent a
semantic shift in later times, always with direct or implied reference to
the courts, which could, however, be secular or ecclesiastical (mainly
the papal ones but also the episcopal). More generally, the terms denoted administrative headquarters (as in the Jesuit order's Curia Gener-
alis), especially with juridical functions and prerogatives, as in the case
of the various chanceries. The sense of "chancery" prevailed in German
linguistic usage through the eighteenth century with reference to the
language of the high and lower courts (*idioma curialis* or *forensis*, *Kan-
zleisprache*, *Geschäftssprache*—language of the court chancery and of
business, i.e., administration).

The courtly code as found in German epics, romances, and lyrics is
fraught with terms that were fully developed semantically even before
French influence. The ideal knight was supposed to exhibit a harmonious mixture of such inner, spiritual qualities as *triuwe* (loyalty), *milte*
(generosity), *tapferkeit* or *manheit* (prowess, courage, Prov. *proeza*,
Fr. *proece*, *hardiment*), and *mâze* (Prov. *mezura*, Fr. *mesure*, self-
restraint or measure), and of outer ones, namely *zuht* (good bearing).
This mixture would ensure that he deserved honor in the world (*ere*)
and *hoher muot*, a state of inner, exalted happiness of heart—what the
troubadours and the French trouvères called *joi*.

As to France, Old French *curteis* is in the *Chanson de Roland*; Provençal *cortes* appears first in William IX, circa 1100. They derive from
Vulgar Latin *cortis* (*curtis* in Frankish times) from the Latin *cohors*,
farm yard, then seigniorial camp or domain, hence court of justice.[55]
Courtois had its counterpart in the *vilain*, as the civil city-dweller
would also be naturally contrasted with the rustic country-dweller in
the culture of the Italian communes.[56]

Concerning Jaeger's claim of German terminological priority vis-à-
vis France, we must observe that *curialis* and *curialitas* (without vernacular equivalents) precede German, French, and Italian vernacular
terms of courtesy by only a few years and become positive only gradually, without ever carrying the clear and full weight of French *curteis*
and Provençal *cortes*. Of Gottfried von Strassburg's (d. ca. 1210) ethical

terms *schöne zuhte* and *schöne sîte*, the first was present in both of
Gottfried's close predecessors, namely Heinrich von Veldeke (b. ca.
1140/50, d. before 1210) and Hartmann von Aue (b. ca. 1160/70,
d. after 1210), and they do not seem to predate those three practically
contemporary poets. To state that these terms, like their Latin equivalent *elegantia morum* (and Otto of Bamberg's *elegans et urbana disciplina*), had no early equivalent in Old French and Old Provençal (Jaeger: 141–143) may bear further consideration: the word *manières*, for
example, which appears perhaps as early as 1175 in the very title of the
Livre des manières by the bishop of Rennes and Lisieux Étienne de
Fougères, sounds very close, and it clearly addressed the world of the
knights. True enough, this difficult text used the term in the medieval
sense of Latin *maneria*, a synonym for *genus* that basically corresponded to the notion of social orders or *ordines*, but at the same time
it introduced the connotation of correct behavior according to one's
status and duties.[57]

Thanks to what they had in common, the ethos of curiality eventually merged with that of courtliness, and so did their respective nomenclatures, the latter being conspicuously characterized by a more marked
reliance on the noble qualities of liberality (Prov. *largueza*, Fr. *largesse*)
and frankness (Fr. *franchise*, "frank bearing"). The key Old French
words *preud, proece* > *preudhomme, prouesse* (Prov. *pros, proeza*;
It. *prode, prodezza*), "worthy, worth," and their numerous synonyms
corresponded to and actually replaced "hero" and "heroic"; in medieval and Renaissance iconography the model heroes of antiquity and of
knighthood were presented as a group of characters (usually nine)
called *les Neuf Preux*, "the Nine Worthies."[58]

The main theme of the present study is that there was a logical as
well as factual connection among curiality/courtliness, courtesy (including courtly love), and speculation on civilized manners—all the qualities, that is, of the knightly character and chivalric gentleman, later to
be generalized into the civilized gentleman. It has been observed that
the most famous treatise on courtly love, Andreas Capellanus's *De
amore* (ca. 1180?), frequently uses *curialitas* to mean courtesy, and that
one early manuscript of it bears the title "Liber amoris et curtesie."
Kenelm Foster declared this a fitting title, since "Andreas's principal
theme is love as the way to acquire the qualities which should distinguish a gentleman."[59] Curiality, courtly love, and civilized manners appear to come together naturally in this crucial text, whose ironic qualities are a symptom that the implied concepts could then already be

taken for granted. Similarly, it has been easily shown that a rich terminology for courtesy and courtly love was, indeed, developed in the
twelfth century (Prov. *domnei* and G. *Frauendienst* are some of the
equivalent terms, along with the recurring terms Prov./Fr. *fin'amor* and
G. *hohe Minne*), so that not only the thing and the concept, but the
words existed, too, without having to wait for Gaston Paris to invent
them.[60]

CHAPTER THREE

Courtliness and Chivalry in France

COURTLY KNIGHTS AND CHIVALROUS PRINCES: FROM REALITY TO IDEATION (AND VICE VERSA)

The nonfictional genres of chronicles and biographies will now assist us in establishing the connection between the evolution of *curialitas* and the standards of chivalry. To the German texts adduced by Jaeger I shall add a number that appear to show how the standards were developing, at the same time or even earlier than in Germany, in the Flanders, northern France, Normandy, and Anjou, thus perhaps invalidating this part of his thesis and confirming the more traditional view of the historical genesis of courtesy. Jaeger suggests that German imperial/episcopal standards might have spread to other areas from the tenth to the eleventh century, but, since he has not managed to supply what appear as missing links, we must assume that the developments we are surveying took place independently.[1]

A pithy portrait of the first Norman Duke Richard I by Dudo of St. Quentin (*De moribus et actis primorum Normanniae ducum*, ca. 1017–1020) provides an example of the summary presentation of an already established code of ethical personal qualities expected of a successful leader. This code was both logical and specific in terms of a tradition that harks back to the classics but with significant application to current needs: "He shone for his noble ancestry, . . . well behaved, . . . endowed with a sparkling appearance, second to none in piety. Of fine complexion and more distinguished than anyone in all his gestures, he stood out for his pleasant speech, even sweeter to all for his gait and dress. He was attractive in his clean speaking and always serene and happy at heart." [2] The text belongs in the epideictic genre, a specific antecedent being Claudian's panegyric of the Roman general Stilicho in the *De consulatu Stilichonis*, but what interests us is the way such topoi did not simply carry on a stale schema, but were obviously used because they fitted the occasion. [3]

Dudo's chronicle was continued after 1070 (hence, after Hastings) by Guillaume de Jumièges (*Gesta Normannorum ducum*) [4] and, again, in 1073/1074 by Guillaume de Poitier (*Gesta Guillelmi II ducis Normannorum et regis Anglorum*). [5] This last author concentrated on a panegyrical biography of William the Conqueror, presented as the perfect ideal of the valorous and pious knight. In all these portraits, the chivalric or knightly ethos, still in its inchoate stage, is vested in the high nobility, the *milites* being presented as an unruly crowd in need of restraint from above. It was only in the next century that the lower nobility, turned "courtois," would assume a leading role to be emulated by its superiors.

Interestingly enough, the portraits keep shifting the emphasis from the subjects' warlike virtues to their being handsome knights dedicated to the protection of the poor and the weak, the clergy and the Church, and to the prevention of injustice, plunder, and the violation of equity and measure. In more religious contexts the *miles Christi* was reminded that he had to serve with *humilitas* and *misericordia*, Christian humility and readiness to help the needy. All three chroniclers, Dudo and the two Guillaumes, agree on attributing to the fierce dukes the pious qualities that the preachers of the Peace of God, in the wake of an ancient tradition based on the Bible, had wanted to see in a ruler and a noble soldier.

In a passage that reminds us of John of Limoges's story of Joseph and the Pharaoh, Dudo tells of the abbot Martin of Jumièges's dissuading Duke William Long-Sword (Guillaume Longue-Epée, ca. 930–942), son of Rollo, from abandoning his life as a warrior and secular leader in order to join the "superior," holier rank of the monks. "Who will protect us monks from the pagans and the plunderers if you leave your calling and your duty? Everyone must stay and serve in his God-assigned social role." [6] Consistent with this view of the divinely-ordained social order, Guillaume de Jumièges, who confirms the story of the abbot Martin, [7] praises Richard II for mercilessly and efficiently crushing a peasant revolt by cutting off the leaders' hands and feet.

Thus, says Guillaume, did Richard teach the peasants a lesson: those whom God appoints to work (the *agricolae*) must work, while others fight or pray.[8]

In this interesting episode of the centuries-long debate on *vita contemplativa* versus *vita activa*, the solution is based not on the search for the perfect state but on everyone doing his assigned job. The clerics perform their self-appointed task as court educators by assigning to the rulers a mission that is both a prefiguration of chivalric ethic and a confirmation of what Jean Flori calls "the royal ethic," which, in the climate of the Peace of God, gradually percolated down from the king to the princes and, finally, to the new knightly class.

The texts abound. Two other examples are Helgaud's life of King Robert the Pious (ca. 1033), where the king's main concern is given as the protection of monks, widows, orphans, and the poor,[9] and Odo of St. Maur's (Eudes de Saint-Maur-des-Fossés) life of Count Burchard of Vendôme, Corbeil, Melun, and Paris (*Vita domni Burcardi*, 1058), where this high vassal, counselor, and intimate friend of Hugh Capet and Robert the Pious, is said to have been marked by piety and eagerness to defend the Church.[10] This "royal ethic" could not play the same role in Germany as in France, given the different relationships between Church and state in the two regions and the more limited role of the Peace of God in Germany.

A different vantage point conditions Guelf speculation on the role of *milites* within a divine scheme, which divided humankind into three broad estates or "orders" (*ordines*), usually identified as: *pugnatores* or *bellatores* (the warriors), *oratores* (those who pray), and *laboratores*; namely, the nobility, the priests, and the workers. In a poem of the late 1020s on Robert the Pious by Bishop Adalbero of Laon we read: "Triplex ergo Dei domus est, quae creditur una. . . . Alii orant, alii pugnant, alii laborant." The eleventh-century *Gesta episcoporum Cameracensium* (Deeds of the Bishops of Cambrai) attributes to Bishop Gerard of Cambrai a division of mankind into *oratores*, *pugnatores*, and *agricultores*—a division which can be dated to 1024.[11] These are the first documents of the doctrine: both Adalbero, a man of royal blood of Carolingian descent, nephew of the already mentioned archbishop of Reims by the same name and cousin-german to the dukes of Lorraine, and Gerard, also a Carolingian by blood, were interested in asserting their authority as *magistri* over Robert, king of France; they clearly placed themselves in such a position as *oratores* above the class of *pugnatores* or *bellatores*, which included the king as first soldier.

Writing between 1090 and 1095 within the framework of the controversy on investiture, the brilliant curialist Bonizo, bishop of Sutri
(ca. 1045—ca. 1096), defined the role of the *milites*, part of the *ordo
laicalis* of the *pugnatores*, as military/political service to the lord to
whom they are sworn (above all, to the governing prince) and to the
Church (including the rooting out of heretics and schismatics), as well
as maintenance of moral justice and social order, including the defense
of the poor, widows, and orphans. They must refrain from plunder
and private violence: "praedae non iniare, . . . pauperes quoque et
viduas et orphanos defensare."[12] St. Bernard of Clairvaux would give
his most authoritative endorsement to such a perspective (*De laude
novae militiae*). In the early years of the twelfth century the influential
theologian and moralist Honorius Augustodunensis (perhaps of Augsburg or Ratisbon/Regensburg) reiterated the injunction to knights to
be ready to defend widows and orphans and help the poor ("viduas,
pupillos defendentes, . . . pauperes pascentes"), sternly warning them to
avoid plunder and fornication: "a rapina et fornicatione vosmetipsos
custodire." Fornication here may refer to rape or to the sort of adulterous living and thinking that would become a standard feature of
courtly love.[13]

In the broader context of what Georges Dumézil has called the "trifunctional" doctrine of social order, it is symptomatic that the idea of
the tripartite division of society into Clergy, Nobility (the soldiers), and
Laborers reappeared in the authoritative *Traité des ordres et simples
dignitez* of 1610 by the Parisian Charles Loyseau, who also designated
these "orders" as "estates" (*estats*).[14]

An outstanding example of the closeness of clerics to the knights at
court is that of Ordericus Vitalis, who in his *Historia ecclesiastica*
(1142) tells of Gerald of Avranches, chaplain to the lively *familia* or
maisnie of Hugh of Chester, spinning out chivalric tales for both the
entertainment and instruction of the assembled court (*ad emendatio-
nem vitae virorum curialium*). Rather surprisingly, the tales studding
Gerald's sermons were exemplary lives of ancient saintly warriors
(*sancti milites*): Demetrius, George, Eustache, Sebastian, Theodore,
Maurice, and the monk/Count Guillaume of Aquitaine (the Guillaume
d'Orange of the *chansons de geste*)—all models of the Christian knight,
fighter for God, Church, and society.[15]

Ordericus is an important witness because, even in the seclusion of
his Norman monastery, he was among the first to define a code of ethical conduct that can be considered clearly chivalric by the principles of

"knightly honor" which we encounter in the romances. When we read how nonchalantly Chrétien's Lancelot releases his once dangerous enemies, simply on their promise to do exactly what he commands, we can think back to Ordericus's story of William Rufus (Guillaume le Roux, William the Conqueror's son and successor). The king had just freed his prisoners on their own word, after treating them as honored guests. When his courtiers objected to this trusting gesture, he lost his temper: "A knight does not violate his word, or he would lose his honor forever, as an outlaw!"[16] Another point dramatically presented by Ordericus is respect for our adversaries. Ordericus cites the nearly bloodless 1119 battle between Henry I Beauclerc and King Louis VI of France, in which nine hundred knights fought but only three were killed, as a result, the author says, of the combatants' sense of "brotherhood of arms" (Flori [1986]: 272). The noble warrior wants to defeat his knightly opponents, not slay them. Here again we are reminded of the knight's reluctance to kill even the most abominable characters in the romances, once they have been duly defeated. This brotherhood extends into a strong sense of class solidarity when we realize how the defense of the weak that we have seen illustrated above was largely limited in practice to members of the higher classes. Lambert of Ardres, for example, commends Baldwin II of Guines for being a strong defender of orphans and widows, but we can assume that only noble ones were meant.[17] Orphans spoiled of their heritage would have it restored to them and would then be married off to noble and rich young ladies.

John of Salisbury (1115/20–1180) provides an important analysis of the role of *milites* in the political and social order.[18] His *Policraticus*, dedicated to Thomas Becket, was written in 1159 while John was secretary to Becket, then Chancellor of England, and when Henry of Anjou, once the idol of the French knights and now king of England as Henry II, was trying to restore royal authority after an interlude of triumphant feudality.[19] In line with his patron's firm Gregorian views on the relationship between the spiritual and the secular, John declares the prince to be the priests' minister, inferior to them in absolute status. John advises the prince to be learned in letters in order to be able to read the law; if he is illiterate he should be guided by the counsel of literate men—presumably the learned clerics at court.[20] Against this background it is easier to understand why and how John represents the ecclesiastical perspective of knights as justified and good, even "saintly" if they serve the prince loyally according to the Christian faith.[21] When, however, they behave, as so many do, as plunderers and pursuers of

their own or their lords' violent private quarrels, they are no better than
criminals, to be restrained and punished by the king. Both positive and
negative statements amount to an important theoretical recognition of
the knightly status and of its inherent unacceptability to the Church, at
least in its *de facto* form. In particular, John's statements severely criticize the practice of knight errantry and the knights' ethos of luxury and
splendor—let alone the inherent sinfulness of courtly love.[22] Just as later
"books of chivalry" would turn out to be derivations of Flavius Vegetius's ancient Roman treatise on military art,[23] so do John's concepts
have a basis in the ancient literature on military life and duties. Yet it is
clear that he has chivalry in mind, as when he specifically criticizes the
method of recruitment, which is not based on merit, as he thinks it
should be, but on individual patronage. It is even clearer when, in
book 6, chapters 10 and 13, he refers to the ceremony of dubbing as
symbolic of the knight's solemnly sworn profession (*consecratio* by
ordinata militia) to serve the altar and God with the very sword he has
laid on the altar. Unfortunately, he sadly interjects, some knights, by a
purely secular interpretation which makes of *militia* a true *malitia*,
come to their consecration in order to swear war on the same altar, its
ministers, and God.[24]

John's austerely qualified recognition of the role of knights in the
feudal state was carried forward by Alan of Lille, the outstanding heir
of the Chartres masters William of Conches, John of Salisbury, and Peter of Blois. Jean Flori sees in Alan's work the coming of age of the
chivalric ideology in the last third of the twelfth century, when it
achieved its triumph in Flanders and the Plantagenet domains, perhaps
not without Alienor (Eleanor) of Aquitaine and her daughters having
played a decisive role.[25] Alan's *Summa de arte praedicatoria* reiterates
the main principles of chivalric behavior: knights must take up defence
of country, widows, and orphans, they must be armed with the faith as
well as the sword, and they must neither oppress the people nor resort
to violence (presumably a reference to private wars). Like John, Alan
also regrets that knightly practice does not correspond to its assigned
function. Instead of protecting against plunderers, knights themselves
do the plundering; they serve for personal profit and, in the end, pros-
titute the military calling.[26]

In the *Livre des manières* (ca. 1175), written in the form of a poetic
sermon, Étienne de Fougères, bishop of Rennes and Lisieux and former
chaplain of King Henry II of England, addresses the knightly class,
which in his mind includes the aristocracy as a whole.[27] The tasks God

has assigned to this class are to govern the people, uphold the noblest causes and moral principles toward God, the king, and the Church, maintain peace and justice, and defend the poor. The treatise goes on to review all other classes: peasants, burghers and merchants, and women of all states, and makes the then commonplace critique of each state or "order" (*ordo*) for its failure to keep their divinely-willed mutual harmony. In line with Plantagenet policy, Fougères implicitly places ruling princes above the clergy, at variance with the intent of Adalbero of Laon and Gerard of Cambrai, the first theorists of the *ordines*. Furthermore, he clearly addresses the court and upholds its interests when he commiserates with the toiling peasants only in order to inculcate the principle that they must meekly accept their misery and their exploitation by the lords as God-willed and healthy for them: they are thus cleansed of original sin and will be rewarded in the other world. The long *planctus* on the sad state of peasants urges the courtiers to assert their mission as leaders and teachers of submissiveness to the lower class, since "knight and clerk must live by the peasant's toil."[28]

The courtois paradigm which came out of the romances of about 1155–1180 had a direct impact on the French nobility's self-image. In 1160 Henry II Plantagenet commissioned Wace to write his family chronicle, the *Roman de Rou* (Rou being Rollo or Hrólfr, the Danish Viking who founded the Norman dukedom in France ca. 911). Wace started it in 1160 and interrupted it in 1174. Also by royal commission a "Benoît," arguably Benoît de Sainte-Maure, the author of the *Roman de Troie*, carried the chronicle further in his own *Chronique des Ducs de Normandie*, written between 1173–1175. Both authors were also romanciers, and both carried on the recognition of a positive knightly function.[29] Wace stressed the leader's duty to ensure the triumph of justice in his realm and picked up the story of the abbot Martin dissuading William Long-Sword from entering a monastery, urging him instead to do his work as leader of his people.[30] Of Richard I, Wace says he loved both the clergy and chivalry: "Richard aima clers e clergie, / chevaliers et chevalerie" (3: vv. 273 f.). He was a paragon of courtoisie, governing with fairness all his subjects, peasants as well as burghers, distributing lands and valuables to his nobles, and surpassing all his ancestors in liberality and good manners.[31] The list of courtly virtues is rather full.

It is even fuller in Benoît's *Chronique*, where William Long-Sword is said to have been *hardi, corajos, franc, douz, large, gentis, sage, proz*, and *prodomme*, and Duke Richard I to have been a noble prince, "chevaler merveillos," "Plein de bonté e de valor / E plein de grand pris e d'onnor," a great raconteur, expert at hunting and playing social games, harsh with the wicked, sweet with the good, of good company, and a lover of good music (vv. 19,547–551; 19,560–616). High nobility, knighthood, and courtliness, we can see, had become close allies. Carrying on the Norman/Angevin propaganda line which all these chroniclers share, Benoît made an unfavorable comparison between Louis VII, who downgraded the nobility by surrounding himself with parvenu bourgeois ministers, and Richard II Plantagenet, who would not tolerate anyone of low birth in his entourage.[32] Clearly, this attribution of chivalrous qualities to Norman ancestors was an anachronistic and retroactive reflection of standards then coming into fashion. Even the marauder Rollo was called *buen chevalier* by Benoît de Sainte-Maure (*Chronique*: vv. 2388–2398).

In straight historical writing, the minstrel author of the *Histoire de Guillaume le Maréchal* gives a vivid portrait of William the Marshal, fourth son of an English baron. After serving under Henry II, Henry the Young, Richard Lion-Heart, and John Lackland, William managed through his brilliant and persistent exercise of the knightly and courtly arts to rise to the status of virtual regent (*rector regis et regni*) for the young Henry III. His knightly prowess had first attracted the attention of Alienor of Aquitaine, who appointed him tutor to her son Henry the Young. He had fought in a well-advertised tournament sponsored by Alienor's daughter and Chrétien de Troyes's patroness, Marie de Champagne, and her husband, Henri de Champagne. As a result, he had enjoyed his share of successful and profitable love affairs. He was a good illustration of Charny's "he who achieves more is the more worthy" as the criterion for the model knight (see below).[33]

Feudal society was a man's world, but especially in the twelfth century, the high period of creative feudalism, the role of women was more prominent in the political and economic spheres than in the cultural one, since in the latter women were essentially relegated to a symbolic role of emotional inspiration when not charged with instigation of base lustfulness. Alienor's and her daughters' widely-spread spheres of influence were particularly impressive but not unique cases: women were often in control as regents during a man's absence or minority, and at times as legal heirs. Occasionally they could even lead armies.[34]

Further documenting the close relationship between cleric and nobleman, Breton d'Amboise stressed the joining of chivalry and literacy— the virtues of the warrior/knight and those of the cleric—in the model ruler. Writing his *Gesta Ambaziensium Dominorum* around 1155 (Halphen and Poupardin opined between 1155–1173), he promoted the literate and chivalric Henry, count of Anjou and duke of Normandy and Aquitaine (who had just become Henry II of England) over King Louis VII of France, whom Alienor had left to marry Henry. Like his predecessor, Louis VI, who had battled to reduce the barons' power, Louis VII was not as inclined as Henry II to appreciate chivalric and literary concerns.[35] His successor Philip II Augustus (1180–1223) carried on a victorious struggle against the Plantagenets, especially Henry II's fiercely independent son and heir Richard I Lion-Heart, also count of Anjou and duke of Aquitaine—a chivalric hero in the eyes of all Europe.[36] As legend has it, Richard lost his horse in a battle against Saladin during the crusade of 1191. In admiration for his valor Saladin sent him two Arabian stallions, which enabled Richard to resume the fight and force Saladin to retreat.[37] He was a shining example of the ideology's contradictory power: the pursuit of his feudal interests by chivalrous means made him a bad ruler but a great knight. The famous family rivalry among Richard, his parents, and his three brothers Henry the Young, Geoffrey of Brittany, and John Lackland, shows how the much proclaimed chivalric standards of "loyalty" and "frankness" were impure rhetorical motives, inherently subjective and ambiguous—an aspect of the duality and tension of feudal realities. Richard was admired as the perfect knight and so extolled in the songs of the troubadours (above all, Bertran de Born's), but he was in fact supremely treacherous and perfidious where it counted most, that is, against those who should have been his best lord and his allies: his king and father and his brothers.

Jean de Marmoutier continued Breton's chronicle in his own *Historia Gaufredi Ducis Normannorum et Comitis Andegavorum* written around 1180 (Halphen and Poupardin dated it 1173), where he portrayed the Plantagenet Count of Anjou, Geoffrey the Handsome (Gaufredus), as a model chivalrous prince, again, like Breton before him, stressing the image of the cultured prince who is fond of vernacular poetry and draws on Vegetius to improve his military strategy.[38] In a remarkably "democratic" episode the "liberal" Geoffrey encounters a peasant, typically described as dirty, hairy, and black. Instead of scorning him, Geoffrey offers the fellow a lift on his horse, and as they ride along he asks him what the people think of their lord. Without recognizing Geoffrey, the peasant says the people think him a great lover of justice, a good warrior devoted to peace and to the defense of the oppressed. The trouble in the land, the peasant avers, comes not from the good count, but from his ministers, the true oppressors of the people.[39] This does not mean that Geoffrey did not share a sense of class solidarity: what the episode expresses is distrust for the *ministeriales*, often parvenu commoners, considered greedy and dishonest. Another episode shows him approving the release of imprisoned knights out of sympathy for his peers.[40]

If we wonder about the meaning of this phase in the development of the chivalric ideology and the reasons for its geographical location, we might turn to Paul Zumthor's observation that the literary genre of the romance, arising between 1150 and 1175, appears more closely related to the historiographic genre than to the epic.[41] In those politically better structured regions a new seigniorial class began to discover the harmfulness of warfare. The implicit ethos of the epic was perceived as artificial, if not intolerable. At the same time, clerics and educated knights developed a taste for the book, which began to find a commercial market. While the epic was an oral phenomenon, structurally based on formulaic juxtaposition on the textual level, the romance was completely written out and was to be read in private or heard from reading, not from public recitation. The cultural proximity between historiography and the *roman* bears a formal marker in that, in the twelfth century, practically all works in both genres are in rhyming octosyllables without caesura. This proximity extends further to the first French literary prose, which, at the beginning of the thirteenth century, also emerged simultaneously and, at first, exclusively in these same two genres.

Lambert of Ardres's (1154–1206) exemplary set of biographies is an advanced case in point, showing the chivalric overlay on a rather different social reality (*Historia comitum Ghisnensium*, 1194 or more likely 1201–1206).[42] Lambert made his patron Arnold, Arnoud, or Arnulf the Young of Guines a courtly knight with all the trappings inherent to the early biographies of German imperial bishops. Arnold was born in the 1160s as Arnold IV of Ardres before he succeeded his father, Count Baldwin II of Guines, as Arnold I of Guines in northwest Flanders, now Pas de Calais. Arnold's quest for tests of prowess had carried his fame to Countess Ida of Boulogne, who, having been left mistress of a large lordly estate, planned a splendid future for her hero. They exchanged secret messages, in which he used courtship as a means to a political end, since his expressions of love toward the lady were highly suspicious: the author states outright that, "whether his love was true or simulated, its goal and his aspiration were the acquisition of the countess's land and the dignity of count of Boulogne, once he would have won the favor of the same countess."[43] Since competition was fierce, Arnold missed out to a rival on that opportunity, but he went bravely on to woo the daughter of the count of Saint-Pol, whom in the end, true Machiavellian knight errant that he was, he jilted for a better match still, the heiress of Bourbourg. Upon the qualities of knight as warrior, Arnold clearly overlaid the refinements of courtly lover, which included the witty and kindly affability of the *courtois* courtier and *largesse* almost to the point of prodigality: "in omni curiali facetia praeclarus, servitio promptus"; "largitate ausim dicere fere prodigus." Note the terms *curialis, facetia, servitium,* and *largitas.*[44] Lambert's lovingly elaborate portrait ends with an emphatic brush stroke: "per omnia et in omnibus ab omnibus dicebatur et erat gratiosus," "he was, as everybody agreed, gracious in everything to everybody."[45] Once again, such courtly qualities are also retrospectively attributed to ancestors: Baudouin II of Guines is portrayed as ready to "serve" and protect widows and orphans[46] and, most remarkably, as having joined, at such an early date as 1060, arms and letters, like a knight/clerk. Being only a layman (*laicus*) he did not master Latin, but having had parts of the Scriptures and even secular scientific texts translated for him into the Romance vernacular he knew ("maximam quoque fisice artis de Latino in sibi notam linguam Romanam translatam accepit"), he retained the clerics' expositions and amazed them with his understanding of the deep, hidden meanings: "Non solum superficiem, sed et mysticam virtutem. . . . Non solum ad litteram sed ad mysticam spiritualis interpretationis intelligentiam."[47]

CHIVALRY COMES OF AGE

Joachim Bumke (1964) uses Lambert's famous text to support the following conclusion, a neat summary of his authoritative interpretation:

> The aristocratic knighthood of courtly literature is not explainable in terms of shifts in the class structure. It is an educational and cultural idea of far-reaching significance, and a phenomenon that belongs far more to intellectual than to social history. The reality of the nobility around 1200 clearly looked quite different. . . . Poets set the ideal of chivalric virtue against this harsh reality, the dream of the gentleman who has tempered his nobility with humility, and who strives to fulfill his worldly duties and to serve God at the same time.[48]

This agrees with Edmond Faral's (1913: 195) observation that "le chevalier amoureux est une invention littéraire du clerc." Even in 1200 the reality of baronial living did not accommodate the image of the polished, loving knight, but we must now add an important genetic factor: this ideal was created not "out of thin air," but as part of the civilizing process contained in the clerical education of curial and courtly candidates. The process, we have seen, started in imperial Germany and continued independently throughout the West.[49]

Our three basic concepts are about to come together at this point and a brief pause is needed to keep these distinctions in mind. Chivalry is a historic phenomenon based on both hard social realities and lofty literary ideals, separate yet somehow convergent. It contains in itself, as essential ingredients, the civilizing factors of both courtliness and courtesy, the former being more social in origin, the latter, at this time, more ideological (including, in particular, an exquisitely literary idea which we shall see emerge in the poetry, namely courtly love as the spring of heroic action, its motive and goal).

Because of the model introduced by French romances, the vulgate view of chivalry and courtesy (*courtoisie*) has tended to confuse the two categories as originally and naturally coextensive, further combining or confusing the proper elements of courtliness with courtly love. Courtesy became an operative principle in literature only when education of the noble/warrior class by clerics became an accomplished fact. At that point the "courtly," later "courtois" knight began to draw inspiration from the life of the court, which had become his psychological *locus*. It was not so before, when the feudal lord lived on his domain without a court of educated clerics and intellectuals. The first point of pressure was at the royal courts, where the need for social polish and regulated behavior was first felt, with the high lords soon starting to emulate the royalty. In due course the progress of royal centralization carried the process further. The literature of romances, first written by clerical *curiales* for a noble audience, completed this "educative" task. That, especially in Germany, we find so little evidence of direct seigniorial patronage of medieval epics and romances would seem to argue that clerical authors usually took the initiative in their composition, ostensibly to "educate" their audiences rather than in response to any aesthetic desire on the part of their public.[50]

A number of documents can be adduced to illustrate more explicitly this process of education through instruction in moral behavioral rules and correction of beastly and rustic instincts, to use the terminology of the time (e.g., Peter of Blois's and others' *instructio* and *correctio* of *bestiales* and *rusticales* attitudes). Around 1168 the abbot of Bonne-

Espérance, Philip of Harvengt (near Mons), wrote two revealing letters to important noblemen. First, addressing the new Count Philip of Flanders, he eloquently argued for the principle that a noble knight's *militia* is enhanced, not hindered, by learning, and that, conversely, letters and the arts are given purpose by the virtues of the good ruler:

> Neither is manly chivalry of prejudice to learning, nor is a fitting knowledge of letters of prejudice to the knightly exercises. Indeed, the union of the two is so useful and so becoming in a prince, that the prince who is not made truly noble by knowledge of letters betrays his status by stooping to the condition of a rustic or even a beast.[51]

Philip of Harvengt's other letter conveyed the same advice to Count Henry the Liberal of Champagne, the husband of Chrétien de Troyes's patroness, Marie de Champagne, explicitly urging court patronage of learned clerics. Such arguments were not uncommon: see, for example, Gerald of Wales's reminders that great warriors of the past were all the more valiant in combat as their knowledge of letters threw light on their moral purposes.[52] We have just encountered this same theme in Breton d'Amboise and Jean de Marmoutier.

In a tract aiming to instruct knights in the art of love, *Der heimliche Bote* (first dated 1180–1190, though more recently 1170–1180 has been proposed),[53] a German cleric argued against the warrior ways of loving in favor of the newfangled style of love based on service through humility. Discriminating ladies now favor the "well-loving man who serves with humility" ("der wol minnende man" who "denet mit demute"), virtue, elegant discourse, wisdom, and sweetness, over the man who only relies on his strong body, physical beauty, prowess, and boldness. The author appears to use the *Facetus* as one of his sources.

The closeness of the cleric to the knight that we have seen so clearly implied in Ordericus Vitalis is stated outright as an established principle in a remarkably perspicuous allegorical poem of the late thirteenth century contained in Bodleian MS. Douce 210 (ff. 1ra—12vb), where the identification of nobility and knighthood is also sanctioned in straightforward terms:

> Et quant prince oiez nomer,
> Entendez-i le chevaler;
> Sanz chevaler ne poet rais estre
> Rien plus ke eveske (poet) sanz prestre,
> Dount ces dous, clerc et chevaler,
> Ount tot le mounde a governer;
> Li clerc ki touz dait bien aprendre,
> Li chevaler pur touz defendre.[54]

(And when you hear the name of prince, / understand it for knight; / a king cannot be without the knight, / no more than a bishop without the priest, / hence these two, the cleric and the knight, / have all the world to govern; / the cleric to teach us all, / and the knight to defend us all.)

Let me now anticipate some of the forthcoming analysis by summarily setting the nascent chivalric code alongside the courtly one: equivalences and similarities may point to the way the two will combine into the new code of courtesy. The courtier's "elegance (or beauty) of manners" had meant self-control, entailing humanity and consideration toward others. Similarly, the victorious knight of the romances often surprises us by resisting the instinct to pursue his victory and exercise his right to kill. He humanely releases his prisoner without conditions, or simply on his word that he will publicize his defeat. Elegance is also personal style, etiquette, and social manners, and the knight always puts on a dignified, even splendid show if circumstances permit, with liberality and a sense of theatrical display. Love for the woman adds the decisive dimension of gentility, refinement, and devotion.

TECHNICAL TREATMENTS OF CHIVALRY

Looking for reliable historical sources on chivalry, Maurice Keen has called attention to a type of document that has not been taken into account by either literary or political historians, namely the treatises on chivalry written by technical secular writers—writers, that is, who were reforming neither clerics nor poets. Keen picked three texts that continued to be widely read, translated, and adapted well into the Renaissance, namely: the anonymous poem *Ordene de chevalerie* (probably before 1250); the *Libre del ordre de cavayleria* (between 1263 and 1276) by the Majorcan mystic Ramón Llull, a dedicated knight before his conversion; and the *Livre de chevalerie* by the French knight Geoffroi de Charny (d. 1356).[55] It is interesting to check the parallels in the ethical framework between the literary texts and these documents which, thanks to, rather than in spite of, their relatively late date, can be taken as conclusive statements. There is also an early document of this kind that Keen has not taken up, namely the *Ensenhamen del cavalher* (ca. 1160–1170) by a nobleman from the Landes in Gascony, Arnaut Guilhem de Marsan, especially remarkable because it offers as models of behavior not only such ancient heroes as Paris, Aeneas, and Apollonius of Tyre but, alongside them, the Arthurian knights. Since

Chrétien de Troyes had just begun composing his romances, this is also one of the many indices of the Arthurian lore's widespread popularity even before Chrétien.[56]

The *Ordene* is the poetic story of a Count Hugh of Tiberias who, having been captured by Saladin, obtains his release by agreeing to dub the latter as a Christian knight according to all the proper forms. The elaborate ceremony is described in detail, and Saladin frees his admired *preudhomme* with a display of chivalrous *largesse* that makes Saladin the equal of the most enviable Christian knights. There is evidence that the *Ordene* was well known in Italy.[57]

In the body of the work and in the final summary, Llull's treatise sketches the knight's character as loyal, truthful, hardy, courageous, liberal, moderate, and humble. He must also be eloquent, of noble bearing, and an elegant dresser. The art of knighthood deserves formal cultivation, hence specialized books are needed as spiritual, intellectual, and technical nourishment, and schools should be set up for the proper training of aspirants to this honorable status. Llull was well ahead of his time, since such institutions only came into being in the sixteenth century in the form of Academies for Knights and Riding Schools, starting with the celebrated school established by Federico Grisone in 1532 in Naples. It was later imitated by the Jesuits in their colleges and universities, where such elective subjects (riding, fencing, etc.) were offered as "exercises and sciences of chivalry" and reserved for the nobility. Other countries followed suit: Richelieu established and endowed the exemplary Académie Royale in 1636, one year after his Académie Française; even the small dukedom of Savoy had a famous military academy for the nobles attached to the Royal Palace in Torino, and in addition to the Royal College for the Nobles (1679), run by the Jesuits. The Jesuits had a number of colleges exclusively for nobles, like the important Collège de la Flèche in Anjou established by order of Henry IV (1603), and several in Italy, the most illustrious of these being the one at Parma, founded by Duke Ranuccio I Farnese (1601, entrusted to the Jesuits from 1604 to 1770).[58]

An active man at arms all his life until he fell at the battle of Poitiers in 1356, Charny found enough free time to write three treatises on the fine points of chivalry, the last and longest one probably in the early 1350s. He was talking about real knights, who hurt when they fall and who know how to enjoy the moments of success and conviviality, keeping lofty ideals before them but quite capable of managing their interests on a day-to-day basis. Love service is an uplifting motive for bravery, since to serve *par amours* increases valor (483–485), but it appears without the hyperbolic and unrealistic garb it was wont to take on in imaginative literature.[59]

Johannes Rothe (*Ritterspiegel*, ca. 1410) reviewed the whole aristocratic hierarchy open to the knighthood (*Heerschild*). Ghillebert de Lannoy (*Instruction d'un jeune prince*, first half of fifteenth century,[60] like the anonymous *Enseignement de la vraye noblesse*) made extensive use of Llull and, like his contemporary, the Castilian knight Diego de Valera (*Espejo de verdadera nobleza*, more widely known in the French version by Hugues de Salves, the *Traicté de noblesse*), showed a typical mixture of medieval anachronistic interpolation and incipient humanistic moods by adducing the ancient Romans as models of true chivalry.[61]

These didactic treatises for the instruction of knights demonstrate the inseparability of social and economic factors from the mental structures produced by the literature of imagination. They share a common ethos with the "mirror of princes" for the education of royal scions—both ranks being called upon to "govern."

GILES OF ROME, OR THE MERGING OF THE THREE CODES

One of the most influential of these mirrors of princes calls for our special attention: the *De regimine principum*, dedicated about 1280 to the young prince, the future Philip IV of France, by the Augustinian scholar, high administrator, and pupil of Thomas Aquinas, Aegidius Columna Romanus (Egidio Colonna or Giles of Rome, ca. 1247–1316).[62] An outstanding specimen of political speculation for its moral and doctrinal setting, this treatise was immediately popular, as attested by the numerous vernacular versions including English and Tuscan (the earliest of the five Tuscan versions dates from 1288).

Aegidius is a good example of the importance and complexity of episcopal appointments even in the France of Philip the Fair (1285–1314). Despite the Concordat of Worms, most of the bishops were still chosen from among the king's close collaborators (about twenty-eight of Philip's officials, mostly high-ranking administrators and trusted advisers, became bishops during his reign). Yet even a high-handed king like Philip could not always have his way: at least twice his own hand-picked Pope Clement V appointed other than the royal candidate.[63] Aegidius had been Philip's high tutor, though too busy on his own to be personally very close to his pupil or to act as a royal courtier. He was also naturally opposed to Philip's policies in the quarrel with Boniface VIII since he was a prominent upholder of Guelf policies and papal rights, as laid down in his *De ecclesiastica potestate* (1301), where all power, ecclesiastical as well as temporal, was said to derive from the pope. Nevertheless, his appointment as archbishop of Bourges in 1295 was welcomed by the king:[64] high personal regard could still be an important part of a future bishop's effective credentials, as it had been in the imperial courts before the investiture contest. Moreover, despite the author's strong Guelf feelings, the youthful *De regimine* was explicit on defining royal authority in ways that a king of France could only find to his taste. "Melius est regnum et civitatem regi rege quam lege," "the king's rule is better than rule by law," he unequivocally stated, since the king is above the law, "supra iustitiam legalem,"[65] although kings were said to be tyrants unless they governed for the common good, "propter bonum communem."[66] This healthy principle notwithstanding, he sounded a strong Augustinian note of caution where he said it was better to obey than to revolt against tyrants if revolt risked the evils of anarchy.[67]

The broad scope of the notion of courtliness is confirmed by the definition of *curialitas* we find in the *De regimine principum*: "curialitas est quodammodo omnis virtus, quia nobilitatem morum quasi omnis virtus concomitari debet," "curiality is in a sense the whole ensemble of virtues, since almost every virtue must accompany the nobility of mores," hence it is to be expected of all royal and princely ministers (2.3.18).[68] In that chapter Aegidius expanded on the traditional list of such curial virtues, lingering on *magnificentia, temperantia, fortitudo, affabilitas, hilaritas,* and *liberalitas.*

What throws a special light on this important text is the way it was rendered into French in a remarkable vulgarization that was more influential than the original, undoubtedly starting at Philip's court.[69] The definition of *curialitas* was dropped in the translation (where this chapter 18 became chapter 16 of the same part), although its meaning was clearly carried in the ensuing discussion, but it is particularly interesting that here and throughout the text, *curialitas* was rendered without any hesitation as "courtesy," *cortoisie* (Molenaer ed.: 261). The text goes on promising to demonstrate by two arguments of "nobility" why the ministers of kings and princes must be courtly or courteous: "nos dirrons quele chose est cortoisie, et qu'il afiert as serjanz des rois et des princes que il soient cortois, por quoi nos poons primierement prover II nobleces" (p. 261 vv. 15–20). There follows a disquisition on the roots and characteristics of true nobility, stating that the *serjanz* need "noblece de mours et de vertuz" (p. 261 v. 20), as distinct from the "noblece de lignie" (vv. 21 f.)—"nobility of manners and virtue rather than by birth." Then the exposition presents a twist: the courtier must be courtly (*cortois, curialis* in the original), not simply in order to do what is pleasant or to obey the law, but in order to be like the noblemen of the court: "ne mie por le delit qu'il a ne por la loi acomplir, mes por ensuivre les mours et les manieres des nobles hommes" (p. 263 vv. 12–14). This because courtesy is nothing but a nobility of good mores: "cortoisie n'est fors une noblece de bones mours" (p. 262 v. 29), and a courtier is one who does good deeds in order to imitate and preserve the mores and manners of a noble court: "quant il fet aucunes bones euvres por retenir les mours et les manieres de la cort as nobles hommes" (p. 263 vv. 15–17). He is truly noble who behaves like a nobleman at court. We can thus conclude in our turn: courtiers are imitators rather than originators of noble manners—which can be assumed to be a reversal of what happened in historical reality.

Nor is this all. The last section of the work (part 3 of book 3) contains an art of war, dealing with government in wartime: it starts with seven chapters on *militia* rendered outright with *chevalerie*, boldly and frankly comparing it with other soldiers, *bellatores*, in governing and defending both castles and towns (*chastiaus, citez*). Knights are called upon to defend the people from external enemies or from internal dissensions and injustices (esp. pp. 372 f.). Proper knights are arbiters of battle, above common soldiers. On Vegetius's authority, Giles says peasants are better fighters—"les vileins sont meillors bataillors"—because they are tougher, more used to physical effort and all sorts of hardships, and, not expecting much from life, they are less fearful of death, whereas the nobles are accustomed to many comforts (pp. 376–379). Vegetius, of course, was speaking of Roman legions, where the generals knew all too well that the bulk of their strength lay with the peasants, not the *equites*. Yet the nobles have a powerful factor in their favor: they are motivated by honor, which can make them better fighters. Besides, knowledge and skill count too, especially on horseback (p. 380).

This exemplary text offers palpable proof that, at the time of their full ripening, the three notions of courtliness, chivalry, and courtesy (in the broadest possible sense, including good social conduct) could be seen as logically coexistent and convergent in their natural habitat at court. They coexisted as the centrifugally active ideology, the ethical core of the power center. The interrelatedness of these three codes being the main theme of the present study, of all the material at hand this text of Giles of Rome may be one that ideally and neatly clinches the argument.

To summarize the complex situation I have been surveying: around the year 1100, once the gains obtained by force of arms became consolidated, the high nobility began to taste the advantages of a more refined way of life which was being defined by the educated clerics for a lay society with a secular culture. A more sophisticated ethical code began to set in, with the help of a literary corpus of tales and precepts. The old military virtues became joined with the new courtly ones, specifying liberality in the use of worldly goods, affability and articulateness in conversation, and elegance of manners: the whole cemented in a sublimated experience of love, proclaimed as the secret of all human value. Nobles and knights were getting ready to advance their full claim to rule.

Imaginative Transformations

CHAPTER FOUR

Troubadours, Trouvères, and Minnesingers

COURTESY AND CHIVALRY IN THE OCCITAN LYRIC

The relationship of Occitan lyric to its society has long been problematic. For Aurelio Roncaglia, an authoritative critic, the inner inspiration of this poetry escapes definition, and it remains a matter of controversy whether one can posit a general theory of courtly love: "rather, we must recognize a complex dialectic of opposite tendencies and seek the individual place of each poet in this dialectic."[1] It is part of my task to underline these inner tensions in the lyric as well as in the epic and the romance. Pierre Bec, among others, has focused on such tensions in his provocative attempts to combine the literary and the sociological, the formal and the thematic: "on the level of the poem's formal construction, the values of courtesy come vigorously forth, becoming 'semicopoetic' centers of attraction around which a whole universe of meanings is organized, and this universe's unavoidable tensions constitute the proper dynamism of the message."[2] A satisfactory interpretation seems possible in terms of a collective consciousness evolved by a disparate yet cohesive group of men gravitating around the regional courts. Indeed, E. Köhler has convincingly employed a sociological schema to explain the canso's nomenclature, structure, character, and system of values (see below). Another outstanding Romanist, Alberto Vàrvaro, argues that a truly comprehensive critical method must encompass more than formal aspects, and stresses the need to integrate the formal with the referential in a sociohistorical sense in order to see the full meaning of medieval lyric and epic.[3]

In an illuminating polemic with Roncaglia regarding the interpretation of Marcabru, Köhler criticized the "history of ideas" approach.[4] Marcabru could not simply have been trying to solve an intellectual puzzle based on fitting together the logical pieces of different ways of loving, abstractly considered. Even while he was confronting universal questions of love and survival, he was speaking to a real social group in a particular historical situation. The conventional nature of the motifs means that the poets were not being autobiographical, and also that they spoke as members of a group, a recognized and conscious collectivity, rather than as mere individuals.

Understanding the sociocultural parameters of knighthood in its early period is a prerequisite for an interpretation of its peculiar expression in the lyric. Arno Borst (1959: 216) opened a new phase of research into this thorny question by defining knighthood as "a combination of lordship and service." The corresponding German terms of *Herrschaft* and *Dienst* point to the two poles of a significant dialectical contrast that lies at the root of knighthood as a historical institution, and that is the underlying cause for the apparent contradictions in its literary representation and the accompanying ideology. We can begin with the words' semantic fields. French *chevalier*, like German *rîter, ritter*, simply denoted the horse-mounted man (at arms). But knights could also be called *knechte*, "servants," in Middle High German, which, like the cognate English "knight," clearly pointed to the bond of service between soldier and master. Thus, in a highly productive paradox, what was to become the paramount linguistic sign of nobility, hence freedom, started out as a mark of servitude: the knight was inherently "unfree" as a liegeman and bond-servant of a master who kept him in his pay and at his orders for military and other services.[5] The duality of functions for the nascent status of knight, namely being servant to a feudal lord and, at the same time, member of the ruling class endowed with power and lofty privilege, lies at the root of the contradictory nature of the knight's ideology and self-expression. He is proud of his exalted position and seeks his own individual growth to full dignity in the free experience of bravery, skill, and actual personal power (sought and tested through adventures), but at the same time he acknowledges the source of his dignity and power in the court where he must serve (Arthur's, Charlemagne's, or others).

This ambiguous state is part of the personal predicament of medieval man. It is widely held that feudalism froze personal relations. Yet the feudal arrangement of society presupposed individual judgment and responsibility, since individuals were constantly reevaluating their dynamic relationship with neighbors and superiors, always using ideological schemas to justify practical decisions. Loyalty meant expectation of protection in exchange for service, and service could be withdrawn when no longer profitable.[6]

Both troubadour lyric and chivalric romance are tied to the nature of their audiences—chiefly courtly. In the state of quasi-anarchy that followed the break-up of the Carolingian order, the counts saw themselves forced to shape their domains into relatively independent military entities, relying on a new class of horse-mounted soldiers to enforce their claims against their equally independent-minded vassals. Knights had to be fashioned into reliable, loyal followers through a suitable education, personal support, and enfeoffment for the worthiest. Thus the lord's house became a "court," the home for these new dependents and helpers. Soldiers turned courtiers and, occasionally, noble knights with some feudal status of their own.

The knight's duty toward the lord developed alongside the need for self-assertion as an independent fighting warrior, since fighting was both part of service and a way to acquire one's own fief as due reward. During the lord's frequent absences, his wife acquired a special status carrying great authority: as the lord's substitute (*midons* < Lat. *meus dominus*, referring to the lady, meant "my lord") she became the center of the court and an object of respect, even veneration, on the part of these often unmarried knights. In courtesy and courtly love service to the lady symbolically replaced the service to the real master. If the two goals of service and acquisition were inherently at odds with each other, they still constituted a unified ideology in the imaginary representation of the man who was both adventurous knight and poet in love. The ideology developed naturally over a large front, since the refined forms of civilized behavior represented by the courtois overlay were conspicuously present not only in the lyric and the romance, but also, we shall see, in the epic. The German epic did not develop out of the Carolingian French epic or as a derivation from French courtois sources, yet it contained some of the same courtly and courtois elements as the French romance, which, in turn, was ostensibly imitated in the German romance. This might be the connecting point with the earlier German courtly tradition. Courtliness and courtoisie could develop naturally and independently in different social and cultural environments, as a result of an education that stemmed from the clerics and arose from the spiritual needs of the courts.

We are not interested here in a definition of courtly love or in a dis-

cussion of its various epiphanies, in response to those who object to the
term as little more than Gaston Paris's coinage (1883).[7] Even if this term
does not occur in the Middle Ages, the phenomena it is meant to cover
show clear distinguishing marks from all other forms of sensual love: it
should suffice here to say that, in A. J. Denomy's phrasing (1953: 44),
courtly love distinguished itself in "its purpose or motive, its formal
object, namely, the lover's progress and growth in natural goodness,
merit, and worth."

Despite repeated assurances of total, unending dedication, the lover's
relationship to the lady remains unstable and ambiguous. Hence the
puzzling changes of mind, like Walther von der Vogelweide's eloquent
"challenge to courtly love." In Bernart de Ventadorn's canso "Lo tems
vai e ven e vire," one of his famous expressions of incipient, yet re-
pented, revolt against the intolerable demands of *fin'amor*, we find an
early revelation of the inner contradictions of the psyche. After declaring his intention to turn elsewhere, Bernart eventually reiterates his devotion: his "vengut er al partimen" (I shall come to the parting of ways,
v. 35) is closely followed (v. 43) by "ja no.m partrai a ma vida" (never
in my life shall I leave her).[8]

The chivalrous code of courtesy became one of respect for the
woman and concern for others' needs and feelings, hence for good manners in public behavior. Such a code could not arise by itself from the
lords, who neither needed it nor really practiced it, but who in the end
gladly adopted it from their subordinates for the sake of order and, as
it were, a feeling of comradeship within the comital household. In
adopting it, the lords implicitly yielded to a sort of ideological black-
mail. In what Leo Spitzer called the *paradoxe amoureux* of troubadour
poetry, we see mirrored the lesser nobility's effort to integrate itself into
the higher nobility, an effort which the latter accepted by historical
necessity and managed to control.[9] This effort toward self-legitimization
(the proclaimed loyalty, *leialtat*, etymologically implied legality, *legali-
tas*) embraced a diverse group of court-dwellers who found this ideology to their common interest. Loyalty was a companion of *fe* or *fes*,
faithfulness.

Courtesy implied a self-restraint that was essential to the knights'
survival. *Mezura* became a key principle of cohabitation, entailing recognition of the limits beyond which one could not go. By its inner logic
the court also became the natural place for an art of loving, whose object was the *domina/domna*, superior by definition and unreachable,

yet desired by all.[10] Obviously mansuetude and humility (*umildat*) were a necessary marker of recognition of the lady's absolute superiority as well as the lover/courtier's readiness to be obedient in all (*obediensa*) in order to qualify as *fis*, a dedicated "faithful of Love"—his loyalty going more to the God of Love than to an individual lord or lady.[11]

The convention of this erotic relationship caused keen competition among "lovers," each of whom naturally saw in all others nothing but unworthy rivals to be exposed and denigrated. The term *lauzengiers* covers all other lovers in the audience, denounced as envious and insincere flatterers. The husband, that is, the lord, accepts this chaste devotion toward his wife and is often reminded not to take on the ridiculous role of *gilos*, "the jealous one." He is also reminded that he must reward his vassal's devotion with generous gifts—possibly land, immunities, and positions of power in the household and the domain—this reward being the real, material one adumbrated in the request for *merce* (Fr. *guerdon*) from the lady. The expectation of a benefice was part of the appeal to *dreitz*, the cardinal virtue of justice the lover proclaimed about himself and demanded of the lord.

Within the literature we are examining, different codes coexist in a state of mutual tension, the contradiction or ambiguity being a source of human and poetic richness. The application of the feudal relationship of lord and vassal to the relationship between lovers, the man becoming, in all humility, the servant, carried with it a high degree of playful ambiguity. Another factor of ambiguity was the introduction of the Christian ideology of mystic love, represented at best by the Marian cult, which became bent to profane love. Ever since it was first postulated by the French literary historian P.-L. Ginguené, it has been argued whether the Marian cult influenced courtly love or, on the contrary, it was in part a by-product of the new literary cult of womanhood. Such complexity is part of the fascination medieval literature exerts to this day, since the tension between contradictory moods results from a degree of (Christian) interiorization that ancient man could not experience.

Eduard Wechssler's and Joachim Bumke's older thesis of the nobleman becoming knight, *Ritter* (Bumke, *Studien zum Ritterbegriff*), has been brought into sharper focus by Duby's and Köhler's distinction between the "young" (*jove*) knight—poor, landless, and even *non-casé* or homeless, hence dependent on the powerful lord as his servant—and the "old" lord he serves but tries to bend to his vital interests. Jean Frappier's "culture du désir érotique freiné et prolongé" ("Vues . . .":

140) is in harmony with Duby's and Köhler's abstraction of the troubadours' code, with a view of the high nobility being "educated" by the low "nobility of spirit," soldiers of fortune of humble origin and cadets of the smaller nobility.

During the early stages, it seems reasonable to assume a coming together of the clerical educational ideals with the needs of the poor knights' class. Thus the Jaeger and the Duby/Köhler theses can be joined to fill each other's gaps. The former did not explain the survival of the curial *mentalité* after the end of the imperial bishoprics; the latter did not ask, let alone answer, why the poor knights developed an ideology that reproduced so much of the language and ethos of the *curiales*. Taken together, the two views help to explain how this unique ideology (absurd, for example, when seen in isolation in Petrarca) could acquire so much vitality as to survive almost intact for several centuries, especially through the realistic and skeptical experiences of the Cinquecento. To this outstanding example of the enduring character of aesthetic forms and themes one could apply György Lukács's argument that, beyond mere sociological relativism or determinism, the superstructure has a dynamic life of its own: as reflection or mirroring of a past reality it can live on in the collective memory for the pleasure of recalling the past.

The ideology of courtly love can be seen as part of a process of social climbing, the poor knights behaving as "marginal men" who sought recognition by the upper social stratum in order to overcome the limitations of the stratum they were trying to leave behind. A more aggressive posture could make the lords the butt of impatient courtiers, who criticized them as the "evil rich" (*rics malvatz*), incapable of true love because they were married (*molheratz*), illiberal, lustful, part of the different, inferior "others." Logical and necessary by the very nature of the ideology, these insults risked becoming counterproductive, since the desired advancement depended on the lords' good will. Yet, overlooking such occasional side effects, the lords welcomed the ideology and even joined it because it ensured the knights' loyalty, which the lords needed. A sort of compromise ensued. Some court poets, like Marcabru, remained skeptical and hostile. But some lords, like Raimbaut d'Aurenga and Eble de Ventadorn (whose "school" Marcabru vocally opposed), professed a strain of courtly love, the elitist and exclusive hermetic style of the *trobar clus*, that implicitly gave them a position of leadership. All this developed only among the second generation of Provençal lyricists:

Guilhelm IX (1071–1127) was the first troubadour only in that he started the lyrical tradition, but without spiritual connection with chivalrous ideology.[12]

Our sociological perspective may be a good way to tackle the difficult problem of the *trobar clus*. The *gaps* written in that style often boast of the poet's cunning in defeating the "folly," *foldats*, of "the others" (be these the rivals, the inferiors, or even the lords). It was an interesting bending of the curial quality of shrewdness for the sake of survival in the treacherous environment of the courts. A revealing document of the *trobar clus* is the tenso "Ara.m plaitz, Giraut de Borneill" between Raimbaut d'Aurenga and Guiraut de Bornelh (variously dated at 1168, 1170, or 1171).[13] For Raimbaut, the *grand seigneur*, the *trobar clus* was a distinctive mark of the aristocrat and a way to keep the message of this lofty poetry within the close circle of the worthy. Guiraut objected that he aimed more at universal appreciation ("qu'es mais amatz / e plus presatz / qui'l fa levet e venarsal," "it is more loved and better appreciated if you make it easy and of universal appeal," vv. 12 f.). Elsewhere he contended that the easy style is easy only in appearance, since it results from mastering the difficult art of being comprehensible to the largest possible public (including the populace gathering around the common spring) even while expressing high universal truths, occasionally sublime ones.[14] Furthermore, clarity and ease of style are the result of happiness in love. Dante was to share that position. It was, after all, the classical principle that hidden art is the best art and that the achievement lies in what Boileau would term *l'art caché*, and the late eighteenth-century German classicists, *überwundene Schwierigkeit*, to wit, in overcoming the resistance of the medium, the linguistic difficulty. Raimbaut, however, was expressing the exclusiveness of the true lord who might also want to distance himself from the common jongleurs and the rabble of the court, not to mention the commoners outside.[15] On their part, the troubadours were all the more interested in keeping the lords from monopolizing, or claiming any special rights over, the style and ideological canons that the lords had adopted but not invented.

With succeeding generations of troubadours, the courts increased in importance as they became the only locus for the poor, landless, and homeless knights. Courtesy was the common bond because of common interests (keeping harmony in the *familia*). As, with time, grants of land and property became less likely, reputation and honor (*pretz* and *onor*) no longer depended on property but on public recognition of this ideal of inner perfection. The critique of power and property, noble or bourgeois as the poets might be, was founded on this perception of a superior nobility of spirit.

The virtues invoked in the poems often betray the economic and social background of the ethical ideology, and this is probably nowhere as clear as in Marcabru, who introduces us to the haunting presences of *largueza* as the virtue of the generous and just lord deserving to be loyally served, its opposite vice being *escarsedat*, *avoleza*, or *avareza* (stinginess from avarice, Lat. *avaritia*). For all their transparent economic layers, these concepts embed the poet's implicit theology and metaphysics.[16] Above all, *escarsedat* is almost synonymous with *malvestat*, supreme wickedness and worthlessness, and the ubiquitous enemy of *proeza*, which in turn is made almost equivalent to *largueza*. Another undesirable type is the lady's guardian (*gardador*), appointed by the lord to make sure that knights do not get dangerously close to his wife. Such guardians might be domestic clerics, acting somewhat in the capacity of the eunuchs of Muslim harems, but the troubadours (like Marcabru and Bernart de Ventadorn) are not impressed with their reliability and accuse them of repaying the trust with treachery, even to the point of giving the lord bastard offspring—one cause of moral and racial degeneracy within the nobility. The troubadours saw such guardians as undeserving favorites who got the *merce*, both sexual and material, that was their own due. It was all part of the relationship between knight poets and clerics, as the poets, from Marcabru to Peire Cardenal, burdened the clergy with the critiques that were more generally aimed at the degeneracy of the Church as a whole, even though the clerics were partly responsible for the civilizing process of courtly education.[17]

The coexistence of variant codes could become outright juxtaposition to be expressed in a specific literary form, such as the *descort*, which is found in Provence, northern France, Germany, and Italy (*discordo*, *contrasto*) as well. For a telling example, compare the trouvère Colin Muset's (fl. 1230) "Quant voi lo douz tens repairier,"[18] where, as is typical of this form, the metrical difference between the strophes is meant to express the inner "discord" in the heart of the lover, his inharmonious experience of different manners of emotional involvement, constantly swinging between exaltation and alienation. This was formally analogous to Dante's expression of Pier della Vigna's inner moral discord by adopting his tortuous rhetorical style (*Inferno* 13).

The literary form of the troubadours' compositions reflects the love situation in a way that joins poetics, economics, and social ethics. The structure of the *canso* corresponds to the set social relationship.[19] Of the customary five or six stanzas, the first usually states the poet's intention, framing it in a natural setting of time and place. The second develops the poet's state of mind. The third, the central one, puts forth the praise of the lady, while the fourth stanza often inveighs against the *lauzengiers*, warning the lady against them. What follows may develop the same motifs or warn of changes of mind or tactics if the lover's worth is not recognized (and the knight's valor is not rewarded by the lord). The *envoi* usually addresses itself directly to the lady, a protector, or the lord himself. Lover, beloved, and rivals thus fill the roles of types, but in the society of the poet/knight they are, rather than simply literary conventions, real antagonists in the flesh. This analysis of the correspondence between metrical form and message exemplifies the aesthetic potential inherent in a sociological reading. Sociological criticism does not exhaust literary criticism and is only occasionally capable of investing the poetic/aesthetic level of the texts, but this is also true of most other now-current methods.

With all its repetitiveness and generic abstractness, the literary/ethical framework we have been confronting expresses the poet's feeling as a member of his society, and his style, conventional and generic as it is, adequately expresses his adherence to that society and his functioning within it. To borrow Reto R. Bezzola's sensible explanation of the peculiar nature of Occitan lyric, "le style qu'il adopte, auquel il se soumet sans en sentir la contrainte, est l'expression de cet organisme [i.e., that society]."[20] Since this literature, like most of medieval literature, was chiefly transmitted orally, the relative impersonality of oral transmission—when the message was basically repeated from memory—imposed a large degree of collectivity and "conventionality."[21]

So, courtly literature had motives. It had an ideological finality to define and clarify the values of the chivalric class. The socioeconomic basis for the noble life was clearly implied. The German terms are picturesquely effective by their internal rhyme. A knight was said to need not only the proper spirit, *muot*, but also the material means, *guot*, since he could not be generous and liberal without having anything to give: see Hartmann, *Erec*: 2263–2265; *Gregorius*: 606–620; *Iwein*: 2905–2908; and Gottfried, *Tristan*: 5648–5712. Knightly virtues are often listed pithily but emphatically by the troubadours. One detects an interesting "southern moral realism": contrary to the perfectionism that will be evident in the French romances with their images of ideal

knights, the troubadours are often aware that their possibilities are
limited, and thus, since not all virtues are attainable by one individual,
only he who is deprived of *all* courtly virtues is unworthy of knighthood. Arnaut de Maruelh (fl. 1171–1190) expresses in precise terms
this moral relativism.[22] With their unending pleas for liberality on the
part of their lords, the troubadours echoed either the hurt feelings of
decayed noblemen yearning for their lost "rights," or the hopes for
ascendance on the part of the poor landless nobility. Putting to use both
sides of the coin, nobility was, alternatively, claimed either as a birth-
right or as a matter of personal worth. Consciousness of the changes
that were taking place in the first half of the thirteenth century is evident, for example, in the troubadour Folquet de Romans's reference to
his contemporary Frederick II, who abandoned his characteristic liberality, reduced his courtiers to bureaucratic functionaries (around 1221),
and kept all the land and money for himself: in particular, his southern
court came to favor ministerial poets over professional minstrels.[23]

On the economic plane *largueza* is true virtue, as *avareza* is the
mother of all vices. But a degree of bourgeois rationality gradually intervenes in the debates on liberality among the late troubadours. The
partimen between Albert de Sisteron (Albertet de Sestaro) and Peire
(Raimon?) contrasts Albert's improvident knight who dissipates his patrimony to win his lady with Peire's reasonable and constant knight who
wins the true esteem of his lady and of society by spending advisedly, as
a warranty of future ability to support her. Similarly, and most eloquently, Sordello:

> Quar per larguesa amesurada
> anc nulz oms larcs non pres baisada,
> mas per larguesa franca e folla
> destrui.l seu e son pretz afolla.
>
> .   .   .   .
> Per qu'om deu, qui tot vol salvar,
> per la mediana via anar.

(By a measured liberality no liberal man ever lowered his status, whereas by
excessive and foolish prodigality a man destroys his patrimony and loses his
reputation. . . . He who wants to save everything must keep the middle
way.)[24]

The accent is, then, on *mesura, via mediana*, to avoid *folhor, foldat,*
"folly." The dangers of prodigality had appeared in the earlier troubadours, though not the earliest ones. Guiraut de Bornelh says that no
lord was ruined by giving too much, yet he could appreciate that foolish

liberality can cause problems.[25] Italian sources speak of the Este family almost ruining itself for excessive liberality, and of a Malaspina having to turn to highway robbery to keep up his "giving" (*donare*).[26]

On the moral plane, Guiraut de Bornelh voiced an idealistic concern for the reputation of the chivalric estate when he criticized the abuse of power by knights who turn freebooters instead of using military service for legitimate causes. In his sirventes "Per solatz revelhar" we read:

> You saw tourneys proclaimed,
> with well-equipped gentry attending,
> and then, for a time, you heard
> talk of those who fought best;
> now there is honor in robbing
> and snatching sheep from the flock.
> Shame to the knight
> who dares court a lady
> after touching bleating sheep with his hands
> or robbing churches and travelers.[27]

On the sentimental plane, the rule is not really love as we would understand it, but desire, an unfulfillable desire that is the root and source of unlimited perfectibility—somewhat like the romantic German *Sehnsucht*. Unsatisfied desire frustrates but also gives the lover the true nobility to which he aspires.[28] Satisfaction might not end the infatuation, but would end the progress toward ever increasing perfection. In the course of the thirteenth century, with the weakening of the social structures that had supported the ideology and literature of chivalry and courtly love, the expression of concrete social situations gave way to more universal and abstract schemata, referentiality being turned to broader groups and becoming more collective, as best witnessed in the German and Italian courtly lyric. The fact that political and social changes emptied the courtly motifs of their precise meaning did not make them mere formal conventions. Theme became style, as it did, conclusively, in Petrarca, with a mood of intense spirituality that was no longer socially bound. Hence, the need for allegory and symbolism, as in Ulrich von Lichtenstein and Burkhard von Hohenfels, in lieu of social definitions, however shifting, tense, and dialectically qualified they might have been.[29]

Yet the social milieu that can be identified as the chief producer and consumer, voice and audience of courtly literature, may appear too narrow for the breadth and scope of the rich poetry that is before us.[30] The attitudes that inspired such diverse writers as the Provençal minstrels, the French vagrant goliards, the Sicilian, Bolognese, and Tuscan notaries, and then Dante, Petrarca, and their cosmopolitan imitators of several countries for generations to come, shared something that went beyond their social station, origin, or function. From a functional "ideology" or *mentalité* it became an abstract one, all the more powerful and lasting.[31] Consequently, the debate on their "conventionality" or sincerity somehow misses the mark, precisely because we are dealing with an ideology rather than with personal sentiments. Understanding chivalry and courtliness as ideological phenomena places them in a clearer light than a simply social or political explanation ever could.

What the more exalted troubadours show is a state of mind that transcended and even denied the values of feudalism: their newly found *sen*, "wisdom" or "knowledge," their *gai saber*, "gay learning," became opposed to the warriorlike *ardimen*, "courage" and "bravery" (Fr. *hardiment*, G. *Tapferkeit*, Lat. *fortitudo*), and *proeza* (Fr. *proece*) of the feudal vassal and the knight. Whereas physical strength is born with us, our wisdom and knowledge are acquired, like the erudition of the clerical courtier.[32] Thus, gradually, as the feudal order started weakening, the themes also shifted in relative emphasis, undermining the original ethical system from within and moving from the *cavalaria* of the loving knight to courtly love without the warrior virtues. The knight's military qualities had been set off against the courtly qualities as valuable assets for winning ladies' favors, but later they began to lose the argument as less important. As we shall see, in the quasi-epic setting of the French and German romances it was the other way around: Erec and Yvain had to leave their ladies to prove their worth by a series of victorious knightly deeds. But in a *partimen* between Guionet (Gui de Cavaillon?) and Raembaut (Raimbaut de Vaqueiras?),[33] Raembaut decides that "Cel q'es adregz, plazenz, de bel estatge, / larcs e cortes e senes villania," "he who is correct, pleasing, of good manners, liberal and courtly and without any boorishness," is worth a hundred times more to his lady than the one who has *ardimen*, because it is not right that for one virtue alone one should possess a good lady. In another *partimen*, already mentioned, between Albert de Sisteron and Peire, the latter insinuates with a delightfully ironic touch of bourgeois common sense that military adventure is a dangerous way to win a lady. Better to have the lady without the battle; better to *be* courtly than to *have been* brave. A dead emperor is not worth very much.[34] So courtesy could now even dispense with heroic prowess. Originally *proeza* had meant military valor, as in Guilhelm IX; it was now becoming synonymous with *cortesia* even without *ardimen*. At the extreme end of such arguments, boorish *ardimen* could become an obstacle to the *cortesia* demanded by love, and even a cause of downright *vilania* when deprived of wisdom and culture (*sen*). *Sen* was originally distinguished from *saber* or clerical doctrine, shunned by the knight as pedantic bigotry (the Germans called it *pfaffisch*), but this distinction later disappeared.

We must therefore pause to ask ourselves whether we may not have to go back to where we started, since the basic meaning of this poetic school still eludes us. For one more paradox keeps staring at us: if these poems express and represent the poets' longing for recognition and reward, they keep saying that they do not attain either. We are then left wondering, as contemporary audiences might have, what is the point of iterating, poem after poem, poet after poet, indeed, from country to country, generation after generation, a message that was familiar before it was restated? It amounted to saying: "I want what I cannot get, I need what I will lack, I ask what must be denied." We are confronted with a poetry that appears conventional because it "expresses" what does not individually and personally "inspire" the poet—to use Vàrvaro's appropriate distinction.[35] The answer could be, this time, that the sociological interpretation must be integrated with the analysis of the forms, as practiced by formalist criticism, to conclude that the peculiar nature of this literature lies precisely in its being, conjointly, a verbal game aimed at the pleasure of listening to itself, as a beautiful courtly show, even while it creates by its message and forms the concrete life and practical salvation of the courtier-poet.[36] This poetry became an integral part of court ritual not in a trivial sense, but as a high-level expression of cultural and social refinement that operated as a cohesive and stabilizing factor within the individual courts and through a vast cosmopolitan network, thanks to the poets/minstrels' errancy.

We can thus answer the challenges of, say, a Roncaglia about the ambiguity and mystery of troubadour poetry as well as Zumthor's insistence on their "verbal play." *Mutatis mutandis*, we can apply to this kind of poetry (of "praise of the lady") the peculiar predicament that Stanley Fish (1988: 239) has recently extracted from Ben Jonson's poems of praise, read as an involved strategy for dealing with his ambivalent relationship to court life: "a Jonson poem always has the problem of finding something to say, a problem that is solved characteristically when it becomes itself the subject of the poem, which is then enabled at once to have a mode of being (to get written) and to remain empty of representation."

Great master of "the boast" (*gab*), his favorite genre, Peire Vidal (fl. 1180–1206) undoubtedly offers the most brilliant performance in the jocular mode of *miles ludens*, playing on the juxtaposition or mixture of heroic and courtly.[37] Even his *vidas* are a fine texture of his own ironic boasts as an outrageously successful warring knight and lover. More generally, the element of playfulness in courtois poetry is an extension of the games of courtly elegance. Such playfulness generated a high degree of casuistry in the subtle intellectual debates on conventional and abstract "cases of love," especially in the genres of *partimen* and *tenso*.[38] The chief intent of these debates may be implied in the fact that the decisions usually point to the harder one of the available choices, thus attesting to the principle of *fin'amor* as an educational process that elevates and refines the lover, spiritually, morally, and socially.[39] The highest goal is *onor*, a public, social recognition of true worth. Since, as Köhler has underlined, the term *onor* originally meant fief, this social and moral honor was a sublimated substitute for feudal benefices.[40]

To conclude, let us look at the exemplary portrait of the Young King as a paragon of knighthood in Bertran de Born's *planh* "Mon chan fenis ab dol et ab maltraire" (Pillet-Carstens 80.26—hereafter P.-C.). He was "larc e gen parlan / e gen cavalgan, / de bella faiso / e d'umil senblan / per far grans honors" (generous, noble in speech, apt on horseback, of graceful person and humble in his way of distributing great honors, vv. 5–9). He was "reis dels cortes e dels pros emperaire" (king of the courtly and emperor of the brave, 15). Hence he justly received the name of Young King, since he was the guide and father to all who were truly young: "que 'reis joves' aviaz nom agut / e de joven eras capdels e paire," 17 f. He was the embodiment of joy and love ("jois et amors," 23); he received his courtiers gently and generously in word and deed: "Gent acuillir e donar ses cor vaire / e bel respos e 'ben-sias-vengut!' / e gran hostal pagat e gen tengut / dons e garnirs et estar ses tort faire," 29–32.[41] Note the central position of *joi*, "joy of living." It went together with the other key term of *solas* (*solaz, sollatz*, OFr. *soulas*, "pleasant company" < Lat. *solatium*): court life demanded to be textured with good disposition and graced with good company. Ordericus Vitalis had said of Guilhelm IX that he had surpassed the gayest minstrels in gaity, using that term *facetus* that we have seen applied to the life of the courts as a curial virtue (*facetos etiam histriones facetiis superans*).[42]

THE FRENCH TROUVÈRES

As we leave the Occitan area we note the widespread similarity of literary expressions, which involves the immediate diffusion of Occitan themes and formal motifs, with minimal original variations in the contiguous French area. I shall restrict myself to a sampling of expressive devices in northern France, in and out of the lyric. The more distant geographic areas of Germany and Italy will yield broader basic divergences reflecting the different social situations. I shall specifically dwell on samples of formal motifs because their quick and early crystallization manifests the depth of penetration of themes that we have assumed were originally socially-bound.

Alongside the moral predicates, the ideology of courtly love also embodied the *topoi* inherited from ancient psychology and physiology, transformed into the metaphors of humors and spirits, which could take on a life of their own. The Italian Dolce Stil Nuovo is known for its use of the various *spiritelli* that stood for emotions and dispositions, but even earlier one could find personifications of parts of the psyche that became separable from the individual. These topical personifications were functional in representing the lover's alienation and his drastic inner conflict. Bernart de Ventadorn (fl. 1150–1180), for example, displayed the ideological framework of Neo-Platonic love in the sophism of the heart and soul leaving the lover. See his canso "Tant ai mo cor ple de joya" (P.-C. 70.44, st. 3 vv. 33–36): "Mo cor ai pres d'Amor, / que l'esperitz lai cor, / mas lo cors es sai, alhor, / lonh de leis, en Fransa" (I have my heart close to Love, and my spirit also runs there, but my body is here, in another place, far away from her, in France).[43] He ends his long canso "Lancan vei la folha" with this envoy: "Domna, mo coratge, / .l melhor amic qu'eu ai, / vos man en ostatge / entro qu'eu torn de sai" (Lady, I am sending you my heart, the best friend I have, as hostage until I return from here).[44]

Similarly, in his poem "Merci clamans de mon fol errement," Le Châtelain de Coucy (d. 1203) had the following: "Et quant mon cors li toil, mon cuer li rant" (When I take my body away from her, I return my heart to her). For an example from Chrétien's own region of Champagne, the trouvère Gace Brulé (fl. 1180–1213) has literally lost his heart (to the lady): "S'ele ne m'en crois, viegne i guarder: / Vez, n.en a mie dedenz mi!" (If she does not believe me, let her come and look: see, there is none inside me!).[45] In his "Ahi Amour! com dure departie," the

French trouvère Conon de Béthune (ca. 1150—1219 or 1220), on the
verge of leaving for the Crusade, protests that he is not departing from
his beloved at all, since he leaves his heart with her: "Las! c'ai jou dit?
Ja ne m'en part jou mie! / Se li cors vait servir nostre Seignour, / li cuers
remaint dou tout en sa baillie." [46] Compare, too, Thibaut de Champagne's (1201–1253) famous poem "Ausi comme unicorne sui": "mes
cuers aloit si tressaillant / qu'il vous remest, quand je m'en mui" (my
heart was startled so, that it remained with you when I moved away). [47]
Shades of Marsilio Ficino!

For even earlier cases of this striking metaphorical way to represent
inner conflict we can turn to Chrétien's *Chevalier de la charrete*. Guenièvre (Guinevere), just saved by Lancelot from a frightening imprisonment, withdraws into a chamber and refuses to speak to her dumb-
founded lover. He is said to follow her with his eyes as far as they can
go, but "while his eyes remain outside with his body, his heart is able
to go further" (vv. 4000 f.). More explicitly still, Lancelot "left but his
heart stayed with Guenièvre" (v. 4700). [48] This clearly shows how the
casuistry of love first introduced by the troubadours found parallels not
only among their imitators in the lyric but in the other courtly genres,
too, and also beyond France. Themes and motifs went together with
corresponding stylistic devices. The specific motif we are momentarily
pursuing shows that here, too, German poets were not far behind. Gottfried of Strassburg, for one, excelled in the exploitation of this stylistic/
ideological mannerism. We may recall Isolt's lengthy monologue when
Tristan leaves for a long absence in France: see verses 18,491–600,
especially the motif of "the soul in the other" at 18,510 f.: "daz ir
min leben vüeret hin / und lazet mir daz iuwer hie" (And you have
taken my life along and left your life behind with me). The most
striking episode of all is probably the humorous and surprising debate
between Hartmann von Aue and Lady Love in Hartmann's *Iwein*
(vv. 2971–3028). The motif was already in Hartmann's source, Chrétien's *Yvain* (vv. 2639 f.), but simply as the metaphor that Yvain had
left his heart behind with his wife, and that it was a wonder how the
body could go on living without it. Hartmann turned this into a major
argument and, furthermore, in developing the theme there and elsewhere, he always made the exchange mutual: see *Erec* 2364–2367 and
Gregorius 653 f. [49]

In an analogous vein, within the scope of expressing the contradictions of the lover's predicament, the rhetoric of courtly love developed
a set of conventions that could be played as a game—part of what was

then perceived as civilized refinement, the style of the élite man. A sort of initiation ritual imposed a language of seeming irrationality that combined endlessly, in elegant and witty paradox, contradictory positions of love and hate, hope and despair, happiness and sorrow. Petrarca turned all this into an enduring style of oxymora that had a serious side (the discovery of the contradictory nature of the psyche). Admittedly his early ancestors included, beyond the Provençal troubadours and the French trouvères, Ovid's *odi et amo* and Augustine's *video meliora proboque, deteriora sequor*. But Petrarca's mark on posterity was part of a general phenomenon involving the drift from live social issues toward set style forms, which eventually led to mannerisms of all sorts: an arsenal of motifs to be used as literary play and social conventions.

In "Quant l'aura doussa s'amarzis," Cercamon (fl. 1137–1152) said he was pleased when his lady made him mad, when she made a complete fool of him, when she laughed at him. He thoroughly enjoyed being full of worries for her sake, and it was up to her to make him faithful or full of tricks, a rustic peasant or a most refined courtier, and so on: "Bel m'es quant ilh m'enfolhetis / e.m fai badar e.n vau muzan; / et leis m'es bel si m'escarnis. / . . . . / Totz cossiros m'en esjauzis, / o drechuriers o ples d'enjan, / o totz vilas o totz cortes." [50] In his canso "Non es meravelha s'eu chan," Bernart de Ventadorn had it thus: "A hundred times a day I die of grief, and I revive of joy a hundred times. My disease has a wonderful appearance, for my pain is worth more than any other good," "cen vetz mor lo jorn de dolor / e reviu de joi autras cen. / Ben es mos mals de bel semblan, / que mais val mos mals qu'autre bes." [51]

For exemplary cases among the trouvères, compare Blondel de Nesle's (second half of the twelfth century) heaping of oxymora in quick succession: "plaisant martire," "a pleasant martyrdom," "douce mort," "a sweet death," "qu'en ceste amour m'est li tourmenz delis," "in this love of mine my torment is a delight" ("Mout se feïst bon tenir de chanter"). The obvious stylistic playfulness does not exclude seriousness of purpose. In Le Châtelain de Coucy's "Li nouviaz tanz" we read: "Tanc con fui miens, ne me fist se bien non, / mes or sui suenz, si m'ocit sanz raison; / et c'est pour ce que de cuer l'ai amee!" (As long as I was my own man, she did me nothing but good; But now that I am hers, she kills me without reason; This because I have loved her truly, with all my heart.) Gace Brulé says he wants what harms him most, and dismay makes him rejoice and laugh: "quant je plus vueil ce dont plus sui grevez, / et en l'esmai m'estuet joer et rire" ("Ire d'amors qui en mon cuer repere," vv. 38 f.). Also compare Conon de Béthune's "L'an que rose ne fueille": "einsi me fait vivre melleement / d'ire et de bien" (thus she makes me live in a confusion of grief and joy). Finally, in "Chançon ferais, que talenz m'en est pris," Thibaut de Champagne raves so: "Dame, por vos vueil aler foloiant / que je en aim mes maus et ma dolor, / . . . que mes granz maus por vos si fort m'agree." (Lady, for you I want to go around like a fool, for I love the grief and pain I have from you, . . . my great suffering for you pleases me so!)

There is another side to this typical and productive use of antithesis, which in its apparent play of unreality expresses the very predicament of the illusory woman represented and invoked in the lyric. The convention was there from the very beginning, and remained canonical even through the various forms of Petrarchism. For the earliest testimony, see Guilhelm IX: "Amigu'ai ieu, no sai qui s'es, / qu'anc non la vi . . . / ni'm fes que'm plassa ni que'm pes, / ni no m'en cau. . . . / Anc non la vi et am la fort." (I have a lady friend but I don't know who she is, since I've never seen her, nor has she done to me anything either pleasing or displeasing, and I couldn't care less. . . . I've never seen her yet I love her heartily.) [52] The lady may be, but does not have to be, a person: she can be the lover's other self, his better, spiritual self, his ideal of inner perfection, his mirror image—Narcissus.[53] In other words, in the specific context we are studying, the woman was the knight's chivalric and courteous self.

This possibility is an aspect of the unreality of the woman's presence in medieval literature, even while she is, conversely, the center of attention of much of the literary and artistic discourse. The apparent paradox results from woman having been symbolically invested with functions that did not literally belong to her—like being the real lord—or that were hers on a purely anthropological level—as, typically, in the common phenomenon of equivalence between biological sex and grammatical gender, *in bono et in malo*: woman as the Church (*Ecclesia*), Wisdom (*Sophia, Sapientia, Philosophia*), lust (*luxuria*), and so on.[54] It it also part of what made courtly love so exemplary and durable, namely a radical crystallization of that biological/anthropological phenomenon defined by Mircea Eliade as (Platonic) "androgynization," meaning that in love "chaque sexe acquiert, conquiert les 'qualités' du sexe opposé (la grace, la soumission, le dévouement acquis par l'homme amoureux, etc.)."[55] We have a revealing testimony to this phenomenon in the fact that the list of virtues attributed to the courtly woman is more or less the same as for the man: she is supposed to be *doussa, bela, genta, fina,* and endowed with *cortezia, pretz, sabers,* and *umildat.*

THE GERMAN *MINNESANG*

On German soil, too, the *courtois* ethos spilled over into several genres. The virtue of wisdom in the form of modesty or moderation, for example, is in the very title of a popular collection of proverbial sentences or "*Sprüche*," namely Freidank's *Bescheidenheit* of circa 1230. But it is in the lyric and the romance that we find the most fertile ground for our inquiry.

The Minnesingers were a good match for their Occitan and French peers. The most extended display of obedience at any cost had been, of course, Chrétien's Lancelot, who began by accepting dishonor when he jumped in the condemned man's chariot (and yet would later be spurned by Guenièvre for having hesitated "two steps"), and then carried on in that humiliating predicament until he outdid himself by fighting "cowardly" in the tourney at Noauz, always for the sake of Guenièvre and at her instigation. In lyrical form, after Cercamon (remember the passage quoted above from "Quant l'aura doussa s'amarzis"), the Austrian master Reinmar der Alte (1150/1160, d. before 1210, believed to be the poet praised by Gottfried as "the nightingale of Hagenau") set up the most radical standard of total *mansuetudo* vis-à-vis a mistress who behaved as a cruel tyrant:

> Of one thing only and no other do I want to be a master as long as I live: I want the whole world to give me praise for having the skill to endure suffering better than anyone. A woman is the cause of this state of mine, whereby I cannot remain silent day or night. But I have such a gentle disposition that I take her hate as joy. Yet, alas, how much it hurts![56]

Compare, furthermore, Reinmar's "waz tuon ich, daz mir liebet daz mir leiden solte?" (What am I doing, drawing pleasure from what ought to pain me?, from "Der lange süeze kumber mîn.") It is particularly significant that such expressions of service to the lady could be voiced by high lords, like the powerful Swiss count Rudolf von Fenis-Neuenburg: "Iemer mêre wil ich dienen mit staete" (I am determined to serve always with constancy).[57] It is an example of the adoption of the non-free knights' and *ministeriales'* ethic of service on the part of the lords who did not need it for survival but were conquered by the image of moral nobility it had projected.

The Minnesingers could go beyond the merely psychological representation of the contradictory nature of strong emotional states: they could use stylistic devices as fitting vehicles to express the conflicts between the competing ideologies that surrounded them. Walther von der Vogelweide is second to none in dramatically shifting between *hohe* and *nidere Minne*. His master Reinmar had said that if his lady died he could no longer go on living ("stirbet si, sô bin ich tôt"). Retorts Walther, wittily yet seriously: If *he* dies *she* is as good as dead too, since she has received her true life and glory from being loved and sung by him: "ir leben hât mînes lebennes êre; / stirbe ab ich, sô ist si tôt."[58] Perhaps even more eloquent is his famous stanza of revolt against Reinmar's unswerving devotion to a lady who is the perfect object of high love, while Walther sets side by side the distant, unreal lady of *hohe Minne* and the real, full-blooded, and truly human women he now thinks he can love: "Wîp muoz iemer sîn der wîbe hôhste name / und tiuret baz danne frowe, als ichz erkenne." (Woman will always be the highest name of women, / and is higher praise than lady, I now hold.)[59]

Close as it remained, all in all, to the troubadour lyric, the *Minnesang* also showed marked differences from it.[60] The absence of the concept of *joven*, "youth," and *joi* in the exalted comprehensive sense it had in southern France—Middle High German *vröide* (G. *Freude*) is more neutral—reflected a different social situation and resulted in the absence of certain literary forms. The fact that German courts were configured with a predominance of *ministeriales* over knights of lineage, imposed a greater respect for the lords and less polemical spirit against them, since the often non-free *ministeriales*, who did not enjoy any mobility, tended to accept their given status. Even a knight of lineage like Walther von der Vogelweide, with all his restlessness, was compelled to place *werdekeit*, "value," in a sense of *mâze*, "measure," that was equivalent to "loyal" acceptance of one's "stable status" (*staete*): see his famous poem "Aller Werdekeit ein füegerinne" to Lady Moderation, *Vrouwe Mâze*, where he says: "So bîn ich doch, swie nieder ich sî, der werden ein, / genuog in mîner mâze hô" (However low my status is, I still am, with regard to my worth, high enough within my status).[61]

The traditional explanation has been that the *Minnesang* was the creation of the higher nobility, hence not possibly polemical against it, but once again, as with regard to the origins of troubadour poetry, this hypothesis is contradicted by documented fact. The reason for the difference is the greater stability of court life and family relations as well as the infrequency of knights errant (*vagantes*) in German lands. Hence *senhals*, the pseudonyms for the beloved, or the practice of "ladies of the screen," as seen in Italy, including Dante's *Vita nuova*, were also not needed: they would simply have made the husbands unnecessarily suspicious. Likewise, the Minnesingers were not inclined to break a spear in favor of inner nobility, nor were they so much interested in combating jealousy: the married lord's trust in his wife was his own business and the German courtier was not about to advise him on how to deal with it. They were content to emphasize envy, *nît*.[62]

Accepting one's state, however, poses another paradox in the practice of courtiership and courtly love, since staying put is not only unproductive, but defeats the very premise of the knight's progress: as courtier or lover he must either aspire to a higher state or decay. Despite the courtly love pretensions of pure love outside matrimony, both hereditary knights and *ministeriales* aspired to profitable marriages above their state or with moneyed ladies. The moment of utility was repressed and transferred in the literature, but the fact was not removed on the level of praxis. After an initial stage of alliance between knights and *ministeriales*, Walther's "revolt" showed that the former could learn how to part ways with the latter, protesting their freedom of choice, as Walther did, and threatening to leave the service of the *vrouwe* if she refused to behave as a *wîp*, that is, as a woman rather than as a mistress. Like Walther, the noble poets could go as far as to claim that she owed them as much as they owed her, or more: since they could *make* her, she could repay by *making* them—or lose them.[63] In the meantime, this bold but just claim constitutes an important chapter in the history of poets' self-consciousness concerning the value and power of poetry to grant status and glory to the powerful.

Many key terms of the *Minnesang* are equivalent to those of the troubadours: *gemüete, sin, tumpheit, kumber, elende, übermuot, senen, sorge, biderbe, wert, leide*, and *mâze* correspond, respectively, to *corage*, "valor"; *sen*, "wisdom"; *foldat*, "folly"; *ira*, "sadness"; *caitiu*, "wretched"; *orguelh*, "pride"; *dezirar*, "to desire"; *cuidar*, "worry"; *pro*, "advantage"; *valor*, "worth"; *sofrir*, "suffering"; and *mezura*, "moderation." But there were new and different terms also. *Vröide* corresponds to *joi* but with an ulterior sublimation into *saelde*, completely lacking in the troubadours. Despite the mystical overtone of sanctity (*saelde/saelic*, like *sâlig* and *sâlida*, is the etymology of G. *selig*, "blessed"), this concept is unlike the troubadours' assimilation of love for the lady to love for the Virgin Mary, as they did when they became affected by the religious involution after the Albigensian Crusade. It meant, rather fatalistically, "happy through good fortune." Similarly, the rendering of *merce* with *lôn* and *gnâde* (benefice, grace) stressed the unexpected character of the reward, coming as a gratuitous, rare act of favor. This further proves a lower social origin, since lords would not expect grace: they could only grant it, not receive it—and they performed neither *dienst*, "service," nor *arebeit*, "work," as the courtiers insisted they did.[64]

The *Minnesang* remained productive, if no longer original, through the next century until, in the fifteenth century, it flowed into the art of the Meistersingers. One latter-day Minnesinger was Hugo von Montfort (1357–1423), a great nobleman from the Vorarlberg who served as intendant of the Austrian Duke Leopold III and governor in Swiss and Austrian provinces. His poetry combines the duties of the Christian knight with the canons of *Ritterdienst* and *Minnedienst*, chivalry and courtly love, and praises, instead of an unreachable lady, the three women to whom he was successively happily married. The process of Christianization is somewhat analogous to that which we can observe in Spain in the same century, but it is interesting to catch a German high aristocrat in the act of transcending the original social functions of courtly love.

The fourteenth and fifteenth centuries witnessed a fashion of erotic allegory (*Minneallegorie*) which did not tire of reproducing a set progress of the knight riding through a forest where he meets a beautiful lady: she leads him to a castle where he makes the acquaintance of a series of female allegorical figures that reproduce such familiar chivalric virtues as Love, Joy, Honor, Chastity, Constancy, and Honesty.[65] *Die Jagd* (ca. 1335) of the knight Hadamar von Laber from the High Palatinate is regarded as the high point in the genre for the early period. It was often imitated both in subject matter and in its way of using the "Titurel-stanza." In the flowery style that often characterizes such compositions, Hadamar has an allegorical hunter pursue a deer with the help of his spiritual forces, the hounds Triuwe, Staete, Fröude, Liebe, Leide, Trûren, Sene, Harre, and more, but to no avail, since this kind of hunt can have no end (*Ende*) except in death.

A related, not always distinguishable subgenre was the *Minnerede*, which established itself in the first quarter of the fourteenth century. After reaching a definite form in the second quarter, it lived on through the remainder of the century and, in newly adapted form, even through the sixteenth century. It was an aristocratic diversion (Heinrich Niewöhner, its most outstanding student, declared it composed exclusively for the nobility, at least in the early stage).[66] In the form of a set rhetorical speech the *Minnerede* discussed the specific virtues (sometimes personified and allegorized) that preside over the exercise of true love, namely Treue, Staete, Ehre, Wahrhaftigkeit, and Verschwiegenheit, together with the classic obstacles interposed by the lady's indifference. It also debated the choice between high love or mere friendship, romantic love or sexual gratification, a married lady or a virgin, and the question whether the lady ought to prefer a knight or a cleric. The medieval court of love and its attendant games and judgments found a new garb which replaced the *Minnesang*'s lyrical expression of personal feeling and experience with abstract theoretical debate on set themes in rhymed oratorical form.

The three discrete codes (the courtly, the chivalric/heroic, and the chivalric/*courtois* or, more simply, the courtly, the chivalrous, and the *courtois*) do not correspond to separate genres. All in all, however, the third code was the staple of the medieval love lyric, whereas the romance, to which I shall turn next, incorporated all three in different stages, often wavering in its uneasy relationship with the second and the third.

CHAPTER FIVE

Courtesy in the French Romance

FROM EPIC TO ROMANCE: THE FIRST GENERATION

The world view of the lyric bears a closer relation to that of the courtly romance than has been commonly recognized in historical expositions.[1] We have seen how the former reflects our theme: let us now look at the latter. We will find there the perfect knight who joins in his exemplary person the leading qualities of *arma, amor,* and *litterae*—the valor of the fighter, the refinement of the true lover, and the sophistication of the educated man of society.

The French epics or *chansons de geste* have been amply analyzed for incipient elements of chivalry and courtesy. I shall therefore start with an example outside the main French cycles and single out a Provençal epic of circa 1150, the ten-thousand-line *Girart de Roussillon*, celebrating the struggle between the French King Charles Martel and his vassal Girart. We encounter there the striking portrait of a chivalrous knight readying for battle whom Maurice Keen has found to be of the same mold as the Arnold of Ardres and William the Marshal of somewhat later chronicles.[2]

> Folcon was in the battle lines, with a fine hauberk, seated on an excellently trained horse. . . . He was most graciously armed. . . . And when the king saw him he stopped, and went to join the Count of Auvergne, and said to the French: "Lords, look at the best knight that you have ever seen. . . . He is brave and courtly and skilful, and noble and of a good lineage and eloquent, handsomely experienced in hunting and falconry; he knows how to play chess and backgammon, gaming and dicing. And his wealth was never

denied to any, but each has as much as he wants. . . . And he has never been slow to perform honorable deeds. He dearly loves God and the Trinity. And since the day he was born he has never entered a court of law where any wrong was done or discussed without grieving if he could do nothing about it. . . . And he always loved a good knight; he has honored the poor and lowly; and he judges each according to his worth."[3]

The 114 lines dedicated to him present Folcon as an ideal knight thanks to courtly virtues (he is *cortes* in the sense of "having the manners of the court," according to Hackett) that, outside the lyric, are perhaps here for the first time attributed to a knight rather than a nobleman. He hates war but enters the field of battle with fierce bravery when loyalty calls. He shows good breeding, liberality, and eloquence as well as skill in the courtly pastimes of hunting and social games. His humanity and sense of justice toward the needy also make him the sort of knight that the Peace of God had been preaching.[4]

Another significant episode in the early epic deserves our attention. The French *Coronement Looïs* is part of the cycle of Guillaume d'Orange, the hero of this poem, within the vast *geste* of Garin de Monglane, which goes back to historic characters of the late eighth century. The high nobility's duty to uphold justice (typically, defend orphans and widows) makes a dramatic entrance in this poem when, at the solemn ceremony prepared in the chapel of Aachen for the crowning of his own son, Charlemagne declares that he will veto the investiture unless the candidate king swears to uphold these high ideals:

If you must, dear son, allow yourself to be corrupted, put on and exalt arrogance (*démesure*), indulge in lustfulness and breed sin, take his fief away from an orphan, subtract even four deniers from a widow, in the name of Jesus, son Louis, I deny this crown to you and forbid you to take it.[5]

As Louis hesitates to come forward and take the oath, Charlemagne, in front of all the high nobility of France, declares him unfit to rule and orders him sent to a convent. The action proceeds with the attempt by Arneïs d'Orléans to take over the throne by offering to save Louis and act as his regent until he shows to be worthy of the succession. Guillaume of Orange, however, intervenes, unmasks Arneïs as an impostor, kills him, and puts the crown on Louis's head. Charlemagne accepts Guillaume's warrant that his son deserves the crown.

This surprising plot illustrates how the epic, though of noble origin within the feudal structures, could transcend a class perspective. Arneïs represents the real interests of the high nobility, namely to limit the monarch's hereditary power, whereas Guillaume (regardless of his historic position) becomes a sympathetic hero by acting in a manner that contradicted his class interests and was consonant with popular sentiment—briefly, the growing spirit of national solidarity under and around the king and his family. The king stands for the nation precisely insofar as he is inherently opposed to the interests of the great lords. Consequently, even while stressing the close connection of this literature with the noble spheres that bred it, as historians we cannot interpret it as a direct expression of class interests.[6] The epic became popular precisely because it elicited sympathy over a broad social spectrum. Its generic "horizon of expectations" was collective to the point of encompassing a wide range of "national" consciousness. It is this broad appeal that made the French legends popular even outside France. In Italy they were recited both in noble circles (as in the Venetia under the Ghibelline lords) and in the streets and public squares of free mercantile communes (as in Florence down to the late fifteenth century, the days of Luigi Pulci). At the same time the rich ideological texture of the early epics reflects a tension between the ideal of the monarchic sovereign and the interests of the great lords, who, as typically in the Guillaume of Orange cycle, can overshadow an occasional undeserving king like Louis. Charlemagne himself could be forced by his rebellious lords to recognize his own impotence. In *Huon de Bordeaux* he ends up having to admit himself unworthy of drinking at the cup of "the pure."[7]

The epics put forth the growing conflict between the image of the king as supreme embodiment of the collectivity, the "nation," and the lords' resistance to the process whereby that higher authority imposed limitations on their own sovereign rights. This kind of internal opposition is also found in the Arthurian romances. With the Plantagenets' either tacit or explicit endorsement, the creators of the Arthurian legend upheld the claims of the feudal lords against the centralizing monarchy embodied in the Plantagenets' enemies, the Capetian kings.[8] Arthur became a sort of anti-Charlemagne. He was an ideal feudal king because he behaved as a *primus inter pares*; his peers' identity and dignity derived from their individual adventures away from the court.

Resistance was a matter of survival. Originally, the epic could be used as a functional form of ecclesiastical propaganda to promote the Crusades as well as those cooperative monarchs who led the marches against the infidels. Now other clerics at feudal courts came to the aid of the threatened lords in much the same way, providing them, through the Arthurian mythology, with an ideological means to resist their annihilation.[9] The romance stepped in to assert in coherent terms the great vassals' resistance against those among the French kings (signally Charles VI, Charles VII, and Philip Augustus) who had become conscious of their antifeudal function. The progress of royalty was to mark the evolutionary parable from feudalism to absolute monarchy, culminating with the triumph of centralized absolutism under Louis XIV, whereas elsewhere, as in Germany and, with the long parenthesis of the Elizabethan period, England, the lords held their ground and kept the kings in check.

The medieval romance (Fr. *roman*) is a hard-to-define genre that stems from early French texts already embodying aspects of chivalry and courtliness, namely the "classical romances"—the various *romans d'Alexandre, d'Énéas, de Troie,* and *de Thèbes,* the first of them (the first version of the *Alexandre*) composed around 1100, the others around 1150/1160.[10] These texts continued to enjoy great popularity even outside France: Heinrich von Veldeke, for example, produced a German version of the *Énéas* in his *Eneit* of circa 1170–1189. As the romances grew, their courtly elements became clearer. The anonymous Picard version of the *Alexandre* (ca. 1270), perhaps the best-known version today, starts with the author's polemical allusion to his inept predecessors who "strive to be prized at court," and with his address to an audience of people who "wish to soften their hearts toward good manners" by reading the story of a great hero who inherited from his mother Olympias "such virtues that he was sweet and humble and full of generosity."[11] In the story, Aristotle is made to advise his pupil Alexander on how to win loyal service through *largesse*—generous giving.[12] Similarly, in their *chansons de geste* Garin le Lorrain and Guillaume of Orange, among others, are shown winning the loyal services of knights by promising lavish gifts.[13] A prolific subgenre commonly labeled *roman d'aventure* (G. *Schicksalroman*) is characterized by a sense of fate, fortuna, or chance—qualities which dominate the interminable strings of adventures the heroes and heroines have to go through before attaining their goal, a happy reunion. The label differentiates these often lively texts from the Arthurian variety, where the adventure follows ethical and aesthetic rules that are part of the chivalric code. A particularly interesting example is the successful *Partonopeus de Blois* (ca. 1170?, anonymous though sometimes attributed to a Denis Piramus), which mixes with great verve antique elements, Arthurian ones, and contemporary historical events within a geographic setting that goes from France to the Byzantine East.[14]

The romances of "ancient" matter borrowed some Arthurian lore and also some features from the courtois lyric. The more literate or "clerical" milieus enlarged the ancestral vision of the world of chivalry by including not only ancient Trojan and Roman heroes—duly interpreted as early knights and regularly represented in knightly garb as in medieval iconography, according to a practice that endured through the Renaissance—but also some military biblical figures. The ambitious knightly ideal was thus given an illustrious ancestry that harmonized the Christian with classical and biblical ascendants: Charlemagne, Arthur, and then the Crusading leader Godfrey of Bouillon found themselves flanked by such monumental personages as Hector, Alexander, and Julius Caesar, plus the hallowed Old Testament figures of Joshua, King David, and Judas Maccabaeus. This impressive sequence, or variant thereof, constitutes the canonical series of the Nine Worthies that we see represented from the late-thirteenth-century Vulgate version of the *Queste del Graal* (Bodmer MS) [15] on through Renaissance literature as well as in popular castle frescoes, tapestries, and manuscript illuminations from France to Germany and northern Italy. The Nine Worthies were often paired with the Nine Heroines, who, however, did not symmetrically parallel the male series since they tended to be mostly ancient figures. Nevertheless the idea could show its enduring vitality through the addition of modern characters in later times: Christine de Pisan (1364—after 1429), for one, placed Joan of Arc among the canonical knightly Heroines. [16]

The apocryphal *Gospel of Nicodemus* was also inserted into this grand repertory of knightly heroes through the story of Joseph of Arimathea, the guardian of the Grail (conceived as Christ's eucharistic cup), whose lineage led directly to Perceval and Lancelot's son Galahad in Robert de Boron's *Joseph d'Arimathie*. [17] Keen (120) recalls that the introduction to a French translation of the Books of Judges, Kings, and Maccabees done for the Knights Templar between 1151 and 1171 points to the principles of "chivalry" to be learned from those sacred books. That Christine de Pisan did not hesitate to configure Paris and Helen as courtly lovers (*Épître d'Othéa*) [18] was only one example of that alluring chivalric disguise of ancient heroes which endured in literature and art well into the Renaissance, and not only in France. [19]

Paul Zumthor (1987: 299–311) has forcefully underlined the "uniquely literary" nature of the medieval romance as opposed to the basic "orality" of the lyric, the epic, and other narrative forms. The epic,

in particular, was originally oral or, if written down, so done only as a
textual basis for a fully oral performance, hence to be recited by a minstrel who was, in the concrete act of delivery and performance, indistinguishable from an author/narrator. The *lai*, contemporary to the romance, also expressly declares its oral derivation, while the *conte* was
written down only after an oral tradition (ibid. 301). In clear opposition
to the other forms, the *roman* was written as a text with a relatively
fixed and independent status, to be read before a live audience, presumably at a court, as the work of an individual, self-conscious author. The
possibility was open for works of mixed status, as exemplified by Gautier d'Arras's *Éracle*.[20] Gautier (fl. 1170–1185), also a cleric, was probably a *compain* of Chrétien at the court of Champagne, and may be the
butt of Chrétien's critiques in the prologue of the *Chevalier de la
charrete*.

Reviewing the genesis of the Breton romance, Jean Frappier has argued for Celtic origin and for the Welsh and Cornish minstrels as channels of transmission through the Norman court in England, then on to
the Continent.[21] Whatever may have been the role of Celtic traditions
in the shaping of the French *courtois* ideology, no doubt they contributed significantly to notions that coincided with those independently
developed earlier at German courts. However, while German courtliness had been decisively centered on loyal service to the emperor, the
French romance served the specific function of vindicating the autonomous, antimonarchic claims of the great feudal vassals.

Geoffrey of Monmouth's *Historia regum Britanniae* (1136) is the
major source of the Arthurian cycle and the "matter of Brittany," and
this "*Énéide* bretonne en prose" (Frappier 1978: 189) already contained clear chivalric and courtois elements, including the all-important
coupling of love and valor, *amor et militia*. This, at least thirty years
before Chrétien and about twenty years before the *romans de Thèbes,
d'Enéas*, and *de Troie*. King Arthur's knights regularly proved their
mettle at tourneys in the presence of ladies with whom they were in
love. No lady worth her honor would think of granting her love to a
knight who had not tested himself successfully three times: this kept the
courtly ladies "chaste" and the knights more noble through their love
for them:

> facetae enim mulieres . . . nullius amorem habere dignabant nisi tertio in
> militia probatus esset. Efficiebantur ergo castae quaeque mulieres et milites
> pro amore illarum nobiliores. (chap. 157, vv. 41–44)[22]

Arthur's court is represented as the most splendid ever and much given to lavish displays and games and is said to have become the envy of the world also for being the realm of *facetia*: "copia divitiarum, luxu ornamentorum, facetia incolarum cetera regna excellebat," "it excelled all other realms in riches, luxury, and the ingeniousness of its inhabitants."[23] This rather uncommon meaning for *facetia* can be rendered with "wit," but Frappier does not hesitate to translate it as *courtois*. Interestingly enough Wace translated *facetia* and *facetae mulieres* in the passage just quoted from Geoffrey's chapter 157 precisely with *curtesie* and *curteise dame*.[24] This term's semantic field will appear all the clearer if we think of the mid-twelfth-century didactic poem *Facetus de moribus et vita* by an anonymous cleric (see my chap. 2 above).

Geoffrey's ample narrative, perhaps a way to impress the Normans with the native dignity of the British Celts, victorious fighters against both Anglo-Saxons and Romans, covered the whole of Arthur's fantastic parable, from triumph to final ruin through the disintegration of the realm on account of infighting between the feudal lordships and the potentially anarchic elements of courtesy, including Lancelot's tryst with Guinevere. The twelfth-century poets picked up only the adventures of the happy period, leaving the *Götterdämmerung* to the thirteenth-century compilers of cyclical prose romances, who felt in tune with this part and carried it on until it reached the capable hands of Sir Thomas Malory. Around 1230 the prose romances would thus seal Arthur's tragic fate, and "l'enchantement finira par devenir désenchantement" (Frappier 1978: 211).

Wace's *Roman de Brut* (dated at 1155, labeled as *romans* at the end of the text, and dedicated to Henry II's wife Alienor of Aquitaine) portrays Arthur thus:

> Servir se fist cortoisement
> Et mult se maintint noblement.
> Tant com il vesqui et raina,
> Tos autres princes surmonta
> De cortoisie et de proesce
> Et de valor et de largesce.

(He had himself served with *courtoisie* and held himself most nobly. As long as he lived and reigned, he surpassed all other princes in *courtoisie*, bravery, valor, and generosity.)[25]

At verse 9655 Wace praises Queen Guinevere as very liberal and eloquent, "mult fu large et buene parliere," besides being the most beautiful lady on the island. After the episode from Geoffrey of Monmouth where Duke Cador welcomes the Roman procurator Lucius's challenge to Arthur by extolling warfare as the way to keep knights from going soft and lazy, Wace adds this illuminating answer from Gawain to Cador:

> Sire cuens, dist Walwein, par fei,
> De neient estes en effrei.
> Bone est la pais emprés la guerre,
> Plus bele et mieldre en est la terre;
> Mult sunt bones les gaberies
> E bones sunt les drüeries.
> Pur amistié e pur amies
> Funt chevaliers chevaleries.[26]

(Sir Count, said Gawain, truly, you have no cause to fear. Good is peace after a war, the land becomes all the more beautiful and better; there is good in pleasant conversations and in love affairs. It is for love and their beloveds that knights perform their chivalrous deeds. Vv. 10,765–772.)

Uther Pendragon, too, is vividly depicted as being madly in love with Ygerne (vv. 8549–8665).[27] If his behavior on this occasion cannot be labeled as courtois or chivalrous, other particulars could not be described otherwise. It is tempting to conjecture that such ideas might have traveled from southern to northern France and England with Alienor having a firm hand in the *translatio*—unless it was a spontaneous generation, with or without Celtic imports.

It is interesting to compare the *Brut* with the *Roman de Horn* (early 1170s), that has been judged as "the most typically English" among the Anglo-Norman romances. Whereas *Brut* presents an idealistic and courtly view of knighthood, with sharp differentiation between *chevalers* and such *gent menue* as *pouners, sergans, gelduners, esquiers, garcuns*, and *archers*, in *Horn* the emphasis is on moral probity, religious faith, and traditional military virtues: "courtesy" is replaced by the adverb *vassalment*, stressing duty toward the lord. Horn, a landless knight who wonders who he is, since he has not yet been tested ("Joe ne sai ke joe sui, ne fui onc espruvez," v. 1167), successfully tests his *valur* by feats of arms while still a *bacheler* deprived of *adobement*. He thus finds his identity and is recognized as a true knight: "Or estes chevalier" (v. 1780).[28]

THE AGE OF CHRÉTIEN

As already stated, the romance was far from a well-defined genre. Most striking in this large production are the differences among authors and

texts. Despite appearances at this chronological remove, the evolution
of themes and forms was quick and intense. The same episodes, plots,
and motifs could assume different, contrasting meanings in contemporary or immediately subsequent authors, as is so apparent in the Lancelot and Tristan legends.[29] Plots and myths were props or literary
pretexts for the treatment of vital moral, psychological, social, and
even metaphysical and religious issues, since the often fanciful and
mysterious-sounding motifs, including ogres, fairies, and magic imple-
ments, were essentially *metaphors*—as was even the relationship between lovers.[30] Chrétien de Troyes (fl. ca. 1165–1190) tackled not only
diverse themes in different poems (love and marriage, love and knighthood, love and loyalty to the liege, knighthood and service to God), but
changed his mind on these interrelated values, since he was constantly
trying to offer a harmonious solution that kept evading him and his
society. Hence the textual features we will observe can seldom be taken
as definitions of their works' general import. In his attitude toward his
subject matter, Chrétien can even be viewed as a cleric who ultimately
rejected both courtly love and chivalry.[31] This may sound like a radical
conclusion about the man who more than anyone contributed to the
crystallization of both sides of that ideological phenomenon. But the
main point is that Chrétien appears to us as a cleric who strove to
understand and resolve the contradictions inherent in his subject matter
while remaining bound by the ethical imperatives consistently raised by
the anticourt critics. Combining the anthropological and the aesthetic,
we could say that in these and other romances the narrative art provides
an illusion of order within a perception of reality that is so fraught with
uncertainties as to border on chaos.

The writers of romances were aware that their novel compositions
did not fit the canonical narrative forms. This is evidenced by the lack
of a set generic style of the kinds inherited from antiquity. From Auerbach to Daniel Poirion, literary critics have studied Chrétien's undefined
style, always stressing its "median" quality that hovered somehow in a
no-man's land between the high style traditional for the epic, including
the *Chanson de Roland*, and the low style of both popular and religious
narrative.[32] Despite strongly "class-determined" restrictions in subject
matter, Auerbach saw this as an abstract and "absolute" genre that
excluded the representation of a social and political reality, since the
authors had adopted an ideal fairy-tale world consisting entirely of
deeds of *arma et amor*, "arms and love," the latter often as motivation
for the former.[33] Nevertheless, all its abstract principles and outward

ritual notwithstanding, the chivalric ethos was an operative one that created "a community of the elect, a circle of solidarity."[34] Auerbach's characterization must be further qualified with the remark that both Chrétien and his German imitators, mainly Hartmann and Gottfried, were aware of this fairy world's limitations, and reacted to them in a productive way. The lingering popularity of these literarily "abstract" tales can only be explained by their disguising a concrete social predicament. Once again, without being a mirror of society, good literature reveals and expresses society's deeper structural truths.

The mysterious quality of characters who do not behave like real people is part of the poetic charm of these literary texts, yet their characters' deviations from the norm clamor for explanation: we cannot assume that they act as they do simply to be "artistically" odd. Arbitrary oddity is not likely to produce the enduring charm of finished poetry, and contemporary readers must have sensed that there was a concrete meaning to such strange stories. Chrétien, for one, alerted them to his hidden *san*.[35]

Auerbach (119) found the ideal of graduated perfectibility through courtly love and knightly adventure analogous to the experiences of mystic love among the Victorines and the Cistercians in the same century—allowing for the difference of the theological setting as well as the absence of class restrictions in the religious experiences of those monastic movements. Chrétien praised a socially oriented code of courtly behavior combined with love as a powerful inspiration enhancing, not impeding the heroic virtues of knightly valor.[36] From the vantage point of its psychological content, the peculiarity of courtly love stands out more clearly when set against the background of ancient erotic literature. The continuous popularity of Ovid even in the lower schools testifies that pagan sexuality remained very much alive in the Middle Ages. Ovid is conspicuously present in many medieval literary texts on love, even when they are marked by a strong *courtois* and chivalric flavor. Suffice it to mention in passing such thirteenth-century French texts— from a period when courtly love had already reached full bloom—as Maître Élie's rendering of the *Ars amatoria*, the anonymous Norman *Clef d'amour*, Guiart's *Art d'amors*, the anonymous Anglo-Norman *De courtoisie*, Robert de Blois's *Le chastoiement des dames*, Drouart de la Vache's *Livres d'amours*, and Richard de Fournival's *Consaus d'amours*.[37] But the need for self-sacrifice, the devotion to a distant ideal, and the satisfaction in chastity and frustration that are such striking features of courtly love were the direct counterpart of the

Ovidian *Ars amatoria*, with its overtly cynical strategies for winning the lady's sensual favors quickly and without afterthoughts.

We can assume that, whereas the French *chansons de geste* must have been close to anticourt clerical milieus, the *matière de Bretagne*, instead, issued from curial clerics, prone to invest knighthood with the ways of *curialitas*. The two mentalities still coexisted in Saxo Grammaticus' *Gesta Danorum* (1186–ca. 1218). With striking contradiction this author extolled the savagery of Starcatherus, who slew the effeminate husband of King Ingellus's sister, yet he also praised King Canute's (Knud, d. 1035) decision to have his wise counselor Opo of Seeland impose the courtly code on the unruly knights who made political order impossible at court.[38] Just as royal chaplains and imperial bishops had been constrained by standards of conduct imposed as conditions for obtaining their offices, so did King Canute need to polish the warriors at court if they were to be turned into a wieldy instrument of government. There was a conspicuous difference between the lesser nobility at court (Canute's court nobles), who needed restraint of the "courtly" type, and the free higher lords (like Starcatherus), who did not, since they survived by remaining aggressively self-sufficient and independent of the king (the French *fronde* could go on even under the heavy hand of Mazarin). The novelty of twelfth-century France was the cultural (not yet the social) adoption of chivalry by the higher nobility—that is to say, in idea and feeling, not in actual behavior. The new standards originally imposed by real life conditions became ideals and mental models.

Among the key narrative themes of the romances that narratology and semiotics have tried to single out, there is the ever-present *aventure*, definable in sociological terms as "an invention of the poor or lower nobleman"[39] who, like the members of a *maisné*, imagines himself striking out for success (a good marriage, eventually, or a stroke of good fortune) in order to (re-)enter Arthur's court with full rights.[40] Since the Arthurian world of chivalry was inadequate to satisfy the lofty needs of the perfect knight, he might have to seek his perfection in an individual experience—possibly, as with Perceval, of a mystical nature. Typically, Chrétien represented Arthur's court as a counterpart of the Capetian attempt to build a truly sovereign centralized monarchy by stifling out the "anarchic" independence of the feudal nobility and its acolytes, even if this meant raising up the ministerial bourgeoisie. Arthur's "weakness" makes him the ideal feudal king, with his court acting like a chivalric switchyard or, as Köhler wittily put it, "a welfare institute for knights."[41] Arthur's Round Table (made to seat 1500 knights!), first introduced by Wace in the *Roman de Brut*, picturesquely symbolized this aristocratic egalitarianism as a palatable alternative to monarchic sovereignty.[42] Working at the court of Alienor's daughter Marie de Champagne, and her husband Philip of Flanders, another count of exemplary feudal background, Chrétien carried on and raised to the sublime level of art the heritage of Provençal courtesy and knighthood that Alienor had probably brought from Aquitaine to Paris and then to England, and which could be identified with the public image of the anti-French Angevin lords.[43]

This propaganda element, as it were, could then work back on reality, as it did when it fostered the fusion of nobility and knighthood and then again when it inculcated the hopeful ideology in the rural nobility resisting central control down through the Fronde (see my chap. 11 on the case of d'Urfé's *Astrée*). But resisting the victorious march of monarchism—in both France and, with healthy compromises, England—was partly utopian, hence subject to fears and occasional despair. It was not without a degree of desolation that Chrétien's epigones down to Sir Thomas Malory perceived the *Götterdämmerung* of Arthur's court.

If somewhat extreme, Chrétien is exemplary in displaying the attitudes of the chivalric class. His world was reserved for the knights, and the despised *vilain*, also identified with the rising bourgeoisie so prominent in the regions of Champagne and Flanders, was its antithesis. Listen to Guiganbresil's sister insulting the burghers of the city: "Vilenaille, / chien anragé, pute servaille" (boors, rabid dogs, despicable slaves—*Perceval*: 5955 f.). In his encounter with a free town's burghers, Gauvain refuses to use his shield as too noble a piece of armor for such rabble (ibid. 5894 f.). He considers it the greatest insult to be taken for a merchant (5091 ff.).[44] In five of the dialogues of book 1 of his *De amore* or *De arte honeste amandi* (1180s), Chrétien's contemporary, Andreas Capellanus, shows awareness of the alliance between the monarchy and the bourgeoisie by introducing burghers as possible rivals of knights in a lady's love, and by stressing that true nobility is a spiritual matter rather than one of rank, since we all have a common origin from Adam.[45] The *chanson de geste Guillaume d'Angleterre* strongly underlines these class contrasts, presenting with a sense of horror the attempt of some merchants to teach the trade of tannery to the king's sons they have adopted (vv. 1342 ff., 3205 ff.).[46] What alarms the poet is the unthinkable association of a nobleman with a manual art—it does not occur to him that those merchants acted more responsibly than the king toward his sons.

All this is typical of northern France;[47] in the south the relationship between the nobility and the merchant class was much less strident. Especially in Toulouse and southwest France, the towns, much like the Italian communes, teemed with *urban* knights who constituted the bulk of the city's defense even against the local lords (in the late 1170s, for instance, knights commissioned by the city consuls barred Count Raimon V of Toulouse from the city). More important still, these knights were actively engaged in the town's main business as outright traders and speculators in land rents and mortgages. As they did in Italy, they lived in fortified houses and built towers within the city walls—an irritating and surprising sight to the northern invaders at the time of the Albigensian Crusade.[48] Accordingly, in the Midi the merchant was not, as he was in the north, the nobleman's natural political enemy, actively allied with the monarchy in trying to curtail feudal privileges.

Chrétien's way of embedding into his works the exclusivism of the high nobility can be profitably compared with the mentality of contemporary chroniclers on the one hand and troubadours on the other.[49] The reader will remember the encounter between Geoffrey the Handsome and the peasant in Jean de Marmoutier's chronicle (my chap. 3). In Chrétien's *Yvain*, when Calogrenant meets a savage, subhuman-looking, monstrously ugly shepherd and asks him whether he is "boene chose ou non," the answer he gets is that "il ert uns hom." He probes further: "Quiex hom ies tu?" And the new answer is: "Tex con tu voiz; si ne sui autres nule foiz . . . sui de mes bestes sire." (Such as you see, I am lord of my beasts, never anything else.) When, in his turn, the shepherd asks Calogrenant "quiex hom tu ies, et que tu quiers," the knight defines himself as "un chevaliers qui quier ce que trover ne puis; assez ai quis, et rien ne truis." (I am a knight who seeks what I cannot find: much have I searched and nothing do I find.)[50] The *vilain* is nothing but a man, and being is doing: a man is what he does—his work—so he is precisely a *vilain*, more specifically, a tamer of wild beasts. Calogrenant, instead, is a man searching for something, but since his search is so far unsuccessful (and will remain so—only Yvain will succeed in the test of the magic fountain), he is, in a way, nothing, as a poor nobleman who has not found his place in the world.[51] A successful knight, however, will be something special, noble, worth fighting and enduring for, higher than the simple, base humanity of the rustic who is identified with his work and no more. Calogrenant's "adventure" has thus explicitly turned into what the knight errant's adventure is supposed to produce: a finding of one's identity by becoming worthy of the court after proving one's capacity to overcome the lower and inferior world of wild nature and quasi-bestial humanity. The search for individual identity is part of a search for the meaning of the world, which, in turn, is the very nature of the adventure as the core of the *roman*, as expressly stated in another similar episode in the prose *Tristan*. There Dinadan answers Agravain so: "I am a knight errant who every day goes in search of adventures and of the sense of the world; but I cannot find any, nor can I retain any of it for my useful service."[52]

In Marcabru's landmark *pastorela* "L'autrier jost'una sebissa," the bold knight confronted a sharp-tongued shepherdess who managed to put him in his place by turning his knightly logic against him. The knight feels it is natural for him to use a lower human being for his pleasure, but the shepherdess retorts that it is natural for her to find her pleasure with her peers. Inferior though they might be, the rustics had their own place and even rights and dignity, which Marcabru, for one, was ready to acknowledge, perhaps with tongue in cheek.[53] Chrétien's social distinctions were sharper and less compromising.

Nevertheless, a closer look shows that a crack in the exclusiveness of Chrétien's socioethical perspective allowed a disturbing but fertile infiltration. For in the Champagne region the bourgeois point of view could be scorned but not ignored. Thanks to its fairs and through Henry the Liberal's enlightened policy, Champagne had become prosperous as a key international center of commerce and finance, a clearinghouse where Henry's *gardes des foires* guaranteed that the merchants could move about and do their business safely, with officially recognized and enforced contracts. Auerbach (120 f.) already speculated that Chrétien must have felt a nagging awareness of the abstractness of chivalry because of concrete conditions at the courts of Champagne and Flanders where he was writing: he must have sensed that the real forces embodied in the fairs of Champagne and the burghers' guilds of the Flemish communes limited, indeed threatened the dominance of feudal structures.

Yet an open recognition of the *mercatores* could only come gradually: if they could not be assimilated to the *agricolae* as one of the three divinely established social orders, another term for the laboring class, *laboratores*, could well include them, even if some moralists balked at crediting them with productive work and chose to look down on them as exploiters of opportunity, mere "usurers." But the influential educator Hugh of St. Victor (ca. 1096–1141), for one, had written a sort of epic hymn to the industriousness of this daring new class: "Commerce penetrates the secret places of the world, approaches shores unseen, explores fearful wildernesses, and in tongues unknown and with barbaric peoples carries on the trade of mankind. The pursuit of commerce reconciles nations, calms wars, strengthens peace, and commutes the private good of individuals into the common benefit of all."[54] It was enough to fill a merchant's heart with pride at being as honorable as the best knight errant, and probably more useful.

In direct contrast with the warrior's view of marriage as a form of conquest or acquisition by force, the mercantile ethic of contractual bond through mutual consent of the participating parties may have contributed to a change in the ecclesiastical definition of the marriage contract. Perhaps these profound changes affected Chrétien's representation of the moral issues involved in the relationship between courtly lovers. If we read the romances in this light, their socioethical dimensions will appear as a counterpart of the ethical world of the epic, where, at least tendentially, the warrior mentality reigned supreme.[55]

In *Erec et Enide* (Chrétien's first Arthurian romance, dated by Anthime Fourrier as not earlier than 1170),[56] despite the mistaken assumption that Erec is dead, Enide does not consent to the Count of Oringle's attempt to assert his rights as a *bellator* by conquering her by force (vv. 4770–4782). Chrétien insinuates that Enide was entitled to posit mutual consent as the only acceptable and fair ground for marriage. In *Yvain* recent critics have seized on the episode of the "Château de Pesme Aventure" for its striking socioeconomic overtones. Yvain frees three hundred maidens who were enslaved as hard-laboring textile workers by two brothers born of the devil and a woman (vv. 5107–5810).[57] The episode may sound like a critique of textile sweatshops in Chrétien's Champagne. But it would be incorrect to read into this famous episode an expression of real sympathy for workers as against their bourgeois oppressors. Rather, Chrétien's social horizon is once again exclusively limited by his allegiance to the feudal nobility. What moves him in the invention of this episode may be a horror of the alliance, imposed by the realities of the growing monetary economy, between high nobility (and monarchy itself) and bourgeois capitalists exploiting cheap labor. Chrétien's fantasy sounds a stern, resentful warning. He neither understands nor appreciates what he sees around him: cities, enfranchised by kings and princes, serve the long-range financial goals of the monarchs, even against the interests of the landed nobility. The ideal of Arthur as a king of *largesce* who associated with none but brave knights contrasted with a world of acquisitive guile where both Capetians and Plantagenets surrounded themselves with low-class clerics, especially school teachers, *magistri*, and burgher-merchants, who replaced the knights as court administrators and public officials. The clerics at court naturally espoused the doctrine of guile and calculation against the knights' ethic of frankness, bravery, and generosity: the courtliness they taught was the nonknightly kind. In the face of these threatening changes, the romances acted as a literature "qui n'est pas une littérature d'évasion, mais de combat," where chivalry could oppose courtliness.[58]

More important for *Yvain*'s central plot is the hero's conversion from the victorious warrior aiming to conquer Laudine, whose husband he has slain, to the loving husband who must earn his wife's affection by proving his love for her. When he fails by forgetting their anniversary, the "liberated" Laudine demands his atonement and compensation, refusing to recognize him as her husband until she is satisfied. Acknowledging his unforgivable "breach of contract," Yvain loses his mind and turns to a wild life in the forest, hunting and eating raw game. A hermit engages him in an intriguing game of progressive barter exchanges, leading him back to a quasi-civilized state. At first the hermit feeds him moldy bread in exchange for the wild game Yvain hunts; next he cooks the game for Yvain; finally he purchases even better food for Yvain in town with the proceeds from Yvain's hunt. A useful mercantile relationship is established between the holy man and the fallen knight.[59] But in this adventure Yvain tests the dangers of abandoning the court for the world of nature and the open forest. Being reduced to eating raw meat is symbolic of his having fallen back into a naturally savage state. His madness consists of being reduced to the life of a brute. Thus the "adventure," which is the test of conquering the anticourtly forces symbolized by monsters and evil magic together with the wild nature of forests and *vilains*, the subhuman peasants and shepherds, is at the same time the quest for identity and self-recognition, as perceived earlier in Calogrenant's dialogue with the shepherd.

The plot of *Yvain* may also confirm Chrétien's overarching concern for the knights' chivalrous duties toward society as a higher moral commitment than love itself, somehow pitching chivalry against courtly love. In this tale helping the helpless gives more significance to chivalric adventure than love does: whereas Laudine remains a rather marginal figure, there is a powerful moral bond between Yvain and Lunete and

also between Yvain and the lion. Lunete, out of gratitude for his kindness toward her when others had spurned her at court, saves Yvain and
is then saved by him when she is in dire need, just as in an equally
symbolic context the lion saves Yvain in gratitude for having been saved
by him. Yet the destiny of the knight is an unending quest. When Yvain
conquers Laudine's love a second time, he returns to where he had
started. He is no longer a great active knight: conquest ends both love
and chivalric value.[60]

Chrétien's *Perceval* is the culmination of the synthesis of *chevalerie*
and *clergie* that the poet had first announced in his early *Cligès*. The
famous lines 30–35 of the prologue of *Cligès* ("puis vint chevalerie a
Rome / Et de la clergie la some, / Qui or est en France venue") proclaimed the transmission of truth and wisdom (*translatio studii*) together with knighthood or chivalry from ancient Greece to Rome and
now to France.[61] The role and function of chivalry had been ennobled,
historically authorized, and universalized by identifying it with the virtues of the ancient heroes. But the anticourt objections of the moral
rigorists like John of Salisbury and Bernard of Clairvaux had to be answered and neutralized by a clear, programmatic wedding of warrior
ethic with Christian mission. The potentially sinful and even heretical
quality of courtesy had to be overcome in a way that took it to higher
metaphysical and theological levels. The Quest for the Grail attempted
to perform this very act of supreme harmonization with the clerics'
highest wishes. It was the alliance of *fortitudo* and *sapientia*, Christian
chivalry and classical wisdom, nourished by both moral heroism and
intellectual refinement. The good and the true were now one and the
same.[62] In medieval Germany the imperial heritage of antiquity could
be perceived as *translatio imperii*, but the French Arthurian romancers
saw the centralizing authority of emperor or monarch as the enemy, and
the individual knights, perilously replacing the impersonal state and
taking over its functions, as the true heirs of ancient wisdom and heroism. The only superior institution those knights were prepared to acknowledge was the universal Church, and even the Church held a tenu-
ous edge. Gornemanz's dubbing of Perceval makes him a member of the
highest divine order, but such secular orders were suspicious to the
Church, since they could feel superior to the established Church. Indeed, Perceval's quest could be seen as entailing heretical overtones. The
dubbing episode emphasizes the superior moral and social quality of
knighthood in a way that seems to imply the superiority of the *milites*
over the other two *ordines*:

> Et li prodom l'espee a prise,
> se li ceint et si le beisa,
> Et dit que donee li a
> la plus haute ordre avoec l'espee
> que Dex a fete et comandee,
> c'est l'ordre de chevalerie,
> qui doit estre sanz vilenie.

(And the wise man took the sword, girded him with it and then kissed him. And said that with that sword he had given him the highest order created and commanded by God. This is the order of knighthood, which must be without baseness. Vv. 1630–1636.)

The *Vulgate Lancelot* carried this message further in the elaborate speech by the Lady of the Lake who explains to Lancelot that the hallowed institution of chivalry is society's only hope against wickedness and violence. The knight is the sole protector of the church, widows, orphans, and all the unjustly oppressed.[63] The exalted view of chivalry that entered Chrétien's oeuvre in its last phase around 1180 responded to a situation of acute tension that saw the great lords, including Chrétien's new patron, Philip of Alsace, count of Flanders, pitched against both the monarchy and the high clergy.[64] Like the feudal lords, the knights attempted to claim for themselves a superior type of *clergie* which was different from that of the clerics but equal to it in dignity: a *clergie* which valued a Ciceronian view of rhetoric for the training of the public man and which taught the virtues and good manners of courtliness. It was to be the result of a sacramental initiation and courtly training, an education akin to that of the priests but no longer imparted directly by them.[65]

All in all, *courtoisie* could perform a metaphysical function analogous to the theological one of divine grace. For Thomas Aquinas the social estates were part of a fixed natural law which mirrors divine law, yet the estates could be transcended through grace. Similarly, the opposition *courtoisie/vilenie* (originally meaning the aristocracy versus both bourgeois and peasant estates) acquired a transsocial value implying secular transcendence of social limitations: thus the poor or landless knights, even when nonnoble by feudal standards, could be redeemed and ennobled by courtesy alone, the *domna* replacing God. This is the meaning of "true nobility" in the debates already contained in certain Provençal *partimens*.[66] The search for perfection had entered a metaphysical, mystical, neo-Platonic sphere that, for all its connection with religious experiences, was thoroughly immanent and secular. The ideal knight could be at the same time—to use the German terms—*gottes ritter*, "God's knight," and a *vrouwen ritter*, "a lady's knight."

Students of Chrétien are familiar with the conjectural theses on his moral goals ever since the lively polemic between Gaston Paris and Wendelin Foerster, centered on the role of marriage in *Erec* and *Cligès* and on Chrétien's position vis-à-vis the Tristan legend as stated in *Cligès*. This "marriage question" is not unlike the marriage question in the *Canterbury Tales*, but the impossibility of settling it convincingly on the sole basis of philological or psychological analysis proves the limitations of any hermeneutical approach that does not bring in the objective social background. Like Chaucer, Chrétien was not simply a psychologist or moralist trying out a formula to reconcile courtly love with the sacrament of marriage. He was a member of a court society that saw literature as a functional part of its cultural self-image. In *Cligès*, Fenice, married to Alis, refuses to be like Iseut by sharing herself with both lover and husband. She wants to belong loyally and truly to one man only, body and soul (or *ceur et cors*, as she puts it: *vostre est mes cuers, vostre est mes cors*, she tells Cligès: vv. 3145–3164, 5250–5263, 5310–5329).[67] But she achieves her end by serving her husband a magic philter that gives him, every night, the mere illusion of possessing her, and agrees to marry Cligès only after Alis's convenient death. The charge of hypocrisy, for the casuistic solution and for adducing scruples that had less to do with morality than with reputation, is really out of place in this context, since in Chrétien's court society there was no separation between morality and social duties: ethical questions could not be independent of courtly mores.[68] *Cligès* is, indeed, an *Anti-Tristan* in the sense that it refuses to recognize the rights of the individual against society on the basis of the inescapable bonds of high passion. Courtly love demands control of irrational forces and animal instincts, rationally channeled toward social ends. Appearances and reputation are not external matters but the essence of social living. The Tristan story as interpreted by Thomas was uncourtly and subversive insofar as it was eminently antisocial.

A passage from *Le chevalier de la charrete* contains an exemplary stroke of the psychological finesse that could enter the representation of courtesy as a civilizing force—even to the point of subtle personal diplomacy in everyday behavior. Lancelot has swooned at the sight of a comb he recognized as belonging to the kidnapped Guenièvre. A maiden tries to help him but, when he comes to, she tells him a "white lie" in order to avoid embarrassing him. The author interjects:

Do not suppose that the girl would reveal the true reason [for her approaching Lancelot to help him]. He would be ashamed and troubled, and it would cause him pain and anguish were she to reveal the truth [to wit, that she thought he needed help for his fainting spell]. Therefore she hid the truth and said with the utmost tact, "Sir, I come to get this comb. That's why I dismounted. I wanted it so much I couldn't wait any longer." (vv. 1446–1456)[69]

All the courtly and knightly virtues were necessary in love, too, and in a harmonious combination. Contrary to appearances based mostly on an excessive exemplarity attributed to the first two books of Andreas Capellanus's *De amore*, the lack of self-restraint made happiness impossible and tragedy inevitable, as was the case with Lancelot and Tristan. It showed lack of self-restraint to pursue the total gratification of sensual attraction, since the courtly lady was perceived as eminently virtuous. The lyric, specifically, portrayed the lady as infinitely attractive but necessarily unreachable, as Petrarca understood and promulgated well after the heroic age of "courtly love." Capellanus's emphasis on adultery is, at best, symbolic of the difference between the freedom of choice in pure love and the practical, contractual nature of marital relations. But Chrétien's Erec, Yvain, and Perceval, like their German imitations Erek, Iwein, and Parzival, all found happiness and true love in marriage. Even Boccaccio's heroes and heroines, it bears noting, would aim at marriage, often with success. In both the romance and the lyric, courtly love demanded this hard degree of self-denial and self-control, even "frustration." The French *fin' amor* and Gottfried's *hohe Minne* were, after the first French romances, a necessary companion of the knight's prowess, its motivating force and purposeful center of inspiration.

CYCLICAL PROSE ROMANCES
AND LATER DEVELOPMENTS

Since courtly love was conceived chiefly for courtly circles, its appeal was at the same time powerful and narrow. This narrowness is brought into focus not only by the moralistic objections of responsible ecclesiastical circles but also by the satirical insouciance of such an apparently marginal genre as the *fabliau*. Recent research has emphasized the importance of this genre as the expression of a naturalistic ethos or "materialistic hedonism." In sharp contrast with the asceticism preached by the Church as well as the rarefied and spiritualized tenets of *courtoisie*, it included a dose of ridicule heaped on the dainty manners and strained style that *courtoisie* imposed. It is remarkable that, lasting from approximately 1190 to 1330, the *fabliau* coincided with the most creative period of chivalric literature. One can isolate within it a first generation that vigorously, uninhibitedly expressed that hedonistic naturalism, a second generation characterized by bitter and hateful cynicism, and a third that gave in to moral indifference and disillusionment.[70] Other critics have interpreted many of the *fabliaux* as "courtly productions designed to mock the bourgeoisie, neutralizing its economic strength by emphasizing the *vilanie* of its *moeurs*."[71]

The form of Arthurian literature that enjoyed the widest circulation was that of the cyclical prose romance, especially the group of texts traditionally referred to as the Vulgate Cycle or Prose *Lancelot/Graal*, probably composed between 1215 and 1230 and constituted chiefly by the *Lancelot del Lac*, the *Queste del Saint Graal*, and the *Mort Artu*.[72] In the first of these three main texts the Dame du Lac crowns the education of her foster son Lancelot by imparting to him solemn lessons on the meaning of chivalry, the origins of knighthood, the symbolic significance of arms and the horse, and especially the moral obligations to defend the needy and the Church. After Lancelot's first adventures the author starts using the narrative technique of interlacing (*entrelacement*, so named by its first analyst, Ferdinand Lot) more intensively than had been practiced before, and that set an example destined to be carried on with much success by Sir Thomas Malory and especially by Boiardo and Ariosto.[73] He does so with a skill that the modern critics have been slow to recognize, just as the classicistic-minded critics of the Cinquecento would be hard put to accept it from their Italian contemporaries. It is most likely that by referring to "Arturi regis ambages pulcerrime," "the fascinating meanderings of King Arthur's tales," Dante had specifically in mind the interlacing narrative technique of the Prose *Lancelot*.[74]

In the *Queste* critics have detected the intervention of a pious monastic spirit of Cistercian hue, which they have tried to relate to the mysticism of St. Bernard of Clairvaux or, alternatively, to the more rationalistic views of William of Saint-Thierry, St. Bernard's friend though not his disciple. "When a hermit expounds the hierarchy of the virtues, he places highest virginity and below it in descending order humility, patience, justice, and last, strangely enough, charity."[75] Among the knights who achieve the conquest of the Grail the only perfect one is Galaad, who was foreshadowed, as we shall see, in Wolfram von Es-

chenbach's Lohengrin (Loherangrîn). Galaad, Lancelot's son, is a fore-
ordained saint untroubled by human frailties and exempt from temptation, a savior whose name derives from the Gilead of the Vulgate
Bible, one of Christ's mystic appellations. The knight has become the
true man of God, and chivalry a supreme ideal of moral nobility.

Tempting as it might be, we must forego an analysis of the foremost
"best-seller" of medieval literature, the *Roman de la rose* (1225–1240
for Guillaume de Lorris's portion, 1275–1280 for Jean de Meung's),
since in that rich masterpiece the assessment of the role of the courtly
and chivalric elements remains subject to the still very controversial interpretation of the authors' central theses.[76] Arthurian matter continued
to show great vitality long after Chrétien in France and elsewhere. For
the sake of its author, it deserves at least a passing mention that the
chronicler and poet Jean Froissart also composed, around 1388, the
Meliador, which has the distinction of being not only the last French
romance of strictly Arthurian matter, but also the longest one in verse
(30,771 octosyllables). Since we are not engaged in a diachronic survey
of our subject matter in all genres and forms, it should suffice to add
here, because of their peculiar experimentalism on social, literary, and
rhetorical levels, the fifteenth-century "grands rhétoriqueurs" of the
Burgundian domains. These court poets served the duke or other great
lords by celebrating their patrons' supposedly incomparable achievements, from their invariably just wars to every private or public event
in their lives: births, marriages, deaths, and all splendid appearances at
banquets and pageants. The critical reader is challenged to look behind
and beyond the practical and stylistic constraints of this highly "pro-
grammed" literary activity, seeking in the text an *hors-texte* that contains the poet's original and personal inner message.[77]

Caxton's Preface to the most splendid swan song of chivalry, Malory's *Le Morte Darthur* (Westminster, 1485), said plainly that chivalry
teaches both the good, to be imitated, and the evil, to be eschewed. The
literature of chivalry taught quite a little evil to a host of knights errant
who meandered in and out of the princely courts of Europe, breaking
spears, challenging, and maiming one another in earnest imitation of
the Lancelots and Gawains. Martín de Riquer (1970) has published and
studied a number of the many documents, literary and historical, that
testify to this lingering popularity of the romantic knight, perhaps more
so in Spain and Burgundy than elsewhere. The fifteenth century is full
of characters who left thousands of letters of challenge and executions
of private wars or personal duels, with minute contestation of fine legal

points of honor—what Spaniards called *letras de batalla*. The historian
of literature and the historian of social customs share a common interest
in literary works that are based on real events and "adventures" as well
as in daily behavior that is inspired by direct imitation of literary patterns. The Spanish *Amadís de Gaula* was a fictional derivation from the
French romances, but, despite the apparent similarities, Antoine de la
Sale's *Petit Jehan de Saintré* and the anonymous *Roman de Jehan de
Paris*, like the Catalan *Tirant lo Blanch* (whose principal author was the
Valencian novelist Johanot Martorell, 1413 or 1414–1468) and the
anonymous *Curial e Güelfa* (note the names, and that the plot was
curiously set in Italy), were based in good part on real events, recorded
and narrated without exaggeration or distortion and with considerable
artistic verve. In this sense, it is hard to tell the difference between these
"novels" and the factual chronicles of the lives of historical military
figures in knightly garb, like the *Livre des faits du bon messire Jehan le
Maingre, dit Bouciquaut*, the *Livre des faits de Jacques de Lalaing*, or
the Spanish *El Victorial* by Pero Niño. All these books told fantastic
stories, yet the story of Jean de Saintré is invented whereas those of
Lalaing and Boucicaut are rigorous historical records of living knights
who acted in imitation of heroes from the books of chivalry.[78] Cervantes's Don Quijote was far from unique, except for being laughable.

These more or less "literary" biographies of chivalrous characters
constitute a real subgenre in the fifteenth century. All in all, they presented to an eager public exemplary portraits of knightly universals:
when the models derived from real historical figures, they had been idealized and generalized. The mixture of fact and fiction that distinguishes
the genre also brought together discrete class modes or codes. In *Curial
e Güelfa*, for example, the knight errant Curial starts on his adventure
trail by leaving his court, or "curia," for Marseille well provided with
money and letters of exchange, like a regular Catalan merchant. In the
fifteenth century, Burgundian biographies of ruling princes also carried
on the twelfth-century mode of assimilation of the nobleman to the
knight: they portrayed their subjects by patterning them after fictional
paladins mixed with historic knights who had become abstract romantic models. Thus Gawain and Lancelot were coupled with Du Guesclin
and Boucicaut in the chronicles of Enguerrand de Monstrelet, Mathieu
d'Escouchy, Pierre Chastellain, Olivier de La Marche, and Jean Moli-
net. Furthermore, such biographies were packed with highly decorative
visual elements through theatrical spectacles of tournaments, pageants,
feasts, and mock or real battles—in Chastellain's terms, the emphasis

was on *voyables*, to enable the audience to *assoir l'oeil sur les choses*.[79] In the romances as well as in the reality of court life, the exquisite though dangerously serious games of frequent tourneys and hunting parties were part of the chivalric contest.[80]

SOME ENGLISH TEXTS

Courtly love and courtly conduct became bound together through the psychological, literary, and social process of amalgamation of behavioral ideas. The bond proved durable. A shining example is *Sir Orfeo*, the charming Middle English poetic text preserved in the Auchinleck manuscript of Edinburgh from 1330–1340, probably composed not many years earlier by an anonymous poet without much culture but with great imagination.[81] The Orpheus of ancient mythology has become an English king who recovers (for good) his lost Euridice (Queen Heurodis in the text) by playing his inimitable harp before the King of the Fairies, who had taken her from the world of the living. This arresting idea of stealing one's dead beloved away from a fairyland afterworld may not be the invention of *Sir Orfeo*'s poet, since it appears in Walter Map's story of the Breton knight (ca. 1182). The charming fairy tale atmosphere does not prevent the characters from behaving according to the most idealized rules of the world of courtesy and chivalry. When he decides he cannot go on living without his beloved wife, the king leaves the throne in care of his steward, but when he returns, made unrecognizable by ten years in the wilderness, the steward professes his loyal devotion to the king he hopes to see again. When Orfeo reveals his true identity, the steward is so overjoyed that he knocks the table over, and all the lords shout their joy, too. The King of the Fairies is also a chivalrous lord who knows how to keep his word against all logic: having promised to grant the minstrel any reward he desires for his inspiring music, he hands Orfeo back his (dead) wife. All behave like members of the best of all possible loving and loyal worlds, according to rules and patterns unthinkable before the age of chivalry and courtesy.

By contrast, a "realistic" representation of court life stands out clearly in such contemporaneous "epic" texts as, for example, *Havelok the Dane*, where the temporary trustees of the kingdoms of England and Denmark betray their oaths and become unscrupulous usurpers.[82] In the end the rightful heirs triumph and the traitors pay dearly for their perfidy. The courtly code prevails and the reader is conscious of the criminality of its violation.

Sir Orfeo and, in its way, *Sir Gawain and the Green Knight* (ca. 1360/1370, commonly characterized as a most "courtly" English poem) may be further exceptions to Jauss's "test of commutation,"[83] proving my contention that social constants (that is, motifs with a heavy, if obscure, social content) can be stronger than literary ones and, at times, can unexpectedly overcome the latter. Those two gems of Middle English poetry are textured with elements from incommutable genres: Arthurian knights become fairy figures in the former case, or epic ones in the latter. The pagan motif of the head-cutting challenge in *Sir Gawain* may derive from a ninth-century Irish narrative, *Bricriu's Feast*, where myth and fairy tale mixed: it then became a heroic-chivalric contest. In *Sir Orfeo* the king's total devotion to his wife, to the point of being unable to govern or even remain in society without her, is emphatically courtly.

One extraordinary merit of *Sir Gawain* is to have concentrated in such a short space the most essential and complex issues of chivalric morality. Morgan le Fay schemes to humiliate Arthur's court by subjecting its most valiant and proud knight to a supreme test of chastity, loyalty to an absurd promise, and humility. She does so by sending the enchanted Green Knight to deliver an awesome challenge: he will allow a rival to strike his head off with an ax while he is unarmed, on condition that a year hence he will have his chance to return the blow. Indeed, his head is cut off by Gawain, but he picks it up and leaves, waiting for Gawain to come after him the next Christmas and receive his own stroke, equally without resistance. Gawain dutifully shows up and is welcomed with the utmost courtesy in three days of magnificent courtly festivities where his chastity is severely tempted by the Green Knight's wife. He is asked to promise that he will yield to his host all he gains in hunting or otherwise during his visit: his host promises to do likewise. But while Gawain receives all the prey from the Green Knight's three days of successful hunt, he returns to him only the kisses he has received from his wife, not the silk sash or girdle she gave him with the assurance it would make him invulnerable. Bertilak de Hautdesert (the Green Knight is only now so named) feigns to strike him three times, then ends by disclosing the purpose of the test, which Gawain has won only partly, since he has not kept his promise to the point of yielding up the girdle. The conclusive lesson is one of humility: no one is perfect, and chivalric pride can be misplaced.

Yet, we must interject, pride was of the essence, since without it there would be no chivalry. In the end, *Sir Gawain* appears as a sort of metatext, a test of chivalry as an impossibility, a proud *velleitas* asking to be proved absurd. The knight cannot be true to his calling without destroying himself by turning over to his enemy the girdle that would make him invincible. On the other hand the Green Knight is not being fair, that is, chivalrous: he is really cheating since he is asking Gawain to risk everything while he himself risks nothing, thanks to Morgan le Fay's backing him with her magic art. In Chrétien's *Chevalier de la charrete* both Gauvain and, more importantly, Lancelot were in a similar predicament, since their open and fair ways could not win out against the ruthlessly treacherous schemes of Meleaganz without the chance help of intervening admirers, like the maid who freed Lancelot from the prison tower.

Sir Gawain clearly marks a high point in the history of the civilizing process we have been following: the curial virtue of humility, a Christian element inspired by the clerical psyche at court, intervenes to check the knight's inherent pride. The ideal knight's basic virtues and their opposite vices are neatly defined where Gawain confesses to his opponent:

> I cringed at your cuts, and my cowardice induced me
> To make an accord with avarice, abandoning my nature,
> Which always leaned toward loyalty and knightly largess.
> Now I am false and flawed.
>
> (Part Three, vv. 2379–2382)

Yet the hard lesson, with the humbling outcome, has revealed his humanity, and his challenger generously recognizes it in the triumphantly conclusive lines:

> But you have a small flaw, my friend: you lack some faithfulness.
> It didn't arise for an artful object or amorous fling—
> No! you just loved your life, and I blame you the less for it.
>
> (Part Three, vv. 2366–2368)[84]

Then again, while confessing that he has learned his lesson, Gawain will define the vices of "avarice, excess, the frailty of the flesh, and, above all, pride" as the destruction of chivalry (stanza 19 of Part Four, vv. 2439–2455). Gawain, nevertheless, *is* the paragon of knightly virtues: the pentangle emblazoned on his shield and coat involves, in "an endless knot," five sets of virtues, the last of which was made up of: "Free-giving, Good Fellowship, Chastity, Courtesy, and Pity" (Part Two, stanza 9, vv. 651–654). He is welcomed at the castle of the Green Knight as one who brings with him "virtue and valor and the very finest manners," and everybody rejoices at the prospect of watching an incomparable display of

> . . . the most subtle behavior,
> The most sophisticated standards of civilized speech,
> . . . the lore of effortless language,
> . . . the paragon of perfect manners.
> An education in etiquette
> This knight shall surely bring;
> And those who listen well
> May gain love's mastering.
> (Part Two, stanza 17, vv. 912–927)

The Lady of Belcirak weaves her tempting tryst with her guest by engaging in polite flirting with that art of gallant conversation that will become the pride of French Classical literature. In affairs of chivalry, she says, the chief thing is the game of love (v. 1512). And so it was, including this supremely sophisticated gem of late medieval poetry, where not only love but chivalry itself becomes an elegant game to be played in earnest for honor, self-esteem, and survival. The ludic element in the acting out of noble ideals had never found a subtler statement, nor had it ever been taken to more dizzying heights.

CHAPTER SIX

Epic and Romance in Germany

INTERGENERIC DOMINANTS

The preceding analysis provides the tools to discriminate among the three codes of behavior addressed to the ruling class in both narrative literature and literature of behavior, the latter eventually resulting in generalized public standards. Once again, the three codes (courtly, chivalric/heroic, and chivalric/*courtois*), all in full bloom around 1200, were seldom isolated from one another, although their degree of mixture varied with time and place. In the south of France, for example, with Guilhelm IX, Bertran de Born, and Peire Vidal, the lively feeling for the rapacious warrior who obtains vital satisfaction at the sight of strife, broken arms, and split heads was still a norm which coexisted with the refinements of love, though without much need for sublimation. I shall now try to gauge how the codes interacted in German literature.

German lyric forms were fragmented into a number of metrical frameworks which had more to do with musical patterns than with ancient examples. In turn the new epic forms, without deriving directly from ancient models, sprang out of a conflation of classical genres and new popular ones. In other words, they grew directly out of indigenous oral narratives, with some limited background of mediated Homeric and Virgilian features and materials. Just as significant, the "dominants" or constants that we see weaving their way in and out of each group of texts were literary phenomena whose genesis was not strictly literary, but moral and social. As a way to gauge their vitality and autonomy, as it were, H.-R. Jauss has proposed "the test of commutation."[1] He asserts that in a synchronic perspective the delimitation of genres "cannot be decided according to one-sided formal or thematic characteristics." The "test of commutation" reveals the true "dominant" that establishes "constitutive genre distinctions." Just as, for example, "if one puts a princess in a fairy tale next to a princess in a novella, one notices the difference," so characters are not interchangeable (they are "noncommutable") between the *chanson de geste* and the romance. So far, so good. Yet the codes we are pursuing cut across genres: they are, should we say, "non-generic dominants." If it is true that Arthurian knights would not fit in a *chanson de geste* or, vice versa, that the paladins of Charlemagne would be out of place around the Round Table (at least before Boiardo and Ariosto), what do we make, for example, of Siegfried and Brunhild in the *Nibelungenlied*? They are certainly heroic characters, but do they not incorporate strong courtly/*courtois*/chivalric elements, as well as fairy tale magic elements?

On the basis of degrees of reality, John of Garlandia's *Poetria* had differentiated the medieval genres as "res gesta or *historia*, res ficta or *fabula*, and *res ficta quae tamen fieri potuit*"—historic fact, fanciful fable, and imagined possibility.[2] But let us think of the magic Cloak of Darkness that Siegfried uses to win the fateful test imposed by Brunhild, and then again to subjugate her for her husband King Gunther. Was this delivered by the poet as fact, fanciful fiction, or realistic fiction? How far does the distinction reach in the body of the actual texts, beyond the realization of the different origins of single features: some epic, some mytho-religious, some from the folklore of fairy tales? Narrative constituents do become commutable between genres by virtue of the way they serve the deeper dominant constituent of, for example, courtly conventions. Since knights are both subservient to the code of their court society and rebellious against, or transcendent to, it—and more so in Germany than in France: witness Tristan, Iwein, and Parzival—their behavior responds to the ethical point to be made.[3]

Jauss has integrated the educational dimension of literary artifacts into his proposed description of "the fundamental model that the medieval genres of epic, romance, and novella have in common." His "Mode of Construction and Levels of Significance" include the presence of an "exclusively aristocratic" social status in the epic and romance (the novella being essentially bourgeois), with opposition, in the ro-

mance, between the nobility and the *vilain* on the one hand, and, on the
other, the "inactive ideal king" and "the knight who alone takes the
field and whose adventure stands in relation to the winning of his lady."
Next, his "Mode of Reception" includes, for the romance, the communication of "the doctrine of courtly education [*Bildung*] through its
ethics of the event." Finally, his "Mode of Social Function" includes,
again for the romance, that "the later function as an entertainment for
the private reader is preceded by the original function as the initiation
into courtly life and courtly love: the legitimate quest for a terrestrial
happiness regulated by a social discipline and a life-style."[4] Such characterizations should clearly confirm the points I am trying to make.

True enough, through the twelfth century the code of courtly conduct
could not be regarded as a coherent whole except for the basic notion
of *dienst und lon*, service and reward.[5] The qualities we encounter in so
many texts are the traditional ones of *ere* (honor), *milte* (generosity),
triuwe (loyalty), *staete* (constancy), *maze* (measure), *zuht* (good conduct), and *tapferheit* (bravery), but the specific role they play varies
with authors and contexts.[6] Similarly, for some scholars the notion of
courtly love implies a collective ideology which does not correspond to
the idiosyncrasies of individual poets and texts. One authoritative skep-
tic was W. T. H. Jackson, whose admirable familiarity with the texts
does not seem to me to vouchsafe his efforts to "deconstruct" (*avant-
la-lettre*) the poets' adherence to a common mythology.[7] For him Chrétien de Troyes's chief purpose was to display the failure of the Arthurian
code of conduct (e.g. 27: Hartmann, in his *Iwein*, "believed in the
courtly mystique," whereas his source Chrétien did not, so that Hartmann "failed to appreciate his predecessor's irony"). The only woman
with a human face in Chrétien's poems, Jackson claims, is Enide, who
was no Arthurian lady, and every one of his heroes learns at great expense that the Arthurian code, superficial and shallow as it had become,
failed to lead to harmony, greatness, and happiness. Erec, in that poem
about love in marriage—a most un-Arthurian and uncourtly notion—
learns to love Enide above *concupiscentia*, with trust and appreciation
for her personal qualities (23–34).

Granted that Chrétien must have had a long and rich oral tradition
behind him, it seems excessive to assume that at his time the Arthurian
code was already worn out and conventionalized to the point of decay.
Yvain's memorable opening lines (1–41) depict Arthur's court in a context where the irony appears aimed less at that court than, trenchantly,

at the inadequacy of Chrétien's villainous contemporaries, who are worth less alive than are the dead knights of Arthur's memory: "Artus ... / la cui proesce nos enseigne / que nos soiens preu et cortois"; "car molt valt mialz, ce m'est a vis, / un cortois morz c'uns vilains vis." In any event, Jackson maintains that passion was generally considered morally wrong in the Middle Ages, which caused a conflict between the needs of society and the needs of pure Christianity.[8] The sacrament of marriage sanctified sex, but only as the means to obey the commandment to grow and multiply; passionate love had no place within marriage, since desire and enjoyment of sex were inherently and inescapably sinful, the fall's tragic mark, as St. Augustine had so eloquently preached. Duby's recent researches basically agree with this definition of the place of love and sex in marriage.[9] A consequence was the apparent impossibility of finding a logical moral place for love literature. The following discussion should help to focus Jackson's strictures and answer some of them.

CHIVALRY AND THE GERMAN EPIC

One reason for the relative dearth of German chivalric literature in the twelfth century is that education, according to customs inherited from the earliest times, was still regarded with a certain contempt among the German nobility. The Ostrogoths had forbidden noblemen to entrust their sons to teachers, who would turn their minds away from the pursuits of the warrior class. Procopius of Caesarea (*The Gothic War*, sixth century) relates such an edict by Theodoric the Great. Thereafter the Goths sought a "barbaric education" for their sons, who should grow up in the company of their peers and accustom themselves to the use of arms and the exercise of force over their subjects, away from the influence of old, effeminate wise men.[10]

Raoul Glaber of Cluny (*Historiae sui temporis* 2.12, written in the 1030s) tells the story of the grammarian Vilgardus of Ravenna around A.D. 1000 as a moral *exemplum* of the danger of falling into heresy from excessive love of letters:

> He nourished for grammar a passion more insane than prudent, as is typical of the Italians, who, for the sake of it, will neglect all the other arts. Filled with pride for his knowledge he came close to madness. So much so that one night the devils appeared to him in the shape of Virgil, Juvenal, and Horace, and thanked him for his enthusiasm in studying their books and extolling their authority among posterity. Thereafter, seduced by the devils' delusion,

he started to teach their dogmas, asserting that the poets' words carry authority on all matters. At last he was judged to be a heretic and condemned by the bishop of the city, Peter. Everywhere in Italy there were found people who embraced this pestiferous belief: they too died from the iron and the fire.[11]

Historians have often referred to the Burgundian cleric Wipo, preceptor of the future Emperor Henry III (1039–1056), for his regretful observation that Germans regarded it as frivolous and shameful (*vacuum et turpe*) for nonclerics to submit themselves to tutors.[12] Nevertheless, no matter how limited and qualified, the appreciation of classical culture had been growing: Wipo held up the example of Italy, where Roman boys rushed to school as soon as they had passed the age of playing with childish toys.

If Italians differed from Germans in their appreciation of schooling, so did the French. In his biography of Count Burchard, *Vita domni Burcardi* (1058), Odo of St. Maur (Eudes de Saint-Maur) registered the French custom of sending the sons of high noblemen to the king's court for education.[13] Marbod of Rennes (ca. 1035–1123) repeatedly pointed out that it was customary for French noblemen to send their sons to grammar school as soon as they reached the right age.[14] As we saw above (chap. 3), at Henry II's English court Gerald of Wales had praised the great princes of the past for joining "toga and armor," literacy and valor.

In Germany, the epic genre had combined the heathen martial spirit with chivalrous civility without the Christian element so prominent in the French epic, although the specifically chivalric brand of piety that the historian Adolf Waas labelled *Ritterfrömmigkeit* was conspicuously present in the religious epics of biblical inspiration, for example, the *Heliand*.[15] Historians have somewhat confused the picture by distinguishing too sharply between a *Volksepos*, or popular national epic (*Nibelungenlied, Gudrun*), and a *höfisches Epos* (the romance), presumably related to the noble class.[16] But both the epic and the romance thrived within the higher classes and may well have been produced mostly by clerics (as seems to be the case with the extant version of the *Nibelungenlied*), even while minstrels and rhapsodes could perform both kinds before receptive popular audiences. It might be more meaningful to distinguish between a heroic/knightly inspiration in the *Volksepos*, based on the ethic of the warrior class, and an essentially clerically-based inspiration in the romance. The chivalric values of bravery, loyalty, and generosity—the French *prouesse, loyauté,* and *largesse*—were already present in the early pagan epics, signally *Beowulf* and the *Hildebrantslied* (both composed around A.D. 800 or even somewhat earlier), and then appeared in the tenth-century *Waltharius* and eleventh-century *Ruodlieb*,[17] together with the ritual testing of the young hero (who even in *Beowulf* fights monsters rather than heathens, in a way that is characteristic of the French romance vis-à-vis the French epic). The coexistence of martial ethos and Christian piety, with the early forms of courtesy eventually acting as a catalyst between the two, is not a paradox but a natural response to conditions in the earlier Middle Ages, when such late pagan invaders as Magyars, Arabs, Turks, and Vikings threatened the survival of monasteries and the surrounding Christian communities. Germanic bellicosity had a positive side when harnessed for defense from outside dangers: the early epic forms grew in and around the monasteries, most often by the hand of clerical rhapsodes, reflecting this genuine need. Messages of this type resounded in *Beowulf* and the *Hildebrantslied*, and a similar sense of mission was carried in the later *Ruodlieb* and the proliferating songs inspired by the crusading spirit of the eleventh and later centuries.[18] Chroniclers represented family conflicts in terms that echoed the poetic myths in spirit and narrative detail.[19] Both the chronology and geography of such literary and historical documents appear to undermine Jaeger's claim that Germany originated these ethical motifs, since they go further back than his quoted sources and are common to both Germany and France.

Ever since Georges Dumézil (1940),[20] cultural anthropologists have attempted to identify the primeval forms of the epic through such binary oppositions as that of the terrible (Varuna) and the enlightened (Mitra), as between Achilles and Odysseus or Nestor. The Greek, Roman, and Germanic epos starts with tragic anger (see Curtius 170)—a heroic but uncourtly moral trait, by our frame of reference. Achilles' anger sets the theme of the *Iliad*, and Hagen's and Kriemhild's frightening anger fills the stanzas of the *Nibelungenlied*. But the hero can be, and most commonly is, either a youthfully impetuous, emotional, and violent warrior, like Achilles, or a wise, prudent, learned, and self-controlled senior sage, like Nestor. Ideally the hero combines the two, thus creating a more complex and somewhat ambiguous, Janus-like figure, like Odysseus, although the emphasis on wisdom was more characteristic of Hesiod than of Homer. The Homeric epic also flanks these types with the educators of warriors and princes, such as Cheiron and Phoenix. Dares Phrygius transmitted to the Middle Ages an Odysseus who was witty, eloquent, and wise,[21] while Fulgentius (ca. 467–532) and Isidore (d. 636) canonized the two ingredients of the perfect hero, namely courage and wisdom, *fortitudo* and *sapientia* (see Fulgentius's interpretation of the Virgilian *arma virumque* and Isidore, *Etimologiae* 1.39.9, where the definition of the hero worthy of heaven prepared the type for Christian treatment). The soldier *fortis et proelio doctus* became a common topos. In Stoic terms *fortitudo* and *sapientia* corresponded to the cardinal virtues of *fortitudo* and *prudentia*, while justice and temperance appeared later as heroic dedication to the service of high causes and as measure or self-control; these, too, were "courtly" elements that entered the chivalric romance. All these schemata were then transferred to rulers and statesmen, starting with the emperors (Curtius 1963: 167–182).

Education and instruction—character formation and training in "rules"—are undoubtedly at the base of the *höfisches Epos* as its courtly element: this is the novel ingredient that stems from social transformations harking back to the early German courts, coupled with the French poets' mediating contributions.[22] The civilizing process of courtly ideology and sensibility acted gradually in capillary ways. Courtliness rested on consciously chosen social roles and notions of personal responsibility induced by education. When it came in contact with such collective archetypes as the epic and the imaginative romance (including the lyrical eroticism of "courtly love"), it set up a tension between contradictory, incompatible elements that forced profound revisions in form and matter alike.

The most "definitive" text of the Germanic epics, the *Nibelungenlied* (probably composed near Passau, ca. 1203–1205) deserves our attention for its paradigmatic value.[23] Of course the poem is of the heroic type. Three words with the highest frequency of recurrence in its vocabulary are *recke*, *helt*, and *degen* (warrior, hero).[24] The conclusive episode, climaxing in Kriemhild's beheading of Hagen with Siegfried's sword, is clearly an excess of savage revenge: it entails the planned destruction of the house of Burgundy including Kriemhild's own brothers, who were treacherously invited to Etzel's court for that precise purpose.[25] Kriemhild too will die, however, cut down by Hildebrand's sword in punishment for her criminal anger.

Because of the relative closeness of the two ruling classes of feudal nobility and high clergy, there was a certain convergence of ideals all along. Even within a truly heroic context, the *Hildebrantslied* already showed the sort of feudal casuistry about the fine points of loyalty to lord and kin that both a high aristocrat and a sophisticated cleric could nurture and appreciate.[26] This short, powerful poem revolves around the conflict between loyalty to king and loyalty to family. After a long separation, father and son meet on the field of battle at the heads of opposite armies. Since he owes it to his king to fight with all his might, Hildebrant hesitates to reveal his identity to his son Hadubrant. Conversely, Hadubrant is so completely engrossed in performing his duty as warrior that he rejects all hints that he is facing his father, who, he insists, must have died in distant lands. Hildebrant's behavior expresses the heroic notion of identification with the tribe, to which the individual owes unconditional allegiance—even to the point of killing his son. The poem has lost its ending, but critics agree that the likely outcome was Hadubrant's death by Hildebrant's hand, possibly followed by the latter's lament and suicide over the son's body.[27]

Somewhat similar to Hildebrant's is Rüdeger's predicament in the *Nibelungenlied*. When he is sent to the Burgundian court with the mission of persuading Kriemhild to marry Etzel, he sways Kriemhild by a momentous offer that puts his own life on the line. As a courtier who is fully dedicated to the service of master and state, he promises her revenge against all wrongdoers and "swears for himself and all his vassals" to "serve her to the death" in achieving "whatever her honor demands." On this condition she marries Etzel. Then, when the Burgundians arrive at Etzel's court—invited by Kriemhild to carry out her revenge against them—Rüdeger must choose between fighting the Burgundians out of loyalty to his king and queen, Etzel and Kriemhild, or refusing to fight because he had promised his help to the Burgundians when they were his house guests (37.11–32).[28] He begs Etzel to release him from his obligation, to no avail. This type of feudal casuistry was the epic background to the subtle "questions of love" in the "courts of love."

Some of the text's apparent contradictions are probably to be explained by the poet's gloomy sense of tragedy, rather than by his treating courtliness only as a somewhat confused court-critic.[29] A good example of the poet's view of his story as determined by an iron necessity is the grimly humorous episode of Hagen putting the mermaids' prophecy to the test. When the mermaids predict that only the chaplain will survive the trip to Hunland, Hagen tries to drown the chaplain (who survives, thus confirming the prophecy). The poet is so confident in his fatalism that he can play it for powerful effects. Furthermore, everything being preordained, he does not hesitate to anticipate the issue of each of his narrative threads. The suspense is made not of surprise, but of the haunting realization that what must happen is happening step by step before our own eyes. This feature was not uncommon in medieval narrative, where the reader is often apprised beforehand of a story's outcome. In the Italian *Tristano Riccardiano* (ca. 1300) the narrator warns the reader that Tristan's decision to marry Isotta dalle Bianche Mani in order to forget Isotta la Bionda will not turn out the way he planned it.[30] In contrast, of all medieval narrators Chrétien de Troyes was probably the one who played most methodically with a calculated element of surprise by surrounding his characters and events with an atmosphere of dense mystery as to reasons and circumstances.

In the French romances, courtliness subdued the heroic need for proud self-assertion and revenge of personal offense. The failure of courtliness to achieve this triumph of "measure" is part of the tragic element in the *Nibelungenlied*, even though some of its key figures do appear conditioned by courtliness. Siegfried and his parents, Kriemhild herself, Gunther and his brothers, even the pagan Etzel and his surrounding vassals, chiefly Dietrich von Bern, Hildebrand, and especially Rüdeger, are guided by a sense of humanity, good breeding (*zuht*), and measure or self-restraint (*mâze*). The numerous *hôchgezîte* or festival banquets are marked by liberality (*milte*), hospitality, and knightly contests. The three contests Brunhild imposes on Gunther and Siegfried (Bartsch/de Boor ed.: 7.37 [425]) are tests of manhood of the type that the chivalrous knight would undergo to prove himself as deserving of his lady's *guerdon*. Even in the Old Norse saga (the one drawn upon by Wagner) Siegfried's freeing of Brunhild from the ring of fire served the same purpose.

Siegfried, in particular, has been interpreted as a chivalric hero: he is knighted in a formal ceremony, his relationship with Kriemhild involves deliberate courtly wooing, and he is seeking *hohe Minne* (e.g., 3.4 [47]: "Do gedâht uf hôhe minne daz Siglinde kint"). It is not unwarranted to assume that the ladies' dominant role in determining the course and fate of the knights' heroic adventures had antecedents beyond the chivalric romances. An outstanding example is Brunhild's behaving as the amazon who would submit only to a victorious hero. Before the right of the stronger man to possess the woman of his choice started to be questioned (perhaps under the influence of the mercantile ethic, as we have observed), the woman could only assert her dignity by fighting on man's own terms, sword at hand, ready to be subdued by force in a fair, manly contest. The code of the French romances, where the woman was not allowed to handle manly weapons, excluded this "heroic" Germanic way.

The reader is struck by an aspect of the narrative that sounds more like a bourgeois way of looking at chivalry than a genuinely heroic one: that is the emphatic element of pompous ceremony, show, and display. Note, for example, in the third *âventiure*, the apprehensive fuss about Siegfried's departure for Worms, which must be impressively planned with all the trappings of knightly honor: finely embroidered suits of sumptuous fabrics, richly laden beasts in the sumpter-train, and so on. When he arrives in Worms the plain folk keep staring at the party, their mouths agape. An irreverent modern reader might almost be reminded of a Disneyland-like spectacle where the shiny armor is tinfoil. Could this be a sign that the poet, a cleric, was awed by the grandeur of courts to which he did not really belong? The aesthetic element of show was an integral part of *curialitas* from very early times; it has continued to surround the life of the mighty down to our own day. Court ceremony was destined to become more and more elaborate as a show of worth among both secular princes and princes of the Church, bishops and, later, cardinals. But we must conclude that this pervasive feature of the poem is part of its being, rather than a realistic representation of the life of the nobility, a courtly reflection on it.[31]

The legends' original versions having been lost in the mist of time, we can only guess as to how and when such elements entered the German sagas. To be sure, we do not find them in earlier texts of French *chansons de geste*. The German poet is clearly no part of that monastic world that would have disdained the conspicuous display of worldly riches and flashy ornaments. Moreover, such elements are related to the epic poet's habit of hyperbole: he overcharges visual details and over-does the elements that will awe his audience. When we find this marked relish in pomp and display in later poets, it may be part of a *gothique flamboyant* sense of *décor*—as in the masterful representations of *Sir Gawain and the Green Knight*, which surpassed anything previously known in fond descriptions of the luxuries of courtly living. The growing force of the mercantile ethic may also have been a factor. This factor is clearly present in an Italian version of the Arthurian cycle, the well known *Tavola Ritonda* or *Tavola Polidori* (early fourteenth century), and it is interesting to observe that the appreciation of worldly luxury, common to both epic and romance, could take on an overt bourgeois coloring in the land of merchant communes. At one point Queen Isotta's (Isolde) garments and personal ornaments are not only described in great detail, but precisely apprised one by one for their monetary value.[32] In a general sense, this taste for the rich display of wealth, re-finement, and comfort is a feature that the German epos shares with the romance, and which clearly reflects not the original epic sense of severe and austere devotion to warlike ideals but the courtly ways acquired by the new, "courtified" nobility. The sumptuous court festivals, often accompanied by hunting parties and tournaments, had become in actual practice keen models of self-image. The poets appreciated them as the best setting for their live performances and consequent reward.

Similarly, the reader is taken by surprise by rather intimate scenes within the privacy of palace chambers, wherein otherwise savage warriors behave politely and exquisitely, according to the best etiquette of educated society. Here again the poet may introduce elements that were not part of the social reality of the class he portrayed. His occasional irony, another possibly "bourgeois" trait, also reveals his personal distance from that class. Think of the humorous touch of the fierce Brunhild's maidens curiously peeking through the windows at the unknown men in Gunther's party (7.7 [395]). Or consider, in the Eighth Adventure, the poet's explaining Siegfried's financial ability to raise an army of one thousand Nibelungs. Again, remember the scene when Hagen's brother gets the key to Brunhild's treasury to spread presents all around, much to Brunhild's horror. The very episode of the taming of Brunhild on her nuptial bed could be read as sheer, snickering comedy.

This discourse of bourgeois distance from the original world of heroic legend should also apply to the element of the marvelous, which plays a diminishing role as it passes from the earlier, mythologically-grounded sagas to the hands of the *Nibelungenlied* poet. The poet reduces the fairy element of the Hoard and Brunhild's enchantment by Odin to mere backgroud, preserving only the magic stratagem of the Cloak of Darkness—a device Siegfried needs in order to trick Brunhild both in the three contests and on her wedding night—and Siegfried's raising of the army of Nibelungs in order to help Gunther get out of Iceland with his hostile bride-to-be Brunhild.

Insofar as they mark departures from earlier epic forms and, particularly, the more austere French epic, all these elements can be viewed as part and parcel of the courtly/chivalric culture. Even the artistic element that is so striking in the personal formation of Tristan and Isolt is far from belonging uniquely to those characters, since it is also found in the epic, including the *Nibelungenlied*, where it did not appear dissonant with the character of a warrior. Volker, who side by side with the unbending Hagen plays a major role in the final battle at Etzel's court, is a minstrel, a poet-musician, and a great warrior. We are reminded of the famous minstrel Taillefer who, reportedly singing the (still unwritten) *Chanson de Roland,* led William the Conqueror's army to battle at Hastings in 1066.[33] Minstrels and musicians are also employed in diplomatic missions, as in the embassy led by Rüdeger and sent by Etzel to extend the fateful invitation to the Burgundians. Other humane (we could even say humanistic) qualities are found among the fighting heroes, who all along indulge in effective displays of oratory. Hagen himself is a persuasive orator, but Rüdeger, in particular, is a master courtier/diplomat/orator in the sense of active practical politics, as he shows in the way he handles his difficult mission to Kriemhild: it is from that act of "diplomacy" that stems the catastrophe of the fall of the house of Burgundy, the poem's tragic resolution.

Though driven by hateful arrogance, the warriors always behave in a formally courteous manner toward one another, both friends and foes (we may recall Ordericus Vitalis's description of King William Rufus's respect for his prisoners). Out of mutual appreciation and regard for their valor, the opposing armies, which will utterly destroy each other in the end, meet with eager mutual courtesy before the fray (beginning of *âventiure* 28). Dietrich's and Hildebrand's troops "welcome" the Burgundians arriving in Hunland even while they expect great trouble from them. Courtesy reaches a climax in the great battle between Rüdeger and the Burgundians, where, in exchange for Rüdeger's gracious gift of his own shield to Hagen, Hagen and Volker refuse to fight him even if he slew all the other Burgundians (*âventiure* 37).

Courtliness accorded with the principles of Christian personal responsibility, which replaced the pagan fatalism of old. God-willed necessity, the basic predicament in the primitive epic, negated personal choice, but now the hero had to be judged as a good or bad person. The poet had abandoned the psychological frame of the heroic, noble heroes, who though savage, had the aura of divinity about them. The negative view of courtly vices pierces through the *Nibelungenlied* in a way that alters the heroic nature of the original (or at least earlier, Nordic) saga. Thus Gunther's court came to harbor characters who possessed the chief canonical virtues of courtliness, that is, bravery and loyalty, but had few scruples in exerting them for ignoble "political" causes. Hagen kills Siegfried treacherously and out of hateful envy; Gunther backs him in his repeated thievery at the expense of a woman, his own sister Kriemhild. One is reminded of the medieval chroniclers who extolled rulers as noble and admirable even while exposing their horrible crimes, apparently without perceiving the glaring moral contradiction.[34]

Indeed, one can find so many parallels and analogies between the heroes of the sagas and those of the romances that we could easily believe they shared common origins, despite the clear genre distinctions. Tristan and Siegfried go through similar stages of apprenticeship. They both arrive at court as little known guests and manage to obtain general favor with their amazing talents and prowess. Both will tragically succumb to the envy their excellence has aroused against them. Both are used by their kings to win wives for them. In their adventures to win brides for their lieges they use force as well as cunning. The suggestion that the hero be sent to win a bride for the king is made by Mark's envious courtiers just as Hagen originates the same idea in Gunther's mind, at Siegfried's expense.[35] On a more general level, the heroic single combat that characterizes the individualism of the chivalric romance is an epic feature that goes back to the Homeric beginnings of the epic genre.

GOTTFRIED'S *TRISTAN*

Knowledge of the Arthurian world must have developed rather early in Germany, since the way Eilhart von Oberge's *Tristrant und Isalde* (ca. 1170) introduced Arthurian characters assumed on the part of the readers some familiarity with the role of the court (e.g., vv. 5046–5058). Eilhart apparently imported the Tristan legend to Germany, having perhaps received it through the intermediary of Alienor of Aquitaine or her daughter Mathilde, who in 1168 married Henry the Lion, Duke of Saxony: in 1182/1186 the poet followed them into exile in Normandy or England.[36]

For W. T. H. Jackson (1971: 35–48) the Tristan cycle entailed a moralizing condemnation of the lovers as socially subversive sinners, with the exception of Thomas and Gottfried, who alone adopted a sympathetic view, Gottfried even declaring himself one of the noble lovers' followers. Tristan's and Isolt's mutual passion thus became, quite exceptionally, an equal union of noble souls: "ein man ein wîp, ein wîp ein man; / Tristan Isolt, Isolt Tristan," "a man a woman, a woman a man, Tristan Isolde, Isolde Tristan" (vv. 129 f.).[37]

The following interpretation of the Tristan story varies from Jaeger's assessment of the role of German romances within the courtly tradition. For Jaeger, the French romances of the twelfth century offered two basic approaches to courtliness: the courtier narrative and the chivalric narrative. In Germany, he sees Gottfried von Strassburg and Wolfram von

Eschenbach (b. ca. 1170, d. ca. 1220, about ten years after Gottfried) as typically representing these two complementary poles. Gottfried's Tristan would be a hero of courtliness as the art of success and survival, whereas Wolfram's *Parzival* (ca. 1195–1210, contemporary with Gottfried's unfinished *Tristan und Isolt*) postulated an ideal of perfect knighthood which Parzival strove to reach but which only his son Loherangrîn, whose sublime chivalry was pure and uncontaminated inner humanity, was destined to achieve. This distinction between the courtly and the chivalric stresses the latter as God-oriented, the former as more thoroughly immanent. To be sure, God is as absent from the more worldly context of Gottfried's poem as He is ever-present in Wolfram's version of the Parzival story, more so than in Chrétien's Perceval. But the following analysis may show such a distinction to be neither fundamental nor always clear.[38] Jaeger (chap. 12) sees the *Verhöflichung der Krieger*[39] in the two great knight poets, Hartmann von Aue and Wolfram von Eschenbach, signally through their respective adaptations of Chrétien de Troyes' *Yvain* (*Iwein*, ca. 1202) and *Perceval*.

Critics have commented on Gottfried's apparent disagreement with Wolfram. Indeed the two poets embody the opposing classes of clerics and knights: Gottfried, not exactly a cleric but probably educated in a monastery school (*meister* he was called, not nobleman, *hêr*), aimed to uphold the worldly, courtly qualities of the civil servant, as distinct from the knightly virtues extolled by *hêr* Wolfram. Gottfried's *Tristan* is not, by and large, a "knightly" statement. We can agree with W. T. H. Jackson (1971) that Gottfried believed neither in the Arthurian world of chivalrous conventions nor in "courtly love," hence he picked up the romance as a matter of opportunity, because it was there, asking, as it were, to be handled "correctly." The thesis that interested him could neither be understood nor accepted as viable in an Arthurian court: it was "Tristan-love," *hohe minne* for the *edele herzen*, the few elect. He believed that the practice of true love as well as the reading of good love stories (i.e., love literature) went together with the noblest virtues: "liebe, triuwe, staeter muot, / ere und ander manic guot" (amiability, faithfulness, constancy, honor, and many other good dispositions, vv. 181–186).[40] Since love produces a richer way of life, we must strive to love (191–200). Only love can assure true honor, praise, and fame: "ere unde lop erwerben / oder ane si verderben" (207–210). Tristan's impassioned example proved that courtly qualities were not necessarily good, and could be downright bad. At Mark's court, envy (*nît*), suspicion (*arcwan*), indecision (*zwivel*), hate (*haz*), cowardice, intrigue, and selfishness prevailed, becoming obstacles to the superior hero like Tristan.[41]

Envy was a particularly powerful obstacle to courtesy. In Chrétien de Troyes's *Chevalier de la charrete*, Meleaganz, one of the most disloyal and treacherous villains of Arthurian literature, was said to be driven by envy. Later on, Dante presented the tragic case of Pier della Vigna as an exemplary victim of this scourge of the courts. Tristan could not survive without yielding to the ways of the world, thus becoming a deceitful, contradictory, and cunning liar.[42] The blame fell on that court society which crushed our heroes because they could not observe its tenets, whereas the romances had presented the court as an ideal milieu in which love provided the motive for the highest and most refined deeds. Thus, for Gottfried, either the education of the knight had failed in its purpose, or the society that harbored that ideal of education fell short of rewarding its own pupils.

Rual li Foitenant, perhaps the most virtuous character in the poem, is a sort of anticourtier. Jackson (1971: 160 f.) sees this as proof that Gottfried did not believe in courtliness, which is part of this scholar's persuasive "deconstruction" of the poem. He reads it as a radical subversion of everything the readership of this literary genre wanted to believe in. Another interpretation may be more plausible. Gottfried had to put Mark's court under an unfavorable light but Rual is measured by no other virtues than the courtly ones, such as loyalty above all (he is even so named) and total dedication to a superior cause (his lord Riwalin's future through his son Tristan).[43] Gottfried's theme is not the representation of courtliness but of the conflict between love and society—specifically, courtly society. He replaces the knight-hero with the artist-hero. Tristan/Tantris in Ireland is *ein höfischer spilmann*, a courtly minstrel, and is received by Isolt's tutor who is also a musically skilled priest. We move in a world of art appreciators. Just the same, it is a world of knighthood, defined according to the basic traditional virtues we have seen—for example, by King Mark at the lavish ceremony of Tristan's dubbing (vv. 5022–5040). Gottfried's ironic attitude toward the warlike side of the chivalric world comes out typically in such episodes as Tristan's gruesome duel with Morolt (see especially vv. 6871–6905: each rival is four men in one, and so on), almost worthy of Ariosto in its humorous way of quoting alleged sources for textual hyperbole.

Just as other texts justify and extol the active virtues of political agents (for example, Peter of Blois's justification of the role of governors and courtiers, Dudo of St. Quentin's and William of Jumièges's stories of the abbot Martin of Jumièges dissuading William Long-Sword from becoming a monk, John of Limoges's story of Joseph and the Pharaoh), so does King Mark warn Tristan not to let the court discourage him from service to his king: "Virtue and envy are to each other like a mother to her child," Mark advises. "Virtue incessantly gives birth to envy and nourishes it. . . . Bliss and fortune are contemptible when they have never faced hatred."[44] Like Joseph in John of Limoges's text, Tristan is won by King Mark's advice to fight back bravely rather than yield to the attacks of envy and hatred. Not only does Tristan overcome his paralyzing fears of his scheming enemies and decide to remain at court, he even outdoes his detractors by shrewdly returning their own devices against them. He thus becomes a triumphant hero of political courtiership by accepting his enemies' scheme to go and win a bride for Mark, but he tricks his enemies by asking them to go with him on that dangerous adventure. They cannot refuse what was their own idea; hence they must exert themselves for a successful expedition by saving Tristan from Isolt's revenge for the slaying of her uncle Morolt.

As we have seen, in consequence of the prerequisites advertised in the doctrine of curiality, the courtier had became a master of disguise. Similarly, in Gottfried's Tristan "what was a virtue has become a stratagem" (Jaeger: 42), as in Castiglione's courtier, who will disguise his art as a second nature under the practice of *sprezzatura*: "true art is what does not seem to be art, and the most important thing is to conceal it" (*Cortegiano*: 1.26).

Gottfried had begun his psychological portrait of Tristan from the outside: "In gestures and beautiful manners nature had been so good to him that he was a pleasure to look at."[45] This was a comprehensive presentation of good manners, coupling mores with gestures or outward comportment. But serious moral substance underlies this doctrine, since it is said that, when Tristan became a tutor to Isolt, he taught her *site* through its true source, to wit, *moraliteit*. While instructing her thoroughly in music, languages, and the reading of formative books,

> besides all his instruction, he also taught her a discipline which we call *moraliteit*, the art which teaches fine behavior. All women ought to practice it in their youth. *Moraliteit*, that sweet pursuit, is delightful and pure. Its study is in harmony with the world and with God. In its commandment it teaches us to please both God and the world. It is given to all lofty spirits as a nurse.[46]

Commenting on these famous lines, W. T. H. Jackson (1971: 76 f.) pointed out that this German neologism, "probably" from Latin *moralitas* (but what else could it come from?), could only have the meaning of the Latin term, to wit, not exactly "morality," but state of mind, character, and habit of praxis. Jackson further suggested that this beautifully moving passage on the power of music (most becoming to the inner circle of *edele herzen*) echoed closely Boethius's *De re musica*, where the *moralitas* of the singer/performer was said to determine the effect of music, precisely as in Gottfried's context. Musical skill was to be part of the education of the courtier down to Castiglione and beyond, and Gottfried played this motif with unusual subtlety. By his musical talent, Tristan casts a truly magic spell on the court (vv. 3588–3597), and Isolt will learn from him the same art (9036–9131).

Tristan appears in Gottfried as a knight with all the courtly trappings in his education, but he was already so in Eilhart von Oberge and, in part, in the Anglo-Norman Thomas.[47] It is worth noting that Tristan's courtly career shows striking parallels with that of Apollonius of Tyre, the hero of a Latin novel of the fifth to sixth century A.D. that enjoyed remarkable popularity in the Middle Ages. Apollonius, abandoned as a youth in a foreign land, managed to attract the king's attention through his athletic skills, thus becoming a favorite at the palace through his unsurpassed talent at playing the lyre. The princess made him her tutor in music and fell in love with him.[48] The peculiar courtierly twist in the vernacular romances is the element of clever calculation. The result of this educated display of liberal arts is that Isolt, before falling in love with Tristan and when she still knew him only as her tutor and a wandering minstrel called Tantris, concluded that such a man deserved wealth and honor: "der solte guot und ere han" (v. 11,129). She reached this conclusion as she watched him bathe and mused about the great worth of this lowly minstrel. Wealth and honor were the just reward for such a master of the humane arts and *moraliteit*. Furthermore, Tantris had also slayed the dragon, thus proving himself a worthy knight while winning Isolt for his uncle Mark and saving her from the hated seneschal. She thought he deserved a kingdom.

Gottfried called Tristan a *hoveman* (= *Hofman*, courtier), while King Mark calls Tristan's modest pose (the *modestia* of the curial ethos) "cunning" or "craftiness" (*kündekeit*, 3576–3583), very close indeed to Castiglione's *sprezzatura*, wherein the secret of success lies in a cleverly calculated underplay of talent which blunts envy and intrigue at court. It is exquisitely "political" and "diplomatic" and it arouses admiration, not disapproval, even though the sharp-eyed among the audience, including the king, do not fail to see it as a mask. Jaeger (239) compares this situation with Alain de Lille's very "moral" allegorical figure of Honestas (to be placed alongside Cicero's concept of *honestas*), who advises the New Man to learn the rare art of leading two lives, "living his interior life for himself and his exterior life for the many; to . . . show himself all things to all men" ("intus sibi vivens, pluribus extra; / . . . ut omnibus omnis / pareat": *Anticlaudianus* 7: 215–218; the advice is loosely adapted from Seneca, *ad Lucilium* 5: 2–3: "Intus omnia dissimilia sint, frons populo nostra conveniat"). This positive dissimulation, which the critics called hypocrisy, was found in Thomas Becket, *vir geminus* (double man), whereas Thomas More, still very much "a man for all seasons," "omnia omnibus factus" in St. Paul's picturesque metaphor, was equally doomed even without being so ready to adopt duplicity.[49] If duplicity could be regarded as a morally debasing form of hypocrisy, Paul's and Seneca's contexts referred to a manner of duplicity that could well be morally exalting and prudently endowed with saving grace.

Höfische minne thrives on deceit, says Gottfried (Jackson: 93), whereas *hohe minne* transcends deceit and cunning, *valsche und akust* (v. 12,239). Yet courtly society breeds precisely these qualities which can be good or bad, according to circumstances. They are good when they allow Tristan to survive envy, bad when Tristan and Isolt use them to serve their love in a struggle against society. So the very qualities that have made Tristan a hero turn negative and pave his path to self-destruction. These have become the same predicaments of adulterous triangles, covered up elegantly and skillfully in the history of courtly societies from King Arthur to Versailles and the Parisian salons, down to the eighteenth-century *cicisbei*, fashionable young dandies who publicly courted and escorted married ladies as surrogate husbands. Society will destroy the true lovers, whom it casts out because they flaunt its rules overtly and dangerously, whereas it will accept, admire, and honor the courtly, prudent, dissimulating, and "diplomatic" lovers and sinners who play the games of elegant society. The high nobility as well as the high clergy would show the way at all times. Gottfried seems to accuse literature of hypocrisy (Jackson: 94) because it produces mere fiction, divorced from reality, whereas he advocates literary myths that should be our guides in action. In other words, the code that at the start was educational and formative, once established becomes a rule of conformity and success at any cost.

Jaeger (237–241) overdoes it when he singles out the element of cunning in the Tristan story as a distinguishing trait of courtly romance—of German curial origin—if this is meant in any exclusive sense. Indeed, that element was strong in German epic literature, too, and we may wonder which genre has chronological priority in this sense. Cunning plays a prominent role in Siegfried's way of helping King Gunther conquer the invincible Brunhild. His deceitful courtship is quite analogous to Mark's courting of Isolt with the help of Tristan. Gottfried's sources were French, but could he not also have learned such stratagems from earlier German sagas? In any event, it seems fair to conclude that *Tristan* is courtly only on the surface: the author is interested in a deeper search for ethical and behavioral values that go beyond courtliness and chivalry. When all is said and done Gottfried's (and Thomas's) *Tristan* is neither courtly nor *courtois,* and this conclusion contradicts Jaeger's interpretation of Gottfried's place in the ideology of courtesy. The most striking absence is that of the essential quality of restraint or measure—all versions of the Tristan story in verse (i.e., before *Tristan en prose* of ca. 1230) are characterized by elements of exasperated, unrestrained violence and passion.[50] The conflict of the codes is extreme there (hence tragic), because each one of them is pushed to radical statement. Gottfried radicalizes the tragic story of the two lovers united against the world and the court. Hence the court can neither understand nor accept them and will act toward them with mean hostility, while they will use all sorts of courtly ruses to survive. Likewise, *Tristan* is not *courtois* in that its pessimism denies the optimistic faith of *courtois* literature (including Chrétien). Tristan's love doubtless civilizes and sublimates, but it also destroys.[51] The naturalism of Gottfried's *hohe Minne* and Thomas's *fin'amour*, unlike and against the socially conditioned *amour courtois*, raises love above human law and social norms to the exalted dignity of a law of nature. The true origin of this phenomenon, admittedly preexisting Thomas, is ostensibly neither courtly nor chivalric. It is an anthropological/psychological fact that seems part of the subgenre and logically and chronologically transcends the birth of chivalry. The court, however, behaves in it not so much as a microcosm of society at large but as a realm of special groups, the rising bourgeoisie and perhaps also the clerical functionaries, who could not hope to achieve chivalric status.[52] It does not seem unwarranted to assume that in the way both Thomas and Gottfried (together with Eilhart) handled their controversial story, and in direct contrast to the way other narrators had handled it (especially Béroul), we see the traces of clerics at work, addressing themselves to a sophisticated audience of noblemen, with their problematic attitudes toward passion, loyalty, and faithfulness.

The place and role of the various codes in the story of Tristan is hard to assess, chiefly on account of the extant versions' fragmentary state, but it seems clear that, though always present, the Christian ethic there plays a secondary role. In Béroul the two lovers consider themselves sinners and recognize their faults of treachery and disloyalty vis-à-vis King Mark, uncle, benefactor, lord, and husband respectively, but impute to the philter their lack of free choice. When the three years of the philter's effectiveness are up, without really repenting, the lovers accept the hermit Ogrin's attempt to reconcile them to society, in the hope that their violations of the social code will be forgiven for the sake of minimizing the damage and restoring harmony. The moral imperative is reduced to the wisdom of saving what can be saved. It is wise to lie ("por honte oster et mal covrir / doit on un poi par bel mentir," "one must lie in order to erase the dishonor and cancel the evil"—ll. 2353 f.); wisdom lies in being "diplomatic" and making the best of a difficult situation, without jeopardizing social order and welfare for the sake of absolute or abstract principles. Which is, within our discourse, the essence of "courtliness."[53]

WOLFRAM'S *PARZIVAL*

Chivalry in Wolfram's *Parzival* has been extensively discussed and does not need much comment here beyond the excellent use Jaeger (esp. 247–253) has made of this poem, often judged the most poetic of German medieval literature.[54] Suffice it to mention the qualities that Gurnemanz (Chrétien's Gornemanz) lists as essential to the good knight— keeping in mind that in this *Bildungsroman* Parzival is chiefly guided by Gurnemanz's advice (and, later, Trevrizent's). The qualities that are most pertinent to the image we are pursuing of the courtier knight are: courtesy, compassion, shame (*schame*, i.e., as noted before, reverence for others' rights and needs), generosity (*milte*), humility, beauty, nobility, moderation (*mâze*), good breeding, leadership, a coupling of manliness and cheerful disposition (*sît manlich und wol gemuot*), and mastery of arms.[55] Somewhat ironically, one of the canonical curial virtues, reticence (*blûkeit*, a form of discretion and respect), turns out to be the cause of Parzival's major mistake: he fails to ask the decisive question that would have saved the Fisher King because, he will repeatedly explain, Gurnemanz had taught him to refrain from speaking when not asked.[56]

To understand Wolfram's attitude toward his subject matter we must first face the problem of his irony. Irony was quite common in the romances, starting with Chrétien, who probably bequeathed it to his imitators as part of the "median" style that characterized the genre. Yet Wolfram uses it so pervasively and personally as to make himself not only the most memorable master of it, but, indeed, even a precursor of such a supreme ironist as Ariosto. Wolfram's being a member of the knightly class is pertinent to the interpretion of this psychological and stylistic feature because his ironic distancing from his subject matter cannot be the reflection of a different social status, as in the case of Gottfried. If, like the Italian poets later on, Wolfram chose to detach himself from his material, it had to be because its most direct users, that public who had embraced it because of ideological affinity, could now perceive it as "literature," a ludic fiction. The changes vis-à-vis Chrétien included an increase in irony and humor. Parzival himself is more clownish than Perceval ever was: when he leaves home, his mother dresses him up as a buffoon, whereas Perceval's mother had simply dressed him in rawhide, Welsh fashion. Perceval's mother had advised him to take kisses and then perhaps a ring from maidens, but only if willingly granted, and no more; Parzival's mother admonishes him to win (*erwerben*) a ring and then kiss and hold the chaste woman, with her consent. In both texts the young hero clumsily forces the maiden to grant him favors in ways that endanger her reputation, but the clumsiness comes closer to actual rape in the German text, where the encounter with Jeschute turns out to be considerably more offensive than in Chrétien, with the hero behaving like a boorish teenager.[57]

Practical aims may also have affected the poem, that is, the praise of the Plantagenet house of Anjou in France and England and, in particular, of an admired Angevin bishop, Philip of Poitou, a fighter/courtier who had become a man of God, like Trevrizent in the poem.[58] These aims could not be as strong a determinant for the orientation of the poem as Ariosto's wish to praise his Este patrons, but they could condition the handling of the particulars. It is also worth noting that Wolfram seemed better inclined than Chrétien de Troyes toward courtly love since, Perceval/Parzival aside, he showed love-service possibly coming to good ends, as in the cases of Gawan and Orgeluse, Gramoflanz and Itonje, and Obie and Meljacanz.[59]

There is, then, the question of Parzival's real mission. He is a bungling young man who is destined for high achievements, but has to find his way by a gradual learning process of inner education and humanization. He unwittingly causes his mother's death, abandons his beloved wife, and fails to ask King Anfortas the decisive question. The realization of his failures plunges him into aimless wandering in a state of "God-hatred." He will emerge from this phase of despair when Trevrizent converts him by explaining to him not only the meaning of the Grail, but also the supreme duties of the good Christian (book 9, 472: 13–17). Parzival then seems ready to enter a life of ascetic dedication to a higher goal than mundane chivalry, having understood those limitations of Arthurian chivalry that Chrétien and then Hartmann had implicitly but effectively criticized. He should now abandon all frivolity (473: 3: "bewart sîn vor lôsheit"), turn the pride of the fighter to the supreme meekness so heroically practiced by his new adviser, and forsake that service of *Minne* and the "God of Love" which had been King Anfortas's ruin: " 'Amor!' was his battle-cry. / But when humility's the test, / Such battle-cries are not the best."[60] The knights who serve the Grail must abjure all love for women (495: 7 f.). Neither that kind of love nor any natural remedies, including the art of herbs or magic that issues from human science, can heal Anfortas's wound. Christian charity is the only remedy. The "question" that was expected of Parzival was to be prompted by humane concern, compassion, and pity. Parzival will succeed in answering his calling, will ask the fateful question and free Anfortas, and will even become King of the Grail. When he has accomplished his task, Trevrizent will once again urge him to turn from pride to humility: "You attained a great success. / Now turn your mind to humility."[61]

Yet, when we read the elaborate subsequent sections of the poem we wonder whether Parzival has really "converted." In what way has he changed, if at all? For our hero does not come out of Trevrizent's retreat to pursue the great quest directly and exclusively. Instead, he goes back to his accustomed life of adventure, more aimless than ever, amid all the usual trappings of beautiful and sensuous maidens and displays of rich, high living. In due course, he will simply, as it were, stumble once again, by good fortune, into the path of the Grail, which will be handed to him without much effort. In what sense, then, is chivalry really transcended?

We might tentatively conclude that, despite all the moral qualms and the intellectual realizations of absurdities and shortcomings, the paraphernalia of chivalrous living, or dreaming, were just too powerful to be, even only temporarily, obliterated, let alone effectively transcended. Literature and fiction were stronger than reality. Wolfram was, after all, a knight. To be sure, there is a transcendent, mystical side to the Quest of the Grail, but there is also, at least implicitly, an ethical and social one: the correction of the shortcomings of knightly and courtly behavior. Only by broadening the horizons could the Christian truth be combined with the knightly one to produce a superior, non-warlike chivalry. Wolfram the knight was educated by the cleric: chivalry became meek, and Wolfram was paving the way for Dante.[62]

This conclusion on Wolfram's hero should remind us of Jean Frappier's (1954) rather severe judgment on the religious element in the Grail cycle as "un masque," religion being exalted there for no deeper purpose than the self-serving intention of better honoring the chivalric class. In a remarkably "deconstructionist" mood *avant-la-lettre*, the eminent medievalist surmised that the inner mystique of the Grail, allowing the knights to see themselves as noble in the highest and purest way they could devise, truly as *homines sibi relicti*, without and outside the Christian *militia* dreamed about by a St. Bernard, was the defense mechanism of a class that felt threatened—mainly by the rising bourgeoisie. This may be a fair assessment of the complex, mysterious phenomenon of the Quest as reflected in the texts examined by Frappier, and certainly, as I read it, in Wolfram's. It is not that the knight poets felt no religious commitment: indeed, one of them, Hartmann von Aue, abandoned the worldly literature he had so brilliantly cultivated and turned to religious themes for his successful and much discussed, hagiographic *Gregorius*, although, if the accepted chronology is correct, he did return to chivalry for his last and supreme poem, *Iwein*. As Frappier put it (1954), the peculiar mystique of the Grail romances as a whole, from Chrétien through Wolfram and on to Robert de Boron and the Vulgate prose romances (the *Lancelot/Graal*), expressed not so much a view of chivalry at the service of religion as, rather, of knighthood as a religion in itself. The old ideal of a marriage of bellicosity and piety, which the clerical milieus had fostered and nurtured, resulted once again in a juxtaposition rather than a full harmonization.

Incidentally, a curious symptom of the feeling for social refinement that both courtliness and chivalry embodied and promulgated can be seen in the frequent semi-ironic allusions to personal hygiene. As often and as regularly as feasible, the sweating heroes bathe and wash their hands and bodies, sometimes in elaborate ceremonial situations where the solicitous assistance of fair maidens makes the ritual erotically exciting. Details are not spared: washing after meals is said to prevent hurting one's eyes by rubbing them with hands still scaly from handling fish (487: 1–4). It is worth recalling that the ritual bath on the eve traditionally preceded the dubbing ceremony.

HARTMANN'S *IWEIN*

The complex case of Hartmann von Aue is fraught with inner contradictions. *Iwein*, his last great work and, as it were, his conclusive statement, has received two alternate readings: 1) the story reveals the failures of the Arthurian court (which might imply a more general critique of courtly life), since Iwein fails until he transcends the exterior rules of the court and becomes a richer human being through experiences dictated by his conscience rather than by the knightly code; or 2) it reveals the hero's individual failure to uphold the courtly virtues: his conversion from an egotistic adventure-seeker to a socially responsible knight, lord, and husband culminates in his reconciliation with his wife Laudine.[63] The two interpretations may not be mutually exclusive; what the hero experiences in his personal story may be the shortcomings of the court ideology and the way to overcome them by reaching for a higher level of true chivalry.

We are more interested in the social aspects of our literature, but critics have also speculated on political motivations. In contrast to Wolfram, who presented Arthur as a prince of justice and peace among rival lords, possibly as "a corrective for the political chaos of Wolfram's own time," Hartmann has been said to have idealized Arthur as a *paterfamilias*, without the tense feudal antagonisms from baronial competition that one sensed in Chrétien.[64] The dialectical picture of courtly behavior has its specific counterpart in the opposite vices: in Hartmann's *Iwein*, for example, the evil conduct of Duke Aliers and of Lunete's older sister is described as "arrogance," *übermuot* (vv. 3410, 7657), which leads to "pride," *hôchvart*. Interestingly enough, this is also the language of the epic: compare *Nibelungenlied* 54: "der kan mit übermüete der hôhverte pflegen," "he can nurture pride with arrogance."[65]

Even more than Chrétien, his source and model, Hartmann uses chivalric themes as an opportunity to build tales of character formation, moral education, and civil manners on the heroic level that is expected of ideal leaders and social exemplars. In *Iwein* a typically worthy knight was "by courage and generosity the finest man who ever entered the ranks of knighthood" ("der aller tiureste man, / der rîters namen ie gewan, / von manheit und von milte," vv. 1455–1457).[66] The growth from the early *Erek* (1190–1192 ?) to *Iwein* (1202 ?) seems to show an increasing interest in the virtues of *mâze*, self-control, decorum, and manners.[67] Lunete, for example, is declared a true lady except for her excessively loud complaining (Enite's problem, too, in *Erek*): "hete sî sich niht verclagt" (v. 1154). The trials of Iwein and Laudine, like but even more severe than those of Erek and Enite, are a necessary path to maturity through error and painful atonement. Iwein shows his exquisite sense of propriety and consideration when he dismounts to avert the inelegance of a duel of swords fought on horseback, once he and Gawein have broken their spears.[68] The Irish seneschal Kay is probably the worst type of courtier, a radical interpretation of Arthur's partly comic figure Kay (Chrétien's Kex, the "ill-mannered Keiî," "zuhtlôse Keiî" in Hartmann's *Iwein*, v. 90). The educational burden of Hartmann's devotional story *Gregorius* is analogous to the main thrust of his previous *Erek*, in which he had expanded on the didactic aspects of Chrétien de Troyes's *Erec et Enide*, stressing the virtuous elements in the knightly code and condemning the disregard for measure (*mâze*) as a violation of self-restraint.

As Hartmann's relationship to Chrétien encompasses some of the latter's concerns with the moral side of knightly behavior, it also includes a critical view of the troubadourlike kind of *Minnedienst*. Hartmann is even more socially-oriented than his French source and his plots and characters are clearly invested with a complex, highly problematical didactic role.[69] The positive conjugal love between Hartmann's Erek and Enite contrasts with the courtly theory of love as *Minnedienst* in the episode of Mabonagrin, displaying toward the prevailing code a critical stance that ties together Chrétien, Hartmann, and Dante. Somewhat similarly, Hartmann's *Iwein* used Chrétien's *Yvain* to good advantage as a model for the harmonious blending of conjugal faithfulness and heroic dedication to the knightly duties of service to society and the needy.

The preceding analysis should show why Germany was better prepared to receive a practical lesson on behavior (specifically aimed at Hartmann's own milieu of the courtly *ministeriales*) than the France of Chrétien, not because of the serious philosophical bent of the German mind, as critics have been wont to assume, but for the moral, social, and political features of circumstantial historical background. Chrétien remained the provider of themes and forms, but the deeper messages were developed independently. The popularity of Hartmann's *Iwein* remained high among the nobility through the thirteenth and fourteenth centuries, and in the fifteenth it also extended to the wealthy merchants, who were striving to imitate the ways of noblemen.[70] Yet even in the Germanic area the continuators of the Yvain story tended to draw upon the French sources, especially Chrétien, with the exception of Ulrich Füetrer's *Yban*, composed around 1480.

If we should wonder why such outstanding poets as Wolfram and

Hartmann exerted themselves in "translating" Chrétien, even with much freedom of interpretation and reelaboration, the obvious answer is that Chrétien was a very great narrator. From a strictly literary vantage, even in comparison with his sophisticated and complex German imitators, he remains the best storyteller all around. Yet his imitators carried further his remarkable gifts for imparting "meanings" to sheer stories (the *sen* Chrétien referred to at the beginning of his *Lancelot*).

Alongside the three great masters, some early texts used Celtic fantasies for mere entertainment. The Swiss cleric Ulrich von Zatzikhoven's rather erotic *Lanzelet* (perhaps 1194, no later than 1200) made of Lancelot a sort of mindless Casanova, while Wirnt von Grafenberg's *Wigalois* (1204–1209 or 1210–1215) emphasized the non-transcendental, non-Grail-like religious theme of sacred royalty and salvation through a just king (Gawein's son Wigalois, not Arthur).[71] In the rich German production of romances that surrounded and followed the three masters, the Arthurian matter generally lacked vitality. Instead of moral concerns, the main business became jousts, feasts, and sundry pastimes, together with the refined pleasures of the table. It was so in Der Stricker's *Daniel von dem blühenden Tal* (1220–1230), Heinrich von dem Türlîn's encyclopedic compilation *Diu Crône* (*Die Krone*, ca. 1230), the anonymous *Wigamur* (ca. 1250), Albrecht von Scharfenberg's *Jüngerer Titurel* (ca. 1272), and Konrad von Stoffeln's *Gauriel von Muntabel* (ca. 1300). Der Stricker and Heinrich von dem Türlîn seem to have been commoners, from Franconia and Carinthia respectively. True enough, the *Jüngerer Titurel*, which stands out with fifty-seven surviving manuscripts in addition to a 1477 printed edition, may have impressed the audiences with its didactic attempt to hold up a mirror of knightly virtue, combining chivalry with Christian conduct. As to the thirty-thousand-line *Diu Crône*, it was an important original version of Arthurian lore, which Heinrich von dem Türlîn, alone among German romancers, centered on the popular figure of Gawein, placing him within the search for the Holy Grail.[72] Dissatisfied with the marginal role of the chivalric Arthurian ethos in the *Daniel*, Der Pleier retorted between 1250 and 1280 with his *Garel von dem blühenden Tal*, *Meleranz*, and *Tandareis und Flordibel*, but he could not keep such high values from turning conventional and rather lifeless.

The learned Rudolf von Ems (d. in Italy 1252/1253) drew upon a lost French original for his very popular *Willehalm von Orleans* (perhaps 1235–1240; at least 76 manuscripts are extant) but in it praised several German poets including Hartmann, Gottfried, and Wolfram (who after 1210 had also composed a *Willehalm* similarly based on a lost French *chanson de geste* unrelated to Rudolf's romance). The hero is an ideal knight striving to survive in a harsh world of practical realities: he believes in what the poet calls "the highest dignity the world has a name for, I mean the title 'knight.' " [73] Interestingly enough, Rudolf, a ministerial who had acquired noble status in the entourage of the Count of Montfort and showed clear pride in this status throughout his work, made a rich merchant commoner from Cologne the hero of his early *Der gute Gerhard* (ca. 1220), a poem of charity and humility told in first person to Emperor Otto I as a warning against excessive pride. Around 1230 Ulrich von Türheim completed Gottfried's *Tristan* and, between 1240 and 1250, Wolfram's *Willehalm*. In midstream, the prolific Konrad von Würzburg (ca. 1225–1287), virtuoso of the *geblümte Rede*, the flowery style, as he labeled it, tried his hand at many genres including the longer romance in *Engelhard* and *Partonopier und Meliur* (derived from the French *Partonopeus de Blois* of ca. 1170). Konrad, too, was a commoner who could count clerics (including perhaps the bishop of Strassburg), city fathers, and high merchants among his avowed patrons in Strassburg and Basel. The *Trojanerkrieg*, Konrad's last work, managed to mix the story of Troy not only with Arthurian themes but also with the saga of Dietrich von Bern. Chivalric love and adventure joined with the crusading spirit in the syncretic romance *Wilhelm von Österreich* by Johann von Würzburg (1314), where the Third Crusade had become a test to conquer the beloved.

Most of the epigones imitated Hartmann, down to Ulrich Füetrer, who closed the cycle. Sharing his friend Jakob Püterich von Reichertshausen's enthusiasm for Wolfram von Eschenbach, Füetrer (connected since the 1460s with the court of Munich, d. after 1492) managed to express his appreciation for German romances by gathering the stories of Merlin, Titurel, Parzival, *Diu Crône*, Lohengrin, Wigalois, Iwein, and others in his 41,500-line *Buch der Abenteuer der Ritter von der Tafelrunde* (ca. 1473–1490).

All the narrative streams had been coming together, but without unity of inspiration or a convincing message. Boiardo and Ariosto would see to it that this mixed recipe produced more inspiring results.

PART FOUR

The Italian Scene

CHAPTER SEVEN

The Origins

ITALIANS AT GERMAN COURTS

I have posited a connection between the military and sociopolitical ethos of the nobility and the education of high civil servants, and I have assumed that this process started with the development of curiality at the German imperial court. Evidence of early Italian connections with Germany at this level is abundant, if scattered.

The history of education in Italy between Charlemagne and A.D. 1000 hinges on the cathedral schools, in addition to the monasteries, the rare private schools, and such notarial chanceries as that of the *notarii sacri palatii* of the royal palace at Pavia, already active under the Longobard kings.[1] An important episode is the presence at the royal court of Pavia of a school of grammar under a deacon named Felix at the time of the Longobard King Cunipert (671–700). Much beloved and honored by the king, Felix left a progeny of teachers: his nephew Flavianus trained Paulus Diaconus (who recorded this information). Cunipert was the first orthodox Catholic king in Italy, his predecessors having favored paganism, Arianism (like the Ostrogoths before them), or the Three Chapters' schismatic observance; as such he started endowing churches and monasteries, thus establishing the kind of regular intercourse between courts and abbeys that would characterize the curial tradition of later times.[2] Liutprand (712–744) enriched his court by setting up, alongside the court school, a royal chapel with its own clergy of the palace, while members of the royal family were being appointed as bishops of Pavia and Milan. The prestige of his thus refurbished court attracted illustrious Italian and foreign intellectuals and grandees like Pippin, who was sent over by his father Charles Martel in 735 to be educated there. Charlemagne hastened to invite Paulus Diaconus (d. 799) to the Frankish court of Aachen, where the Longobard scholar and courtier spent five years (782–786). While there Paulus inaugurated the genre of episcopal biographies with his *Gesta episcoporum Mettensium*, on the pattern of the *Liber pontificalis.*[3]

The Carolingian revival of grammatical instruction continued to have an impact in the ninth and tenth centuries. In the tenth century "the guiding model for education remained, as in the previous century, the learned bishop."[4] When the German emperors began shaping policies for episcopal training and behavior, there may have been German influences on Italian bishops, too. By the year 1000, however, the lay notaries, versed in the law and later on in the *dictamen* version of rhetoric, were clearly replacing clerics in both communal and episcopal chanceries (Witt 1988: 38). Between 1000 and 1400 the Italian communes employed lay *litterati* whose training, the notarial art, combined the study of law with the study of rhetoric in the form of *ars dictandi*, although after 1350 the two branches started to separate and the *studium iuris* became divorced from the *studia litterarum* or *humanitatis.*[5]

Maria Picchio Simonelli has recently suggested that the impressive Latin poem *Waltharius Manufortis* once attributed to Ekkehart of St. Gall (d. 973) might have originated, instead, around Berengarius I Marquis of Friuli (874), king of Italy since 888 and emperor after 915, holding court mainly at Verona.[6] Classical influences are at work in this poem in Virgilian hexameters about heroic/romantic adventures involving the Aquitanian Walther and his bride Hiltgunt, who escape from captivity among the Huns and survive a series of frightening encounters with the Burgundians Gunther and Hagen, who covet their treasure.

In the cosmopolitan high society of the Middle Ages it is no wonder that at the distant courts of northern Germany one could also find Italians. Italian scholars and clerics who acquired curial ideals in German imperial and episcopal courts included such prominent courtier prelates as Liutprand of Pavia, Gunzo (of Novara ?), Leo of Vercelli, Anselm of Besate, Benzo of Alba, Siccardo of Cremona, Acerbo Morena, and, as far down as the fifteenth century, Aeneas Silvius Piccolomini. The cathedral school of Würzburg (962), one of the earliest to be vitalized by the Ottonian educational policies, flourished under an Italian master teacher, Stephen of Novara (Stephanus Grammaticus), called there by Otto I (962–973) and the local bishop, Poppo.[7] Liutprand, born in Pavia of noble Longobard ancestry, first served at the courts of the Italic kings Hugh of Provence and Berengarius, until he was made bishop of Cremona by Otto I in 961, as a reward for his support and services since 956. He traveled widely, twice as ambassador to Constantinople (949–951 and 968), and in Germany he learned enough German to act as interpreter between Otto and Pope John XII (963) in Rome. He praised his high protector in the polemically lively *Liber de rebus gestis Othonis imperatoris*.[8] The mysterious and cantankerous grammarian Gunzo, perhaps a deacon from Novara, turned up at the Saxon court, too. Leo of Vercelli, a cultured diplomat and man of law with ties to the school of Pavia, became bishop of Vercelli in 998 after having been archdeacon of Otto III's sacred palace (*iudex sacri palatii*). His influence was felt in the organization of the chancery after the significant unification of the chanceries of Germany and Italy decreed in 998 under the aegis of the *archilogotheta* Eribertus, archbishop of Cologne.[9] Gerbert of Aurillac (d. 1003), the famous teacher and bishop of Reims and then tutor to Otto III, is connected with the history of Italian education as he later influenced it when he became Pope Sylvester II: his mark was to be felt long thereafter in France insofar as the "Twelfth-Century Renaissance" at Chartres still kept a fresh memory of the work done there by Gerbert's pupil, Bishop Fulbert.

At the court of Henry III (1039–1056), alongside such luminaries as Wipo, Anno (later bishop of Cologne), and Adalbert, bishop of Bremen, there was also the Italian (?) Anselm of Besate known as the Peripatetic, educated at the cathedral school of Milan, and the author of the manneristic *Rhetorimachia* (ca. 1050). Henry III's court also enjoyed the services of Bishop Benzo of Alba, perhaps the most interesting Italian figure at the north German courts thanks to his numerous writings addressed *ad Heinricum IV imperatorem*, purportedly for the emperor's instruction and originally composed in the third quarter of the eleventh century but recompiled between 1086–1090.[10] Benzo was an eager participant in the struggle over investiture, and his polemic writings were aimed at lending support to the cause of Henry IV against Pope Gregory VII, royal chaplains having much at stake in defending imperial prerogatives in the naming and controlling of bishops and high ecclesiastics. Without meaning censure, Benzo could objectively portray the royal chaplains "as drawing long sighs after the benefice of an episcopal ring," "regales capellani longa suspiria trahentes pro anuli beneficio"

(*Monumenta Germaniae Historica* SS 11: 599, v. 44). For him the court was an impressive assemblage of noble characters who could have graced the ancient senate with their political and rhetorical Ciceronian skills: "Multi quidem nobiles et sapientes viri morantur in curia domini mei, qui Ciceronicis amministrationibus valuissent sedare commotiones imperii" (ibid. 614, vv. 11 ff.). Indeed, he did not hesitate to model the king's council on the Roman Senate: the court itself he called *senatus* and the courtiers, *senatores*, whom he addressed as *patres conscripti* (*MGH* SS 11: 622, v. 47; 631, v. 7; 671, v. 48). In his verses he vividly reflected a humanistic spirit by reviving classical imagery in order to invest the new imperial court with the glories of ancient Rome:

> Transcendens Fabios et Cicerones,
> Cunctos Fabricios atque Catones,
> Das populis iura cum Salomone.

As Jaeger puts it (123), "over Henry [IV]'s shoulders Benzo casts the mantle of the divine emperor, the successor of Julius Caesar and other noble Romans."

It seems appropriate to presume that at least some of these prelates contributed to the diffusion of ideas of courtliness around Italian episcopal courts and cathedral schools. We can add that Benzo, for one, addressed many of his humanistically-slanted remarks to Italian bishops. He praised the bishop of Turin for "finding his place in the annals of illustrious men by following Cicero and Sallust": "Imitaris Ciceronem, sequeris Salustium, / In katalogo virorum es scriptus illustrium" (*MGH* SS 4.4: 639, vv. 21 f.). He urged Archbishop Theobald of Milan to come to the aid of the emperor, citing the previous cases of *barones episcopi* under Otto III, including Leo of Vercelli (ibid. 4.1: 634–636). To persuade imperial appointees to perform according to their lord's expectations, he tried to stir up the noblest instincts in them by composing a praise of man (ibid. 4.12: 654, vv. 33–36) which Jaeger (124–125) finds worthy of a Renaissance humanist. Elsewhere (ibid. 7.3: 673, vv. 20 f.) he produced an interesting allegory of Virtue that Dante could have accepted as a good definition of inner nobility: "Virtue is dignity of mind and nobility of soul, that makes man an object of wonder and, even more, deifies him":

> Virtus est mentis dignitas et animi nobilitas,
> Quae homines mirificat, insuper et deificat.

In Benzo's allegorical "Palace of Virtue," the sun in the firmament of worldly life is *amicitia*: "Huius virtutis gratia sol est in mundi patria" (ibid. 674, v. 13). Elsewhere he had postulated a bond of love between king and courtiers, in terms that Castiglione might have found fitting for his ideal court (ibid.: 600, vv. 31 f.).

Benzo cultivated another motif with a humanistic ring to it: the lessons of history. He admonished Henry IV to study the records of his predecessors in order to imitate their imperial customs: "legat quantulumcunque de historiis patrum praecedentum, ut inde sibi assumat bonae imitationis emolumentum. Legere enim aliorum annales plurimum valet ad instruendos ritus imperiales" (ibid.: 600, vv. 35 f.). Machiavelli and Guillaume Budé would have agreed, too.

We encounter in Italian biographies the same personal dispositions and educational features we have seen prescribed for the curial cleric or courtly diplomat as well as the chivalrous ruler. Gaufred of Malaterra, a monk of Norman descent who shortly after 1099 was commissioned by Robert of Sicily to write a history of the conquest of Sicily by his brother Robert Guiscard (d. 1085), described the Norman warrior race in terms that incorporated courtly qualities: "Their princes spare no expense in cultivating fame and good report. This people knows the art of flattery, practicing the study of eloquence to such a degree that even their young boys appear rhetors. . . . They delight in rich clothing, horses, and other instruments of warfare."[11] The apotheosis of the heroes of Norman Italy involves a different slant from that of the partisans of the Germanic empire. For the Normans of Italy and particularly Robert Guiscard shared a grand scheme of Christian knighthood which included the Spanish *reconquista* and came under the aegis of the papacy (of which the Normans were avowed vassals), in direct opposition to German imperial policies. Among the later Normans of Italy, Roger II of Altavilla, king of Sicily (1130–1154), was probably the most learned ruler of his time. He called to his court outstanding intellectuals, including Arab poets and scientists who translated a large number of theretofore unavailable Greek masterworks, like Plato's *Meno* and *Phedo*. Yet, in contrast with such centers as Oxford, Reims, and other northern cathedral schools, the lack of regular schools limited the impact of this splendid court to isolated sectors of specialists.[12]

Writing shortly after his subject's death, one of his three biographers reported that Bernard of Parma, who died as bishop of that city in 1133 and had been a friend of the powerful Countess Mathilde of Canossa, grew up with a good education in letters and was "handsome, strong of character, generous in giving, skilled in arms, pleasantly eloquent, devoted to his mother, eager to win honor, . . . and gracious and dear to all those who knew him."[13] In a long poem completed in 1115 Donizo, a Benedictine monk in St. Apollonius of Canossa, praised the Countess Mathilde for her generosity toward minstrels and for gracing with a rich library a court that was a paragon of courteous living.[14]

Siccardo da Cremona applauded Frederick Barbarossa as "illitera-tus, sed morali experientia doctus," stressing the difference between literary instruction (which Barbarossa allegedly lacked) and moral edu-cation (which he possessed in a high degree), the latter being sufficient to educate the good courtier even in the absence of the former (Jaeger: 216 f.).

Another Italian, Acerbo Morena, drew a comprehensive series of portraits of Barbarossa's court around 1164 (Jaeger 171–173). The dominant personal characteristics of both the emperor and his entou-rage, including the empress Beatrix, are physical and psychological rather than moral, starting with physical beauty. Barbarossa himself was "so cheerful that he always seemed ready to break into laughter," "hilari vultu, ut semper ridere velle putaretur." All personages at court displayed an eminently cheerful disposition (*hilaritas, iocunditas, laeti-tia*), a curial and courtly quality that was obviously of great value in social intercourse and was regularly found among the chivalrous knights and rulers of twelfth-century romances, even though it clashed with the ascetic ideals sternly advocated by Peter Damian and Bernard of Clairvaux; for the latter the pursuit of *laetitia* was an aspect of pride, and laughter a sign of downright stupidity (see my chap. 2 at passage with note 38).

The choice of language in the Middle Ages for literary purposes de-pended as much on the genre as on the writer's native language.[15] Like several of his Italian contemporaries who used Occitan for the lyric, French for didactic verse, and Franco-Venetian for chivalric romance and epic, so did a courtier from Cividale del Friuli, Tommasino dei Cerchiari (ca. 1185—before 1238) use German for an interesting poem on court manners, *Der Wälsche Gast* (1215–1216), dedicated "to the stout knights, good ladies, and wise clerks." Tommasino became part of medieval German literature under the Germanized name of Thoma-sin von Zerclaere (or Zirclaere, Circlaere, Cerclaere). He had been a priest at the court of Wolfger von Ellebrechtskirchen in Aquileia, where Wolfger, formerly a German bishop, was serving as patriarch. It was at that court that Tommasino learned the principles of French chivalry. The title of his poem meant "the Italian guest among Germans."[16] The northeastern region of Italy was particularly imbued with both German cultural elements and feudal traditions,[17] but it is notable that an early poem on manners and courtliness composed in Italy would use the German language as a natural medium not only for the audience it addressed but also for the subject matter.

Together with such ideally related works as Vincent of Beauvais's *De eruditione filiorum nobilium* and Gerald of Wales's *De principis instructione*, this fourteen-thousand-line didactic poem marks the birth of a new genre of princely education at a time when the teaching of courtly virtues had shifted away from the cathedral schools to the secular and ecclesiastical courts. Tommasino meant to convey to his aristocratic courtly audience the educational message of civic humanism that was first formulated in the Ottonian bishops' biographies and then passed on to the cathedral schools of the eleventh and early twelfth century. It was now ready to become the staple of treatises of princely or courtly education as well as treatises of manners. The first of the poem's ten books contains advice to young men and women, including instruction on table manners; courtly epic poetry is declared to be an educational genre. The moral doctrine is laid out in the following books and focuses on *staete*, constancy of mind, condemning the evils of its opposite, *unstaete*. *Mâze* (conceived as moderation), *milte* (generosity), and *reht* (respect for law) are the principal attendant qualities. Once again, as in the pedagogy inculcated by the masters of the cathedral schools leading to Fulbert of Chartres, William of Conches, Bernard Silvestris, and John of Salisbury, teaching remained inherently conservative, since the cult of the great teacher and the imitation of his exemplary life was an essential part of the educational process, which transcended the search for truth *per se*. For Tommasino change is a form of corruption, and a good society is stable in its aristocratic order. Most noteworthy is that in stressing the courtly content of the romances he recognizes for that genre the right to allegorical exegesis, normally reserved for biblical literature: romances "contain representations of courtliness [*zuht*] and of truth: in them truth is clothed in lies" (for higher purposes).[18]

TROUBADOURS, *DICTATORES*, AND POLITICAL THEORISTS IN ITALY

Even while they also participated in the life of the communes, the ubiquitous minstrels, those vagrant professionals of oral literature who freely roamed all parts of medieval Europe from the Iberian peninsula to Russia, made their presence felt at Italian courts.[19] It is interesting that among his samples of letters for all occasions, Buoncompagno da Signa (d. ca. 1240) included a set of letters from around 1200 recommending jongleurs and minstrels (both male and female) who could perform at court as well as at dubbings and nuptials (*militia atque nuptiis*).[20] That authoritative master of *ars dictaminis* taught mostly at the flourishing school of Bologna but was also active throughout Italy and claimed to have been in Constantinople. Francis of Assisi dignified that class of homeless artists by calling himself and his followers *joculatores Domini*, "minstrels of God." For a festivity in 1324 the Malatesta lord of Rimini was said to have gathered at his court no fewer than fifteen hundred minstrels.[21]

The first surviving Italian poem in the Occitan vernacular is probably the sirventés by Peire de la Caravana (or Cavarana, Cà Varana near Verona ?) exhorting the Lombard communes to put up a common front against the Germans. It has been dated 1157 or 1194.[22] The tenso between the Marquis Alberto Malaspina and Raimbaut de Vaqueiras (after 1195) is the first example of an Italian lord writing in Provençal: the marquis adopted the troubadour's conventions and dealt with him on a level of social parity even to the extent of exchanging burning insults.[23] In those years Raimbaut was once again a guest of the powerful Marquis Boniface I of Monferrat, nephew of Emperor Conrad III (he had first been the guest of Boniface around 1180). The two remained together and participated in military undertakings in Piedmont and then Sicily, where Boniface dubbed Raimbaut a knight in 1194. They then departed for the fourth Crusade, Boniface I having been elected general of the army. After the conquest of Constantinople they both disappeared in 1207 in a battle against the Bulgars. Raimbaut wrote of assisting Boniface in his *joven fagz*, youthful knightly deeds in defense of young ladies in distress. Together they rescued Saldina del Mar from a Malaspina and returned her to her lover; then they freed Giacomina di Ventimiglia, daughter of the Count Guido Guerra of Dantesque memory, from the tyrannical tutelage of her uncle Otto, restored her to her patrimony, and handed her over to a suitable husband.[24]

Rambertino Buvalelli was a typical Italian troubadour insofar as he combined the culture of the courts with that of the bourgeois communes, having served as podestà between 1201–1221 in Brescia, Milan, Padua, Mantua, Modena, Genoa, and Verona. An adventurous Italian troubadour, the Mantuan Sordello (1200–1269 ?), gave a comprehensive definition of the courtly man in his famous *ensenhamen d'onor*, "Aissi co'l tesaurs":

> Amesuratz e ver disenz,
> francs e de bels acuillimenz,
> be respondenz en totz mos ditz,
> netz en mos faitz granz e petitz,
> ben acuillenz e gen onranz,
> umils e ben aparianz,
> de bon aire, gent ensengnatz.

(Moderate and sincere, affable and hospitable, elegantly articulate in all my words, neat in all my deeds big and small, ready with my hospitality and with doing honor, humble and sociable, of good appearance and well educated—vv. 187–193.)

In this poem *gent ensengnatz* refers to the *bos noirimenz*, "good education," that makes an educated and well-mannered knight (*gent noirit* and *be acostumat*) preferable to one well endowed by nature (*ben aibit*). Whether or not this was a self-serving definition privileging the jongleur over the born nobleman, as Köhler chooses to interpret it,[25] it neatly synthesizes much that the curial tradition had been teaching.

Partisans of the imperial party could prosper even in the shadow of the papal throne and at the height of the investiture struggle during the Gregorian reform. In his *Orthodoxa defensio imperialis* of around 1112, Gregorius of Catina, a monk at Farfa, recognized the emperor alone as logical leader of armed *defensores* for all just causes, with the right to head not only the empire but the Church itself and the Crusade.

Despite its being addressed to a foreign monarch, Italians could find the influential *De regimine principum* of Egidio Colonna (Giles of Rome, ca. 1280) consonant with their needs too, since, for example, on Aristotle's authority it grounded all principles of civilized organization in the towns—thus misinterpreting, but not by much, the Greek notion of *polis*, explicitly rendered in Tuscan with "ville e città."[26] In this tract of Guelf orientation that praised monarchic rule above republican order, Giles says that cities and realms are healthy when they abound in people of median state ("mezzane persone," "abbondanza di gente di mezzo," which we could interpret as pointing to the middle class of burghers). The statement made particular sense in highly urbanized Italy.[27]

When Fra Salimbene Adami da Parma (1221–1287 or shortly thereafter) praised Frederick II for his "cunning" (*calliditas*) in "dissimulating," so as not to hear offensive personal remarks and thus spare incautious court jesters, he did so by referring to biblical proverbs of wisdom rather than to the literature on curiality.[28] Yet it is precisely this Franciscan chronicler who has given Georges Duby an opportunity to obtain clear testimony of the force of courtly cultural models.[29] A study of Salimbene's vocabulary by one of Duby's students shows how this third-generation follower of St. Francis evaluated and praised human character only in courtly and chivalric terms, ignoring any virtues that would smack of Franciscan spirituality. All the laymen he approved of were "handsome and noble," all the men of the Church, "saintly and learned." The former he praised for being "docti ad proelium," well versed, that is, in the arts of the knight; also courtly, liberal, adept at writing good songs, and rich (no apparent appreciation for poverty, chosen or not). This terminology with which we are by now familiar reflects the relative unavailability of cultural and ethical models other than those of the knight and the cleric, which, together with the model of the king/prince, were the only ones admired by the masses. Duby goes on (307) to speculate—and this corresponds to the assumptions of our study—that the point of origin of such collective models could only be the princely courts, where the two coexistent and competing groups of clerics and knights exerted their influence on each other and on the remainder of society. We could add that the court games which so often included debates on whether a lady should prefer a cleric or a knight are proof that the competition between the two orders was not just a literary matter or a joke for Andreas Capellanus to make, but part of the serious question of relative preeminence. Since they were of clerical origin, such literary debates naturally tended to give the advantage to the cleric.[30]

A systematic and authoritative treatment of chivalry within the established orders of Christian society appears in the *De insigniis et armis* by the prominent jurist and theorist of canon law, Bartolus of Sassoferrato (1314–1357), who distinguished among "theological nobility" due to God's grace, "natural nobility" due to birth, and "civil nobility" issuing from the will of the sovereign, hence formally recognized by law. Natural and civil nobility were thus to be understood as necessitating a degree of wealth, since generosity (Fr. *largesse*, free spending to reward one's dependents), a concomitant of nobility, is impossible without something to give. Aristotle had rightly postulated the need for wealth for the free members of human society, and Bartolus also agreed with Aristotle's distinction between men who are naturally free—hence born with the capacity to rule—and those who are only apt to serve. Indeed, the French term *franchise* meant the moral attitude of the naturally free, who consequently bear themselves as free persons.[31] Bartolus' thoughts on nobility, framed within a commentary on Justinian's Code and using the ancient juridical notion of *dignitas* as implying the modern concept of nobility, remained a major source for four centuries.[32]

FIRST POETIC SCHOOLS
AND EARLY PROSE NARRATIVE

When, in 1220, the twenty-five-year-old Frederick of Swabia, the future "stupor mundi," entered Italy to claim his imperial crown, the troubadour Aimeric de Peguilhan (1190–1221) saluted him as the one who would bring back the knightly ideal: "I thought that Valor and Liberality were dead. . . . Never did a man see a physician of such youth, / so handsome, so good, so generous, and so knowledgeable, / so courageous, / so firm, so conquering, / so apt in speaking and understanding. / . . . See how much valor in a mere boy!"[33]

Giacomo da Lentini, the most important poet at Frederick II's court, where the Italian poetic tradition started, was a notary, as was the court's most significant prose-writer, the *protonotario*, "first notary" or chancellor, Pier della Vigna. Imitating the Provençal lyric and the Bolognese notarial *dictamen* as well as the Roman *stilus rhetoricus* of the chancery of Honorius III, these courtiers carried on the civilizing trend that had imposed the patterns of *cortesia* on the urbanized knighthood. A striking novelty of this school is the practical deletion of the political context: love reigns supreme at a court where the centralizing will of the sovereign obviates the charged dialectical play of interests and special pleadings that characterized the careers of free agents at the feudal courts. From the status of a symbolic and allusive cover, courtly love could now turn to purely psychological and spiritual considerations. Frederick II's poets were no longer spokesmen of warrior knights but high bureaucrats who had to eschew all references to social, political, or economic claims.[34]

As we have seen (chap. 5), *courtoisie* could perform a metaphysical function analogous to the theological one of divine grace; the opposition *courtoisie/vilenie*, originally meaning aristocracy versus both bourgeois and peasant estates, came to imply secular transcendence of social limitations whereby the poor or landless knights, even when nonnoble by feudal standards, could be redeemed and ennobled by courtesy alone, the *domna* replacing God. This meaning of "true nobility" could find its place in the Provençal *partimens* or in the thoroughly secular neo-Platonic mysticism of the Perceval figure.

Moving along such lines, in the subsequent doctrine of the Dolce Stil Nuovo the argument for spiritual refinement played a key role, stressing personal inner nobility versus social privilege. Dante's *Convivio* would soon lend powerful support to this thesis. True nobility was, for these poets, gentleness of heart, and the "gentleman" was inescapably marked by the capacity for love. The motif of the noble heart as source of true nobility reminds us of Gottfried's *edele herzen*: it implied a happy yet tragic conspiracy, like that of Tristan and Isolt, individuals isolated by their virtuous superiority to the intrigue, dishonesty, baseness, raw ambition, and material impulses of the crowd at court. Cavalcanti was known, even as late as Boccaccio's *Decameron*, for his aristocratic will to stay aloof from the materialistic crowd of his fellow Florentine merchants, and Dante's own scorn for the bourgeois ideals of his fellow citizens was tied to his despair about the future of Florentine policies. All this notwithstanding, we must bear in mind that the Stil Nuovo is essentially a bourgeois movement, numbering among its leaders lawyers (like its "founder" Guinizelli and Dante's admired friend, Cino da Pistoia) and high merchants (Cavalcanti issued from a merchant Guelf family). It was not without social reason that it flourished in areas with strong popular bases, namely Bologna and Tuscany. The unashamed espousal of the vernacular, as most consciously with Dante, was an explicit act of faith in the *popolo*. In his *Convivio* Dante meant to share science with the common man, a goal that required the vernacular.

Popular sentiments were vocal all around on the political and cultural levels. The chroniclers of the bourgeois commune, typically Dante's contemporaries Dino Compagni and Giovanni Villani, could not hide their sympathy for the *comune del popolo*. Their keen analyses of events displayed the mentality and sense of values that characterize bourgeois rather than aristocratic societies, namely: a taste for parliamentary and free representative electoral procedures; respect for the rule of law; and concern for the cost of government—all matters of little concern to high noblemen and their acolytes. They criticized the very things that marked aristocratic life styles and their imitators among the high merchants, namely conspicuous consumption, sumptuous dress, and aggressively heroic individual postures.[35] These same chroniclers and their communal predecessors held the view that noblemen tended to be bellicose, unruly, hard-headed, and arrogant in their unbounded ambitions—Starcateruses *in potentia*. The nobles could only survive by banding together and forming collective *consorterie* around their own families and their allies. Deep down, their morals were those of the Nibelungs. Yet the environment of the city also acted on them as a civilizing force, though their resistance compelled the burghers to do their best to either tame them completely or oust them beyond city walls.

Cavalcanti reminded his audience of the Christian virtue of humility as a requirement for courtliness and courtesy when he attributed *umiltà* to his lady ("donna d'umiltà") in "Chi è questa," a sonnet that, for a textual competition with Guinizelli's "Io voglio del ver la mia donna laudare," is textured in a sort of "parodia-analogia sacrale" of biblical terminology, as G. Contini put it.[36] It was an idiosyncratic example of the blending of secular and religious mysticism that characterized late courtly lyric from Provence on. Courtly love had been the romantic side of that broad sense of love, compassion, human sympathy (*reverentia*), and ultimately "humanity" that made up courtliness as a whole. Gottfried, we remember, had closely bound together nobility and morality: "[moral teaching] is given to all noble hearts as a nursemaid," "[moraliteit] sist edelen herzen allen / zeiner ammen gegeben" (8014 f.). Around the same time that Cavalcanti wrote the *Novellino* (end of the thirteenth century), the prolific Florentine translator and moralist Bono Giamboni defined moral virtues as "courteous habits and beautiful, pleasing manners."[37]

The other genre that concerns us, the primer of conduct or treatise on social manners and mores, which may be ideally related to the early episcopal biographies, started in Italy with the Florentine Brunetto Latini and the Milanese Bonvesin da la Riva, *popolani* both (aside from the case just mentioned of Thomasin von Zerclaere, who wrote in German for a noble audience). This genre, too, like the lyric, developed by bending for a burgherly society standards that originally derived from the chivalric society and that had to be tamed and adapted—often by sheer transposition without transformation. Brunetto (1220 or after–1294) is the more striking case: a citizen of the most mercantile-minded commune, he adopted all the paraphernalia of chivalric education for the edification of his burgher citizens and city leaders. In the 1260s, Brunetto's portrait of a knight whose bearing befits his status as he rides through the city, comprised the advice to proceed with restraint—the traditional *mesure*—and an easy yet distinctive and dignified self-assurance:

> Consiglioti che vade
> molto cortesemente:
> . . . . . .

ch'andar così 'n disfreno
par gran salvatichezza.

. . . .

Guarda che non ti move
com'on che sia di villa;
ma va sicuramente.

(Go . . . in a stately manner [*cortesemente*], . . . for to ride without restraint
betrays great boorishness. . . . Guard against moving like a man from the
country; but go self-assuredly.) (*Tesoretto* vv. 1806–1817) [38]

Latini's *Tesoretto* describes a court inhabited by canonical chivalric
figures allegorically representing, at first, the four cardinal virtues (the
foundation of civic education in Cicero's *De officiis*). Among these he
assimilates the traditional "temperance" to the more chivalric term of
"*mesure*" ("Qui sta la Temperanza, / cui la gente talora / suol chiamare
Misura"—vv. 1284–1286). *Fortezza* is defined as "Valenza-di-corag-
gio" (v. 1298). Virtue, the "Empress" of the court, is said to be "capo e
salute / di tutta costumanza / e de la buona usanza / e d'i' bei reggimenti / a che vivon le genti" (vv. 1239–1244)—in other words, all the
qualities of good social conduct. Then follow the more specific chivalric
virtues of Cortesia, Larghezza (Liberality), Leanza (Loyalty), and Prodezza (Prov. *proece*) (vv. 1343–2054). Brunetto advises his reader (vv.
1350–1356) that more virtues related to these are treated on a loftier
level in his *Trésor*. Cortesia declares Larghezza to be "il capo e la grandezza / di tutto mio mistero" (vv. 1587 f.). We are reminded that in
speaking we need "provedimento [care, circumspection], . . . lingua
adorna, . . . detto soave," avoidance of "gravezza" [something like Castiglione's *affettazione*], since it ingenerates "noia," and finally, once
again, "misura" (vv. 1559–1622). As the poem proceeds, we meet Fino
Amore with Ovidio intervening in the discussion.

Brunetto's *Rettorica* dealt more specifically with the art of government, in accordance with a false etymology that related rhetoric to *re-
gere*, the art of the city's *rettori*.[39] It is not clear whether his major work,
the French *Trésor*, was earlier or later than the *Tesoretto*, but both
stemmed from his period of exile in France (1260–1266). The *Trésor*
was based on the *Nicomachean Ethics*, Guillaume Perrault's *Summa
aurea de virtutibus* (vulgarized in Cavalca's *Pungilingua*), the *Moralium
dogma philosophorum* attributed to Guillaume de Conches and well
known in Germany, and, for the last book on rhetoric and politics,
Cicero's *De inventione* and some unidentified Italian political tracts reflecting communal democratic ideas.[40]

Bonvesin (ca. 1250–1315) was a successful and apparently prosperous "magister" or, as in his epitaph, "doctor in gramatica," owner of property including his private school. He implemented his role of educator of the Milanese high burghers by composing in the regional dialect a treatise in alexandrines, *De quinquaginta curialitatibus ad mensam* (before 1285 ?), where the *curialitates* of the Latin title correspond to the fifty rules of "cortesie da desco" indicated in the second line, namely "rules on civilized table manners." It was an early and rather lively example of the genre that would culminate in Della Casa's *Galateo* and that was preceded by the *Liber Faceti*, which in turn was meant as a supplement to the popular medieval schoolbook *Liber Catonis*. Bonvesin's fifty rules of "cortesie" include the general principle that moderation or measure is necessary in everything ("mesura e modho," v. 179, analogous to the Tuscan expression "modo e misura").[41]

The qualities of noble bearing that were traditionally attached to the civilized nobility were denied to the *vilan* upstart who has "climbed from lowliness to great prosperity" and political status: he is, in the words of Brunetto's and Bonvesin's contemporary, the Anonimo Genovese writing in the 1290s, devoid of "measure, grace, and kindness"—the virtues demanded of noble courtiers from Otto I to Castiglione.[42] The vigorous versifier known simply as Anonimo Genovese offers an interesting mixture of aristocratic prejudice, mercantile experience (probably from his belonging to a prominent shipping family), and devout religious asceticism and moralism. A semantic shift from the courtly connotations of "convenience" to that of "responsibility and accountability" appears in his use of the term *honesty*: "for only honest works and virtues / are merchandise of quality."[43] The mercantile lexicon was still in its infancy, but the bourgeois ethic was clearly operative as a matter of survival.

In the nomenclature that resurfaced in Italy, after Occitan and French precedents that included Andreas Capellanus's identification of the noble and loving soul in his canonical *De amore*, "gentleness" (*gentilezza*), "nobility" (*nobiltà*), and "courtesy" (*cortesia*) could be used as synonyms, but certain distinctions must be kept in mind. The ideology and the accompanying terminology were pervasive in Italian literary texts from the very beginning, and *gentilezza* was synonymous with civility even without losing its connotation of class nobility. But the lively debates on nobility, from Guinizelli,[44] Dante, and on to such exemplary humanistic texts as the tracts by Buonaccorso da Montemagno,[45] Giannozzo Manetti, and Pico della Mirandola, reflect a different social situation from that of France, Germany, or England. Since in Italy the burghers' communes were the social and political centers, the aristocracy never attained the relatively homogeneous strength it enjoyed in those other regions. In Florence, in particular, the nobility was uneasily tolerated and constrained by the power of the burghers' guilds, which it had to join. That freedom from involvement in any form of manual labor which usually distinguished the nobleman was replaced by mercantile activities that Florentine noblemen came to share with the entrepreneurial class. Thus the theoretical debates on nobility that thrived in Guelf urban environments and around the universities retained a more abstract character and were aimed at a philosophically persuasive definition of the subject, based on spiritual and intellectual excellence rather than inherited feudal privileges and outward signs of distinction (Dante's *antica ricchezza e belli costumi, Convivio* 4). The theme of courtesy, on the contrary, retained its practical basis of ethical, behavioral casuistry, what the Germans referred to as *schöne site* or *zuht*, and was particularly popular in areas of seigniorial rule, like the hinterland of Venice (the area of the Franco-Venetian *cantari*) and Ferrara.[46]

At the time of Dante, *cortesia* began to be felt as a sublime moral attitude within a religious context in the Franciscan circles. Compare the *Fioretti*:

> questo gentile uomo sarebbe buono per la nostra compagnia; il quale è così . . . amorevole e cortese al prossimo e ai poveri. . . . La cortesia è una delle proprietà di Dio, il quale dà il sole suo e la sua piova a' giusti e agli ingiusti, per cortesia, ed è la cortesia sirocchia della carità, la quale spegne l'odio e conserva l'amore.[47]

Remarkably, here courtesy is assimilated to charity and attributed to God himself. The most inspired collection of popular tales, known as the *Novellino* but entitled *Libro di novelle o di bel parlar gentile* in the Panciatichiano manuscript (ca. 1290), used the word as denoting effective speech—a sense it still carried markedly in Boccaccio.

Confirming the fact that from its earliest documents Italian prose narrative reflected courtly ideals, in the *Novellino* story after story mirrors a nostalgic longing for the gentle manners of a courtly society that the Florence of wealthy and self-conscious burghers could only dream about. The story of Prester John introduces Emperor Frederick II, a favorite character, as a paragon of courtly manners and speech, who answers the question of what is most precious in the whole world by saying: "The best thing in this world is measure" (*misura*).[48] It had been a virtue of great prize all along. The story of Tristan and Isolde in the *Novellino* (no. 65 in Contini's edition) includes an exemplary illustration of courtly cunning in the deception of King Mark by the two lovers. It is the incident of King Mark watching their assignation from a pine tree and Isolde dispelling his suspicions through a clever trick.

Another text from the end of the Duecento that was close to the *Novellino*, *I conti di antichi cavalieri*, possibly of multiple French origin, contains, among others, charming stories about Saladino, starting with the first of the collection.[49] There the Saladin is portrayed thus: "El Saladino fo sì valoroso (= *prode*), largo (liberal), cortese signore e d'anemo gentile (*courtois*)" that he was reputed perfect. The troubadour Bertran de Born visited him and discovered his secret: every day he sought advice on what to do and say from the best experts (*conoscenti*)—in other words, he used his courtiers to the best advantage (548). The woman whom Bertran advises Saladino to love with high love, so that he will be inspired to even nobler deeds, imposes the condition that he depart from her town (just besieged in order to reach her), taking only her heart with him and leaving his heart with her (once again the motif of the severed heart). *Conto* 19 about Brunor and Galetto (Gallehault) moves on an equally high level of chivalry. A king owes his honor to good deeds, not to his possessions and power: a knightly king prefers to give away his kingdom (as Lancelot and Tristan did) in order to dedicate himself to chivalrous pursuits.[50] *Onore* comes from *valore*, and *valore* from *vertù*. So Arthur is defined as "king only in his virtuous deeds of love, chivalry, courtesy, loyalty, and liberality."[51]

Francesco da Barberino (1264–1348) is remarkable for his knowledge of Provençal poets, of whom he mentions no fewer than twenty-one (all from the twelfth and early thirteenth century) in his didactic prosimetric poem *Reggimento e costumi di donna* (before 1309–1318/ 1320), as against the merely six quoted by Dante and the fifteen by Petrarca.[52] His didactic-allegorical poem *Documenti d'Amore* (before 1309–1314) treats the theory of love in awkward but learned terms.[53] Scholarly familiarity with Provencal literature remained more operative in Italy than elsewhere, and in the Cinquecento, especially through Bembo, it would contribute to the establishment of Petrarca as the model of poetic practice. It was part of the continuity of a rich tradition of moral and behavioral sublimation that permeated the lyrical, ethical, and practical codes even in social environments largely dominated by the middle class.

After the Sicilian School, the high lyric thrived outside the courts, but there was also a "court poetry" by professional courtiers—who, it must be said, did not show a high level of poetic inspiration. These Trecento poets are sometimes referred to as *curiali, curtensi,* or *cortigiani.*[54] Such were the Sienese Bindo di Cione del Frate, the Ferrarese Antonio de' Beccari (1315–ca. 1370), the Paduan Francesco di Vannozzo di Bencivenne, Braccio Bracci from Arezzo (second half of fourteenth century), and the Sienese Simone Serdini, called Il Saviozzo.[55] They gravitated around the Milanese Visconti court, the principal court of northern Italy, and moved about a lot, mirroring their wandering nature through the chameleonlike opportunism of their shifting political stances, though other themes were more common to their verse, from the amorous to the burlesque. Vannozzo's work is the richest document of courtly literature extant from northern Italy. While Vannozzo showed some satirical verve in condemning current corruption and loss of courtly virtue,[56] Braccio Bracci did not hesitate to flatter his lord Bernabò Visconti with a fictional letter of praise from the Sultan of Babylon.

The intensive use of the paradigm of *servizio d'amore* will disappear in the Quattrocento.[57] *Cortesia* became a commonplace term, with an ever more vague meaning, still carrying along *villania* as its antonym. Yet the term was ready to enter the semantic field of etiquette, since as early as the second half of the fourteenth century it could be employed in the external sense of behavioral patterns that come immediately under the senses, as in the proverb "cortesia di bocca assai vale e poco costa" cited in Paolo da Certaldo's *Libro di buoni costumi* (79).[58] A Tuscan merchant who may have held office in the Florentine commune, Paolo (fl. ca. 1360) had offered this interesting definition: "cortesia non è altro se non misura, e *misura dura*: e non è altro misura se non avere ordine ne' fatti tuoi"; "*measure endures,* and courtesy is nothing but measure, to wit, orderliness in your business." Hence we may interpret the implicit values of parsimoniousness and accountability.[59] His text is a witness to the popularity of several current manuals on conduct upon which he drew, specifically Le *cinque chiavi della sapienza* (a compilation of didactic sentences by various authors), *L'Albertano* (a summary of Albertano da Brescia's Latin works), Le *quattro virtù morali* (attributed to Seneca), *Il libro di costumanza* (a vulgarization of the *Vulgarium dogma*), and *La pìstola di Santo Bernardo della masserizia e reggimento della famiglia.* The *courtois* morality of the communal bourgeois is contrasted by Paolo with the "beastly," irrational, and potentially criminal behavior of the peasant (still the uncourteous *villano, rustico*, or *pagano*), whom the landowner must handle with shrewdness and circumspection.[60] The aristocratic quality of loyalty to one's liege has been turned into a bourgeois virtue: the peasant's good service toward the landlord.[61]

In more general terms, we have seen the beginning of an Italian development that responded to transalpine cultural suggestions under the peculiar conditions of a lively burgherly society. The combination of social structures and cultural thrusts, namely, feudalism and curiality/courtliness, that elsewhere generated the chivalrous ideals, was also a fact in Italian regions, but with a necessary adaptation to the vital conditions of mercantile forces either resisting or dominating. Chivalry thrived in Italy, too, but took peculiar forms of defense of spiritual values that were not bound to aristocratic milieus. The feudal nobility did retain a pervasive force in Italy, but was tempered, checked, and transformed by the assertive presence of the high merchants even while the new ideals were tinged by themes and motifs that originally issued from the same circles of clerical educators around episcopal and secular courts that also operated north of the Alps.

CHAPTER EIGHT

Dante, Petrarca, and Boccaccio

DANTE (1265–1321)

That Dante, descended from a family of poor nobles, would be sensitive to questions of nobility and chivalry is not surprising. His ancestry took him back to the "martyred" crusader Cacciaguida, whom the Emperor Conrad III had "girded with his knighthood" for "good deeds" performed in a Crusade in 1147: "Poi seguitai lo 'mperador Currado, / ed el mi cinse della sua milizia, / tanto per bene ovrar li venni a grado" (*Paradiso* 15: 139 f.). Dante can hide chivalric ideals in short episodes and rather marginal figures: when Trajan agrees to delay his battle march in order to render justice to a poor widow insistently presenting her grievance to him, he behaves in the chivalrous manner expected of a prince or knight of the twelfth century, rather than of an ancient ruler (*Purgatorio* 10: 73–78). For that act of humility and justice, Dante reports, the pagan Trajan was saved. This image of defenders of widows, orphans, and the weak, we have seen (chap. 3), was frequently propagandized under the "royal ethic" that became part of the knightly ethic.

Dante's ethic incorporated much of the chivalric ideal but excluded from it feudal militarism, which concurred neither with his being the citizen of a merchant commune nor with his personal espousal of the royal ethic's antifeudal policies. His striking emphasis on "sweetness," including the denomination of his "school" as the Sweet New Style, is a semiotic index of his departure from the rough, warlike edges of militant chivalry and the heroic mode. In this sense he was carrying further than ever the process that brought the late troubadours to question and occasionally condemn the heroic elements in the knights' behavior, the *ardimen* as a necessary ingredient of *proeza*.[1] Yet his animosity toward the Capetians, whom he indicts as usurpers in the process of unifying France, reflects not only his "Ghibelline" support of the emperor against the pope and his ally the king of France, but also Dante's feudal sympathies for the French barons resisting national policies.

In the *Fiore* attributed to Dante and derived from the *Roman de la rose*, the allegorical character of Cortesia looms large and Larghezza operates as Cortesia's close ally. Cortesia is the mother of Bellaccoglienza, who plants the Fiore in the Garden of Piacere. She is charged with keeping the Vecchia at bay and is the first to enter the castle of Gelosia after killing Malabocca, whereupon she and Larghezza can free Bellaccoglienza and plead with her on behalf of Amante.

Dante's harmonization of *vita activa* and *vita contemplativa* carried to sublime fruition the intellectual and moral desiderata of twelfth-century Chartres.[2] It is also rewarding to contrast Dante's idiosyncratic conservatism with the anticourt sentiments of reactionary clerical spheres (see my chap. 2). Dante praised the simple, austere customs of virtuous ancestors (Cacciaguida) and accordingly criticized women's sumptuous dresses and lustful ways (see Forese's indictment of shameful feminine fashions, *Pg* 23: 98–111, and Cacciaguida's invective against contemporary mores, *Pr* 15: 97–135). These were topoi of court criticism, yet Dante also nostalgically praised the courtliness of old. His *laudatio temporis acti*, linked to the identification of courtliness and courtesy with virtue, contrasts with his condemnation of courtly love as sinful and immoral (Francesca). Dante resolved the conflict by embracing courtesy without the "adulterous" kind of love it had postulated (Francesca), and grafting his own theologized, Beatrice-centered love on the courtliness of old-fashioned knighthood (Borsiere, Cacciaguida).[3]

There is a striking closeness between the troubadours' invectives (especially in such conscious moralists as Marcabru, Guiraut de Bornelh, and Peire Cardenal) and Dante's moralism—all pivoted on the ethical, social, and theological notions of *cortesia*, avarice, and envy.[4] But Dante regarded wealth as inherently corrupting, a scourge of good mores, whereas the troubadours, much as they could occasionally echo the monastic, anticourtly, reformist critique of ecclesiastical greed and conspicuous consumption, criticized wealth only when it was not shared with them. They inveighed against the wicked rich, the *rics malvatz*, mostly to enrich their own pots by persuading them to reward the knight/poets as they thought they deserved.

As a citizen of a nonfeudal society, Dante, like the Stilnovisti before him, had to abandon the Provençal themes whose precise meanings were part of the feudal order. Both in his behavior and in his ethic he remained a son of the commune and never adopted the canonical ways of courtiers, even when exile forced him from court to court. Surely his oeuvre reflects none of the attitudes of typical courtiers. To begin with, *largueza* and *liberalidat* could no longer play a key role as synonymous with courtesy and nobility, since only the emperor could still make the sort of gifts the knights expected, and obviously not within the confines of free communes. In *Convivio* 2.10.7–8 Dante specifically objected to the identification of *cortesia* with *larghezza*, and this emargination of *larghezza* implied criticism of the Occitanic insistence on it. The help Dante received from the lords was no longer the remuneration for courtly service but simply a humiliating bread that tasted bitterly salty ("Tu proverai sì come sa di sale / lo pane altrui, e come è duro calle / lo scendere e 'l salir per l'altrui scale," *Pr* 17: 58–60). For him *avareza* no longer referred to the relationship between a courtier knight and his lord; he bent that moral concept completely into an argument about the state of the world and particularly the Church. The lover's *guerdon* no longer counted for much after Dante discovered that he could be satisfied with a greeting alone or even the mere chance of praising his lady. Beatrice was no court *domna*! And of course the *lauzengiers* and the hated guardians were all gone, replaced by evil, degenerate parvenus and wealthy rascals. The troubadours' satirical spirit could be turned to loftier, less self-centered, more universal causes. All this even while the violent, "vulgar" style of, say, a Marcabru could be put to good use: for example, when Dante called the Church the king's "harlot" and represented the harlot and the giant in a lewd mutual relationship. Similarly in *Purgatorio* 32: 149 f.: "una puttana sciolta / m'apparve con le ciglia intorno pronte," kissing the giant (Philip of France); and the "puttaneggiar" referring to the Church of Rome in *Inferno* 19: 108 may remind us of Marcabru's "per que domneys ar puteia," "courting has now become harlotry."[5] *Mezura* becomes the Aristotelian middle point between two vices, as with the avaricious and the prodigals, the only case of Dante's using the paradigm of two extremes as vices. We have seen how the notion of prodigality as a dangerous excess had appeared only late among the troubadours. In Italy it made sense to regard the rational use of property as a virtue and prodigality as folly: Dante's Sienese spoiled brats who, having joined the club of the *brigata spendereccia*, squander their fathers' hard-won patrimonies, are figures of excess and ridicule.

In the *De vulgari eloquentia* Dante gives an interesting definition of *curialitas* to explain his use of the epithet *curiale* as one of the four prerequisites for the *vulgare illustre* or standard Italian language—another being *aulicum*, which also points to a place with noble tenants, since it literally refers to the royal hall or court. His language, he says, is rightly to be called "curial" because, even though Italians do not *de facto* have a royal court at which to gather and use their most excellent national language, as Germans have, they have the equivalent of it insofar as they use such a language, regardless of place, whenever they speak by the light of reason. For "curiality" is nothing but a well-balanced, self-imposed regularity in whatever we perform.[6] In light of the German background of the ideology of curiality, it is noteworthy that Dante singled out the Germans as the people who, alone, had the right kind of physical *curia*. Since the *librata regula* of *VE* 1.18.4 entails "inner orderliness" and "measure," critics have commented on Dante's focusing on "rationality" as an index of curiality and on the possible connection of his *curialitas* with the rhetorical *dictamen curiale* and *curialitas loquendi* of John of Garlandia and Boncompagno da Signa.[7]

Aulicum and *curiale* could be interchangeable in the language of Dante's time. While *aulicum* unequivocally referred to the royal hall, the synonym *curiale* could also refer to the royal chancery as well as all lesser tribunals and courts of law or to the papal chancery specifically.[8] *De vulgari eloquentia* 1.12 connected the birth of Italian high lyric to Frederick II's and Manfred's southern court. The ideology of courtesy also shows its impact where, rather than *amor* or *charitas*, Dante chooses *venus* to denominate the theme of love as one of the three that fit the illustrious vernacular (*salus*, *venus*, and *virtus*; "salvation, love, and virtue"—*VE* 2.2.8).

Dante's oeuvre, including the *Divina commedia*, abounds in references to *cavalieri* and *cavalleria*: one of the most intriguing is the charming allusion of *De vulgari eloquentia* 2.13.12 to the youthful excitement of the knight who feels entitled to special privileges on the day of his ceremonial dubbing.[9] Through this analogy Dante hopes to be forgiven for his own excess in challenging his formidable predecessor Arnaut Daniel while trying to outdo him by writing a double sestina, "Amor, tu vedi ben che questa donna," which required the unprecedented technical feat of a heavily repetitive rhyme scheme, "nimia eiusdem rithimi repercussio." The famous reference to the Arthurian legends ("Arturi regis ambages pulcerrime," *VE* 1.10.2) needs no elaboration here: it is one clear testimony of Dante's appreciation of the style of the romances. As already suggested in chapter 5, the term *ambages* must refer to the prose *Lancelot*'s interlacing technique, which Dante found most beautiful. Of all Arthurian literature, that was undoubtedly the text that Dante knew best: beside the passage just mentioned from *De vulgari eloquentia*, he alludes to it three times in the *Commedia* (*If* 5: 127–138; *If* 32: 61 f.; *Pr* 16: 13–15) and once in the *Convivio* (4.28). The case of *Paradiso* 16 is particularly suggestive. Beatrice turns her smile on Dante when he begins to address his ancestor Cacciaguida with the honorific *voi*, and Dante compares this smile to the cough with which the Dame de Malehaut had accompanied Lancelot's avowal of his love to Guenièvre. Some critics have seen both smile and cough as signs of encouragement,[10] but it is more plausible that both were an ironic warning of trespassing. Lancelot was fatally violating his duty of loyalty to his king, and Dante was uneasy about his vainglorious complacency in his illustrious descent.

An important philosophical influence on Dante may have been Fra Remigio de' Girolami, a Dominican lector at Santa Maria Novella (d. 1319). In his *Via Paradisi* Remigio quoted the apocryphal *Invectiva contra Sallustium*, attributed to Cicero, where Cicero purportedly held that it was better to shine through our own deeds than through our ancestors' fame and that anyone could attain true nobility by following virtue. This coincided with both Brunetto Latini's (*Trésor*) and Dante's definition of nobility (*Convivio*).[11] Dante was following an Italian poetic tradition dating to the earliest Stil Nuovo texts. Compare *Convivio* 4.19–21 at 20: "Therefore, let not any scion of the Uberti of Florence or of the Visconti of Milan say: 'Since I have such ancestry, I am noble,' for the divine seed does not fall upon a race, that is, a stock, but on the individuals.... Lineage does not make the individual noble; it is the individual who ennobles the stock."[12] Similarly, in the *Commedia* he inquired why noble scions often degenerated ("com'esser può, di dolce seme, amaro," *Pr* 8: 93). Here the ruling King of Naples Robert of Anjou, brother of Charles Martel, is taken to task for the ignoble vice of stinginess, despite his descent from a generous father: "La sua natura, che di larga parca / discese" (*Pr* 8: 82 f.).

It would be wrong, however, to infer that Dante rejected noble birth. Not only did he confess to taking pride in his noble ancestry when meeting Cacciaguida in Paradise ("nel cielo io me ne gloriai," *Pr* 16: 6), he also admitted in the *Convivio*, even while he was arguing for the nobility of spirit, that inheritance plays its role, since God implants the seed of true happiness ("seme di felicitade") only in those who are naturally well formed: in those, that is, who have "l'anima ben posta, cioè lo cui corpo è d'ogni parte disposto perfettamente" (*Cv* 4.20.9)—a question of genes, we might say.[13] And in *Monarchia* 2.3.4–7 he accepted Aristotle's definition of nobility as necessitating wealth, usually inherited: "est enim nobilitas virtus et divitie antique iuxta Phylosophum in *Politicis*," despite Juvenal's Stoic identification of nobility with virtue alone ("nobilitas animi sola est atque unica virtus"). There are two valid kinds of nobility, Dante concluded, the inner one (*propria*) and the inherited one (*maiorum*), as in Aeneas's exemplary case.

In defining nobility, Dante related it to cowardice (*viltade*) as its opposite. *Convivio* 2.7.3–4 gives reason as the noble part of the accomplished human being—when, to borrow Aristotle's term, man has achieved his entelechy. This notion is confirmed in 3.7.6 within a neo-Platonic context of grades of nobility, and then again in 4.7.11–12, while 4.10.10 states that riches cannot grant nobility because they are essentially ignoble (*vili*). Finally, 4.16.4–8 defines nobility as perfection of form or nature, be it in a human being or in a stone or animal. Noble is equal to *non-vile* (4.16.6). This perspective throws light on the striking episode of the Ante-Inferno (remember "colui / che fece per viltade il gran rifiuto," *If* 3: 60).[14] Indeed, the Ante-Inferno is the place of the *vili* or, better still, *pusillanimi*—the coward or small-souled ones, as against the great-souled ones or magnanimous that Dante, among others, identified as chivalrous or noble. Thomas Aquinas (*Summa Theologica* 2.2, Qu. 44 a.4) had distinguished *timor* or fear, cowardice, as the opposite of *fortitudo*, the cardinal virtue that was the main ingredient of true nobility.

The now familiar distrust of the *villano* as the antithesis of the man of nobility comes to the fore in *Convivio* 4.14.3 as part of the argument about nobility. The aristocratic scorn for the merchant's wealth pierces the discussion of true knowledge (*scienza*): the perfection granted by *scienza* cannot be diminished by desire for more, which is the curse of riches, as merchants know, who tremble like leaves when they have to go through the hazards of travelling while carrying goods (*Cv* 4.13.11).

Convivio 2.10.7 f. states that "courtesy and honesty are but one thing: this term derived from the courts, meaning 'courtly habit,' because virtues and beautiful manners used to be practiced at court, just as they have now been forsaken for their opposites."[15] This Dantesque conception of curiality and courtesy has recently been connected with Aristotelian *megalopsychia*, magnanimity or heroic virtue, which can also be seen as underlying the chivalric sense of *aventure* that is marked by *hardement* and *proesce* in the French romances.[16] At 4.26 we read that the chivalric and courtly virtues of *temperanza, fortezza o vero magnanimitate, amore, cortesia*, and *lealtade* must guide our youth. Here again, Dante employs the analogy of the horseman, *buono cavaliere, cavalcatore*, who uses both the spur (*sprone = fortezza*) and the rein (*freno = temperanza*).

We realize the full impact and precise meaning of Dante's moral terminology if we keep in mind its classical context. His "la fretta / che l'*onestate* ad ogn'atto dismaga" (*Pg* 3: 11), for example, obviously does not refer to inner moral uprighteousness, which could not be affected by hasty motion, but to the decorous outer behavior that becomes a sage. In other words, his *onestà* is Cicero's *honestas*, the standard of the public man. Similarly, Beatrice's *onestà*, which strikes every passer-by when she walks down the street (sonnet "Tanto gentile e tanto *onesta* pare"), is an outer disposition which is a sign of inner qualities.[17] True enough, Cicero had been mediated by closer authorities within the circles affected by the ideals of *curialitas*, including Hugh of St. Victor, who spoke of *moralis composicio* having an inner aspect (the cultivation of virtue) as well as an outer one that faithfully mirrored the former: this outer manifestation of virtue consisted of a dignified bearing at all times.[18] Cicero's *decor*, Hugh's *decens disposicio*, and Dante's *onestà* are all akin. In the *Commedia*, too, *onesto* means "dignified" rather than "morally good." Compare Sordello's shadow sitting lion-like, "nel mover degli occhi onesta e tarda" (*Pg* 6: 63), and the similar "l'accoglienze oneste e liete" (*Pg* 7: 1): all semantically contiguous to *onorato, onorare*, or *onorevole* (cf. *If* 4, nine times in the episode of the pagan sages).[19]

Both in the *Convivio* and the *Commedia* Dante's definition and arrangement of moral qualities is known to depend on Aristotle. As noted with regard to the Ciceronian moral scheme, however, the use of the Aristotelian scheme must be set against the background of the chivalric ethical nomenclature in order to see the differences in definition, emphasis, and application that the classical framework underwent in the Middle Ages. When in *Convivio* 4.17.4−7 Dante recalls the virtues according to the *Nicomachean Ethics*, his verbal texture entails subtle distortions, which give his listing a "chivalric" sound. He enumerates the virtues as eleven (Aristotle did not have a number, and his complex listing involved several subdivisions), namely: *fortezza* (defined as the middle between foolhardiness and timidity), *temperanza* (measure in the use of food), *liberalitade* (measure in the use of material goods), *magnificenza* (advantageous use of wealth), *magnanimitade* (rational thirst for fame), *amativa d'onore* (measured ambition), *mansuetudine* (moderation of anger), *affabilitade* (sociability), *veritade* (avoidance of boasting), *eutrapelia* (wit), and *giustizia*. Prudence, the missing cardinal virtue, is kept outside this group of "moral" virtues as one of the "intellectual" virtues, as Aristotle indeed had it, and as a necessary general guide of the former (*Cv* 4.17.8). Dante dropped "shame" or "fear of dishonor," given by Aristotle as a quasi-virtue (and different from the Ciceronian notion of *reverentia* that we find in medieval curiality and, for example, in Castiglione's *vergogna*, implying considerateness). The prominence given to liberality, as middle ground between avarice and prodigality, is clearly in tune with a genuinely chivalric discourse. The long Aristotelian section on liberality and magnificence (*Nicomachean Ethics* 4.1–2 1119b-1123a) could sound to a medieval ear like an appropriate exhortation to chivalrous behavior. While the systematic appeal to the happy medium is thoroughly Aristotelian, affability (*affabilitade*), a traditional curial and courtly quality, replaces Aristotle's friendship (Lat. *amicitia*), leaning on Thomas Aquinas's commentary (*in Ethicam Nicomacheam* 2, lect. 9, n. 354, referring to Aristotle's *NE* 2.6.1108 26–28). *Amistade* does find its place in *Convivio* 3.3.11, where reference is made to *Nicomachean Ethics* 8.4, but a typical coupling with "honesty" is suggested by the intervening scholastic commentaries: Dante's "la vera e perfetta amistade de l'onesto tratta" recalls Aquinas's "amicitia propter honestum" (*in Ethicam Nic.* 8 lect. 3 n. 1563) and Albertus Magnus's "honestum" (*Ethica* 8.1.3—see, also, *Cv* 3.9.14 and 4.21.1). Dante's definitions of fortitude and temperance (the curial/courtly bravery or prowess and measure) also leaned on Aquinas.[20] Generally speaking, Dante's naming of the basic virtues (for example in *Cv* 4.17) was fairly standard by his time, and remained so throughout the Renaissance: it is strikingly close, for example, to Tasso's dialogue on the court (1585).[21]

In the *Commedia* Ciacco charges the Florentines with harboring pride, envy, and avarice—three traditional vices according to the courtly code: "superbia, invidia e avarizia sono / le tre faville ch'anno i cuori accesi" (*If* 6: 74 f.). The stern judgment is repeated by Brunetto Latini: "gent'è avara, invidiosa e superba" (*If* 15: 68). In a few scattered lines Dante makes much of the loss of *cortesia* in Italy, while, he says, it graced the good society of old. In mid-thirteenth-century Florence it went together with virtue and valor in such leaders as Guido Guerra,

Tegghiaio Aldobrandi, and Jacopo Rusticucci. Guido Guerra, Dante says, "fece col senno assai e con la spada," "achieved much with his wisdom and with his sword" (*If* 16: 39), which is the classical and medieval topos of joining the two heroic virtues of *sapientia* and *fortitudo*. These three honorable Florentine statesmen are in the circle of the violent against nature, where Brunetto also dwells. Jacopo asks Dante if *cortesia e valor* still dwell in Florence as they used to in their time, since they hear a recent arrival, Guglielmo Borsiere, insistently mourn the departure of those two virtues ("assai ne cruccia con le sue parole," *If* 16: 67–72). Dante answers that, indeed, they have forsaken a city that is now ravaged by the opposite vices of pride and excess, "orgoglio e dismisura," sadly brought along by the "gente nuova e i sbiti guadagni," the quickly enriched upstarts who have come in from the countryside (*If* 16: 73–75). Let us note that the derogatory reference to the parvenus as nouveaux riches reflects the nobility's century-old effort to close ranks and harden class barriers in order to preserve inherited privileges threatened by the mercantile classes. Similarly, the critique of fancy dresses and conspicuous consumption without *misura*, as in Cacciaguida's discourse (*Pr* 15: 97–129), implies the nobility's defense of its traditional privilege of distinctive dress, not to be outdone and nullified by the nouveaux riches' right to display their wealth, which the sumptuary laws futilely attempted to stem.[22]

In *Purgatorio* 14: 109–111, Guido del Duca nostalgically reminisces on the beautiful customs of arduous tests and pleasing deeds once inspired by love and courtesy in the Romagna:

> le donne e' cavalier, li affanni e li agi
> che ne 'nvogliava amore e cortesia
> là dove i cuor son fatti sì malvagi.

The complaint was, after all, commonplace in Italy: compare Folgòre da San Gimignano: "Cortesia, cortesia, cortesia chiamo, / e da nessuna parte mi risponde."[23] Once again, in *Purgatorio* 16: 115–117 Marco Lombardo regrets the disappearance of that "valore e cortesia" that could still be found in northern Italy before Frederick II's defeat:

> In sul paese ch'Adice e Po riga
> solea valore e cortesia trovarsi,
> prima che Federigo avesse briga.

Dante's sense of chivalric virtues was central to his conception of the moral roots of the present world's political, social, and economic imbalance.[24] The binomium of *valore e cortesia* in *Inferno* 16: 67 and

Purgatorio 16: 116, echoing the *proz et curteis* of the French epic ever since the *Chanson de Roland*, is opposed by Dante to *orgoglio e dismisura* (*If* 16: 74, besides *viltà* and *villania* elsewhere). The roster of the basic virtues which Dante sadly missed can be summarized as: *cortesia, valore, misura, prodezza, nobiltà, senno, gentilezza, leggiadria*, and *belli costumi* (remember MHG *schöne sîte*)—all of them typical of the medieval knightly code. To these we must add the Aristotelian magnanimity we also found mentioned in the *Convivio* Dante's Farinata had been a great-hearted leader of his party (*magnanimo, If* 10: 73).

Given Dante's closeness to the Provençal poets and the presence of some of them in his works, we must pay attention to his treatment of four leading figures, namely Guiraut de Bornelh, Arnaut Daniel, Bertran de Born, and Sordello (we can forego Folquet of Marseille from *Pr* 9).[25] It is fitting that in *De vulgari eloquentia* 2.2 he would praise Guiraut de Bornelh (fl. 1165, d. after 1211) as the poet of moral rectitude (*directio voluntatis, rectitudo*, P. *dreitura*) by quoting from his canso "Per solatz revelhar, / que s'es trop endormitz," a complaint about the disappearance of courtly virtues (*solatz* is usually translated there as "courtly pleasures") from a corrupt world now given to base material pleasures. A similar mood rings through Dante's own complaints concerning the disappearance of courtly values from present-day northern Italy (Marco Lombardo in *Pg*), even though Guiraut was speaking of southwest France a hundred years earlier. In that same passage of *De vulgari eloquentia*, calling himself "the friend of Cino da Pistoia," Dante placed himself alongside Guiraut as a kindred poet of the theme of *rectitudo*: he exemplified by quoting his own canzone 106, "Doglia mi reca ne lo core ardire," a poem of th time of exile, in which the poet indicted men and women for having abandoned virtue ("Omo da sé vertú fatto ha lontana; / omo no, mala bestia ch'om simiglia").

In both *De vulgari eloquentia* and the *Commedia* (*Pg* 26: 115–148) Dante shows his great appreciation for Arnaut Daniel (fl. 1180–1210) as chief master of the *trobar clus*. In *De vulgari eloquentia* 2.2.9 he had placed him below Guiraut de Bornelh, but in *Purgatorio* 26: 117 f., Guido Guinizelli declares him the "miglior fabbro del parlar materno," who "versi d'amore e prose di romanzi / soverchiò tutti." Historically, Marcabru and Raimbaut d'Aurenga were the original and more influential practitioners of the "closed" style, but Dante could no longer understand the cultural implications of that rather mysterious phenomenon, best illustrated by the tenso "Ara.m platz, Giraut de Borneill" between Raimbaut and Guiraut de Bornelh (see chap. 4 above). Just as Raimbaut's position was to be echoed later by Petrarca's equally

elitist belief that serious literature was unsuitable for large and unini-
tiated audiences, so was Guiraut's position in that polemical exchange
similar to Dante's with regard to the merits of the vernacular for high
literary and cultural purposes. Guiraut had defended the *trobar leu* or
plan ("plain" like the "comic," "low," or "humble" style of the *DC*) as
the most apt to reach a universal audience. Likewise Dante protested
that his vernacular poetry (like his preceding vernacular prose of the
Cv) aimed to reach, in a fitting style, the largest public. Nonetheless,
Dante was attracted to Arnaut's difficult style as part of his lifelong
experimental interest in testing all styles and pressing them into service
in order to express deeply hidden allegories.

Equally significant is the episode of Bertran de Born (*If* 28:
113–142) as a clear sign of Dante's attitude toward courtliness. Bertran
(b. ca. 1140 ?, d. ca. 1200) had been the most outstanding spokesman
of the ideal of the knight-warrior, while Dante had made the momentous shift from the combination of war and love to an exclusive espousal
of love/charity. He had definitively rejected feudal bellicosity in favor of
that "peace"—the necessary condition and very goal of the Empire—that could jeopardize the knights' livelihood. An antimilitarist by
choice, Dante never boasted of his military experiences, citing them either in humorous contexts or as matter-of-fact incidents; still more important, he declined to do what the feudal code regarded as a family
duty, to wit, to avenge his relative Geri del Bello. Paramount in Dante's
mind was the logical necessity of espousing the cause of the emperors,
which had been the cause of peace ever since the Ottos identified their
interests with the meekness of good curial administrators. Thus Dante
had to condemn Bertran's role as a sower of discord between Henry II's
son Richard Lion-Heart and his eldest son, *el rei jove* (*il re giovane* of
If 28: 135). That role had made sense in the environment of the class of
landless knights of which Bertran was a spirited leader and most eloquent poet, but what was logical and positive among the courtly poets
had become criminal from Dante's vantage point.[26]

Indeed, Dante's unqualified espousal of the cause of peace amounted
to a reversal of the feudal ethic of chivalry, which he had to transcend
in order to lay a new foundation for his doctrine of the imperial order.
Seen from this angle, the contrast betweeen his treatment of Bertran and
that of Sordello (*Pg* 6) is paradigmatic. Dante does not hesitate to dis-
tort the image of Sordello, certainly no partisan of peacefulness, who
differed from Bertran only in that the latter unashamedly advocated
violence for the sake of the resulting loot. Sordello's *planh/sirventes* for

the death of Blacatz, a fitting echo of Bertran's *planh* for the death of *el rei jove* and an anticipation of Dante's gloomy picture of the unworthy rulers of his own day, sarcastically rebuked the ruling princes of Europe for their sloth and cowardice in the face of loss of their inherited lands. This motif of chivalrous condemnation of contemporary moral decay runs from Dante through Petrarca and even, for different yet convergent reasons, to Machiavelli. Sordello appears in a memorably dignified courtly posture in *Purgatorio* 6 and 7, where he has a surprise encounter with the fellow poet and fellow Mantuan, Virgil, as a paragon of brotherliness among neighbors. This leads to Dante's invective against Italy, a land divided into warring factions and regions.[27]

Cacciaguida's *laudatio* of the sober and happy old days (*Pr* 15: 97–135) fills in the picture anticipated by the eloquent hints we picked up in Guglielmo Borsiere's, Guido del Duca's, and Marco Lombardo's episodes. Searching for the sources of Dante's representation of Florence's past, Charles T. Davis (1984) has continued Arnold Busson's, Raffaello Morghen's, and others' studies on the *Cronica* attributed to Ricordano Malispini. This research has shown the continuity among chroniclers and poets on the matter, but, against Morghen, Davis agrees with Paul Scheffer-Boichorst's (1870) and Giovanni Aquilecchia's (1955) argument that the Malispini *Chronicle*, instead of a late thirteenth-century source of Dante and Villani, is a much later compilation from Villani's text, done after 1350.[28] Consequently, Davis claims that Dante's views on the progressive corruption of Florentine mores did not echo the chroniclers but were his own. It was the chroniclers who somewhat clumsily and contradictorily repeated his views, regretting Florence's civil strife and political excesses but without seeing its economic prosperity as a sign of impending doom. Dante's condemnation of Florentine greed, on the other hand, was an integral part of his philosophy of history and political order, whereby human happiness could be based only on harmonious acceptance of the monarchic regime by all elements of the empire. This original assessment was strongly colored by the particular context of courtois ideology within which Dante's thinking still moved. Curiously enough, the "burgher" Villani seemed to borrow from Dante a view of Fiesolan wickedness as an element of dissent and disorder within Florence, as part of the Fiesolani's "racial" constitution, whereas Dante, the "aristocrat," vigorously insisted that nobility is not based on "blood" and is not inherited, but consists of our virtuous deeds alone.

The nostalgic critique of contemporary moral decay and the conse-

quent invidious comparison with the good old virtues was commonplace between 1250 and 1350, in Tuscan writing and elsewhere, and
although Dante did not invent it, he powerfully contributed to it. Compare Matteo Frescobaldi's (d. 1348) canzone "Cara Fiorenza mia"
("Dear Florence mine"): "As long as you were still adorned, O Florence, / by good and ancient citizens and dear, / people far and near /
admired the Lion and its sons. [The lion was another symbol of Florence.] / Touted even among Muslims, whore you are now the world
round."[29]

It may seem surprising that Dante, without textually coupling the
terms, would associate *cortesia* and sobriety of customs in the golden
age of Florence (Cacciaguida's time, ca. 1150), followed closely by the
similar picture given by Giovanni Villani (but with chronological displacement of the *buon tempo antico* to ca. 1250). Textually, Dante and
Villani are close, and both are very close to Ricordano Malispini, but
with the difference that Ricordano (like his supposed immediate con-
tinuator, his nephew Giacotto, covering the years 1282–1286) eschews
the moral judgment that disapproves the present and praises the past
(Davis 1984, chap. 4). Dante's judgments reflect an aristocratic, anti-
bourgeois vantage point where, typically, wealth, hence luxury, are associated not with civilized refinement, as in the tradition of *curialitas*,
but with decadence, as, traditionally, among knightly and monastic
circles.

If the anticourtly tradition is the distant background of Dante's sense
of values, he also lent the most powerful poetic voice to the court critics'
ultimate cause, that is, Church reform, even while he sublimated courtly
love into a theological idea that could only be his. Dante was on the
side of court critics insofar as he was on the side of Church reformers
with some of the same arguments: those which aimed at both the life-
style of the *curiales* and the state of the Church; both *curiales* and
Church prelates were guilty of excessive worldliness. To illustrate this,
Dante hit upon the allegory of Lady Poverty as Francis's means to attain
virtue by chasing *avaritia*, the she-wolf of the *Commedia*. For Dante
the welfare of mankind depended on whether the Church and its prelates could accept Caesar's authority and divest themselves of all
worldly possessions.[30]

Dante felt that the emperor should have complete jurisdiction over
all temporal possessions; the Church, none. The mendicant orders,
spearheads of Church reform, had preached and practiced apostolic
poverty: like Christ before him, Dante's Francis had "married" Lady
Poverty, and Bonaventura spoke of Dominic as being of the same ilk in

this as Francis. Yet Dante went further than Francis and Dominic by advocating total poverty not only for the mendicant friars but for the whole Church and clergy. In this Franciscan state of affairs there would be little room indeed for any trappings of *curialitas*.

Immediate sources of Dante's moral views were Bonaventura's *Legenda maior* and the radical literature of the Franciscan Spirituals, especially Pietro di Giovanni Olivi and Ubertino da Casale, who in the stirring prophecies of their mystical tracts had advocated the reform of the order and of the Church through the literal adoption of Francis's injunction of total poverty. Dante's political system was, however, his own, since neither the Spirituals nor the Joachites, who in part also inspired both the Spirituals and Dante, had room for any imperial role in their vision of Church reform. Dante was truly a Ghibelline at least in his expectation of a new Augustus who would restore universal authority for the empire and force the clergy to give up their economic privileges. Only this would cleanse the world of the curse of universal cupidity, since even the Mendicants, as both Aquinas and Bonaventura bitterly pointed out in *Paradiso* 11 and 12, had gone astray and could not be expected to reform themselves. Frederick II's manifesto to the princes of Europe (1245), *Illos felices*, professing as his life-long purpose the restoration of the clergy to its pristine evangelical state of poverty, sounded ominously like Dante's warnings to the high clergy. Salimbene Adami da Parma had attributed to Frederick the wish that "the pope and the cardinals should be paupers and go on foot" (Davis 54 f.).

Dante's political views are a landmark in the evolution of ideas and feelings concerning the role of government and public officials, in a sense that is an integral part of our discourse about the ethical framework of the man of court. I can best summarize a complex history of interpretation with some well-phrased definitions by Lauro Martines (1979), which are based on the research of A. Passerin d'Entrèves, C. T. Davis, J. R. Hale, Nicolai Rubinstein, J. K. Hyde, and others.[31] Martines goes over the literature on the role of public officials, especially the podestà, according to Brunetto Latini's *Trésor* and *Tesoretto*. He then discusses the role of St. Augustine's *De civitate Dei* on one side and Aristotle's *Politics* and Cicero's rhetorical treatises on the opposite side in the shaping of these ideas, but with a strong emphasis on the determining value of communal experiences. He goes on as follows:

> To see the birth of the state in a divine judgment, or to root it in the nature of man himself without any pejorative suppositions regarding his fallen condition: these were the rival views, even if they were not seen in this guise, and Aristotle best represented the latter. In the first view, the state is a re-

pressive force, as much a punishment as a remedy for sin, and certainly a monstrosity unless circumscribed by a Christian framework; in the second, the state is a positive institution, which not only regulates and protects men but also perfects their companionship and makes possible their most worthy enterprises. In the former view, public service can have nothing good about it unless it is related, in some manner, to the Christian vision of loss and redemption; in the latter, public service is a manifest good in itself, requiring no mystical act of enablement or ennoblement.

Dante, for one, parted ways with St. Augustine in that he firmly conceived of the state and the empire as the foundation of virtuous action and indeed of the temporal happiness of civilized man—*beatitudo huius vitae* as distinct from but collateral to *beatitudo vitae aeternae* (*Monarchia*). At the same time, he clearly reflected the environment of a communal society by referring to citizenship in a city as the *conditio sine qua non* for civilized living when, for example, Charles Martel asked him whether there can be civilization outside the city (*Pr* 8).

> It may seem remarkable that the change [from the Augustinian to the secular view] took so long in coming, but this is to underestimate the force of the Christian lexicon. The transition from one view to the other was not in the first instance a process of abstract cerebration, as historians of ideas like to imagine, but one of action and feeling, experience and attitude. [It] involved a community process and a fund of expressive attitudes from which any gifted individual might fitfully draw new insights.
>
> Such a man was . . . Remigio de' Girolami. . . . Yet his idea of the common public good was not necessarily pinned to Aristotle; it had welled up from local feeling and was lodged in the statutes of the communes, the speeches of the podestàs, and the musings of poets.

The episode of Pier della Vigna plays an important role in Dante's representation of the order of divine justice.[32] I wish to call attention to the relevance, for the correct understanding of that episode, of the role of Envy, scourge of the courts—a key concept in the structure and message of the *Commedia*, together with its symmetric parallel, Avarice, scourge of the Church. We have already noted that envy as the demon of court life was a standard topos in medieval narrative and didactic writing. John of Salisbury had warned: "Ubique autem qui illustrioribus clarescunt meritis acrius invidiae toxicato dente roduntur" (*Policraticus* 7: 24; Webb ed.: 2: 215). In Walter Map's *De nugis curialium* (James ed.: 1: 12, 16 f.) the "unknown youth" who finds favor at the King of Portugal's court is ultimately brought down by the courtiers' envy. In the *Nibelungenlied* Siegfried arouses the envy of King Gunther's courtiers, who will successfully plan his undoing. Gottfried's Tristan is persecuted by the envious courtiers, and their envy will bring about both his and Queen Isolt's death. One can appropriately add the biblical precedents of Joseph at the Pharaoh's court and Daniel at the courts of Nebuchadnezzar, Belshazzar, and Darius (Jaeger 236 f.). We also recall how, after a lively and contrasted career as a courtier, Peter of Blois had spoken of envy and avarice as the scourges of courts, and of himself as envy's victim. Dante's figure of the unhappy courtier/chancellor had a tragic predecessor of sorts in another exemplary victim of envy, the powerful Bishop Adalbert of Bremen. There is a remarkable parallelism between these two careers. Both men were beset by unforgivable faults of character and behavior, yet both were exemplarily driven by unwavering loyalty to their king as the pivot of their private and public careers.[33] Dante seems to blame Piero, implicitly yet forcefully, for lacking the courage of the good courtier to resist courtly vices, including jealousy and hateful envy: a modern reader of medieval romances is reminded here of Gottfried's Tristan, when, after a moment of despair, he heeded King Mark's advice (vv. 8353–8366).

Dante's Ulysses also comes into this discourse as an example of successful courtier-counselor, whom Dante, however, condemned for his *desmesure* in worldly curiosity and in counseling cunning.[34] Jaeger (95–100) has located a text that he considers unique, the *Ars versificatoria* by Matthew of Vendôme, where a portrait of Ulysses appears as third, after two others of a pope and of a ruler named Caesar, and in a capacity that Jaeger, without any reference to Dante, thinks could have been labelled *curialis* or *consiliarius*. Two manuscripts titled "Causa Aiacis et Ulixis I-II" (edited by P. G. Schmidt, 1964) present a debate between the two heroes that, Jaeger believes, can be attributed to Matthew himself or one of his students, and where Ulysses successfully argues for the superiority of the courtier (himself) over the knight (Ajax). This appears to be the only medieval case of identification of Ulysses as a pedagogic model for the courtier cleric (Jaeger 99). Cicero, *De officiis* 1.113, had contrasted the characters of Ulysses and Ajax by pointing to the former's endurance of insult for the sake of his long-range plans, and to the latter's impatience of any contradiction.[35]

As a dissimulating, fraudulent counselor, Ulysses is in the company of his modern counterpart, Guido da Montefeltro, who represents Dante's rejection of cunning or duplicity ("lunga promessa con l'attender corto," Guido's counsel to Pope Boniface—*If* 27: 110) as a necessary quality of both the military leader and the politician, the knight and the courtier.[36] For Dante the statesman must be a lion, not a fox

("l'opere mie / non furon leonine ma di volpe," says Guido, *If* 27: 74
f.). We can anticipate here the shift in emphasis and function between
Dante's view and Castiglione's appreciation of non-knightly *mansuetudo* in the courtier (*Cortegiano* 2.7), even though Castiglione recom-
mended it as a way to avoid the ostentation of military arts. *Mansuetudo*, we shall recall, was a traditional requirement in the court
chaplain, a non-military man. Incidentally, Castiglione sided with the
moderns in the running arguments concerning the comparative virtues
of ancients versus moderns, and accordingly rebuked the *laudatores
temporis acti* who kept complaining about the disappearance of the
good old courtly virtues (2.1–3).

The ongoing controversies concerning the deep meanings of Dante's
characters and their structural role within his orthodox Weltanschauung could receive better light through a greater awareness of the poem's
inner tensions and multiple orientations. Perhaps it is time to outgrow
the recently triumphant emphasis on a supposedly absolutely consistent, rigorously unitary theologism on the poet's part. Some non-
American critics, in particular, have been voicing uneasiness with such
approaches. Robin Kirkpatrick (1987), for example, criticizes the excessive emphasis on the philosophical character of the poem and favors
greater attention to language and structural tension,[37] and Peter Dronke
(1986) as well as Jeremy Tambling (1988) react against what they consider reductively allegorical readings.[38] The main thrust of American
Dante critics has been to privilege the theological at the expense of other
cultural factors and of the inner tensions of expression and style. The
factors I have been stressing should contribute to a better balance
among the rich elements that Dante inherited. For he was not only a
reader of theological manuals: his political and moral views, which
were just as central to him, were derived from traditions that exalted
the worldly duties, the ones that St. Augustine had purposely downplayed but which the needs of society and of government had forced
upon many a Christian conscience. Semiotically, the Dante critics who
have overemphasized theologizing allegorism are naive readers because
they assume their deep reading will discover the only true meaning of
the text. Their interpretation is methodologically contradictory because, while they speak of irony and ambiguity, they aim to discover a
true meaning that is a priori neither ironic nor ambiguous at all, namely,
that Dante's *intentio auctoris* is really to deliver nothing but a perfectly
consistent and conformist theological message.

PETRARCA (1304–1374)

The "prince of humanists," Francesco Petrarca, was not only, as a lyrical poet, the most illustrious heir of the Provençal troubadours, he was also a product of the curial tradition. After all, much as he came to loath it in his mature years, the highly corrupt yet equally sophisticated curial court of Avignon was Petrarca's nurturing ground, with close personal association with some of its leading figures. At the same time he also embodied in a unique and eloquent form the medieval anticourt tradition in seeking refuge from the cares of the court and the world in Vaucluse, his villa outside Milan, and Arquà, as well as in the therapeutic value he derived from his writing. We might think especially of his meditations on solitude (*De ocio religiosorum De ocio religiosorum* and *De vita solitaria De vita solitaria*). Petrarca's method of working was also shaped by certain important modifications that his Italian predecessors introduced into the methods of literary production. The consequences were far-reaching, with a decisive impact on the literature of the courts.

Life at court was especially conducive to oral literature. We have seen how, like new incarnations of Socrates, the early bishops and the educators at imperial and episcopal chapels and cathedral schools often did not care to put their teaching down in writing, since their efficacy rested on their live voice. One of the greatest medieval poets, Wolfram von Eschenbach, stated outright that he was not one who could write. Literary life at court had been based on live performance, and verse compositions were usually delivered with musical accompaniment. Yet, even at a time when oral transmission in all genres (including those of science and philosophy) was still the general rule, remaining so until close to the end of the fifteenth century, writing started to play a more decisive role in Italy. This means that recitation at court went hand in hand with the use of the manuscript, which circulated and propagated motifs and forms beyond the courts to the more literate among the burghers.[39] The change was soon to affect the whole Italian cultural scene, preparing the ground for making written literature the core of humanistic education.

Typically, Dante invented the difficult form of the terzina also to make sure that the scribes would be restrained from their customary rewriting of texts—a natural and perfectly legitimate aspect of the transmission of a live culture that was normally tied to a verbal, hence

constantly moving and evolving delivery. In a terzina it was not possible
to introduce any substantive verbal changes without rewriting a whole
canto—at least if any rhyme was affected. Any accidental dropping or
interpolation of lines would have been immediately apparent by disturbing the tight movement of the rhyme structure.

The new habit of paying scrupulous attention to the precise wording
of a poet's written text—a habit that was to lead to the great achievements of humanistic philology—was started by Petrarca above all others. He did so by leaving to his disciples a painstakingly accurate record
of his work, page by page, word by word, variant by variant, many of
the variants often marked by glosses and specific annotations as to the
exact time and circumstances they were entered into a draft. He was
making sure, for the first time in medieval Europe, that his writings
would be regarded as *ne varietur* editions. His rather novel desires were
heeded by the succeeding generations, and autographs of his final drafts
(including the *Canzoniere*) were religiously preserved, together with
many a preliminary draft. This was unprecedented at a time when no
autograph was ever destined to survive. Zumthor (1987: 165) notes
that "we possess no autograph manuscript of poetry before the end of
the fourteenth century: this means that, up to that date, of all our texts,
without exception, what we perceive in our reading is the stage of reproduction, not of production." Zumthor ignores Petrarca's case, indeed a hard one to overlook, and when he mentions Boccaccio (166) as
the first to show "un véritable souci d'authenticité auctoriale," he
thinks only of his autograph corrections to the scribal copy of the *Decameron* (for Boccaccio, too, we have many autographs, including the
Teseida complete with his glosses).

This degree of attention to form and style, composition and structure, was formerly limited to Latin writing, and only occasionally practiced. Petrarca and his Italian predecessors methodically extended it to
the vernacular, starting perhaps with Provençal. It is remarkable that
this phenomenon occurred in a country relatively poor in both Latin
and vernacular poetry compared with Germany, France, or England before, say, 1230. At the same time, in their respect for the letter of the
literary text the Italians were guided by the invigorating example of the
ancients.[40]

Italian was to become the language of diplomacy, hence an interna-
tional medium of communication, replacing Latin in this function.
Knights as well as clerics had been cosmopolitan classes in the Middle
Ages, but only the clerics possessed an international language, kept rela-

tively invariant and universal by its being constrained within fixed
grammatical structures that were dead for the man of the street. The
knights, instead, had at their disposal only regional, unstable dialects
for both their everyday life and their cultural expression. Even Occitan
literature, so successful internationally, had barely faced the problem of
standardization, overcoming the motley situation of sharply variant dialects simply by relying on the early models from the Limousin. The
Italians were the first to confront the problem squarely and to become
seriously preoccupied with a "national" standard: even before Dante
intervened with his *De vulgari eloquentia* and the doctrine of the
vulgare illustre, the Sicilians had already profited from the cosmopolitan ambiance of Frederick II's court to begin a process of linguistic
homogenization.

The change toward standardized wordings, carefully handed over in
a strictly written record, also affected the use of ideas and forms associated with chivalric ideology, including the literature of courtesy,
courtly love, and formation of the courtier, until Castiglione crystallized
it in an exquisitely structured formal discourse. Petrarca's personal contribution amounted to a consolidation of much of the heritage of courtesy in a fairly fixed form within vernacular poetry, replete with standardized imagery and figures of speech: "Petrarchism" became both a
lyrical mode and a behavioral ideal.

In dealing with troubadours and Minnesingers I have noted the apparent contradiction of constantly protesting total devotion while
threatening a change of heart if reward was not forthcoming; I concluded that this was part and parcel of that "game of love" that was
conventionally and artificially verbal and yet, at the same time, an earnest strategy for survival. In·a way, we can say, Petrarca conclusively
sealed that contradiction for subsequent imitators by framing his whole
Canzoniere—the most consistent and prolonged expression of total
dedication to an evanescent and elusive, even physically absent, ideal
woman—inside the recantation of his passion as "a youthful error" in
the first poem and the transcendent hymn to the Virgin in the closing
poem, number 366. Beyond the Provençal heritage, this inner ambiguity
was perfectly consonant with the personality of that supreme lyricist,
who embedded in his lifetime's work a "discovery" of the inner tensions of the self and the contradictory nature of the psyche.[41] What had
been a witty and elegant game of survival (in the knight courtier's
career) became a symbolic expression of man's ambiguous, dialectic
predicament.

Despite its incompatibility with Christian love, courtly love had imposed itself on court life because of its social function. But when the amatory lyric outgrew its social boundaries, as was the case, for instance, with the early Bolognese and Tuscan poets who had no contact with any court of the Provençal or French type, the conflict stood out clearly enough to demand a solution. The Stil Nuovo doctrine of the *donna angelicata* came to the poets' rescue and, just as Dante had profited from that new departure for his sublime ends, so did Petrarca proceed within the new intellectual framework that had transcended the Provençal context. In other words: despite the fact that the sociological settings had become incompatible in the transition from the feudal courtly environments to the republics and signories of fourteenth-century Italy, the Stil Nuovo managed to codify the ideology of the former to the taste and understanding of the latter in a language that eventually became Petrarchan. A similar situation characterized Catholic Spain in that and the following century, where the adulterous definition of courtly love was commonly deemphasized: the lover, aristocrat or no, could look to a love within marriage, or the writer could attack the implications of a sinful passion, as did the author of the *Celestina* (1499).[42] The case of Castilian and Portuguese amorous poetry is interesting for the use of Petrarchism in establishing a firm context of psychological analysis of a moral predicament, in a tense polarization between a rational sublimation of love and the condemnation of an alienating passion, futile at best, destructive at worst. In that poetry a universal ethos filled the forms inherited from a court setting that could no longer be operative, since it no longer existed.

Petrarchism grew steadily in Quattrocento Italy, and it was in courtly environments that it produced potentially aberrant forms. The outstanding example is Serafino Aquilano (d. 1500), a page at the Neapolitan court in his youth and then an acclaimed court entertainer at Urbino and northern Italian courts. In line with the progressive Christianization and Platonization of erotic poetry after Petrarca, the virtues of the lovers came to sound more and more like the standard Christian virtues. *Onestade, temperanza, vergogna, continenza,* and such, dominated both in stanzas of European love poetry like the *Cantos de amor* of the fifteenth-century Catalan poet Augias March and in pages of philosophical speculation on love like Mario Equicola's successful *Libro de natura de amore* (1509).

Finally Bembo managed to canonize Petrarca along classicizing lines. Thanks mostly to Bembo's authoritative endorsement in his 1525 *Prose della volgar lingua*,[43] Petrarca's model of frustrated love as the noblest form of love, his latter-day interpretation of courtly love taken out of its social context, became archetypal for much of the subsequent European lyric. His success must not make us oblivious to the availability of other options both at his time and before, as if it had been a foregone conclusion. For not only could a frankly uncourtly view of love be presented (or perhaps advocated) even in such an extended treatment as the *Roman de la rose*, but a chivalric dressing could be used for transparent *uncourtois* allegories disguising daydreams about subduing a woman with knightly force instead of worshipping her lofty resistance. Typically, at least as early as 1214 a festival at Treviso included a victorious siege by young males of a Castle of Love held by fair maidens.[44]

Petrarca brought to its most consummate level the habit of composing "logically" rather than by succession of lyrical moods—a habit which has been observed in the passage from the earlier Provençal, French, and German lyric to the more mature Italian lyrical modes, especially with the Stil Nuovo. But above all Petrarca should also enter our discourse for his more technical contribution of turning some typical chivalric and *courtois* clichés into a method of lyrical expression—what became the main ingredients of European Petrarchism in the lyric, including the conventionalized uses that can be termed "manneristic."[45] I am referring, first, to his adoption of *courtois* motifs in the form of stylistic antitheses and oxymora as well as the symmetries of his "correlaciones plurimembres," to use Dámaso Alonso's terms. An impressive example of the compositional structures that Petrarca canonized is Giacomo da Lentini's (fl. 1233–1240) "Lo basilisco a lo speco lucente." There, the first known Sicilian poet exploited the form of the sonnet, which he invented, for the most architectonic compositional format it could encompass. He did so by using not only a correlative pattern (in the quatrains) but also a recapitulation of its members (in the tercets), all of it in the midst of continuous antitheses.[46] Antithesis abounds in Giacomo as well as its most concentrated form, the oxymoron: see, for example, the sonnet "Chi non avesse mai veduto foco," ending with a most effective pre-Petrarchan antithetical treatment of his relationship to Love and the beloved: "Certo l'Amore fa gran vilania, / che non distingue te che vai gabando; / a me, che servo, non dà isbaldimento," "Surely Love does wrong: / he does not subdue you, who only mock, / he has no reward for me, who truly serve," reminiscent of the close of more than one of Petrarca's most memorable sonnets.[47] Likewise in Rinaldo d'Aquino's canzone "Amorosa donna fina": "d'uno foco che non pare / che 'n la neve fa 'llumare, / ed incende tra lo ghiaccio," "with a fire that does not show, / that shows its light in the snow, / and flares up inside the ice"; and in Guido delle Colonne's (b. ca. 1210) "che fa lo foco nascere di neve," "which makes fire arise out of the snow" (canzone "Anchor che l'aigua per lo foco lassi").[48] These are paradoxical antitheses in the form of *adynata* of a kin with Petrarca's "icy fire."[49]

We have noticed that such figures were also common in the earlier French, Provençal, and German poets. One more striking, final example is the famous passage in Gottfried's *Tristan* (vv. 60–64) where the poet espouses the true love of his tragic couple, and where we find even the equivalent of Petrarca's neologism *dolceamara*, "bittersweet":

> ir süeze sur, ir liebez leit,
> ir herzeliep, ir senede not,
> ir liebez leben, ir leiden tot,
> ir lieben tot, ir leidez leben:
> dem lebene si min leben ergeben.
>
> (Their sweet bitterness, their loving sorrow,
> their hearts' love, their yearning misery,
> their loving life, their wretched death,
> their loving death, their wretched life:
> let my life be devoted to that life.)
>   (W. T. H. Jackson's trans., 1971: 54)

And again

> daz honegende gellet,
> daz süezende siuret,
> daz touwende viuret,
> daz senftende smerzet.
>
> (love's gall, with honey fraught,
>   bitterness, sweet though tart,
>   pain, soothing though it smart,
> fire, quenching though it burn.)
>   (vv. 11,884–11,887 Ranke ed.,
>   11,888–11,891 Zeydel 1948 trans.)

Indeed, Gottfried favored antitheses and oxymora throughout, climaxing in the definitional one he adapted from Thomas: "Isot ma drue, Isot mamie, / en vus ma mort, en vus ma vie!" (19,409 f., in French in his text).[50] He had called Isolt Tristan's "living death," "sin lebender tot" (14,468).

I have picked up (in chap. 4) a few precedents for the conceit of the heart or soul detached from the lover, which Petrarca transmitted to his Quattrocento imitators and beyond. In sonnet 16, "Io mi rivolgo indietro a ciascun passo," he is away from his beloved and wonders how it can be that his limbs are detached from the spirit that sustains them: "come posson queste membra / da lo spirito lor viver lontane?" Besides Provençal, French, and German antecedents, he had Italian ones as well. Listen to Rinaldo d'Aquino ("Amorosa donna fina"): "che vita po l'omo avere, / se lo cor non è con lui? / Lo meo cor non è co' mico, / ched eo tutto lo v'ho dato." (How can one live without a heart? Mine is not with me, since I have given it entirely to you.) Of course, the roles could also be reversed, and Guido delle Colonne, in the canzone already quoted, could say that "he thought the soul happily dwelling inside his body was really his lady's own": "Lo spirito ch'i' aggio, und'eo mi sporto, / credo lo vostro sia, / che nel meo petto stia / e abiti con meco in gran diporto."[51] Traditional motifs that embody the notions of sweet enslavement and liberation through poetic singing come down from the troubadours all the way to the most recent models, like Guittone d'Arezzo (ca. 1253–1294): "come l'augel dolci canti consono, / ch'è preso in gabbia e sosten molti guai," "I sing sweet songs like the bird who is kept in a cage and suffers much woe" (sonnet "Dolcezza alcuna," ending with the antithesis "credendomi appressare, io m'allontano," "in the illusion of coming closer I drift further away"). Or take the motif of the pilgrim who looks for the sacred relics as the poet looks for the likes of his beloved (see Petrarca's "Movesi il vecchierel"), as in Lapo Gianni's (ca. 1250–1328 or later) sonnet "Sì come i Magi a guida della stella": "Sì come i Magi a guida della stella / girono inver' le parti d'Oriente / per adorar lo Segnor ch'era nato, / così mi guidò Amore a veder quella." (Just as the Magi, guided by the star, / turned toward the East / in order to worship the newly born Lord, / so Love guided me to behold that woman.)[52]

As Dante had done, so did Petrarca often couple *cortesia* with *onestade*. See, for example, *Canzoniere* 338: 1–5: "Lasciato ài, Morte, . . . cortesia in bando et onestade in fondo," and again in 351: 5 f.: "Gentil parlar, in cui chiaro refulse / con somma cortesia somma onestate." Similarly, the frequent occurrence of *convenevole* and *decoro* as attributes of true beauty in Renaissance critical theory reminds us of Cicero's key concept of *decorum*, with the applications we have noted.[53]

I shall conclude by summarizing the main threads of my argument on Petrarca's specific role. Seigniorial courts had been a fitting environment for oral culture both in the curial setting of clerical teaching for ecclesiastical and administrative instruction and in the social relationships that fostered troubadour poetry as live singing of the lady's praises. In Italy the new political setting of the Frederician court of Palermo as well as the new social and professional setting of notarial circles that produced the Stil Nuovo brought about a decided privileging of the written text, fixed and transmitted by copying and reading rather than reciting and singing. Petrarca inherited the curial and courtly traditions in this new "grammatological" form, and radically crystallized it by making the Petrarchan lover part of a written elitist culture with canonized, universalized motifs of high love—a trademark of the new educated man of the world.

BOCCACCIO (1313–1375)

Boccaccio's allegiance to the social and political ways of republican and bourgeois Florence was always ambiguous. Even while breathing the air of Florentine mercantilism and occasionally serving the Florentine republic, he never outgrew his early experiences at the Neapolitan court; for the remainder of his life he went on hoping to become once again a courtier, preferably again at Naples under the aegis of Niccolò Acciaiuoli, or else at such minor courts as that of Francesco Ordelaffi at Forlì. His hopes were all in vain, but not for want of trying.[54] It was the courtly environment of Naples that prompted him to fashion for himself a background of nobility by pretending to be the illegitimate issue of an affair between a Tuscan banking agent and a Parisian lady of royal blood, and then to create the elaborate, prolonged fiction of his romantic involvement with Maria d'Aquino, the king of Naples's illegitimate daughter who allegedly married a count of the Aquinas house. Boccaccio reflected his intoxication with the charms of the Neapolitan court in what is perhaps his first work, the *Caccia di Diana* (1333 ?, 1339 at the latest), a celebration of Venus in a courtly atmosphere where sixty ladies behave like noble courtiers, obliviously hunting and jousting away in the name of love.

Boccaccio's life is shot through with medieval readings, and the romances left their mark on his fervid imagination. In the *Filocolo* (1336 ?)—a massive, meandering novel in which all the characters are noble—the lengthy digression of the Questions of Love (book 4, chaps. 17–72) clearly echoes French court habits (at least from literature). The love story of the *Filostrato* (1335 ?, 1339 ?) is grounded in courtly love: Troiolo's total devotion owes much to that tradition, rather than to an anachronistically romantic exaltation in an overpowering passion. The *Teseida* (1339–1341) is an original mixture of classical epic and medieval romance, with heavy emphasis on disguising ancient warriors as chivalrous knights. Arcita and Palemone, the two rivals for the love of Emilia, conduct their wooing in knightly style by testing their prowess in an elaborate, bloody tournament. While they wait for the decisive test, they entertain lavishly to display their virtue and wealth. Before the battle Theseus formally dubs them both. Finally, on his deathbed the victorious Arcita magnanimously yields Emilia to his rival. The *Amorosa visione* (1342) lists Arthurian knights and ladies in the triumph of Fame (Canto 11), Lancelot and Tristan in the Triumph of Love (Canto 29). In the *Elegia di Madonna Fiammetta* (1343–1344) Fiammetta compares herself to Isolde (chap. 8). Instead of prayer books, the *Corbaccio*'s (1355 ?) lusty widow reads Lancelot's story and is sexually aroused by it. The *De casibus virorum illustrium* (1355–1362) asserts that the story of King Arthur, apparently drawn from Geoffrey of Monmouth, deserves mention because of its popularity, but is of doubtful historicity: it can serve as an example of the fragile nature of immodest conquest.

As to the *Decameron* (1349–1353 ?), the men of business who studied the pages of that "epic of the Florentine merchant" with their daring forays into unknown and dangerous lands and their often triumphant, sometimes puzzling displays of *ingegno*, would have delighted in the description of their fate and praise of their achievements that Hugh of St. Victor had given more than two centuries earlier (see my chap. 5). It took all this time for a fully conscious representation of mercantile psyche and ethos, first by the pen of Boccaccio, then by the equally able one of Chaucer.[55] Likewise we can see registered in the *Decameron* the fully autonomous presence, also, perhaps, for the first time, of women as real characters with their own personalities, needs, desires, and points of view. Whereas women had been rather regularly represented before as no more than other selves of the masculine observer or mere allegorical symbols, such characters as madonna Beritola (2.6), Alatiel (2.7), Zinevra (2.9), Bartolomea (2.10), Monna Filippa (6.7), and a score of others, not to speak of Fiammetta in the *Elegia*, cannot be dismissed as such—even if their artistic representation is loaded with irony and symbolism. It was no mean achievement.

Much speculation has verged on the exact meaning of the *Decameron*'s subtitle "libro soprannominato il Galeotto," a reference to Sir Galehault of the Lancelot Vulgate cycle also alluded to by Dante in *Inferno* 5. The "stories of adventure" of the Second Day are patterned after the sense of adventure that informed the French *romans d'aven-ture*, but with the decisive difference that Boccaccio's stories fit perfectly the experiential mercantile world: the medieval merchant was no less adventurous than the knight errant, and perhaps more successful in taking his chances.

Courtly love was thought to have transcendent redeeming qualities; the lady could perform miracles, substituting for God's Grace. Boccaccio presents this medieval idea in a classical garb in the striking story of Cimone, the boorish character who is turned into a paragon of utter refinement by the sight of Iphigenia's naked beauty (*Decameron* 5.1). In the *Caccia di Diana* Boccaccio first used this chivalric motif of "the civilizing influence of sexual love" that would emerge again in the *Filocolo*, in the *Commedia delle Ninfe Fiorentine* (1341–1342), and in the story of Cimone.[56] In this favorite allegory the uncouth young man owes his "education" to beauty and love, thus emerging from a rustic state of nature to one of social refinement. The theme turned to a Dantesque philosophical discourse in the *Amorosa Visione* (1343). The *Filocolo*, the *Ninfale fiesolano*, and several stories of the *Decameron* dwell on a love that irresistibly draws two young people together despite legal, social, or economic barriers.[57] It is as though Boccaccio, born to a more open society, were struggling against the feudal social fetters that had shaped an illustrious literary tradition.

We find exemplary cases of *cortesia* in the *Decameron* stories of Federigo degli Alberighi (5.9), Bergamino (1.7), Guglielmo Borsiere (1.8), Neerbale (3.10), Ghino di Tacco (10.2), Natan and Mitridanes (10.3), Gentile de' Carisendi (10.4), messer Ansaldo and madonna Dianora (10.5), Tito and Gisippo (10.8), and the Saladin and messer Torello (10.9). In the stories of Natan, Gentile, Ansaldo, and Tito the lordly virtue of *liberalità* acquires the higher connotation of moral generosity even to the level of true magnanimity. In the story of Ansaldo, in particular, madonna Dianora has imprudently tried to get rid of an unwanted lover, Ansaldo, by promising to yield to him if he can pass the impossible test of producing a flowering garden in January, which Ansaldo unexpectedly achieves with the help of a necromancer. When, after consulting with her husband Gilberto, Dianora comes to Ansaldo ready to fulfill his wish, he sends her back, untouched, to her husband. But note the subtly ironic touch of social realism in the differentiation between the two men. Ansaldo is *un nobile e gran barone*, a noble knight who sets out to outdo in liberality and *cortesia* his rival Gilberto, who, being only *un gran ricco uomo*, a very rich commoner, is both

motivated by a sense of fair play and concerned about the necromancer's power of revenge. All the stories of this last day of the *Decameron*
stage splendid displays of courtly generosity, in richly variant forms.

Even there, however, Boccaccio looks at the most conspicuous tests
of aristocratic patterns of behavior through the eyes of a burgher's son.
In the story of Griselda (10.10) the Marquis of Saluzzo is determined to
marry a humble woman to make sure he has a perfectly obedient wife.
Griselda patiently endures a series of cruel tests. In the last, the marquis
pretends he has taken a noble-born new wife and asks Griselda what
she thinks of her. Griselda praises the new wife but advises the marquis
not to test her in the same way, for the daughter of a count could not
have the strength of a humbly-born woman. So Griselda becomes the
noble heroine of the Aristotelian fortitude that Cicero had defined as
"the virtue of one who can advisedly accept and endure all tests and
hardships, and that is made of a great heart, loyalty, patience, and per-
severance."[58] In Boccaccio's own words of comment, it is a peasant
woman who gives a lesson in humanity and reason to an absurdly proud
and cruel great lord. Although critics have been reluctant to identify
sources for this stunning novella, Chrétien's *Enide* also comes naturally
to mind as the exemplary victim of a knight's somewhat high-handed
will to test wifely obedience and submission (though noble, she had also
been forced by poverty to dress in tattered rags when first seen by Erec).

My main point here is that the *Decameron* shows side by side, in a
state of inner tension, the two contradictory ethics of the knightly class
and the merchant class. Aside from its more abstract, or spiritualized,
version that we have witnessed in the story of Dianora and other stories
of the Tenth Day, the key virtue of "liberality" is still extolled in its more
pecuniary connotations of feudal memory in the stories of the rich and
generous abbots of Cluny (1.7, 10.2). In this traditional knightly form
it is also the virtue that has reduced Federigo degli Alberighi to poverty
(5.9). When, however, Federigo's courtly behavior won him the love of
the wealthy madonna Giovanna and they finally married, Boccaccio
tells us that, having attained his goal, Federigo changed his ways and
started behaving more wisely, no longer as a knight but as a merchant,
hence a prudent and efficient manager of his patrimony, "miglior mas-
saio fatto." He thus exemplified that mercantile ethic that would make
Leon Battista Alberti speak of "questa santa masserizia" in *Della famiglia* (1441), his treatise in dialogue form on family economy. *Massaro*
was a common Italian term for financial responsibility and accountability: in fourteenth-century Mantua, for example, the commune's chief

fiscal officer was called *massaro*. In a feudal society, if the sources of income turned out to be inadequate to run the noble house as was fitting and "honorable," the nobleman hoped to make up his deficits with new grants from the sovereign, military conquests, or downright plunder. But as a spendthrift nobleman converted to the virtues of good patrimonial management, Federigo degli Alberighi shows the juxtaposition of the two codes in the Florentine society of merchants who lived side by side with the decayed nobility. In that society, no grant could be expected from monarchic or feudal sources.

Boccaccio was familiar with both the mentality of the merchants, among whom he had been nurtured, and that of the nobility, whom he had observed at the court of Naples. He was among the first to present a critical view of the chivalric ethos from an economic vantage point. It is not surprising that economic concerns were also conspicuously present in the literature of chivalry, fraught as it was with sharp allusions to wealth and the ways to attain it. Wealth was to be gained not by work but by benefices, grants, or conquests, and then spent freely. Unlike the bourgeois ethos, the chivalric ethos ignored any principle of saving, investment, and capital accumulation. From any list of a nobleman's honorable ways of acquiring riches, thrift was always notably absent. Indeed, the nobleman was marked by conspicuous "liberality," since the noble way of both living and dying was expensive. It is symptomatic that heraldic treatises gave much space to descriptions of lavish funerals with thousands of Masses to follow for the benefit of the departed noble soul. In a way, rich merchants ended up imitating the nobles more after death than in life, since they could make peace with God and their consciences by bequeathing their wealth, or large portions of it, as the nobles were wont to do, to good causes like churches and charities.

I noted above (chap. 2) Cicero's coupling of *decorum* and *honestum*, the outwardly honorable and inner virtue. By extension, in the high ranks of the nobility, from the Middle Ages all the way to the French Revolution, and especially in the French *ancien régime*, what was "honest," meaning "honorable," was also fitting and becoming—not only in moral terms but in the derivative area of economic ethic, too. The lord or master spent, on principle, according to his rank, social status, and hierarchic obligations, not according to his income—of which he had no idea, since it was the responsibility of his *intendant*, and it was beneath his dignity and status to concern himself with such non-aristocratic matters. Hence it might well be "honest" for him to overspend and, as a "liberal" lord, behave in what the bourgeois code of financial responsibility would regard as outright dishonesty.[59]

Likewise, in a feudal environment it was not dishonorable, indeed it was a way to avoid embarrassment and dishonor, for a member of the warrior class—or a high ecclesiastic to the extent that he too had adopted the warrior's ways—to circumvent the pressures of creditors through the use of physical force or by simply ignoring their claims. A massive experiment in this method of resolving budgetary impasses resulted in the widespread bankruptcies of the large financial concerns in the 1340s, with ensuing depression, famine, and plague. The *Decameron*'s first story cleverly illustrates the point: the banker Musciatto Franzesi had to hire a disreputable character like ser Ciappelletto in order to collect what could still be salvaged from the defaulting noble debtors of Burgundy. The story must have rung a familiar bell with Boccaccio's merchant readers, who, amused though they might be, could not laugh too loud.

Despite the triumph of the burgher class in the city states of the late Middle Ages and Renaissance, the aristocratic mentality and ethos continued to affect the behavior of ruling classes through the eighteenth century. Even Diderot's enlightened *Encyclopédie* clearly showed how the aesthetic sense, which controlled expenditures on private buildings, remained relative to social rank or posture. Architectural style was strictly subjected to the criterion of fitting the building to its social, hence cultural function.[60] Elias (*The Court Society* 67) recalls the story of the Duke of Richelieu who intended to give his son a lesson in lordly prodigality rather than bourgeois frugality. He gave him a full purse for a day on the town, and when the boy returned with a portion unspent, the duke disdainfully tossed it out of the window. Such attitudes were typical of noblemen everywhere: in 1590 the Florentine Orazio della Rena observed that in refeudalized Ferrara all gentlemen "live off their rents and have no respect for those who do not spend to the limit; they regard commerce and trade, even wholesale, as shameful and unworthy of a gentleman; they consider themselves much superior to the gentlemen of mercantile cities [read: Florence or even Venice], they gladly spend all their income and more, so that they are always in debt up to their ears."[61] The frugality that was preached to commoners and burghers contrasted with the conspicuous consumption and outright prodigality that were deemed a necessary sign of noble behavior.

CHAPTER NINE

Renaissance Transformations: I

THE PAIDEIA OF HUMANISM

One of our underlying themes is the continuity between medieval chivalry and Renaissance civic service within both republican communes and seigniorial courts. We shall find a first example in a widely circulating French text by Jean Miélot, derived from a free interpretation in Latin by Giovanni Aurispa (ca. 1376–1459) of an ancient story recorded in the Latin Livy and the Greek Lucian. This text superimposed the chivalrous mold over classical heroes in an underworld debate among Hannibal, Alexander, and Scipio Africanus, who argued before Minos about which of them had most excelled "by his knightly deeds." It is a striking case of our themes coming together despite their being identifiable with apparently incompatible mentalities. It is also an eloquent example of the way stories and texts can be bent to timely use in different cultural climates. Contrary to Lucian's text, where Alexander and Hannibal won first and second places for military glory, in Aurispa's and Miélot's renderings Minos ruled in favor of Scipio because his achievements were inspired not by a search for personal honor and glory but by the will to maintain the dignity of the Roman name. In other words, at the same time that Miélot presented Scipio as a chivalrous hero, his preface stressed the point, also made by Aurispa, that Scipio acted out of duty to the fatherland.[1] While tracing this intriguing text incorrectly, M. Keen (235) finds "a back-handed dig here at the quest for vainglory, which had inspired Hannibal and Alexander and had been their ultimate undoing, and which the critics constantly identified as one of the besetting sins of knighthood. The general moral is clear, and its emphasis is on the value of public service, whose aim is to uphold not the fame of an individual, but the honor and fortune of a people." In sum, we could hardly find a better example of civic humanism at work within the legacy of chivalric ideology.[2]

Aurispa brought Lucian's dialogues and many other Greek manuscripts to Italy from Constantinople. In his free rendering of the competition between the three generals before Minos (1425–1427) he gave the story a completely new twist by introducing into it the humanistic principle that true virtue consists of service to the public good (mostly indicated with the term *patria*, rendered in Miélot's version as *chose publique*). Miélot's version, executed for Philip the Good in 1449–1450, was usually transmitted under the title "Débat entre trois chevalereux princes," which carried a strong Burgundian flavor. The often accompanying translation of Buonaccorso's text was entitled, in turn, *Controversie de noblesse*. (The French version of Llull's *Ordre de chevalerie* also accompanied those two texts in B.R. MS. 10493–10497 of Brussels.)

What deserves all our attention is that the virtues of Aurispa's and Miélot's Scipio are not theological but cardinal (mainly prudence and fortitude), hence secular, and we have noted that this shift already characterized the medieval tradition of curiality on the supporting ground of its Ciceronian component (see my chap. 2). Aurispa identified this ethical strain with *humanitas*, rendered by Miélot with *vertus*— chivalric virtues which thus became equivalent to the humanistic ideal of service to the fatherland (*la chose publique*).[3]

We could trace our steps even further back and find continuity and implicit alliance between *curialitas* and humanism, starting with Petrarca and his immediate predecessors. Petrarca's idea of education and Vittorino da Feltre's pedagogical practice were closer to the image of the early medieval teacher of curiality and courtliness than to that of the scholastic dialectician.[4] For, even more than the ascetic monastic circles, the courtly ethic's sternest enemies were the thirteenth- and fourteenth-century dialecticians who remained the target of most humanists' arrows down to the beginning of the sixteenth century. Those dialecticians had replaced a concern for humaneness and affability with an unswerving quest for pure truth. The Battle of the Seven Arts had started in mid-twelfth century France on the level of psychological and ethical habits affecting personal careers as much as on that of methods of teaching, learning, and thinking.

I have noted the contrast between the cult of personal greatness, establishing patterns of imitation on the ground of the teacher's charisma, and a desire to prove one's point in purely scientific terms.[5] Stephen of Novara, the Italian master called to Würzburg by Otto the Great, saw his authority challenged when his brilliant pupil, Wolfgang of Regensburg, promised a commentary on Martianus Capella that would outdo his teacher's critical powers. Such a breach of etiquette was to be repeated in other clamorous incidents, as when, in 1028, the Lombard grammarian Benedict of Chiusa appeared in Limoges and without any regard for his hosts' sensitivities proceeded to dispute their belief that their patron St. Martial had been an apostle. Then again, and most sensationally, in mid–twelfth century Abelard criticized the expertise of his teachers, Anselm of Laon and William of Champeaux, after having brashly offended the monks of St. Denis by challenging the true identity of their patron saint. This was not the way the pupils of *curialitas* were supposed to behave toward their teachers, who were unprepared for the philosophical principle "amicus Plato, sed magis amica veritas." The avenues to worldly success were, instead, respect, obedience, deference, and diplomatic tactfulness. Abelard, for one, paid dearly for his love of truth above human respect. He never would have risen into a bishopric or a high court. His letter to his son Astrolabe concerning his idea of a correct relationship between teacher and pupil tells much about the new mentality.[6]

No matter how boldly innovative, the early humanistic schools of Vittorino da Feltre at Mantua and Guarino Veronese at Ferrara were still the kind of court schools that trained young knights and sons of princes. They contributed to bringing the ideals of courtly education to fruition. Despite Petrarca's and, among genuine educators of the youth, Vittorino's religious motivations, the new culture was, like that of the medieval knight, generally world-oriented. It sought to refine mind and manners for the secular ends of achieving honor at court and wealth in society, skill in chancery administration, and eloquence in public oratory, including the notarial art. It managed to endow the mind with high humane values even while it fitted its possessors with the credentials for the ruling élite in the city power structure. For such training, ethics was the central and almost exclusive branch of philosophy, and literature the foundation of value and effective communication. Many humanists were at the same time men of action and men of learning, active and occasionally leading citizens of city states, like their proclaimed models from ancient Athens and Rome. True enough, while the chivalric knight had represented the sublimated ideal of medieval clerics and noblemen, the new burgher tried to see himself as a reincarnation of the ancient hero. Yet the goal was similar: to become a civic-minded leader. Pietro Paolo Vergerio's *De ingenuis moribus* (ca. 1402) addressed this type of humanist as a whole man, scholar and citizen when, citing Aristotle, it warned that "the man who surrenders himself completely to the charm of letters or speculative thought may become self-centered and useless as a citizen or prince."

Humanistic education ideally aimed at a coupling of eloquence with civic and moral virtues. The actual school practice emphasized the grammatical, rhetorical, and philological aspects of reading the *auctores*; the extant manuals and commentaries do not generally reflect an equal concern with the formation of moral and social character.[7] In a way, the curial, courtly, and chivalric literature we have been considering embodied such concern more concretely than the statements and exercises of humanistic persuasion. It can be assumed that, as in the best tradition of the medieval royal chapels and cathedral schools, much of the practical impact on students was taking place in the form of the teacher's direct influence by charisma and communication.

At the same time the more worldly side of both medieval and Renaissance educational training, to wit, the rhetorical curriculum (including the *ars dictandi*), was directed at what looked like useful preparation for the art of the practicing lawyer. "The critical figures in the origins of humanism," Lauro Martines reminds us, "were lawyers and notaries, the most literate members of lay society and among its most active in public affairs." Just as Brunetto Latini had been a notary in Florence, "nearly the whole school of Paduan pre-humanists hailed from the administrative-legal profession," and the two early leading figures, Lovato Lovati (ca. 1237–1309) and Albertino Mussato (1261–1329), were notaries as well as politicians.[8] The value of rhetoric was stressed not only in special treatises on the art, but also in humanistic political tracts, like the *Re repubblica* by T. L. Frulovisi (ca. 1400–1480), who held eloquence basic for all members of the city government, including the prince. In his *De institutione reipublicae* the Sienese Francesco Patrizi da Cherso (1413–1494) reiterated this notion, stressing the government agent's need to persuade others to action. The study of history, especially ancient heroic history, was similarly urged as *magistra vitae*, a guide to action as an essential part of humanistic education, as in Leonardo Bruni's *De studiis et litteris* (ca. 1405). Ancient historians were valued as a repository of eloquence as well as practical wisdom.

Toward the middle of the sixteenth century Peter Ramus produced a large number of school manuals, particularly successful in France, England, and Germany, that contributed to a more practical orientation of educational methods in the sense of pursuing socially attractive positions rather than simply scholarly and intellectual sophistication. But medieval and early humanistic education had been typically concerned with what was regarded as "formation of the mind" rather than with the imparting of directly useful skills: the Trivium Arts were eminently formal rather than professional. This included, to a large extent, rhetorical training, whose relevance to the purpose of forming the lawyer and public man was limited to the development of the "power of persuasion."

Civic humanism had a counterpart in what one historian has labeled as "courtly humanism" and another one as "subdital humanism," with reference to the use of the renovated classical ethos to support, praise, and illustrate the new seigniorial rulers.[9] Indeed, humanists could be courtiers, too, and their fashionable panegyrical displays distilled a heady brew of old and new ideals that applied some of the features of the medieval knight and courtier to the new uses of the modern warrior statesman. A most successful funeral oration by the Venetian patrician Leonardo Giustinian for the Venetian leader and general Carlo Zeno (1418, at least sixty-four manuscript copies and six printed editions are extant) praised Zeno as a model captain, even more excellent than the Athenian Themistocles, for having been victorious not by force of arms but through the humanistic virtues of authority, humanity, clemency, affability, civility, and eloquence (*auctoritas, humanitas, clementia, affabilitas, comitas, eloquentia*). The Ciceronian matrix, put to a new use, had helped to transform the image of the chivalric leader and refined courtier into that of the modern condottiero in the garb of a humanistic orator.[10] But the widespread enthusiasm for learning that characterized the Renaissance also provided new channels to the aristocrats who had lost the opportunity to achieve power by force of the sword. They became refined courtiers.[11]

If the humanists' public was basically the new oligarchic bourgeoisie in the republican cities and the new aristocracy in the princely signories, it is interesting to see the old topoi of liberality and avarice turned to new purposes and adapted to new social uses.[12] Informed by a taste for democratic values, Poggio Bracciolini's *De avaritia* (1428) and *De infelicitate principum* (1440) both indicted the powerful for their greed and praised them for their patronization of public causes, artists, and humanists.[13] In the dialogue *De avaritia* Poggio attributed to his character, Antonio Loschi, the bourgeois thesis that avarice could be a source of temperance and happiness in the wise use of fortune. It was a sign of mercantile appreciation for industriousness and thrift—the economic sides of fortitude and prudence.

Humanistic treatises on the nobility and dignity of man invariably emphasized virtue against birth as the true root of nobility, as eloquently argued in Lapo da Castiglionchio il Vecchio's (d. 1390) famous letter to his son Bernardo (1377–1378),[14] Coluccio Salutati's (1331–1406) *Tractatus de nobilitate legum et medicinae* of 1399/1340, and then, most unequivocally, Buonaccorso da Montemagno il Giovane's (d. 1429) influential tract *De nobilitate* (1429). This philosophical idea, based on ancient, mostly Stoic speculation, had received the powerful support of Dante's *Convivio*, which reflected a point of view developed by the new poetic schools for reasons that had to do with the use of courtly love in an alien social setting. When they had to cope with current realities, both Lapo, a jurist of the old landed nobility, and Coluccio, known for his shifting sense of political values, recognized nobility by descent or by holding public office—as did Bartolo da Sassoferrato, translated by Lapo in the first part of his letter.

In Poggio's *De nobilitate* (1440) the interlocutor Niccolò Niccoli defined nobility as personal virtue, identical to a wise use of assets instead of the simple possession of them, and found only the exercise of virtue a convincing trademark of nobility. His opponent Lorenzo de' Medici objected that a virtue without social purpose is useless and sterile.[15] By vividly examining the behavior of noblemen in different Italian and foreign regions, the dialogue elicited the resentful reaction of some Venetian erudites. Poggio gave more currency to the established distinction that wealth entitles us only to be called "rich," not "noble." Replying to Poggio in 1449, Leonardo Chiensi founded nobility in *sapientia* and *virtute*.[16] Platina also rejected the equation of nobility and riches (*De vera nobilitate*, 1471–1478; 1540 ed., p. 43). In book 2 of L. B. Alberti's *Della famiglia* we read a hymn to *mercatura* within a eulogy of wealth as reward not for love or force, but industriousness: noble and great achievements are grounded in strenuous and risky work carried out with liberality and magnificence. Writing in the shadow of a princely court, Guarino Veronese's son Battista Guarino (*De ordine do-*

cendi et studendi, 1457) declared that only those who could write elegant Latin verse were well educated. This was obviously beyond the reach of the average burgher, busy with other things, but close enough to the training of such refined courtiers as Castiglione, a Latin poet of note.

The best-known texts of this humanistic genre, namely Giannozzo Manetti's (1396–1459) *De dignitate et excellentia hominis* (1452) and Giovanni Pico della Mirandola's (1463–1494) *Oratio de hominis dignitate* (1486), were more concerned with the philosophical underpinnings of the humanistic view of man's inner dignity than with the specific social context I am pursuing here. Similarly, Cristoforo Landino's *De vera nobilitate* (after 1481) repeated what had become standard humanistic motifs, without Manetti's freshness and Pico's philosophical sweep. At the end of the century, in an *Epistola de nobilitate*, Antonio De Ferrariis, known as Il Galateo (1444–1516), once again submitted an equation of nobility with rationality: "nobiles sunt . . . qui vere philosophantur" (Colucci edition, pp. 140–411). This general theme had been carried on eloquently by P. P. Vergerio, Bartolomeo Fazio, Giannozzo Manetti, Flavio Biondo, Giovanni (Gioviano) Pontano, and the great Pico. The *De principe liber* (1468) of Pontano (1426–1503), a humanist statesman particularly well versed in court life, was a manual of advice to a young prince. Others of his numerous moral tracts dealt with specific qualities of the public man.[17] His *De sermone* raised the quality of *facetudo*, the *facetia* of medieval memory, to the status of a trademark of the good speaker, namely the one who pleases and avoids offense by clothing his moral judgments in a humorous garb: this distinguishes the man of court from the rustic.[18] In a different vein, Sannazzaro's *Arcadia* (1480–1496, published 1501, 1504), a successful work fraught with enormous potential for later imitation in many literatures, introduced shepherds and shepherdesses as a counterpart to the Neapolitan court. This model remained the groundwork for generations of pastoral novels, including Honoré d'Urfé's *Astrée* (1607–1628).

Even on the level of pure poetry, texts that we admire as distillations of the humanistic revival of ancient forms and themes might also, at the same time, respond to solicitations from chivalric customs of medieval origin. Poliziano's poetic masterpiece, the *Stanze per la giostra del Magnifico Giuliano*, was occasioned by the 1475 tournament in which the burghers' scion Giuliano de' Medici joined in a noble knightly sport to celebrate a diplomatic achievement by his illustrious brother Lorenzo.[19]

PAPAL CURIA AND COURTIER CLERICS

Aeneas Silvius Piccolomini's (1405–1464) *De curialium miseriis* did not proscribe courtly service for the man of piety, but warned him of the extraordinary difficulties of remaining pure among the soiled: "si potest ignem ingredi et non uri, non illum curiam sequi prohibeo; nam meritum tanto grandius assequetur, quanto periculosius militavit."[20] This warning found an echo in Castiglione's dialectical notion that true virtue needs testing and stands out clearly only in the midst of vice. Piccolomini had profited from a long, intense experience of court life in Italy and central Europe. As to the term he used in this letter, it is worth noting that the vernacular *curiali* for "courtiers" was also current in Quattrocento Italy.[21] In tune with the negatively polemical radicalism of the traditional subgenre, however, the pamphlet turned the ambiance of the court into a den of vices that stifled all moral and psychological freedoms, even denying the virtues of eloquence and learning that the idealistic tradition had regularly posited: "in princely courts it is a fault to know letters and dishonorable to be called eloquent," since "no good art and no love of virtue rule there, but only avarice, lust, cruelty, debauchery, envy, and ambition."[22]

The field is still wide open for research and, rather than in the Roman social world, I suspect we shall have to search for evidence of the continuity of *curialitas* in the antipapal documents of conciliary debates. Yet the genre of episcopal biographies, once thriving in medieval Germany, continued its productive life in the Renaissance, including such outstanding papal biographies as that of Nicolas V by Giannozzo Manetti (1459), Julius II and Leo X by Raffaele Maffei, Paul II (1474) by Gaspare da Verona (1400–1474), and those of several popes by Jacopo Zeno (1418–1481) and Platina (Bartolomeo Sacchi, 1421–1487).[23] The great Lorenzo Valla expounded his views on the role and nature of the Curia in his inaugural lecture at the University of Rome, the *Oratio in principio sui studii* (1455), where he proposed the Curia as the logical center of the renaissance of the Latin language and culture. Even earlier, in 1438 the Florentine humanist Lapo da Castiglionchio il Giovane (1405–1438) had written a short *Dialogus super excellentia et dignitate Curiae Romanae* where, in a somewhat ambiguous context, the Curia was discussed as a locus for humanistic undertakings.[24]

Given the ecclesiastical connections of the ideological framework we have been pursuing, it is pertinent to recall the relative frequency of personal association with the Church. With Piccolomini we are in the presence of a future pope. Many important historical characters in Castiglione's *Book of the Courtier* held (in 1507) or were about to hold important ecclesiastical positions. Bembo was ready to embark on a successful and fruitful ecclesiastical career which saw him secretary to Leo X and then, after 1539, cardinal. Federico Fregoso became bishop of Salerno and almost a cardinal, Bibbiena a cardinal, and Ludovico di Canossa bishop of Tricarico (1511) and then Bayeux. Michael de Silva, Castiglione's Portuguese dedicatee, was then bishop of Viseu and in 1541 a cardinal. Castiglione himself died as bishop of Avila, having been a cleric since 1521 and a candidate for a cardinal's hat since 1527, before publishing his book in 1528.

Dionisotti has estimated that in the first half of the sixteenth century about half of the high literati in Italy moved within the Church as priests, monks, bishops, cardinals, or holders of important ecclesiastical benefices. Even such an apparently unlikely candidate as Ariosto was not only, for a time, secretary to Cardinal Ippolito d'Este, he was himself a cleric and, for a while, hopeful of a bishopric from Leo X.

Rome was teeming with intellectual clerics who gravitated about the cardinals' *familiae* and the papal Curia,[25] but in secular republics, too, clerical positions were sought for social and political advancement by all sorts of intellectuals. In late Quattrocento Florence, among the leading humanists Angelo Poliziano held minor orders, Marsilio Ficino was a priest, and Pico della Mirandola an apostolic protonotary with minor orders. A prominent humanist who combined high-level philological activity with a full politico-curial career was Niccolò Perotti (1429–1480), archbishop of Siponto and governor of Viterbo, Spoleto, and Perugia.[26]

Against this background, the connection between Castiglione's oeuvre and a contemporary treatise by a leading humanist, Paolo Cortesi's (1465/1471–1510) *De cardinalatu*, is worth exploring, dealing as it does with the figure of the cardinal as an ideal courtier.[27] Dedicated to Julius II and published posthumously in 1510, it derived from the author's 1504 *Sententiarum libri*, in turn part of a projected but never accomplished treatise about the prince (*De principe*). Castiglione's dialogues are placed in 1507 but were ready in 1516 (first redaction), hence chronologically and ideally close to Cortesi's work as well as to the famous *Commentarii urbani* of Raffaele Volaterrano, a friend of Cortesi who had grown up in the same circle of the Roman Curia. The main point is that, to put it as does Dionisotti (68), "the cardinal is for

Cortesi more or less what the courtier is for Castiglione: an ideal figure of a man who stands close to the center of a real social sphere, the center, that is, of the ecclesiastical, curial society of the early Cinquecento." In Italy cardinals were, like Castiglione's courtiers and like chaplains and bishops around German imperial courts, at the point closest to the center of power. Cesare Borgia, for a striking example, had turned himself from a cardinal into a prince.

In the Renaissance, the Roman environment provided little incentive to keep alive the basically Ghibelline tradition of medieval *curialitas*; moreover, the humanistic climate made it more expedient to lean on the paradoxically less dangerous patterns and motifs of ancient Roman glory. Humanism rings in Cortesi's manner of referring to his cardinal as cardinal/senator, even though he conducted himself more as a cardinal/prince. Furthermore, it was more prudent to deal with style of life and speech than with moral substance and deep-seated merit. Images of once admired courtier bishops could not be safely invoked in an age of rampant absenteeism from pastoral duties. A couple of glaring examples will suffice. Although bishop of two English sees, the active humanist Cardinal Adriano Castellesi never visited England; while bishop of Aquino and Cavaillon, and despite the urgings of his close friend Jacopo Sadoleto, Mario Maffei, another humanist among high prelates, lived in Rome, Florence, and his hometown of Volterra.

Cortesi's encyclopedic work is also somewhat analogous to Castiglione's in the arrangement of subject matter. Book 1, entitled "liber ethicus et contemplativus," deals with personal character and moral qualifications, education, and cultural aptitudes; the second, the "liber economicus," deals with the management of the cardinal's princely court; and the third, "liber politicus," with the cardinal's function as an advisor to the pope, supreme prince of the church, and as a subordinate ruler at his nominal service. The elaborate listing of the virtues required of the cardinal is a conflation of Christian, classical, and courtly prerequisites, including *prudentia, memoria, providentia, intelligentia, ratiocinatio, docilitas, experientia, circumspectio, cautio, consilium,* and *judicium.*

In book 2 Cortesi prescribes in detail a magnificent life style for princes of the Church, precisely defining a standard in line with what had been the prerequisites of the high aristocracy and would become the mark of high social status under Louis XIV. The household of the cardinal, Cortesi says, must be ample and imposing, requiring support to the tune of 12,000 *aurei* or ducats per year on the average. For comparison, let us note Cortesi's specification that major officials should earn about fifty gold florins or ducats per year.[28] The College of Cardinals was expected to supply such funds and, should the College run short, the pope was to help. According to the census of 1526/1527 each court or *familia* of the twenty-one contemporary cardinals averaged 134 servants, administrators, and protégés (the papal *familia* then numbered seven hundred). Other incomes derived from other benefices, including bishoprics.

This and other tracts on Church government show a distinct similarity to secular political treatises. *Del governo della corte d'un signore in Roma* by the Florentine humanist Francesco Priscianese (1495–1549) described in detail the management of a Roman princely court of the secular kind with duties and functions corresponding to Cortesi's description of a cardinal's *familia*.[29] Cortesi himself held a court of sorts in his own house, in what is usually referred to as the Roman Academy (variously conducted by Pomponio Leto, Cortesi himself, Angelo Colocci, and Johannes Goritz, with rather dramatic vicissitudes).[30] Vincenzo Colli, known as il Calmeta (d. 1508), the famous proponent of the *lingua cortegiana* referred to by Castiglione, was a prominent member of Cortesi's Academy and left a valuable account of it in his biography of the poet Serafino Aquilano.[31] Calmeta makes intriguing comments on the courtly behavior of Cortesi's house circle, ascribing Ciceronian influences to a humanistic discussion centered on decorous public behavior as well as on the principle of decorum in literature and poetry, especially in vernacular works. As to Serafino's career, Calmeta places the court and its patronage system at the centre of that poet's work, despite the lack of appreciation on the part of Cardinal Ascanio Sforza, Serafino's lord.[32] It is an important sign of the realization that courtly environments had become vital for poetic and literary creativity.

Later in the Cinquecento, the literature on the formation, duties, and social status of the bishop gradually started to reflect the shift toward less worldliness and a greater sense of clerical responsibility which was dictated by the Counter-Reformation. Early treatises go from the important *De officio viri boni ac probi episcopi* (1516) by Gaspare Contarini (1484–1542) to Pier Francesco Zini's (ca. 1520—ca. 1575) *Boni pastoris exemplum ac specimen singulare* (1555).[33] These Venetian citizens forcefully advocated a type of high ecclesiastic who, consonant with the clergy's way of life in the Venetian republic, purposely eschewed the imitation of princely display of wealth and mundanity that characterized the Roman Curia. Contarini specifically excludes *magni-*

ficentia as a necessary or desirable attribute of a bishop's life (1571 ed., p. 407).[34] For one thing, the princely courts held by cardinals and bishops, as splendidly illustrated by Cortesi, were made anachronistic, at least on principle, by the Council of Trent's injunction to the high clerics to reside in the places of pastoral assignment. De facto, bishops and high prelates were affected much more by the new sense of austerity than were the cardinals, who continued to live and rule like ostentatious princes holding court. The new priests, foremost among them the Jesuits, were less like courtiers than were their predecessors. Yet the pendulum swung back when, in the course of the Italian wars, the secular courts lost much of their importance and autonomy, while the diplomats who felt superior to the princes started to gravitate toward the only effective court in Italy, the Roman Curia, thus consummating a process of "desecularization" that would have important and lasting consequences for Italian society. As we have seen, this was typically the destiny of several of the *Cortegiano*'s interlocutors.

CASTIGLIONE'S COURTIER

The reader looks to the *Cortegiano* (1508–1528) for signs of changing times, new standards, and renewed social attitudes. Burckhardt made us see the Renaissance as a cultural revolution, the civilizing effect of literature and the humanities bringing about social refinement and a new spiritual sophistication. The courtier was the new model for the future *honnête homme* and *gentleman*, replacing the feudal hero whose power and authority were more apt to be based on the accidents of birth and social position.[35] The Italian courts became the centers of a new "civilization of good manners" (N. Elias), whether this meant the foundation of a new secular leadership or, rather, as Francesco De Sanctis held, the sterile and artificial separation of a new élite from those popular layers of society that in the Middle Ages had been the source of productivity and cultural vitality.[36]

Castiglione's question, "what is a courtier?" was, after all, similar to the one affecting the ruling classes from the twelfth century on, namely: "what is a nobleman?" The similarity rested in the nobleman's inherent right to be close to the centers of power and to be at court, just as nobility could be granted as a reward for successful service at court. Castiglione did refer to "noble knights" (*nobili cavalieri*) as his specific audience.[37] Urbino was the right setting for a marriage of humanism and chivalry: Federigo da Montefeltro (1422–1482), a paragon of humanistic patronage on the largest scale, also sympathized with his northern contemporary the Duke of Burgundy in his appreciation of old chivalry, and had his court painter, the incomparable Piero della Francesca, portray him in full knight's armor at the feet of the Virgin and Child (the portrait, of around 1475, is now in the Brera Gallery). After all, that founder of public museums and public libraries, who had hundreds of scribes copying away precious ancient and medieval manuscripts at his court, endowed his library and museum with money he had amassed from serving as a condottiero, like his illustrious ancestors.

The thread that ties together the three main subjects of our inquiry—courtliness, chivalry, and courtesy—should by now be clear: just as knighthood and courtliness were intimately interrelated in the Middle Ages, so was the Renaissance courtier the direct descendant of the medieval knight. With regard to courtesy, our third ingredient, while discussing Wolfgang Mohr's (1961) description of the twelfth-century *courtois* lover/courtier as "servant of love," *Minnes Dienstmann*, E. Köhler (Mancini ed., p. 276) offered a sociological transcription of it which, *mutatis mutandis*, could still apply to Castiglione's courtier over three hundred years later:

> To be recognized as a powerful lord's *Dienstmann* already meant much for the knight: having once obtained this goal he must persevere in his service with loyalty, constance, and without hesitation. He must know how to be patient and to endure disillusionment. A great psychic, ethical, and spiritual effort was necessary to advance in the service of the lord. His effort aimed at the ultimate goal of becoming integrated into the rank of lords, but the aspirant took great care not to make his wishes too obvious.

We could say that the Renaissance *cortegiano*'s submissiveness placed him even closer to the *curialis* than to the knight, and even the "aestheticizing" of manners and conduct that makes *cortegiania*, in Burckhardtian terms, a work of art, had clear medieval precedents.[38] Furthermore, both *curialis* and chivalrous knight possessed a high degree of polite refinement (including affability in elegant conversation, musical training, respect for women, humility toward superiors, and dedication to helping the needy and the weak) which distinguished them from the heroic knight of the epic, and which continued to engage the theorist down to the *Cortegiano*. There may be some irony in the fact that a text which to a De Sanctis or a Burckhardt was a paragon of Renaissance secularism would in fact turn out to be so closely tied to long-standing ecclesiastical perspectives. Classical qualities that Castiglione derived directly from Cicero and Horace were also reflected in the medieval portrait of the *curialis*, that is, a combination of *decus, honestas,* and *mediocritas*: we find in Castiglione "certa onesta mediocrità" (1.41) and "certa mediocrità difficile e quasi composta di cose contrarie" (3.5).[39] The criterion of decorum would extend to what became known in the seventeenth century as *un homme comme il faut*, a term still current today. Conforming with the social standards of one's status, no matter how modish and irrational they might be, was a sign of respect for other members of the social group, a sign of deference and *vergogna*. One would avoid censure and ridicule by adopting set ways of dressing, gesturing, moving, and speaking.[40]

Some strikingly specific instructions remind us of the ethos of the knight errant. Federico Fregoso, in open disregard for contemporary reality, warns the courtier who is engaged in a military action to keep to himself, go to battle in the smallest company possible, and not mingle with the crowd of common soldiers (2.8)—in other words, to behave on the battlefield like a knight of King Arthur or a paladin of Boiardo or Ariosto, rather than in ways that were more likely to save his skin and render him useful.[41] This and other passages point to the concern with personal honor which, we shall see, would soon be defined as the mainspring of chivalric behavior, even above loyalty to prince and country: granted that arms hold first place in the hierarchy of courtly values, Federico Fregoso specifies that the courtier's motivation on the battlefield is principally his own honor: "dee esser solamente l'onore" (2.8).

While dealing with the imposing educational baggage the courtier has to carry, the dialogue enters some differences of opinion on primacy of arms or letters, although all interlocutors agree that the knowledge of letters is relevant. Curiously enough Ludovico di Canossa takes the French to task for "recognizing only nobility of arms with no esteem for anything else, so that they not only do not appreciate letters, but abhor them, holding all lettered men as most base, so that among them it is a great insult to call anyone a *cleric*."[42] Count Ludovico, who against Pietro Bembo was a firm partisan of the primacy of arms over letters (he had trenchantly decided that "questa disputazione . . . io la tengo per diffinita in favore dell'arme" 1.45), nevertheless blames the French for their uncivilized attitude and holds firmly that being lettered befits no one better than a man of arms ("tengo che a niun più si convenga l'essere litterato che ad un om di guerra" 1.46). We have seen how important early chroniclers and clerical advisors considered a liberal education to be for princes as well as for knights at court. It will suffice to recall Lambert of Ardres on Baldwin II of Guines and Philip of Harvengt's letters to Philip of Flanders and Henry the Liberal (chap. 3 above). It was also important in the romances: just let us think of Gottfried's delineation of Tristan's character and role. The old theme of the primacy of arms or letters spilled over into dozens of treatises of all kinds, and included the clerical argument on whether a cleric could be a better lover than a knight.[43]

Despite these medieval antecedents to the requirement of literacy in the clerics and courtiers, Castiglione's emphatic statement is clearly a reflection of Renaissance humanism: his courtier needs "more than an average degree of erudition . . . at least in these studies that we call humanities," meaning "familiarity with the poets, the orators, and the historians," music and the arts, Latin, Greek, and the vernacular, too. All this because "letters are the true and principal ornament of the soul," and not only for courtiers.[44]

If Castiglione's pages appear to reverberate with echoes of medieval portraits of courtiers, an earlier humanistic text will also ring a bell for its remarkable specificity, while it helps us to tie the literature of courtliness to that of chivalrous love: it is L. B. Alberti's *Ecatonfilea* (1428), with its portrait of the ideal lover:

> neither poor, uncleanly, dishonorable, nor cowardly . . . which will require prudence, modesty, patience, and virtue . . . ; studious of the good arts and letters. . . . Deft, physically strong, courageous, both bold and meek at the right time, poised, quiet, modest, given to wit and playfulness when and where it was fitting, he was eloquent, learned and liberal, loving, compassionate and respectful, cunning, practical-minded, and more loyal than anyone, excellent in courteousness, adept with the sword, horse riding, archery, and whatever similar sport, and expert in music, sculpture, and any other most noble and useful art, and second to no one in all such worthy activities.[45]

In his *Ragionamento d'amore* of 1545, Francesco Sansovino repeated these epithets of *astuto* and *pratico* in another lover's portrait: "of medium height, well to do, noble both by inner worth and by birth, versed in letters and music, . . . prudent, attractive, courageous, practical-minded and cunning, well-received and of loving disposition, affable, pleasing and sweet."[46] We can readily note the persistence of so many specific terms.

On the verbal level we must not be deceived by the partial absence of the traditional moral terminology, replaced by Castiglione's personal nomenclature. It is significant that the term "courtier" was rendered as *curialis* and *aulicus* ("man of the palace") in Bartholomew Clerke's Latin translation of the *Cortegiano* under the title *De curiali sive aulico* (London, 1571, 1577, 1585, 1593, 1603). The Latin terminology was both more precisely connotative and more enduring. If it is true that the crucial term *cortesia* is missing, it should be evident that Castiglione's three key terms *sprezzatura*, *grazia*, and *affettazione* are recognizable reinterpretations of measure (G. *mâze*), good bearing (like G. *zuht*), and the opposite of reticence as part of *mansuetudo*—this last quality encompassing the "naturalness" that is part of the game of noble deportment, associated with the kind of dissimulation that we found, for example, in Gottfried's young Tristan. Ever since Quintilian and through the medieval period, *urbanitas* included elegant and witty speech, hence also *facetia*—and here we immediately think of the famous section of *Cortegiano* 2.42–83 on witty speech. Nor should we forget the presence of clowns or minstrels at Castiglione's court: besides being the traditional carriers of literature (mainly oral), they contributed that ingredient of courtly gaiety that we have seen among curial qualities as *facetia* and among courtly/*courtois* ones as *joi* and *solaz*. The extensive treatment of wit and humor in speech (including *facezie*) is part of this.

Though a neologism, *sprezzatura* is obviously close to the modest pose shrewdly displayed by the young Tristan at King Mark's court, when he coyly underplayed his extraordinary talents. Castiglione explains it further with the synonymous *sprezzata disinvoltura*, a nonchalantly poised self-assurance designed to impress the observer with the feeling that "the man masters his art so thoroughly that he can obviously make no mistake in it," like the dancer who talks and laughs while he performs, seeming to pay no attention to his complicated movements (1.27). It is all part of the standards of external conduct, the *mores* (MHG *sîte*). The seeming disregard for behavioral technicalities, whereby we look like noble gentlemen rather than manual craftsmen or professionals, is not only an elegant attitude but the result of the fact that the courtier's instruction in the arts is, precisely, not professional, as Castiglione emphasizes early on.

Sprezzatura recalls the *Nicomachean Ethics*' rather ambiguous treatment of "irony" as the counterpart of boastfulness, somehow corresponding to Castiglione's opposition of *sprezzatura/affettazione*. For some critics the dissimulation that is inherent to both irony and *sprezzatura* is "a trick, . . . a discrepancy between being and seeming"; it seems to reveal "an attitude to class values that we must call aristocratic": in Aristotle "the magnanimous man will have recourse to irony

in his dealings with the generality of men, the masses." It also involves
a complex, difficult, and risky balancing act: if we are caught dissimulating, our game will be over—like courtiers, diplomats, or orators in
front of a jury.[47]

There are closer antecedents for this notion of an art that looks like
nature. In his treatise on the managing of the household (*De iciarchia*),
L. B. Alberti advised his readers to handle important things

> with much modesty joined with gracefulness and a certain gentlemanly air,
> so as to delight the observer. Such matters [requiring maximum concentra-
> tion] are horseback riding, dancing, walking in public, and so on. Above all
> we must moderate our gestures and our bearing, the movements of all our
> person with the greatest care and with such thoroughly controlled art, that
> nothing will seem to be done with calculated artifice; whoever sees you must
> feel that this excellence is an inborn, natural gift.[48]

Similarly Castiglione:

> Having long considered whence this grace may come, I find a most universal
> rule, to wit, . . . to eschew affectation as much as possible; and, to coin what
> may be a new term, to make use in everything of a certain *sprezzatura* that
> conceals art and makes whatever we do and say seem effortless and almost
> unconscious. I feel that grace derives above all from this: and this is because
> we all know the difficulty of things that are rare and well done, so that we
> tend to marvel at witnessing ease in such matters. Therefore we can say that
> true art is that which does not appear to be art; nor must we put our effort
> in anything more than in hiding it. . . . I remember having once read of ex-
> cellent orators of antiquity, who . . . pretended not to have any knowledge
> of letters; and while dissimulating their knowledge.[49]

This gift of concealed art, echoing Ovid's *Metamorphoses*, remained
a trait of noble behavior until at the court of Louis XIV Boileau defined
it as the peak of art, calling it *art caché* (translation of Longinus's Ch.
22). We know that the same milieu had become accustomed to the identification of reason and nature or naturalness. The, shall we say, deceiv-
ing function of such fashioning of character through the appropriate
use of *misura* and *mediocrità* lies in being not "like the others" but
better than they, but without offending them and, we could add, without causing reactive "envy": "he must strive to surpass all others in
everything at least a little, so that he will be known as the best."[50]

Alberti's antecedent to the supreme requirement of dignity, poise,
and ease that Castiglione summarizes in *sprezzatura* can also be recognized in what has been called the "poetics of ease" (*poetica della facilità*) with reference to the controversy over comparing Raphael's Olym-

pian style to the "difficulty" of Michelangelo's art. Alberti's *De pictura* (1435) had enjoined that the motions of the figures be "moderate and sweet, so that they will rather inspire grace to the onlooker than wonderment out of difficulty," and that virgins, young men, or adults should all be represented as moving with strong but sweet gracefulness ("una certa dolcezza").[51] The term and the concept were destined to enduring success. Merely six years after the appearance of the *Cortegiano*, Agostino Nifo da Sessa (ca. 1470—ca. 1540), the Aristotelian philosopher at Padua who was also known for his un-Platonic view that love is driven by sensitive appetite (*De pulchro et Amore*, 1531), published a treatise on courtliness (*De re aulica*, 1534, translated into Italian by Francesco Baldelli in 1560) where he advised spontaneity and naturalness but gave examples that sounded quite artful, so that, we can interpolate, he was teaching a Castiglionesque art that tried to look like nature.[52]

In sum, the ideal portrait encompasses the principal requirements of: nobility; military art (but only the basic principles, not the "mechanical" technical skills, and including the knightly art of horseback riding); knowledge of humanistic disciplines, including dance and music; and, as for mores, the *sprezzata* gracefulness of a second nature, in addition to that discretion that avoids or blunts envy and that sense of measure which avoids passing the mark. Since the Renaissance interpreted the traditional virtue of *sapientia* as essentially knowledge of literature, within the courtly frame of reference the traditional heroic symbiosis of *fortitudo* and *sapientia* became a binomium of arms and letters. (Of all Europe, Siglo de Oro Spain witnessed the most intensive and productive coupling of *armas y letras*.[53])

The theme of knight versus cleric, *miles an doctor*, a matter of practical as well as theoretical choice, was destined to remain alive, as witnessed, for example, in Girolamo Muzio's *Il gentiluomo* (1564) and Annibale Romei's *Della nobiltà* (1586). But Castiglione no longer separates the two poles: he smoothly merges them into his ideal courtier, a refined military man, statesman, and, if called for, a man of the Church too, the way the medieval bishop had to be statesman and armed ruler in one. Duke Ercole of Ferrara had to implore his son, Cardinal Ippolito d'Este, not to doff his spectacular suit of white armor in order to go off to war against Louis XII of France on the side of Ludovico il Moro.

His sources, Castiglione avers in the prefatory letter to Miguel de Silva, are Plato, Xenophon, and Cicero (meaning Cicero's *De oratore* for the idealized image of the orator, but also perhaps the *De officiis* for the moral portrait of the public man). To these models we must add Plutarch and Aristotle,[54] as evidenced by his numerous derivations from their texts. But we must not overlook relevant medieval ingredients, like the pre-humanistic medieval image of the pupil imitating the teacher: see Castiglione's statement that "whoever would be a good pupil must not only do things well, but must always make every effort to resemble and, if that is possible, to transform himself into his master."[55]

The courtier's functional requirements include the traditional cardinal virtues. Although princes often "abhor reason and justice" ("alcuni hanno in odio la ragione e la giustizia" 4.7), it is the courtier's role to make them practice them in spite of themselves, together with fortitude, prudence (*prudenza* and *discrezione*), and temperance (defined as harmony through reason).[56] In performing this difficult task, *grazia* must temper the severity of the philosopher and moralist, who would otherwise anger an impatient prince. The courtier thus becomes a subtle and dissimulating diplomat, indeed, the foundation of modern diplomacy.

Feeling that the closest specimens of the perfect courtier are his contemporaries, Castiglione protests against the nostalgic *laudatores temporis acti* who, as Dante and the court critics had traditionally done, use the courtly models to criticize contemporary moral decadence. The image of Castiglione as a nostalgic dreamer after good things irreparably lost is a rather Romantic way of reading him. Pride in the ripeness of the present is Castiglione's primary mover. Nevertheless, the courtier lives in a state of tension in the book as well as in the real life of those years of supreme uncertainty: while trying to save his neck, he must also strive to serve his prince in such a way as to achieve the good of the state and of his subjects. The *virtù di cortegiania* was conceived by Castiglione as a means to a moral political end.

While discussing Petrarca's position within the modes of literary transmission, I stressed the relative novelty of the early Italian poets' concern for a standardized language, pointing out the ideal connection between such concerns and the nature of life at court. Castiglione's position on the Questione della Lingua was in harmony with his perception of the nature and role of the courtier class, which was to be the most unified and responsible segment of Italian society. The active debate on the national language, destined to have a prolonged impact in many countries,[57] started precisely at Italian courts (Rome, Urbino, Mantua, and Milan).[58] It was not only natural and fitting, but supremely logical that in that setting the question of a standard means of communication would be seen from a vantage point of administration and official acts rather than literature and high culture, especially since courts were interregional and courtiers, moving about a lot, had to communicate in some lingua franca.

A common language was of paramount importance among people who daily could witness the tragic consequences of the lack of any other strong national bond. Calmeta, cited by Castiglione, and a denizen of all the courts just mentioned, was probably the originator of the theory of a *lingua cortegiana*, with a book called *Della volgar poesia* (ca. 1503, dedicated to the Duchess of Urbino) that is now lost.[59] Mario Equicola (1470–1525), another courtier and secretary to the Marquises of Mantua, proposed the usage of the Roman Curia, rejecting current spoken Tuscan as plebeian.[60] So did Gian Giorgio Trissino (*Il Castellano*, 1529), the major theorist of the "courtly language," while one more proponent of this thesis, Piero Valeriano, found current Tuscan wanting on account of excessive regionalism. Clearly, Castiglione had company, but Bembo's doctrine of Trecento Florentine prevailed, thanks to the prestige of the Three Crowns. Bembo had plenty of allies in all camps in his distaste for anything that smacked of popular parlance, which contributed to downgrading Dante and elevating Petrarca and the expurgated Boccaccio to the status of canonical models. The aesthetic criterion played a dominant role in rejecting from the literary lexicon any part of the language that was not "fitting and decorous"—another echo of established courtly behavioral patterns. Beyond language itself, the new classicism canonized decorum above all.

The issue of a common language was a central one in the life of the courts and it remained so in other countries, too. The emergence of French as the "universal language" of the civilized world from the end of the seventeenth to the beginning of the nineteenth century and beyond was a court phenomenon. Intellectuals, scientists, and diplomats read and wrote French (as well as Latin) all over Europe, but it was only the court societies, from Lisbon to St. Petersburg, that made wide and regular use of spoken French.

The special use of language at court was affected by the style, terminology, and moods of Petrarchist/Platonic love as a way of feeling, speaking, behaving, and living. On its highest level, that philosophy of love had become a form of mystical rapture, and indeed the *Cortegiano* ended in an emotional climax with Bembo's speech on Platonic love. It was a religion for an age of religious skepticism. The fact that Petrarca

fitted into this need for a Platonic idealism was another reason that
Laura became the universal model of the beloved. No room was left for
Dante's Beatrice, who was not only sublime and divine but lead directly
to God Himself. Platonic and courtly love found a major authority in
the learned courtier-philosopher Mario Equicola thanks to his successful treatise *Libro de natura de amore*, published in the vernacular in
1525 and 1526 (Venice) as a translation of the Latin original of 1495.
Equicola perceptively discriminated between the ancient way of loving
and writing about love and the Provençal way of, as he put it, "concealing through courteous dissimulation any lustfulness in their af-
fections."[61] Platonic love was the inspiration of another authoritative
Ficinian philosopher of those years, Leone Ebreo (*Dialoghi d'amore*,
Rome 1535).

Should we still wonder how Bembo's lengthy digression on Platonic
love squares with the main theme of the *Cortegiano*, another answer
might be that it fits as a conclusive moment of mystical exaltation filling
the role of *joi* in *fin'amor*, with which it has in common the striking
feature of unsatisfied longing for a superhuman reward: courtly love
itself functioned as an ideal form of training for service to the lord or
prince. Bembo's speech is thus at the intersection of courtliness and
courtesy, while courtly love was chivalry's poetic expression. Auerbach
(*Mimesis* 122) recalled Castiglione for his fusion of Platonism with the
courtly ideal but concluded that this Platonism was little more than "a
superficial varnish," whereas the true role of courtly culture, "with the
characteristic establishment of an illusory world of class (or half class,
half personal) tests and ordeals," remained "a highly autonomous and
essentially a medieval phenomenon." The preceding has shown somewhat closer connections between Renaissance developments and an operative medieval heritage. It bears recalling that Ficino had adapted medieval techniques, including the special intellectual devices that, as we
have seen, Petrarca inherited from the troubadours. Furthermore, his
sophisticated and somewhat sophistical mysticism of love was the instrument whereby he created at the Medici court his own inner court or
"academy" of intellectuals who expressely bound themselves to one another by this Platonic love. P. O. Kristeller has reminded us that Ficino
is the only thinker of modern times who tried to found a philosophical
school on both an intellectual and a moral bond between teacher and
pupils—this bond being his successful brand of "Platonic love."[62]

Ferroni and Quondam, among others, have stressed (perhaps overstressed) the "laceration" and the forced "suture" that occurs between book 4 and the other three books of the *Cortegiano*.[63] Other critics have speculated that Castiglione, having described a self-sufficient court that seemed elegantly aimless and useless (to the "subjects"), decided that his courtiers needed a redeeming social and political function, so he put their rare qualities and talents to the good use of impressing the prince and making him receptive to good advice.[64] But rather than being a possible afterthought, perhaps this "suture" reflects a real duality in western civilization. The gentleman—useless, as we shall see, for a Machiavelli—remained for a long time an object of attention, admiration, and emulation, a center of real power, hence a being with a social function, even when economically unproductive. This bipolarity lived on in literature as it lived on in society. The foregoing exposition should have made clear that this tension between "service" and personal dignity, being a lord's liegeman and at the same time one's own master, is not a unique problem for Castiglione, but the common predicament of the medieval and Renaissance knight and courtier.

We might also wonder whether this suture or inner tension was not analogous to the tensions we found in the medieval epics and in the chivalric romances, especially between, on the one hand, the image of an Arthurian court that was divorced from social and moral reality, and, on the other, the poets' (Chrétien, Hartmann, Gottfried, or Wolfram) need to find a useful moral purpose for wandering knights. Far from being conclusive and satisfied codifications of a self-sufficient imaginary world, those poems were live attempts to frame and resolve open socioethical problems through the fiction of beautiful tales. None of those authors, from Chrétien to Castiglione, felt they were closing a discourse by providing definitive answers. Hartmann, for one, was not even sure he wanted to go on lending allegiance to his chosen genre, as his about-face, later to be once again reversed, showed in the writing of *Gregorius*.

What some observers of Castiglione's *Courtier* have perceived as a contradiction between the real forces of court life and the need for moral satisfaction is in fact a noble effort to reconcile reality with moral imperatives. In Gottfried's *Tristan* and Wolfram's *Parzival* we noted a tense confluence of sublime aspirations to moral aesthetic perfection and a realistic perception of civilizing forces at work. Tristan was at the same time, in an uncanny combination, a hero of purity and an artist of survival. Somewhat similarly, the myth of Prometheus and Mercury in

Il Cortegiano 4.11 contains in a nutshell Castiglione's concepts of "viver moralmente," "sapienza civile," "virtù civile," and "vergogna": Jove symbolizes an aboriginal ruler, and Mercury an educator through eloquence and learning, this process involving progress from (individual) art to (collective) civilization.[65] Like Tristan, the courtier too has to face the divergence between full and free development of personal qualities and service to society.

In a passage that reminds us of King Mark's advice to Tristan in Gottfried's *Tristan* (8353–8366), Castiglione presents a dialectical view of the role of courtly vices in setting off courtly virtues:

> Evil being the contrary of the good and vice versa, it is almost necessary that by the law of opposition and compensation the one sustain and strengthen the other, so that if one decreases or increases, the other must increase or decrease, since every term is not without its opposite. Who does not know that there would be no justice in the world if there were no wrongs? No magnanimity, if none were pusillanimous? ... No truth if there were no falsehood? Hence Socrates well says, according to Plato, that he marveled that Aesop had not made up a fable in which he imagined that God, realizing the impossibility of combining pleasure and pain, had joined them by their extremities, so that the beginning of one was the end of the other. Indeed, we can see that no pleasure can ever be truly appreciated unless it is preceded by some displeasure. ... Therefore, virtues having been given to the world through grace and gift of nature, by immediate necessity vices became their companions, according to that law of chained contrasts. So, as soon as either one grows or abates, perforce the other must also grow or abate.[66]

In this remarkable piece of pre-Hegelian dialectic the existence of opposites is explained as a psychological and ontological necessity, an answer to the existential question mark that had troubled every moralist from Job through Augustine and on, about the justness of divine providence and the reason for the existence of evil. Castiglione even adds a theoretical insight that is tantamount to a doctrine of the balance of opposites—a doctrine which would continue to be popular among moralists and produce a lively debate in the late seventeenth- and eighteenth-century theory of *bonheur*, especially in France.[67]

Another feature the *Cortegiano* shares with chivalric literature is the element of play in the form of contests and formal games—not only in the first chapters, where various typical forms of entertainment are proposed before selecting the game of portraying the ideal courtier, but in the postulate that court life must be entertaining throughout, even in the conduct of serious business.[68] We have noted how in the romances, too, all contests, like tourneys and hunting parties, were perceived as exquisite games even when they had a serious and dangerous side, as they often did. The fourteenth-century *Sir Gawain* had carried this aspect of chivalry to extreme consequences.

Castiglione's reception is a signal case of evolution in the form of productive dislocation or even distortion: a work that was a continuous question mark, a problematic meditation on something dynamic, *in fieri*, to be discussed dialectically because it was still moving and partly undefined, an act of life and a fervent, partly nostalgic reminiscence, was happily misread into the static canonization of a supposedly perfect state, a universal model. Quondam (19) gives a concentrated description of this reception: the work assumed (my translation) "the proportions of an anthropological manifesto (a true cultural typology, a generative model), . . . which activated, above all, other grammars . . . , e.g., that vast body of treatises on dance, games, duel, hunting, horse riding, dressing, eating, being a secretary, etc."—all literature which was related to the life of the court, explicitly or implicitly.

In conclusion, the specificity of the *Cortegiano* vis-à-vis the more generic ethics of other treatises on conduct and princely education lies in a combination of military aptitudes, humanistic training (liberal arts), and behavioral patterns—all to be directed to the civic function of influencing the prince by winning his trust and favor. It is this combination of factors that finds its specific antecedents in curiality and courtesy, if we understand the latter as a combination of martial arts and moral purpose with a psychologically strategic method of pleasing refinement. Of course one must take into account the more secular setting of the courtier vis-à-vis the curial cleric (to take the other extreme of the medieval parable). But even here we must bear in mind the closeness of high ecclesiastical spheres to knightly milieus at the chronological beginning of our story—since the bishops were often temporal rulers and warriors as well—and then, at the other end of it, the closeness of Renaissance courtiers to high ecclesiastical milieus, as personally witnessed by the protagonists of the *Cortegiano* and its Roman counterpart, Cortesi's *De cardinalatu*.

The *Cortegiano* was the lofty expression of the humanistic intellectuals' effort to find their place in a changing society at the closest point to the peak of power. The ensuing "curialization" of the courtier was an implicit acknowledgment of defeat, since the ideal of a responsible lay counselor to the prince had hardly been attained. Ironically closing the circle from its medieval beginnings, the courtier was soon to become either a *curialis* or a *ministerialis* as a minister, secretary, or bureaucratic functionary to a prince.

MACHIAVELLI (1469–1527) AND THE COURT AS ARTIFICE

We have begun to see better the complexity and ambiguity of social allegiances in Renaissance Italy. I shall now turn to the telling case of Machiavelli in order to show that this so consistently Florentine observer of human behavior is no exception to the fact that even in the most bourgeois environments the aristocratic ideologies that had dominated medieval literature and thought continued to affect perspectives and judgments.

Castiglione's perception of moral values in the world of politics has often been contrasted with Machiavelli's. Patently, Machiavelli's "realism" clashes with his contemporary's idealizing will to form a "perfect courtier" who embodied all that was most admirable and morally respectable in a member of the governing élite. For Machiavelli, we all know, the ordinary moral virtues are more a hindrance than a help to effective political action. Although the well-endowed statesman is conscious of the need to *appear* virtuous, he is able and ready to depart from moral rules when it is expedient to do so, since he aims not at the good but at the useful. Castiglione was not prepared to see how the good and the useful could be separated. But more relevant for us is how, beyond personal attitudes, both writers mirror the reality of a shattering crisis, involving the agonizing realization that the fragmented individualism of Italian political behavior had been a high price to pay for the splendors of the Renaissance. When foreign armies supported by socially unified national states appeared on the scene, the impossibility of a common policy among the Italian states spelled general ruin. The spectacle of men in unstable governments scrambling for improvised means to save their skins and privileges in the wars of 1494–1559 revealed not only the weaknesses of social and political structures but also the decisive nature of the basic moral imperative: the fateful choice between "good" government in the interest of all subjects and expediency in preserving personal or group privileges.

Both Castiglione and Machiavelli had to face the alternative of justice or power, deep honesty or hypocritical preservation of form, virtue as moral value or "virtue" as, in Machiavelli's peculiar acceptation, efficient inner energy. Along with the traditional virtues of private morality, the "curial" ethic was now revealing more clearly than ever both its relevance and its profound ambiguity. The questions and the choices were: leading or seeming to lead, governing or oppressing and exploiting.

The "Florentine secretary" was particularly disinclined to appreciate the role of the social layer that made up the courts. As a true citizen of bourgeois and republican Florence, he did not hesitate to define the *gentiluomo* as one who lives abundantly off revenues without work, "senza fatica"; hence he is inherently outside that true "vivere in civilità" that Machiavelli identified with the free cities, and is particularly dangerous when he possesses castles and dominates working people who have to obey and serve (*Discorsi* 1.55).[69] That "vivere senza fatica" that irked Machiavelli as parasitism unwittingly echoes Castiglione's image of the gentleman whose most impressive behavioral feature is grace in concealing his artfulness, so that he seems to do whatever he does without effort and almost without thinking: "senza fatica e quasi senza pensarvi." Besides being a supreme mark of elegance, that easy manner was also a correlative of "living without effort" on the economic level. The very abstractness and unproductiveness of knightly games in the literature of the romances was a necessary sign of the knights' "nobility"—not quite without effort, to be sure, but without "use." Even in the epics there were as many tournaments and games as real battles.

To Machiavelli, military exercises were justifiable neither as elegant games nor as a form of superior service to God, but only as necessary means to political ends—a shift that even the Church was compelled to accept. Hence his little regard for the usefulness of the knightly class extended to the military sphere, where he held infantry more valuable than cavalry. Compare, besides his *Arte della guerra, Discorsi* 2.18, "come si debba stimare più la fanteria che i cavagli," where he blames the condottieri for a special interest in keeping armies of horsemen and, typically, appeals to the Roman model, where infantry had the major role. He cites the modern example of the battle of July 5, 1422 at Arbedo near Bellinzona, where Carmagnola, acting for Filippo Visconti, managed to prevail against the Swiss infantry only after dismounting all his horsemen.

Just as he distrusted courtiers, noblemen, and knights, Machiavelli appreciated the potential virtues of "the people" (*la moltitudine*, he says, indiscriminately) in terms as explicit as were ever heard before or long after. One of his most rewarding essays, *Discorsi* 1.58, is titled "La moltitudine è più savia e più costante che uno principe." There he takes a firm stand against public opinion, "contro alla commune opinione," including, mind you, the hallowed authority of *his* Livy, by protesting that the people are more prudent, more stable, and of better judgment than the prince: "dico che un popolo è più prudente, più stabile, e di migliore giudizio che un principe." They are also more reliable in their choice of elected public officials, usually worthier men than the choices of absolute rulers: "Vedesi ancora nelle sue elezioni ai magistrati fare di lunga migliore elezione che un principe." The people will never be persuaded to put in office a corrupt and infamous person, something princes do easily. In sum, popular governments are better than despotic ones: "sono migliori governi quegli de' popoli che quegli de' principi." If, as was the thesis of *Il Principe*, princes are better at organizing new states, popular governments are superior at maintaining a state once organized: "se i principi sono superiori a' popoli nello ordinare leggi, formare vite civili, ordinare statuti ed ordini nuovi, i popoli sono tanto superiori nel mantenere le cose ordinate." The superior wisdom of the *popolo* is reaffirmed in *Discorsi* 3.34. We have come a long way from the hateful distrust of the *vilain*: even if Machiavelli's close paradigm was bourgeois Florence, which did not include peasants as citizens, his universal model was republican Rome, with plebeians a majority among the voting population.

All this notwithstanding, it is particularly interesting in our context, and it may come somewhat as a surprise, that in a literal sense Machiavelli's ethical framework owed more to the courtly tradition than to the classical and Christian canons. Analyzing the virtues that are profitable to the prince in the ethical section of *Il Principe* (chaps. 15–24), he criticizes above all the notions of *liberalità* (all of chap. 16), *generosità*, and *lealtà*. The choice and sequence of qualities should have a familiar ring to us. When Machiavelli advises the prince to be a "gran simulatore e dissimulatore" (chap. 18), we are reminded once again of the familiar courtly environment, including the literary one of Tristan.

Machiavelli's review of the prince's moral traits begins with this listing (chap. 15):

> alcuno è tenuto liberale, alcuno misero . . . ; alcuno è tenuto donatore, alcuno rapace; alcuno crudele, alcuno pietoso; l'uno fedifrago, l'altro fedele; l'uno effeminato e pusillanime, l'altro feroce et animoso; l'uno umano, l'altro superbo; l'uno lascivo, l'altro casto; l'uno intero, l'altro astuto; l'uno duro, l'altro facile; l'uno grave, l'altro leggieri; l'uno relligioso, l'altro incredulo, e simili.

IX. THE CASTLE OF DINAN SURRENDERS; WILLIAM KNIGHTS HAROLD AND THEY RIDE TO BAYEUX, WHERE HAROLD SWEARS ALLEGIANCE TO THE DUKE.

1–2. William of Normandy knights Harold of England; The Battle of Hastings: details (sections 21 and 58, last) of the Bayeux tapestry (ca. 1073–1083). Courtesy of the Town of Bayeux.

XXVI. THE BATTLE OF HASTINGS. THE NORMAN CAVALRY CHARGE FORTH.

3. Ruins of Castle Aggstein on the Danube, Austria. A point of encounter for many troubadours. Courtesy of Austrian Tourist Office, New York.

4. Imperial Palace in Goslar, Germany. Courtesy of German Information Center, New York.

5. Castle Gutenfels on the Rhine. Courtesy of German Information Center, New York.

6. Elz Castle, near the Moselle River. Courtesy of German Information Center, New York.

7–8. Two views of ruins of Les Baux-de-Provence, a leading Provençal feudal court carved out of the rock in the thirteenth century, destroyed by order of Richelieu as a focal point of feudal resistance to the centralized monarchy. Courtesy of French Government Tourist Office, New York.

9. Giant Roland in front of Bremen City Hall. Erected in 1404 by the burghers in defiance of the archbishops' authority, using chivalric ideology as a symbol of communal freedom. Courtesy of German Information Center, New York.

10. Jan van Eyck (fl. 1422–1441), *The Last Judgment.*
Tempera and oil on canvas. The angel-judge appears in
the garb of a knight. Courtesy of the Metropolitan Museum of Art, New York, Fletcher Fund, 1933 [33.92b].

11. Pol de Limbourg, The Fall
of the Rebellious Angels as
knights in armor. *Les très riches
Heures du Duc de Berry,* Musée
Condé, Chantilly. Courtesy of
Musée Condé/Art Resource,
New York.

12–13. Two views of Carcassonne. Outstanding example of medieval military architecture and planning of a fortified town that coincided with the castle and an extended lordly court. Courtesy of French Government Tourist Office, New York.

14. Camera degli Sposi, frescoes by Mantegna, with Ludovico Gonzaga consulting his secretary Marsilio Andreasi (1465–1474). Ducal Palace, Mantua. Courtesy of Scala/Art Resource, New York.

15. Knights in the shield of the City of Frankfurt on the Römer, 1404. Courtesy of German Information Center, New York.

16. Corner of Urbino Palace, built under Federico da Montefeltro, ca. 1480? Note blending of medieval and Renaissance features. ANSA photo from Italian Cultural Institute, New York.

17. Carlo Crivelli, *St. George and the Dragon*. A saint in knightly garb, or a saintly knight: another example of the coupling of the religious and the profane. Courtesy of the Isabella Stewart Gardner Museum, Boston, and Art Resource, New York.

18. Castle of Heidelberg. Courtesy of German Information Center, New York.

19. Jacopo Vignola, Palazzo Farnese (1550–1559), Caprarola (Viterbo). Courtesy of ENIT, Italian Government Travel Office, New York.

20. Palazzo Farnese, Caprarola, Sala dei Fasti. Pius III and Charles V in battle against the Lutherans. Courtesy of ENIT, Italian Government Travel Office, New York.

21. Palazzo Farnese, Caprarola, Sala dei Fasti. Francis I welcoming in Paris the Emperor Charles V accompanied by Cardinal Alessandro Farnese (Taddeo Zuccari and helpers, 1562–1565). Courtesy of ENIT, Italian Government Travel Office, New York.

22. Lorenzo Bregno, St. George and the Dragon, from the facade of Buora's Dormitory, Isola di San Giorgio Maggiore (Venice). Courtesy of Giorgio Cini Foundation, Venice.

23. Villa Lante, Bagnaia (Viterbo). Courtesy of ENIT, Italian Government Travel Office, New York.

24. The Great Hall of the Hradshin Imperial Castle, Prague, engraving by Aegidius Sadeler, 1607. The court as a center of wide-ranging social and even commercial activities, including trading in art works. Courtesy of the Metropolitan Museum of Art, New York, Harris Brisbane Dick Fund, 1953 [53.601.10(1)].

Is this not a list of chivalrous qualities, positive and negative? It seems clear that Machiavelli did not have in mind some moral treatment of classical or Christian virtues but one of the kind that would be at home ina "mirror of princes" based on the chivalrous ethic.

Let us now take another look, reordering the pairs which Machiavelli inverts five times. He opposes liberality to miserliness, generosity to thievery, pity or mercy to cruelty, loyalty to treachery, manly spirited-ness (Fr. *franchise*) to duplicity (a courtly though not a *courtois* virtue), indulgence to hardness, dignity to plainness, and respect for religion to indulgence to hardness, dignity to plainness, and respect for religion to irreverence. The "great soul" that is made to loom large among the valuable strategic qualities (chap. 21) derives from both classical and medieval ethics, as we have observed, and Ferdinand the Catholic is declared to be its most striking example. The reference to greatness of character or soul that was implied in the *animoso* (contrasted to *pusil-lanime*) is fully developed in chapter 21, where *grandezza* (*grande imprese, rari esempli*) is commended as a way of winning fame (*egregius habeatur* in the Latin title rubric) and conquering the admiration of subjects and rivals. Once again, Machiavelli had the ancient Romans in mind, but the belligerent policies he regarded as a sign of vitality in the state and an almost biological law of politics had been a trademark of the chivalric ethic. Aristotle's *megalopsychia* was destined to play a con-tinuous role through the Middle Ages and humanistic education as well, including, in the new context of militant Christianity at the service of the Church, the Jesuit schools. The ideal of magnanimity would remain part and parcel of Jesuit pedagogy, since Ignatius of Loyola (himself a heroic professional soldier before his conversion) characterized the true Christian as a militant soldier of Christ, the new *miles Christi*.[70] Ma-chiavelli's heroic view of political leadership falls within this continuous tradition.

Indeed, at opposite poles, as it were, both the secular thinking of a Machiavelli and the planning of educational patterns for the Counter-Reformation disclose the presence of the combined ideologies of chiv-alry and courtliness. As an eloquent example of the latter I shall men-tion only the case of the most important college for the nobility in Italy, that of Parma. The Duke of Parma, Ranuccio I Farnese, took pains to ensure the functioning of the Ducal College for the Nobility (1601) as a bulwark of his policies of firm orthodoxy within a program of outspo-ken loyalty to the Roman Church and to Spain. It is interesting that in so doing he spelled out the guiding principles for his college in terms of the ideologies of chivalry and courtliness. Its pupils were to be instructed not only in piety and letters—which was also the explicit pro-gram of all Jesuit educational institutions—but also "in those other ex-ercises that are proper to the Nobility and necessary to Knights," namely dance (a healthy sport and a social grace), mathematics (for military engineering), fencing (for the use of arms in the service of God), and horseback riding.[71] The College was soon entrusted to the Jesuits (1604–1770).

The presence of the courtly ethic in Machiavelli's oeuvre extends be-yond the *Principe*. Besides the image of the virtuous prince using the art of "the fox" (like Caesar Borgia in *Il Principe*, chaps. 7 f.), the theme of *astuzia*, analogous to the familiar "cunning" of successful courtiers and such devious courtier/lovers as Tristan, conspicuously invests the whole plot and characterization of the *Mandragola*, a triumph of unscrupu-lous pursuit of personal ends.[72] In a properly political context, *Discorsi* 2.13 and 3.40 treat *fraude* (fraud) as advisable strategy rather than *forza* (force) in appropriate circumstances, especially at war, when one deals with an enemy ("parlo di quella fraude che si usa con quel nimico che non si fida di te," 3.40): again, the fox rather than the lion. *Discorsi* 3.30 confronts the problem of avoiding envy (*invidia*). Three chapters of the *Discorsi* (1.28–1.30) deal extensively with the question of loyalty and attendant gratitude that recalls the feudal tenets of mutual service and response to favors. In 1.29 the modern example is again Ferdinand of Aragon, who in 1507, suspicious of the acquired reputation and power of his victorious captain, Gonzalo Fernández de Córdoba (Con-salvo di Córdova), confined him to Spain instead of rewarding him for his Neapolitan victories against the French. Machiavelli presents the case in a feudal mode of reasoning, political actors being moved by personal considerations rather than by impersonal ones. The following chapter 30 addresses the question of ingratitude by analyzing what amounts to the change from feudal to absolute government (translated into our code, *ingratitudine* is lack of proper reward, or withholding of it without good reasons). The prince must prevent a subordinate from gaining glory for himself: he can do so by participating personally in the campaigns. A victorious captain, in turn, must no longer expect grateful reward (as his knightly predecessors did). He must either aban-don the army, to avoid suspicion of ambitious aims, or be bold enough to hold onto his conquests for himself. We have gone from feudal de-centralization and delegation of power to a radical individualism of pri-vate wills and interests, yet the new background is the Roman type of state, with impersonal relationships through law and office, instead of personal privileges and rights. The chivalric mentality, in other words, still appears in the background of Machiavelli's reasoning on moral issues, but it has been left behind for a new mental environment of calculated realism.

Machiavelli's tenacious republicanism in the face of his deep realization that the days of liberty were numbered stands out even more clearly when we note the readiness of leading citizens to cooperate with the Medici in institutionalizing absolutism. Typically, Ludovico Alamanni authored a cynical discourse of advice to the Medici ruler on how to corrupt republican leaders by turning them into subservient courtiers, so as to cut them off from any community of interests with the governed. It was precisely what Duke Cosimo I formalized by instituting the Order of Santo Stefano (on which more later). After the leaders have been attracted to the new court as servants of the new prince, and thus converted and bound to his destiny, Alamanni suggests that they will not only renounce the ideals of the republic, but will never again aspire to popular favor as champions of the subjects' common interest.[73]

The preceding has shown how, leaning on the virtues of a new courtesy, the ideals of chivalry found a fresh operating ground in both lay and ecclesiastical courts of the Italian Renaissance, while they remained part of the mental processes whereby even a republican-bourgeois observer like Machiavelli could frame his own analysis of the ways to achieve and maintain power.

CHAPTER TEN

Renaissance Transformations: II

EDUCATORS AT COURT

Partly because of historical conditions, partly by influence of the *Cortegiano*, treatises on the education of princes were frequently given a courtly setting. Prominent among these treatises in Castiglione's time was Erasmus of Rotterdam's *Institutio principis christiani* (1515), dedicated to the future Emperor Charles V. The prince, Erasmus says, carries in his person the image of the eternal prince: as the sun is God's image in heaven, so is the prince God's living image on earth, and all the ritual, iconographic, and formal paraphernalia of power are necessary expressions of this exalted status.[1] Thus Erasmus, appearing in the manual as the educator-philosopher, did not hesitate to invest the prince with the high role of a representative of God on earth by using the image-making metaphor of the sun—the traditional metaphor that Dante had recalled in the *Monarchia* but that Machiavelli had rejected as implying a symbolic/metaphysical superiority of monarchic over republican government. The concept would live on down to Louis XIV, the Sun-King. *Curialitas* was becoming adoration. Once advisors, collaborators, and administrators, the courtiers began to yield to a new role as ornaments of the god's palace.

Another successful writer, the master of *estilo culto* Antonio de Guevara (1480–1545), was a high courtier in Charles V's service in Spain. Having been brought up at court as a page under Isabel, he then turned

Franciscan friar, but Charles V recalled him to court as his official preacher and historiographer. He later became bishop. His most famous book is the *Libro áureo de Marco Aurelio* (The Golden Book of Marcus Aurelius, 1528), revised as *Relox de príncipes* (Dial of Princes, 1529), a seven-hundred-page manneristic repertory of preaching topoi written in a Euphuistic style *avant-la-lettre*, as Eduard Norden and then Morris W. Croll characterized it.[2] It was an instant best seller throughout Europe. In Italy both versions, *Libro aureo* and *Relox*, received two translations each.[3] In two later works, the *Aviso de privados ó despertador de cortesanos* (Warning for Favorites and Awakening-Bell for Courtiers, 1539)[4] and the *Menosprecio de corte y alabança de aldea* (Scorn of the Court and Praise of the Country, Valladolid, 1539), both published ten years after the *Relox*,[5] Guevara managed to reverse and subvert both classicism and Renaissance humanism in a vigorous revival of medieval anticourt criticism, set in a context that the Counter-Reformation would soon welcome and that was reminiscent of medieval *mesure* in its focusing on *aurea mediocritas* or *mensura*. These revisited anticourt sentiments were now expressed by turning the "mirror of princes" into a theater of the topsy-turvy world. The court implicitly appeared as a mirror of the world of Satan, Prince of Darkness, versus the good prince as Prince of Light (the light of the Sun as in Erasmus). A new asceticism and mysticism were aiding political absolutism. Guevara's *Menosprecio*, whose main sources were John of Salisbury's *Policraticus*, A. S. Piccolomini's *De curialium miseriis*, and Petrarca's *De vita solitaria*, used the world of the pastoral to praise life in the country as a corrective for the mad and ungodly corruption of the courts, urging courtiers to abandon both court and city for the virtuous countryside. Of course, that countryside was populated not by real peasants but by gentlemen turned shepherds who conducted themselves by none other than that genuine courtly code which the court was taken to task for having betrayed.[6] The shift of locus had not displaced the code. Such pastoral references to court motifs, which fill Renaissance and baroque literature, brought back Virgil's way of donning the Arcadian veil to clothe political allegories and even personal economic allusions (like his complaints to Augustus on his loss of the family farmland).

A history of the social implications of the pastoral and Arcadian myth (the topos of the Golden Age) remains to be written.[7] It would demand an assessment of anthropological, religious, and historiographic functions, not only by surveying the myth in its literary uses, but by explaining, for example, why so many authors associated with court life treated the myth in a spirit of wishful, utopian withdrawal from the realities of the court. At times it was used as an act of escape or refusal, at others as a reform from within. Although it was basically outside the medieval *pastorela*, the myth was ubiquitous even before the birth of the pastoral as a classical genre. Brunetto Latini, for one, had expressed his bourgeois communal background by rejecting the myth's implication that primitive man was virtuous and happy: only rationality, culture, and the city provide human conditions for what is, without them, only a beast.[8] Dante may have been impressed by Latini's argument, which recurred often in the democratic environment of the communes, as it did in Fazio degli Uberti (*Dittamondo*: 1.12:52–91) and then again in the Florence of Cosimo de' Medici, in the famous "realistic" painting of Piero di Cosimo studied by Panofsky.[9] In that environment the pastoral happiness of a perfect idleness was consciously opposed by a firm notion that social values are the result of human industry, "work," including the work of agriculture versus the *otium* of shepherds. For noblemen, instead, including the courtly milieus as well as the high merchants on their way to a seigniorial state, like the Medici, the Golden Age of human happiness coincided with the idyllic life of pastoral *otium* (e.g., Lorenzo il Magnifico's *Selve d'Amore*: 2.84–2.112).[10]

An Italian counterpart of Guevara was, in his odd way, Pietro Aretino (1492–1556), an intellectual who created his literary market by selling fame while buying ephemeral influence and earthly success. His *Ragionamento delle corti* (1538) was a radical anti-*Cortegiano* where the court was picturesquely styled "a hospital of hope, burial of life, . . . market of lies, . . . school of fraud, . . . paradise of vices and hell of virtues, . . . more wretched than the most horrid and bestial cave or tomb."[11] The court he knew best was that of Rome, although he was writing from the safety of Venice.

Saba (or Sabba) da Castiglione's *Ricordi* (Bologna 1546; expanded edition Venice 1554; published twenty-six times before the end of the century) drew on Guevara, though in a more manageable and orderly mood. A monsignor and knight of Malta, Saba introduced Tridentine dogmas and catechist prescriptions into the education of the prince, with the addition of the prescribed behavioral qualities of "maestà, gravità, modestia, maturità e decoro."[12] He carried forward Guevara's court criticism by denouncing contemporary courts as dens of vices and degeneracy (37v). In the chapter of his *Ricordi* that dealt with "La cortegiania dei nostri tempi," he reversed all the traditional virtues of the courtiers, now all degenerate, into their opposites, since they are all "vili, ignoranti, adulatori, assentatori, parasiti, lenoni, per non dire ruffiani, malcreati, buggiardi."[13] Yet, once again it is important to be aware of a new twist to this way of handling court criticism. Whereas medieval court critics operated outside the courts and looked to an alternative way of life—the life of the monastic orders and a reformed Church— such critics as Guevara and Saba could not easily get out of their milieu, since the court was their real world. What they proposed was little more than a disguised or reformed court. Saba also recouped Castiglione through the notion of "giusto mezzo" between "affettazione" and "naturalità"—a new dressing for *sprezzatura*. In Saba's readily apparent, conformist Christianization of the genre the courtier, the prince and the knight (*cavaliere*) have become thoroughly clericalized.[14] The key virtues of the gentleman courtier were to be *modestia, magnanimità*, and *umiltà*.

Some didactic treatises had begun even earlier to assimilate courtly values to the ideals of the Counter-Reformation. The pious anonymous author of the *Novo corteggiano de vita cauta e morale* (probably issued in Venice by an unknown publisher in 1530 or 1535) attempted to educate an aristocratic ruling class according to principles of *aurea mediocritas* that were inspired more by ideals of retreat from the dangers of the world than by a positive appreciation of court life.[15] The author's praise of the agreeable solitude of country living, "amene solitudini," sounds like the later pastoral appeal to the theme of country versus city/ court in Guevara's *Menosprecio*. Similarly, the Genoese Pellegro Grimaldi Robbio wrote a successful book of *Discorsi ne' quali si ragiona di quanto far debbono i gentilhuomini ne' servigi de' lor signori per acquistarsi la gratia loro* (1543), where the echoes from Castiglione are as evident as the attempt to clericalize him by shifting the main reference point to the Roman Curia.[16] In these borrowings from Castiglione we note the generalization of both the approach and the subject matter, now covering the broad educated classes of "gentlemen." In his way, Stefano Guazzo would continue this trend in his *La civil conversatione* (1574). It is a literature that expresses a malaise growing out of acute disillusionment with life at court.

The growing disenchantment with the moral life of the leading classes, from the high clergy to the new princes and courtiers, brought about a semantic drift. As the terms *cortegiano, homme de cour*, and *courtier* gave way to their synonyms *galantuomo, honnête homme*, and *gentleman*, in Italy *cortegiano* acquired a negative connotation. Castiglione had avoided the feminine of *cortegiano*, using instead *donna di palazzo*, because *cortegiana* already had the negative connotation of English courtesan and French *courtisane*.[17] The more derogatory views come forth in the literary genres of satire and *lirica giocosa* à la Berni, where, however, the prevailing cynicism must be partly discounted as a generic prerequisite in this attempt to exploit social observation for purposes of facile comedy. Here as elsewhere the most common reproach was of avariciousness and illiberality; this revived the medieval motif of liberality as a trademark of true *courtoisie*, which the new bourgeois ethic had not managed to sweep away. Typically, a Matteo Bandello mirrored the new skepticism in a demystifying perception of ladies who no longer rewarded virtue in their admirers, but only wealth.[18]

THE COURTESY BOOK

Self-fashioning after a chivalric image is analogous to the acquisition of manners, insofar as both impose a personality and a behavior from the outside through social pressures and education. These two civilizing forces—that is, chivalry and manners—must be ranged side by side because the chivalrous habit included an imposition of social manners in both feeling and gesture. A subgenre of the treatise of manners is the manual of etiquette, especially table manners, which enjoyed great popularity in the sixteenth century. It grew out of earlier educational treatises that often contained sections on such matters, and it signaled changes in the consciousness of civilized behavior.[19]

Although specific precepts started to be voiced as early as the twelfth century as the expression of collective awareness rather than a result of original speculation, the first broad compilation of such rules was Erasmus's enormously successful *De civilitate morum puerilium* of 1530. Immediately translated into several languages, it was reprinted in its original form thirty times within the remaining six years of the author's life and 130 times through the eighteenth century. Its seven chapters dealt successively with bodily cleanliness, care of the body, manners at church, at the table, in public gatherings, at games, and in the bedchamber. Its direct impact was felt in the popular *Colloquiorum scholasticorum libri quatuor* by the Calvinist Mathurin Cordier (1564; 1568).[20] Both Erasmus and Cordier had a close antecedent in Johannes Sulpicius's *De moribus in mensa servandis*.

The Erasmian title provided the common term for approved behavioral attitudes in many languages, such as French *civilité* and English *civility*, later extending into the more general and abstract French and English *civilisation*, Italian *civiltà*. Protestant educational manuals, like Cordier's *Colloquia*, contributed to the wide diffusion of the new terms, which for a time were practically interchangeable with "courtesy," *courtoisie*, and *Hübescheit*. This last term had appeared perhaps for the first time, in the form *hüfscheit*, in the German title (*buoch von der hüfscheit*) that Thomasin von Zerclaere reported in his *Wälscher Gast* (ca. 1210) for his now lost Italian treatise on the subject. It was akin to German *Hofzucht* (courtly manners), title of a book attributed to the courtly poet Tannhäuser (ca. 1200—ca. 1270).[21] A similar early treatise was Bonvesin da la Riva's *De curialitatibus*, where the "curiality" of the Latin title was equivalent to *cortesia* in the body of the Italian text. German *hübsche Leute* (the fine people) meant the court nobles, just as *Höflichkeit* (courtliness) was their ethical code, allied to the etymologically and semantically related *Höfischkeit*, still current for "courtesy." Gradually, French *civil* and *civilité*, alongside *poli, politesse*, and the even more popular *honnête* and *honnêteté* (which in France also acquired the connotations of Italian *cortegiano*, like the nominal French *gentilhomme* and English "gentleman," more explicitly denoting nobility), displaced *courtois* and *courtoisie*. In other words, "civility" replaced courtesy as the name for politeness, as pointedly noted by Dominique Bouhours in 1675.[22] The two terms *courtoisie* and *civilité* were still used interchangeably in Jean du Peyrat's translation of Della Casa's *Galateo* in about 1562, where the term *gentilhomme*, too, appeared in the very title: *Galatée ou la maniere et fasson comme le gentilhomme se doit gouverner en toute compagnie*.[23]

Castiglione died a bishop. Giovanni Della Casa (Mugello 1503—Rome 1556), another leading writer of treatises on social manners, was archbishop of Benevento for the last dozen years of his life. He had been first clerk to the Apostolic Chamber since 1538 and then archbishop of Benevento and papal nunzio to Venice in 1544. Made secretary of state to the Vatican in 1555 by Paul IV, he hoped for a cardinal's hat in the last year of his life. His *Galateo*, published posthumously in 1558, is one of the most important exemplars of the subgenre of etiquette or courtesy books, and is also of particular interest for its references to high clerical spheres. The title came from the Latinized name of Galeazzo Florimonte, bishop of Aquino first and then of Sessa Aurunca, who appears in the story as a paragon of courtliness.

Della Casa was a steady student of Cicero, whose *De officiis*, that crucial text for the tradition of curiality, he adapted in part of his *De officiis inter tenuiores et potentiores amicos*, a treatment of friendship between the powerful and their dependents, hence close to the principal concerns of court life. It was published in a vernacular version as *Trattato degli uffici comuni fra gli amici superiori e inferiori* by Giovanni Antonio degli Antonj (Milan, 1559).[24] The Aristotelian/Ciceronian/Horatian notion of virtue as *medietas* or *mediocritas*, middle point between extremes, which we encountered as a key ingredient of medieval courtesy under the rubrics of Latin *moderamen*, French *mesure*, and German *mâze*, returns as the supreme ideal in the *Trattato*. One achieves this *certo mezzo o certa misura* (middle point or measure), which is *convenevole*, "decorous," when one manages to please and captivate the powerful. Chapter 7 gives an interesting aperçu on the role of the addressee with clear understanding of the communicative relationship between speaker and audience: "conoscere chi noi siamo e con cui parliamo" is proposed as the key to *amicizia* or (with a Greek term) *filía*.

The text of the *Galateo*, too, shows the proximity of Cicero's *De officiis*, particularly for the constant presence of the paradigm of measure. See, for example, the eloquent passage in the second part of chapter 13: "even the good, when excessive, displeases. . . . Those who make themselves humble beyond any sense of measure and refuse the honors they deserve, display in this more pride than those who arrogate to themselves what is not due to them."[25] Chapter 20 derives "good manners" from *misura*, a happy medium which consists of avoiding both the excess of deferring to our interlocutor (this is *giocolare e buffone*, demeaning buffoonery and downright flattery) and the opposite excess of being unconcerned with the effect we make on others (this is for the *zotico e scostumato e disavvenente*). The string of three insistent terms: *bellezza, misura*, and *convenevolezza* (beginning of chap. 26) appears to echo the Ciceronian as well as the courtly appeal to moral beauty, measure, and honesty in the sense of mores that are becoming to our social status and function. Later on (start of chap. 28) we find an echo of Castiglione's emphasis on *grazia*: "Gracefulness is nothing other than a certain light that shines forth through the fittingness of things that are discreetly and harmoniously composed all together: without this degree of measure even the good is not beautiful, nor is beauty truly pleasing."[26] Next, manners are compared with food: gracefulness and a sweet lightness of touch are to manners what flavor is to food, which will not be pleasing just by being wholesome and nourishing.

The work characteristically concentrates on manners and mores, as indicated in the very title *Galateo ovvero dei costumi*, and this narrower focus reminds us of the *schoene sîte* or *zuht* of the German traditional nomenclature. Notice the emphasis in chapter 1:

> I shall begin with . . . what is pertinent to the purpose of being well mannered and pleasing: which nevertheless is either a form of virtue or very similar to virtue. . . . Good manners are no less important than greatness of soul and mastery of the self, since they need to be exercised many times in the course of every day, . . . whereas justice, fortitude, and the other nobler, major virtues are put into practice more seldom.[27]

He repeats later on that he has been treating not virtues and vices intrinsically but "fitting or unbecoming ways of dealing with each other."[28] Likewise, he had gone over the matter of making dress and speech appropriate to social status and local custom for the sake of not displeasing our audiences unnecessarily in matters of no moral substance. Here again we could think of Cicero's treatment of *honestas* as the virtue of fitting behavior to occasion and circumstance.

The elegant little treatise insists on a pattern of civic behavior that will ensure respect toward others' interests and rights, sensitivity to others' wishes and well-being, and, in one word, the beauty and sacredness of individual "liberty." See the prolonged critique of false display of respect, which offends the recipient as insincere and inappropriate if not downright adulatory with ulterior motives. The author designates this insincere adulation with a relative neologism, *cerimonie*, implicitly attributing it to foreign influences (read: Spanish; it has not taken deep roots in Italy, he says). Such obnoxious "standing on ceremony" hinders that freedom which we all desire more than anything else, and derives from an annoying overemphasis on nobility as mere social status. It is an excess of formality that either covers up for moral vacuity or conceals a base character.[29] Della Casa advises against using social status as a basis for judgment of personal character.

Della Casa's overarching concern is with being "pleasant," but this pleasantness is not based on conformism and indifference to underlying moral issues: it is a necessary aspect of a way of life that takes into account the need to communicate and interact with others, in full respect for their feelings and interests. In other words, it is the outer veneer of that urbanity that we have seen attributed to the city dweller, the *asteîos anér*, both in ancient Greece and Rome and in the medieval centers of curiality. This form of urbanity was particularly at home in the Italian communes, as part of a city-bound society: "nella città e tra gli uomini."[30] From the very beginning of his dialogue, Della Casa explicitly stresses the distinction between morality and sociality, the heroic ethic of pure virtue, which comes into play only seldom, and the compromise with others that makes the worldly city human and operative. The *moraliteit* that Tristan was teaching the young Isolt, and that Gottfried of Strassburg extolled as the most profound message of courtly education, was, we can extrapolate, closer to this sociality than to a pure, abstract, and heroic morality. For Della Casa this concrete virtue of "comune conversazione" is part of social intercourse: it is not at home in the solitude of hermitages ("non per le solitudini o ne' romitori").[31]

THE HUMANISTS' ETHICAL VIEW
OF MAN AS CITIZEN

Della Casa's theme of "conversation" implemented humanism's commitment to civic-minded allegiance to the community, excluding the recluse, the misanthrope, and the hermit. This bias invested much of the philosophical moral literature of the Italian Quattro- and Cinquecento, from Leonardo Bruni to Lorenzo Valla and on to, say, the Sienese Alessandro Piccolomini, a reader in philosophy at the University of Padua. In two versions of a lifetime work running from 1543 to 1582, Piccolomini spoke of the "animale civile e comunicativo" that thrives in the society of the city, whereas the hermit ceases to be truly human. Social living requires manners (*costumi*) that are developed by education through literature and poetry, history and eloquence, the natural sciences being only instrumental.[32] Similarly, another Piccolomini, Francesco (1520–1604), stressed the *scienza civile* over and against the heroic virtue worthy only of heroes.[33] It was all part of that humanistic concern with the *viver civile* which runs through both Castiglione and Della Casa, continuing some specific themes of the medieval curial tradition and applying them to social conduct in new environments.[34]

Other ethical treatises embodying mature humanistic views were due to Sperone Speroni, Pietro Pomponazzi, Agostino Nifo, Giambattista Gelli, and Paolo Paruta.[35] In his *Capricci del bottaio* and *Circe* (1541–1548) the spirited Florentine shoemaker/philosopher/littérateur Gelli (1498–1563) dramatized the motif of man's freedom to choose between rising to the nobility of angels or stooping to the materiality of brutes—a motif that had been made famous by Pico della Mirandola's *Oratio de hominis dignitate* (1486).[36] Speroni was radical in his defense of the active life (in the second part of his *Dialoghi*, Venetia 1552, new ed. Venezia 1596: 180–215). Marc-Antoine Muret's Roman oration *De moralis philosophiae laudibus* (1563) extolled ethics above the natural sciences and the contemplative life, as the philosophy of the active man in the full blossoming of the civic community. In his *Della perfezione della vita politica* (1579) Paruta proclaimed that a goal of philosophy was preparation for the active life, incomparably superior to the works of the solitary man who lives only for himself. On a more professional philosophical level, a host of commentaries on Aristotle's *Nicomachean Ethics* carried on the message of the superiority of praxis to pure contemplation, as part of civic humanism's stress on the citizen's duty toward the social group: we are human only by being an active part of society. Referring to the works of Bernardo Segni, Agostino Nifo, Crisostomo Javelli Canapicio, Felice Figliucci, A. Scaino, Antonio Brucioli, Pietro Pomponazzi, Simone Porzio, and Torquato Tasso (*Dialoghi*), one of the most authoritative students of this literature, Eugenio Garin (1965: 204), found it to be generally lacking in originality and ultimately sterile, even while it perpetuated an important message of Quattrocento humanism. Yet, for all its relative platitude, what interests us in this once successful production is the continuous vitality of specific motifs of chivalric and courtly virtues, which, rather than being overtly brought forth in treatises with a specific chivalric/courtly theme, were generalized, disguised, and eventually assimilated to classical virtues.

COURT AND WORLD AS ACTOR'S STAGE

The motif of sociality as the truest form of morality that is shared by much of Cinquecento ethical speculation becomes a true leitmotif in Stefano Guazzo's (Casale Monferrato 1530–1593) *La civil conversatione*, where it insistently recurs even ad nauseam.[37] This treatise is remarkable for its impact abroad, which in distant England was almost equal to that of Castiglione. It is significant that Guazzo's rather modest book enjoyed greater influence abroad than the more substantial treatises by Speroni, Piccolomini (Alessandro), Pomponazzi, Nifo, Gelli, and Paruta, which it rather unimaginatively summarized. This was because it explicitly put the accent on those criteria of social conduct that observers of Italian life wanted to hear about.

   A Piedmontese courtier, ambassador, and writer, Guazzo came from a noble and wealthy family of courtiers to the marquises of Monferrato and the dukes of Mantua. He continued in his forefathers' footsteps by serving the same lords as secretary and courtier at different times, following Ludovico Gonzaga of Mantua to France for seven years when the latter became duke of Nevers, then serving as ambassador to Charles IX of France and, in 1566, to Pope Pius IV. Enjoying no fewer than thirty-four Italian editions (twenty-five of them between 1574–1603, but none after 1631), his major work was soon translated into French (ten versions), Latin (fourteen versions), Dutch (two versions), Spanish, and German; of the six English versions (last, London, 1788), most influential was the one by George Pettie (1581, first three books), continued by Bartholomew Young for book 4 and published in complete form in 1586.[38]

Guazzo's title made "conversation" a term for social behavior throughout Europe. It echoed Della Casa's "comune conversazione," but its twofold acceptation of "pleasant, civilized social intercourse" and "using language as a civilized and civilizing means" was already established, as shown in the "cosmological" thesaurus *La fabrica del mondo* (1546–1548) of Francesco Alunno (1485–1556). The notion of "civil conversation" and the association of the city with courtesy, urbanity, and civility was manifest in Alunno's definition of *urbanità*: "*urbanità, la civilità*"; "*urbanità*: Lat. *urbanitas, facetiae, dicteria, ioci, sales, lepores, cavillatio, dicacitas, argutiae, delitiae*; è gratiosa conversatione di cittadini."[39] It was a list of rhetorical figures covering all forms of wit. Alunno defined *conversare* as "conversare per praticare insieme,"[40] and *cortesia* as "beneficence, gift, humane and gracious liberality, with a becoming habit of moderation; so denominated from the courts of good princes where such virtues always shine."[41]

Although conversation for Guazzo meant social intercourse, his dwelling on verbal civility contributed to the spreading of "conversation"'s more modern acceptation.[42] The lexical choice is an important echo of the humanistic emphasis on language as the foundation and carrier of civilization—"language as the basis of social intercourse," as Burckhardt recalled with reference to the large section dedicated to linguistic matters and the effective use of language in Castiglione's book 2.[43] Humanists conceived of speech as the essence of humanity, and language as action in dialogue, hence truly "the art of conversation." "He who wishes to engage successfully in civil conversation," says Guazzo, "must consider that language is the mirror and portrait of his soul; and that, much as we can tell a coin by its sound, so from the sound of our words we see deeply inside a man's character and his behavior."[44]

After Castiglione, his earnest concern for the moral substance of the man of court came to take second place to the art of speaking charmingly and effectively in public. The art of the courtier became a sort of court rhetoric and elegant conversation. Guazzo well represented this narrowing of the horizon according to a widespread trend that was perhaps more pronounced in Spain than elsewhere, as clearly shown by Luis Milán's Spanish translation of *Il Cortegiano* in *El libro entitulado el Cortesano* (1561), dedicated to Philip II. Milán's hero must speak well but mostly, it seems, about pleasant, witty, and harmless things: he must be a good *motejador*. Although this emphasis on orality was to be further developed in France, the Spain of Philip II provided a new breeding ground for the medieval virtue of reticence: besides knowing how to speak well, the new hero, *el cortesano*, that is "el caballero armado virtuoso, la mejor criatura de la tierra," has to know when it is more appropriate to keep silent: "bien hablar y callar donde es menester."[45] We sense here a new twist away from Castiglione's individualistic and comparatively independent agent toward a mere servant at court, prudent master of diplomacy and self-effacement. This twist was already apparent in Pellegro Grimaldi, who in his *Discorsi* (1543) did not want to discuss the virtues of a complete courtier but only the art of survival, to be summed up in the advice "to keep your mouth shut, as the saying goes," "tenete (come si dice) la bocca chiusa," after doing all that pleases the prince—and no more.[46] One of the more than one hundred proverbial sentences that stud Guazzo's *Civil conversatione* has the same ring: "il tacere a tempo è più lodato che il ben parlare," "keeping mum at the right moment wins more praise than eloquence." Guazzo also differs from Castiglione by focusing on real conditions and practical applications. Furthermore, he extends the area of Erasmian "civility" and deemphasizes the service to the prince and the imperative of pleasing the prince with a willful search for a broader social grace that will satisfy the inner man, too.

The dialogue sets Annibale Magnocavalli, a doctor, against the author's brother Guglielmo, who, disappointed by the futility of courtly life, is thinking of retirement from the world. Appearing as Guazzo's spokesman, Annibale argues for a good life in service of society but away from politics and the court. One senses here a disenchanted echo of Guazzo's difficult relationship with the rulers of Monferrato and their ruthlessly absolutist disregard for the statutory freedoms of the recent feudal past. His patron Ludovico Gonzaga was distrusted by Duke Guglielmo of Mantua, whose cousin Vespasiano Gonzaga Marquis of Sabbioneta, his *longa manus* and strongarm man in Casale, at one point even ordered all followers of Duke Ludovico of Nevers out of town.[47]

Guazzo basically follows Castiglione in the ordering of topics, even down to the digressive theme of love, although in formal presentation he echoes the *Cortegiano* only in book 4, which enacts an actual conversation in the course of a banquet, whereas the preceding three books are more like a treatise.[48] Nevertheless, he makes a brave attempt at originality in departing from the established generic patterns. The result is an idiosyncratic nomenclature that strikes the reader as plainer and more down-to-earth than Castiglione's, especially since the discussion divides the topic into public and domestic behavior, including relationships between spouses (as in treatises on the management of the household), and presents a set of virtues and vices that does not remind us specifically of the received schemes. Guazzo's love is a civilizing force whereby a man "waxes more wise"; an honest love makes us capable of finer things; it inflames us with virtuous thoughts and even "stirs up to Poetry" (book 2, vol. 1: 238 of Pettie's 1581 translation). *Sprezzatura* has become *negligenza o sprezzamento*, based on avoidance of *affettazione* (p. 161 ed. Venice: Robino, 1575) and on hiding that *arte* which is the cultural basis of the elect behavior: "faccia il tutto con arte, ma in maniera che l'arte sia nascosta e paia il tutto a caso" (ibid.: p. 20).[49]

The city, larger setting of the court, is regarded as the seat of civilization and virtuous living, "albergo di virtù," although it can also be "albergo de' vizi" (book 1). Hence the sphere of civility goes beyond the walls of both the court and the city: "Civile conversation is a vertuous kinde of living in the world . . . [but] to live civilly is not said in respect of the cities, but of the qualities of the mind: so I understand civile conversation not having relation to the citie, but consideration to the manners and conditions which make it civile" (Pettie 1: 56).[50] Thus, beyond the taste for a plainer style, Guazzo's originality vis-à-vis Castiglione lies mainly in this broader scope than that of the man whose whole career is centered on currying favor with superiors and the powerful. Consequently his art of conduct becomes, in the end, potentially incompatible with the dissimulation, the insincerity, the theatrical display, the cultural dilettantism, and the outward ornamentation that life at court seemed to require and that court critics found so objectionable even in Castiglione, regardless of that author's lofty moral concerns.[51] Only transcending the world of the court would satisfy the other protagonist of the dialogue, his brother Guglielmo, at whose instance the dialogue was presumably engaged. His appeal to the broader common sense and freer manners of the educated gentleman rather than the professional courtier is similar to Della Casa's impatience with insincerity in all forms.

Yet, the centrifugal force of court patterns was such that, while Guazzo was trying to transcend the narrow boundaries of the court, his views of good behavior remained conditioned by the court. Standards of conduct at court were based on a relationship between individual worth and public image. Accordingly, Guazzo's willful advice to be what we want to appear, "tale dee procurar l'uomo d'essere, quale desidera d'apparere,"[52] remained wishful thinking. What the French would later call *le qu'en dira-t-on*, similar to the punctiliousness of the Spanish *pun de onor*, is a special dimension of a society that recognizes the importance of our public image: the man of court is all reputation, next to which inner worth is nonexistent or irrelevant. Regretfully, Guazzo had to recognize that "the jugement which wee have to know our selves is not ours, but wee borrow it of others" (Pettie). An attentive critic (Frank Whigham [1983]: 637) has underscored this statement as a sign that reputation had replaced virtue for all practical purposes, and was therefore "radically dependent on the eye and voice of the audience." Thus, "the ideal courtier is *never* off-stage" and "public opinion takes precedence over one's own moral perception" (Whigham 634 f.). On this ground Stanley Fish (1988: 260) makes a remark which could be a summary conclusion on the general drift of that courtly ethic we have seen unfolding from the beginning: "so self-consciously rhetorical is courtly life that moral categories themselves are realized as various performative styles." Fish (261) quotes Heinrich F. Plett's further observation (1983: 613) that "the courtier lives only as a social being and is in private 'retreat' . . . a cipher." The literature of the sophisticated court society of Louis XIV compels us to agree with these characterizations. From his angle, Fish was trying to define Ben Jonson's (1572–1637) poetically productive attempt to protect himself from the cannibalistic nature of the court by reversing roles and offering the truly moral and honest man a way to form an inner society away from the court, within "the tribe of Ben." This interpretation offers an understanding of Ben Jonson's difficult predicament in reconciling inner honesty with successful adjustment to the ways of the world, especially in the hothouses of princely courts.

Guazzo's attempt to broaden the social scope of good manners was a latter-day index of Renaissance humanism, and was destined to be lost in the reversion to a top-heavy social makeup that came about in the baroque age. Emanuele Tesauro (1592–1675) typically expressed this need for a select speech that in its witty urbanity (*arguto, urbano*) would operate as a status symbol, privileging the élite gathered around the prince by sharply differentiating them from the hoi polloi: "differenzia il parlar degli uomini ingegnosi da quel de' plebei."[53] The motif of urban versus rustic that we have often encountered is here intensified into an explicit defense of the theatricality of court manners and gestures as a functional semiotic pattern, consciously sought and accepted as part of necessary class distinctions within an aristocratic society.

THE NOVELS OF CHIVALRY, 1300–1600

Though politically and socially diverse, all regions of Italy welcomed the courtly culture issuing from northern and southern France. Monferrato and the Venetia were particularly receptive to Occitan poetry. During and after the Albigensian Crusade (1208–1228) several troubadours were attracted to the court of the powerful Marquis Boniface I of Monferrato, and after his death their frequent reproaches to his unworthy successors were an eloquent example of the troubadours' court function of education and moral judgment. The principal area of diffusion of Occitan literature was the Venetia, particularly near Treviso at the court of Ezzelino da Romano's brother Alberico after 1236, and thanks mainly to Uc de Saint-Circ (Faidit). Between 1220 and 1240 Uc authored many of the *vidas* and *razos* of Occitan poets and their poems as well as the *Donat Proensal*, the first grammar of a European vernacular.

It was in that area of northeastern Italy between Trieste and Padua, including the territory of Ferrara, that a Franco-Venetian literature of chivalry flourished in prose and verse from at least the end of the thirteenth century through the beginning of the fifteenth. Its *Mischsprache*, a hybrid language that, for all its local elements, was basically French, testifies to the vitality of the subject matter, since it was widely enjoyed by illiterate yet diglossic popular audiences in public squares. In that literature a felicitous juxtaposition of the two *matières* of France and Brittany found its roots, leading to the famous "fusion" (the term goes back to Pio Rajna) or "contamination" of the two rival and somewhat incompatible matters of Charlemagne and King Arthur which has long been credited to Boiardo and Ariosto.

This Franco-Venetian literature, much discussed by Vincenzo Crescini, Adolf Mussafia, Pio Rajna, Giulio Bertoni, and others,[54] reflected the presence in that region of a strong contingent of aggressive feudal families that controlled the land and dominated the communes. Rolandino of Padua's thirteenth-century chronicle of the March of Treviso maps out the history of the region, including the Venetian hinterland all the way to Verona, as a history of four great families: the Marquises of Este, the Da Romano, the Camposampiero, and the Da Camino.[55] The situation was similar in most of northern Italy including the northwest, in the hands of the Savoy, the Marquises of Monferrato, and those of Saluzzo. Their hold on local communes was much like that of the feudal lords of, say, the duchy of Burgundy, the earldom of Lancaster, and the archbishopric of Cologne.[56]

The successful *Entrée d'Espagne* of around 1320, the work of a learned and inspired Paduan poet, displayed a mixture of Carolingian warlikeness and Arthurian adventurousness: Roland abandons Charles out of pique and embarks on Oriental wanderings that also entangle him in an erotic situation. Around 1330 the *Entrée* found its continuation in *La prise de Pampelune*, dedicated to Nicolò I d'Este (d. 1344) by Nicolò da Verona, a court poet who was probably a doctor of laws at Padua.[57] The text geographically closest to Boiardo and Ariosto was perhaps *La Guerra d'Attila*, a vast poem of the second half of the fourteenth century. Niccolò da Casola, a Bolognese notary in exile in the Venetia and then Ferrara, composed it by encouragement from his Ferrarese friend Simone Bisone and left it unfinished after more than 37,000 lines in sixteen cantos, with the intended dedication to Count Bonifacio Ariosti, uncle of the Marquis of Ferrara, Aldobrandino d'Este.[58] It shared with both Boiardo and Ariosto not only the clear courtly intent of celebrating the Este family by recalling the brave stand against the Huns of their mythical ancestor, Prince Forest, but also the mixing of knightly valor and romantic love in the story of another legendary ancestor of the Este, the handsome Accarino. Thus was the wedding of the two *matières* handed over to the later Ferrarese poets.[59]

Both directly and through the intermediary of the Franco-Venetian tradition, the stories of chivalry also filtered into Tuscany by way of the popular jongleurs known as *canterini di piazza*, or *cantimbanchi*, the best of whom was Andrea da Barberino (ca. 1370–after 1431). Andrea skillfully used Franco-Venetian as well as Tuscan sources for his several prose romances, including the extremely popular *Reali di Francia* and *Guerino il Meschino*. Franco-Venetian and Tuscan traditions came together once again in *La Spagna in rima* (mid–fifteenth century), where the Tuscan octave was used to clothe the matter of the *Entrée d'Espagne*

and of the Tuscan *Rotta di Roncisvalle* in verse. *La Spagna* also had a
shorter Emilian version, surviving in a miniatured codex prepared for
Borso d'Este in 1453. Through the Tuscan *Orlando* and *La Spagna in
rima* the medieval matter transmitted in the Franco-Venetian texts provided a fertile background for the *Morgante* by Luigi Pulci, a sort of
communal court poet who was a member of the *salon* of Lucrezia Tor-
nabuoni, Lorenzo de' Medici's mother.[60]

Italians performed the remarkable feat of saving lively medieval traditions in both genres of manners and of chivalry when France and
Germany tended to abandon them. Except for the prose *Lancelot*,
Chrétien himself and his other French contemporaries and immediate
followers ceased to be read after 1400 even in France: they were in any
event linguistically unapproachable. After 1500 the glorious stories of
medieval knights continued to be of vital importance in European literature thanks, chiefly, to the new Italian versions.

Distortions and original interpretations contained in popular texts
became part of the Italian chivalric tradition. The legend of Tristan in
particular was reworked into cyclical compilations, foremost among
them the *Tristano Riccardiano* of around 1300, and the still broader
summation of Arthurian matter, the *Tavola Ritonda*, usually dated between 1320 and 1340; both of these were Tuscan. The *Tristano* shows
that the story had taken roots in Italy in a form that was clearly outside
the mainstream of courtly love. The adventure between Tristan and the
(married) Dama dell'Agua della Spina (chaps. 41–44) is overtly sexual
and entails the consummation of avowed desire at the first private encounter. Starting with King Mark, who aggressively rivaled Tristan but
hid his jealousy like a courtly dissimulator, the men at court acted en-
viously and treacherously, Ghedin openly scheming to destroy Tristan.
This way of handling Arthurian lore confirms that Petrarca's decisive
contribution to the crystallization of courtesy in the love lyric drew directly from the Provençals through the philosophically-bent Stil Nuovo
poets, whereas the *cantimbanchi* who operated in the mixed climate of
northern Italian courts and burghers' communes could hardly appreciate the tense purity of erotic sublimation underlying the ideals of
chivalry.[61]

L'Entrée d'Espagne, La prise de Pampelune, and *La Guerra d'Attila,*
we have seen, acted as precedents for the "fusion" of genres, but the
fusion also had such French precedents as the thirteenth-century *Huon
de Bordeaux.* Pulci's *Morgante,* too, mixed some characteristics of both
genres, though somewhat superficially: his main characters, Orlando
and Rinaldo, spent most of their time running after personal adven-

ture, in disregard for Charlemagne's needs. In terms of aesthetic value and impact on future reception, however, Boiardo's and Ariosto's "fusion" was indeed a signal achievement that changed the nature of the genre. H.-R. Jauss ("Theory of Genres": 82) has neatly commented on the phenomenon in a way that combines his "test of commutation," designed to discriminate genre from genre, with the relevance of reception or reader-response to determine values and meanings within literary forms.

> Despite the gradual assimilation of the heroic epic to the knightly romance in the French tradition, heroes like Roland or Yvain, ladies like Alda or Enide, and lords like Charlemagne or Artus [sic in trans.] were not brought from out of the one genre into the other; a reception through another tradition, the Italian one, was first called for, so that through a fusion of the two French genres into a new one, the so-called romance epic, the originally distinct groups of characters could be transposed into a single structure of action.

The fusion involved more than merging the textual characteristics of two French genres in their mature form; it also brought back some early Celtic elements which had been downgraded or brushed aside altogether. The marvelous of Boiardo and Ariosto gave new life to the giants and fairies of the original Celtic lore, which Chrétien and his followers had replaced with tall knights and sensuous maidens. Together with the fairies, numerous and powerful in intrigue—especially Morgan-le-Fay, (very busy in the background of, say, *Sir Gawain and the Green Knight*)—Merlin and his acolytes also came back in full glory. They had played a major role in Geoffrey of Monmouth's *Vita Merlini*, but only the thirteenth-century prose romances found room for them within their cyclic treatment of Arthurian matter.

Despite the bold humor of his narrative, critics have attributed to Boiardo (1441–1494) the only true revival of medieval *cortesia* in a serious vein.[62] Boiardo did feel that the virtues of true chivalry were still gracing the court of Ferrara:

> Se onor di corte e di cavalleria
> può dar diletto a l'animo virile,
> a voi dilettarà l'istoria mia,
> gente legiadra, nobile e gentile
> che seguite ardimento e cortesia,
> la qual mai non dimora in petto vile.[63]

Boiardo's revival of chivalry was made possible by the new climate of refeudalization that was part of the successful Este policy, consciously pursued, according to recent historical investigation, as an instrument of social and political control.[64]

Croce's elegant formula, which defined Boiardo's poetic inspiration as "il gusto dell'energico e del primitivo" (a taste for primitive energy), can be reset within the framework of our inquiry by correlating such instincts to the traditional military qualities (*militia*—the theme of the Germanic sagas, vigorously espoused by the reactionary clerical circles), now freshly felt as knightly *vis vitalis*. But Boiardo's characters are more than just warriors: they can be courtly and courteous knights. Beyond the enjoyment of the supremely entertaining spectacle of tall tales, the more serious part of Boiardo's attitude includes a perception of chivalric *virtù* that is internal, made of inner control of the will, relying on force but with the help of more courtierly *astuzia*, and resulting from an eager quest for self-discovery. It implies subordination of the individual to the rules of the ideal chivalric code, serving others (lord or lady) rather than individual interest, and it includes *pietà* prevailing over *ira*, humane compassion above soldierly anger. At the conclusion of a duel the winner will show respect for the dignity of his worthy rival. Both Christians and pagans can possess this *virtù*, whose *perfect* hero is Brandimarte (first a pagan, then a Christian): "un Saracin, che un altro sì perfetto / non ha la terra che è dal mar voltata / . . . / ma sopra tutto la persona umana / era cortese, il suo leggiadro core / fu sempre acceso da gentile amore."[65]

One of the most memorable passages of the *Orlando Innamorato* is the friendly argument between Orlando and Agricane when they are resting for the night before resuming their mortal duel (1.18.41–45). Orlando contrasts Agricane's barbarous version of knighthood as mere rule of force with his own courtly view of it as made of arms and studies—the ancient epic topos of *sapientia* and *fortitudo* in a Renaissance setting, but well anticipated by the medieval image of the literate knight at court. In his spirited way of tackling old stories and his own fitting inventions, Boiardo coupled *cortesia* with *allegrezza* (e.g., *OI* 2.1.2), reminding us of the *hilaritas* the *curiales* expected in their successful leaders, despite the frowns this caused among ascetic reformers.

Ariosto continued Boiardo's juxtaposition of knightly "manliness" to true courtesy in the form of joining *sapientia* to *fortitudo* (see *Orlando Furioso* 20.1–20.2, extending it to women who have also excelled, some in arms, like Camilla, and some in letters, like Sappho: "Le donne antique hanno mirabil cose / fatto ne l'arme e nelle sacre muse").[66] A synthesis of the basic themes of the medieval lyric, epic, and romance, added to the ironic echo of Virgil's and Homer's exclusive references to their hero's deeds, is programmatically achieved by Ariosto from his very first octave, a lucid index of his power of concentration in a deceptively plain-sounding "median" style. "Le donne e i cavalier, l'arme e gli amori, / le cortesie, l'audaci imprese io canto": the deeds of prowess performed by knights out of *courtois* love for their ladies will be the subject of his singing, he says—military valor (*militia*), that is, aimed at winning a high lady's love.[67] The double chiasmus ties together the traditional ingredients.

Title notwithstanding, from the vantage point of the poem's courtly function, namely of winning the favor of the Este patrons, the main character is Ruggiero:

> Ruggier, come in ciascun suo degno gesto,
> d'alto valor, di cortesia solea
> dimostrar chiaro segno e manifesto,
> e sempre più magnanimo apparea.
>   (*OF* 41.4.1–4)

The career of this paragon of chivalry makes a true *Bildungsroman*, a novel of education of the hero who, like Perceval, gradually finds his way. From its beginning Ruggiero's career is mapped on the pattern of the Perceval story. He starts out bumbling, like Perceval/Parzival, then takes, or tries to take Angelica, just as Parzival had symbolically "raped" Jeschute in Wolfram, and finally goes through the perilous experience of Alcina's Garden of Pleasure.[68] Perceval's mother had kept him in the wilderness in order to avoid his falling victim to the same passion of chivalry that had caused the deaths of both his father and his brothers. Likewise Ruggiero is isolated by his tutor or adoptive father, Atlante, within the impassable walls of a magic castle: this is meant to forestall his destiny, which Atlante knows will lead him to become a Christian in order to marry Bradamante. His life is surrounded by magic, like the mysterious events that studded Perceval's growth into manhood. Ruggiero has to overcome this string of enchantments by going through several wrong moral choices (like his entrapment in Alcina's garden) and recovering from their consequences; he then finds his way painfully by winning many tests of chivalric prowess, and finally attains the necessary degree of wisdom. It is precisely in Alcina's garden that Ruggiero makes a formal profession of courtliness and chivalry (6.80):

> Ruggier rispose: "Non ch'una battaglia,
> ma per voi sarò pronto a farne cento:
> di mia persona, in tutto quel che vaglia,

> fatene voi secondo il vostro intento;
> che la cagion ch'io vesto piastra e maglia
> non è per guadagnar terre né argento,
> ma sol per farne beneficio altrui,
> tanto più a belle donne come vui." [69]

Even Orlando's madness was not entirely a novel idea, since it had precedents in both Yvain/Iwein and Perceval/Parzival. Yvain went mad when his wife abandoned him for an unintentional infraction of the code (forgetting his appointment with her); Parzival when, out of self-pity for having failed to ask the pertinent question of the ailing Anfortas, he renounced his saintly adviser Gurnemantz and even God, thus entering upon his period of *Goteshaz*, "hatred of God." Inner moral substance and sense of purpose constitute true humanity, and they are the consequence of suffering and the realization of error, as again in the cases of Ruggiero and Orlando. Rodomonte himself, a new Starcatherus, brutal hero of pure *militia*, and in feudal terms the very image of the great lord who recognizes no superior and goes it alone, shares with Ruggiero and Orlando the fate of the warrior who will find out that he needs, above all, love, but that love must be won by loving truly, loyally, and through hard tests.

The French and German poets of romances, especially Chrétien, Hartmann, and Gottfried, had often taken a critical view of Arthur's court as guilty of formality of manners and superficiality of ethic. *Mutatis mutandis*, this theme surfaces again in the *Orlando Furioso*. One glaring case is Rinaldo's dogged and ill-humored defense of Gabrina in full awareness of her perfidy (apparently a derivation of the complicated episode of the "demoiselle toute chenue" in the prose *Lancelot*, the obnoxious hag who obliges Lancelot to abandon the rescue of Guenièvre in order to pursue all sorts of unpalatable services to her).[70] The reader is struck by this supremely humorous example of empty formalism in the performance of courtly rules, which result not in justice but only in absurd constraints on behavior. In Boiardo and Ariosto, Doristella, Origille, and Gabrina echo the unworthy ladies Perceval and Gauvain served in Chrétien's poem, where one of them was declared to be worse than Satan ("pire que Sathanas," *Perceval* v. 7456). Such episodes also easily remind us of *Yvain* (and Hartmann's *Iwein*): Arthur's court was unable to recognize Yvain in the Knight of the Lion and gave aid to the devious Meleaganz and to Lunete's undeserving older sister, while it denied it to the virtuous Lunete as well as to Gauvain's brother-in-law. In the same story the seneschal Kay was typical as a bad and dishonest judge of right and wrong, although even the most exemplary knights could act quite irresponsibly.

Ariosto's famous irony has seldom been traced further back than to Boiardo or, perhaps, to Pulci, but recent criticism has stressed (perhaps overstressed and overread) Chrétien's irony and that of succeeding poets of Arthurian romances (signally Hartmann and Gottfried) as part of that critical stance they often seemed to share toward the moral irresponsibility of the Arthurian court. In the prose cycles this irresponsibility became a cause of the court's downfall. We cannot tell whether Ariosto could detect such signs of ironic treatment in his French sources, or rather, if he did, he could attribute it to authorial intentions. Yet it is reasonable to assume that, rather than by his personality alone, his own unmistakable mood was induced at least in part by the very nature of his sources as he read them. The genre was ready for full parodic treatment of the kind we find in Teofilo Folengo's (d. 1544) burlesque *Baldus*, an inspiration to Rabelais for the way it echoed the popular spirit of reversal of roles and subversion of sociocultural hierarchies (in Bakhtin's sense).

On a more general level bordering on the metaphysical, this way of burlesquing the knight (an inherent aspect of the representation of the hero from the earliest romances) marks an artistic distancing from an idealized self-image which ostensibly does not coincide with a given social reality. The chivalrous and courtly knight is not simply a warrior or an aristocrat: his nobility is more ideal than social.[71] Ariosto was the supreme master of this expression of ironic detachment, but it was characteristic of the genre to encourage the knight to look at himself critically. In a sense, all literature holds up an ideal dream of beauty and perfection at the same time that it contains the artistic consciousness of it as a fictional, though powerfully functional, dream. Lancelot, Gawain, Yvain, and Tristan are monumental embodiments of the divergence between ideal and reality: their sublime troubles are those of the inner incoherence of that very dream.

Ariosto's relationship to his society was one of both acceptance and resistance: he accepted the chivalric interests of the refeudalized Ferrara but he also knew that he had not been born to be a knight. In his humorous reference to Ippolito turning him from a poet into a knight ("di poeta cavallar mi feo," *Satire* 6: 238) the choice of the deprecatory form *cavallaro*, "horseman," betrays his protest at being forced to forego the sublime pleasures of his poetic vocation for the unwanted burdens of courtierly activities. Laying to rest De Sanctis's and Croce's image of a poet willfully unconcerned with social realities, recent Ariosto criticism has brought forth the image of a man who brilliantly expressed his complex Weltanschauung by bending the received literary forms to his advantage. His "cosmic harmony" is a controlled form for a bitter view of the human condition.[72]

The reception of Ariosto's masterpiece includes the invidious comparison with Tasso's *Gerusalemme liberata* and vice versa, in a far-flung controversy that unfolded largely at the Este court of Ferrara. One aspect of the classicistic reaction to the *Furioso* is particularly relevant here. After Giraldi Cinthio's (1504–1573) and Nicolucci Pigna's (1530–1575) defenses of Ariosto's narrative format in 1554, the influence of the growing Aristotelianism persuaded many a critic, from Sperone Speroni (1501–1588) to the young Torquato Tasso (1562 preface to the *Rinaldo*), Antonio Minturno (1563), Ludovico Castelvetro, Alessandro Piccolomini, and Filippo Sassetti (1575/1576), to voice a lively string of demurrers against elements of Ariosto's narrative method that contradicted basic Aristotelian norms. The polemic surrounding the *Furioso* had to do with the classicistic notion of regular genre, namely a literary form based on rational rules authorized and exemplified (possibly, also theorized) by ancient models and authors. This definition of genres and attendant rules was, as modern scholarship has increasingly emphasized, nothing but an invention of the Italian Cinquecento critics. Giraldi Cinthio, for one, first labeled the *Furioso* as a *romanzo cavalleresco*, a new, modern type of work with its own privileges.[73] The ensuing classic-minded critics insisted on classifying the romances as a form of epic (as Tasso continued to do until his *Discorsi* of 1594), hence subject to the typical strictures of that genre, with the resulting exclusion of some of the most salient features of such works as the *Furioso*—and just about all of the most valid works of imagination, including, first and foremost, the *Divina Commedia*.

Specifically at issue were, first, the frequent authorial interventions in the form of (ironic) moral judgments on action and characters, especially in the exordia to the cantos; second, the constant interruptions of the action in order to shift from one to another of the plot's numerous threads. Chapter 24 of Aristotle's *Poetics* was the authority the classicists repeatedly invoked against authorial comments and infractions of narrative continuity, stigmatized as violations of verisimilitude and unity, respectively. In our own time Wayne Booth (*The Rhetoric of Fiction*, 1961) first pointed out the modern narratological bias against authorial presence, tracing it back to Flaubert and Henry

James, but it must be further historicized as a neoclassic Aristotelian norm, not shared by medieval narrators, who, *qua* narrators, were surely no less "credible" for breaking that norm.[74] As noted, such medieval epics as the *Nibelungenlied* also shared the medieval habit of ironic intervention.[75]

Ariosto clearly knew some of his medieval antecedents, at least through the Franco-Venetian versions, but the intentional obliteration of medieval lore that characterized the Renaissance induced the Cinquecento critics to ignore all that matter. Thus, typically, Sperone Speroni (probably shortly after 1560) rejected Giraldi Cinthio's claim that Ariosto's addresses to the reader carried on the oral minstrels' need to address their audiences at the beginning of each new episode in the course of their recitations. For Speroni such exordia were inventions of Boiardo and it was madness, "una pazzia," to assume that they were a function of the recitation, just as Dante's or Petrarca's addresses to the reader at the beginning of cantos (in the *Commedia* and the *Trionfi*) had nothing to do with such compositions being sung.[76] Being part of the argument against the *romanzi*, this discourse invested the whole of that glorious episode of medieval literature.

As to the second critique, directed to the structural interruptions, Giraldi and Pigna felt that these much discussed incidents of "interlacing" enhanced the general suspense and held the reader's attention, whereas the more classic-minded critics considered them nothing but violations of the hallowed Aristotelian principle of unity, frustrating to the reader and unredeemable on any ground.[77] Jacques Peletier du Mans (1517–1582), however, sagaciously defended the technique as early as 1555 in his *Art poétique*, specifically mentioning the French *romans* and their imitator Ariosto, and adducing the argument that the interruptions both provided a welcome suspense and heightened the readers' interest.[78]

We remember that ironic authorial comments as well as the interlacing technique that is characteristic of Boiardo's narrative and, more spectacularly still, Ariosto's, had a well-tested antecedent in Chrétien, Gottfried, Wolfram, and, especially for the practice of interlacing, the authors of the anonymous prose romances of the Vulgate Lancelot/ Grail cycle. Both features also distinguished the romance from the classical epic. Eugène Vinaver has masterfully analyzed the precedents of interlacing, with particular regard to their landmark outcome in Sir Thomas Malory's (d. 1471) *Le Morte Darthur*.[79] The matter is related to the structural and formal character of the romance which, starting with Chrétien, involved a basic bipolarity—a much debated subject ever since the pioneering study of Wilhelm Kellermann.[80] Chrétien's romances are built on a dual set of adventures involving two heroes or two couples: Alexandre/Soredamors and Cligès/Fenice in *Cligès*, Gauvain and Lancelot in *Le chevalier de la charrete*, Gauvain and Yvain in *Yvain*, and Gauvain and Perceval in *Perceval* (in *Erec* the division consists in the two phases of the hero's career). In some instances the two heroes occupy the two parts of a poem, in others their adventures intertwine. This structural duality further developed into a constitutive multiplicity of juxtaposed and integrated stories of individual knights which extended into their full genealogies—a narrative schema that became characteristic of the thirteenth-century prose cycles. The individual found his place in society by discovering his identity in a series of adventures *outside* society, specifically, outside Arthur's court. In the early romances the hero could learn to live without, above, or against Arthurian society, but this produced either an uncourtly opposition that the society could not abide (this was Tristan's case) or the discovery of a transcendental, mystical salvation higher than the ways of ordinary society (as in Perceval).

More generally, the Aristotelian critics blamed the romances still available to them, namely the cyclic compilations in prose and then Boiardo's and Ariosto's poems, for lack of unity in the plot and unconcern for the reader's ability to keep track of the plot as a whole.[81] This remained Tasso's main objection in his *Discorsi del poema eroico* (1594).[82] Nevertheless, in both *Innamorato* and *Furioso* the specific feature of interlacing, although carried to extreme consequences, contained a basic finality and order. The heroes find their goal at last by overcoming the dispersive obstacles interposed by moral and military enemies. In so doing they either return to their point of origin, like Orlando and Rinaldo returning to the war after the pursuit of Angelica, or they find their true goal, like Ruggiero and Bradamante achieving their fateful union.

TASSO AND THE COUNTER-REFORMATION

Tasso's (1544–1595) difficult predicament vis-à-vis the chivalric tradition and his personal difficulties in writing his masterpiece, including his obsessive need for the Inquisitors' approval, can be better understood if we take into account the widespread criticism against the genre he had chosen. The arguments against court and chivalry continued to be voiced in the new climate of the Counter-Reformation with specific reference to the later chivalric literature. One of the most authoritative critiques within ecclesiastical milieus was the *Bibliotheca selecta* (1593) by the Mantuan Jesuit, polymath, and diplomat Antonio Possevino. In this ponderous, systematic assessment of the vast bibliographic material available to contemporary teachers of every academic subject, Possevino specifically proscribed all chivalric literature, including the *Orlando Furioso*, for its immoral, heretical influence on the nobility.[83] In addition to the moralism of medieval memory, Possevino reiterated the classicistic recourse to the "Aristotelian" rules of imitation of nature, verisimilitude, and regularity of plot.

Besides their historic derivation from the ancient pastoral, Tasso's *Aminta* (1573) and Battista Guarini's *Pastor Fido* (definitive edition 1602), respectively historic models for the pastoral drama and the "tragicomic" genre, are ideally linked to the Provençal *pastorela* and French medieval *pastourelle* in the introduction of shepherdesses engaged in a possibly equal relationship with courtier/knights. This kind of pastoral could occasionally be set in a rarefied dream-like climate, the best examples of which are possibly Gavaudan's two *pastorelas* "Desamparatz, ses companho" and "L'autre dia, per un mati" as well as Walther von der Vogelweide's "Nemt, vrouwe, disen kranz."[84] Whereas the *pastorela* usually represented the shepherdess as a plaything to be taken advantage of as a member of the subhuman peasant class, the *vilans*, Marcabru turned it into a confrontation between the absurd arrogance of the knight and the subtle cleverness of the peasant girl, who sends him packing as out of place and out of turn. Gavaudan (fl. ca. 1195–1220) is remarkable for giving the genre a further twist: the knight finds consolation for the disappointments of the court in a relationship with a shepherdess who becomes his true love. Gavaudan considered himself unusual: "eu no sui pars als autres trobadors," "I am not like other troubadours." Indeed, he went both beyond the pastoral genre and beyond courtly love itself. Walther, in his turn, presented the motif of love for a shepherdess as the dream of a pleasant and wholesome sexual adventure—a dream because the reality of a class-conscious society made such a solution preposterous. Somewhat similarly, the dreamlike world of the *Aminta*, with its escapist thrust away from the strictures of the court, expresses the consciousness that the reality of a necessarily repressive society does not allow us such harmoniously natural behavior—and that we are the worse for it.

The nostalgic dream of a gentle chivalrous existence that still inspired Boiardo returns for a moment in Tasso, who, however, was deeply troubled by the remoteness of chivalrous virtues from the realities of court life. After dreaming about bygone ideals in his youthful *Rinaldo*, in the great work of his maturity, the *Gerusalemme liberata* (1581), he represented the knightly type in the romantic isolation of Tancredi, and the courtier type in Gernando. The planned contrast between the gentle Tancredi and the savage Argante is also a contrast between the true chivalrous knight and the barbarous warrior who recognizes no rule but his own strength (*militia* in its pure state). See how Tancredi addresses his opponent (6.36, 1–4):

> Anima vile,
> che ancor nelle vittorie infame sei,
> qual titolo di laude alto e gentile
> da modi attendi sì scortesi e rei?

And Argante dies as a Starcatherus would have wanted to die (19.26, 6–8):

> Minacciava, morendo, e non languìa,
> superbi, formidabili e feroci
> gli ultimi moti fur, l'ultime voci.

The sentimental rejection of the court is best represented by powerful indirection in the episode of Erminia among the shepherds: just as she gives up (temporarily, as Tasso himself was only ever able to do) by withdrawing from the real world of the court, she listens to the disenchanted courtier who has found wisdom and peace in the wilderness, where he now leads the life of a shepherd (*Gerusalemme liberata* 7.12 f.). The Christian form Tasso newly imposes on the chivalric epic involves once again the fusion of Carolingian and Arthurian in the juxtaposition of centralized authority under loyalty to Godfrey, the leader selected by heaven, and the knights' centrifugal instinct to wander off on their own search for honor and individual happiness (signally, Rinaldo and Tancredi).[85] The order implied in the submission to the collective Christian ideals and goals is threatened by the anarchic thrust of sensuality and passion, love and honor. This is the new aspect of the joining of the epic and the romantic, the new predicament of the "fusion" of genres, which in Ariosto had achieved a sort of happy harmony, but again showed its inherent, almost irreconcilable tension in Tasso, the poet of the manneristic culture of the Counter-Reformation.

Much as he dreamed of achieving a reconciliation of the culture of the knight and the culture of the prince, the feudal dream of independence and the orderly centralization under a benevolent and beneficent monarch, he ultimately failed in his professed purpose since what he did express was, above all, the inescapable disjunction between will and instincts, faith and desire, intellect and heart. The need for authoritarian order that was sanctioned by the Counter-Reformation went together with the developing need for a classicism based on the Aristotelian rules. The *Jerusalem Delivered* gave poetic voice to both.

Although he never managed to publish them as a whole, Tasso originally conceived his *Dialoghi* in 1578 as a comprehensive treatment of the *vita activa* in the form of the basic moral values affecting the life of the man of court—a crucial question for this life-long courtier, son of a diplomat courtier, and recipient of the best schooling a courtier's son could hope for.[86] The first dialogue, *Il Forno overo della nobiltà* (1580, second version 1585),[87] spoke of the high nobility as made of the *illustrissimi* (the princes, together with the *molto illustri*, i.e., their grand feudatories and the noblest knights of court) and the *illustri* (the higher city magistrates and the high office holders at court).

Tasso's lucubrations on courtly life come forth most significantly in another dialogue, *Il Malpiglio overo de la corte* (probably 1585), where he also discusses whether Castiglione's portrait of his subject is limited by the historical vicissitudes that affect and change all human affairs. He concludes that Castiglione had provided a Platonic, transcendentally philosophical, and universal image of ideal value for all times and places.[88] When he summarizes his conclusions, Tasso lists the basic virtues with terms that are significantly close to Aristotle's list as Dante had translated it: *fortezza, magnanimità, magnificenza, liberalità, cortesia, modestia, verità, affabilità*, and *piacevolezza*.[89] He defines courtliness as exercise of chivalry in order to win the favor of the prince while avoiding the envy of courtiers. These two goals are mutually exclusive, so real skills must be downplayed. Chivalry consists of physical aptitudes for riding and fencing as well as spiritual virtues, good mores and sociable manners. Knowledge of all disciplines and arts elicits esteem, hence favor. Fortitude and liberality must be exercized with extreme prudence and humility in obeying the prince, so as to avoid both envy and the prince's suspicion. Hence *modestia* is also necessary as a constant concealment of our true excellence: "Dunque appari il cortigiano più tosto d'occultare che di apparere," "the courtier must sooner learn to conceal than to seem."[90] This twist in the argument reveals a disenchantment from the earlier faith in the potential inherent in the man of court or public figure. The prince was becoming more of a tyrant, and the courtier an opportunistic social ornament. Differently from Castiglione's more sanguine approach, this new portrait, where Dante's and Aristotle's "intellectual" virtue of prudence, a necessary guide to all the "moral" virtues, has become the paramount consideration ("la principal virtù delle corti"), is said to apply to Tasso's time, since dissimulation has become a major virtue: "in questi tempi, in cui l'infinger è una de le maggior virtù."[91] Not only is the new courtier reduced to the role of humble servant to the prince—serving even by writing court poetry—he has also been denied access to the political realm that was his predecessors' true vital space. In Tasso's pages that refer to the court, there is no suggestion of political involvement.[92]

We are now approaching the end of the Italian segment of our complex subject, and it is time to take stock of some crucial threads in our story. By tracing the progress of literary forms and themes through the social ambience of the Italian courts and their centrifugal impact on the life of the public squares, I have singled out some typical elements that remained constant as part of an underlying ideology and that take us back to the early manifestations of courtly chivalry, even including some original ingredients of the magical setting of wandering knights and their relatives, the charismatic men of court. We have witnessed the continuity of the courtly heritage in such basic literary attitudes as irony and moral distancing. In a similar pattern of continuity, the early anticourt arguments have kept coming back in new settings and with a renewed sense of purpose.

PART FIVE

The Shift to Absolutism

CHAPTER ELEVEN

From Courtly Knights to Noble Courtiers

THE MODEL CONSOLIDATES

Whereas the feudal lord could rely on his privileged position by birth alone, Castiglione's courtier fashioned a code for a new nobility which, being mostly of middle class origin, needed distinguishing traits in its outward appearance and behavior. The medieval nobleman had a use for manners only when he had to prove himself at court; the Renaissance nobleman needed them in all circumstances, since he often derived his power and status solely from having held office or having officeholders among his forebears. This gave rise to a relatively fixed political class—a phenomenon that had started in Venice early in the fourteenth century. Historians have pointed out that in the middle of the sixteenth century politics in Italy came to be formally associated with noble lineage.[1] Although it was only in the relative stability of the years 1550–1560 that this situation became crystallized, Castiglione's portrait of the courtier reflects this incipient shift where it prescribes nobility and the imitation of the feudal knight by acquiring the martial arts (e.g., 1.14).[2]

Since the new nobility no longer lived through feudal grants, the ethic of feudal rewards had outlived its function. Absolutist centralization tended to reserve land and fiscal rights for the state: the rewards for service were now offices, favor, and influence. Accordingly, traditional "liberality" acquired the bright new function of making the prince shine through a splendid theatrical display of wealth and power which wrapped the whole court within its glow. Through the *ancien régime*, this life of conspicuous consumption became the trademark of princes and their acolytes, while courtiers looked on that style of life as a flattering backdrop for their own social preferment. Recent scholarship has stressed the element of "play" in the life of Castiglione's courts,[3] but it might be more appropriate to speak of "theatricality." The courtier sees himself as constantly on stage. Since he is what he seems to be, his social status is based on appearance.[4] Shakespeare's generalization "the world's a stage" was clearly inspired by the spectacle of the court, and the baroque insistence on "the theater of the world" was motivated likewise. Recent critical focusing on the "mystification of power" and the process of "self-fashioning" implied in the court life of Elizabethan England and its literature points to a phenomenon that had common roots beyond those confines.[5] The courtier had to be able to use his public image to his advantage, almost "pushing it ahead of his true self": "whenever he has to go where he is not yet known, he must send there first, before his own person, a good image of himself, making it known that in other places, at the courts of other lords, ladies, and knights, he enjoys good esteem."[6]

The progress toward absolutism altered the nature of the courtier-prince relationship: the excellence of the courtier as Castiglione describes it was of great value in laying a solid foundation for the deification of the prince, whose authority owed much to the convenient services of such public "educators." Ottaviano Fregoso put it eloquently: "Helped by the instruction, education, and artfulness of such courtiers and formed by them to such prudence and goodness, . . . the prince will be glorious and most dear to men and God, acquiring by God's grace that heroic virtue that will enable him to exceed the boundaries of humankind, so that he will be regarded more as a demigod than a mortal man."[7] The court becomes a functional backdrop for absolutism, preparing the ground for the transition to the state of an Elizabeth I or a Louis XIV, where the courtiers' relationship with the monarch will be the carefully managed stage for the monarch's exalted status. This assumed role of the new sort of princes will make them objects of "more than love, quasi-adoration" not only for the courtiers but for the citizenry as a whole, out of gratitude for a pattern of remuneration that by principle exceeds personal merit. Even while the rulers are expected to observe impartiality, equality, and merit in distributing justice and basic freedoms, their quasi-divine favors will be received as though imparted in ways that transcend objective merit.[8] This special role also applied to monarchs who, like Elizabeth, were effectively restrained by the aristocratic constitutionalism that was typical of England.

The new circumstances forced a process of adaptation for the traditional mix of courtly qualities. "Modesty," for example, became the acknowledgment of the gratuitous nature of princely reward, whereas the feudal vassal's contractual relationship with his lord had once put him in a position to insist on such reward as a right—a right constantly proclaimed in troubadour poetry.

This fateful turning point in the conception of state power was grounded in the doctrine of the king as *lex animata*, law in form of a person possessing *summa legibus soluta potestas*, hence a supreme authority unbounded by law. Jean Bodin theorized as much, although he somewhat duplicitously yet diplomatically disapproved of Machiavelli's alleged agreeing with the doctrine—which, however, went back to medieval theology and institutional jurisprudence. The prince's arbitrary power was thus explicitly justified by the principle of the transcendence of sovereignty, according to the doctrine of "the king's two bodies" illustrated in a famous study by Ernst Kantorowicz (1957). Even in our time the principle can be invoked in relevant contexts, and not only for the most radical applications (like Hitler's theory of the *Führerprinzip*, declaring the person of the leader the only true source of right and law), but in democratic societies too (as when President Nixon's counsels invoked the principle of inherent power and executive privilege in the Watergate controversy).[9]

The courtier does not claim the right to influence the prince by personal merit: he only relies on the prince's unpredictable pleasure and arbitrary, uncensurable choice. Castiglione was clear on the matter. The power relationships at court had grown beyond the encounter of competing personal rights of feudal times, when the king's attempts to establish himself as true sovereign had to overcome the feudal lords' resistance in the name of customary rights and privileges. The doctrine of the *rex legibus solutus* had to override the feudal notion of the king as simply suzerain, just enforcer of customs and laws. *Lex facit regem*, "the king issues from the law," had been the rule, and the king who betrayed his mandate deserved his subjects' rebellion.[10] We have seen that the doctrine of absolutism was potentially implied in the kings' thrust against feudalism, and I pointed to Giles of Rome's *De regimine principum* as exemplary in this respect (end of chap. 3).

At a time when authoritarian regimes were on the verge of crowding out the last surviving forms of representative government, Castiglione

attempted to map out a morally defensible type of princely state that
was based on a well-groomed court of administrators and advisors. His
formula might have satisfied the popular longing for justice, order, and
peace by bracketing tensions and personal struggles within the enclo-
sures of the courts and keeping in check the despots' irresponsible arbitrariness. Still, the people would have been excluded from any direct
form of participation.[11] Machiavelli's sympathies for effective republicanism were already discounted in Castiglione's experience, which corresponded to the patterns prevailing outside Florence and Venice.

Thus, around the middle of the sixteenth century the new sociopolitical situation forced a major shift in the self-image of the nobleman/
gentleman. The ideals of courtliness and chivalry underwent a momentous reduction that centered the new idea of nobility on personal
"honor," with an accent on the duel as the definitive test of truth and
merit. This produced a flowering of treatises on a new "science of
chivalry," dealing specifically with honor and duels. There had been a
pioneer essay in the Neapolitan Paride dal Pozzo's (Paris a Puteo) *Libellus de re militari ubi est tota materia duelli* (ca. 1471, most successful in the often printed Italian version, *Il duello*). Then came such
often-reprinted works as Andrea Alciato's *De singulari certamine* (Paris,
1541; Lugduni: Antonius Vincentius, 1543); Girolamo Muzio's *Il duello*
and *Risposte cavalleresche* (1550), *Il cavalier* (Rome, 1569) as well
as *Il gentilhuomo, trattato della nobiltà* (1571);[12] Sebastiano Fausto
da Longiano's *Il duello regolato a le leggi dell'honore* (Venice: Vincenzo Valgrisi, 1551); the *Eversiones singularis certaminis* by Antonio
Bernardi della Mirandola (1503–1565, Averroist philosopher at Bologna and then bishop of Caserta); Giambattista Possevino's (Mantua,
1520–Rome, 1549, brother of the Jesuit polymath and diplomat Antonio, and a participant at Bernardi's lectures) *Dialogo dell'honore . . .
nel quale si tratta a pieno del duello* (Venice: Gabriel Giolito de' Ferrari,
1553); Pompeo della Barba's *Due . . . dialoghi . . . dei segreti della
natura . . . sull'armi e le lettere* (Venice, 1558); Annibale Romei's *Discorsi divisi in sette giornate, . . . quinta della nobiltà, . . . settima della
precedenza dell'arme e delle lettere . . .* (1585; ed. Marco Antonio Pa-
lazzolo, Verona: Gerolamo Discepoli, 1586; Venice, 1594); and finally,
in the next century, Camillo Baldi's ponderous and somewhat conclusive tome on challenges (*mentite*, 1633).[13] In book three of his *Risposte
cavalleresche*, Muzio, official advisor on matters of chivalry to the successive governors of Milan, the Marquis of Vasto and don Ferrante
Gonzaga, defined the laws of chivalry by the key principle that honor

supersedes all other values, including loyalty to the prince and the laws of the country.[14]

I have mentioned (in chap. 1) the *letras de batalla* and *pasos de armas*, to wit, the endemic challenges and duels among Catalan and Aragonese noblemen. A similar study for Italy is still lacking: it would reveal no less obsession there with such practices of latter-day chivalry, despite widespread proscription by various authorities attempting to stem the tide of fashion.[15] After a spate of severe edicts against duels in the 1540s, a series of duels took place publicly in the 1550s with much fanfare through various parts of Italy, including Milan and Rome. One eloquent example of related documentary material of the kind studied by Martín de Riquer should suffice here, namely the *Cartelli e manifesti passati tra M. Perseo Boninsegni e M. Francesco Baldinaccio detto il Mancino d'Agubbio* published in 1560.[16] New restrictions came in the 1560s, aiming at least at superficial peace, not to mention conformity with Christian morality as demanded by the Counter-Reformation.

After 1560 definitions of nobility began to appear that were inspired by those of the humanists but were technically dependent on the newly published works of Jerónimo Osorio, professor of Sacred Scriptures at Coimbra and future bishop, André Tiraqueau (d. 1558), a member of the *parlement* of Paris, and Barthélemy de Chasseneux (d. 1541), president of the *parlement* of Aix-en-Provence.[17] The two French authorities were interested in putting forward the viewpoint of the *noblesse de robe*, the new nobility that was playing an increasingly important role as representative of the high bourgeoisie and ally of the monarchy against the ancient nobility of the sword (but reserving the right to oppose the monarch when he infringed the privileges of this new corporate group).[18] The Portuguese author submitted an impressive Christian codification of nobility with clear political overtones: nobility is based on the inheritance or direct exercise of qualities that serve the common good in public life. Though we are all born free, we still owe obedience to the power of the best, *optimatum potestas*, or their descendants, no matter how unworthy (and the progeny is often sadly unworthy of its ancestors), since social order and man's desire for peace demand it, while popular governments spell the ruin of their cities.[19] Similarly in Muzio's 1571 *Il gentilhuomo*, after the first book's generic definitions based on ancient and humanistic authorities (the Stoics, Seneca, Boethius, Dante, etc.), the second book faced the tricky problem of nobility not by virtue but by social position, and concluded that *de facto* nobility comes from having held important political office: this entails the progeny's right to continue exercising such honorable social func-tions. Political power has become the prerogative of noble status—a notion implying a return to Bartolo da Sassoferrato's still authoritative equivalence between *officium* and *nobilitas*.[20]

All this went hand in hand with a new surge of sumptuary laws that completed the separation of nobles and commoners. The 1560s wit-nessed a formal legitimization of nobility as an officially identifiable, separate physical entity: widespread decrees institutionalized specific orders of knighthood and prescribed their ways of dressing in public.[21] One example should suffice. In 1562 Cosimo I instituted the Order of Santo Stefano, whose nobles were to be the new ruling class of Florence and Tuscany, personally issuing from the duke's will and dependent upon him. Only families of officeholders and members of the new no-bility, not the members of the older nobility, were exempted from the restrictions of new sumptuary laws of the same year, which were meant to regulate dress and conspicuous consumption.[22] All other states had or would soon have similar provisions.

Francesco Sansovino's 1566 *Origine de' cavalieri*, appropriately dedicated to Cosimo I, was a brave attempt to trace the growing multi-tude of precepts governing the religious orders of knighthood, starting with the Hospitallers of Saint John of Jerusalem, who had become the Knights of Malta, down to Cosimo's Order of Santo Stefano. The rules of Malta became particularly rigorous in 1599, sanctioning the will to increase cloture of the new aristocracies. New Italian postulants had to prove two hundred years of nobility, with no involvement in either com-merce, agriculture, or professional trades, including the notarial art, for a period of four generations, and without having held a public office of the sort that was also accessible to commoners. Such rules were particu-larly out of step with past social reality in Italy, and exceptions were made for four cities only: Genoa, Florence, Siena, and Lucca. Although restrictions applied to all members, special attempts were made to en-force them for the highest of the three grades of knighthood, starting with that of knight proper, with some leniency for the lower ones of chaplains and servants or sergeants at arms.[23] This intended separation of the higher classes affected the style of the man of court, whose behav-ior was now meant to seal the prince's distance from his subjects. It has been noted that the new concepts of majesty and decorum definitively chased the quotidian, the lowly, and the popular from the courts, to-gether with all once accepted forms of benevolent mixing with the populace.[24]

It is not my purpose to survey the large body of literature on the concept of nobility: at least for Italy we possess an excellent such study by Claudio Donati (*L'idea di nobiltà in Italia*, 1988). But it seems fitting to close these notes on the Late Renaissance with a mention of Giovanni Botero (1543/4–1617), the Piedmontese political theorist, former Jesuit, and secretary to Archbishop Carlo Borromeo of Milan, whose late years were largely spent at the court of the Savoy Duke Emanuel Philibert. In a *discorso* published in 1607 and written for the instruction of the duke's third son, the paramount virtues as foundation of true nobility were declared to be, in order: religious piety, military fortitude, justice, and civil prudence, together with mastery of humane letters and liberal arts.[25]

The ethos of curiality and courtliness had come about originally through an interpretation of the classical cardinal virtues with the addition of Cicero's *decorum*: this peculiar formula had become a prop for the image of true nobility. As we approach the end of the Renaissance, we observe that this heritage was adapted to a theatrical show of Castiglionesque gracefulness as the foundation of a new nobility, whose chief function was to serve the prince in his public display of splendor. After having become a courtier, the medieval knight had turned into a docile servant of princes in a hothouse where the court had replaced nature.

NEW ORIENTATIONS IN FRANCE (AND ENGLAND)

One of the first influential figures in French Renaissance poetry, Clément Marot (1496–1544), was a court poet, "valet de chambre" to Marguerite d'Alençon, and close to the royal entourage. The "school" of his followers kept close to him as well as to Francis I's court, starting with Mellin de Saint-Gelais, king's "aumonier" and "garde de la librairie," first French practicing Petrarchist, and critic of the Pléïade. In his *Amye de court*, an episode among many in the lively *querelle des femmes*, Bertrand de la Borderie, Marot's and Saint-Gelais's friend, contrasted the habits of court ladies with the noble love that was then to be located in the Platonic mysticism of a Bembo rather than in the earlier tradition of courtly love. It started a parrying of pros and cons, with Antoine Héroët (1492–1568) coming down on the side of pure love as supreme good (*La parfaicte amye*, 1532). Héroët was in the entourage of Marguerite de Navarre, who imbued her own *Heptaméron* with Platonic love according to the fashion of the day, in and outside the courts. It was a way to turn courtly love into a philosophical experience.

Although I have paid particular attention to literature that grew in and around the courts, the ideas that concern us had become ubiquitous. In Rabelais, Frère Jean's utopian Abbey of Thélème welcomes guests who fit a courtierly description rather well. They must be "gens libères, bien néz, bien instruictz, conversans en compaignies honnestes," conditioned by what had traditionally been regarded as the prerogative of the nobility: they were guided by instinctual dispositions to act nobly and honorably through ancestral example—"par nature un instinct et aguillon, qui tousjours les poulse à faitz vertueux et retirés de vice, lequel ilz nomment honneur" (1.57.159).[26] Occasionally acting as the king's unofficial publicist, Rabelais was the protégé of such highly located personages as Jean and Guillaume du Bellay and Marguerite de Navarre. In the creation of his *Pantagruel* (1532) he respected the traditional plot structures of the heroes of such *chansons de geste* as *Fierabras, Huon de Bordeaux*, and *Les quatre filz Aymon*. It bears mentioning that Mikhail Bakhtin singled out the Thélème episode as a reflection of the utopian climate of the humanistic feast at court rather than the popular feast, since it owed more to the aristocratic spirit of the Renaissance than to that popular sense of utopia that nevertheless invests the bulk of Rabelais's masterpiece.[27]

The impact of the Italian treatises on conduct was felt as far as England, from Thomas Elyot's *The Boke named the Governour* (1531) to Roger Ascham's *The Scholemaster* (1570) and on to John Milton's celebrated essay "Of Education" (1644), even while in Italy Castiglione's treatise ceased being reprinted in 1562.[28] Each country had its popular manuals, one of the most successful being Baltasar Gracián's *Oráculo manual y arte de prudencia* (Portable Oracle on the Art of Prudence, 1647), a collection of maxims that Norbert Elias labeled "the first handbook of courtly psychology."[29] It was also often reprinted in Nicolas Amelot de la Houssaie's French version *L'homme de cour* (Paris, 1684).

Hoby's successful translation of *Il Cortegiano* as *The Book of the Courtier* (1561) provided the basis for the future ideal of the English "gentleman," well-versed in both arms and letters, "tam Marti quam Mercurio," and accustomed to disguise his knowledge with elegant *sprezzatura* (hence, e.g., the still current objection to "talking shop" in social conversation). Soon thereafter (1576) Robert Patterson Anglicized Della Casa's *Galateo*. The French term *honnête-homme* that replaced *cortegiano* at the time English was replacing "courtier" with "gentleman," *cortegiania* with "civility," and courtly with "courteous," combined the implication of a superior élitist model with the traditional Ciceronian *honestas* that we have seen associated with the ideal of *curialitas* from the beginning.

The New Historicists have called attention to the nonliterary motives of some Elizabethan literature that grew around the court of Elizabeth I, just as in his masterful study of Petrarchism (*The Icy Fire*, 1969; 1978) Leonard Forster had pointed out how Queen Elizabeth could exploit the political and diplomatic dimensions of the cult of Petrarca. Since this rich field lies outside the geographic area of our investigation, I shall limit myself to some brief remarks on fundamental aspects that have recently attracted attention. It seems clear that until at least the 1580s court poetry under Elizabeth I was also a way to seek preferment by displaying "a rhetorical virtuosity specifically identifiable with the sophisticated manners of the courtly elite" (Javitch 1982: 225 f.). Puttenham's *Arte of English Poesie* (1589) explicitly drew "affinities between poetic style and court conduct" (ibid.), while George Gascoigne (ca. 1539–1577) provided an outstanding example of a knight-poet who skillfully used the pen as well as the lance to promote his courtly ambitions. Both Puttenham and Gascoigne make clear reference to the art of dissimulation ("cunningly to be able to dissemble") as a means of survival and advancement at court, in an interesting analogy with the literary use of *allegoria* (Puttenham's term).[30] Puttenham also called allegory "the figure of faire semblant," essential to the courtier because "in any matter of importance his wordes and his meaning very seldom meete." He included the political extension by explicitly associating dissimulation with the art of government: "qui nescit dissimulare nescit regnare."[31] A variant was offered by Sir Philip Sidney, who advocated what Castiglione had styled *sprezzatura* as a sign of true art as well as true aristocratic breeding, concealing artifice in both poetry and conduct: see "so smooth an ease" in *Astrophil and Stella*, sonnet 74 verse 9. *Sprezzatura* thus set off the high courtier's social superiority as against the mannerisms of would-be courtiers who were unable to hide their (for Sidney, misplaced) ambitions in speech or deed. It was also the appropriate personal marker whereby the former could keep the latter in their place, as they well deserved.[32]

The shift from the medieval knight's individualistic ethos—analogous to Castiglione's ideal of a self-sufficient courtier—toward a docile and diplomatically adroit servant of princes found a clear statement in the

preface to Jean du Peyrat's translation of the *Galateo* (1562). The very
title stressed the generalizing bent of this reading (. . . *comme le
gentilhomme se doit gouverner en toute compagnie*), and these generalized social manners were expressly yet contrastively tied to the habits
of the knight: "the entire virtue and perfection of a gentleman . . . does
not consist [merely] in correctly spurring a horse, hauling a lance, sitting
straight in one's armor . . . ," including the correct ways of loving ladies,
but also in serving kings and princes at the table, performing the chores
of court, talking and gesturing appropriately, and so on. The knight
had thus accomplished his transformation into a courtier to princes, but
the standard had also extended to all who wanted to be gentlefolk.
Courtierly and chivalric manners had been a social and cultural distinguishing trait, a sign of belonging to privileged groups, and of superior
prerogatives when deployed toward inferiors. Now they amounted to
pleasing the powerful, the new lords, to fit elegantly at their courts as
embellishments of the palace, or to impose on the populace with a
public show. The restraints and compulsions of good conduct were extended to the inferiors who must keep their place and not offend their
squeamish superiors with coarse manners.[33] In other words, the knight/
courtier had become a model for both his social superiors and his
inferiors.

The new courtly ideology was bound to provoke further reactions,
both subtle and strong, either deviously masked or frontally direct. We
have seen the willfully radical rejection by Guevara, whose oeuvre's
deep reverberations in England favored his *Marco Aurelio* also as an
exercise in style. A provocative case is that of Philibert de Vienne's *Le
philosophe de cour* (Lyons, 1547; Paris, 1548), a perceptive, tongue-in-
cheek satire of court behavior which, curiously yet not too surprisingly,
seems to have been read in England (in George North's translation:
London, 1575) as a normative manual.[34]

Philibert was pointing to a chronic irreconcilability between court
ethic and classical ethic, which he identified with the Socratic tradition.
"Socrates forbids such masking and general disguising, because we
should not appear to be others than we are; and we also allow the
same. . . . But Socrates letteth us not, that having no desire to show
ourselves contrary to that we would be esteemed, notwithstanding we
dissemble, and accommodate ourselves to the imperfections of everyone." The satirical garb of the presentation turns the problem around
by pretending that Socrates was wrong and *we* are right, since this is
the wise way to live in the real world. Indeed, overlooking the exempla-

riness of his execution as a martyr of straightforwardness, Philibert declares Socrates himself a master dissembler through the deceptive maieutical method of his philosophical pedagogy: "Himself doeth serve us for example, for although he was ever like unto himself, yet was he the greatest dissembler in the world" (North's trans.: 97 f.).[35]

By a brilliant stroke of psychological observation, Philibert makes us face the paradoxical opposition between private and public morality by exposing the pragmatic coincidence of the theoretically incompatible criteria of being and seeming (the fundamental dilemma of classical ontology and metaphysics), hence sincerity and insincerity, knowing and pretending, meaning and dissimulating. Even the most formidable symbol of the knight's status and power, the sword, had become little more than an ornament, since it was used mostly for duels in matters of personal honor. Success rested no longer on bravery and military prowess, but on playing the courtly game gracefully and cleverly. Molière's *Misanthrope* would present the dilemma in the very midst of the most organized exercise in dissembling in western history, Louis XIV's court.[36] Like Molière's Alceste, Philibert's gentleman is taught that "the virtue of man consisteth not in that which is only good of itself, following the opinion of Philosophy: but in that which seemeth to them good" (12). "In so doing he shall be accounted wise, win honor, and be free of reprehension everywhere: which *Proteus* knew very well, to whom his diverse Metamorphosis and oft transfiguration was very commodious" (101).

Philibert was familiar with the ethical background of his "new philosophy of court" and brought Cicero's *De officiis* into the argument: from the adoption of the virtues and attitudes of courtiers "proceedeth the *decorum generale*, general comelinesse, that Cicero speaketh so much of in his Offices" (15). The *Philosophe de cour* was divided according to Cicero's categories of cardinal virtues: Prudence, Justice, Magnanimity, and Temperance, culminating, however, in a broadly treated new category that carried no Ciceronian flavor but clearly a Castiglionesque one, to wit, Good Grace, to which all other virtues are subordinated.[37] Thus the new courtly "virtue . . . differeth from the Philosophy of the Auncientes, in that their vertue . . . is to live according to the instinct of Nature; and ours is to lyve according to the manner of the Courte" (17). The ancients "would have us, without any hope of honour to embrace and follow vertue for the love of hir selfe," whereas the new philosophy of court teaches us "to live vertuously to the ende to obtayne honour and reputation" (20).

The critical reading of Castiglione is clear in the mock eulogy of a
man who has "some pretie sprinckled iudgement in the common places
and practizes of all the liberall sciences, chopt up in hotchpot togither,"
just for the sake of spicing social conversation "and no more," and so
that "with the more assured cunning to couche our credite, it shall not
be amisse to interlace our discourses with certeine suddaine lyes and
inventions of our owne forging." Similarly for "the knowledge of fence,
of vaulting, of tennis, of dauncing, and other sportes of exercise: and
some understanding of the state and affayres of the Realme, as of
warres, of practizes, of merchandize, and howe we maye honestly
robbe, deceyve, and make our best profite" (30 f.). It was a program,
one can see, of unashamed dilettantism for the sake of mere make-believe. In the same chapter the treatment of Prudence bends the traditional norm of measure into counseling the avoidance of excess even in
knowing too much of these arts or taking them too seriously. Dealing
with Justice, the next chapter intimates "that it is tollerable to beguile,
filch, and cogge, and do the worst we can, so that neither lawe, judge,
nor iustice may touch or catch hold of us for it."[38] In other words, laws,
private or public, are of no consequence as long as we manage to get
away with mischief and succeed in our endeavor, that is to curry favor
of the powerful and be esteemed by society. This is a sort of Machiavellian courtliness or, more precisely, an indictment of Machiavellianism if
the text is, as appears inevitable from its very brashness, a Lucianic
satirical encomium.[39]

Such acute sensibility to deep moral questions reflects the climate of
religious crisis that would lead France into the wars of religion, while
the apparent unawareness of the true meaning of this text in Tudor
England is due to the climate of compromise and acceptance of Elizabeth's glorious image as the Virgin Mother of a new nation at peace
with itself.[40] The Elizabethan acceptance of these moral games of court,
however, must not blind us to the fact that it was precisely in England
that the feudal spirit lived on and, indeed, prevailed against the temporary experiment in authoritarianism by imposing the constitutional parliamentary solution.[41] Neither in England nor in France was the aristocracy yet facing the sort of neutralization that characterized the Italian
nobility at court. Long ago J. H. Hexter authoritatively rectified the
notion of a "monstrous nobility" turned "half court insect, half bucolic
vegetable" by the Renaissance despots, but his corrections threw light
on the contrast between the Italian situation and that of other lands
where, as in France and England, the sons of the gentry were still eagerly

sent to school to be instructed in the arts of serving the commonwealth rather than the prince.[42] Montaigne, for one, urged the nobleman to give his scion a tutor who "shall frame his charge's will to be a most loyal servitor of his prince, very well affected and courageous, but he will dampen in him any desire to attach himself to the court except out of a sense of public obligation." The boy will thus retain that sense of liberty that is impossible in "a man waged and bought, . . . a courtier who can have neither the right nor the will to speak or think otherwise than favorably of a master who has chosen to foster and raise him up from among so many other subjects. Such favor and usage dazzle a man's eyes and corrupt his freedom."[43] In a famous letter of advice on education of the nobility Queen Elizabeth's great councilor Francis Walsingham spoke repeatedly of the duty to serve the commonwealth, but not of serving the prince.[44] Much as the feudal lords could withdraw their loyalty when their interests were not preserved, so was obedience to the prince reconsidered at the time of the revolt of the Netherlands, the French civil war, and the English Puritan revolution. But few courtiers were in such a position in Italy.

Prose novels of chivalry remained highly popular, and a principal source of revenue to French printers: about eighty adaptations of romances and *chansons de geste* (only three of them Carolingian) saw the light between 1478 and 1549 in France, some of them enjoying several printings. In the enthusiasm for things Italian that sparked the French Renaissance, even such a genuinely French genre made use of Italian ingredients, and courtly themes were also drawn from Italy, as in the *Treize élégantes demandes d'amour* (1523), a translation of the episode of the court of love in Boccaccio's *Filocolo*. I have mentioned Antonio Possevino's blanket indictment of the romance, on the basis of the Aristotelian criteria of unity and verisimilitude. His attack was in tune with the classicistic critics who felt uneasy with the *Orlando Furioso*. In France an early expression of such concerns combined with the new Catholic rigorism was the preface to the translation of *L'histoire éthiopique d'Héliodore* (1547) by the courtier and clergyman, later bishop, Jacques Amyot.[45] By setting the norms for a Counter-Reformation literature that satisfied the classical prerequisites of unity and verisimilitude while being entertaining, that is, aesthetically pleasing, Amyot, followed by Bishop Jean-Pierre Camus and then Bishop Huet, started a new phase of clerical intervention in the education of court audiences and the setting of literary and humane standards. I have also noted (chap. 10, end of section on "Novels of Chivalry") the dissenting voice of the learned poet-theorist Jacques Peletier du Mans, coming in 1555 to the defense of interlaced narratives. Since neither an extended discussion of the epic or narrative genres nor the mention of interlacing or other ordering techniques appear as part of the poetic arts of the time, such as Thomas Sébillet's and Joachim Du Bellay's, it is tempting to hypothesize that Peletier's introduction of a defense of the *romans* and specifically of Ariosto's narrative mode may have been prompted by Amyot's critique of the romances.

Between Amyot's influential preface and Possevino's text the specific butt of the new moralistic condemnation was the fashionable tale of Amadis of Gaul, which had invaded France in the form of a Spanish imitation of an older French tale, and had also been Italianized by Bernardo Tasso (Torquato's father). The popularity of the *Amadis* was also due to a new element vis-à-vis the older chivalric matter: an erotic taste for voluptuous and sentimental love scenes. These elegant affairs of the heart, immediately frowned upon by concerned moralists, were to develop into the literature of *galanterie* which also had an impact in other countries. Amyot's *Histoire*, a version of Heliodorus's *Theagenes and Chariclea*, was an attempt to replace the fantastic tales of the medieval romances with the matter of Hellenistic and Byzantine novels that Amyot, in his humanistic orientation, considered closer to nature and truth. What the new models lacked, however, was the heroic mold of the tales of knights errant, so that the translators and elaborators of the huge Amadis cycle, though shaken by Amyot's censures, were not subdued to the point of giving up. The French versions had started with Nicholas Herberay des Essarts, who expanded the Spanish original by Garci Ordóñez Montalvo (four books in one volume, ca. 1508) into eight successive books (1540–1546). Further elaborations continued to appear, with book nine by Claude Colet (1553) and books ten, thirteen, and fourteen by Jacques Gohory (1555, 1571, 1575).[46] The prefaces pointed out, apologetically, that the frivolity of the subject matter was offset by the need to cater to audiences that demanded light entertainment as well as an uplifting spectacle of heroic *grandeur*, fit for noble warriors.

While in Italy Torquato Tasso bypassed the new objections by offering a serious poem on crusading Christian chivalry, in France the whole group of the Pléiade poets came to the aid of the continuing translators of the *Amadis*. Jacques Gohory prefaced his translation of book 13 (Paris, 1571) with a reminder that Francis I had rightly appreciated the very similar *Girone il Cortese* by the Italian poet Luigi Alamanni: the

beautiful veil of poetic lies hid "good moral instruction for the nobility." It did so "by exalting virtuous deeds and condemning vicious
ones, always recommending the adoration and reverence of God and
the defence of good justice, principally of pitiful persons, such as maidens, widows, and orphans."[47] We do know how traditional these arguments were. As to the open-ended, multiple narrative plots, they had
advantages over the greater tightness of the Hellenistic models: Ariosto
had proved how delightful and instructive such techniques could be to
the reader.

   We cannot engage here in a detailed examination of the complex
question of Cervantes's attitudes toward chivalry and the chivalric novel
or romance, but when all is said and done concerning that rich and
puzzling masterpiece, it is relevant to bear in mind that *Don Quixote*
(first part 1605) was "still, for the general public of the period, one of
the manifestations of the Catholic Reformation applied to literature."[48]
As to the general perception of the courtier's role, such symptomatic
observations as those by Philibert of Vienne show how the courtier's
dignity vis-à-vis a potentially tyrannical prince could be preserved only
by remaining true, in the new surroundings, to the time-honored aristocratic view of reciprocal obligations between sovereign and feudal
lords. This "resistance" that Castiglione had so subtly and poignantly
represented won out only in post-Tudor England. The courtier who
started to seem clearly hypocritical was the one who had given in to
absolutism.

THE SCHOOL OF COURTLY MANNERS
IN THE AGE OF LOUIS XIII

Historians have long recognized in the romances of the French Renaissance a "school of civility."[49] Contemporaneous readers appeared to
appreciate the psychological and social nourishment of what Étienne
Pasquier referred to as "vraye courtizanerie." A learned critic, Pasquier
was determined not to allow the new humanistic standards to chase into
oblivion the glorious past of medieval French literature, including the
troubadours and the romances. The old chivalric romances (though no
further back than the prose *Lancelot*) went on being read, always as a
favorite genre of the higher and lower aristocracy and their imitators
among the high bourgeoisie. Jean Chapelain countered the Aristotelian
classicists' theoretical objections by suggesting that Aristotle himself,
had he been confronted with such texts as the *Lancelot*, would have

adjusted his principles to accommodate the new works alongside the *Iliad* and the *Odyssey*. Yet, the romance decayed into a genre of mere entertainment to be enjoyed as pure fantasy, in full consciousness of its being divorced from present reality: at the height of the "classic" period, Louis XIV's court nobles knew full well that they were no longer Gawains and Lancelots.

In the meantime, France had acted as a mediator in the Renaissance fashioning of the ideal gentleman as social canon. Italian definitions were transmitted almost literally within a broadened context that made the ideals once developed for the knight and the courtier universally valid for all educated people, all *honnêtes gens*. This last term appeared in the programmatic title of a text that remained crucial throughout its century, Nicolas Faret's *L'honeste homme ou l'art de plaire à la Cour* (1630).[50] There the art of the courtier seemed to become, in essence, the art "to please," specifically to please at court. For the remainder, Faret leaned heavily on the *Galateo*, the *Civil conversatione*, and of course Castiglione's *Cortegiano*, whose key term *sprezzatura* he rendered with *negligence* (as in Guazzo's *negligenza o sprezzamento*): one must above all avoid *l'affectation* and use "une certaine negligence qui cache l'artifice, et tesmoigne que l'on ne fait rien que comme sans y penser, et sans aucune sorte de peine" (1970 ed.: 20).[51]

The change from *courtois* to *honnête* and *civile* was more than a matter of linguistic fashion. It reflected a gradual change from the image of a knight who drew his authority and legitimacy from a court but acted as a relatively independent agent in his adventurous endeavors, to that of the man of court who saw himself and was seen by the whole society as the acme of civilized living, regardless of his having become completely dependent on that same court, to the point of seeing his nobility practically equated with the status of successful bourgeois courtiers. This process spanned the twelfth through the seventeenth century, the moment of transition coming at the time of Henry IV of France (1594–1610), who, as Henry of Bourbon, Prince of Navarre, had been one of the last heroes of the chivalrous ideal of resistance to monarchic centralization, but upon becoming king felt compelled to execute "those who resisted, those who did not understand that from free lords and knights they were to become dependent servants of the king."[52]

Later on, the school of *politesse mondaine* that the romances had become kept attracting readers to the otherwise hardly readable tomes of such popular heroico-sentimental novels as Madeleine de Scudéry's *Le Grand Cyrus* (1649–1653, 10 volumes). The most popular of its

century, Honoré d'Urfé's (1567–1625) pastoral novel *Astrée* (1607–
1628, including Baro's edition of the posthumous fourth part in 1627
and "conclusion" in 1628) was eagerly received as a civilizing manual
of manners and polite conversation, especially among the courtiers—
and the ladies, who delighted in finding themselves so flatteringly idol-
ized, as the ladies of courtly love had once been. Critics have recognized
the book's practical civilizing impact, reflecting a new taste for noble
sentiments and refined behavior.[53]

Elias offers a rewarding analysis of the *Astrée* as an expression of the
mentality of the lower, noncourtly nobility vis-à-vis the higher nobility
that had yielded to royal pressures and become a court aristocracy.[54]
Belonging to a leading group of rural provincial noblemen, d'Urfé had
been a militant member of the Catholic League against the Protestant
armies led by Henry of Navarre, to whom, in a gracious gesture of
surrender, he dedicated the second part of his novel after Henry became
king. D'Urfé's personal background, from a prosperous and prominent
southern family close to the Savoy house and to the high clergy, had
exposed him to a refined courtly education without making him an active courtier. The *Astrée* is the imaginative work of a nobility that recognizes its defeat without joining the victors in adopting the ways of the
ruling court, hence it remains cut off from the rewarding yet humiliating
conformism of the courtly aristocracy dominated by the absolute monarch. Despite lingering resistance, the new court represented an irre-
versible new situation. The price of heeding Montaigne's demurrers was
too high for most.

In the *Nibelungenlied* Kriemhild had sought revenge not because
Siegfried was the most lovable man, even though he was the perfect
warrior hero, but because *her* man had been taken away from her in an
act of personal injury to her honor. Both in the Middle Ages and at the
time of Louis XIII "romantic" troubadourlike devotion in a framework
of absolute fidelity was not the modus operandi of the higher but of the
middle nobility. By taking this sublimated posture the "poor nobles"
made up for their inferiority to the true masters, who could afford to
love freely (as the first troubadour, William IX, had done, and as the
court nobility of eighteenth-century France would continue to do). Reflecting the ideal standpoint of this middle nobility, the sentimental
novel of which the *Astrée* was the most successful example extolled a
pure, chaste, marriage-oriented love of constancy, fidelity, and reason-
ableness. Compare the titles of some of the most popular sentimental
novels of the time: *Chastes amours d'Eros et de Kalisti*; *Le triomphe de*

la constance où sont décrites les amours de Cloridons et de Melliflore;
and so on. D'Urfé explicitly opposed the love of Céladon for the shepherdess Astrée to the libertine mores of the high nobility and the
"nymphs." "The simple, good, free life of the lower-ranking shepherds
and shepherdesses is contrasted again and again to the customs and
morals of the higher-ranking lords and ladies of the court, the actual
wielders of power in this world."[55] It was d'Urfé's way of carrying on
the struggle at the vicarious level of imagination by nostalgically roman-
ticizing a feudal nobility which thought it could go on living on the
land, away from the central court, even while it depended on the central
government for its survival. This pattern of absolute romantic fidelity
recalled not only the chivalrous manners of old, but also their most
radical interpretation, Dante's love for Beatrice.

The general orientation of d'Urfé's meandering narrative comes forth
in the letter to Céladon at the beginning of the second part, which
praises the traditional (read: feudal) moral values of sincerity, loyalty,
honor, and purity of mores still to be found (in the book) among the
bergers of the land of Forez. The perfect love of the shepherds, which
was the feudal love of twelfth-century knights, is called *l'honnête amitié*
since its radical sublimation leaves little room for sex. It does involve,
however, a lot of sensitive casuistic conversation. The formula also contains an interesting echo of the Ciceronian term *honestum*, that d'Urfé,
the pupil of a Jesuit school, had learned to apply to his *honnêtes
gens*—courtly though not of The Court. "Amour," that is, sensual love,
the novel avers, has disturbed the peace of Forez by introducing rivalry
and dissension, just as ambition had done at court.

The revealing formula of the preface, "vivre plus doucement et sans
contrainte," refers to the ethic of a "dual-front class": the freedom of a
romantic, utopian, idyllically rustic life—at the country homes of the
feudal nobility. This meant freedom from the humiliating constraints
and high etiquette of the centralized court, while accepting the exhila-
rating constraints of a romantic, constant, and refined Petrarchan love
that placed its upholders above the coarse lower classes of foul-smelling
real rustics (remember the medieval *vilains*).[56]

The consciousness of rank is peculiarly acute in this seemingly abstract pastoral world, because it addresses a specific audience. These shepherds and
nymphs are understood for what they really are on the basis of their line of
descent: "Only if one knows the social origin and thus the social rank of a
person does one know who and what this person really is. . . . For descent
and social rank are keystones of the social existence of the nobility. *Astrée* is

> an aristocratic novel that puts variously disguised aristocrats on the stage for
> an aristocratic audience. That was—and is—the first question that interests
> nobles when they meet another noble: "From what house, from what family
> does he or she come?" Then he can be classified.
>
> (Elias 1983: 255)

We are reminded of Farinata's arrogant question to Dante: "Who
were your ancestors?" ("Chi fuor li maggior tui?" *Inferno* 10.42). The
firm sentiment for keeping one's place and holding inferiors to theirs
was not to be challenged until the French Revolution. In one of Goldoni's masterpieces, *La locandiera* (1753), the progressive and demo-
cratically inclined yet firmly bourgeois Venetian playwright has his
charming protagonist Mirandolina, a paragon of adroitness, wit, and
solid common sense, vigorously wooed by a count, a marquis, and a
knight, only to turn them all down elegantly and decide to "keep her
place" by marrying her valet, Fabrizio.

The theory of love embedded in the "Douze tables des lois d'amour"
read by Silvandre and contested by Hylas (book 2 of second part) is a
Petrarchist/Neo-Platonic summation of the medieval code of courtly
love, just as the behavior of both the shepherds on the one hand and the
princes and knights on the other (*bergers, princes, chevaliers*—namely,
the lower and higher nobility, respectively), including the warriors at
Mérovée's court, is said to be constantly informed by *courtoisie*.[57] Playing the role of advisors and educators, the high priests (*les druides*), for
their part, signally among them Adamas, interject long disquisitions on
the ideology of love and virtuous living that supplement those tables.
The obverse of this is conveniently supplied, in a nice dialectical coun-
terpoint, by the libertine Hylas: he manages to counterfeit the text of
the tables, declaring in his new version that, in love as elsewhere, *ex-
trème* and *infini* are signs not of *fidelité* but of *imprudence*, and *raison*
is the supreme criterion for a wisely selfish, practical use of love for
pleasure rather than mere *honneur*. It is an echo of the troubadours'
and Minnesingers' occasional moments of revolt against the frustrating
constraints of the code of love.

The critique of monarchic absolutism comes to the fore in the case
of Childéric.[58] Before being finally deposed by the unanimous assembly
of the Celts and Franks, he not only had planned to take a married
noblewoman by force, as he had done with others, but had allowed
himself to be persuaded by flattering courtiers that "toutes choses
étaient permises au roi; que les rois faisaient les lois pour leurs sujets, et
non pas pour eux, et que, puisque la mort et la vie de ses vassaux étaient

en sa puissance, il en pouvait faire de même pour tout ce qu'ils possé-
daient." It sounds like a clever exposure of the doctrine of inherent
power and of the king as *lex animata*.

The intriguing prefaces to the novel's first three parts contain precious insights into the author's attitudes. The first one ("Épître de l'au-
teur à la bergère Astrée") recalls Tasso's *Aminta* for the convention, that
d'Urfé is carrying out, of introducing refined characters (his peers and
Tasso's courtiers) in the garb of shepherds. But he makes sure to remind
his readers that they are not real shepherds. In the second one, in the
form of a letter "au berger Céladon" the author warns his character
that his way of loving is "aimer à la vieille Gauloise," as the knights of
the Round Table did, a way no longer appreciated in an age when lovers, like Hylas in the novel, want concrete reward rather than mere
obedience, constancy, fidelity, honor, sacrifice, and suffering: "aimer et
jouir de la chose aimée sont des accidents inséparables." The author is
conscious of going somehow against current, in a state of nostalgic retreat. The third preface (to the river Lignon) recalls the scholastic dictum, of Ficinian ring we might say, that "the lover's soul is more inside
the beloved than inside the lover to whom it gives life," "magis est ubi
amat quam ubi animat," as, d'Urfé claims, the etymology indicates:
"*aimer* que nos vieux et très sages pères disaient *amer*, qu'est-ce autre
chose qu'abréger le mot d'*animer*, c'est-à-dire, faire la propre action de
l'âme. Aussi les plus savants ont dit, il y a longtemps, qu'elle vit plutôt
dans le corps qu'elle aime, que dans celui qu'elle anime."[59] We know
that this had been a favorite topos among troubadours, trouvères, and
Minnesingers.

IMITATION AND TRANSFORMATION IN GERMANY

France and England are notable for the close connections with the standards that were set in the Italian Cinquecento. For Germany I shall
extend my rapid survey of the literature of chivalry, courtliness, and
courtesy up to roughly 1700 in order to reflect delayed echoes of Italian
and French developments.

In the fifteenth century the first imports from Italian humanism
joined the Flamboyant Gothic romanesque coming out of Burgundy in
the literature patronized at the courts of two latter-day emulators of
Alienor of Aquitaine and Marie de Champagne, that is, the Countess of
the Palatinate Mechthild von Vorderösterreich (co-founder of the humanistic Universities of Freiburg, 1455, and Tübingen, 1477) at Rotten-

burg on the Neckar, and the Duchess Eleonore of Austria at Innsbruck (whose husband Duke Sigmund of Tyrol had befriended Aeneas Sylvius Piccolomini in his youth). The chivalric revival that characterized this literature mixed ancient and modern elements in the works of the Swabian knight Hermann von Sachsenheim (1365–1458: see his *Des Spiegels Abenteuer*, 1451, and *Die Mörin*, 1453,[60] love allegories dedicated to Mechthild), *Der Elende Knabe*, and perhaps Elbelin von Eselberg (or Elblin von Eselsberg, dates uncertain). Eleonore, herself perhaps the author of a prose romance adapted from the French, *Pontus und Sidonia*,[61] sponsored such works as the *Reisen nach der Ritterschaft* (after 1450) by the adventurous crusading knight Georg von Ehingen, and *Melusine* (1456, also from the French) by the Swiss Thüring von Ringoltingen (d. 1483).[62] *Melusine* is the story of a knight who unknowingly marries a sea-fairie and, somewhat as in the story of Psyche, loses her by breaking the injunction not to watch her bathing. Ulrich Füetrer,[63] mostly active at the court of Duke Albrecht IV the Wise of Bavaria in Munich, was also in touch with both Mechthild's and Eleonore's courts.

The medieval romance continued its desiccated life. The prolific Georg or Jörg Wickram (1505-ca. 1561), founder of a school of Meistersingers in his native Colmar in Alsace, is best remembered as the author of sundry romances. If his *Ritter Galmy* (1539) and *Gabriotto und Reinhart* (1551) still echoed the courtly romance closely enough, in *Der Jungen Knaben Spiegel* (1554) and *Der Goldtfaden* (1554, published 1557) the new social reality pierced through by pitching the merchant class against the old nobility.[64] *Der Jungen Knaben Spiegel* unfavorably sets a prodigal young nobleman against the virtuous son of a burgher. In *Der Goldtfaden*, sometimes regarded as the beginning of the German novel, Leufried, a shepherd's son adopted by a merchant, finds menial employment in a count's castle. Having fallen in love with the count's daughter Angleana, he embarks on a series of adventures for which he is knighted and rewarded with Angleana's hand. One can readily see how, despite the willful drift toward recognition of moral superiority for the lower classes, the life pattern remains that of the medieval knight: the class gap is bridged only by emulation of the traditionally ideal modus vivendi of the nobility. One wins by joining them, not by fighting them or by asserting substantive differences.

The *Amadis de Gaule* was highly popular in Germany, too. It saw the light in successive German renderings based on the French versions and published by the trendy publisher and bookseller Sigmund Feyerabend, starting in 1569 and soon reaching thirteen books in 1583, finally twenty-four in 1595.[65] Public demand prolonged the life of this extravagant mélange of heroic adventurism and gallant eroticism replete with Greek, Byzantine, and medieval sources, inspiring Christoph Martin Wieland to put forth his longish *Der neue Amadis* as late as 1771. The taste for this type of high-class exotic sentimentality was akin to the taste for the "gallant literature" (*galante Dichtung* and *galanter Roman*) that leaned on the refined stylized eroticism flourishing in the second half of the seventeenth century in the French aristocratic salons. It was merely an imitative literary phenomenon, since Germany lacked the social environments where such a way of life could thrive. Nonetheless, the *Amadis* ran strong as part of the modified survival of medieval romances.

Andreas Heinrich Buchholtz (or Bucholtz, 1607–1671) is often considered the author of the first original *höfischer Roman* or court novel with his *Des christlichen teutschen Großfürsten Herkules und des böhmischen königlichen Fräulein Valiska Wundergeschichte* (1659), which had a sequel in 1665.[66] These works were meant to entertain court nobility and gentry while instructing them through the edifying discourses that studded the narrative plot. It was a new twist in the narrative pattern that meant to supersede the vogue of the gallant—and the *Amadis* itself in what it contained of gallant willfulness.

The shattering experiences of the Thirty-Years War (1618–1648) enabled Germany to develop further than any other region the dramatic potential of ascetic reflection on human destiny. As indicated earlier (at beginning of chap. 10), the baroque theme of the topsy-turvy world, where values are the opposite of what they seem, fed fruitfully on the long tradition of court critique, signally on Guevara's recent authority, and turned the fate of the courtier into a symbol of the human predicament. The lesson it taught was: the shinier, the shallower; the higher they rise, the harder they fall. This realization was made to invest the whole of mankind: Guazzo, for one, had contributed to the generalization from courtier to gentleman by extending the idea beyond the court.

The lyric flowering of the German baroque was closely related to the life of numerous learned societies, which largely thrived around various princely courts and under the patronage of ruling princes. From the beginning of their existence the "academies," which started in Italy with the Platonic Academy of Marsilio Ficino under the aegis of the Medici in Florence, and then spread to other countries in imitation of the Italian models, were extensions and at times even instruments of aristocratic governments. This was particularly true in Germany, starting with the most important German academy, the Fruchtbringende Gesellschaft. Prince Ludwig of Anhalt-Köthen (Dessau 1579—Köthen 1650), who became its president until his death, founded it in 1617 in Weimar in direct imitation of the Florentine Academy of the Crusca (1583, sponsored by the Medici dukes), of which he had been a member while in Florence (1610–1612).[67] Gueintz, Harsdörffer, Schottel, Stieler, Kramer, Leibniz, and Steinbach became members of it.

Literary historians have used the expression *Hofpoeten*, "court poets," for poets who, while participating in the varied lyrical and narrative forms of their age, also produced verse that was specifically aimed at entertaining and flattering princes and high courtiers. Such poets were, for example, the Berliner Friedrich Rudolf von Canitz (1654–1699), diplomat and state functionary in Prussia; the Courlander Johann von Besser (1654–1729), son of a country clergyman who in 1690 became a courtier, diplomat, and master of ceremonies (Zeremonienmeister) at the Prussian and then the Saxon courts; the Silesian Benjamin Neukirch (1665–1729); and the Saxon Johann Ulrich König (1688–1744), who in 1729 succeeded Besser in Dresden as court poet to Augustus II, Elector of Saxony and King of Poland. Their works remained popular and somewhat influential at least through the middle of the eighteenth century.

Anton Ulrich, Duke of Braunschweig-Lüneburg (1633–1714), was a great prince who by long family tradition exerted a remarkable personal influence on literary activities around his court and himself authored important works of a courtly nature. His five-volume *Die durchleuchtige Syrerinn Aramena* (1669–1673) and six-volume *Die römische Octavia* (1677–1707) were literature for nobles, declared manifestos for an aristocratic mission painstakingly set in a massive structure of quasi-mathematical hierarchies, which attracted Leibniz, the duke's librarian at Wolfenbüttel.[68] In Anton Ulrich's *Aramena* the Stoic virtues of constancy and faithfulness, *Standhaftigkeit* and *Treue*, triumph in a large web of characters paired by love and centered around the prince and his court. The attending ministers and state functionaries are arranged in cooperating groups or power centers to be controlled or conquered. As in the medieval romances, the love stories do not develop alongside the social and political power game but are an integral part of it. The setting is ancient, Oriental and Roman, but the issues are transparently modern. The novel as a genre has become a noble school for the court, *Hof-* and *Adelsschule*. The classicism in the choice of forms and plot material bequeathed by humanism to the heroic novel combines with the chivalric heritage to produce a grand design, all meant to present the high issues of the day from the perspective of a nobility that feels destined to rule the world and set it right.

In the century of absolutism, lyric, drama, novel, sermon, epistle, pamphlet, and sundry tractates were all full of concepts of nobility and its accompaniment of grandeur or *Großmütigkeit* (= *magnanimitas*), heroes (*Helden*), courage (*Tapferkeit*), and every other chivalric virtue. These by now traditional qualities show the tenacity of a terminology that had been imposed by medieval usage: *mâze*, for example, was the ideal of the poet from Memel/Königsberg Simon Dach (1605–1659). Such virtues were said to establish the noble hero as the divinely appointed leader by setting him above and apart from the common humanity of the subjects. H. J. C. von Grimmelshausen's (1622?–1676) 1666 *Der keuscher Joseph*[69] and Casper von Lohenstein's (1635–1683) 1683 *Arminius*[70] are, among others by less eminent writers, some exemplary texts of this attitude that spanned literature and social behavior.[71]

As to the literature of conduct, Castiglione's work was translated by Lorenz Kratzer in 1565/1566 as *Der Hofmann*, and again with the same title by Johann Engelbert Noyse of Augsburg in 1593.[72] In 1578 in Rostock, Nathan Chytraeus published his often reprinted Latin translation of Della Casa: *Galateus, seu de morum honestate et elegantia*, followed in 1597 and 1607 by Chytraeus's own German version, *Galateus: Das ist das Büchlein von erbarn höflichen und holdseligen Sitten*.[73] In 1582 the printer Bernard Jobin of Frankfurt, who also published the Latin *Cortegiano*, brought out Wolfgang Unger's first German version of Antonio de Guevara's *Aviso de privados* with the title *Aviso de privados: Der Hofleut Wecker*. Starting with a preface to the second edition of the Latin *Galateus* (1579), Johannes Caselius (1533–1613) presented a positive use of manners and courtesy as key to the art of *prudentia politica*, the secret of success in ethical matters.[74] In a version of the metaphorical "sugar-coated pill," the courtier advises the power holder through the pleasant entertainment of games (*joci, ludi*) in order to hide the bitter truth of duties and hard tasks. The *Cortegiano* had indeed spoken of court games as the flower whose fruit is the education of the prince ("quasi il fiore . . . il vero frutto della cortegiania," 4.5).

It is remarkable that all fourteen Latin editions of Guazzo's text were published in Germany, between 1585 (Köln) and 1673.[75] The German public was accustomed to looking for treatments of this genre in Latin, starting at least with Erasmus's *De civilitate morum puerilium*. A special development and a valuable document for the history of manners is *Grobianus sive de morum simplicitate libri duo* (Frankfurt, 1549) by Friedrich Dedekind (1525–1598, after 1551 a Protestant pastor in Neustadt and then Lüneburg). In this classic satire of bad manners in Latin distichs, Dedekind ridiculed coarse, vulgar, and self-centered behavior in social intercourse and especially at table by ironically praising boorishness. It became popular in Caspar Scheidt's 1551 rendering in German rhymed verse (*Grobianus, von groben sitten und unhöflichen gebärden*), and Dedekind felt encouraged to give it a sequel in a third book dealing with feminine behavior under the name of the character Grobiana.[76] His late *Der christliche Ritter* (1590) drew inspiration from Erasmus.

It was particularly in Germany that speculation on the conduct and function of the courtier was extended to the formulation of proper ethico-economic attitudes in running the household in what is called *Hausväterliteratur*—a literature that began in the late sixteenth century and developed briskly in the seventeenth.[77]

Despite the numerous translations from Italian and French, however, original speculation was late in coming to Germany: the poet Georg Philipp Harsdörffer (Nürnberg 1607–1658) as well as the philosopher Christian Thomasius (Leipzig 1655–1728) in his *Discours* of 1687, are known for having lamented the lack of manners among their fellow countrymen despite the rich literature available on the subject and the fashion of French imitation. In addition to his translation of Eustache Du Refuge's (d. 1617) *Traité de la cour* (1616) as *Kluger Hofmann* (1655),[78] Harsdörffer made an early contribution with his series of *Frawenzimmer Gesprächspiele* (1641–1649),[79] dialogues on intellectual divertissements and parlor games addressed to high society, followed by a *Discurs von der Höflichkeit* appended to his *Mercurius Historicus* of 1657.[80] Thomasius keenly theorized on the divergences between absolute values and the moral compromises that seem necessary to make them acceptable to society under the rubrics of courtesy, *politesse*, affability, friendliness, pleasant disposition, the Italian categories of the *galantuomo giudizioso, prudente, discreto*, and the Spanish ones of Baltasar Gracián's *Discreto* and *Oráculo manual y arte de prudencia*—the latter work being also available in Germany in Nicolas Amelot de la Houssaie's translation of 1684.[81] *Klugheit* became a key word covering both prudence and discretion, and *Ton* rendered both "style" and "manner" (as in French *bon ton*). Being witty—having *esprit*, as the French put it—was essential for survival, and worldly-wisdom was a surer secret of success than stern Stoic virtues.

It was at this time that Germans developed a lively literature on "ceremonial" (*Zeremonial*), that is, on ways to fit our behavior and our style of life, manners, gesture, speaking habits, and even feeling and thinking to social circumstances, according to the French insistence on *bienséances*. All this came specifically from the imitation of the ways of nobility at court. It was, so to speak, a new universal knighthood, and it led to the development of an interesting terminology of elegant verbal "compliments" denoting urbanity and civility. German *Kompliment* was analogically related to a peculiar German neologism *Complement*, referring to the polished outer "complement" to our inner civility, and harking back to the poet Georg Greflinger (Regensburg, ca. 1620– ca. 1680, settled in Hamburg as a notary) in his *Ethica complementoria* (1645).

Etiquette books in the vernacular continued their course, and they would culminate in the *Über den Umgang mit Menschen* (1788), about the only work by which one still remembers Adolf F. F. Freiherr von Knigge (1752–1796), a prolific author of satirical novels and travel stories. The proverbial phrase "nach Knigge" can still be heard in Germany when people discuss proper social conduct. While readable as a prescriptive text on manners and etiquette, *Über den Umgang* displayed broad humanity and practical common sense according to the principles of the golden mean in a series of such essays as "Über den Umgang mit sich selbst," "Von dem Umgange mit Eheleuten," "Über den Umgang mit Gelehrten und Künstlern," and so forth. Knigge's observation that to live well in the world one must adjust and be governed by the others' customs, feelings, and manners—which was in line with the long tradition of *cortegiania*—elicited a lively reaction in the age of Romantic emphasis on the honest individual who must stay away from the crowd in order to preserve his or her purity as well as intellectual and moral superiority.[82]

Indeed, the new Romantic hero was to be an anticourtier who rejected rules and conventions even to the point of being unwilling or unable to adjust to social realities; he was ready to go under rather than compromise with the rules for power and worldly success. Goethe's Werther was the first symbol of this uncompromising attitude toward the principles put forward by the tradition we have been following: he was an adversary of those who had succeeded by adopting the ways of the world even in the form of being chivalrous, *courtois*, and courtly.

Conclusion

The connection between the image of the chivalrous knight and that of the courtier should now be apparent, and the broad cultural scope of these images should also be obvious. Toward the end of the Renaissance there came a literary genius who provided the best testimony to the power and pervasiveness of the courtly ideology, since his works were undoubtedly the most penetrating representation of the world of court. It is a paradox of literary history that this man, William Shakespeare, left no record of his exposure to the world that inspired him so deeply and so creatively.[1]

The alliance of knightly and courtly mentality, with the occasional Tassoesque drift (which we observed in the *Astrée*) toward the Arcadian never-never land of noble shepherds as transparent disguises of the nostalgic lower nobility, has continued in shifting forms, down to our own day. The individualistic streak of chivalrous culture survived the centralization of state authority and the shift in military techniques, including a heavier emphasis on well-armed infantry as well as the replacement of knights with trained professional officers (who often were members of the nobility of knightly rank in different dress but similar spirit).[2] At home that individualistic streak of chivalry sustained the spirit of independence, resistance, and occasionally rebellion in the various *frondes* to the very threshold of the French Revolution. The same chivalric individualism contributed to the adventurous urge that drove legions of Europeans into the "errantry" of exploration and conquest in the eras of discovery and colonization. Colonization, a strictly European phenomenon (adopted by Japan as part of its westernization), can be regarded as an extension of the chivalric tradition. "The legacy of the cult of errantry in the age of chivalry" survived in individual "odysseys" that kept driving new adventurers abroad, in quest of gain and honor (*vide*, e.g., Lope de Aguirre's *mas valer* in Peru), in a mixture of ruthless rapacity with the noble cause of carrying "faith, civilization, and the flag of loyalty" to faraway lands and peoples (M. Keen 1984, 250). Dress changed more than the underlying spirit.[3]

This lingering of the chivalric heritage is Maurice Keen's conclusion (1984) as well as my own. Where I part ways with him is in stressing different outcomes. Whereas Keen sees the enduring vitality of chivalry in the notion that the memory of ancestral achievement carries the high educational worth of personal example, my coupling of chivalry with courtesy and courtliness lays stress on the close connection between chivalry and a universal behavioral model to be admired and imitated by all members of society who aspired to acceptance, respect, and success. This remained operative until the great behavioral changes that have occurred in our own century.

If a detailed survey beyond 1625 were desired, for its Italian section it would have to make appropriate room for the discovery of the heroic ethic in Giambattista Vico's (1668–1744) *Scienza Nuova* (1725, definitive version 1744). Cultural historians have analyzed the way Italians perceived the historical role of Germanic customs, leading to Vico's doctrine of the Germanic Middle Ages as a type of heroic culture. The evidence shows a rather surprising gap in the knowledge of German literature even while historical material pertaining to German and Scandinavian lands was being evaluated from the Renaissance on by such erudite archeologists as Scipione Maffei and Ludovico A. Muratori. In this sense Maffei's *Della scienza chiamata cavalleresca* was typical of the Enlightenment: Germanic behavior was regarded as based on sheer force, as opposed to the southern peoples' reliance on a sense of reason and justice.[4] Had Vico been familiar with the Germanic heroic literature from the *Hildebrantslied* to the *Nibelungenlied*, he would have found there the most fitting confirmation of his theory that Achilles' murderously resentful wrath was also in keeping with the morality of the feudal age. Vico's concomitant theory of history's cyclic courses and recourses would have found solid ground there for the assimilation of the Middle Ages to the Homeric age. For the Neapolitan philosopher was well aware of the "universal nature" of feudal forms of social organization (the "natura eterna de' feudi"). He clearly saw the underlying psycho-

logical connection between the forms of feudalism that still dominated
in Naples as well as in other European regions and the ancient structures of clientele, through the medieval institutions of vassalage. He envisaged all such phenomena as cases of "ricorsi," postulating a correla-
tion between conscious, high-level ideas and collective mentalities on
the deep, dark level of popular beliefs.[5]

One of our themes has been the way the ideology of the aristocracy
operated at court and generated a school of high manners there. The
literature of French Classicism brought that refinement of manners to
fruition within the court, radiating out from it through the upper layers
of the surrounding society. But the ideology underlying that social paradigm had been changing, as exemplified by the tragic genre. The avowed
intent of French tragedy was to restore the classical coordinates of this
high genre, signally the sense of fate and of loyalty to family and country.
Yet these very coordinates had been replaced by the typically courtly
ones of a code of honor founded on loyalty to the king. The stage was
no longer occupied by the ancient conflicts between moral duty toward
religious laws or the family and the will of the lord—the conflicts that
one saw at work, say, in the myth of Antigone and Orestes in opposition to Creon and Aegysthus—but by the sort of feudal conflicts that a
Corneille could borrow from the medieval opposition of the knightly
Cid to his king.[6] Orestes and Electra had killed the usurper Aegysthus
and their own mother, Clytemnestra, to revenge their father Agamem-
non; feudal heroes like the Cid, instead, protested the sovereign's violation of their rights. To eighteenth-century audiences, however, especially in Italy, even these more "modern" standards had lost much of
their meaning.[7] Active chivalry had been pushed to a marginal position,
and on the level of consciousness its days were numbered. The mock-
heroic and the burlesque had driven out the heroic, the martial, and the
chivalrous. After trying his hand in the *Henriade* (1723/28), Voltaire
could conclude—oblivious to the *Chanson de Roland*—that "les Français n'ont pas la tête épique"—and he turned to *La Pucelle d'Orléans*.

As centralized absolutism was taming knights and courtiers, the idea
of nobility was also being weakened, sapped at the very roots of its
actual or perceived functionality. Noblemen began to be seen as parasites without sufficient objective merits to support their privileges. In
1710 the polymath Scipione Maffei from Verona, himself a marquis,
published a scathing attack on the ideas of chivalry and nobility in his
satirical *Della scienza chiamata cavalleresca*.[8] Savagely ridiculing the
most esteemed authorities on duels, from Paride dal Pozzo to Girolamo

Muzio, Sebastiano Fausto da Longiano, and Camillo Baldi (see chap.
10 above), Maffei proposed that the laughable modern punctilio on
knightly honor, which he traced to the Longobards' barbarous custom
of private vendetta (*faida*), be replaced with a newly classical sense of
true human virtues, which he wanted to see grounded on a philologically correct knowledge of antiquity.[9] This new classicism would act as
a corrective to false notions of nobility and reveal where human greatness truly lay. The nobles could once again become honorable by turning to useful functions instead of vegetating as expensive parasites who
spurned on principle all productive activity. Maffei was thus closing the
circle of the history of courtliness, which had started out with the Ottonian thrust toward education with a social content. His attack was to
be echoed in a vast literature in the Age of Reason, of which it should
suffice to mention, for Italy, Giuseppe Parini's (1729–1799) spirited
and radical *Dialogo sopra la nobiltà* (1757, published posthumously
1801), in addition to his better known satirical poem, *Il giorno*.[10] The
leaders of the Risorgimento, who numbered many noblemen, placed
among their heroes both Parini and, even more, Vittorio Alfieri, who,
not content with the clamorous antiestablishment statement of re-
nouncing his Savoy countship, went around European courts refusing
to bow before kings.

Despite such ominous forebodings of changes to come, the ethos of
chivalry continued unabated on the level of daily practice. The novel/
memoir by Giacomo Casanova, *Il duello ovvero saggio della vita di
G. C. Veneziano* (1780), is a picturesque example of the power of the
mental image of a noble character who asserts his right to be a leader
by fighting a dangerous duel for honor's sake.[11] When, in Warsaw in
1766, the powerful royal courtier Francis Xavier Branicki insulted Ca
sanova, the protagonist felt compelled to challenge Branicki to a duel.
Though both men came out of the fight badly mangled, both behaved
according to the most exquisite chivalric rules before, during, and after
the duel. It was a telling case of risking everything—not only one's life
but condemnation by laws and authorities, since duels were illegal—for
the sake of proving to oneself—hence, implicitly, to society—that the
man of high status deserved his position because he possessed personal
qualities that distinguished him from the populace. To Branicki, this
evidence was worth risking his career as one of the most powerful men
of the kingdom; to Casanova it was a way to assert himself as a worthy
member of the élite.

The Romantic revolt was an attempt to transcend what had been a court-oriented aristocratic culture. In the introductory discourse to her 1810 *De la littérature considérée dans ses rapports avec les institutions sociales*, Madame de Staël, a forerunner of sociological criticism, aroused Napoleon's ire and the ensuing censorship of her work by upholding the exemplary value of German literature over the French partly on the ground that the latter had succumbed to the domination of an aristocratic élite, thus producing an art that "consisted essentially in the fostering of good manners."[12]

Yet, both the French Revolution and the Romantic movement fell far short of obliterating the aristocratic tradition and in particular chivalry, which, aside from its continuous impact on personal behavior among the nobility and others imitating its ways, enjoyed a broad cultural revival in the nineteenth century. Mark Girouard (1981) has written an elegant study of the way the two codes of chivalry and courtliness continued to affect both the public image and the personal behavior of gentlemen in Victorian and Edwardian England. His prefatory remarks point out that an equally productive study could be made for Germany and even America in the same period.[13] In America the idea was strong enough to provoke Mark Twain's *A Connecticut Yankee in King Arthur's Court*, that "by no means light-hearted piece of fooling" in which he "attacked mediaeval knights as superstitious, snobbish and ignorant exploiters of the rest of society" (i–ii).[14] The revival of chivalry that enjoyed such a fashion between the end of the eighteenth century and 1918 produced, before 1900, a model of the gentleman in which chivalry was superimposed on earlier traditions. The romantic gentleman became a chivalrous figure who was brave, honorable, frank, true to his word, loyal to country, monarch, and friends, ready to defend women, children, and the downtrodden. He was worthy of ruling the country in all honorable employments not because of wealth or social position, but because of moral superiority. He was well removed from the eighteenth-century gentleman, essentially a privileged man of landed property. Furthermore, his sexual attitudes bore the mark of a new courtly lover, pure as Galahad while absolutely devoted to his wife, whom he had married for love.

To return to our starting point in order to sum up the trajectory we have covered, we can agree with C. S. Jaeger (6) that, rather than arising from a change within the French lay nobility, "courtesy and 'chivalric' ideals were nurtured in the conditions of court life." This was also N. Elias's thesis, although the two historians part ways where Elias seeks the roots of the changes in the collective needs of courtly life, whereas

Jaeger points to individuals and their ideas. My own focus has been on the special needs and feelings of a rather restricted category of people (like Duby's and Köhler's poor knights) within and around the courts—these needs having first been voiced by clerical members of the same groups. More particularly, the foregoing analysis of apparently disparate expressive forms has stressed an underlying common theme that ties together social needs, ideological attitudes, and imaginative narratives. We have seen knight/courtiers constantly operating under the creative stress of a need to justify their social function by serving the power structures at the same time that they were seeking their own personal ennoblement by rising to a privileged status of free, refined agents. The knight, etymologically a servant, became the most exalted model figure of his society. The courtier saw himself not only as a knight but also as a paragon of human perfection and the aesthetic ornament of his society, sitting on top of a decorative power structure. Words, concepts, and institutions have thus shown their close mutual ties even while they contained insoluble contradictions. The knight in Charlemagne's army and the knight/courtier at Arthur's court or, later, at the court of Urbino, were torn between their sense of individual worth, dignity, and freedom, on the one hand, and, on the other, their function as loyal servants to a lord or collective order—a state. This existential dialectical ambiguity characterizes the history of western civilization.

Of that dialectical ambiguity we have seen a growing awareness in literature, and the story of our manifold subject matter should have contributed to the discovery of an intriguing yet disturbing aspect of public life: that what succeeds is not necessarily truthfulness, righteousness, and goodness, but rather a persuasive agreeableness, *grazia* perhaps. It is necessary to hide one's feelings and smile in the face of adversity, be respectful and kindly toward our enemies even at the moment of confronting them, be calculating and diplomatic, even to be or to seem to be hypocrites in order to survive and perhaps, in the end, to win in the real world. The patterns of public behavior rest on an inherent duplicity, and virtues are at times indistinguishable from vices. To start from the tail end of my story, the history of the reception of the *Cortegiano*, including Guazzo's landmark work, shows the problematic nature of this literature, which earnestly attempted to face the question of whether the public man can be inherently honest or only superficially so. The virtues of the *curialis* and then of the loving chivalrous knight were similarly ambiguous. This discovery goes beyond political observation, since it invests the general question of the nature of the psyche, of society, and of values.

The historically trained reader may feel that the enduring quality of the ideological nomenclature has masked or distorted the uniqueness of each historical experience, or at best failed to recognize it and valorize it. This lies within the nature of ideologies, which, just the same, *are* real conditioners of human behavior. To close this summary defense of the surface continuity we have been following, I quote a pithy definition recently given by a sagacious observer of this type of mental and cultural phenomena. Human culture, says Virgil Nemoianu, "is single-minded and exclusionary. Power, growth and progress, creativity and control, economic interest and ideological vision, complex as they may be, take monolithic shapes and foster streamlined uniformities. . . . They all concentrate on the principal or the main, they all confer a decisive priority on what is central over what is marginal." The themes we have encountered kept being reiterated despite the hidden differences because they were part of the main rather than the marginal.[15]

Circumstantial differences may be what some historians most care about, but the episodes I have extracted from the flow of time illustrate the persistence of a characteristic phenomenon that modern man is hard put to appreciate, namely the puzzling insistence on a seemingly contradictory code of conduct that made men both worship and despise women, and left women teetering on the precarious and dangerous tightrope of flirtation and wiles. Setting different genres alongside one another has shown an enduring correspondence between woman as object of a sublime devotion, mixing sexual desire and Platonic renunciation, and the image of the woman of court as the bearer of aristocratic blood, hence necessarily chaste even while she served as a stimulus to other men's bravery and eloquence. The knight fights bravely and the courtier speaks artfully for the sake of the chaste and unattainable woman they faithfully yet hopelessly love. This predicament combines the ethic of knighthood and the ethic of courtliness even while it shows us the relationship between the conduct of courtiers and the code of the romances.[16]

The knight, radically yet typically, always moved in a fairyland, isolated from the world of the "rustics," the "real" world. At the same time, Tristan and Lancelot could not survive because they could not help but be disloyal to their king in the closest quarters of their private and public lives. Perhaps one way to appreciate the special contribution of chivalry to western culture is to realize that it enabled the sharpest representation of something literature and art represent inherently by their own constant nature: the divergence between the outside world and our inner world, between objective reality and our perception of it, between the given and the desired. Art always holds up a mental image and a dream even while it exposes both its outer and inner tensions, namely the tensions between the dream and the outside reality on the one hand and, on the other, the dream's incoherence with its own operational rules.

Albrecht von Eyb and the Legend of St. Alban

Two medieval legends that strike us for their radical exemplariness provide interesting points of contact with the culture of courtliness in its diverse ramifications. I refer to the Germanic versions of the convergent legends of St. Alban (Albanus, "*Albanuslegende*") and Saint Gregory (Gregorius). The former is extant, besides its Latin originals, in at least a German and a Dutch version, and was later included in the *Ehebuch* of Albrecht von Eyb (1420–1475), the humanistically educated German cleric best remembered for the first German manual of rhetoric, the Petrarca-based *Margarita*. The Albanus legend has been expertly studied in its Latin, German, and Dutch versions by Karin Morvay (1977), but without much attention to the analogous, though literally unrelated story of Gregorius.

The widespread hagiographic motif of Gregorius reverberated in several versions from an anonymous twelfth-century French text, the entirely fictional *Vie du Pape Grégoire* (no reference to any of the historical popes by that name), to Hartmann von Aue's (b. 1160–d. after 1210) four-thousand-line poem, *Gregorius* (probably 1187–1189, or 1195 at the latest), for which the motif is principally known, and finally Thomas Mann's novel *Der Erwählte* (1951), acknowledging Hartmann as immediate source. Neither the well-known British legend of St. Gregory the Great from the abbey of Whitby,[1] nor the St. Alban associated with the monastery of St. Alban in England, nor the Sant'Albano of a fourteenth-century Tuscan manuscript (Riccardiano 2734) bears any relation to our stories.[2] The *Albanuslegende* is a much more articulated

elaboration of the motif inherent in the Gregory legend, without reference to the life of any pope. In narrative richness it is superior to any
other version, including the celebrated one by Hartmann.[3] The name,
Alban, which curiously enough appears only at the very end of the text,
is clearly related to the contiguous citation from Psalm 50,9: "et supra
nivem dealbabo" ("dealbari" in the text).

What makes the two legends worthy of attention within the context
of the foregoing investigation is the presence of important courtly and
chivalric elements, both in the patterns of external behavior and in the
deeper moral and religious motivation.[4] Our legendary texts share the
combination of these elements with a body of literature which spans
the hagiographic and the genuinely literary, in a way that exemplifies
the deep moral and even theological concerns lying in the background—
and sometimes coming directly into the foreground—of some of the
most vital literature of courtliness and courtesy. Furthermore, some elements of Eyb's version in particular testify to the continuity of the medieval tradition which underlies the Renaissance treatises of manners,
so that it appears relevant for the study of both sides of our dual subject
insofar as our subject joins chivalry and manners.[5]

The Gregorius/Albanus core stories were *exempla* of God's infinite
mercy, since the most horrible sins can be forgiven after sincere repen-
tance and proper atonement. Their theme displayed the most tragic
criminal infractions on the canvas of the classical Oedipus complex.
Hartmann's Gregorius (named both Grigorss and Gregorius in Mann's
novel) is born of the incestuous union of brother and sister, who are
presented as models of courtly conduct and serve as examples of the
danger of yielding to the demands of the courtly code without a sense
of discretion and restraint by measure, as the deeply moral Hartmann
often attempted to demonstrate in his romances. The father is overcome
by remorse and departs on a Crusade, meeting his death on the way.
The mother decides to entrust the child to God's care and sends him
floating downstream in a little boat. An abbot finds him and raises him
with loving care, but, like Perceval, Gregorius feels an irresistible calling
to become a knight, and his chivalrous wanderings will bring him to
save a lady who has been robbed of her domain. She rewards him with
her love and they marry, only to discover that she is his mother. We
have, thus, a situation of double incest. Gregorius embarks on a life of
penance and spends seventeen years with fettered feet on a rock set in a
lake in a wild region (hence the title of the later Volksbuch version,
"Gregorius auf dem Steine"). Two Roman wise men arrive with the

mission of fetching him for the papal throne, since God has manifested His choice of this holy hermit as His next vicar on earth. The mother comes to Rome seeking absolution from the new pope and both spend the remainder of their lives in deep piety, thus obtaining divine forgiveness for their sins and those of the father.

The educational burden of the story is analogous to that of the previous *Erek*, in which Hartmann, expanding on Chrétien de Troyes's *Erec et Enide*, had stressed the virtuous elements in the knightly code and condemned the disregard for measure (*mâze*) as a violation of self-restraint. Shortly after its composition, *Gregorius* was translated into Latin under the title *Gesta Gregorii peccatoris ad penitenciam conversi et ad papatum promoti* by the abbot Arnold von Lübeck, who imitated the German meter. One can wonder whether this abbot's text was known to his later fellow-Lübeckian, Mann. A fourteenth-century manuscript at Munich preserves another free Latin translation in hexameters. The legend became popular once again in a new German prose version that produced a Volksbuch, first published in 1471 as *Gregorius auf dem Steine* and reprinted several times thereafter.[6] The date of printing is witness to its respected position in the public eye, since at such an early date printers would not easily risk commercial failure by picking less than sure sellers. In Mann's version the chivalrous motivation is once again played up as psychological setting for the adventurous instincts that lead Grigorss, first to save his unknown mother, lady Sibylla, from her enemies, and then to marry her, with most of the principal events adhering closely to Hartmann's plot.

While factually quite different and more complex, the Albanus legend of Eyb's *Ehebuch* carries the same moral and theological message, inserted into an ample discourse on marriage. It is therefore not too surprising that sometimes Eyb's Albanus has been mistakenly identified as Gregorius-related: a fourteenth-century manuscript already used the title *De Albano* for the legend of Gregorius (Morvay 161). The story is entered as one of three novellas, which include the *Marina-Novelle*, a story of hard-won fidelity between husband and wife, and that of the tragic love between Ghismunda and Guiscardo from Boccaccio's *Decameron* ("Guiscard und Sighismunda" in Eyb).[7]

In this story of Christian salvation through the example of a "Christian Oedipus," Eyb declares his *intentio auctoris* thus: "I shall write about a certain *hauptsünder* who killed father and mother, wife and sister, and having unknowingly committed the sin of incest with his mother and sister did in the course of time perform such great penance as to be numbered among the saints. . . . By this story everyone is to understand that no sinner, however great and enormous his faults may be, should give himself up to despair."[8]

The characters are the emperor's family, in a central European setting. The original incest (recorded in detail in the *Gesta Romanorum*) is " 'trimmed and pruned' in order to emphasize the motive of penance in the second part of the story all the more,"[9] but from the narrative point of view the situation is completely reworked. The protagonists of the first incest are not brother and sister, as they were in some preceding versions, but the emperor and his daughter. As the story goes, a widowed emperor falls in love with his beautiful daughter, who reminds him of his lost beloved wife. The father wants to kill the child of this ill-fated union, but the mother persuades him to send the infant out of the country, to be abandoned with a purse at his neck containing a precious ring. A peasant couple finds him on the road in Hungary and delivers him to the king's court, where he grows up as a favorite courtier and knight.[10] When the news spreads that, to ensure the succession to the throne, the aging emperor is seeking a spouse for his daughter, the king of Hungary sends Albanus as the most suitable bridegroom. Only on his deathbed does the king of Hungary reveal to Albanus that he is his adopted son. He gives him the purse with the ring, which soon will prove his true identity to his wife/mother/sister. Together with the emperor himself, the couple decide to retire from the world and lead a life of atonement. The bishop sends them to a holy hermit, who assigns them to a hermitage on top of a deserted mountain. After seven years they descend in search of the hermit to terminate their period of seclusion but they lose their way and have to spend the night in the wilderness, Albanus perched in surveillance on top of a tree. As daylight breaks he is horrified to note that his parents have not been able to resist the temptation and are once again joined in an incestuous embrace under the tree. He climbs down in an uncontrollable rage and slays them both. Overcome with grief and shame, he returns to the mountain for seven more years of penance. But the legend of his tragic destiny and saintly atonement has spread over the land, and when a new ruler is to be chosen the people ascend the mountain and beg him to be their leader. He declines and decides to end his life as a holy hermit, but is finally slain by a party of bandits. His corpse, floating down a river, is caught under the wheel of a mill, and when lepers come to cleanse themselves by the waters nearby, they are miraculously healed. The corpse is discovered and Albanus's saintly nature is thus revealed to all the people.

We have noted that the two legends share common motifs. At Eyb's hands what had been in Hartmann a devout Christian poem of salvation, a *christliche Erlösungsdichtung*, became an equally exemplary though differently plotted novella of salvation, *Erlösungs-Novelle*. Hartmann's version is close to the later Volksbuch as well as a host of tales, both folkloric and literary, extant in many languages, including Latin, French, Spanish, Italian, German, Middle English, Polish, Russian, Bulgarian (the legend of Paul of Cesarea), Serbian (the story of Simeon, of which Jacob Grimm pointed out the relationship with the Gregorius legend), and Coptic (the story of Armenios).[11]

All, except Hartmann's, were apparently derived from a prose story embedded into chapter 81 of the *Gesta Romanorum*, which A. van der Lee found to hark back to an original Latin moral *exemplum*. There are three other early versions, two in fourteenth-century French and one in Italian in a Florentine manuscript of 1399.[12] The widely circulating *Gesta Romanorum* was first published in Germany (Cöln: Ulrich Zell, 1473, followed by two other editions within the next three years), precisely when Eyb was working on the different version of the story. The compilation, originally put together toward 1300, was characterized by a *moralizacio* appended to each story and containing a multilayered, fancifully shifting set of mystical allegorizations. Under the title "De mirabili divina dispensatione et ortu beati Gregorii papae," chapter 81 offered an exegesis of the emperor and his sister as representing Christ and the soul, with the son Gregorius standing for mankind: again, Christ is the knight who frees the mother from the devil and then marries her, that is, the Church. The knightly and chivalric element plays a large role in Gregorius's career.

The abridged version of the St. Alban legend contained in chapter 244 of the *Gesta Romanorum* is noteworthy for the lower stylistic quality, the pervasive ungrammaticality, and the lack of clarity in the narrative. The *moralitas* that concludes it is particularly inept and confused, without the appeal to Christological symbols that marks so many of the earlier chapters, including chapter 81 on St. Gregory.[13] The running moralizations of this theme combine Christian motifs with the more universal Oedipal matter of the son replacing the father at the side of the earth mother, in the anthropological cycle of life and death, fertility and regeneration.

The literature on this extensive body of ideally related texts is large, and much of it of difficult access. The texts can be grouped by independent clusters of variations, all stemming from a prehistoric concern with incest. Eyb's version shows similarities with the Italian legend of Vergogna, studied by Alessandro D'Ancona. Reinhold Köhler (1869) called attention to the Latin *Vita Sancti Albani* by the papal chancery secretary Transmundus as the source of a German poem of shortly after 1186, from the Moselle region, extant only in fragments.[14] The most widespread text was the somewhat streamlined one that appears in the *Gesta Romanorum* (chap. 244 of the Oesterley edition).

Let us now take a look at Eyb's career.[15] Born August 24, 1420, in Schloß Sommersdorff near Ansbach (Franken), he died July 24, 1475 in Eichstätt. In the fall of 1444 he began to study law at Pavia, where he received his doctorate *utriusque iuris* on February 7, 1459, and where he met Gasparino Barzizza, Manuel Chrysoloras, Maffeo Vegio, Lorenzo Valla, and Francesco Filelfo. His mentor, the law teacher Baltasar Rasinus, introduced him to ancient rhetoric and moral philosophy. The intervening years also brought him to Bologna, Padua, and back to Bologna. Eyb moved about in the circle of the famous humanist Pirckheimer, a fellow Franconian, who was in Bologna at that time. He returned to Bamberg in 1451 in order to seek a term of residence in view of a canonry and archdeaconry in the local cathedral. The pursuit of such benefices was to cost him severe harassment from the hostile bishop of Würzburg, John III, in the fall of 1462, but it was crowned with success three or four years later, after the bishop's death. In 1460 he returned for good to Eichstätt, by now an established center of humanistic studies. Late in 1462 he embarked on a fourth journey to Italy to plead for his rights as a canon. As a cleric in lower orders he practiced canon and civil law while canon (Domherr) in the cathedral chapters of Bamberg and Eichstätt, cubicularius of Pope Pius II after 1458, and archdeacon of Iphofen after 1465, in addition to other minor ecclesiastical benefices.

In his younger years, Eyb translated two Plautine comedies, the *Bacchides* and the *Menaechmi*, as well as Ugolino da Parma's Latin comedy *Philogenia*, into German. From Italy he brought back extensive notebooks with ancient and humanistic literary and juridical materials, some of which are extant in manuscript form. Of the several works that he composed, starting in 1451, some appear to be the earliest humanistic writings in Germany. The following tracts have remained unpublished, except for excerpts (especially in Herrmann): *De Eucharistiae Sacramento laudatio*; *Tractatus de speciositate Barbarae puellae* (Bamberg, 1452, leaning on Piccolomini's *Euryalus et Lucretia*); *Appellatio mulierum Bambergensium* (a satire leaning on Leonardo Bruni); *Ad laudem et commendationem Bambergae oracio* (reputed to have opened the German tradition of city-praise in humanistic form);[16] and *An uxor viro sapienti sit ducenda* (Bayrische Staatsbibliothek München, Cod. Lat. Mon. 650, fols. 47–72; first nucleus of his later *Spiegel*). His major works were printed during his lifetime, namely: the *Margarita poetica*, the *Ehebuch* or *Ehebüchlein*, and the *Spiegel der Sitten*.[17] The *Margarita* (1459–1464) was published in 1472, with a last, fifteenth edition, in 1503. A good handbook on rhetoric, it comprises some thirty discourses, some of them from Petrarca's *Re remediis* in the third part. The *Ehebuch* (1471), also printed in 1472, leaned on the "Ehekapitel" in *Der Ackermann aus Böhmen* and Francesco Barbaro's *De re uxoria*. Compared with the *Margarita*, basically a compilation, the *Ehebuch* displays a notable degree of originality, and is regarded as one of the finest texts of German prose for its century. It is this work that makes of Eyb the originator of the typically German literary genre of treatises on marriage (cf. R. Koebner 1911). Eyb's last work was the less successful *Spiegel der Sitten*, a compilation in the guise of a mirror of manners but with a definitely moralistic orientation. Composed in 1472–1474, it was printed in 1511.

German scholarship has generally been inclined to interpret Eyb's works as part of the earliest German humanism. The most extensive non-German study on this prolific writer, by J. A. Hiller, has given a contrary interpretation that stresses his medieval, moralizing tendencies and sources. This is not the place to discuss Eyb's role in the growth of German humanism, but it seems otiose to deny a strong humanistic influence in a man who was so close, and for so long, to such leading authorities of humanism, including Pius II. The matter that concerns us specifically may be an example of the moral and religious commitment that kept both early and mature German humanists clinging to certain medieval traditions, as is typical of much of northern Christian humanism.

The Latin sources carefully traced by K. Morvay for the Albanus legend hail back to around 1300, with the extant manuscripts coming mostly from the fourteenth and fifteenth centuries, but the German versions, probably translations at their point of origin, go back to around 1200. The legend was fortunate enough to receive the attention of a master editor of the stature of Karl Lachmann, who first entered the field of scientific research on the subject by publishing in 1836 a verse fragment of the legend from the Lower Rhine, without being able to identify the legend any further. Around 1400 Andreas Kurzmann, a poet presumably from the Salzburg area, composed an elaborate Ger-

man poem on the legend which offers what is perhaps the most extensive presentation of the material. Eyb's prose text, about half the length
of Kurzmann's poem, remains quite close to the earliest prose versions
in Latin.

K. Morvay speculates (esp. p. 154) that the legend may have originated in the milieu of the Roman Curia around 1186, at the time of the
confrontation with Barbarossa concerning Church versus state rights,
and that the exemplary sinfulness at the imperial court as depicted in
the legend may be meant to reflect on Barbarossa's court. Practically all
the principal versions, identified by Morvay as MS. groups A, B, and C
(C being the basis for chap. 244 of the *Gesta Romanorum*), begin textually with the phrase "Habitavit quidam aquilonis in partibus imperator," which would clearly refer to the German imperial court, seen as
a "northern" one from Rome. Important early versions are traceable to
Italy and perhaps to the circle of the first teachers of *cursus* as a trademark of the papal curia, namely Albertus de Morra (Pope Gregory VIII
in 1187, the last year of his life) and especially magister Transmundus,
a papal protonotary under Pope Alexander III (d. 1181) who wrote a
summa dictaminis in the form of a collection of letters which included
the heterogeneous text of the Albanus legend. Critics have speculated
on the stylistic connections of the legend with the Roman Curia on the
basis of its strict textual adherence to the Roman *cursus*.[18] In her apparently well documented analysis of this notarial material, Sheila J.
Heathcote concludes that the Albanus legend did not belong to the
original Transmundus collection, but according to Morvay (152) this
does not exclude the possibility that Transmundus was also the author,
at a later time.[19]

The dates of Albertus de Morra's and Transmundus's activity at the
Curia, to wit, 1178–1187, would provide a time frame of 1178–1190
for the legend, on the basis of its close adherence to those *dictatores'*
rules about the use of the *cursus*. An additional dimension of the narrative lies in the theological point made about the practice of sacramental confession by the three imperial characters involved in the common
sin—a powerful motif at a time of frequent excommunications and
public atonements by German rulers. Furthermore, we note that while
the legitimate rulers are in spiritual retreat carrying out the penance
imposed on them by the bishop and the hermit, two bishops take over
the political authority as acting rulers, for both the empire and the kind-
gom of Hungary. This was obviously an attractive solution for the Guelf
ecclesiastical circles. At a somewhat later time, the legend became popu-

lar in Czechoslovakia, a phenomenon recently studied by Emma Urbánková and related to the aggressive policies of the Bohemian King and
Roman Emperor Charles IV, also possibly in connection with the
planned marriage of his son Sigismund (Morvay 155).

The legend of St. Alban as we have it has served a multiple function,
ending with universal moral preaching but possibly starting with a political context, while it never bore a genuine hagiographic stamp (no
cult of such a saint is documented, and the legend never entered into the
ritual). The possible political aim, which interests us as part of the struggle between the secular ideals of proper education for public servants
and the contrasting ones from ecclesiastical circles, might have been to
expose the dangers of grave moral corruption in high temporal (indeed,
imperial) spheres at the time of the alliance between the Hohenstaufens
and the house of Norman Italy through the betrothal and then marriage
of Henry VI and Constance of Sicily (Dante's "Costanza imperatrice").
This union was to bring the Hohenstaufens to Italy and to a position of
hedging in the papal state from both sides. Thus the reference to the
"partes aquilonis" meant exactly the German emperor, with Hungary
being his close neighbor and eventual ally. This heightened ecclesiastical
awareness of Guelf inspiration and background may have found its
veiled polemical form in a fable of multiple incest in very high places,
with powerful moral overtones couched in the effective literary garb of
the Roman *cursus*.[20]

In the *Ehebuch* we note a moral terminology that echoes some basic
concepts of courtesy. *Zucht*, good breeding, is coupled with *erberkeit*
(= *Ehrbarkeit*) in *zucht und erberkeit*, to mean "chastity and honor"
(17, 32, 63, 92). *Messigkeit* (MHG *mâze*), *weysheit*, and *stetigkeit*, all
often recurring terms, are also combined in the expression *messig stete
weyse menschen* (90) for temperate, loyal, and prudent at the same
time. Magnanimity (*grossmuetigkeit*) is invoked, too (22, 57, 70, 90,
92), at least once with reference to the ruler. It is to be noted that the
moral terminology in question was then undergoing a semantic shift
from the medieval emphasis on external qualities to more inner ones:
from the denotation of manners indicating good breeding, *zuht* (*zucht*)
was becoming a sign for inner purity (equal to *Keischheit*, *Reinheit*,
"chastity"), and *erberkeit* was similarly turning from respectability as a
consequence of social approval to a sign of true "honor" by purity of
conscience.

The *Spiegel der Sitten* is arranged according to the capital sins and
has strong words against avarice and greed, whose opposite virtues are

generosity (*miltigkait*), kindness, compassion, and affability (fols. xiii–
xiv of the "Vorred"). It also reviews the qualities required of the civil
servant and statesman, as part of the detailed analysis of each social
class. *Gute sitten*, "good mores," are declared to be the overarching
goal of the ruling classes; knights in particular ought to distinguish
themselves by magnanimity, honesty, good manners, modesty, sobriety,
and devotion to the cause of peace and unity (fol. 108). Modesty
(*scham*), we have seen, generally carried a meaning similar to Castiglione's *vergogna*, that is, consideration toward others, though in Eyb
the frequent term *shemig* generally has the connotation of Christian
modesty.

Being apparently aware of the lesser role of knighthood at a time of
ascendancy for the burgher class, Eyb entered a typical debate between
the nobleman Celerius and the commoner Flaminius competing for the
hand of the noble virgin Lucretia whom they both woo. Eyb declares
that the commoner deserves victory because he can show himself more
noble, *edel*, by being possessed of greater virtue, wisdom, and public
spiritedness. Lucretia, who wanted to marry the "nobler" of the two,
appears to agree and makes her choice even without need of her father
and the Senate's concurring opinions (fols. 103–110).

In 1470, just a couple of years before Eyb started composing this
Spiegel der Sitten, there came to light the earliest vernacular compilation of selected Italian humanistic writings in German, the *Translati-
onen oder Teutschungen* by Niclas von Wyle. It included a rendering of
Buonaccorso da Montemagno the Younger's *Disputatio de nobilitate*
(perhaps shortly before 1429, the year of the author's death at the age
of thirty-seven or thirty-eight), in which Lucretia, after listening to the
pleadings by an ancient Roman patrician and a plebeian, gives her hand
to the latter as the "nobler" of the two, because he had pursued the
path of virtue by studying letters and Greek philosophy and had then
decided to use his acquired excellence by serving the commonwealth in
public office and on the battlefield. As Hans Baron has reminded us,[21]
the enormous success of this exemplar of civic humanism growing out
of Leonardo Bruni's circle did not prevent its imitators outside Italy
from expressing their hesitation toward what, in less burgherly climates, could sound downright subversive. In the 1481 English version
by John Tiptoft (printed by Caxton) and in the earliest English secular drama, Henry Medwall's *Fulgens and Lucres* (ca. 1497), the audience was warned not to take the outcome of this debate as a critique of
the excellence of hereditary nobility. Similarly, Wyle's German version

ended the debate without a conclusion, leaving the decision to the addressee, Graf Eberhard of Württemberg, a true lord endowed with the true qualities of a nobleman, that is, the author spells out, wealth, virtue, and a pedigree of humanistic imprint, going back to no less than Abraham, Aeneas, and Romulus. Baron does not mention Eyb, but clearly the Lucretia of the *Spiegel* is no other than Buonaccorso's disputed young lady, and it is remarkable that Eyb shows to have overcome the northern tendency to disregard or downplay the Italian original's popular, antiaristocratic sympathies.

The systematic moral catalog of the *Spiegel der Sitten* can be compared with the analogous vernacular texts of the genre of *specula morum* and its German derivative, *Standeslehre*, or rules of social life, including the popular "bürgerliche Sittenlehre," *Der Renner* (1300), by Hugo von Trimberg (ca. 1230–ca. 1313), schoolmaster in the abbey school of St. Gandolf near Bamberg; the Thuringian priest Johannes Rothe's (1360–1434) *Ritterspiegel* (after 1410); and the South Tyrolean knight Hans Vintler's *Die Pluemen der Tugent* (*Die Blumen der Tugend*, 1411, printed 1486), derived, as the title indicates, from the anonymous Italian *Fiore di virtù* (Bologna, 1313–1323). Although Vintler's *Pluemen* displayed a particular severity against the vices of the nobility, the author must have been exposed from his youth to the charms of the chivalric tradition: his family's castle, Runkelstein (near Bolzano), was famous for its frescoes illustrating Tristan and other romances.[22] Another work by Rothe, which was given the title *Von der stete ampten und von der fursten ratgeben* by its nineteenth-century editor A. F. C. Vilmar, deals with the organization of state councils and the duties and functions of counselors.

The texts we have glanced at, even so cursorily, manifest the inextricability of social, political, religious, and ethical motifs in enduring literary traditions that crossed so many chronological and geographic boundaries; these multiple dimensions cannot be fairly analyzed without taking into account their everpresent chivalric elements.

Notes

INTRODUCTION

1. Sir Ector to Sir Launcelot in Thomas Malory's *Le Morte Darthur*, chap. 13.

2. William of Wykeham's motto. Wykeham (1324–1404) was Chancellor to Edward III and Richard II.

3. Ludovico Sforza (1452—27 May 1507) was taken prisoner at Novara in 1500 by Louis XII. The graffito is somewhat similar to a famous drawing by Leonardo now in the British Museum, once also regarded as a self-portrait. Leonardo, another unlikely subject for portrayal in military accoutrement, had worked for Ludovico in Milan. See G. Touchard-Lafosse, *La Loire historique, pittoresque et biographique*, 5 vols. (Tours: Lecesne, 1851): 4: 209; Jean Vallery-Radot, *Loches* (Paris: Henry Laurens, 1954): 38 f.; Ian Dunlop, *Châteaux of the Loire* (London: Hamish Hamilton; New York: Taplinger, 1969): 17.

4. On the news of Castiglione's death, Charles V declared to his court in Toledo: "Yo vos digo que es muerto uno de los mejores caballeros del mundo." The emperor could find no better word to praise the illustrious courtier and papal nuncio than by calling him "one of the best knights in the world."

5. Foucault, "The Dangerous Individual," in Lawrence D. Kritzman, ed., *Michel Foucault: Politics, Philosophy, Culture* (New York, London: Routledge, [1978] 1988): 125–151.

6. *Theory of Literature* (New York: Harcourt, Brace; Harvest Books, 2d ed. 1956).

7. This is a summary statement quoted by Umberto Eco from his own *Opera aperta. Forma e indeterminazione nelle poetiche contemporanee* (Milano: Bompiani, 1962) in "*Intentio lectoris*: The State of the Art," *Differentia* 2 (Spring 1988): 147–168 at 152 f. The paper cogently presents, in a semiotic

key, the development of current perceptions of reader response in literary theory, history, and criticism.

8. Reviewing Robert Alter and Frank Kermode, eds., *The Literary Guide to the Bible* (Cambridge, MA: Harvard University Press, 1987), the British poet Donald Davie voiced the concerns of religious fundamentalism by objecting that to treat the Bible as literature is tantamount to calling it "a fabrication," since it might reduce it to an aesthetic experience shorn of directly relevant moral content. ("The Literary Guide to the Bible," *The New Republic* 197, 26 Oct. 1987: 28–32.) The critics included in the *Guide* could counter that, on the contrary, through a competent literary reading they fastened on the crucial fact of reader response, revealing "what the text does to the reader" rather than what it simply says, thereby bringing forth and explaining how the moral contents become effective through other means than plain statement or preaching. Hence literary criticism itself becomes a moral act when it invests an intrinsically moral text. Davie's feeling of shock might have been abated through better information on the history of biblical scholarship, which for more than half a century has seen a fruitful application of literary perspectives and has even become, in this very form, a model for more socially grounded literary studies. This began with the so-called "form-historical school" of Protestant theology (H. Gunkel, M. Dibelius, R. Bultman), Catholic scholarship soon following the lead. Hans-Robert Jauss, *Toward an Aesthetic of Reception*, translated by Timothy Bahti (Minneapolis: University of Minnesota Press, 1982), "Theory of Genres and Medieval Literature," 76–109 at 100, reminds us that as early as 1943 Pope Pius XII recognized the modern theory of literary genres as an aid in biblical exegesis (encyclical *Divino afflante spiritu*).

9. See, for example, Dominick LaCapra, "On the Line: Between History and Criticism," *Profession 89* (New York: MLA, 1989): 6: "One common complaint is that deconstruction has often seemed to parallel, if not replicate, New Criticism and formalism in general."

10. A clear statement of the problem with regard to the Tristan legend is in Joan Ferrante (1973): 11–23.

11. Köhler, Mancini ed.: xxx, xxxiii, 21. I shall often refer to this Italian edition, Köhler, *Sociologia della fin'amor*, with a valuable introduction by Mario Mancini, because it conveniently gathers into a single volume numerous essays that were scattered in miscellanies and journals. Interesting early discussions of Köhler's method are in Mario Mancini, "Problemi di sociologia romanza," *Studi di letteratura francese* 1 (1967): 127–134; François Pirot, "L'idéologie' des troubadours. Examen de travaux récents," *Le Moyen Age 74* (1968): 301–333; and Ursula Peters, "Niederes Rittertum oder hoher Adel?," *Euphorion* 67 (1973): 244–260. Bezzola's opus (*Les origines*, 1944–1963) has laid the groundwork for Köhler's general orientation but has often been criticized for a rather rigid sociologism. For Köhler's position on chivalry in French literature and society, see especially his *Ideal und Wirklichkeit*; on troubadour lyric, especially his *Trobadorlyrik* and *Esprit und arkadische Freiheit*. As a variant to Köhler's analyses, the sociological approach is also examined and used by Ursula Liebertz-Grün, *Zur Soziologie des "Amour courtois": Umrisse der Forschung*, Beiheft zum *Euphorion* 10 (Heidelberg: C. Winter, 1977).

12. This phenomenon in its dual aspect has been well documented by Martín de Riquer (1970), whose research involves mostly Catalan texts.

13. This desideratum underlies Lauro Martines's recent *Society and History in English Renaissance Verse* (Oxford, New York: Basil Blackwell, 1985), a challenging study even though methodologically rather problematic *in bono et in malo*.

14. Stephen Greenblatt, "Introduction" to Greenblatt, ed., *Representing the English Renaissance* (1988): viii.

15. Louis Adrian Montrose, " 'Shaping Fantasies': Figurations of Gender and Power in Elizabethan Culture," in Greenblatt, ed., *Representing the English Renaissance* (1988): 56.

16. While noting (without being sure of it) that "new historicism, at least as a general trend, now seems to be in the ascendant," and that "the program of the MLA's 1988 convention might seem to indicate that deconstruction is in retreat and that the new historicism—at least as a topic of controversy—is in the ascendant," Dominick LaCapra, "On the Line: Between History and Criticism," *Profession 89* (New York: MLA, 1989): 6, critically tries to relate the two modes which, he asserts, may coexist in the same critic.

17. "Als ein Schritt weg von einer zwar notwendigen, aber die Ästhetik kaum tangierenden 'Soziologie der Literatur,' die es längst gibt, zu einer 'soziologischen Literaturwissenschaft,' die Hugo Kuhn zufolge noch nicht existiert." Köhler in Borck and Henss, eds. (1970): 75; Mancini ed.: 296. For Hugo Kuhn's definition of "subjective" versus "objective" (including sociological) aspects of the *Minnesang*, cf. Kuhn in H. Fromm (1961): 167–179.

Much scholarship of different hues has recently verged on the definition of this now growing method, often including theoretical discussion of the particular Marxist applications ever since such landmarks as György Lukács's well known studies. See, for example, Lucien Goldmann's *Pour une sociologie du roman* (Paris: Gallimard, 1964), "Introduction aux problèmes d'une sociologie du roman," 21–57, and untitled postscript 365–372. The notion of the "problematic hero" that Goldmann derives from Lukács certainly applies to the knight errant of the romances much earlier than Don Quixote, and with different implications from the hero of the nineteenth-century novel. Tempting as it is because of the applicable concepts of *dégradation* and tension between individuals and collective consciousness, we cannot engage here in a theoretical discourse concerning structural criteria that have been based on modern literary forms, with reference to the members of a quantitative market economy (of exchange) rather than a qualitative economy of usage. For Italy see, for example, Fernando Ferrara et al., eds., *Sociologia della letteratura*, Atti del 1° Convegno Nazionale, Gaeta 1974 (Roma: Bulzoni, 1978). The recent issue 14.3 of *Critical Inquiry* dedicated to "The Sociology of Literature" (1988) contains surprisingly little scholarly material.

18. This conclusion agrees with Cesare Cases, "La critica sociologica," in Maria Corti and Cesare Segre, *I metodi attuali della critica in Italia* (Torino: ERI [Edizioni Radio Italiana], 1980): 19–34.

19. Auerbach, *Mimesis: The Representation of Reality in Western Literature* (1953; 1957): 117–121, discussed in my chap. 5, "The Age of Chrétien."

Auerbach's sociologism, especially in his *Literary Language and Public in Late Latin Antiquity and in the Middle Ages* (1958), verged chiefly on literary reception.

20. See Elias, *Über den Prozess der Zivilisation* (1939); idem, *Die höfische Gesellschaft* (1969); Jaeger, *The Origins of Courtliness: Civilizing Trends and the Formation of Courtly Ideals 939–1210* (1985). I shall refer to this 1985 book simply by author and page numbers, whereas I shall quote Jaeger's supplementary 1987 paper with the added date.

21. Jauss, "Theory of Genres," especially pp. 80–83.

22. See Evelyn B. Vitz's perceptive review of Zumthor's *La lettre et la voix* (1987) in *Envoi* 1.1 (1988): 185–191 at 190. For Zumthor's extended discussion of the implications of historical research and literary history seen from his basically formalist vantage point, see his *Parler du Moyen Age* (Paris, 1980), trans. by Sarah White as *Speaking of the Middle Ages* (Lincoln, NE: University of Nebraska Press, 1986). Recent scholarship on medieval literature has been opening up this rich field to innovative interpretative methods: for a recent collection of disparate approaches see, for example, Kevin Brownlee and Stephen G. Nichols, eds., *Images of Power: Medieval History/Discourse/Literature* (*Yale French Studies* 70, 1986).

23. In this mode of artistic production the text enjoyed no special privilege outside the actual performance "here and now," and the texts lived through a continuous evolution of "féconde intertextualité orale." What this view of things amounts to is a type of global "deconstruction" of the whole history of western literature on the premise that (differently from figurative art and even poetry) written literature as we know it is neither a perennial human activity nor, as the humanists firmly held, the highest product of civilization and the very foundation of humanity: it would be a temporary affair, largely confined to the modern period, and perhaps already extinct. We are now witnessing a type of paraliterature (mass literature, what the Germans call *Trivial-Literatur*) which tends to merge with "true" literature as indistinguishable from it, in a process of confusion that some German theorists decry with the heavy yet telling term of *Entdifferenzierung*, "de-differentiation." Medieval "literature" looks to us more like our own mass culture than like the "classical" literature of 1500–1900: see Zumthor (1987) 319–322.

Zumthor's perspective is basically anthropological. In a specifically anthropological context the third and conclusive volume of Claude Lévi-Strauss's "Mythologiques" trilogy, after vol. 1, *Le cru et le cuit* (1964), and vol. 2, *Du miel aux cendres* (1967), is titled *L'origine des manières de table* (Paris: Plon, 1968). This third volume, dealing with "l'origine des manières de table . . . et . . . du bon usage" (422), exemplarily shows how the anthropologist's outlook on phenomena far removed from western civilization does not discover the kind of principles we shall encounter in the course of this study. This should confirm that the western phenomena we are analyzing enjoy a peculiar, though not unique, status.

24. M. M. Bakhtin, *Rabelais and His World*, trans. Hélène Iswolsky (Cambridge, MA: M.I.T. Press, 1968; 1988; Bloomington: Indiana University Press, 1984; Russian original *Tvorchestvo Fransua Rable*, Moscow: Khudozhestvennia Literatura, 1965): 270 f. of 1984 ed.; It. ed. *L'opera di Rabelais e la cultura*

popolare, trans. Mili Romano (Torino: Einaudi, 1979, 3d ed. 1982): 296 f. Also
M. M. Bakhtin, *The Dialogic Imagination: Four Essays*, ed. Michael Holquist,
trans. Caryl Emerson and Michael Holquist, University of Texas Press Slavic
Series 1 (Austin: University of Texas Press, 1981); idem and P. N. Medvedev,
*The Formal Method in Literary Scholarship: A Critical Introduction to Socio-
logical Poetics* (Cambridge, MA: Harvard University Press, 1985).

25. *European Literature* 167–170, "Heroes and Rulers."

26. For example, Tony Hunt in *Forum for Modern Language Studies* (1981):
93, with frequent references to the researches of G. Duby, J. Flori, L. Génicot,
and others.

27. N. Elias, *Power and Civility* (1982): 274, and the whole section "The
Muting of Drives: Psychologization and Rationalization," 270–291.

28. Cf. the definitions of Elias's method in his *The History of Manners, Power and Civility*, and *The Court Society*, and see *The Court Society*
(1983): 16.

29. See Duby, *Hommes et structures* (1973): 363: "Il faut partir de l'idée
que l'homme en société constitue l'objet final de la recherche historique dont il
est le premier principe. L'histoire sociale, en fait, c'est toute l'histoire."

30. See Elias, *The Court Society*: 280, and all of Appendix A, "On the notion that there can be a state without structural conflicts," 276–283, regarding
the structural contradictions in the government of the Third Reich, viewed not
as a sign of disorganization and ineffective leadership but as the "logic" of dic-
tatorial power government. Hitler kept his agencies and cohorts in check by
pitting them against each other. These had been the inner workings of the Prussian aristocratic court, just as Louis XIV maintained his absolute power over
the groups of high noblemen and high bourgeois administrators by playing
them against one another, thus preventing their opposition from congealing
into a common front. Each in its own time and situation, those contrasting
groups represented real interests at stake in the play for power and privilege.
Likewise, within a democracy or representative form of government, the apparent disorder of personal and collective "lobbying" represents the play of real
forces in a more overt and public form, with procedures controlled by laws,
elections, and organization into parties and guilds. The German public felt uncomfortable with the visible show of squabbling among the groups and parties
because it was not accustomed to overt displays of contrasting interests. Hitler
exploited this psychological unpreparedness to bring down the Weimar Republic, and then moved those tensions into his inner court, where he could keep
them out of the public eye and play them against one another to his own
advantage.

The debate on this question started with a series of articles featured in *Der
Spiegel* by the editor Heinz Höhne in 1966–1967, under the title "Der Orden
unter den Totenkopf," and Elias confronts the traditional historian's reaction of
Hans Mommsen, which, Elias claims, prevents us from understanding the
events because it ignores the issue of necessary structural tensions in any given
society, including the most monolithic despotism. On the Prussian political system see now Robert M. Berdahl, *The Politics of the Prussian Nobility: The
Development of a Conservative Ideology, 1740–1848* (Princeton: Princeton
University Press, 1989).

CHAPTER ONE: NOBLEMEN AT COURT

1. For example, G. Duby, *Hommes et structures* (1973): 344, and F. Cardini (1976). Summarily stated, the complex question of the social, legal, and political nature of knighthood is given a chronological locus by Duby, *The Three Orders* (1980): 293, with the conclusion: "in the eighth decade of the twelfth century, at the end of Louis XII's reign, . . . knighthood became a genuine institution."

2. P. Zumthor (1987) 72–76.

3. The implications of literary references to social condition are complex, hence it is problematic to think of "classes" in medieval society. The term "class" is used hereafter for its convenience, but with the caveat that its sense differs from its modern use, since the term *ordo* of the sources referred to functions rather than fixed and uniform social estates. "Estate" is probably a good rendering for the Latin *ordo* in its broadest acceptation: cf. H. Fuhrmann (1986): 177. J. Flori (1983; 1986), a student of Duby and, indirectly, of Génicot, while reiterating Génicot's warnings that generalizations are difficult because social situations varied greatly from region to region, denies that the state of knight was recognized at all before the year 1000. See, for example, Flori (1986): 3 and passim for numerous citations of uses of the term around the year 1000 with varying connotations sometimes implying noble status. On the question of chivalry and knighthood see F. Cardini's (1982) bibliographic study. Bumke (esp. 1964, and chap. 7 added to 2d ed. 1977, "On the State of Research into Knighthood" in 1982 trans. 124–161) insists on necessary distinctions and on the non-existence of a knightly "class" as such. He points out approvingly (1982: 140) that in Fleckenstein (1972) the term *Ritterstand* does not even appear. Linda Paterson, *Forum for Modern Language Studies* 17 (1981): 126, resumes Flori's argument thus: "before 1180 a knight in the eyes of French epic poets and their audiences is not a member of some 'order of chivalry' or homogeneous social class, but a professional horseback warrior with special equipment." Hence, when it appeared—through literary and cultural impact rather than social change—the chivalric ideology had a novel significance. Compare G. Duby, *The Three Orders* (1980) 294: "Thanks to the vocabulary of the charters, we can fix two chronological markers in a very fluid evolution: beginning in 1025, the word *miles* slowly came into usage to distinguish the members of one social group from other men (whereas in German-speaking Lorraine this term penetrated only after 1170 and really became established only after 1200). After 1175 the title *miles* regularly preceded the patronymic of all knights and was connected, as a rule, with the title *dominus*, 'messire.'" See M. Keen (1984), chap. 8 "The Idea of Nobility," especially p. 148, on the problematic character of the aristocratic status in the later Middle Ages.

4. For recent contributions to a still wanting history of the practice of dubbing see M. Keen (1984) chap. 4, "The Ceremony of Dubbing to Knighthood," 64–82, and the more extended J. Flori (1986), especially 319–329, together with Flori's previous "Les origines de l'adoubement chevaleresque. Étude des remises d'armes dans les chroniques et annales latines du IXᵉ au XIIIᵉ siècle," *Traditio* 35 (1979): 209–272.

Liturgical acts and symbolism varied greatly and their practice is still largely unclear. For the German area see an expert discussion of the social implications of dubbing in J. Bumke (1964) chap. 5, especially 83–96, with rich bibliographic references. Pierre Bonnassie, *La Catalogne du milieu du Xe à la fin du XIe siècle: croissance et mutation d'une société* (1975) 31, 805–807, 875, assumed, perhaps too hastily, that such ceremonies existed in Catalonia from the end of the eleventh century. A significant early figuration of the ceremony is in section 21 of the celebrated Bayeux tapestry (see figures 1–2): Edward the Confessor of England had purportedly sent Harold Godwinson, son of the earl of the West Saxons, to William of Normandy with the message that William would be Edward's successor. To impress on Harold, a powerful pretender to the throne, the symbolic meaning of being invested as a liegeman to his new lord William, the latter dubbed him knight—an investiture act not yet current in England—and exacted from him a solemn oath of fealty. When at Edward's death two years later Harold succeeded to the throne, William invaded England and killed Harold at Hastings. The inscription over the figures in the tapestry reads: "Hic Willelmus dedit Haroldo arma."

An example of the elaborate nature of the ceremony, once it became established, was the great court festival at Mainz in 1184 for the initiation of Barbarossa's sons. The *Hennegau Chronicle* (*Chronica Hanonia*) of Gislebert de Mons reports that seventy thousand *milites* assembled for the occasion, including noblemen and *ministeriales* (Bumke 1982: 142). See an extended study of that festival and another one held in 1188, again at Mainz, in J. Fleckenstein (1972): Barbarossa's imperial court "had adopted chivalric norms for itself" (1029), and Fleckenstein relates this phenomenon to French cultural impulses by tracing it back to Barbarossa's having held court at Besançon in Burgundy in 1157 (1040–1041). Dubbing might or might not confer aristocratic status. Barbarossa had also been dubbed knight, and he derived from his family a habit of chivalrous ceremonials: the first recorded chivalric tournament was held in Würzburg in 1137 by Dukes Frederick and Konrad of Swabia, Barbarossa's father and uncle (Otto of Freising, *Gesta Frederici* 1.27). See J. Bumke (1982): 93 f., 143.

5. Like the decisive oath by the *senior* to defend the vassal, the practice of *immixtio manuum* is known in Italy, too, but some historians consider it ended by the middle of the tenth century within the Italic Kingdom: see *Storia d'Italia*, eds. Romano and Vivanti, 5.1: 263, 277.

6. B. D. Lyon (1957), especially 243 on *fief-rentes* as new forms of enfeoffment by annual money grants rather than land grants.

7. G. Duby, *The Three Orders* 299, with reference to the Cistercian monk Hélinand de Froidmont's *On the Correct Princely Conduct*, of those years (*Patrologia Latina* [henceforth *PL*] 212: 743 f.). The type of dubbing that marked the investiture of a knight derived from the ceremonial granting of feudal nobility as part, in turn, of the ritual recognition of authority in the emperor, king, pope, or bishop. The ritual climaxed in the tapping with the sword on the shoulder and girding with the sword belt as symbol of power: see Robert de Blois, *Ensoignement des princes*, ed. J. H. Fox (1948): 94, ll. 73–78: "Senefie que toz li mons / Doit le chevalier honorer, / Quant le voit espee porter / Cinte, que nus

ne la çognoit / Jadis, se chevalier n'estoit." (It signifies that the whole world must honor the knight when he is seen carrying the sword at his waist, which no one used to wear without being a knight.) The first detailed description of a dubbing ceremony seems to be the knighting of Geoffrey the Fair of Anjou in 1128 at Rouen on the eve of his marriage to Matilda, the daughter of Henry I of England, as related in [Jean de Marmoutier's] *Chroniques des Comtes d'Anjou*, eds. Halphen and Poupardin (1913): 179 f. See M. Keen (1984) 64 f. But P. van Luyn, "Les *milites* dans la France du XIe siècle. Examen des sources narratives," *Le Moyen Age* 77 (1971): 5–51, 193–238, has discovered eleven more cases from the period 1070–1125. Cf. Bumke (1982): 133 f.

8. A good presentation of the matter is in M. Keen (1984): 144 f. As to the cost of horse and armor, see H. Fuhrmann (1986): 177: "in the eighth century a full set of equipment for a cavalryman was equivalent in value to forty-five cows or fifteen mares. In the eleventh century a horse was worth five to ten oxen, and a mail-shirt anything from twenty to a hundred oxen. When in 1100 Count Robert of Flanders undertook to provide 500 knights, it was assumed that each would have three horses, and this seems to have been normal for the Staufer period: one to travel on, one to fight on and one to carry baggage. It has been calculated that an estate would have to be a minimum of 400 acres in order to support a knight who was ready to fight at all times."

9. Duby, *Hommes et structures* (1973): 347–352.

10. Génicot, *L'économie namuroise* (1960). It deserves stressing that for our purpose the specialist's insistence on local peculiarities and circumstances as the only scientific way to understand reality is not completely helpful where general causes should be invoked, since broad historical phenomena do have general causes.

11. Given the state of our knowledge of medieval society, the social status of freedom that plays a striking role in Génicot's researches is still rather unclear. Serfdom meant different things in different areas and different times, and the relationship between serf and master could vary radically. The widest divergences probably obtained between western and eastern parts of Europe, especially Russia, as Suzanne Massie has brilliantly illustrated, perhaps in a somewhat generalized manner, in her celebrated *Land of the Firebird* (New York: Simon and Schuster, 1980). See J. Flori (1986) 223–230 for a description of different situations as to the status of knights vis-à-vis the nobility in the main regions of France, Flanders, England, and Germany in the twelfth century.

12. Duby, *Hommes et structures* (1973): 160.

13. Our knowledge of administrative and fiscal practices in Catalonia 1151–1213 is now solidly documented through the archival researches of Thomas N. Bisson, *Fiscal Accounts of Catalonia under the Early Count-Kings (1151–1213)*, 2 vols. (Berkeley, Los Angeles, Oxford: University of California Press, 1984). Ramon Berenguer IV's (Count of Barcelona 1131–1162) first fiscal officer was the able knight Bertran de Castellet. The vicars of royal domains were usually of baronial or knightly class. The bailiffs, operating under temporary tenures of one to three years, could be rich peasants or Jews. The best general historical survey of this geographic area is now T. N. Bisson, *The Medieval*

Crown of Aragon: A Short History (Oxford: Clarendon Press, 1986). Pierre Bonnassie's numerous studies are also valuable for this area and southern France.

14. John T. Noonan, Jr., "The Power to Choose," *Viator* 4 (1973): 419–434; J.-B. Molin and P. Mutembe, *Le rituel du mariage en France du XIIe au XVIe siècle* (Paris: Beauchesne, 1974); Marie-Odile Métral, *Le mariage: les hésitations dans l'Occident* (Paris: Aubier, 1977); G. Duby, *Le chevalier, la femme et le prêtre: le mariage dans la France féodale* (1981); Jean Leclercq, *Le mariage vu par les moines au XIIe siècle* (Paris: Cerf, 1983).

15. The policy was meant to counter the feudal thrust toward hereditariness of royal benefices, which resulted in eventual independence for the vassals. "Bishops are given the secular office of count. This appointment of high ecclesiastics without heirs was intended to put a stop to the tendency of functionaries of the central authority to turn into a 'hereditary, landowning aristocracy' with strong desires for independence": N. Elias, *Power and Civility* (1982): 20. It did not quite work out that way, however, since the count-bishops tended to become just as independent as the secular princes, and could also turn their domains into hereditary ones.

16. See beginning of my chapter 7 on the Italian cathedral schools.

17. Also Fleckenstein, *Early Medieval Germany* (1978) chaps. 9–13, pp. 131–176, on Otto I's imperial and educational policies. At Magdeburg Anno of St. Maurice founded a famous school on the king's orders, and Würzburg flourished under the celebrated scholar Stephen of Novara, called there by Otto I (Fleckenstein 155). Schools started at Cologne in 953 (under Brun), Hildesheim in 954, and Trier in 956.

18. Jaeger (1987): 574 f. For Jaeger (1985: 67–81 and passim) the administration of Archbishop Adalbert of Bremen (1043–1072) and the reforms of Bishop Azelinus at Hildesheim (1044–1054) are clear examples of this activity at its moment of full maturity.

19. *The Letters of Gerbert, with his papal privileges as Sylvester II*, trans. Harriett (Pratt) Lattin (New York: Columbia University Press, 1961), Letters 153 and 154; see Frova (1973): 65 f. Text in J.-P.-E. Havet, ed., *Lettres de Gerbert (983–997)* (Paris: Picard, 1889): 173, no. 187: "Nescio quid divinum exprimitur cum homo genere Graecus, imperio Romanus, quasi hereditario iure thesauros sibi Graecae ac Romanae repetit sapientiae." See also ibid.: no. 186 p. 172, and *PL*: 139 col. 159. Compare A. Roncaglia, "Le corti medievali" in A. Asor Rosa, ed., *Letteratura italiana* 1 (1982): 82. Gerbert had taught liberal arts at Reims for ten years (972–982) while counselor and secretary to the local bishop, and the chronicle of his pupil Richer, a monk at the monastery of Saint-Rémy in Reims, dedicated twenty-three chapters of book 3 to Gerbert's school, thus making it probably the best documented school of the early Middle Ages (Pierre Riché 1979: 180 f., 358 f.). See Richer de Saint-Rémy, *Histoire de France (888–995)*, ed. Robert Latouche, 2 vols. (Paris: Champion, 1930–1937). Stephen G. Nichols, Jr., *Romanesque Signs: Early Medieval Narrative and Iconography* (New Haven: Yale University Press, 1983) 1–7, discusses Richer's historiographic method and his relationship

to Gerbert. It may not be purely accidental that Richer's manuscript came back to light in 1833 in Germany, in the library of St. Michael's monastery in Bamberg.

20. Havet, ed., *Lettres de Gerbert*: 145, no. 163.

21. Lauro Martines (1979): 24–26.

22. After 1122 investitures were often made by the local lay princes rather than by the pope or by the emperor, as, for example, in the case of the bishops of Cambrai, who after 1167 were chosen by the counts of Flanders or Hainaut. See Henri Platelle in Louis Trenard, ed., *Histoire des Pays-Bas Français* (Toulouse: E. Privat, 1972): 88.

23. I quote from the good summary of a complex secular situation in William Shirer, *Twentieth Century Journey, A Memoir of a Life and the Times, II: The Nightmare Years, 1930–1940* (Boston: Little, Brown, 1984; New York: Bantam Books, 1985): 155 f. Shirer tries to explain the ineffectiveness of the Protestant churches' resistance to Hitler in the years 1934–1938 and the role of Pastor Martin Niemöller, who had been a conservative, anti-Weimar, pro-Hitler patriot but ended up in Sachsenhausen and Dachau for seven years until the liberation.

24. After all, the pagan ethic of the Germanic warrior did not exhaust its appeal in the Middle Ages; it remained operative in limited but significant ways both under and on the surface of European culture, and not only in Germany. It could even be brought back brutally and quite specifically in a religious context in our century, when the official Nazi ideologue Alfred Rosenberg, as "Führer's Delegate for the Entire Intellectual and Philosophical Education and Instruction for the National Socialist Party," brazenly proclaimed the little-known Thirty Articles for the new "National Reich Church," which included: "5. The National Church is determined to exterminate irrevocably . . . the strange and foreign Christian faiths imported into Germany in the ill-omened year 800; . . . 19. On the altars there must be nothing but *Mein Kampf* (to the German nation and therefore to God the most sacred book) and to the left of the altar a sword." Articles 18 and 30 prescribed the banning of all crosses and Bibles from all churches. See W. Shirer, *Twentieth Century Journey* (1985): 157. The Nazi connection with the ethics of the medieval sagas was not limited to enthusiasm for Wagnerian opera.

25. J. Bumke, *Ministerialität und Ritterdichtung* (1976). M. Keen (1984): 34–37 gives an up-to-date survey of the German situation.

26. J. Flori (1986): 27 f., 264 for an evaluation of these German historians' researches. On the basis of the emergence at court of the new classes of *ministeriales* and burghers, Horst Fuhrmann (1986 Engl. trans.) ranges over the cultural, political, economic, and social transformations occurring between 1050–1200 in Germany, contrasting them with contemporary developments in France, England, and Italy.

27. "Aus den Reitersoldaten ist das Rittertum nicht entstanden." Bumke (1964: 59; 1982: 44), citing Otto Frh. von Dungern, *Der Herrenstand im Mittelalter. Eine sozialpolitische und rechtsgeschichtliche Untersuchung* 1 (Papiermühle: A.-S., Gebr. Vogt, 1908): 342.

28. J. Bumke (1964), chap. 3 "Der Ritter als Soldat," 35–59; (1982) especially 36–44. Bumke's evidence is largely made of German sources.

29. See, for example, P. Contamine (1980) on the way technological changes in methods of warfare affected the role of the knight.

30. "Abelestrier et meneour / et perrier et engeneor / seront de or avant plus chers." *La Bible* vv. 183–185, in *Oeuvres de Guiot de Provins*, ed. John Orr (Manchester: Publications de l'Université de Manchester, 1915; Genève: Slatkine Reprints, 1974). See Flori (1986): 335 f.

31. Köhler, Mancini ed. (1976): 18.

32. For a pithy, authoritative treatment see Duby, "Les laïcs et la paix de Dieu," *Hommes et structures*: 227–240 on the growing literature concerning this difficult question.

33. Tony Hunt in *Forum for Modern Language Studies* (1981): 97.

34. *Vita Sancti Geraldi*. Cf. C. Erdmann (1935): 78 f.; E. Köhler, Mancini ed. (1976): 98; and B. H. Rosenwein and L. K. Little, "Social Meaning in the Monastic and Mendicant Spiritualities," *Past and Present* 63 (1974): 4–32. See *St. Odo of Cluny; being the Life of St. Odo of Cluny by John of Salerno, and the Life of St. Gerald of Aurillac by St. Odo*, ed. and trans. Gerard Sitwell (London-New York: Sheed & Ward, 1958).

35. St. Bernard, *Ad milites Templi de laude novae militiae* in *S. Bernardi Opera*, eds. Jean Leclerq, C. H. Talbot, and H. M. Rochais, vol. 3 (1963): 207–239; also, with the title *De laude novae militiae*, in *PL* 182: 921 ff. Bernard lent a powerful impulse to the development of the Templars, whom he considered true Christian knights as compared to the *militia saecularis*, the purely worldly military service of ancient origin that was now to be condemned. See, in that text, his bitterly contrastive portrait of the "malicious" secular knight, all concerned with his attractive physical appearance, versus the Templar, shaven of his hair and bearded, looking like an ascetic man of God. Cf. F. Cardini, "Il guerriero e il cavaliere" (1987): 98.

Nobles who entered a monastery, as they often did for atonement in their advanced age, could occasionally be accepted as true monks and called *milites Christi*, a title they deserved as *personae generosae*. This was the case with the fierce warrior lord and leading troubadour Bertran de Born, who before 1196 entered the Cistercian monastery he and his family had generously endowed in the course of their stormy careers. Other laymen entering the religious life would not become Cistercian monks and would simply be called *nobiles laici*. Cf. William D. Paden et al., eds., *The Poems of the Troubadour Bertran de Born* (Berkeley, Los Angeles, London: University of California Press, 1986): 25, with the apt comment that the term *generosus* evoked both noble birth and generous beneficence toward the Church.

36. Duby, *Hommes et structures*: 339 f.

37. Duby, *Guerriers et paysans* (1973); *Terra e nobiltà nel Medioevo* (1971). Also, J. Fleckenstein, *Early Medieval Germany* (1978), chaps. 3 and 7 on "The Economic Basis" and "The Rise and Diffusion of Feudalism."

38. There are analogous phenomena through history, and the extreme case of the Mafia in Bourbonic southern Italy may come to mind as groups that tried

to fill the vacuum of a weak and irresponsible central government by taking justice into their own hands.

39. Duby, *Guerriers et paysans* (1973): 190. See M. Keen (1984), chap. 12 "Chivalry and War," 219–237, on the general question of the ambivalent role of the warrior-knight, both supporter of legitimate authority on ideal grounds, and self-seeking, lawless pursuer of private gain. On a practical level, the ruthlessly destructive violence of mercenary soldiers was often hardly distinguishable from the behavior of the most admired heroes of chivalry. Cf. Honoré Bonet (fl. 1378–1398), *L'arbre des batailles* (ca. 1382–1387), ed. Ernest Nys (Bruxelles: C. Muquardt, New York: Trübner, 1883), translated as *The Tree of Battles*, ed. and trans. G. W. Coopland (Liverpool: Liverpool University Press; Cambridge, MA: Harvard University Press, 1949): 189: "the man who does not know how to set places on fire, to rob churches and usurp their rights and to imprison the priests, is not fit to carry on war." See M. Keen: 233, and M. H. Keen, *The Laws of War in the Late Middle Ages* (London: Routledge & Kegan Paul, 1965), chap. 2. Bonet was also translated in 1456 by Sir Gilbert Hay or "of the Haye" as *The Buke of the Law of Armys*. See this text in vol. 1 of *Gilbert of the Haye's Prose Manuscript* (A.D. *1456*), ed. J. H. Stevenson, 2 vols. (Edinburgh, London: W. Blackwood for the Saxon Texts Society, 1901–1904). Volume 2 of this edition includes Sir Gilbert's *The Buke of Knychhede*, a translation from the French of Ramón Llull's manual already published as *The Buke of the Order of Knychthood, translated from the French by Sir Gilbert Hay, Knight, from the MS. in the library at Abbotsford* (Edinburgh, 1847), and the same author's *The Buke of the Governaunce of Princis*, a translation of a French version of the *Liber de secretis secretorum*.

40. For example, Maurice Keen, *The Outlaws of Medieval Legend* (London: Routledge and Kegan Paul, 1961).

41. Jaeger quotes both Duby and Köhler approvingly, even though his interpretations do not quite accord with theirs. Both Duby and Köhler aim to interpret the courtly ideology as a function of the social and mental structures of the feudal society; Jaeger's point is that courtesy does not evolve naturally and spontaneously inside the feudal class: it is imposed on it, as it were, from the outside, by the clerical class as part of its educational mission. For him it was a particular clerical ideology that produced chivalry, not feudalism by itself.

42. See a not too frequent example of this recognition in *Hommes et structures*: 346: "au plan des attitudes mentales," that "valorisation de la figure exemplaire du chevalier" performed by the literature of Arthurian romance and courtly love may have contributed to the merger of the rank of knight with that of high nobleman. Martín de Riquer (1970) is a good example of the conditioning force of literature.

43. Michel Stanesco, "Le dernier âge de la chevalerie," in T. Klaniczay et al., eds., *L'époque de la Renaissance* (1988): 405–419 at 405, with references to Huizinga.

44. Enguerrand de Monstrelet, *Chroniques*, ed. Douet d'Arcq, 6 vols. (Paris: Société de l'Histoire de France, 1857–1862) 1: 43 ff., 4: 219. See J. Huizinga, *The Waning of the Middle Ages* (1924; Eng. ed. London, 1927; New York: Doubleday, 1954), chap. 7; Jean Miquet, "Les épopées chevaleresques en

prose," in T. Klaniczay et al., eds. (1988): 420–431 at 429. In 1528 it was Francis I who started the private quarrel with Charles V, and Charles asked "the best knight in the world," Baldassar Castiglione, to draw up the riposte. Castiglione, then a papal nuncio, declined the honor, diplomatically alleging that it did not suit a man of the Church to take part in affairs that could end in bloodshed.

45. Ludwig Schmugge, "Ministerialität und Bürgertum in Reims. Untersuchungen zur Geschichte der Stadt im 12. und 13. Jahrhundert," *Francia* 2 (1974): 152–212, against the thesis that ministerials were a uniquely German phenomenon. J. Bumke, *Ministerialität* (1976), limits the ministerials' quantitative role within the courtly literature audience.

46. Köhler, Mancini ed.: 237 f.

47. "Si tuit li dol e.l plor e.l marrimen," no. 80.41 in A. Pillet and H. Carstens, *Bibliographie der Troubadours* (1968) [hereafter P.-C.]; ed. C. Appel (Halle, 1932): no. 43, ll. 9–11. See Köhler, Mancini ed.: 241. The attribution of this famous *planh* on Henry the Young to Bertran de Born has been contested: it is not included in the recent edition by William D. Paden, Jr., et al. (1986), which does include the other *planh* on Henry the Young "Mon chan fenis" (P.-C.: 80.26).

48. Köhler, Mancini ed.: 242.

49. Duby, *Hommes et structures* (1973): 214: "entre l'adoubement et la paternité."

50. J. Bumke (1964): 93.

51. Duby, "Les 'jeunes' dans la société aristocratique dans la France du Nord-Ouest au XIIe siècle," *Annales* 19 (1964): 835–846 at 838, rpt. in *Hommes et structures* (1973): 213–225 at 216.

52. Besides Duby's studies see, especially, Köhler's "Sens et fonction du terme 'jeunesse' dans la poésie des troubadours," *Mélanges R. Croiset* (Poitiers: Éditions du CESCM, 1966): 569 ff.; Mancini ed.: 233–256.

53. A precious portrait of an Italian condottiero being presented as a model knight is the detailed story of the Milanese condottiero Galeazzo of Mantua in the long allegorical *Le Chevalier errant* that the Marquis Thomas III of Saluzzo composed in 1394/1395 during his captivity under the Count of Savoy. The text is in the still unpublished, splendidly miniatured Manuscript B.N. Fr. 12559. See M. Keen (1984): 18 f., with color plates nos. 28, 29. It was studied by Egidio Gorra, *Studi di critica letteraria* (Bologna, 1892): 3–110 and partly summarized in Thomas F. Crane (1920): 45 f. Gorra opined that it was probably composed in Paris around 1403–1404.

54. Duby, *Hommes et structures* (1973): 223: "une meute lâchée par les maisons nobles pour soulager le trop plein de leur puissance expansive, à la conquête de la gloire, du profit, et de proies féminines."

55. Cf. Bakhtin, *Rabelais and His World*, trans. Hélène Iswolsky (Cambridge, MA: M.I.T. Press, 1988; Russian original *Tvorchestvo Fransua Rable*, 1965): Introduction.

56. Duby, "Les origines de la chevalerie," *Hommes et structures*: 325–341.

57. On all this see Duby, "Situation de la noblesse en France au début du XIIIe siècle," *Hommes et structures*: 343–352. The dating of Lambert's work

was challenged and pushed forward into the fourteenth century by W. Erben (1922), whose opinion still finds some supporters despite an authoritative refutation by F. L. Ganshof (1925): cf. Flori (1986): 14. J. Bumke (1982: 126–132) agrees with Duby's conclusions and finds that independent German research has confirmed them despite the differences in the social conditions and chronological terms.

58. J. Flori (1986): 32 warns that there is also evidence to the effect that part of the nobility, for instance in Picardy, refused this identification, and that the assimilation between nobility and knightly class was no clear-cut matter before 1269. The evidence he has gathered, Flori (1986, passim) reiterates, supports the conclusion that chivalry did not really come of age before the twelfth century, which was also the age of its full flowering.

59. G. Duby, *The Three Orders* (1980): 295.

60. Theodore Evergates, "The Aristocracy of Champagne in the Mid-Thirteenth Century: A Quantitative Description," *Journal of Interdisciplinary History* 5 (1974): 1–18; idem, *Feudal Society in the Bailliage of Troyes under the Counts of Champagne, 1152–1284* (Baltimore, London: Johns Hopkins University Press, 1975).

61. For example, Anthony Richard Wagner, *Heralds and Heraldry in the Middle Ages* (London: Oxford University Press, 1956); Rodney Dennys, *The Heraldic Imagination* (London: Barrie and Jenkins, 1975); and M. Keen (1984), chap. 7 "Heraldry and Heralds," 125–142.

62. Text and French translation in Henri Waquet ed. (1964). See J. Flori (1986): 274–277 on Suger.

63. Köhler, Mancini ed.: 152 f.

64. Listing his prerogatives over one of his twenty-four castles, the bishop of Vicenza declared himself "rex, dux et comes," recognizing no lord above himself but the emperor: "nullum dominum, neque parem nec socium nec consortem praeter imperatorem." *Storia d'Italia*, eds. Romano and Vivanti: 5.1: 290.

65. L. Martines (1979): 8 and 13.

66. L. Martines (1979): 50 f. For an authoritative recent analysis of sociopolitical structures in the Italian city states see Giovanni Tabacco, *The Struggle for Power in Medieval Italy* [1979], trans. Rosalind Brown Jensen (Cambridge: Cambridge University Press, 1990).

67. M. Keen (1984): 38–41 for a strongly critical stance against the common view of a bourgeois patriciate as the effective ruling class in medieval northern and central Italy.

68. Donald E. Queller, *The Venetian Patriciate: Reality versus Myth* (Urbana, Chicago: University of Illinois Press, 1968); Margaret L. King, *Venetian Humanism in an Age of Patrician Dominance* (Princeton: Princeton University Press, 1986).

69. Published Rome: Antonio Blado, 1540. See D. Giannotti, *Opere politiche*, ed. Furio Diaz, 2 vols. (Milano: Marzorati, 1974): 1: 29–151.

70. Published posthumously in Paris, 1543, and read mostly in Ludovico Domenichi's translation (Venice, 1544).

71. On these texts by Giannotti, Contarini, and A. Piccolomini see C. Donati, *L'idea di nobiltà in Italia* (1988): 56–58, 60–62.

72. L. Martines (1979), especially chap. 3, for an up-to-date survey of recent findings concerning the complex social structure of Italian communes.

73. To put these figures into perspective, at the fateful battle of Bouvines (1214), a turning point in the fortunes of the French monarchy, Philip II Augustus of France victoriously confronted the assembled forces of the German emperor, the counts of Flanders and Boulogne, and the king of England with a feudal host of no more than thirteen hundred knights (plus eight hundred kept on the side for the southern defense), "summoned from Philip's entire feudal resources at the most critical moment of his reign." The allied army facing him is estimated to have counted thirteen to fifteen hundred knights. See John W. Baldwin, *The Government of Philip Augustus: Foundations of French Royal Power in the Middle Ages* (Berkeley, Los Angeles, London: University of California Press, 1986): 285 f. The total number of knights in England is estimated at circa six thousand at the time of the Domesday Book, and for several reasons that number declined from the end of the eleventh century, so that by 1258 there were no more than three thousand actual knights and potential knights, that is, landowners of knightly state, and only some 1,250 actual knights, including earls and barons. It is believed that at that time the king of England could not field an army of more than five hundred knights. See N. Denholm-Young, "Feudal Society in the Thirteenth Century: The Knights," *History* 29 (1944): 107–119; R. F. Treharne, "The Knights in the Period of Reform and Rebellion, 1268–67," *Bulletin of the Institute of Historical Research* 21 (London: University: Institute of Historical Research, 1946): 1–12; and Tony Hunt in *Forum for Modern Language Studies* (1981): 104. For such statistical conclusions it is usually assumed that knighthood cannot be sharply separated from horse-mounted and heavy-armed men at arms of the mercenary kind.

74. *Cronica* 7.120, cited by Daniel P. Waley, *The Italian City-Republics* (London: Weidenfeld & Nicolson, 1969): 222, 228. See D. Waley, "The Army of the Florentine Republic from the Twelfth to the Fourteenth Century," in Nicolai Rubinstein, ed., *Florentine Studies: Politics and Society in Renaissance Florence* (Evanston: Northwestern University Press, 1968): 93.

75. For example, L. Martines (1979): 51–55. See Sergio Bertelli, *Il potere oligarchico nello stato-città medievale* (Firenze: La Nuova Italia, 1978); idem, *I ceti dirigenti nella Toscana del Quattrocento* (Firenze: Papafava, 1987).

76. Daniel P. Waley, *The Italian City-Republics* (1969), chap. 3, "Government."

77. Poem 7, stanza 3: see Köhler, "Reichtum und Freigebigkeit," *Trobadorlyrik* (1962), Mancini ed.: 54.

78. The emulation of the ways of the nobility was more than psychological. The popularly "elected" communal lords in the age of the rising signories were usually of noble origin, and their governing councils naturally attracted the neighboring nobility also because they acted like noble courts: "le casate minori . . . avevano finito con il gravitare intorno alla corte dei signori cittadini, che . . . erano tutti più o meno di origine feudale, e disposti a configurare le loro

corti ed il loro modo di vivere su quello delle classi e delle corti feudali, cui una lunga tradizione . . . conferiva il carattere di 'modello.'" *Storia d'Italia*, eds. Romano and Vivanti, 5.1: 293. On the relationship between *signori* and the nobility, see Ernesto Sestan, *Italia medievale* (Napoli: Edizioni Scientifiche Italiane, 1968), "Le origini delle signorie cittadine: Un problema storico esaurito?" 209 ff.

79. L. Martines (1979): 97–102.

80. See Christian Bec, "Lo statuto socio-professionale degli scrittori (Trecento e Cinquecento)," in A. Asor Rosa, ed., *Letteratura Italiana* 2 (1983): 228–267; and idem, "I mercanti scrittori," ibid.: 269–297 on the merchant writers especially within the communes and then the signories.

81. A productive scholar issuing from the school of Buoncompagno da Signa, Rolandino was also an important regional chronicler: see my chapter 10 with note 55 on his *Chronicle*.

82. Riquer (1970): 236–251, 251–258, 259–268 on these three episodes.

83. Above all, Garrett Mattingly, *Renaissance Diplomacy* (1955; 1970).

84. N. Elias, *The Court Society*: 158 f. Elias reiterates the above facts in the wake of the still relevant research of the French historian Henri Lemonnier: *Charles VIII, Louis XII, François Ier et les guerres d'Italie* (Paris, 1903; rpt. ibid.: Tallandier, 1982).

85. For a detailed analysis of the Italian scene in the fifteenth and sixteenth centuries see Francesco Cognasso, *L'Italia nel Rinascimento* (Torino: Unione Tipografica Editrice Torinese [UTET], 1965), especially part 3, pp. 459–698 on Italian society.

86. On the social situation in the Byzantine empire in those centuries see Speros Vryonis, Jr., *The Decline of Medieval Hellenism in Asia Minor and the Process of Islamization from the Eleventh through the Fifteenth Century* (Berkeley, Los Angeles, London: University of California Press, 1971; 1986): 70–80.

87. Vryonis 76: "The single most fateful development leading to the defeat of Byzantium in Anatolia was, then, this vicious contest for political power between the bureaucrats and the generals, consuming as it did all the energies of the state in a destructive manner at a time when the external pressures were becoming dangerous."

88. Vryonis: 78.

89. See Takeshi Takagi (1879–1944), *A Comparison of bushi-do and Chivalry* (Tòzai bushidò no hikaku [1914]), trans. Tsuneyoshi Matsuno (Osaka, Japan: TM International Academy, 1984).

CHAPTER TWO: THE ORIGINS OF COURTLINESS

1. ". . . ipsa scola, quae interpretatur disciplina, id est correctio, dicitur quae alios habitu, incessu, verbo et actu atque totius bonitatis continentia corrigat." Hincmar, *Epist. syn. Karisiac.* 12, *Monumenta Germaniae Historica* [hereafter *MGH*], Leges 2, Capit. 2, p. 436, ll. 2–6, cited by Jaeger (1987): 609. For a magisterial presentation on medieval courts, especially in Italy, see Aurelio Ron-

caglia, "Le corti medievali," in A. Asor Rosa, ed., *Letteratura italiana* 1 (1982): 33–147.

2. But on Ottonian government see, notably, Karl J. Leyser, *Rule and Conflict in an Early Medieval Society: Ottonian Saxony* (1979; 1989), and idem, "Ottonian Government," *English Historical Review* 96 (1981): 722–753.

3. For a fuller appreciation of medieval humanism Jaeger brings forward, for example, Erdmann's rich surveys and editions of letters from the period of Henry IV, remarking (119) that a study of "the motifs of these letters as forerunners of the main themes at the French humanist schools in the earlier twelfth century is still to be written. It is a rich topic." See Carl Erdmann, *Studien zur Briefliteratur Deutschlands im 11. Jahrhundert*, MGH, Schriften 1 (Leipzig: Hiersemann, 1938); C. Erdmann and N. Fickermann, eds., *Briefsammlungen der Zeit Heinrichs IV*, MGH, Briefe der deutschen Kaiserzeit 5 (Weimar: Böhlau, 1950).

4. Jaeger (1987): 587. See Margaret T. Gibson, "The *artes* in the Eleventh Century," in *Arts libéraux et philosophie au moyen âge*. Actes du 4ᵉ Congrès international de philosophie médiévale, Montréal, Institut d'études médiévales, 1967 (Paris: Librairie philosophique J. Vrin, 1969 [c1968]): 121–126; idem, "The Continuity of Learning circa 850—circa 1050," *Viator* 6 (1975): 1–13.

5. Fleckenstein, *Early Medieval Germany* (1978): 154 f.

6. Similarly, while investigating this ideal of a harmoniously literate and moral education in the teaching of the fifteenth- and sixteenth-century humanists, A. Grafton and L. Jardine (1986) have found that it was effected by "lived emulation of a teacher who projects the cultural ideal above and beyond the drilling he provides in curriculum subjects" (27, with specific reference to Guarino Veronese). This was achieved, these historians claim, despite the absence of an explicit moral content in a curriculum that insisted chiefly on careful, philologically correct reading of classical authors.

7. *Vita Angelrani* 3 in *PL* 141: 1406a. Jaeger (1987): 586, note 62.

8. Jaeger (1987): 581 f., quoting from *Ioannis Saresberiensis episcopi Carnotensis Metalogicon*, ed. Clemens Webb (1929), 1, Prol., p. 4, and 1.24, p. 55: "Illa autem que ceteris philosophie partibus preminet, Ethicam dico, sine qua nec philosophi subsistit nomen, collati decoris gratia omnes alias antecedit"; and from Onulf of Speyer, *Colores rhetorici* (1071–1076), ed. W. Wattenbach, Sitzungsberichte der Preussischen Akademie der Wissenschaften (1894) 361–386 at 369: ". . . arti rhetoricae: morum elegantiam, compositionem habitus, vitae dignitatem amplectere," which Jaeger translates as "elegant manners, composed bearing, and dignity of conduct," given as goals of rhetorical instruction.

9. The exemplary text is *De sui ipsius et multorum ignorantia* 4: see F. Petrarca, *Opere latine*, ed. Antonietta Bufano, 2 vols. (Torino: UTET, 1975) 2: 1106–1108. See Jerome Taylor, "*Fraunceys Petrak* and the *Logyk* of Chaucer's Clerk," in A. Scaglione, ed., *Francis Petrarch, Six Centuries Later: A Symposium* (Chapel Hill, NC: University of North Carolina Department of Romance Languages; Chicago: Newberry Library, 1975): 364–383 at 372–374.

10. "Onde i buon pedagoghi non solamente insegnano lettere ai fanciulli, ma ancora boni modi ed onesti nel mangiare, bere, parlare, andare, con certi

gesti accommodati." *Cortegiano* 4.12, trans. Singleton 297; see Jaeger: 231.
John W. Baldwin, "Masters at Paris from 1179 to 1215: A Social Perspective,"
in Robert L. Benson and Giles Constable, eds., *Renaissance and Renewal* (Cambridge: Harvard University Press; Oxford: Oxford University Press, 1982;
1985): 151–158 shows the linkage between advanced education and the attainment of governmental and ecclesiastical high careers around 1200.

11. Jaeger: chap. 8, "The Language of Courtesy," 127–175.

12. N. Elias, *Power and civility* (1982): 258–270, "The Courtization of
Warriors" (*"Die Verhöflichung der Krieger"*). For the German area, see J.
Bumke, *Knighthood in the Middle Ages* (1982): 156 on the study of rulers'
ethic; the texts edited by W. Berges; and the studies by K. Bosl, G. H. Hagspiel,
U. Hoffmann, E. Kleinschmidt, H. Kloft, W. Störmer, and H. Wolfram in my
References.

13. See *Andreae Capellani Regii Francorum De amore libri tres*, ed. E. Tro-
jel (Copenhagen: Gad, 1892; rpt. Munich: 1972); Andreas Capellanus, *The Art
of Courtly Love*, trans. John Jay Parry (New York: Columbia University Press,
1941; Frederick Ungar, 1957; Norton, 1969): 159–162, 241, 285 f.

14. Jaeger: 153 f., 160, and 147–149.

15. "A letter of the authors expounding his whole intention in the course of
this worke" in *The Works of Edmund Spenser: A Variorum Edition*, eds. Edwin
Greenlaw et al. (Baltimore: Johns Hopkins University Press, 1932–1957). See,
on the broad historical context of this famous passage, S. Greenblatt (1980):
"To Fashion a Gentleman: Spenser and the Destruction of the Bower of Bliss,"
157–192.

16. See word frequency count and semantic history in Jaeger: 129–133. The
lack of a true Provençal or Old French equivalent for the given acceptation of
Medieval Latin *disciplina*, Middle High German *zuht*, and Middle English *discipline* points to the German origin of this central notion for the code of courtesy (Jaeger: 132). It will help to clarify the exact import of *zuht*, a very common term in Middle High German literature, if we bear in mind that its modern
form, *Zucht*, still carries the complex and variable meaning of good breeding,
including both education and good family origin, culture, discipline, honesty,
chastity, and modesty, while its old antithesis *unzuht, unzucht*, meant lascivi-
ousness and lechery.

17. On the "twilight of the Gods" climate of the late cycles down to Sir
Thomas Malory's (d. 1471) *Le Morte Darthur* (or *d'Arthur*) see, for example,
Eugene Vinaver, *The Rise of Romance* (1984).

18. I quote from Testard's edition of *De officiis* as *Les devoirs* (1965),
where, interestingly enough, this *comitas* is translated with "courtoisie."

19. "Sequitur ut de una reliqua parte honestatis dicendum sit, in qua uere-
cundia et quasi quidam ornatus uitae, temperantia et modestia omnisque seda-
tio perturbationum animi et rerum modus cernitur. Hoc loco continetur id quod
dici latine decorum potest, graece enim *prepon* dicitur decorum. Huius uis ea
est ut ab honesto non queat separari; nam et quod decet honestum est, et quod
honestum est decet. . . . Similis est ratio fortitudinis. Quod enim uiriliter ani-
moque magno fit, id dignum uiro et decorum uidetur, quod contra, id ut turpe,
sic indecorum."

"Quocirca poetae in magna uarietate personarum, etiam uitiosis quid conue-
niat et quid deceat, uidebunt, nobis autem cum a natura constantiae, modera-
tionis, temperantiae, uerecundiae partes datae sint cumque eadem natura doceat
non neglegere quemadmodum nos aduersus homines geramus, efficitur ut et
illud quod ad omnem honestatem pertinet, decorum quam late fusum sit, ap-
pareat et hoc quod spectatur in uno quoque genere uirtutis."

"Omnes participes sumus rationis praestantiaeque eius qua antecellimus bes-
tiis, a qua omne honestum decorumque trahitur et ex qua ratio inueniendi officii
exquiritur." (Translations in the text are mine.)

20. Jaeger (1987): 592–598, with supporting quotations from Richard W.
Southern, *Medieval Humanism and Other Essays* (New York: Harper & Row,
1970), and Beryl Smalley, *The Becket Conflict and the Schools: A Study of
Intellectuals and Politics* (Totowa, N.J.: Rowman & Littlefield; Oxford: Basil
Blackwell, 1973).

21. *MGH*, Scriptores [hereafter *MGH*, SS] 20: 562, ll. 9 f., cited by Jaeger
(1987): 593, note 90.

22. Discussing Edward Pechter, "The New Historicism and Its Discontents:
Politicizing Renaissance Drama" (*PMLA* 102, 1987: 292–303), Ben Ross
Schneider, Jr. (Letter to the Editor, *PMLA* 103, 1988: "Forum," 60 f.) recalls
Karl Marx's somewhat nostalgic denunciation of the capitalistic bourgeoisie
of the Renaissance for sweeping away feudal and patriarchal family ties, religious and chivalric idealism, and respect toward "natural superiors" and time-
honored occupations, while it replaced them inexorably with the cold monetary
rewards and the irresponsible freedoms of free trade (*Communist Manifesto*,
Chicago: Regnery, 1954: 12 f.). Renaissance texts, Schneider contends, must be
interpreted by understanding the ideology of the ruling class that they rational-
ized. He suggests that "this ideology is to be found very close to home, in the
European idea of a gentleman, so much admired by Conrad, Hemingway, and
Faulkner," claiming that this ideology "originates in the Christian doctrine of
self-sacrifice melded with the ancient concept of honor." One crucial text that
both old and new historicists have neglected, Schneider adds, is Cicero's *De
officiis*, "the most important moral authority of the period, well known to every
schoolchild," whereas, according to Schneider, "they prefer to fix on such details as the apparently self-serving aspects of Castiglione's *sprezzatura*, while
ignoring the thrust of his book as a whole. . . . The task of assembling the ideology of the ruling class in the Renaissance is still before us," concludes
Schneider.

23. On the use of Cicero within the perspective of "civic humanism" see
Baron, "Cicero and the Roman Civic Spirit" (1938).

24. The motif, Jaeger (237) reminds us, had a long life in European literature: even Stendhal's Fabrizio del Dongo serves the Prince of Parma precisely
with the intent of obtaining a bishopric.

25. R. E. Latham, ed., *Dictionary of Medieval Latin* (London: Oxford University Press, 1975–[Letter C 1981, Letter D 1986]), gives as basic meanings
for *curialitas*: "a) courtliness, refinement, sophistication; b) courtesy, favor, (act
of) graciousness; c) gratuity, free gift"; and for *curialis*: "municipal official (Isidore, *Etymologiae*: 9.4.24), courtier of royal or magnate's court, subordinate."

26. *Weitere Briefe Meinhards* no. 1 in C. Erdmann, ed.: *Briefsammlungen der Zeit Henrichs IV* (1950): 193. See Jaeger (1987): 598, with more texts.

27. Jaeger (1987): 596 f., with texts and examples. Hugh's text is from *De institutione novitiorum, PL* 176: 925–952 at 935B–D: "disciplina . . . est membrorum omnium motus ordinatus et dispositio decens in omni habitu et actione, . . . frenum lasciviae, elationis jugum, vinculum iracundiae, quae domat intemperantiam . . . et omnes inordinatos motus mentis atque illicitos appetitos suffocat. Sicut enim de inconstantia mentis nascitur inordinata motio corporis, ita quoque dum corpus per disciplinam stringitur, animus ad constantiam solidatur." The term *disciplina* looms large in Hugh's text: chaps. 10 through 21 deal with "disciplina in actu et in gestu, in loquendo, in mensa, in cibo."

28. "In quo ergo animae decor? An forte in eo quod honestum dicitur? . . . Cum autem decoris huius claritas abundantius intima cordis repleverit, prodeat foras necesse est . . . pulchritudo animae palam erit." *Sermo super Canticum* 85: 10–11, in *Sancti Bernardi Opera*, eds. Jean Leclerq and H. M. Rochais (1957–1977): 2; (1958): 314; quoted by Jaeger (1987): 599.

29. Jaeger: 128 f., 136. Herbord's text is now in the Warsaw edition by Wikarjak and Liman (1974).

30. In the Middle Ages the basic text for all this was, once again, Cicero's *De officiis* (Jaeger 103–116), but the opposition *urbanus/rusticus*, underlying the distinction between the literate and the illiterate registers of speakers of Latin, was a constant of ancient culture. Even in Rome it went back to archaic times: Quintilian, *Institutio oratoria* 6.3.105, relates Cato's definition of *homo urbanus* as the one who speaks correctly, aptly, and wittily—*facetus* and *lepidus*, to use Plautus's adjectives. See Eugène de Saint-Denis, "Évolution sémantique de *urbanus-urbanitas*," *Latomus* 3 (1939): 5–24, and Edwin S. Ramage, *Urbanitas: Ancient Sophistication and Refinement* (Norman, OK: University of Oklahoma Press, 1973). For the broad sociological implications, see, for example, Richard Sennett, *The Fall of Public Man* (New York: Vintage Books, c1976, 1978).

31. *Joannis Lemovicensis abbatis de Zirc 1208–1218 Opera omnia* (1932): 1: 71–126. Johannes, abbot of a Cistercian monastery at Zirc in Hungary for a time, addressed his work to Count Theobald IV of Champagne. For Jaeger (91–95) this impressive text, which "deserves a new critical edition and a serious and informed commentary," has been regularly misunderstood by historians and critics.

32. Jaeger: 55; see Damiani's text in *PL*: 145: 463–472.

33. Flori (1986): 158 f. Flori's whole chapter 15 "Critiques de la chevalerie," 331–338, goes over the abundant literature inspired by the spirit of ecclesiastical and social reform.

34. See this in Thomas Wright, ed., *The Anglo-Latin Satirical Poets and Epigrammatists of the Twelfth Century* (London: Longman, 1872).

35. Jaeger: 58 and note 279.

36. John of Salisbury's *Policraticus* contains two chapters on the definition of *civilitas* (book 8, chaps. 10–11; Webb ed.: 2: 284–306). See, also, *Policraticus* 1.4 against courtly culture, specifically the practice of hunting, as aestheti-

cally attractive but little more than an expression of frivolity and vanity (Webb: 1: 21–35).

37. *Aeneae Silvii de curialium miseriis epistola* (1928). Peter of Blois's text is his epistle 14, *PL*: 207: 42–51. See, also, the "Dialogus inter dehortantem a curia et curialem," st. 7, in Peter Dronke, "Peter of Blois and Poetry at the Court of Henry II," *Medieval Studies* 38 (1976): 208. For Jaeger (58) the existence of such polemical literature is proof that the type of court cleric portrayed in the episcopal *vitae* was not a literary fiction but a social reality.

38. *De gradibus humilitatis et superbiae* chap. 12.40, in *S. Bernardi Opera*, eds. Jean Leclerq and H. M. Rochais, 3 (1963): 1–59 at 46. Jaeger: 171.

In the tenth and eleventh centuries the Cluniacs had been in the forefront of the movement for Church reform, consequently, of resistance and opposition to courtliness, seen only negatively as hypocrisy, worldliness, corruption, and effeminacy. But in due course Cluny became widely regarded as a center of refinement (see, typically, Boccaccio's stories on the abbot of Cluny as a paragon of liberality and good living: *Decameron* 1.7; 10.2), and so it was seen by the Carthusians and Cistercians: the history of architecture is a running commentary on the critical stance of the Cistercians' stern, spiritual Gothic versus the worldly, earth-bound, and ornate Romanesque of the Cluniacs. The order of Cîteaux became the leader of austere reform when St. Bernard took over the center of Clairvaux in Champagne in 1115.

39. "Mimos et magos et fabulatores, scurrilesque cantilenas atque ludorum spectacula, tanquam vanitates et insanias falsas respuunt et abominantur." *De laude novae militiae, PL*: 182: 926. See his definition of a good bishop's true virtues as essentially chastity, charity, and humility in the letter "De moribus et officio episcoporum ad Henricum Senonensem archiepiscopum" of circa 1127 (*PL*: 182: 809 ff.), addressed to the archbishop of Sens, who had come to his office from a career at court.

40. Marc Bloch, *La société féodale* (1939–1940): 2: 152.

41. "Fateor quidem, quod sanctum est domino regi assistere" (440D); "Principibus placuisse viris non ultima laus est" (441B; see Horace, *Epistolae*: 1.17.35); "non solum laudabile, sed gloriosum reputo domino regi assistere, procurare rempublicam, sui esse immemorem, et omnium totum esse" (441C: see Jaeger: 84).

42. *Facetus*, edited by A. Morel-Fatío, *Romania* 15 (1886): 224–235. See Ingeborg Glier, *Artes amandi* (1971): 18–20.

43. I differ from Jaeger's translation (167): "Retain your modest restraint even when speaking falsehoods."

44. I. Glier, *Artes amandi* (1971): 18–20.

45. Günter Eifler, ed., *Ritterliches Tugendsystem* (1970); Gustav Ehrismann, "Die Grundlagen des ritterlichen Tugendsystems" (1919): 137–216; idem, *Geschichte der deutschen Literatur* (1972); E. R. Curtius, *European Literature and the Latin Middle Ages* (1963): 522–530. See, now, Jörg Arentzen and Uwe Ruberg, eds., *Die Ritteridee in der deutschen Literatur des Mittelalters: eine kommentierte Anthologie* (Darmstadt: Wissenschaftliche Buchgesellschaft, 1987).

46. Holmberg 82: see Curtius, *European Literature* (1963): 529.

47. J. Flori (1986) 17, 277–280. Flori concludes that the polemic between Curtius and Ehrismann was satisfactorily resolved in a sort of compromise by Daniel Rocher's studies (1964, 1966, 1968).

48. For example, Daniel Rocher's and Gert Kaiser's studies (1966; 1986).

49. Jaeger's relationship to Elias's work raises questions that involve the method of "history of ideas." Jaeger (9) claims that, although his own presentation issues from Elias's, "Elias sees courtesy as a product of certain social changes, a response to conditions. I maintain just the contrary: courtesy is in origin an instrument of the urge to civilizing, of the forces in which that process originates, and not an outgrowth of the process itself." Thus, he sees the birth of the curial ethic as essentially a matter of conceptual thrust in a civilizing movement, and blames Elias for grounding this ideology in social circumstances. Yet, the real matter is one of convergence of experience and culture, so that Jaeger may be faulted for what Lauro Martines (1979: 126–128) calls "the [occasionally] abstract cerebrations of [some] historians of ideas" (my additions). As I read it, Jaeger's later paper of 1987 seems to come around to a different assessment of his research's methodological import where he says: "I stress that this type, the ideal educated bishop, the courtier bishop, was not in its origins a product of shaping ideas, but rather of political and social circumstances which favored the rediscovery and revival of those ideas. An office in the Ottonian imperial church system required a statesman/orator/administrator to fill it, and from that office and its requirements, an educational program, the cultivation of virtues in the old learning, took its major impetus in our period [i.e., 1000–1150]" (594 f.; Jaeger also refers to his "The Courtier Bishop in *Vitae* from the Tenth to the Twelfth Century," *Speculum* 58 [1983]: 291–325). He thus seems to have moved from an essentially "history of ideas" position to a practically sociological one—in substance, Elias's very own.

50. See the review of Jaeger's book by Gerald A. Bond, *Romance Philology* 42.4 (1989): 479–485 at 483.

51. Jaeger (1987): 599–601, citing P. G. Walsh, "Alan of Lille as a Renaissance Figure," *Studies in Church History* 14 (1977): 117–135; Michael Wilks, "Alan of Lille and the New Man," *Studies in Church History* 14 (1977): 137–157; and Linda Marshall, "The Identity of the 'New Man' in the *Anticlaudianus* of Alan of Lille," *Viator* 10 (1979): 77–94.

52. *Secretum Secretorum: Nine English Versions*, ed. M. A. Manzaloni, Early English Texts Society no. 276 (Oxford: Oxford University Press, 1977): 1: 79 f.

53. "Ipse etiam fratrum commoda sepius amplius decrevit. . . ." *Chronicon Hildesheimense* [*Chronicon episcoporum Hildesheimensium*], MGH, Scriptores 7 (Hannover: Hahn, 1846): 845–873 at 853 par. 16. "Eo . . . presidente irrepsit ambitiosa curialitas, quae . . . disciplinae mollito rigore claustri claustra relaxavit." *Fundatio ecclesiae Hildesheimensis*, ed. Adolf Hofmeister: MGH, SS 30.2: 939–946. Second text quoted by Jaeger: 153 f., 160, from this latter edition: chap. 5, 945, 12 ff.

54. "rex filium suum . . . beato Thomae cancellario commisit alendum, et moribus et curialitatibus informandum," in [Matthew Paris (1200–1259)] *Matthaei Parisiensis, monachi Sancti Albani, Historia Anglorum, sive, ut vulgo dicitur, Historia minor. Item, ejusdem Abbreviatio chronicorum Angliae*, ed.

Frederic Madden, Rolls Series no. 44, 3 vols. (London: Longmans, Green, Reader, & Dyer, 1866–1869): 1: 316, cited by Jaeger (1987): 612, n. 126. Each term has its individual history: the important term *disciplina*, for example, had a pertinent connotation in France as early as in Hincmar of Reims, while Jaeger (130–131) finds the first occurrence of it in a context of good manners in the *Ruodlieb*, commonly dated between 1030 and 1050, although Jaeger (122) prefers Karl Hauk's later dating between 1042 and 1070.

55. *Cortes*, it is worth noting, appears in Arnaut Daniel's speech in Dante's *Purgatorio* 26: 140.

56. There has recently been a lively interest in lexical and semantic studies concerning the extent and value of terms relating to knighthood, chivalry, and courtesy, with results still to be assessed on a comparative basis. For the Provençal epic language see, for example, Linda Paterson, "Knights and the Concept of Knighthood in the Twelfth-Century Occitan Epic," *Forum for Modern Language Studies* 17.2 (1981): 115–130, who takes her point of departure from Jean Flori's studies and quantitative methods.

Similarly, the ethical and the juridical vocabulary deserve parallel study for the light they can throw on each other. The feudal "mentality" has been reconstructed in part by analyzing the changes in Latin and vernacular terms referring to property and interpersonal attitudes: see, for example, the semantic studies by K. J. Hollyman, *Le développement du vocabulaire féodal en France pendant le haut moyen âge* (Genève, Paris: E. Droz, 1957). The nomenclatures of the "virtues" of the lords, their vassals, their courtiers, the knights, and so on, appear largely interchangeable with those advocated for the courtly lover and the chivalric hero of literature, but with significant semantic shifts, some of which I shall pursue. See G. Duby's strictures about Hollyman's important study in "La féodalité? Une mentalité médiévale," *Annales* 14.4 (1958): 765–771, reprinted in *Hommes et structures* (1973): 103–110.

57. Du Cange gives *maneria, maneries* for *modus, ratio*, with Abelard's logical acceptation of *genus* (*De generibus et speciebus*: "genera id est manerias"). See Adolf Tobler and Erhard Lommatzsch, *Altfranzösisches Wörterbuch* 5 (Wiesbaden: F. Steiner, 1963): *maniere, meniere* < Medieval Latin *man(u)arius* with the still current meanings of *guise*, "properly set mode," and "habit and mores" documented since the twelfth century as in "mout cuidoit chanter par maniere," "les ges et la maniere," and "n'avoir meniere" = to be immoderate, extravagant, without sense of proportion: "tant qu'il n'avoit meniere."

58. For example, M. Keen (1984): 121–123.

59. K. Foster, *The Two Dantes* (Berkeley, Los Angeles, London: University of California Press, 1978): 20.

60. See, out of an abundant literature, Joan M. Ferrante, "*Cortes'amor* in Medieval Texts," *Speculum* 55 (1980): 686–695.

CHAPTER THREE: COURTLINESS AND CHIVALRY IN FRANCE

1. Whether it is an afterthought or an initial motivating force, Jaeger's study ends with an indictment of the age-long polemics invidiously pitting the myth of French *civilization* against that of German *Kultur* (cf. Nietzsche's alleged

admiring endorsement of Wagner's claim that, before his art, civilization would
"dissipate like fog before the sun"—Jaeger: 271). The French origin of courtesy
would play the role of an opening chapter in this story of France as the source
of western civilized living.

2. "Nitebat enim pro generum [sic] nobilitate, florebat bonitatum agalmate
[sic]. Moribus erat illustris, sublimiorque merito astris. Effigie rutilabat, nul-
lique pietate secundus erat. . . . Vultu clarus erat, omnique actu clarior cunctis
exstiterat, dulcis emicabat eloquio, habitu et incessu omnibus suavior. Nitidus
ore mellifluo, serenus semper corde jucundissimo." *PL*: 141: 607–758 at 724,
discussed in Nino Scivoletto, *Spiritualità medievale e tradizione scolastica nel
secolo XII in Francia* (Napoli: Armanni, 1954): 218–221, also cited by Vallone, (1955): 55 f. Jaeger (198 f.) quotes a longer passage from Dudo on the
same prince from *PL*: 141: 740a-c. See [Dudon de Saint-Quentin,] *De moribus
et actis primorum Normanniae ducum, auctore Dudone Sancti Quintini de-
cano*, ed. Jules Lair (Caen: F. Le Blanc-Hardel, 1865).

3. Vallone (1955): 56 for Claudian's text.

4. Guillaume de Jumièges [Guilelmus Gemeticensis], *Gesta Normannorum
ducum*, ed. Jean Marx (Rouen: A. Lestringant; Paris: A. Picard, 1914). See Flori
(1986) 146–148.

5. Guillaume de Poitier [Guilelmus Pictaviensis], *Histoire de Guillaume le
Conquérant*, ed. and trans. Raymond Foreville (Paris: Les Belles Lettres, 1952).
See Flori (1986): 148–150.

6. "Defensor hujus patriae, cur talia rimatus es facere? Quis fovebit clerum
et populum? Quis contra nos ingruentium paganorum exercitui obstabit?"
Cited by Flori (1986): 145, from Dudo, ed. J. Lair (1865): 201.

7. Guillaume de Jumièges, *Gesta Normannorum ducum*, ed. Marx (1914):
3.8: 39 f.

8. Flori (1986): 147.

9. Flori (1986): 151 f., citing from Helgaud de Fleury, *Vie de Robert le
Pieux; Epitoma vitae Regis Rotberti Pii*, ed. and trans. Robert-Henri Bautier
and Gillette Labory (Paris: Centre National de la Recherche Scientifique, 1965):
par. 30, p. 139. Helgaud was a monk at Fleury-sur-Loire (d. ca. 1050).

10. Flori (1986): 152–158. See the *Vita domni Burcardi* in Eudes de Saint-
Maur, *Vie de Bouchard le Vénérable: comte de Vendome, de Corbeil, de Melun
et de Paris (Xᵉ et XIᵉ siècles)*, ed. Charles Bourel de la Roncière (Paris: A. Picard, 1892), esp. p. 9.

11. On the tradition of the *ordines* see Duby, *Les trois ordres* (1978); idem,
The Three Orders (1980); J. Bumke (1982): 115; and Flori (1986): 331–338.
See Duby (1980): 13–20 on ideological background, authors, and dates of the
two documents. A student of Georges Dumézil, J. H. Grisward, *Archéologie de
l'épopée médiévale* (1981), esp. p. 20 and chap. 1: 38–48, has imaginatively
applied Dumézil's anthropological hypothesis of a primordial Indo-European
mythic pattern of trifunctional division of society to explain the role of the
ordines idea in the epic of *Aymeri de Narbonne*. See Dumézil's preface to this
work, pp. 9–15, and G. Duby, *The Three Orders* (1980): 6–8 on the broader
implications.

12. *Liber de vita christiana*: 7.28: 248 f. See M. Keen (1984): 5, and Flori

(1986): 249–253. On Bonizo, see Walther Berschin, *Bonizo von Sutri* (Berlin, New York: de Gruyter, 1972).

13. *Speculum Ecclesiae, PL*: 172 (1895): 807–1108 at 865; see sections "ad milites," col. 865, "ad mercatores," cols. 865 f., and "ad agricolas," cols. 866–876. See Flori (1986): 253–257.

14. G. Duby, *The Three Orders* (1980): 1–4.

15. Ordericus Vitalis, *Historia Ecclesiastica*, in *The Ecclesiastical History of Orderic Vitalis*, ed. and trans. Marjorie Chibnall, Oxford Medieval Texts, 6 vols. (Oxford: Oxford University Press, 1969–1980): 3: 216 (vol. 6.2 of Chibnall ed.). See Duby, *Hommes et structures* (1973): 158 f., 222; also Jaeger: 231. Duby was using the study by Hans Wolter, *Ordericus Vitalis: Ein Beitrag zur kluniazensischen Geschichtsschreibung* (Wiesbaden: F. Steiner, 1955).

16. "Absit a me ut credam quod probus miles violet fidem suam! Quod si fecerit, omni tempore, velut exlex, despicabilis erit." Ordericus Vitalis, *Historia ecclesiastica*, ed. M. Chibnall, vol. 4, book 10, p. 49, cited by J. Flori (1986): 273.

17. "orphanorum quidem consolator, viduarum in tribulationibus pius adiutor," *Historia, MGH,* SS 24: chap. 24, p. 573; ed. Denis Ch. de Godefroy-Ménilglaise, chap. 24, p. 61. The point that only members of the nobility were the beneficiaries is made by Flori (1986): 294 f.

18. J. Flori, "La chevalerie selon Jean de Salisbury," *Revue d'Histoire Ecclésiastique* 77 (1982): 35–77, and Flori (1986): 280–289.

19. G. Duby, *The Three Orders* (1970), declares the *Policraticus* "the first systematic description of a medieval state machinery and its workings" (287); "the first systematic formulation of a secular ideology of power and social order. As it was the work of a clerk—and not a servile one, but a man convinced of the superiority of his estate—the system it proposes is, of course, strongly marked with the imprint of ecclesiastical thought" (264).

20. *Policraticus*: book 4, chap. 3: "princeps minister est sacerdotum et minor eis" (Webb ed.: 1: 239); and 4.6: "debet peritus esse in litteris, et litteratorum agi consiliis" (Webb ed.: 1: 250).

21. "nam et haec agentes milites sancti sunt et in eo fideliores principi quo servant studiosius fidem Dei." *Policraticus*: book 6, chap. 8; Webb ed.: 2: 23.

22. *Policraticus*: 6. 5–10, 13, 19, 25 for statements on duties of the military class. See Hans Liebeschütz, "Chartres und Bologna. Naturbegriff und Staatsidee bei Johann von Salisbury," *Archiv für Kulturgeschichte* 50 (1968): 3–32. *Policraticus*: 1.6 (Webb: 1: 41–42) contains a thinly veiled condemnation of courtly love literature as frivolous and sinful while criticizing knights for being interested more in success with women than in fulfilling their moral duties toward society—a critique that J. Flori (1986): 332 declares "extremely rare."

23. M. Keen (1984): 5, 31, and passim (see his Index), and J. A. Wisman, "L'*Epitoma rei militaris* de Végèce et sa fortune au moyen âge," *Le Moyen Age* 85 (1979): 13–31. Vegetius's *Epitoma de re militari* (between A.D. 383 and 450) was the only manual of Roman military institutions to have survived intact.

24. "Inoleuit consuetudo solennis ut ea ipsa die, qua quisque militari cingulo decoratur, ecclesiam solenniter adeat gladioque super altare posito et ob-

lato quasi celebri professione facta seipsum obsequio altaris deuoueat et gladii, id est officii sui, iugem Deo spondeat famulatum." *Policraticus*: 6.10 (Webb ed., 2: 25). Bad soldiers must be punished by taking away their right to carry the sword: "Sunt autem plurimi qui . . . quando militiae consecrandi cingulum altari obtulerunt, uidentur protestari se eo tunc animo accessisse ut altari et ministris eius, sed et Deo, qui ibi colitur, bellum denuntiarent. Facilius crediderim hos malitiae execratos quam ad legitimama militiam consecratos." *Policraticus*: 6.13 (Webb ed.: 2: 37). The text is also in *PL* 199: 602–608.

   25. Flori (1986): chaps. 13 and 14, pp. 290–330; on Alienor, Rita Lejeune, "Rôle littéraire d'Aliénor d'Aquitaine et de sa famille," *Cultura Neolatina* 14 (1954): 5–57, and Régine Pernoud, *Alienor d'Aquitaine* (Paris: A. Michel, 1965; 1980).

   26. "Nil violenter exigant, neminem concutiant, sint defensores patriae, tutores orphanorum et viduarum, . . . interius armentur lorica fidei." "Suam militiam prostituunt." Chaps. 39 and 40; *PL* 210: 185 f.

   27. Duby, *Hommes et structures* (1973): 347. J. Flori (1986) 18 finds that John of Salisbury and Étienne de Fougères were the first authors to turn their attention directly and explicitly to chivalry. He adds that S. Painter (1940, 1967) was skeptical of the influence of such literature on the knights' actual behavior. M. Keen (1984): 4, declares Étienne's treatise "the first systematic treatment of chivalry," with the term *chevalerie* being identified with the warrior estate and free, hence noble birth: "*de franche mère né.*"

   28. *Le livre des manières*: vv. 677–710. See G. Duby, *The Three Orders* (1980): 282–285.

   29. On Wace and Benoît see J. Flori (1986): 308–315. The *Roman de Rou* contributed to the valorization of the lay status that we have seen in the form of recognition of a positive role for the knighthood as part of the class of *bellatores*, defenders of the state and the Church. See Benoit de Sainte-More (sic), *Chronique des ducs de Normandie, publiée d'après le manuscrit de Tours avec les variantes du manuscrit de Londres*, ed. Carin Fahlin, 4 vols., vol. 4, "Notes," by Sven Sandqvist (Uppsala: Almqvist & Wiksell, 1951–1979).

   30. *Roman de Rou*, ed. A. J. Holden (Paris: A. et J. Picard, 1970): 3: 72, vv. 1710–1717.

   31.   Li quens de Normandie fu moult prouz et cortoiz,
              Bien maintint sez villainz, bien out chier sez borjoiz,
              A sez barons donna terres, fieus et conrois,
              As fiz as vavasours donna dras et hernois,
              Armes et pallefroiz et chevals espanois.
                                                    (2: 4124–4129)

              . . . .
              De largesce e de nobles murs
              Surmunta tuz ses ancesurs.
                                                    (3: 2297–2299)

   32. "Unques vilain nus ne d'eus nez / Ne fus granment de lui privez." *Chronique*: 28,832–834. See Flori (1986): 314. Susan Crane (1986) has attempted a socio-political interpretation of Anglo-Norman literature on the line of Duby's reading of French medieval *mentalités*.

33. M. Keen (1984): 20–22. On the chronicle of William the Marshal see Sidney Painter, *William Marshal* (Baltimore: Johns Hopkins University Press, 1933), 44–46 on the tourney, and G. Duby, *William Marshal* (1985).

34. See M. Bloch, *Feudal Society* (1968): 200 f.; Andrée Lehmann, *Le rôle de la femme dans l'histoire de France au Moyen-Age* (Paris: Berger-Levrault, 1952).

35. Breton's text in *Chroniques des Comtes d'Anjou et des seigneurs d'Amboise*, eds. L. Halphen and R. Poupardin (1913); see Duby, *Les trois ordres*: 348; *The Three Orders*: 289 f., and Flori (1986): 304 f. Also Duby, *The Knight the Lady and the Priest*: chap. 12, "The Lords of Amboise," 227–252 (where the author of this first chronicle of the Amboise house is said to be unknown) on the presentation of marriage in these texts. See the picturesque anecdote of Louis VII's entourage laughing at Count Fulk the Good after catching him in a posture of devout prayer: the once great lord, now a canon at Saint-Martin of Tours, looked like "an ordained priest." But Henry of Anjou, without uttering a word, right away penned a note to the king which read: "An illiterate king is a crowned ass." The king, Breton reports tendentiously, was compelled to acknowledge that *sapientia, eloquentia*, and *litterae* were becoming not only to kings but counts, too (like Henry), for they all have a duty to excel "in both morals and letters." *Chroniques des Comtes*: 140–142.

36. On Philip Augustus's historical role vis-à-vis the French great lords and the English king, see John W. Baldwin, *The Government of Philip Augustus: Foundations of French Royal Power in the Middle Ages* (Berkeley, Los Angeles, London: University of California Press, 1986).

37. James A. Brundage, *Richard Lion Heart* (New York: Scribner's, 1974): 170–172.

38. *Chroniques des Comtes d'Anjou* (1913): 194–196, 218; see Keen (1984): 31; Flori (1986): 306–308.

39. "liberalis Gaufredus, non ut pauperem dives contempsit, sed, ut homo hominem reconoscens. . . . 'Nam juris amicus, custos pacis, hostium debellator, et, quod plurimum in principe nitet, oppressorum benignus auxiliator est. . . . Hostes nostri sunt prepositi, villici ceterique ministri domini nostri consulis.'" *Chroniques* (1913): 184 f. See Flori (1986): 305–308.

40. "Inhumani, inquit, cordis est qui sue non compatitur professioni. Si nos milites sumus, militibus debemus compassionem, presertim subactis." Ibid.: 196. On the Plantagenet chronicles after 1216 see Elizabeth M. Hallam, ed., *The Plantagenet Chronicles* (1986), and the same editor's companion volume, *Chronicles of the Age of Chivalry*; preface by Hugh Trevor-Roper (1987): both lively presentations including only extracts of sources and derivative narratives.

41. "Genèse et évolution du genre," in J. Frappier and R. R. Grimm, eds., *Le roman jusqu'à la fin du XIIIe siècle, Grundriß der romanischen Literaturen des Mittelalters* 4.1 (1978): 60–73 at 63 for this and the immediately following remarks. Also Robert W. Hanning, *The Vision of History in Early Britain: From Gildas to Geoffrey of Monmouth* (New York: Columbia University Press, 1966), on the connection between historiography and romance.

42. Lambert of Ardres, *Chronicon Ghisnense et Ardense*, ed. Godefroy-Ménilglaise (1855) 198. This early edition was superseded by Johann Heller's

edition under the title *Historia comitum Ghisnensium* in *MGH*, Scriptores 24 (1879): 550–642. See Heller: 556, on the 1855 edition.

43. "ad terram tamen et Boloniensis comitatus dignitatem, veri vel simulati amoris objectum, recuperata ejusdem comitisse gratia, aspiravit." *MGH, SS 24*: 603–605 chaps. 90–93 for this episode, 605 chap. 93 for quote. This important chronicle has been much studied by Duby: see, for example, *Terra e nobiltà*: 146–148, *Hommes et structures*: 161 and 221–223; *The Chivalrous Society*: 143–146; and especially *Medieval Marriage*: chap. 3, "A Noble House: The Counts of Guines," 83–110; and *The Knight the Lady and the Priest* (1988): "The Counts of Guines," 243–284. Also see Jaeger: 207 f. and Flori (1986): 294–297 on Lambert's portrait of Arnold. "The Young" in Arnold's name refers to his being then a knight errant, hence a *jeune* (P. *jove*).

44. Ed. Godefroy-Ménilglaise (1855): 198. Also, on the counts of Flanders and Hainaut (Hennegau) in that period, *Iacobi de Guisia Annales historiae illustrium principum Hanoniae*, ed. Ernst Sackur, *MGH, SS* 30.1: 44–334, and [Gilbert of Mons, 13th c.,] *Gisleberti Balduini V Hanoniae Comitis Cancellarii Chronica Hanonia (1040–1195)*, ed. Denis Ch. Godefroy-Ménilglaise (Tornaci: Typis Malo et Levasseur, 1874; Genève: Slatkine Reprints, 1971); *La Chronique de Gislebert de Mons*, ed. Léon Vanderkindere (Bruxelles: Kiessling, 1904). For the tormented history of this region of French Flanders see, besides such classics as Henry Pirenne, L. Vanderkindere, and F.-L. Ganshof: Louis Trenard, ed., *Histoire des Pays-Bas Français* (Toulouse: E. Privat, 1972): especially chapter 3.

45. *MGH, SS* 24: 603, vv. 39–42, chap. 90.

46. Chap. 24, ed. Godefroy-Ménilglaise: 61; *MGH, SS* 24: 573.

47. Chaps. 80 f. p. 598; 1855 ed.: 170–173. Lambert reminds his readers that Arnold's father Baldwin II had been dubbed by Thomas Becket around 1165; likewise he describes at length Arnold's dubbing (resulting in his being turned into a "perfect man") on Pentecost 1181—the only event he precisely dates: "in die sancto Pentecostes ... militaribus eum in virum perfectum dedicavit sacramentis dominice incarnationis anno 1181." *MGH, SS* 24: 604, chap. 91. See G. Duby, *The Three Orders* (1988): 300. Similarly, Lambert emphasizes Arnold's having been entrusted to Count Philip of Flanders for his military and moral education: "moribus erudiendus et militaribus officiis diligenter imbuendus et introducendus," *MGH, SS* 24: 603. At times of leasure, Arnold indulged in listening to his elders telling edifying Carolingian and Arthurian stories: "senes autem et decrepitos, eo quod veterum eventuras et fabulas et historias ei narrarent et moralitatis series narrationi sue continuarent et annecterent, venerabatur et secum detinebat. Proinde militem quendam veteranum dictum Costantinensem, qui de Romanis imperatoribus et de Karlomanno, de Rolando et Olivero et de Arturo Britannie rege eum instruebat et aures eius demulcebat." Ibid.: 607.

48. "Das adlige Rittertum, von dem die höfische Dichtung erzählt, kann nicht aus Verschiebungen in der Ständeordnung erklärt werden; es ist ein Erziehungs- und Bildungsgedanke von weitreichender Bedeutung und ein Phänomen der Geistesgeschichte viel mehr als der Sozialgeschichte.... den Traum vom adligen Menschen, der die Demut in seinen Adel aufgenommen hat...."

Bumke, *Studien zum Ritterbegriff im 12. und 13. Jahrhundert* (1964; 2d ed. 1977): 147 f. I have slightly modified Jaeger's translation 208 f. to make it more literal. W. T. H. Jackson's translation (1977: 120) somewhat obscures the meaning (e.g.: "cannot be explained by shifting it into the social hierarchy"). Bumke's thoroughly documented study shows how, more than for other literatures, the sociological interpretation of German medieval literature has long been established in Germany. But although Jaeger cites it approvingly, it does not appear to confirm his general thesis: it implicitly shows that the German concept of knighthood must have owed much to France, since, contrary to French *chevalier* and so on, even the pertinent German terms (*rîter, ritter*, etc.) appeared in significant contexts only at the end of the twelfth century. Bumke's main point is that the lexical and semantic history of the basic terms denies the existence of the notions of nobility, knighthood, and chivalry as a unified class or status as well as unified mental constructs before 1250 except in literature. This would support the conclusion that chivalry was an idea that became a social fact through the influence of literature, which in turn reflected a growing ideology.

49. Jaeger's thesis (209) is that the process involved a direct "assimilation of the imperial tradition of courtesy to the archaic values of feudal nobility."

50. J. Bumke, *Mäzene im Mittelalter* (1979), and Jaeger: 234. Chrétien, for example, mentions prompting from Marie de Champagne, but such suggestions must usually have referred to no more than theme and plot: the way the material would be used and the meaning it would be given were presumably the poet's prerogative. Also Karl J. Holzknecht, *Literary Patronage in the Middle Ages* (University of Pennsylvania Diss., Philadelphia, 1923; New York: Octagon Books, 1966), and Mary Dominica Legge, *Anglo-Norman Literature and Its Background* (Oxford: Clarendon Press, 1963; Westport, CT: Greenwood Press, 1978).

51. "Non enim scientiae fortis militia vel militiae prejudicat honesta scientia litterarum, imo in principe copula tam utilis, tam conveniens est duarum ut, sicut praedictus Ayulfus asserebat, princeps quem non nobilitat scientia litterarum non parum degenerans sit quasi rusticanus et quodammodo bestialis." Epistola 16, *PL* 203 (1855; rpt. Turnhout: Brepols, 1979): 147–151: see 149–B–C, quoted by Jaeger: 224 f. and Flori (1986): 304. This letter, of uncertain date, has been placed between 1130 and 1183: see Flori (1986): 304, note. The letter to Henry of Champagne is Ep. 17, *PL* 203: 151–156. See, also, Philip of Harvengt's *De continentia clericorum, PL* 203: 811–820, on the comparative status of the *ordines* of clerics and *milites*, and the remarks in J. Flori (1986): 235–239.

52. "quanto litteratiores erant et eruditiores, tanto in rebus bellicis animosiores . . . et strenuiores." *De principis instructione liber*, ed. George F. Warner (London: Eyre & Spottiswoode, 1891): 1, praefatio, 21.8.7. By praising the great princes of the past for joining "toga and armor," literacy and valor, Gerald of Wales was sounding a hope of restoration of ancient imperial glory.

53. Jaeger: 223 f., quoting the H. Meyer-Benfey ed. (1909) and the studies by Helmut de Boor (1964): 394 for the 1180–1190 date as well as Ingeborg Glier (1971) for 1170–1180.

54. Tony Hunt in *Forum for Modern Language Studies* (1981): 105 f.
(Trans. mine.)

55. Keen (1984): 6–17: 6 f. on the *Ordene,* 8–11 on Llull's *Libre,* and
11–17 on Charny's and later similar treatises; and F. Cardini, "Il guerriero e il
cavaliere" (1987): 100 f. Keen draws extensively from these three treatises
throughout his study. See *Ordene de chevalerie* in Étienne Barbazan, ed., *Fabliaux et contes des poètes français des XIᵉ, XIIᵉ, XIIIᵉ, XIVᵉ et XVᵉ siècles,*
new ed. vol. 1 (Paris: B. Warée, 1808), and Raoul de Houdenc [ca. 1165–ca.
1230], *Le roman des ailes / The Anonymous Ordene de chevalerie,* ed. Keith
Busby (Amsterdam: John Benjamins, 1983). Llull's tract was translated into
many languages through the sixteenth century, including Caxton's English edition. Charny's *Livre de chevalerie* is in tome 1 (1873), part 3 of Jean Froissart's
Chroniques in Froissart, *Oeuvres,* ed. Kervyn de Lettenhove, 25 vols. (Bruxelles: V. Devaux for the Académie Royale de Belgique, 1867–1877).

56. Rita Lejeune, "The Troubadours," in R. S. Loomis, ed. (1959, 1961):
393–399 at 394.

57. Keen (1984): 39, with references, p. 258 n. 73, to the *Novellino, L'avventuroso ciciliano,* and Folgòre da San Gimignano.

58. Scaglione, *The Liberal Arts and the Jesuit College System* (1986): 91,
113. On Llull's career see the masterly study by Anthony Bonner, ed., *Selected
Works of Ramon Llull (1232–1316),* 2 vols. (Princeton: Princeton University
Press, 1985), which does not include the book on chivalry.

59. In light of the exemplary and morally well-motivated presentation of the
chivalric state they contain, it is interesting to note that the author of these
treatises is the same Charny who has been recently in the news as the first
exhibitor of the Holy Shroud in his newly built church in the 1350s. The
"Shroud of Turin," Christendom's most hallowed relic, soon passed into the
hands of the Savoy dukes. After long controversy, it has now been carbon-dated
to 1260–1380, hence not far from the time Charny exhibited it with such dramatic impact.

60. Ghillebert de Lannoy (1386–1462), *Oeuvres,* ed. Charles Potvin (Louvain: Imprimerie de P. et J. Lefever, 1878) 443–472. See J. H. Hexter, *Reappraisals in History* (1979): 64, on Ghillebert and his younger contemporary
Jean de Lannoy exhorting the young to learn: Ghillebert urges the study of the
ancients, especially the historians, who teach how our ancestors loved honor
and yearned to serve the public good.

61. Because it was better known outside Spain, I presume, M. Keen uses a
complete French manuscript version of Valera's *Espejo,* while a partial one was
printed in 1497 and a different manuscript has been edited in 1981: see Keen:
256, n. 48.

The standard medieval confusion between ancient heroes and medieval
knights was not as absurd as it may strike us, since phenomena analogous to
knightly practices belong to many cultures, with the ancient Thracians offering
perhaps the most interesting early cases. See Zlatozara Goceva's several studies:
Monumenta orae Ponti Euxini Bulgariae (Leiden: E. J. Brill, 1979); *Corpus
cultus equitis Thracii (CCET)* (Leiden: E. J. Brill, 1979–); *Monumenta inter
Danubium et Haenum reperta* (Leiden: E. J. Brill, 1981–1984); and "Les traits

charactéristiques de l'iconographie du chevalier thrace," *Bulletin de Correspondance Hellénique* n.s. 14 (1986): 237–243. See the detailed study of the "prehistory" of chivalry from the earliest times to the ninth century by Franco Cardini, *Alle radici della cavalleria medievale* (Firenze: La Nuova Italia, 1981), where the Thracians are not mentioned.

62. The original received numerous editions, like the 1498 one (Venice: Simon Bevilaqua) and the 1607 one (Rome: apud Bartholomaeum Zannettum).

63. Philip Strayer, *The Reign of Philip the Fair* (Princeton: Princeton University Press, 1980): 93 f.

64. Strayer, ibid.

65. Bk. 3, pt. 2, chap. 29 in 1498 ed. (pages unnumbered); pp. 523–533 in Rome, 1607 ed. In the French version (Molenaer ed.) this became chap. 27 of same part: see pp. 353 f.

66. Ibid. bk. 3, pt. 2, chap. 12 in 1498 ed. and (at pp. 482–484) 1607 ed. Same chapter number in French version, pp. 324 f.

67. Ibid. bk. 3, pt. 2, chap. 34 in 1498 ed.; p. 549 of 1607 ed. See Strayer 7 f.

68. The title of this "capitulum 18 tertiae partis libri secundi" is: "Quid est curialitas et quod decet ministros regum et principum curiales esse." In the Venice 1498 edition I read "omnis virtus quia" instead of Jaeger's (161) "qua." Jaeger: 286 f., note 47, reports Konrad von Megenberg's free adaptation from Aegidius's coupling of curiality with military qualities: "ministri minores imperatoris duo in se debent habere milicie bona, videlicet curialitatem morum et armorum industriam. . . . Congruit igitur ministros Cesaris tanto curialiores esse, id est bonis moribus splendidiores, quanto curia eius sublimior est curiis omnium secularium miliciarum." *Yconomica*: 2.4.12 in *Ökonomik (Buch II)*, ed. Sabine Krüger, *MGH*, Staatsschriften des späteren Mittelalters 3.5 (Stuttgart: Hiersemann, 1977): 199.

69. *Li livres dou gouvernement des rois: a XIIIth century French version of Egidio Colonna's treatise De regimine principum*, ed. Samuel P. Molenaer (New York: Columbia University Press and Macmillan, 1899; rpt. New York: AMS Press, 1966).

CHAPTER FOUR: TROUBADOURS, TROUVÈRES, AND MINNESINGERS

1. Roncaglia, "*Trobar clus*: discussione aperta. I: Identità o contrasto d'ideologie? *Fin'amors* e *trobar naturau* in Marcabruno," *Cultura Neolatina* 29 (1969): 5–51 at 7.

2. "Sur le plan de la construction formelle du poème, [les valeurs courtoises] deviennent des éléments extraordinairent valorisés, des centres d'attraction 'sémico-poétiques,' autour desquels s'organise tout un univers de signification dont les indispensables tensions constituent le dynamisme propre du message." P. Bec, *Nouvelle anthologie* (1970): 20.

3. Vàrvaro (1985), esp. chaps. 3 on Occitan lyric and 4 on French epic. See Vàrvaro's assessment of sociological and anthropological interpretations of Oc-

citan lyric by R. Nelli (1963), Köhler, Duby and J. Le Goff (pp. 6 and 214, note 134). See J. Bumke's reactions to E. Köhler's thesis and his further questions on the matter in *Knighthood in the Middle Ages* (1982): 158–161 (from 2d ed. of *Studien zum Ritterbegriff*, 1977), as well as a critical assessment of Köhler's work by Ursula Peters, "Niederes Rittertum oder hoher Adel? Zu Erich Köhlers historisch-soziologischer Deutung der altprovenzalischen und mittelhochdeutschen Minnelyrik," *Euphorion* 67 (1973): 244–260.

4. "Marcabru und die beiden 'Schulen'" (1970), Mancini ed.: 264. The collective quality of the troubadours' themes does not diminish their profound originality even if we were to accept the highly speculative connection with some striking antecedents in Arabic love lyric, which included the common themes of the lover's humility, the need for secrecy, hence the *senhal* (the hiding of the true identity of the beloved behind an allusive conventional name, usually male), the scorn for the unworthy rival lovers, that is, the *maudisants* always ready to ridicule and degrade, the condemnation of jealousy, and others. See a lively presentation of the thesis in Henri Davenson (pseudon. for Henri Irénée Marrou), *Les troubadours* (Paris: Éditions du Seuil, 1961): 109 ff. In the absence of sufficient documentary evidence of direct influence, such analogies are likely to remain part of anthropological universals, like the equally striking similarities between Zen Buddhist Neo-Confucianism and the European phenomena of Socratic teaching through personal relationships rather than transmission of written doctrine (we have observed them among the cathedral school teachers of 950–1150), or the ethical system of education for the Japanese daimyo and that of the European knight (see my chap. 1).

5. J. Bumke, *Studien zum Ritterbegriff* (1964): chap. 4, "Der Ritter als Dienstmann," 61–87, esp. 72; trans. Jackson (1982): chap. 4, "The Knight as Retainer," 46–71, esp. 59 on the epos. Also the following chap. 5, "Der adlige Ritter," 88–129; "The Noble Knights," 72–106. Bumke (72 and 59 respectively in the two editions) observes the rarity of the word *dienestman* (MHG for *dienstmann*, "retainer") before 1200 even in the epic, which did not derive from French sources, whereas its perfect equivalent *ministerialis* is the common term for court service, administrative or military, in non-literary documents. He concludes that the reason must have been the perceived "unpoetic" nature of the word, whereas *ritter*, "rider" (serving by being able to cover the whole feudal territory thanks to his mobility—as in modern English, "to ride" implied the use of a conveyance, not necessarily a horse) could be perceived as evocative of a colorful condition, even without direct pressure from the French *chevalier*. Whether or not we find this explanation satisfying, the fact remains that the three terms are equivalent through the twelfth century. But at the end of that period, in spite of and in effective contrast with the etymological sense, the connotation of noble status had taken over, implying freedom and high social position. See, also, W. H. Jackson, "The Concept of Knighthood in Herbort von Fritzlar's *Liet von Troye*," *Forum for Modern Language Studies* (1981): 131–145. The *Liet von Troye* is dated circa 1200–1210.

6. Walter Ullman, *The Individual and Society in the Middle Ages* (Baltimore: Johns Hopkins University Press, 1966).

7. See end of my chapter 2 with note 60.

8. Alfred Pillet and Henry Carstens, *Bibliographie der Troubadours* (Halle/Saale: Max Niemeyer, 1933; rpt. New York: Burt Franklin, 1968): 70.30; Hill and Bergin ed.: 1: 55–57. Whenever therein included, I shall identify Provençal poems by the number in that standard bibliography (as P.-C.), and whenever therein included, I shall also refer to R. T. Hill and Th. G. Bergin, eds., *Anthology of the Provençal Troubadours*, 2 vols. (New Haven: Yale University Press, 2d ed. 1973), even though textual references and interpretations are based on critical editions of individual poets. Except when otherwise indicated, translations will be mine. See Bernart de Ventadour, *Chansons d'amour*, ed. Moshe Lazar (Paris: Klincksieck, 1966). See the ample study (bibliographically not as up-to-date as the publication date would imply) by Michael Kaehne, *Studien zur Dichtung Bernarts von Ventadorn*, 2 vols. (München: Finck, 1983), largely sympathetic to E. Köhler's interpretations.

9. Spitzer, *Romanische Literaturstudien* (1959): "L'amour lointain etc." 364; Köhler, Mancini ed.: 228.

10. Köhler, "Die Rolle des niederen Rittertums bei der Entstehung der Trobadorlyrik" (first in French as "Observations historiques et sociologiques sur la poésie des troubadours," *Cahiers de Civilization Médiévale*, 1964: 27–51, then in *Esprit und arkadische Freiheit* 1966: 9–27); Mancini ed.: 1–18 at 14–18.

11. On "obedience" in the troubadours see Aurelio Roncaglia, "*Obediens*," in Jean Renson, ed., *Mélanges de linguistique romane et de philologie médiévale offerts à Maurice Delbouille* (Gembloux: J. Duculot, 1964): 2: 597–614. I wish to add here a striking example of the motif of obedience as a sign of true love to be respected implicitly within the *courtois* world. In the Tuscan-Umbrian *Tristano Riccardiano* (ca. 1300) Tristan, having just saved King Arthur from impending death after an imprudent foray into the Fontana Avventurosa, has to cope with the King's request that he reveal his name. For his own unexplained reasons, Tristan invents the pretext that he cannot oblige because his lady has commanded him to keep his identity secret. The unquestionable argument immediately persuades the curious Arthur to desist. See C. Segre and M. Marti, eds., *La prosa del Duecento* (Milano, Napoli: R. Ricciardi, 1959): 647. In the romances, too, the motif was played *ad absurdum* in innumerable situations as an unquestioned law of courtesy. In the prose *Lancelot* it reached heights of almost comic sublimity, and there the motif of hiding one's name is also given full swing: for the first one third of the long romance nobody knows Lancelot's name even while everybody is desperately looking for him.

12. "It is just a question of convenience to regard Guillaume IX as the first troubadour": Paul Zumthor, *Essai de poétique médiévale* (Paris: Éditions du Seuil, 1972): 59; It. trans. *Semiologia e poetica medievale* (Milano: Feltrinelli, 1974): 60.

13. P.-C.: 242.14 and 389.10a—respectively under Guiraut and Raimbaut, the latter being named Lignaura in the poem. See Köhler, Mancini ed., 178–187. The most recent critical edition of Guiraut is *The cansos and sirventes of the Troubadour Giraut de Borneil*, ed. Ruth Verity Sharman (Cambridge: Cambridge University Press, 1989): 394–398 for the tenso. For Raimbaut see, also, *The Life and Works of the Troubadour Raimbaut d'Orange*, ed. Walter T. Pattison (Minneapolis: University of Minnesota Press, 1952).

14. Qu'eu dic qu'en l'escarzir / non es l'afans, / mas en l'obr'esclarzir," "be-cause I say that the hardest toil lies not in making our work obscure, but in making it clear": Adolf Kolsen, *Sämtliche Lieder des Trobadors Giraut de Bor-nelh*, 2 vols. (Halle/Saale: Max Niemeyer, 1910, 1935): 1: no. 48 vv. 8–10; "e l'auch a la fon portar," "and I hear my song being taken to the spring to be sung there": Kolsen ed.: 1: no. 4 v. 14. Ulrich Mölk, *Trobar clus—Trobar leu. Studien zur Dichtungstheorie der Trobadors* (München: W. Fink, 1968), ex-pands on this interpretation by his teacher Köhler, opposing the two styles as expression of the opposition between the aristocratic views of a Guilhelm of Poitier or a Raimbaut d'Aurenga and the "democratic" stand of a Marcabru or a Guiraut de Bornelh. Text of the *tenso* in *The Life and Works of the Trouba-dour Raimbaut d'Orange*, ed. W. T. Pattison (1952). For Köhler's analysis of the tenso see Mancini ed.: 183–187.

15. On the uses and meanings of the various terms *jongleur, minstrel*, and their numerous analogues, see P. Zumthor (1987): 60–62.

16. Köhler, "Reichtum und Freigebigkeit in der Trobadordichtung," *Tro-badorlyrik* (1962): 45–72; Mancini ed.: 39–79.

17. S. Thiolier-Méjean, *Les poésies satiriques et morales des troubadours* (1978), provides a rich organic repertory of the moral themes as found in *vers* and *sirventes* through the whole of Occitan literature, illustrating the conscious-ness of divergences between Christian values and the *éthique courtoise* of courtly love.

18. Karl Bartsch and Leo Wiese, eds., *Chrestomathie de l'ancien français* (Leipzig: F. C. W. Vogel, 12th ed. 1920, 1927).

19. See Köhler's paradigmatic analysis of Bernart de Ventadorn's "Can vei la lauzeta mover" in his article "Zur Struktur der altprovenzalischen Kanzone," Mancini ed.: 19–37 at 30–37. Also Vàrvaro (1985): 202–206 and Moshe Lazar, "Classification des thèmes amoureux et des images poétiques dans l'oeuvre de Bernart de Ventadour," *Filologia Romanza* 6 (1959): 371–400. Köhler's analysis of the sequence of themes in the canso must, however, be qualified with the caveat that the order of stanzas in the vulgate version of a medieval lyric, including this particular one, was not fixed. The order chosen by the editor (Bernart von Ventadorn, *Seine Lieder*, ed. Carl Appel, Halle/S.: Max Niemeyer, 1915, 250–254) is found only in two of the twenty manu-scripts, only the order of stanzas 1–2 being constant and that of 6–7 frequent (11 times), yet not even regularly at the end of the poem. As is well known, and illustrated, for example, by Rupert Pickens's edition and study of Jaufré Rudel, minstrels exercised great freedom in their own arrangement of parts of poems at the moment of singing or recitation. The stability of ordering is more char-acteristic of the Italian manuscript tradition, typically bound to written trans-mission, than the French one, which remained tied to oral delivery. See, on the importance of the various modes of transmission and the different manuscript traditions, D'Arco Silvio Avalle, *La letteratura medievale in lingua d'oc nella sua tradizione manoscritta* (Torino: Einaudi, 1961).

20. Bezzola, *Le sens de l'aventure et de l'amour*: 82 f., cited by Köhler, Mancini ed.: 21. Vàrvaro (1985: 209; see note 3 above) seems to concur with this definition of Occitan "conventionality."

21. On the ways and forms of oral transmission see, above all, P. Zumthor (1987). On the systematic repetition of grammatical and "formulaic" items as a common compositional device in all medieval oral genres, including the lyric, see, for example, Zumthor's (1987) chaps. 9 and 10. The practice will be continued by Petrarca as part of his use of symmetry and balance.

22. Köhler, *Trobadorlyrik* (1962): 54; Mancini ed.: 53.

23. P.-C.: 156.6: Folquet de Romans 6, stanza 3. See Köhler, *Trobadorlyrik* (1962): 53; Mancini ed.: 51; text of "Far vuelh un nou sirventes," in Vincenzo de Bartholomaeis, ed., *Poesie provenzali storiche relative all'Italia* (Roma: Tipografia del Senato, 1931): 2: 3–4 and 9. See A. Asor Rosa, ed., *Letteratura Italiana* 2 (Torino: Einaudi, 1983): 181–183, and A. Roncaglia, ibid. 1 (1982): 124.

24. Sordello, *Ensenhamen d'onor*, "Aissi co'l tesaurs es perdutz," vv. 713–720; see Köhler, "Reichtum und Freigebigkeit," *Trobadorlyrik*: 72, Mancini ed.: 78 f. See Sordello, *Poesie*, ed. Marco Boni (Bologna: Palmaverde, 1954). Marco Boni, *Sordello, con una scelta di liriche tradotte e commentate* (Bologna: Riccardo Pàtron, 1970), is a good general study, and *The Poetry of Sordello*, ed. and trans. James J. Wilhelm (New York: Garland, 1987), is a new complete edition with translation. On the tradition of the troubadour lyric in courts of the Venetia, including Sordello, see Gianfranco Folena, "Tradizione e cultura trobadorica nelle corti e nelle città venete," *Storia della Cultura Veneta*, 6 vols. (Vicenza: Neri Pozza, 1976–1986): 1: 453–562.

25. Guiraut, sirventes "Solatz, ioys e chantar," P.-C.: 242.75, no. 73, ll. 14–17 in R. V. Sharman ed. (1989): 464–467: "Et anc per trop donar / Senes autras foudatz / Rix hom no fon cochatz, / ni per son gent-estar," "And no rich man, innocent of other foolish acts, ever suffered through giving too generously or through his gracious manners"; sirventes "S'es chantars ben entendutz," P.-C.: 242.67, no. 65, ll. 36–39 in Sharman 426–429: "Rics ia vitz decazegutz, / Pus foron larc donador, / Quar per agrey de folhor / Remania lur pretz nuts," "you have surely seen rich people ruined by giving [too] generously, for the folly of their actions stripped their reputation bare" (Sharman's translation).

26. Giosuè Carducci, *Della poesia cavalleresca*, from sources in L. A. Muratori, *Antiquitates Italicae Medii Aevi*, 6 vols. (Mediolani: Ex Typographia Societatis Palatinae, 1738–1742; rpt. Bologna: A. Forni, 1965): 1: 606.

27.   Vos vitz torneis mandar
               E segre.ls gen garnitz
               E pois dels melhs feritz
               Una sazo parlar:
               Er'es pretz de raubar
               E d'ebranchar berbitz.
               Chavalers si'aunitz
               Que.s met en domneiar,
          Pos que tocha dels mas moltos belans
           Ni que rauba gleizas ni viandans!
         (P.-C. 242.55; Hill and Bergin ed., 1: 74 f.)

The *razo* connects this poem with the Viscount Gui of Limoges having robbed Guiraut's castle of Excideuil of books and belongings in 1211 (see Hill and Bergin: 2: 24), in which case Guiraut's indignation might lose some of its universal, objective ring. The dates of Guiraut's life are uncertain: he is supposed to have lived between circa 1138 and 1212, with his poetic production falling mainly between 1165 and 1200 (Hill and Bergin ed., 2: 22). This *razo* is also in Martín de Riquer, ed., *Los trovadores: Historia literaria y textos*, 3 vols. (Barcelona: Planeta, 1975; Editorial Ariel, 1983): 1: 490–494, where the dates "1162–1199" are given as Guiraut's.

28. Arnaut de Marueil, "Mas am de vos lo talen et.l desir / que d'autr'aver tot so c'a drut s'eschai," "Just to desire you pleases me more than having from another all that is due to a lover," canso "Si cum li peis an en l'aiga lor vida," P.-C.: 30.22. See R. C. Johnston, ed., *Les poésies lyriques du troubadour Arnaut de Mareuil* (Paris, 1935; Genève: Slatkine Reprints, 1973): 45. Echoing René Nelli, Jean-Charles Huchet, *L'Amour discourtois: La 'fin'amors' chez les premiers troubadours* (Paris: Bibliothèque Historique Privat, 1987): 149, attributes "pure love" to the second generation of troubadours who, being of *paubra generation*, that is, lower origin than such early masters as Guilhelm of Aquitaine, could not afford the high ladies that a Guilhelm could easily treat as his erotic playthings. See Nelli, *L'érotique des troubadours*, 2 vols. (2d ed. Paris: Union Générale d'Éditions, 1974, 1984): 1: 22: "L'amour courtois fut un pis-aller—ou une revendication minima—avant d'être un idéal." Nelli (ibid.: 2: 201–328) speaks of *affrèrement*, involving a degree of fictional substitution of the values of male friendship by extension to heterosexual love. Similarly, Huchet's study hinges on a conception of troubadour love as essentially androgynous, with the woman in a metaphorical or subsidiary role.

29. It is worth noting that this shift could occur even within the knightly class. Ulrich von Lichtenstein came from a family of *ministeriales*, was *dapifer*, "steward," and then marshall of Styria, and was knighted in 1222 along with 250 other squires at the wedding of the daughter of Duke Leopold of Austria in Vienna. See J. Bumke (1964): 93 f.

30. Applying the method of reception aesthetic, M. L. Meneghetti, *Il pubblico dei trovatori* (1984), focuses on the problem of the troubadours' public, audience, or recipients (the implied readers). Chapter 2, 41–97 attempts to identify the specific courts and places of reception for Occitan poetry and its jongleurs.

31. Alexander J. Denomy, *The Heresy of Courtly Love*.

32. Köhler, "Über das Verhältnis von Liebe, Tapferkeit, Wissen und Reichtum bei den Trobadors," originally published in 1955–1956, then in *Trobadorlyric* (1962): 73–87, and as "Sui rapporti fra amore, ardimento, sapere e ricchezza nei trovatori" in Mancini ed.: 81–99.

33. P.-C.: 238.2: "En Raïmbaut, pro domna d'aut paratge"; *Trobadorlyrik* (1962): 78–80; Mancini ed.: 88 f.

34. "En Peire, dui pro cavalier": P.-C.: 16.15, st. 4. Köhler, Mancini ed.: 76–78.

35. Vàrvaro (1985: 209) distinguishes "expression," which entails collective ideological referentiality, from "inspiration" understood as personal and individual—which in that poetry was rather limited. Bernart de Ventadorn's typical

coupling of *joi* and *chantar*, for example, "implica una ragione . . . non soltanto tecnica e non soltanto formale, ma appunto espressiva (che non vuol dire d'ispirazione)."

36. Starting from the premises of a chiefly formalist approach, P. Zumthor (1987: 81) stresses the "verbal" and more specifically "oral" quality of courtly love, "a verbal game" that irked the more serious-minded clerical observers, like Walter Map, as going counter to the Augustinian view of a love that necessarily carries an intellectual content of more intimate knowledge of God. Courtly love was too much verbal sound, frustratingly sophisticated and even obscure, with too little semantic content (*sen*). The element of ironic playfulness is stressed in Simon Gaunt, *Troubadours and Irony* (Cambridge: Cambridge University Press, 1989).

37. A recent, sociologically-slanted study of Peire as upholder of the interests of the feudal nobility is Ariane Loeb, "La définition et l'affirmation du groupe noble comme enjeu de la poésie courtoise? Quelques analyses des textes du troubadour Peire Vidal," *Cahiers de civilization médiévale* 30.4 (1987): 303–314.

38. Ilse Nolting-Hauff, *Die Stellung der Liebeskasuistik im höfischen Roman*, Heidelberger Forschungen no. 6 (Heidelberg: C. Winter, 1959).

39. G. Duby, *Mâle moyen âge* (1988): "A propos de l'amour que l'on dit courtois," 74–82, attempts an interpretation of *fin'amor* from the vantage point of a historian of medieval society, also stressing the (somewhat devious) civilizing process it entailed.

40. See Köhler, "Der Frauendienst der Trobadors, dargestellt an ihren Streitgedichten," first in *Germanisch-Romanische Monatsschrift* 41 (1960), then in *Trobadorlyrik* (1962): 89–113 at 102–104; Mancini ed.: "Il servizio d'Amore nel *partimen*," 101–138 at 122, and the eloquent examples at 120 ff.

41. I quote from *The Poems of the Troubadour Bertran de Born*, eds. William D. Paden, Jr., Tilde Sankovitch, and Patricia H. Stäblein (Berkeley, Los Angeles, London: University of California Press, 1986): 215–232. Numerous textual variants in other editions do not affect the meaning: M. de Riquer, *Los trovadores*: 2: 702–705 reads: "Mon chan fenisc . . . larc e gen parlan / e be chavalgan, / de bela faisso / e d'umil semblan / per far grans onors"; "Reis de.ls cortes e de.ls pros emperaire"; "quar 'reis joves' aviatz nom agut / e de joven eratz vos guitz e paire"; "Gen acolhir e donar ses cor vaire / e bel respos e 'besiatz-vengut' / e gran ostal paiat e gen tengut, / dos e garnirs et estar ses tort faire."

Paden and his co-editors (11 f.) conclusively declare Bertran the conscience of the times and the voice of the knightly ethic that set the time's standards and values, but they object to Köhler's identification of this ethic with that of the poor knights, since Bertran was de facto a baron and a great lord (44 note). Köhler had already answered such objections by showing that the lords found nobler-sounding motives for their feudal interests in the adoption of their knights' rhetoric. Loyalty was a matter of life and death for a knight at service, whereas a lord could turn it around as his wind shifted, as Bertran did with Henry the Young, Richard Lion-Heart, Geoffrey of Brittany, and Henry II.

42. Zumthor (1987): 65, 75 f.

43. Text in Hill and Bergin: 1: 42 f. and M. de Riquer, *Los Trovadores*: 1: 372–375.

44. P.-C.: 70.25. I quote this canso from Frederick Goldin, ed., *Lyrics of the Troubadours and Trouvères: An Anthology and a History* (Garden City, NJ: Doubleday Anchor Books, 1973), and the improved new ed. (Gloucester, MA: P. Smith, 1983).

45. *Gace Brulé, trouvère champenois, édition des Chansons et étude historique*, ed. Holger Petersen Dyggve (Helsinki, 1951; rpt. New York: AMS Press, 1980): no. 44, vv. 43 f., and the new edition, *The Lyrics and Melodies of Gace Brulé* (New York: Garland, 1985).

46. For the French trouvères I use the convenient anthology by Frederick Goldin, ed., *Lyrics of the Troubadours and Trouvères* (1973), cited. Once again, the translations are mine except when otherwise indicated.

47. Count Thibaut IV of Champagne was King of Navarre from 1234 to his death: he was a liberal protector of artists, poets, convents, and universities and a great traveler, moving between Reims, Blois, and Pamplona, always in search of good tourneys and real battles, including a crusade overseas.

48. In his wide-ranging search for the theme of "the soul in the kiss," which included medieval lyric and romance as well as mystical and theological writings, Nicolas J. Perella, *The Kiss Sacred and Profane* (Berkeley, Los Angeles: University of California Press, 1969), missed these and other clear antecedents of his subject.

49. Christian Gellinek, "Zu Hartmann von Aues Herzenstausch: *Iwein*: vv. 2956–3028," *Amsterdamer Beiträge zur älteren Germanistik* 6 (Amsterdam: Rodopi, 1974): 133–142.

50. P.-C.: 112.4, vv. 37–39, 49–53: Hill and Bergin ed.: 1: 27 f.

51. P.-C.: 70.31, st. 4, vv. 3–6; Hill and Bergin ed.: 1: 38–40. Even Petrarca's troubled hints at attempted suicide, prevented only by the fear of divine punishment, find their authoritative antecedents: Raimbaut de Vaqueiras (b. 1155/60, fl. 1180–1205) has a canso-sirventes, "No m'agrada iverns ni pascors" (P.-C.: 392.24), where we read: "e, si no.m sembles fols esfreis, / anc flama plus tost non s'esteis / q'ieu for' esteins e relinquitz" (And if it did not seem a mad and desperate act, no flame was ever snuffed out faster than I would have been, all destroyed—vv. 19–21). Text in F. Goldin 268–274 from Joseph Linskill Hill, ed., *The Poems of the Troubadour Raimbaut de Vaqueiras* (The Hague: Mouton, 1964), and in Hill and Bergin ed., 1: 162–164, with slightly different reading (the initial verse in P.-C. adds a last word "alegra").

52. No. 4, st. 5–6 in *Les chansons de Guillaume IX, duc d'Aquitaine (1071–1127)*, ed. Alfred Jeanroy, Classiques Français du Moyen Age no. 9 (Paris: H. Champion, 2d rev. ed. 1972): 1.

53. See Frederick Goldin, *The Mirror of Narcissus in the Courtly Love Lyric* (Ithaca: Cornell University Press, 1967); Richard W. Hanning, "The Social Significance" (1972): 11 f. On the myth of Narcissus and the theme of androgyny in several French romances, such as *Narcissus* of circa 1200 and the slightly later *Floire et Blancheflor*, see Joan M. Ferrante, *Woman as Image* (1975): 74–97.

54. On the woman as "androgynous" lord (*midons, domna*) and unsexed human being see Christiane Leube-Fey, *Bild und Funktion der dompna in der Lyrik des Trobadors* (Heidelberg: Carl Winter, 1971). On gender exchanges, Caroline Walker Bynum, *Jesus as Mother: Studies in the Spirituality of the High Middle Ages* (Berkeley, Los Angeles, London: University of California Press, 1982). Joan M. Ferrante, *Woman as Image* (1975), is a perceptive analysis of some typical groups of medieval literary works from the point of view of the representation of the woman (chap. 3 on lyric and romance in France). It shows that, in general, the woman is not distinguishable as an independent presence in that literature. See, also, the anthology by Marcelle Thiébaux, *The Writings of Medieval Women* (New York, London: Garland Publishing, 1987).

55. Cited in Honoré d'Urfée, *L'Astrée*, ed. Jean Lafond (Paris: Gallimard, 1984): 30.

56.   Des einen und dekeines mê
        wil ich ein meister sîn, al die wîle ich lebe;
        daz lop wil ich, daz mir bestê
        und mir die kunst diu werlt gemeine gebe,
        daz niemen sîn leid alsô schône kan getragen.
        Dez begêt ein wîp an mir, daz ich naht noch
        tac nicht kan gedagen.
        Nu hân eht ich sô senften muot
        daz ich ir haz ze vröiden nime.
        Owê, wie rehte unsanfte daz mir doch tuot!

Reinmar 10.5 in Carl von Kraus, Hugo Moser, and Helmut Tervooren, eds., *Des Minnesangs Frühling*, nach Karl Lachmann, Moriz Haupt, und Friedrich Vogt, 3 vols. (36th ed. Stuttgart: Hirzel, 1977–1981): 1: 315 (trans. mine).

57. Quoted from Carl von Kraus et al., eds. *Des Minnesangs Frühling* (Leipzig: S. Hirzel, 1944): 81.14. See J. Bumke (1982): 160.

58. "Saget mir ieman, waz ist minne?," vv. 24 f. in *Die Gedichte Walthers von der Vogelweide*, eds. Karl Lachmann and Carl von Kraus, 13th ed. revised by Hugo Kuhn (Berlin: W. de Gruyter, 1965). More recent editions are: Walther von der Vogelweide, *Die Lieder*, ed. Friedrich Maurer, 2 vols. (Tübingen: Max Niemeyer, 3d and 4th eds. 1969, 1974); and idem, *Werke, Text und Prosaübersetzung*, ed. Joerg Schaefer (Darmstadt: Wissenschaftliche Buchgesellschaft, 1972).

59. Frederick Goldin, ed., *German and Italian Lyrics of the Middle Ages* (Garden City, NJ: Doubleday Anchor Books, 1973): 96–101, gives a good summary of the controversial interpretation of Walther's poetic stance mostly on the basis of an imaginative essay by Renata Karlin, "The Challenge to Courtly Love," in Joan M. Ferrante and George Economou, eds., *In Pursuit of Perfection: Courtly Love in Medieval Literature* (1975): 101–133.

60. Especially Köhler, "Vergleichende soziologische Betrachtungen zum romanischen und zum deutschen Minnesang," in Karl H. Borck and Rudolf Hensss, eds., *Der Berliner Germanistentag 1968* (Heidelberg: C. Winter, 1970): 61–76; Mancini ed.: 275–297.

61. Köhler, Mancini ed.: 281 and 285 f., citing from *Die Gedichte Walthers von der Vogelweide*, eds. Karl Lachmann and Carl von Kraus (Berlin: W. de Gruyter, 12th ed. 1959): 66, vv. 37 f.

62. Köhler, Mancini ed.: 293.

63. Köhler, Mancini ed.: 292.

64. Köhler, Mancini ed.: 282 f., with reference to Herbert Kolb, *Der Begriff der Minne und das Entstehen der höfischen Lyrik* (Tübingen: Max Niemeyer, 1958): 39 ff. For a plainer sociological interpretation see N. Elias, *The Civilizing Process* 2 (1982): 1.1.2, pp. 66–90, "On the Sociogenesis of *Minnesang* and Courtly Forms of Conduct."

65. Lucie Brind'Amour in T. Klaniczay et al., eds. (1988): 454–456.

66. "vor 1340 ist Minne Sache des Adels": see Heinz Otto Burger, ed., *Annalen der Deutschen Literatur* (Stuttgart: J. B. Metzlersche Verlag, 1971): 219–222.

CHAPTER FIVE: COURTESY IN THE FRENCH ROMANCE

1. "E' questo il mondo che si esprime originariamente nella lirica trovatoresca e nel romanzo cortese: due manifestazioni connesse tra loro assai più di quanto non appaia dalle correnti storie letterarie." Aurelio Roncaglia, "Nascita e sviluppo della narrativa cavalleresca," in Accademia dei Lincei, *Convegno Internazionale Ludovico Ariosto, 1974*; Atti dei Convegni dell' Accademia dei Lincei no. 6. (Roma: Accademia dei Lincei, 1975): 229–250 at 240.

2. Vv. 4958–5009. Keen (1984): 42 f. I quote from Linda Paterson's translation cited by Keen. See L. Paterson in *Forum for Modern Language Studies* 17 (1981): 115–130 for other textual citations from *Girart*, with bibliographic references.

3. Original text in *Girart de Roussillon, chanson de geste*, ed. W. Mary Hackett, 3 vols. (Paris: Picard, 1953–1955). Hackett places the poem either in the area from Bordeaux to Poitiers or between Lyon and Vienne. It long remained popular, and in 1447 it enjoyed a French version by Jean Vauquelin, the prominent calligrapher and translator at the Burgundian court of Philip the Good. See *Girart de Roussillon*, ed. Edward Billings Ham (New Haven, CT: Yale University Press, 1939).

4. Hackett ed., 3: 537–539. See Linda Paterson (1981): 123 f., quoting J. Flori, "La notion de chevalerie dans les chansons de geste du XIIᵉ siècle. Étude historique de vocabulaire," *Le Moyen Age* 81 (1975): 420; P. Bonnassie, *La Catalogne* etc. (1975–1976): 656 ff.; and Jean-Pierre Poly, *La Provence et la société féodale, 879–1166. Contribution à l'étude des structures dites féodales dans le Midi* (Paris: Bordas, 1976) 195, 361. See, also, J.-P. Poly, *La société féodale en Provence du 10ᵉ au 12ᵉ siècle* (Paris: Hachette, 1972).

5.   Se tu deis prendre, bels filz, de fals loiers,
        Ne desmesure lever ne essalcier,
        Faire luxure ne alever pechié,
        Ne orfe enfant retolir le suen fié,
        Ne veve feme tolir quatre deniers,
        Ceste corone de Jesu la te vié,
        Filz Looïs, que tu ne la baillier.

Le Couronnement de Louis, chanson de geste du 12ᵉ siècle, ed. Ernest Langlois, Classiques Français du Moyen Age no. 22 (Paris: Champion, 1920, 2d ed. 1925): vv. 80–86. (My trans. in text.)

The extent to which the notion of "measure" is operative in the *chansons de geste* cannot concern us here. It appears as a positive imperative in the text quoted, and we have seen it as one of the key terms in the definition of curiality. Its role in determining Roland's tragic character flaw in the *Chanson de Roland* has been much discussed, with some critics regarding it as a superimpositon on the actual context: see, for example, Larry S. Crist, "A propos de la *desmesure* dans la *Chanson de Roland*: quelques propos (démesurés?)," *Oliphant* 1 (1974–1975): 10–20, surveying the question and trying to dismiss it as a weary old critical *poncif.*

6. For a similar interpretation, see Vàrvaro (1985): 229–243.

7. After the monumental work of Reto R. Bezzola, the most comprehensive presentation of this interpretation of the French epic and romance is perhaps Erich Köhler, *Ideal und Wirklichkeit in der höfischen Epik* (1956; 2d ed. 1970), esp. chap. 1; see a spirited summary of the thesis in Jacques Le Goff's Preface to the French ed., *L'aventure chevaleresque* (1974): xiii f.

8. As part of Henry II's propaganda campaign against the French centralized idea of monarchy, "the writers in his employ exploited the 'British material' [the Arthurian legends], pitting against the image of Charlemagne that of King Arthur": G. Duby, *The Three Orders* (1980): 287.

9. This is Joseph Bédier's well-known thesis on the origin of the Roland epic. See Köhler, *L'aventure chevaleresque* (1974): chap. 2, "Chevalerie-clergie," 44–76, on the development of the new mythology, and ibid., esp. 11–15 for the definition of King Arthur's role as upholder of feudal rights in Chrétien de Troyes's *Erec.*

10. On the history of the word *roman* or *romanz* for the narrative genre, see Aurelio Roncaglia, *Tristano e Anti-Tristano. Dialettica di temi e d'ideologie nella narrativa medievale* (Roma: Bulzoni, 1981): 92–115, and for the narrative matter of the genre, Roncaglia, "Nascita e sviluppo della narrativa cavalleresca nella Francia medievale" (1975): 229–250, as well as the learned and broadly gauged "Introduzione" by the editor in Maria Luisa Meneghetti, ed., *Il romanzo* (1988): 7–85, a rich volume that also includes reprintings of studies on this matter by Maurice Wilmotte, "La fondazione del romanzo: nostalgia dell'antichità e attualità politica e culturale," 107–122, Cesare Segre, "I problemi del romanzo medievale," 125–145, and others.

11. Translation in R. S. Loomis and L. Hibbard Loomis, eds., *Medieval Romances* (1957): 236.

12. Lambert li Tors and Alexandre de Bernay, *Li romans d'Alixandre*, nach Handschriften der Königlichen Büchersammlung zu Paris, ed. Heinrich V. Michelant (Stuttgart: Literarischer Verein, 1846; rpt. Amsterdam: Rodopi, 1966): 17. For a much better, critical edition see *The Medieval French Roman d'Alexandre*, eds. E. C. Armstrong et al., 7 vols. (Princeton: Princeton University Press; Paris: Presses Universitaires de France, 1937–1942; New York: Kraus Reprints, 1965).

13. *La Mort de Garin le Loherain, poème du 12ᵉ siècle*, ed. Édélestand Du Méril (Paris: Franck, 1846; Genève: Slatkine Reprints, 1969): 74; *Le Couronnement de Louis*, ed. Langlois (1925): vv. 2254–2266.

14. See *Partonopeu de Blois, A French Romance of the Twelfth Century*, ed. Joseph Gildea, 2 vols. in 3 (Villanova, PA: Villanova University Press, 1967, 1968, 1970).

15. Text in F. Vieillard, "Un texte interpolé du cycle du *Graal* (Bibliothèque Bodmer MS. 147)," *Revue d'histoire des textes* 4 (1974): 289–337.

16. A splendid sample of such illustrations is in the manuscript of Thomas of Saluzzo's *Chevalier errant* (1395), Bibliothèque Nationale MS. Fr. 12559 (see my chap. 1), and in the frescoes Thomas himself ordered for his castle of Saluzzo. See M. Keen (1984): chap. 6, "The Historical Mythology of Chivalry," 102–124; also 18 f., with color plates nos. 28 and 29.

17. Pierre Le Gentil, "The Work of Robert de Boron and the *Didot Perceval*," in Roger S. Loomis, ed., *Arthurian Literature in the Middle Ages* (1959; 1961): 251–262; M. Keen (1984): 60, 62, 118–120. The Lady of the Lake in the Vulgate *Lancelot* answers Lancelot's query concerning historical examplars of perfect chivalry by naming Maccabaeus, David, and Joseph of Arimathea as ancient models: see H. O. Sommer, ed., *The Vulgate Version of the Arthurian Romances*, 8 vols. (Washington, DC: Carnegie Institute, 1909–1916): 3: 116 f.

18. Christine was also the author of more technical treatises related to our subject, like the *Livre des faits d'armes et de chevalerie* (1408–1409), published by William Caxton in translation as *The Book of Fayttes of Armes and of Chyvalrye*, 1489 (eds. H. Milford and A. T. O. Byles, Early English Text Society, London: Oxford University Press, 1932); and *Le livre des fais et bonnes meurs du sage roy Charles V* (Paris: H. Champion, 1936). Her love poetry, too, is remarkable for confronting the role of the woman in the ambiguous situation of courtly love: see her *Livre du duc des vrais amants*, followed by the *Cent ballades d'amant et de dame*. The casuistry of love generated by the courtly conventions found eloquent expression in the numerous works of Christine's influential younger contemporary Alain Chartier (ca. 1385–ca. 1429): see his *Quadrilogue invectif* (1422), *La belle dame sans merci* (1424), *Débat des deux fortunés d'Amour* (1425?), and other works, where the cases of lovers are loaded with psychological, moral, and socio-political overtones.

19. For one rather singular example from Italy, the thirteenth-century *Istorietta troiana* offers a gem of contamination of medieval mores into the reading of the most hallowed ancient myths: the abduction of Helen by Paris is rendered as a model raid of a community (assembled in a temple for a festival), with systematic plundering of property, killing of all that resisted, and abduction into slavery of able bodies, including women, all rather unnecessarily, since Helen had agreed beforehand to follow Paris. Text in Egidio Gorra, *Testi inediti di storia trojana, preceduti da uno studio sulla leggenda troiana in Italia* (Torino: C. Triverio, 1887): 371–403, comments pp. 152–166; new ed. in Alfredo Schiaffini, *Testi fiorentini del Dugento e dei primi del Trecento* (Firenze: G. C. Sansoni, 1954): 151; and in C. Segre and M. Marti, *La prosa del Duecento* (Milano, Napoli: R. Ricciardi, 1959): 535–545 at 540–542. Boccaccio has "ancient" characters behave in similar "knightly" ways in the story of Cimone's

conquest of Iphigenia (*Decameron* 5.1): see A. Scaglione, *Nature and Love in the Late Middle Ages* (Berkeley, Los Angeles: University of California Press, 1963; rpt. Westport, CT: Greenwood Press, 1976): 80 f., 85.

20. Zumthor has dedicated prolonged research to this work: see his "L'écriture et la voix: le roman d'Éracle," in Lee A. Arrathoon, ed., *The Craft of Fiction* 1 (Rochester, MI: Solaris Press, 1984): 161–209, and idem (1987): 308–310. See Zumthor's reconstruction of the original meaning of *mettre en roman*: "l'expression *mettre en roman*, fréquente dans le français du XIIᵉ siècle, désigne le processus permettant d'atteindre cette fin: opérée par un individu frotté de culture livresque, la *mise en roman* a pour destinataire quelqu'un du milieu chevaleresque et noble" (1987: 300 f.). Also, Per Nykrog, "Two Creators of Narrative Form in Twelfth Century France: Gautier d'Arras—Chrétien de Troyes," *Speculum* 48 (1973): 258–276.

The oral nature of the epics is tied to their closeness to the popular layers on the assumption that they developed mainly along the pilgrimage routes. An intriguing hypothesis would, instead, surprisingly tie such a key text as the *Chanson de Roland* to courtly milieus in Norman Italy: see A. Roncaglia, "Le corti medievali" in A. Asor Rosa, ed., *Letteratura italiana* 1 (1982): 95–97.

21. J. Frappier, "La matière de Bretagne: ses origines et son développement," *Grundriß* 4.1 (1978): 183–211, esp. 209. A different slant, favoring transmission through the minstrels of Bretagne rather than from the English isles, is in R. S. Loomis, "The Oral Diffusion of the Arthurian Legend," in R. S. Loomis, ed., *Arthurian Literature in the Middle Ages* (1959; 1961): 52–63.

22. *Historia regum Britanniae*, ed. Edmond Faral (1929): chap. 157, vv. 41–44. See Frappier (1978): 190. See, also, Geoffrey's chaps. 154, v. 2; and 157, v. 39.

23. *Historia regum Britanniae* (1929): 3: 238, 246. See Jaeger: 166.

24. *Le roman de Brut de Wace*, ed. Ivor Arnold (1938–1940): 2: vv. 10,493 ff., 10,511 ff.

25. *Le Roman de Brut*, ed. I. Arnold (1938–1940): vv. 9260–9265. See vv. 14,865 f. for date and generic labeling: "Mil et cent cinquante et cinc ans / fist mestre Wace cest romans." For the Brut legend see, also, Alexander Bell, ed., *An Anglo-Norman Brut (Royal 13.A.XXI)*, Anglo-Norman Texts 21/22 (Oxford: Blackwell, 1969), from British Museum MS. Royal 13.A.XXI.

26. MS. H has for the last two lines: "Par la noblesce de s'amie / fait jovenes hom cevalerie."

27. Frappier, "La matière de Bretagne: ses origines et son développement," *Grundriß*: 4.1: 200 f. on these points.

28. I cite from the excellently informed Tony Hunt, "The Emergence of the Knight in France and England, 1000–1200," *Forum for Modern Language Studies* (1981): 104 f., with references to Thomas A. McGuire, *The Conception of the Knight in the Old French Epics of the Southern Cycle, with Parallels from Contemporary Historical Sources* (East Lansing, MI: The Campus Press, 1939), and J. D. Burnley, "The *Roman de Horn*: Its Hero and Ethos," *French Studies* 32 (1978): 385–397. Text in Mildred K. Pope and T. B. W. Reid, eds., *The Romance of Horn by Thomas*, Anglo-Norman Text Society 9–10, 12–13, 2 vols. (Oxford: B. Blackwell, 1955–1964): 1: 6–15.

29. See Joan M. Ferrante (1973) for a comparative study of all basic motifs at the hands of the authors of five of the major texts within the Tristan cycle. Also Daniela Delcorno Branca, *I romanzi italiani di Tristano e La Tavola Ritonda* (Firenze: L. S. Olschki, 1968), and idem, *Il romanzo cavalleresco medievale* (Firenze: Sansoni, 1974).

30. For a pithy discussion of the anthropological meaning of the marvelous elements, see F. Cardini, "Il guerriero e il cavaliere" (1987): 102.

31. This is, for example, Joan M. Ferrante's conclusion in "The Conflict of Lyric Conventions and Romance Form," in J. M. Ferrante and G. D. Economou (1975): 135–178 at 159. A student of W. T. H. Jackson, Ferrante extends further her teacher's distrust of love as a positive factor in Arthurian romance by sharply distinguishing that genre from the lyric, where love was conceived as the root of chivalry—a stand that would be systematically carried to a metaphysical and even theological fruition by the Italian lyrical poets. Chrétien kept searching for a solution and, unable to find a settlement for courtly love as socially positive and harmonious with chivalric duty, he eventually gave up—leaving both *Lancelot* and *Perceval* unfinished—(Ferrante, ibid.: 145). Chrétien was not alone in finding in chivalry an open question, rather than a closed book with all the answers.

32. Erich Auerbach, *Mimesis: The Representation of Reality in Western Literature*, trans. Willard Trask (Princeton: Princeton University Press, 1953; Garden City, NY: Doubleday Anchor Books, 1957): 121; Daniel Poirion, "Théorie et pratique du style au moyen âge: le sublime et la merveille," *Revue d'histoire littéraire de la France* 86.1 (1986): 15–32.

33. Auerbach, *Mimesis*: 117–121: "Calogrenant . . . has no political or historical task, nor has any other knight of Arthur's court. Here the feudal ethos serves no political function; it serves no practical reality at all; it has become absolute. It no longer has any purpose but that of self-realization. . . . It would seem that *corteisie* achieved its synthetic meaning only in the age of chivalry or courtly culture, which indeed derives the latter name from it. The values expressed in it—refinement of the laws of combat, courteous social intercourse, service of women—have undergone a striking process of change and sublimation in comparison with the *chanson de geste* and are all directed toward a personal and absolute ideal—absolute both in reference to ideal realization and in reference to the absence of any earthly and practical purpose." See my Introduction, p. 5.

34. Auerbach: 119, borrowing the latter term from the Orientalist Hellmut Ritter.

35. This is also, more or less, Eugene Vance's conclusion to his challenging analysis of *Yvain* (*Mervelous Signals* 1986)—although, I must confess, I find it somewhat stretched in its insistence on commercial dimensions which, furthermore, he endows with far-reaching metaphysical and anthropologically symbolic supra-meanings.

36. On Chrétien see the extensive sections by Jean Frappier and others in *Grundriß* 4.1, especially Alexandre Micha: 231–264. Also Jaeger: 196, on the preceding point.

37. All these texts are excerpted and translated in *The Comedy of Eros: Medieval French Guides to the Art of Love*, trans. Norman R. Shapiro, notes

by James B. Wadsworth (Urbana: University of Illinois Press, 1971), an anthology of scarce scholarly value that I cite here for its convenience. See, for *La clef d'amour* and Élie de Winchester: *La clef d'amour*, ed. Edwin Tross (Paris: Librairie Tross; Lyon: Perrin, 1866), and *Maître Élie's Überarbeitung der ältesten französischen Übertragung von Ovids* Ars Amatoria, eds. H. Kühne and E. Stengel, in Edmund Max Stengel, ed., "Ausgaben und Abhandlungen aus dem Gebiete der romanischen Philologie 47" (Marburg: N. G. Elwert, 1886). This edition also included Elie's, Everart's, and an anonymous author's translations of the *Disticha Catonis*.

38. Jaeger: 185–190. Saxo's book 10 contains an extensive summary of King Canute the Great's "Lex castrensis sive curiae," an attempt to civilize the unruly and barbarous knights attending his court (Jaeger: 136–138). Note the terms "saluberrimum castrensis disciplinae tenorem, qua tantae varietatis discordiam rumperet"; "rex verecundiam a suis servari voluit." We may recall Castiglione's notion of *vergogna*, akin to Latin *verecundia*, considerateness or respect for others' rights. See Saxo Grammaticus, *Danorum regum heroumque historia*, Books 10–16: the text of the first edition with translation and commentary in three volumes, ed. Eric Christiansen (Oxford: British Archaeological Reports, BAR International Series, 1980–1981).

39. E. Köhler, "Literatursoziologische Perspektiven" (1978): 89: "Der fundamentale und so folgenreiche Gedanke der Aventüre ist primär eine Schöpfung des niederen bzw. des armen Rittertums."

40. The key term "adventure" is a curious derivation from a Latin future participle (*adventurus*), expressing the instability of knight-errantry, the knight waiting for something to come that will affirm his identity. See Zumthor (1987): 102 f. G. F. Beneke, *Zeitschrift für deutsches Altertum* 1 (1841): 49–56, had already studied the term *aventiûre* in Middle High German. For broad studies of the question see E. Köhler, *L'aventure chevaleresque* (1974): chap. 3, "L'aventure: Réintégration et quête de l'identité," 77–102, and Michael Nerlich, *Ideology of Adventure: Studies in Modern Consciousness, 1100–1750*, trans. Ruth Crowley (Minneapolis: University of Minnesota Press, c1987) [original title *Kritik der Abenteuer-Ideologie*].

41. "ein ritterliches Versorgungsinstitut": Köhler, "Literatursoziologische Perspektiven": 90. Arthur was indeed conceived as just another knight with a special status as king, and could even behave like a wandering knight in search of adventure. A specific instance of such a dangerous and, ultimately, irresponsible search for individual adventure on his part is seen in the Italian *Tristano Riccardiano* (ca. 1300): he goes off alone to the Fontana Avventurosa, where after a year of enchanted imprisonment he would have been killed had not Tristan showed up in the nick of time to save him. Text in Segre and Marti, eds., *La prosa del Duecento* (1959): 647.

42. In the thirteenth century this social connotation gave way to more abstract cosmological and metaphysical considerations: Robert de Boron's *Queste du Saint Graal* makes the Round Table symbolic of the roundness of the world. See J. Frappier, ed., *Grundriß*: 4.1: 199.

43. On the court of Champagne as historical background to Chrétien's representation of the fictional court of Arthur, see John F. Benton (1961; 1990).

44. Köhler, "Zur Diskussion der Aldelsfrage bei den Trobadors," *Troba-*

dorlyrik (1962): 115 ff., "I Trovatori e la Questione della Nobiltà" in Mancini ed.: 139–162, esp. 150–153.

45. Köhler, ibid. G. Duby, *The Knight the Lady and the Priest*: 216–219, attempts to place Capellanus at the court of Philip Augustus as a humorous teacher of bachelor knights. The pleasures of courtly life could satisfy the knights' lust outside the bonds of marriage, thus keeping them under the control of an elegant sport. In this manner, though paradoxically, courtly love could coexist with the serious institution of marriage even in the face of the Church doctrine of the sacrament, which excluded passion from conjugal love.

46. Köhler, ibid.

47. Chrétien was showing himself a member of the clerical class in this, too. The clerical administrators were less flexible and more bureaucratic than secular lords in their scorn for merchants, whose moral code they could not adapt to their own code, conceived for a rural society. Accordingly, in northern France the communes were more likely to elicit understanding and cooperation from the secular lords than from the bishops. Thus revolt spread to such towns as Beauvais, Noyon, Soissons, Laon, Cambrai, and Reims.

Despite a rather unconvincing focusing on "nascent capitalism," Fredric Jameson (1975: 158) has put his finger on the manifold emargination of the knight and the courtly poet in his narratology of the romance:

> Romance as a form ... expresses a transitional moment, yet one of a very special type: its contemporaries must feel their society torn between past and future in such a way that the alternatives are grasped as hostile but somehow unrelated worlds.... The archaic character of the categories of romance (magic, good and evil, otherness) suggests that the genre expresses a nostalgia for a social order in the process of being undermined by nascent capitalism, yet still for the moment coexisting side by side with the latter.

48. Especially Jean-Pierre Poly, *La Provence et la société féodale, 879–1166. Contribution à l'étude des structures dites féodales dans le Midi* (Paris: Bordas, 1976): 142–144, 286–317, 362 f., and Linda Paterson, "Knights and the Concept of Knighthood in the Twelfth-Century Occitan Epic," *Forum for Modern Language Studies* (1981): esp. 118–121.

49. This exclusivism extended to the contemporary epic, too. See K.-H. Bender, "Un aspect de la stylisation épique: l'exclusivisme de la haute noblesse dans les chansons de geste du XIIᵉ siècle," *Société Rencesvals*, Actes du IVᵉ Congrès International, Heidelberg 1967 (Heidelberg: C. Winter, 1969) 95 ff.; idem, "Des chansons de geste à la première épopée de croisade. La présence de l'histoire contemporaine dans la littérature française du 12ᵉ siècle," *Société Rencesvals*, Actes du VIᵉ Congrès International, Aix-en-Provence 1973 (Aix-en-Provence: Université de Provence, 1974): 485–500.

50. *Yvain*: 327, 329 f., 355, 357–360.

51. E. Köhler, "Literatursoziologische Perspektiven," in Frappier et al., eds., *Grundriß* (1978): 87 f.

52. "qui chascun jor voiz aventures querant et le sens du monde; mais point n'en puis trouver, ne point n'en puis a mon oes retenir." See Eugene Vinaver, *A la recherche d'une poétique médiévale* (Paris: Nizet, 1970), "Un chevalier errant à la recherche du sens du monde," 163–177 at 166. On this theme of the search

for identity of the self in medieval romance see, also, A. Roncaglia, "Nascita e sviluppo della narrativa cavalleresca nella Francia medievale" (1975): 249 f.

53. Köhler, "Marcabrus *L'autrier jost'una sebissa* und das Problem der Pastourelle," *Trobadorlyrik* (1962): 193 ff.

54. *Didascalicon*: 2.8, trans. J. Taylor (1961).

55. On the role of the mercantile ethic in Chrétien, see the provocative semiotic analyses in E. Vance, *Mervelous Signals* (1986): chap. 5, "Chrétien's *Yvain* and the Ideologies of Change and Exchange," 111–151.

56. Anthime Fourrier, *Le courant réaliste dans le roman courtois en France au Moyen Age*, 1 (Paris: A. G. Nizet, 1960).

57. There is an unexplained relationship between the two devilish brothers—said at verse 5271 to be the ones who hold the maidens captive—and a very beautiful damsel who reads a romance to her parents in the garden (5362–5370). Her father declares that he who defeats his two "soldiers" (the brothers) will own "his" castle and his daughter (5488–5491).

58. J. Le Goff in the Preface to Köhler, *L'aventure chevaleresque*: xv.

59. Peter Haidu, "The Hermit's Pottage: Deconstruction and History in *Yvain*," in R. Pickens, ed., *The Sower and His Seed* (1983): 127–145; E. Vance (1986): 142–145. Vance's analysis of *Yvain* goes further, starting out with a more conjectural interpretation of the relationship between Lunete and Yvain as a well calculated exchange of services loaded with deep monetary symbolism (see his pp. 125–138).

60. Joan M. Ferrante in Ferrante and Economou (1975): 158. Other critics have underlined this tension between love and chivalry: cf. T. Ehlert and G. Meissburger, "Perceval et Parzival," *Cahiers de civilization médiévale* 18 (1975): 197–227: "[in Perceval] courtly love is no longer seen as a force that ennobles and educates the knight but on the contrary as a power that threatens his very existence."

61. The complex story of this motif has been expertly examined and convincingly assessed, in a critical dialogue with Gaston Paris, Étienne Gilson, and E. R. Curtius, by E. Köhler, *L'aventure chevaleresque* (1974): chap. 2, "Chevalerie-clergie," 44–76.

62. Marc Bloch, *La société féodale* (1939–1940): 2: 55.

63. H. O. Sommer ed. (1910): 3: 113 ff.

64. Philip of Alsace (Count of Flanders 1168–1191, dead at St. John of Acre in the Third Crusade) protected and strengthened the burgher towns while he reduced the power of the *châtelains*, feudal lords who had hereditarily exercised the higher administrative functions, replacing them with *baillis*, who issued from the lower nobility and acted as simple functionaries at the mercy of the prince. His struggle with Philip Augustus, whom King Louis VII had confided to him as his pupil, ended disastrously with his former pupil inheriting large portions of Flanders, including the Artois and Vermandois in 1185 and 1191. See Louis Trenard, ed., *Histoire des Pays-Bas Français* (Toulouse: E. Privat, 1972): 91–93.

65. G. Duby, *The Three Orders* (1988): 303–306 on this ideological and sociopolitical background to Chrétien's late work (but with incorrect citation of Chrétien's passage).

66. E. Köhler, "Zur Diskussion der Adelsfrage bei den Trobadors," *Trobadorlyrik* (1962): 115 ff., Mancini ed.: 139–162 at 154.

67. E. Köhler, *L'aventure chevaleresque* (1974): 172–182, and the whole chap. 5, pp. 160–207 on the moral question of love and marriage in Chrétien.

68. Köhler, ibid.: 175 with n. 21.

69.
> Ne cuidiez pas que le porcoi
> la dameisele l'an conoisse,
> qu'il an eüst honte et angoisse,
> et si li grevast et neüst,
> se le voir l'en reconeüst;
> si s'est de voir dir gueitiee,
> einz dit come bien afeitiee, etc.
> (Mario Roques ed., 1983, 45.)

I have quoted J. Wilhelm's translation (1984).

70. This "thesis" underlies, for example, Charles Muscatine, *The Old French Fabliaux* (New Haven: Yale University Press, 1986), but its definition and chronological limitations as outlined above are brought out more sharply by the major authority on the subject, Per Nykrog, in his review article "The Fabliaux in California," *Romance Philology* 42.3 (1989): 285–292.

71. Tony Hunt, "The Emergence of the Knight in France and England, 1000–1200," *Forum for Modern Language Studies* (1981): 93–114 at 100. See, besides Per Nykrog, *Les fabliaux* (Genève: Droz, new ed. 1973); Reinhard Kiesow, *Die Fabliaux. Zur Genese und Typologie einer Gattung der altfranzösischen Kurzerzählungen* (Bensberg/Rheinfelden: Schäuble, 1976), esp. 79 ff.; Marie-Luce Chênerie, "'Ces curieux chevaliers tournoyeurs . . .' Des fabliaux aux romans," *Romania* 97 (1976): 327–368; and R. Howard Bloch, *The Scandal of the Fabliaux* (Chicago: University of Chicago Press, 1986).

72. The texts are in the eight-volume edition by H. O. Sommer (Washington: Carnegie Institution, 1908–1916). See Ferdinand Lot, *Étude sur le Lancelot en prose* (Paris: Honoré Champion, 1918; 1954); Jean Frappier, "L''institution' de Lancelot dans le *Lancelot en prose*," *Mélanges de philologie romane et de littérature médiévale offerts à Ernest Hoepffner* (Paris: Les Belles Lettres, 1949): 269–278; Elspeth Kennedy, "Social and Political Ideas in the French Prose *Lancelot*," *Medium Aevum* 26 (1957): 90–106; the expert synthetic study by J. Frappier, "The Vulgate Cycle," in R. S. Loomis, ed., *Arthurian Literature* (1959; 1961): 295–318; and Alexandre Micha, *Essais sur le cycle du Lancelot-Graal* (Genève: Droz, 1987). A. Micha has recently re-edited the *Lancelot del Lac* in nine volumes of the series "Textes Littéraires Français" (Genève: Droz, 1978–1983). The dating for the *Lancelot/Graal* is as proposed by Frappier in Loomis's 1959 vol., but Zumthor (1987: 310) proposes 1225–1235.

73. F. Lot, *Étude sur le Lancelot en prose* (1918): chap. 2, and Frappier in Loomis (1959; 1961): 298 f.

74. J. Frappier in Loomis (1959; 1961): 318, with reference to Pio Rajna in *Studi Danteschi* 1 (1920): 91–99.

75. Frappier in Loomis (1959; 1961): 305 f., with bibliography.

76. G. Duby, *Mâle moyen âge* (1988): 83–117, attempts an interpretation of the *Roman*'s relationship to its historical and social setting, but without adding much to the vast secondary literature by literary historians and critics.

77. Johan Huizinga gave a celebrated analysis of this literature and culture in his landmark *The Waning of the Middle Ages, a Study of the Forms of Life, Thought and Art in France and the Netherlands in the XIVth and XVth Centuries*, trans. F. Hopman (London: E. Arnold, 1924; 1970), but see Paul Zumthor's *Le masque et la lumière: La poétique des grands rhétoriqueurs* (Paris: Éditions du Seuil, 1978) and *Anthologie des Grands Rhétoriqueurs* (Paris: Union Générale d'Éditions, 1978) for a fresh and authoritative new look at the whole field, though not entirely convincing in his attempt to read between the lines and beyond the text in order to attribute to the poets a dynamic transcendence of their social fetters.

78. Martín de Riquer (1970): 5–8. For *Le Livre des faits du bon messire Jehan le Maingre, dit Bouciquaut, mareschal de France et gouverneur de Jennes*, see the recent critical edition by Denis Lalande, Textes Littéraires Français no. 331 (Genève: Droz, 1985). Lalande dates the text, extant in only one MS. (BN Fr. 11.432), between 1406–1409.

79. After Huizinga's classic description of this literature in *The Waning of the Middle Ages*, see, for example, Michel Stanesco in T. Klaniczay (1988): 405–419.

80. More often than with actual warfare, the life of the knight was taken up with theatrical shows in the form of tourneys and jousts, the folly of which met with opposition from moralists in the Church. Hence from early times on, the vast literature on such forms of ritualistic chivalric "tests" was underpinned by a need to allegorize in mystical keys: Huon de Méry's (fl. 1234) *Le tournoiement de l'Antéchrist*, for example, staged a formal joust between Christ and Satan, with the eager participation of archangels, the cardinal and theological virtues, and the chivalric virtues of *Prouesse, Largesse, Courtoisie*, and *Debonnaireté* [Good Humor] as well as the knights of the Round Table, all on the good side. The old edition by Prosper Tarbé (Reims: P. Regnier, 1851) has been reprinted by Slatkine Reprints (Genève: 1977), but there is now a critical edition by Margaret O. Bender: Huon de Méri, *Le torneiment Anticrist* (University, Mississippi: Romance Monographs, 1976). See Larry Benson, *Malory's "Morte Darthur"* (Cambridge: Harvard University Press, 1976): "Knighthood in Life and Literature," 163–185; idem, "The Tournament in the Romances of Chrétien de Troyes and *L'Histoire de Guillaume le Maréchal*," in L. Benson and J. Leyerle, eds., *Chivalric Literature* (1980): 1–24; F. Cardini, "Il guerriero e il cavaliere" (1987): 113; Juliet R. V. Barker, *The Tournament in England, 1100–1400* (Wolfeboro, NH: Boydell Press, 1986); and Alan R. Young, *Tudor and Jacobean Tournaments* (Dobbs Ferry, NY: Sheridan House, 1987).

81. A. J. Bliss, ed., *Sir Orfeo* (Oxford: Oxford University Press, 1954), contains all three extant manuscripts. This text is commonly regarded as one of the extant "Breton lays" from the thirteenth and fifteenth centuries, ending with Chaucer's *Franklin's Tale*. See the texts in Thomas C. Rumble, ed., *The Breton Lays in Middle English* (Detroit: Wayne State University Press, 1965). Donald B. Sands, ed., *Middle English Verse Romances* (New York: Holt, Rinehart & Winston, 1966), is a selection of lays and verse romances including a version of our text as *King Orpheus*.

82. G. V. Smithers, ed., *Havelok* (Oxford: Clarendon Press, 1987).

83. See "Intergeneric Dominants" in my next chapter.

84. J. R. R. Tolkien and E. V. Gordon, eds., *Sir Gawain and the Green Knight*, 2d ed. by Norman Davis (Oxford: Clarendon Press, 1967). I am using Wilhelm's translation in James J. Wilhelm and L. Z. Gross, eds., *The Romance of Arthur* (1984). Incidentally, irony appears in this text, too, for example, in the authorial intervention at verses 1991 f.: "I won't venture to vouch for a sound sleep or a vexed one, / For he had much to mull over," concerning Gawain's forthcoming encounter with the Green Knight, where he expects to lose his head. On irony and criticism of knightly failure in *Sir Gawain*, see W. R. J. Barron, "Knighthood on Trial: The Acid Test of Irony," *Forum for Modern Language Studies* (1981): 181–197.

CHAPTER SIX: EPIC AND ROMANCE IN GERMANY

1. Jauss, "Theory of Genres": 82 f.
2. Jauss, "Theory of Genres": 96, for the meaning of such categories for John of Garlandia's contemporaries. See the survey of this terminology in Heinrich Lausberg, *Handbuch der literarischen Rhetorik* (München: Hueber Verlag, 1960): paragraphs 290–334.
3. It is remarkable that Jauss never adduces examples from Germanic literatures for the medieval epic and romance. I feel that this broadening of the horizon would enrich and perhaps modify his definitions.
4. Jauss, "Theory of Genres": 83–87.
5. W. T. H. Jackson, *The Anatomy of Love: The Tristan of Gottfried von Strassburg* (1971): 144, for a denial of a unified and identifiable code. A summary of research on the matter in Eduard Neumann (1951).
6. *Staete* can also be close to *triuwe* insofar as it can be equivalent to Latin *fides*, just as *mâze* was felt to be equivalent to Latin *moderatio* or *temperantia*: see H. Fuhrmann (1986): 180.
7. See, especially, Jackson's 1971 *The Anatomy of Love*.
8. Jackson (1971): chap. 1, 1–30, esp. 13.
9. G. Duby, *Medieval Marriage* (1978) and *Mâle moyen âge* (1988).
10. Carla Frova (1973): 74. See A. Scaglione, "The Classics in Medieval Education," in Aldo S. Bernardo and Saul Levin, eds., *The Classics in the Middle Ages*, Medieval & Renaissance Texts & Studies (Albany: State University of New York Press, 1990), forthcoming.
11. Frova: 64 (trans. mine). See Rodolphus Glaber, *Historiarum sui temporis libri quinque*, in Migne's *PL*: 142, and Stephen G. Nichols, Jr., *Romanesque Signs: Early Medieval Narrative and Iconography* (New Haven: Yale University Press, 1983): 7–14 and 35–41 on some implications of Raoul's account of Vilgard's "heresy" and its alleged spreading as far as Orléans.
12. Wipo, *Tetralogus*, in *Die Werke Wipos*, ed. Harry Bresslau, *MGH*, Scriptores rerum germanicarum in usum scholarum 61 (3d ed. Hannover, Leipzig: Hahn, 1915; rpt. 1977): p. 81, vv. 187 ff., 199 ff. (cited by P. Riché 174, 387). See James W. Thompson, *The Literacy of the Laity in the Middle Ages*: 90 ff.
13. "Curie regali, more Francorum procerum, a parentibus traditus est; . . .

in aula regis, cunctis tam celestibus quam militaribus imbueatur institutis." Eudes de Saint-Maur, *Vie de Bouchard le Vénérable, comte de Vendôme, de Corbeil, de Melun et de Paris,* ed. Charles Bourel de la Roncière (Paris: Picard, 1892): 5. For Jaeger (215, he spells his name Eudes de St. Maure) this text indicates instruction not in courtly ethics but in military and divine matters, as is stipulated in Germanic sources with reference to clerical training in episcopal centers.

14. "Cum ergo ad pueritiam pervenisset, qua primum aetate mos est nobilium liberos in disciplinam dare, traditus est magistro." *Vita sancti Magnobodi, PL:* 171: 1547–1562 at 1549a; similar remarks in Marbod's *Vita sancti Licinii* and *Vita sancti Gualterii.* See Jaeger: 224.

15. A. Waas, *Geschichte des Kreuzzuges* (Freiburg: Herder, 1956): 1: 33 ff. and 451 ff., referred to by M. Keen (1984): 51–57.

16. I spoke in chapter 5 of the special "literary" or "written" nature of the romance, and this consideration must extend to Germany, too.

17. Gordon B. Ford, Jr., trans., *The Ruodlieb. The First Medieval Epic of Chivalry from Eleventh-Century Germany* (Leiden: E. J. Brill, 1965). Ford dates this fragmentary poem, possibly by an unknown German monk at the Bavarian monastery of Tegernsee, at about 1070. Though earlier datings have been proposed, this later dating would explain the apparently chivalric aspects of the story. See my chapter 2 at passage with note 50.

18. M. Keen (1984): 52 f.

19. Keen (1984): 54–56. See Karl J. Leyser, *Rule and Conflict in an Early Medieval Society: Ottonian Saxony* (1979; 1989).

20. Dumézil, *Mitra-Varuna. Essai sur deux représentations indo-européennes de la souveraineté,* Bibliothèque de l'École des Hautes Études: Sciences religieuses, [56] 16 (Paris: Gallimard, [1940]; 2d ed. 1948).

21. *Daretis Phrygii de excidio Trojae historia,* ed. F. Meister (Leipzig: Teubner, 1873): p. 16, v. 19. This extant Latin version may be from the fifth century.

22. Jaeger does not mention the early "court" poetry of Norway (so called in the original Old Norse language), namely the *dróttkvaett,* a poetic genre praising living kings or their ancestors (from *drótt,* Anglo-Saxon *dryht,* meaning a court or a lord's household). It was written in a formal metrical stave of eight six-syllable lines with rather regular alliteration and rhymes, and was theoretically and practically examined by the great Icelandic saga writer and poet Snorri Sturluson (1178–1241) in his *"Prose Edda."* Most of the poetry, some of it going back to the ninth century in written form, is contained in the *"Poetic"* or *"Elder Edda"* of the rich Codex Regius of Copenhagen of ca. 1270, and the parts that deal with the Nibelungs stories (including the tales of Atli/ Attila, Gudrun/Kriemhild, and Sigurd/Siegfried) are supposed to have Germanic sources. This court poetry has been known and appreciated by medievalists at least as far back as W. P. Ker's spirited 1904 references to it in his landmark work *The Dark Ages* (New York: Mentor Books, 1958): 193 f. It should be interesting to relate it to continental court poetry.

23. The standard aid for orientation in the large literature on the poem is Willy Krogmann and Ulrich Pretzel, *Bibliographie zum Nibelungenlied und zur Klage* (Berlin: Erich Schmidt, 4th ed. 1966), while Friedrich Panzer, *Das Nibe-*

lungenlied: Entstehung und Gestalt (Stuttgart: Kohlhammer, 1855), still provides a useful guide to research up to its date. See a recent analysis in English from a vantage point of historical and generic context in Edward R. Haymes, *The* Nibelungenlied: *History and Interpretation* (Urbana, Chicago: University of Illinois Press, 1986).

24. J. Bumke (1964; 1977: 33; 1982: 20) gives the following statistical counts for the *Nibelungenlied: recke* 492 times; *helt* 390; *degen* 363. *Ritter* (knight) appears only 170 times. MHG *ritter, rîter* appeared only late in the twelfth century.

25. True enough, Kriemhild's purpose grows gradually and darkly, since at the beginning she would have liked to find a way to single out Hagen for punishment.

26. As is well known, the sixty-eight-line extant fragment of the poem is found on the first and last leaves of a theological manuscript, copied there by two monks of Fulda at the beginning of the ninth century. It may have traveled there from Bavaria, where it had allegedly arrived from its place of origin, the Longobards' royal court in Italy. Hildebrand may not have been an Ostrogoth but a Longobard; in the saga he was, as he still remained in the *Nibelungenlied*, the trusted lieutenant (*der Gefärte, Waffenmeister*) of the Ostrogoth king Dietrich (Theoderic).

27. A detailed presentation of scholarly opinion is in Max Wehrli, *Geschichte der deutschen Literatur von den Anfängen bis zur Gegenwart* 1 (Stuttgart: Philipp Reclam Jun., 1980): 27–35. Wehrli, 31, adds that of the many epic encounters of father and son the *Hildebrantslied* is the only one where the father knowingly kills the son.

28. Quotations from the *Nibelungenlied* will be based on the Bartsch/de Boor edition (1979).

29. Confused court criticism is Jaeger's judgment (190–193), which in my opinion does not do justice to the role of courtliness in the poem.

30. Segre and Marti, eds., *La prosa del Duecento*: 630: "ma tutto in altra maniera addiverrae, che Tristano non hae divisato, di questa aventura."

31. Jean Miquet's analysis of the later epic tradition, especially in the *dérimée* (prose) versions 1300–1500, in T. Klaniczay et al., eds. (1988), underscores the static nature of the genre before the Italian poets took it over. I find this survey somewhat misleading where it states that the mixing of the austere, typical of the epic tradition, with the refined and elegant spectacle, that was typical of the romance, remained rare in the epic. The mixing of elements could be very lively in the epic, especially in Germany.

32. Chapter 94 in Segre and Marti, eds., *La prosa del Duecento*: 666–735 at 709: her corset had around the neck and cuffs buttons worth more than 1000 *agostani* (Frederick II's gold coin); in her belt, made of gold thread, were encased about 800 stones worth 100 gold deniers each; her two gloves were worth more than 300 gold *bisanti* (Byzantine *solidi*); and so on. The text has multiple sources, mostly Italian, with some derivations from Thomas and the French prose *Tristan* and *Roman de Lancelot*.

33. Zumthor (1987): 74. Seven of the ten extant chronicles of the battle, approximately dating between 1070 and shortly after 1200, mention him, and three of them name him.

34. In his translation of *The Lay of the Nibelung Men* (1911): xv, Arthur S. Way quoted Matthew Arnold's pertinent association of the ethic of the *Nibelungenlied* with the chronicles of Froissart and Philippe de Commines (*Lectures on Modern History* 2).

35. Hugo Kuhn, "Tristan, Nibelungenlied, Artusstruktur," *Sitzungsberichte der bayerischen Akademie der Wissenschaften*, Phil.-Hist. Klasse 5 (1973), seems to have been the first to stress the parallels between Tristan and Siegfried. Theodore M. Andersson, *A Preface to the* Nibelungenlied (Stanford: Stanford University Press, 1987), is the most informed treatment to date of the relationship between the *Nibelungenlied* and the French and German romances, in addition to earlier Germanic sagas. Aside from the author's debatable stand against the oral-formulaic interpretation of sources, this study analyzes the characters of Siegfried and Hagen within the rich tradition of the bride-quest theme and the *Spielmannsepen*, including French sources for the context of the marital romances. Siegfried's career is interpreted as a "growth from innocence" tale characteristic of the courtly romance (141); "Hagen too is in some sense a romance hero" (143). In the poem chivalric loyalty and friendship rise to heights unseen in Hartmann, Wolfram, or Gottfried (131).

36. Guy Raynaud de Lage in *Grundriß*: 4.1: 212–230 at 214. See the recent Eilhart von Oberge, *Tristrant*, trans. J. W. Thomas (Lincoln, NE: University of Nebraska Press, 1978), the translation into modern German in Eilhart von Oberg, *Tristrant und Isalde, neuhochdeutsche Übersetzung*, trans. Danielle Buschinger and Wolfgang Spiewok (Göppingen: Kümmerle Verlag, 1986), and the Old Norse version: *The Saga of Tristram and Isönd*, trans. Paul Schach (Lincoln, NE: University of Nebraska Press, 1973).

37. It deserves mention, however, that in Béroul's *Tristan*, too, the author/ minstrel showed overt sympathy toward the lovers and full scorn for their villainous and treacherous enemies: see, for example, Evelyn B. Vitz, "Orality, Literacy and the Early Tristan Material: Béroul, Thomas, Marie de France," *Romanic Review* 78.3 (1987): 299–310.

38. Using a different frame of reference which focuses the chivalric ideal on the hero's conflict between his duties as a knight and his duties as a lover, W. T. H. Jackson (1971) denies that *Tristan* is a courtly romance and calls it, instead, a chivalric romance.

39. The phrase comes from N. Elias (see the English version *Power and Civility*, 1982, "The Courtization of Warriors," 258–270).

40. References are to the Ranke/Weber edition of Gottfried (1967). Chrétien's story of Lancelot already contained the exaltation of High Love that Gottfried would incorporate into his story of Tristan as a religion of *hohe Minne*.

41. Jackson (1971): 144, 158.

42. Jackson (1971): 159, and Gisela Holland, *Die Hauptgestalten in Gottfrieds Tristan: Wesenszüge, Handlungsfunktion, Motif der List*, Philologische Studien und Quellen 30 (Berlin: Erich Schmidt, 1966), on skill and cunning (*List*) as part of Tristan's rejection of courtois and moral values.

43. See the definition of Rual's character at verses 2186–2190: "Dar an tet er der werlde schin, / wie wollekomener triuwe er pflac, / was tugende und eren an im lac." "And thus by all it can be seen / how true and kind was Rûal's way, / what virtue, honor in him lay." Zeydel's translation in *The "Tristan and*

Isolde" of Gottfried von Strassburg, trans. Edwin Hermann Zeydel, Princeton: Princeton University Press, 1948, p. 44.

44. "The promise of honor, virtue, and dignity to be gained in the fight against court vices places Mark's speech in a tradition of defense of state service which began in antiquity, continued faintly in the Middle Ages, and was revived by Castiglione." (Jaeger: 86 f., with his translation of Gottfried 8353–8366.)

45.   an gebaerde unde an schoenen siten
                 was ime so rehte wol geschehen,
                 daz man in gerne mohte sehen.
                                  (vv. 3348–3350)

46.   under aller dirre lere
                 gab er ir eine unmüezekeit
                 die heizen wir moraliteit,
                 diu kunst diu leret schoene site:
                 da solten alle vrouwen mite
                 in ir jugent unmüezic wesen.
                                  (vv. 8002–8007)

I have slightly modified Jackson's translation (1971): 77, 176, 181.

47. The mutual relationship of the various extant versions of the Tristan story is difficult to assess, since their chronological order (starting around 1165) is unclear: see, for example, Jackson (1971: 35, with the "usual" dating of Thomas ca. 1170 and Béroul ca. 1190). Whether Béroul preceded or followed Thomas (both apparently falling between 1150 and 1191 as extreme poles), he seems to show the illiterate minstrel performing his story before a live audience, the transmitted text containing a high degree of "orality," whereas Thomas, either dictating or writing, speaks from a more detached and intellectual standpoint which may disclose the cleric at work. See E. B. Vitz, "Orality, Literacy and the Early Tristan Material: Béroul, Thomas, Marie de France" (1987), already cited. See Béroul's and Thomas's *Tristan* texts in *Tristan et Yseut*, ed. J. C. Payen (Paris: Garnier, 1974), and [Thomas,] *Les fragments du roman de Tristan, poème du XIIe siècle*, ed. Bartina H. Wind (Genève: Droz, 1960).

48. Laura A. Hibbard, *Mediaeval Romance in England: A Study of the Sources and Analogues of the Noncyclic Metrical Romances* (New York: Oxford University Press, 1924; 2d ed. Burt Franklin, 1960): 166, n. 4; Helaine Newstead, "The Origin and Growth of the Tristan Legend," in R. S. Loomis, ed. (1959; 1961): 122–133 at 132. Text of *Apollonius of Tyre* in A. Riese's edition (Leipzig: Teubner, 1871; 1893). Scholars differ on the possible derivation from a Greek original of the second to third century A.D.

49. In its context, the epithet "a man for all seasons" attributed to Thomas More in Robert Whittinton's (ca. 1480—ca. 1530) school manual echoes Paul's dictum well, without being a literal translation, and it admirably recalls the language of courtesy: "More is a man of angel's wit and singular learning; I know not his fellow. For where is the man of that gentleness, lowliness and affability? And as time requireth, a man of marvelous mirth and pastimes; and sometimes of as sad a gravity; a man for all seasons." See John Bartlett, *Familiar Quotations*, 15th ed. (Boston: Little, Brown, 1980): 155.11.

50. See K. Peter, "Die Utopie des Glücks. Ein neuer Versuch über Gottfried von Strassburg," *Euphorion* 62 (1968): 317–344, a forceful statement of the

case for both Thomas and Gottfried as anticourtly subverters of the courtois Weltanschauung. Also J. C. Payen, ed., *Tristan et Yseut* (Paris: Garnier, 1974): viii–ix: "Les *Tristan* en vers sont des poèmes de la violence. Tout s'y révèle exaspéré: les élans amoureux comme la vengeance. Constante est l'hyperbole. Ni Béroul ni Thomas ne pratiquent l'art de la litote. Chez eux, le langage ne cherche pas à masquer le scandale. . . . Le public féodal et le public courtois . . . souhaitent . . . cette formulation brutale qui manifeste les contradictions entre la *fin'amors* et la fidélité vassalique, entre la générosité de l'amour et les interdits de la loi, entre les devoirs de caste et les exigences de la passion."

51. Bartina Wind, "Éléments courtois dans Béroul et dans Thomas," *Romance Philology* 14 (1960): 1–13 at 7: "l'oeuvre de Thomas n'est courtois que dans la conception des personnages secondaires, dans l'ambiance où baigne le drame, qui par lui-même échappe à l'influence courtoise. Tristan et Iseut unis dans la douleur autant que dans l'amour ont une grandeur qui manque à la poésie courtoise." This largely applies to Gottfried, too.

52. See, on the preceding, Köhler: "Literatursoziologische Perspektiven," 94 f.

53. A full discussion of this problematic predicament of Béroul's text is in Alberto Vàrvaro, *Il Roman de Tristan di Béroul* (Torino: Bottega d'Erasmo, 1963): 103–123.

54. Also, J. Bumke, *Wolfram von Eschenbach* (Stuttgart: J. B. Metzlersche Verlagsbuchhandlung, 1964), and idem, *Die Wolfram von Eschenbach-Forschung seit 1945* (München: W. Fink, 1970).

55. Book 3, 170:21 f., 25–28:

> ir tragt geschickede unde schîn,
> ir mugt wol volkes hêrre sîn,
>
> . . . .
>
> iuch sol erbarmen nôtec her:
> gein des kumber sît ze wer
> mit milte und mit güete:
> vlîzet iuch diemüete.

Also the references to *mâze* and *manlich und wol gemuot* at 3.171:13, 172:7.

References hereafter are to the G. Weber (1963) edition, which after the text gives a full modern paraphrase ("Nacherzählung"). I shall use Zeydel's not very precise but spirited translation for these lines from which I have extracted some of the terms: cf. Wolfram von Eschenbach, *Parzival*, trans. Edwin Hermann Zeydel, Chapel Hill: University of North Carolina Press, 1951:

> You've beauty and nobility,
> A people's leader you can be.
>
> . . . .
>
> Compassion show to men in need,
> Assuage their grief by word and deed,
> With kindness, generosity,
> And cultivate humility.

56. *blûkeit* occurs at 14.696:20: "âne blûkeit wart er vrô," "he was joyful without reticence." Old High and Middle High German *blûkeit* (*blûcheit, bliukeit, blwecheit*) is defined as *diffidentia, Schüchternheit, Bedenkenheit*.

57. *Perceval*, ed. F. Lecoy: 1, vv. 544–546: "De pucele a mout qui la beise; / s'ele le beisier vos consant, / le soreplus vos en defant." See the whole passage, vv. 529–554, for the mother's injunction; 665–778 for the encounter with the damsel. *Parzival*, ed. G. Weber: book 3, st. 127, vv. 25–32; st. 129, v. 132 to st. 132, v. 24.

58. For a summary of the critics' conjectures on such aspects of the work, see E. H. Zeydel's Introduction to his edition and translation (Chapel Hill, 1951): 12–15.

59. J. Ferrante in Ferrante and Economou (1975): 160 f. Ferrante 160–164 interprets Wolfram as exposing the inadequacies of courtly love in the stories of Gawain in the service of Orgeluse—a complex and fascinating plot of multiple tests laden with symbolic meanings.

60. "Amor was sîn krîe. / Der ruoft ist zer dêmuot / iedoch niht volleclîchen guot." (478: 30 to 479: 2)

61. "sich hât gehoehet iwer gewin. / nu kêrt an diemuot iwern sin." (798: 29 f.)

62. Such questions cannot be asked of Chrétien's version because it is interrupted at the point where Perceval decides to seek the holy hermit's advice, after his period of religious crisis.

63. See McConeghy's informative survey of critical opinions in the Introduction to his edition of *Iwein*: xiii–lvii (with rich bibliography), esp. xxii. J. W. Thomas has recently produced valuable translations of both Hartmann's *Iwein* (Lincoln, NE: University of Nebraska Press, 1979) and *Erec* (ibid., 1982). The latter is commonly regarded as the first Arthurian romance in German. See, also, *"Erex Saga" and "Ivens Saga": The Old Norse Versions of Chrétien de Troyes's "Erec" and "Yvain,"* trans. Foster W. Blaisdell, Jr. and Marianne E. Kalinke (Lincoln, NE: University of Nebraska Press, 1977). See Gert Kaiser, *Textauslegung und gesellschaftliche Selbstdeutung. Aspekte einer sozialgeschichtliche Interpretation von Hartmanns Artusepen* (Frankfurt/M.: Athenäum, 1973); and Ursula Peters, "Artusroman und Fürstenhof. Darstellung und Kritik neuerer sozialgeschichtlicher Untersuchungen zu Hartmanns 'Erec,'" *Euphorion* 69 (1975): 175–196.

64. Karin R. Gürttler's article on "German Arthurian Literature" in Norris L. Lacy, ed., *The Arturian Encyclopedia* (New York, London: Garland, 1986): 215–221, with bibliography.

65. Edward R. Haymes, *The* Nibelungenlied: *History and Interpretation* (1986): 98, regards *übermuote* in the *Nibelungenlied* as equivalent to the Christian notion of *superbia*, of which he declares it the standard German translation for the period, and adds: "Although Christianity plays almost no role in the epic, there is no question that the Christian value system was a part of the horizon of expectations into which the *Nibelungenlied* was projected."

66. J. Bumke, *The Concept of Knighthood* (1982): 108, for more examples of the use of epithets (*der höfschte, der küneste, der schöneste, der tugende rîcheste*, "the most courtly, bravest, most elegant, richest in virtue, worthiest . . .").

67. H. Sparnaay in R. S. Loomis, ed. (1959): 430–442 for an expert assessment of Hartmann's originality as well as his debt to Chrétien.

68. Sparnaay, ibid.: 435.

69. René Pérennec, "Adaptation et société: l'adaptation par Hartmann d'Aue du roman de Chrétien de Troyes 'Erec et Enide,'" *Études Germaniques* 28 (1973): 289–303. The German poets' social sensitivity vis-à-vis their French counterparts included the Minnesingers, who accordingly emphasized chivalric values as part and warrant of social order and marriage as logical culmination of mutual love.

70. McConeghy's edition: xxxv–xxxviii. Werner Fechter, *Das Publikum der mittelhochdeutschen Dichtung* (Frankfurt/Main: Diesterweg, 1935, rpt. Darmstadt: Wissenschaftliche Buchgesellschaft, 1966), and J. Bumke, *Mäzene im Mittelalter* (1979), provide detailed surveys of the history of the manuscript tradition and of patronage.

71. Ulrich was probably a *capellanus* from the Swiss canton of Thurgau. On most of the following texts, see K. R. Gürttler in Norris L. Lacy (1986). Sparnaay, too, in R. S. Loomis, ed. (1959), typically characterizes this multiple genre of the German romance after the great masters as lacking a point or inner coherence.

72. See *"The Crown": A Tale of Sir Gawein and King Arthur's Court*, trans. J. W. Thomas (Lincoln, NE: University of Nebraska Press, 1989).

73. "In die hohsten wirdekait / Die diu welt mit namen trait, / Ich maine ritterlichen namen"—a dignity that is conferred by formal dubbing: vv. 5611– 5613. See *Rudolfs von Ems Willehalm von Orleans; hrsg. aus dem Wasserburger codex der Fürstlich Fürstenbergischen Hofbibliothek in Donaueschingen*, ed. Victor Junk, Deutsche Texte des Mittelalters 2 (Berlin: Weidmann, 1905; rpt. 1967).

CHAPTER SEVEN: THE ORIGINS

1. Charles Radding, *A World Made by Men: Cognition and Society, 400–1200* (Chapel Hill: University of North Carolina Press, 1985): 175–186 on the notarial school of Pavia.

2. On the medieval Italian courts see the rich survey by A. Roncaglia in A. Asor Rosa, ed., *Letteratura Italiana* 1 (1982): 33–147; 53 on King Cunipert, Felix, and Stephanus Monachus (or Magister), a monk probably stemming from Bobbio who praised Cunipert's policies.

3. Roncaglia, ibid.: 54–57.

4. Ronald G. Witt, "Medieval Italian Culture etc.," in *Renaissance Humanism: Foundations, Forms, and Legacy* (1988): 1: 29–70 at 36. On the Italian cathedral schools and their decline around 1100 see Ronald G. Witt's forthcoming study, anticipated in the paper just cited, especially 41: "as an institution the cathedral school lost its leading role in Italian education after 1100." On the schools of Verona see Rino Avesani, "La cultura veronese dal secolo IX al secolo XII," in Manlio Pastore Stocchi et al., eds., *Storia della cultura veneta*, 6 vols. (Vicenza: Neri Pozza, 1976–1986) 1: *Dalle origini al Trecento* (1976): 240–270 at 251–257. The brilliant and scholarly Ratherius (d. 974) was bishop of Verona in the late tenth century.

5. Franco Gaeta in A. Asor Rosa, ed., *Letteratura Italiana* 1 (1982): 186 f.
6. See A. Roncaglia in A. Asor Rosa, ed., *Letteratura Italiana* 1 (1982): 65.
7. Luigi Foscolo Benedetto, "Stephanus Grammaticus da Novara," *Studi Medievali* 3 (1908–1911): 499–508; J. Fleckenstein (1956); Jaeger (1987): 572.
8. See A. Roncaglia in A. Asor Rosa, ed., *Letteratura Italiana* 1 (1982): 73 f.
9. Ibid.: 81.
10. Text arranged in seven books in *Monumenta Germaniae Historica*, Scriptores 11 [= *MGH* SS 11] (1854) 591–681. On Benzo see Max Manitius, *Geschichte der lateinischen Literatur des Mittelalters*, Handbuch der Altertumswissenschaft 9.2.2–3 (Munich: Beck, 1923–1931): 3: 454–457; Percy Ernst Schramm, *Kaiser, Rom und Renovatio: Studien zur Geschichte des römischen Erneuerungsgedankens vom Ende des karolingischen Reiches bis zur Investiturstreit*, 2 vols. (2d ed. Darmstadt: Gentner, 1957): 1: 258 ff. See Jaeger: 56, 122–125, 171, 228, 278n., 284n. Jaeger: 122 says he was "probably an Italian, possibly a Greek."
11. "Principes vero delectatione bonae famae largissimi; gens adulari sciens, eloquentiae in studiis inserviens in tantum ut etiam ipsos pueros quasi rhetores attendas. . . . Equorum ceterorumque militiae instrumentorum et vestium luxuria delectatur." *PL*: 149: 1102b-c; Jaeger: 200 f. (his trans.). See the thoroughly courtly context of the praises of the Norman rulers in the poem of 2,500 lines in five books by William of Apulia (Puglia), *Gesta Roberti Wiscardi*, in *La geste de Robert Guiscard*, ed. M. Mathieu (Palermo: Istituto Siciliano di Studi Bizantini e Neoellenici, 1961), usually dated between 1090 and 1111.
12. A. Roncaglia in A. Asor Rosa, ed., *Letteratura Italiana* 1 (1982): 97–105.
13. Second of *Vitae prima et secunda s. Bernardi episcopi Parmensis*, ed. E. P. Schramm, in *MGH* SS 30.2 (Leipzig: K. W. Hiersemann, 1926): 1114–1127 at 1323 f.: "Erat enim aspectu formosus, animo robustus, distribuendo largus, armis edoctus, conversatione iocundus, genitrici sue subiectus, honore avidus, . . . et ideo cunctis eum agnoscentibus gratiosus et carus."
14. "Copia librorum non defuit huicve bonorum / libros ex cunctis habet artibus atque figuris"; "Timpana cum citharis stivisque lirisque sonant hic / ac dedit insignis dux premia maxima mimis." *Vita Mathildis* (or *De principibus canusinis*) 2: 1370 f. in *MGH* SS 12: 405 f. and ibid. 1: 830 f. in *MGH* SS 12: 368. See A. Roncaglia in A. Asor Rosa, ed., *Letteratura Italiana* 1 (1982): 94.
15. For example, A. Vàrvaro, *Letterature romanze del Medioevo* (1985): chap. 1.
16. Middle High German *Wälsch*, German *Welsch*, originally meaning "Celtic," probably from the Celtic tribe of the Volcae (like Eng. Welsh, Wales, and Cornwall), had come to mean Roman, Romance, or Italian—and also "foreigner," as in *Walloon* and Irish Gaelic *gall*.
17. As a relevant example, as late as circa 1400 the castle of Runkelstein near Bolzano was richly decorated with frescoes apparently inspired by Wirnt von Grafenberg's *Wigalois* (1204–1209 or 1210–1215), Rudolf von Ems's

popular story of *Willehalm* (from ca. 1235–1240), and Der Pleier's *Garel von dem blühenden Tal* (ca. 1260).

18. *Der Wälsche Gast*, ed. H. Rückert: vv. 1124–1126. Jaeger: 266.

19. Corrado Bologna, "La letteratura dell'Italia settentrionale nel Duecento," in A. Asor Rosa, ed., *Letteratura Italiana* 7.1 (1987): 101–188; 123–141 on minstrels operating within the burghers' communes. Aurelio Roncaglia, "Le corti medievali," ibid. 1 (1982): 33–147 on literary activities at medieval Italian courts, and Franco Gaeta, "Dal comune alla corte rinascimentale," ibid. 1: 157 on the social shifts from communes to Renaissance courts.

20. P. Zumthor (1987): 73, citing from Daniela Goldin's course notes *Boncompagno da Signa: Testi* (Venezia: Università; Centrostampa, 1983): 45 f., but see full text of these letters in D. Goldin, *B come Boncompagno: Tradizione e invenzione in Boncompagno da Signa* (Padova: Centrostampa, 1988): 83–88, from the largely still unpublished *Boncompagnus* chapter 7, with ample critical analysis on pp. 53–78. On the love letter as a formal genre in Buoncompagno and the other masters of *ars dictaminis*, see Ernstpeter Ruhe, *De amasio ad amasiam: zur Gattungsgeschichte des mittelalterlichen Liebesbriefes*, Beiträge zur romanischen Philologie des Mittelalters 10 (München: Fink, 1975).

21. Zumthor (1987): 72, based on Constance Bullock-Davies, *Menestrellorum multitudo: Minstrels at a Royal Feast* (Cardiff: University of Wales Press, 1978): 67–173.

22. Aurelio Roncaglia, ed., *Antologia delle letterature medievali d'oc e d'oïl* (Milano: Accademia, 1973): 367–371, with bibliography p. 630, including the dating by Rita Lejeune.

23. Text in Joseph Linskill Hill, ed., *The Poems of the Troubadour Raimbaut de Vaqueiras* (The Hague: Mouton, 1964): 108–116, no. 4.

24. A. Roncaglia in A. Asor Rosa, ed., *Letteratura Italiana* 1 (1982): 108–113.

25. Köhler, Mancini ed., 157 f.: see n. 34. On the troubadour tradition at courts of the Venetia, including Sordello, see Gianfranco Folena, "Tradizione e cultura trobadorica nelle corti e nelle città venete," *Storia della Cultura Veneta*, 6 vols. (Vicenza: Neri Pozza, 1976–1986): 1: *Dalle origini al Trecento* (1976): 453–562.

26. The Latin original's numerous vulgarizations in all vernaculars included no fewer than five Tuscan versions, the earliest of them dating from 1288. The Tuscan texts derived from the French translation, *Li livres dou gouvernement des rois* (see my chap. 3, end), rather than from the Latin original, hence Italian *villa* for French *ville* and *ruga* for "street": see 3.1.1 in Cesare Segre and Mario Marti, eds., *La prosa del Duecento* (Milano, Napoli: R. Ricciardi, 1959): 267, based on the manuscripts.

27. 3.30; Tuscan version in *La poesia del Duecento*: 290 f.

28. "Iste imperator derisiones et solatia et convicia ioculatorum sustinebat et audiebat impune et frequenter dissimulabat se audire. Quod est contra illos qui statim volunt se ulcisci de iniuriis sibi factis. Sed non bene faciunt, cum dicat Scriptura *Ecclesiastici* X: 'Omnis iniuriae proximi ne memineris et nichil agas in operibus iniuriae.' Item *Proverbiorum* XII: 'Fatuus statim indicat iram

suam; qui autem dissimulat iniuriam, callidus est.'" Gianfranco Contini, ed., *Letteratura Italiana delle Origini* (Firenze: Sansoni, 1970) 25, from *Cronica*, ed. Ferdinando Bernini, 2 vols. (Bari: Laterza, 1942).

29. Duby, "La vulgarisation des modèles culturels dans la société féodale," *Hommes et structures* (1973): 299–308 at 306–308.

30. On the general matter of clerical presences among the literati see Roberto Antonelli and Simonetta Bianchini, "Dal *clericus* al poeta," in A. Asor Rosa, ed., *Letteratura Italiana* 2 (1983): 171–227.

31. Not surprisingly, secular courtiers thought likewise, as did in the following century the eminent *maître d'hôtel* of Charles the Bold of Burgundy and tutor to Philip the Handsome, Olivier de La Marche (1422–1502): see M. Keen (1984): 148–151. Olivier de La Marche authored the important *Chronique* and the bizarre allegorical/moral *Triumphe des Dames*.

32. C. Donati, *L'idea di nobiltà in Italia* (1988): 3–7, 18 n. 1. Bartolus's commentary dealt with Justinian's book 12, "De dignitatibus": *dignitas* corresponds to "nobilitas secundum volgare nostrum," so that, Bartolus opines, although we do not have technical juridical treatises on nobility, we can rightly treat it under this heading: "licet sub nomine nobilitatis non habeamus aliquem specialem tractatum, tamen habemus hunc librum de dignitatibus," hence "de nobilitate recte tractare possumus." Cited by Donati, p. 18 n., with reference to the text in Bartolus a Saxoferrato, *In Secundam Codicis Partem* (Venetiis: n. p., 1585): 45v-48v. See Anna T. Sheedy, *Bartolus on Social Conditions in the Fourteenth Century* (New York: Columbia University Press; London: P. S. King and Staples, 1942; rpt. New York: AMS Press, 1967): esp. 105–125.

33.   Ladonc cugei que fos mors Pretz e Dos,
            . . . .
            Anc hom no vi metge de son joven,
            tan belh, tam bo, tan larc, tan conoissen,
            tan coratjos, tan ferm, tan conqueren,
            tam be parlan ni tam be entenden.
            . . . .
            . . . Guardatz valor d'enfan!

William P. Shepard and Frank M. Chambers, eds. and trans., *The Poems of Aimeric de Peguilhan* (Evanston: Northwestern University Press, 1950): 146, poem no. 26.

34. See Alberto Vàrvaro, "La curia fridericiana," in A. Asor Rosa, ed., *Letteratura Italiana* 7.1 (1987): 86–98.

35. Lauro Martines (1979): 65 f.

36. Contini, ed., *Letteratura Italiana delle Origini* (1970): 163 f.

37. "I cortesi costumi e li belli e piacevoli riggimenti." *Il libro de' vizi e delle virtudi*, in C. Segre and M. Marti, eds., *La prosa del Duecento* (1959): 756. Also Bono Giamboni, *Il Libro de' vizî e delle virtudi e il Trattato di virtù e di vizî*, ed. Cesare Segre (Torino: G. Einaudi, 1968). Note the emphasis on outer conduct, as in the courtly tradition, and the hendiadys *costumi e reggimenti*, which returned in Francesco da Barberino's *Reggimento e costumi di donna*. See a lively description of court life in Verona at the time of Cangrande in

Immanuel Giudeo's *Bisbidis*, edited by Vincenzo de Bartholomaeis, *Rime giullaresche e popolari d'Italia* (Bologna: Zanichelli, 1926; rpt. Bologna: A. Forni, 1977): 68–71. De Bartholomaeis also explored the documentary value of Provençal poetry as a source for Italian history in his edition *Poesie provenzali storiche relative all'Italia*, Fonti per la storia d'Italia 71/72 (Roma: Tipografia del Senato, 1931).

38. Text of the *Tesoretto* in Gianfranco Contini, ed., *Poeti del Duecento*, 2 vols. (Milano, Napoli: Ricciardi, 1960): 2: 169–277. Also, Brunetto Latini, *Il Tesoretto*, ed. and trans. Julia Bolton Holloway (New York, London: Garland, 1981).

39. See Contini, ed., *Poeti del Duecento* (1960): 2: 170 for Giovanni Villani's characterization of Brunetto as the first educator (*digrossare*) of the Florentines in the art of speaking and governing.

40. Treatises and manuals on ethic abound in medieval literature both in Latin and the vernaculars, and often the versions redacted in Italy were based on French originals. Well known among such compilations are Domenico Cavalca's *Pungilingua*, a vulgarization of the French Dominican Guillaume Perrault's (or Peyraut, Peraldus or Paraldus, Paraldo in Italian: ca. 1200–ca. 1261) *Summa aurea de virtutibus* or *Summa virtutum et vitiorum*, a casuistic tome after pagan and Christian sources (printed Lyon 1546), and the Pisan Dominican Bartolomeo di San Concordio's (ca. 1262–1347) popular *Summa casuum conscientiae*, also available in the vernacular as the *Maestruzzo* or *Pisanella* by Giovanni dalle Celle. Excerpts from these and other authors in *Prosatori minori del Trecento*, 1: *Scrittori di religione*, ed. Giuseppe De Luca, La Letteratura Italiana: Storia e Testi 12.1 (Milano, Napoli: Riccardo Ricciardi, 1954). On Peraldus in Italy and the whole tradition of the *exemplum* see Carlo Delcorno, *L'exemplum nella predicazione volgare di Giordano da Pisa*, Venezia, Istituto veneto di scienze, lettere ed arti, Memorie, v. 36, fasc. 1 (1972); idem., *L'exemplum e la letteratura tra medioevo e rinascimento* (Bologna: Il Mulino, 1989).

41. See the annotated text in Contini, ed., *Poeti del Duecento* (1960): 1: 703–712, or in Contini's comprehensive edition *Le opere volgari di Bonvesin da Riva*, 1 (1941).

42. Anonimo Genovese, *Poesie*, ed. Luciana Cocito (Roma: Edizioni dell'Ateneo, 1970). Also the annotated selection in Contini, ed., *Poeti del Duecento* (1960): 1: 713–761. Cf. Lauro Martines (1979): 85.

43. "Le ovre dirite e le virtu(t)e / son merze bonne e zernue; / de fin da or in quele inpiega": vv. 161–163 of "Exposicio de modo navigandi," a long poem on the art of navigation (no. 145 in Cocito ed.: 621–639). See L. Martines (1979): 87–93 for an interesting analysis of this Genoese poet.

44. Paola Mildonian, "Strutture narrative e modelli retorici: Interpretazione di *Novellino* I–V," *Medioevo romanzo* 6.1 (1979): 63–97 on new sense of nurtured nobility in Guinizelli and the *Novellino*.

45. On Buonaccorso's impact see the detailed analysis in Hans Baron's seminal *The Crisis of the Early Italian Renaissance*, 2 vols. (Princeton: Princeton University Press, 1955): 1: 365 f.; 2: 623–628 (abridged in 1 vol. 2d ed., ibid., 1966).

46. Maria Corti, "Le fonti del *Fiore di virtù* e la teoria della 'nobiltà' nel Duecento," *Giornale Storico della Letteratura Italiana* 36 (1959): 77.

47. Cited by Vallone (1950): 10, from *I Fioretti di San Francesco*, ed. Giovanni Getto (Milan: A. Martello, 1946): xxxvii, 119.

48. Contini, ed., *Poeti del Duecento* (1960): 259–261 with complete text. See P. Mildonian, op. cit. (1979).

49. Text in C. Segre and M. Marti, eds., *La prosa del Duecento* (1959): 548–554.

50. Ibid.: Conto 19 at 551–554: "Tristano e Lancelotto e altri assai ei regni loro lassaro e diero altrui, volendo cavalieri tali divenire: che quelli è re che en bontà ben se regge" (553); and the virtue that qualifies one as a true knight and king lies "in operare onne bontà d'amore de cavallaria de cortesia de larghezza de lealtà de fermezza [constancy] e de ciascun valore" (552).

51. "Re e signore solamente in operare ordinato e in fare e inviare; in operare onne bontà d'amore de cavallaria de cortesia de larghezza de lealtà de fermezza e de ciascun valore" (552).

52. Antoine Thomas, *Francesco da Barberino et la littérature provençale en Italie au moyen âge* (Paris: E. Thorin, 1883). See the critical edition by Giuseppe E. Sansone (Torino: Loescher-Chiantore, 1957).

53. A. Parducci, *Costumi ornati* (1928), and the semidiplomatic editions of the *Reggimento* by Carlo Baudi di Vesme (Bologna: G. Romagnoli, 1875) and of the *Documenti* by Francesco Egidi, 4 vols. (Roma: Società Filologica Romana, 1905–1927).

54. Emilio Cecchi and Natalino Sapegno, eds., *Storia della Letteratura Italiana* 2: Il Trecento (Milano: Garzanti, 1965, 1973): 688–697, and 701 for Bindo, not included among the *curiali*.

55. Some of the texts of Bindo di Cione, Antonio da Ferrara, Francesco di Vannozzo, and Simone Serdini in Natalino Sapegno, ed., *Poeti minori del Trecento* (Milano, Napoli: Ricciardi, 1952): 1–278, and *Il Trecento, dalla crisi dell'età comunale all'Umanesimo*, eds. Raffaele Amaturo et al., La Letteratura Italiana, Storia e Testi, 2.1, ed. Carlo Muscetta (Bari: Laterza, 1971): 527–568.

56. For example, Vannozzo's canzone of 1374 on the states of the world, "Correndo del Signor mille e trecento / anni settantaquatro," in Sapegno ed. (1952): 218–222. Of course, this tradition of court poetry continued in the following centuries: see Carlo Dionisotti, "Niccolò Liburnio e la letteratura cortigiana," *Lettere Italiane* 14 (1962): 33–58; Eugenio Garin, "La cultura fiorentina alla corte dei Medici," in Emilio Cecchi and Natalino Sapegno, eds., *Storia della Letteratura Italiana* 3: Il Quattrocento e l'Ariosto (Milano: Garzanti, 1966): 310–317; Domenico De Robertis, "Poesia delle corti padane," ibid.: 614–631; Paola Vecchi Galli, "La poesia cortigiana tra XV e XVI secolo. Rassegna di testi e studi (1969–1981)," *Lettere Italiane* 34 (1982): 95–141.

57. An interesting comparative survey of the transformations of the chivalric and *courtois* ideas in fifteenth-century European literature is T. Klaniczay et al., eds. (1988), especially the contributions by Michel Stanesco, Jean Miquet, Hana Jechová, and Lucie Brind'Amour, pp. 405–459. The scholarly usefulness of the volume is, however, impaired by the lack of precise bibliographic refer-

ences for all quotations, and the Italian material is particularly unreliable in detail.

58. After A. Schiaffini's edition see this text also, together with other memoirs by Florentine merchants, in Vittore Branca, ed., *Mercanti scrittori: ricordi nella Firenze tra Medioevo e Rinascimento: Paolo da Certaldo, Giovanni Morelli, Bonaccorso Pitti, Domenico Lenzi, Donato Velluti, Goro Dati, Francesco Datini, Lapo Niccolini, e Bernardo Machiavelli* (Milano: Rusconi, 1986): 84, par. 351.

59. Branca ed.: par. 82, p. 13, with reference to Morelli, *Proverbi* in *Ricordi* (1969): 47, for the proverbial phrase *misura dura*. Other passages with admonishments to use measure in Paolo's *Libro* paragraphs 3, 81, 232, 243, 375, 377, and 383 (Branca ed.: 5, 12, 45, 46, 92, 93, and 96).

60. Schiaffini ed.: 91–93; Branca ed.: 19 f., par. 103. See Remo Ceserani and Lidia De Federicis, eds., *Il materiale e l'immaginario*, 10 vols. (Torino: Loescher, 1979–1988): 3: 134 f., 597–600, 633.

61. Schiaffini ed.: 211–214. See Ceserani and De Federicis, 3: 599. Paolo da Certaldo (83 f.) is one of the many witnesses of the bourgeois practice of marrying off the daughters as early as possible, on the average around the age of fifteen, since unmarried women could be a greater burden and a less disposable commodity than they had been in feudal families. Consequently, Florentine fathers regularly falsified their declarations for the fiscal *catasto* in order to make their daughters appear younger. See Anthony Molho, "Deception and Marriage Strategy in Renaissance Florence: The Case of Women's Ages," *Renaissance Quarterly* 41 (1988): 193–217 at 205. Similar advice in Giovanni di Pagolo Morelli (1371–1444), *Ricordi*, ed. Vittore Branca (Firenze: Felice Le Monnier, 1956): 210. As evidenced by the memoirs conveniently available in V. Branca's *Mercanti scrittori* (1986), from Paolo da Certaldo's *Libro* to Francesco Guicciardini's *Memorie di famiglia*, the family was the vital structure and real center of the merchants' life and ethos, as it had been, in different ways, in early feudalism.

CHAPTER EIGHT: DANTE, PETRARCA, AND BOCCACCIO

1. Especially E. Köhler, "Uber das Verhältnis von Liebe, Tapferkeit, Wissen und Reichtum bei den Trobadors," in *Trobadorlyrik und höfischer Roman* (1962) 73 ff.

2. See Jaeger's (1987) interpretation of the philosophy of the Chartres masters.

3. A. Vallone (1950) has attempted to trace the poetic background to Dante's notion or, rather, "sentiment" of *cortesia* without any reference to social motivations but with clear awareness that the concept spans the whole period from the Provençals to Castiglione.

4. For example Köhler, Mancini ed. 4 f., 41.

5. *Poésies complètes du troubadour Marcabru*, ed. J.-M.-L. Dejeanne, Bibliothèque Méridionale . . . Faculté des Lettres de Toulouse, Sér. 1 vol. 12 (Toulouse: Édouard Privat, 1909) 187. This is poem 38, st. 6 v. 7 in MS. R5[a]; Dejeanne, 190, translates: "aussi galanterie tourne maintenant en libertinage."

6. "[Vulgare illustre] est etiam merito curiale dicendum, quia curialitas nil aliud est quam librata regula eorum que peragenda sunt; et quia statera huiusmodi librationis tantum in excellentissimis curiis esse solet, hinc est quod quicquid in actibus nostris bene libratum est, curiale dicatur. Unde cum istud in excellentissima Ytalorum curia sit libratum, dici curiale meretur. Sed dicere quod in excellentissima Ytalorum curia sit libratum, videtur nugatio, cum curia careamus. Ad quod facile respondetur. Nam licet curia, secundum quod unita accipitur, ut curia regis Alamaniae, in Ytalia non sit, membra tamen eius non desunt; et sicut membra illius uno Principe uniuntur, sic membra huius gratioso lumine rationis unita sunt. Quare falsum esset dicere curia carere Ytalos, quanquam Principe careamus, quoniam curiam habemus, licet corporaliter sit dispersa" (*VE* 1.18.4 f.). Cf. Emilio Pasquini, "cortesia," and P. V. Mengaldo, "curiale," *Enciclopedia Dantesca* 2. I quote the *De vulgari eloquentia* from the *Enciclopedia Dantesca* (henceforth *ED*), Appendice 763.

7. Mengaldo, *ED* 2: 288 on Aristide Marigo's pertinent comments in his edition of the *VE*, lxxx-lxxxvi, 154–157, and Francesco Di Capua, *Scritti minori*, 2 vols. (Roma, Parigi: Desclée et Co., 1959) 1: 286–288. Incidentally, in an interesting discussion of the *De vulgari eloquentia*, the British poet Donald Davie (*Purity of Diction in English Verse*, Oxford, London: Oxford University Press, 1953: 82–90 at 87 f.) connects Dante's notion of courtliness in *De vulgari eloquentia* with "the modern notion of urbanity"—a judgment that Robin Kirkpatrick, *Dante's* Paradiso *and the Limitations of Modern Criticism: A Study of Style and Poetic Theory* (Cambridge, England, and New York: Cambridge University Press, 1978) 74, cites approvingly. As we have seen, urbanity was already a traditional ingredient of curiality in the Middle Ages.

8. Compare P. V. Mengaldo, "aulico" and "curiale" in *ED*. Also, *De vulgari eloquentia* 1.16.5, 1.17.1, and 1.18.2 f. See the medieval meanings of *curialis* and *curialitas* as courtly, refined, bureaucratic, and appropriate to civil servants, in Latham's *Dictionary of Medieval Latin* (chap. 2 above, note 25).

9. "nisi forte novum aliquid atque intentatum artis hoc sibi preroget; ut nascentis militie dies, qui cum nulla prerogativa suam indignatur preterire dietam."

10. A. Viscardi in R. S. Loomis, ed. (1959; 1961) 423.

11. Charles T. Davis (1984), chap. 8 on Fra Remigio: see p. 203.

12. "Sì che non dica quelli de li Uberti di Fiorenza, né quelli de li Visconti da Melano: 'Perch'io sono di cotale schiatta, io sono nobile'; ché 'l divino seme non cade in schiatta, cioè in istirpe, ma cade ne le singulari persone, e, sì come di sotto si proverà, la stirpe non fa le singulari persone nobili, ma le singulari persone fanno nobile la stirpe." (*Cv* 4.19–21 at 20.)

13. Nicola Zingarelli, "La nobiltà di Dante," *Nuova Antologia* 332 (1927): 412: "La nobiltà di sangue Dante non la nega," since virtue can also be transmitted from father to son.

14. Cf. Maria Picchio Simonelli's forthcoming volume on *Inferno* 3 in the "Lectura Dantis Americana" (University of Pennsylvania Press).

15. "Cortesia e onestade è tutt'uno; e però che ne le corti anticamente le vertudi e li belli costumi s'usavano, sì come oggi s'usa lo contrario, si tolse quello vocabulo da le corti, e fu tanto dire cortesia quanto uso di corte."

16. Emilio Pasquini, *ED* 2: 227b.

17. *Onesta* in this Dantesque sonnet has precedents that point up its aesthetico-moral context rather than a more restricted moral one. *Adorna* is close to Dante's *onesta* in Guinizelli's "Passa per via adorna e sì gentile" ("Io voglio del ver la mia donna laudare"). See G. Contini, ed., *Poeti del Duecento*, 2 vols. (Milano, Napoli: R. Ricciardi, 1960) 2: 472. The subtext to Dante's sonnet was Cavalcanti's *ballata grande* "Veggio negli occhi della donna mia" (*Poeti del Duecento* 2: 521).

18. "decens composicio membrorum," which imposes a "membrorum omnium motus ordinatus et disposicio decens in omni habitu et actione." Jaeger (1987): 614 n. 132.

19. For a discussion of Dante's use of Sordello's poetry with particular regard to Sordello's *Ensenhamen d'onor*, see Ruggero M. Ruggieri, *L'umanesimo cavalleresco italiano da Dante al Pulci* (Roma: Edizioni dell'Ateneo, 1962) ch. 3, "Tradizione e originalità nel lessico 'cavalleresco' di Dante: Dante e i trovatori provenzali."

20. The popular *Nicomachean Ethics*, which began by defining politics as the science of the good, became available only in the twelfth century in three partial renderings from the Greek by an anonymous translator, and then in the thirteenth century in the complete translations by Robert Grosseteste and William of Moerbeke from the Greek, in addition to one from Arabic. Dante drew on Moerbeke's text and occasionally on Grosseteste's but leaned occasionally on Aquinas's and Albertus Magnus's commentaries.

21. Dante's polemical portrait of nobility as based on intellectual and moral excellence sounded offensive to aristocratic readers when the nobility of stock became the pillars of authoritarian regimes. See an exemplary case of political use of the *Convivio* in a *Lezione accademica* of 1732 by the Pisan Angelo Poggesi, recently brought to light by Domenico Pietropaolo in "Dante's Concept of Nobility and the Eighteenth-Century Tuscan Aristocracy," *Man and Nature / L'homme et la nature* 5 (1986): 141–152. It is interesting to find that the *Convivio* could be so instrumentalized to attack the degenerate and conceited Tuscan aristocracy.

22. M. Keen (1984) 146. Other interesting reminiscences from times gone by include "il gran barone" mentioned by Cacciaguida (*Pr* 16: 128), to wit Hugh the Great of Brandenburg, Otto III's Imperial Vicar who died in Florence in 1001, and William II of Sicily (1166–1189) in *Paradiso* 20: 64 f., who sees in Paradise how heaven appreciates a just ruler: "come s'innamora / lo ciel del giusto rege." Jacopo della Lana (1328) praised William II as liberal and his court as a hospitable place for arts and pleasure:

> liberalissimo. Non era cavalieri né d'altra condizione uomo, che fosse in sua corte o che passasse per quella contrada, che da lui non fosse provveduto; ed era lo dono

proporzionato a sua vertude. . . . In essa corte . . . erano li buoni dicitori in rima di ogni condizione, quivi erano li eccellentissimi cantatori, quivi erano persone d'ogni sollazzo che si può pensare virtudioso e onesto . . . li abitanti e sudditi nôtavano in allegrezza.

Rather than an objective reflection of the state of affairs in twelfth-century Sicily, this was a remarkable projection of the image of the court that had established itself in northern Italy. See A. Roncaglia, "Le corti medievali," in A. Asor Rosa, ed., *Letteratura Italiana* 1 (1982): 105, citing *La Comedia di Dante degli Allagherii col Commento di Jacopo della Lana, Bolognese*, ed. L. Scarabelli (Bologna: Tipografia regia, 1866) 3: 310.

23. Sonnet "Cortesia cortesia cortesia chiamo" in Mario Marti, ed., *Poeti giocosi del tempo di Dante* (Milano: Rizzoli, 1956) 391. All grace, the sonnet goes on, has been chased by *avarizia*, and those who have do not give. A younger contemporary of Dante's, Folgòre died in or before 1332.

24. Ruggero M. Ruggieri has adeptly highlighted this central concern in Dante's opus: see his article, "Cavalleria," in *ED* 1: 897–899, to which I refer the reader for the pertinent bibliography.

25. See Teodolinda Barolini, *Dante's Poets: Textuality and Truth in the Comedy* (Princeton, NJ: Princeton University Press, 1984), esp. 96–100, 108–112 on Guiraut and 164–173 on Bertran, as well as the philological studies on single troubadours by Michelangelo Picone: "I trovatori di Dante: Bertran de Born," *Studi e problemi di critica testuale* 19 (1979): 71–94; "Giraut de Bornelh nella prospettiva di Dante," *Vox Romanica* 39 (1980): 22–43; and "*Paradiso* IX: Dante, Folchetto e la diaspora trobadorica," *Medioevo romanzo* 8 (1981–1983): 47–89, in addition to his "Dante e la tradizione arturiana," *Romanische Forschungen* 94 (1982): 1–18. *Tenso, Bulletin of the Société Guilhem IX* 5.1 (1989) is a special issue on the theme of "Dante's Influence on (Our Reading of) the Troubadours." In particular it focuses on the way Dante has accustomed us to underline the troubadours' exalted sense of the lady's value and the absoluteness of love.

26. On Bertran see the ample commentary in *The Poems of the Troubadour Bertran de Born*, eds. W. D. Paden et al. (Berkeley, Los Angeles, and Oxford: University of California Press, 1986).

27. On the contrastive parallel between Bertran and Sordello in the *Divina Commedia* see T. Barolini, *Dante's Poets* (1984), "The Poetry of Politics: Bertran and Sordello" 153–172. It is not known whether Dante also knew Sordello's moral composition "Ensenhamen d'onor."

28. Davis (1984): chap. 4, "*Il buon tempo antico* (The Good Old Time)," chap. 5, "The Malispini Question" with further supportive arguments from detailed analysis of the manuscripts, and the Appendix "Recent Work on the Malispini Question."

29.　　　　　Mentre che fusti, Firenze, adornata
　　　　　　di buoni antichi cari cittadini,
　　　　　　i lontani e' vicini
　　　　　　adorârno el Lione e' suoi figliuoli;
　　　　　　ora se' meretrice pubblicata
　　　　　　in ogni parte insin tra' Saracini.

Text in Natalino Sapegno, ed., *Poeti minori del Trecento* (Milano, Napoli: R. Ricciardi, 1952) 28–30. See L. Martines (1979) 84.

30. Davis, chap. 3 "Poverty and Eschatology in the *Commedia*."

31. Martines 126–128 and the literature cited in his notes and bibliography, esp. pp. 340 and 347.

32. See A. Scaglione, "Dante's Poetic Orthodoxy: The Case of Pier della Vigna," *Lectura Dantis*, ed. Tibor Wlassics, 1 (Charlottesville, VA: Bailey Printing, 1987): 49–60, rpt. in Paolo Cherchi and Michelangelo Picone, eds., *Studi di Italianistica in onore di Giovanni Cecchetti* (Ravenna: Longo, 1988) 57–66.

33. On Adalbert of Bremen see Jaeger, esp. 67–81.

34. See *Convivio* 4.13.6–9, where a sense of self-restraint even in seeking the highest goals is stressed as part of wisdom, and specifically discipline and measure in seeking knowledge beyond the possible and the useful: "Nel primo de l'Etica dice che 'l disciplinato chiede di sapere certezza ne le cose, secondo che [ne] la loro natura di certezza si riceva.' . . . E però Paulo dice: 'Non più sapere che sapere si convegna, ma sapere a misura.'"

35. ". . . cum et mulieribus . . . inseruiret et in omni sermone omnibus affabilem esse et iucundum se uellet; domi uero etiam contumelias seruorum ancillarumque pertulit, ut ad id aliquando quod cupiebat, ueniret."

36. Sources for the theological aspect of the episode (Pope Boniface's promise to absolve Guido for his yet uncommitted sin of deceitful counseling) do not seem to have been located, but there is a similar story in a thirteenth-century French poem, *Valentin et Orson*, successful enough to have received a printed edition in 1489, where an archbishop attempts to seduce King Pepin's sister by promising her absolution beforehand for the sin of fornication.

37. R. Kirkpatrick, *Dante's* Paradiso *and the Limitations of Modern Criticism* (1978); idem, *Dante's* Inferno: *Difficulty and Dead Poetry* (Cambridge, England, and New York: Cambridge University Press, 1987). It may sound like a coincidental confirmation of the preceding analysis that, in his 1978 study, Kirkpatrick phrases his conclusion on "The Organisation of the Canto in the *Paradiso*" thus: "[Dante is,] within *the code of a divine courtliness*, the lover of Beatrice. And in the Twenty Third Canto, which, in portraying the place of the Blessed Virgin in Heaven, is the *supreme representation of the courtly life*, Dante proves his claim to participate, according to his own peculiar *virtues and abilities*, in the celebration of ultimate *civility*" (p. 177, emphasis mine).

38. Peter Dronke, *Dante and Medieval Latin Traditions* (Cambridge: Cambridge University Press, 1986); Jeremy Tambling, *Dante and Difference: Writing in the* Commedia (Cambridge: Cambridge University Press, 1988). The methodological impasse that is evident in recent Dante criticism may be highlighted by the fact that, convincing as these objectors may sound, they have not exploited alternative methods in a satisfactory manner. For critical assessments of Dronke's, Tambling's, and Kirkpatrick's works see the reviews by Teodolinda Barolini in *Renaissance Quarterly* 41.2 (1988): 293–294; 42.3 (1989): 537–540; and *Comparative Literature* (forthcoming, 1991); also, Richard H. Lansing on Tambling, *Italica* 67.4 (1990): 520–522.

39. Aurelio Roncaglia, "Per il 750° anniversario della Scuola poetica Siciliana," *Atti dell'Accademia Nazionale dei Lincei, Rendiconti della classe di*

scienze morali, storiche e filologiche, Serie 8ª: 38 (Roma: Accademia dei Lincei, 1983–1984) 321–333, has made an intriguing hypothesis about the manuscript copy of the Provençal corpus that Frederick II may have obtained from Ezzelino da Romano in Verona and made available to his court poets around 1232. But see Alberto Vàrvaro's strictures in A. Asor Rosa, ed., *Letteratura Italiana* 7.1 (1987): 92. See Zumthor (1987) 164–166 on the first methodical uses of written documents for literary transmission.

40. R. G. Witt (1988) 52.

41. On this aspect of Petrarca's poetic and moral psychology see my "Petrarca 1974: A Sketch for A Portrait" in A. Scaglione, ed., *Francis Petrarch, Six Centuries Later: A Symposium* (Chapel Hill: University of North Carolina Press; Chicago: Newberry Library, 1975) 1–24; idem, "Classical Heritage and Petrarchan Self-Consciousness in the Literary Emergence of the Interior 'I,'" *Altro Polo* 7 (Sydney, Australia, 1984): 23–34, rpt. in Harold Bloom, ed., *Modern Critical Views: Petrarch* (New York: Chelsea Press, 1989): 125–137.

Petrarca's appreciation for Occitan poetry needs no further arguing here; his taste for the "matter of Brittany," on the other hand, is not largely documented beyond such statements of awareness, tinged by condescendence for its sheer amenity and popular appeal, as in *Trionfi* 2: "Tr. Cupidinis," vv. 79–81: "quei che le carte empion di sogni: / Lancillotto, Tristano e gli altri erranti / onde convien che 'l vulgo errante agogni" (ed. C. Appel, Halle, 1901).

42. Lucie Brind'Amour in T. Klaniczay et al., eds. (1988): 450–453. The key texts and authors for Castille are *El cancionero de Baena* (1445), Juan de Mena, the Marquis of Santillana, Juan del Encina, Jorge Manrique, and Hernando de Ludueña (*Doctrinal de gentileza*); for Catalonia, especially Ausias March.

43. On the codification of Petrarchistic practice in the lyric after Bembo, especially with regard to the influential work of Girolamo Ruscelli, see Amedeo Quondam, "Livelli d'uso nel sistema linguistico del Petrarchismo," in Fernando Ferrara et al., eds., *Sociologia della letteratura*, Atti del 1º Convegno Nazionale, Gaeta 1974 (Roma: Bulzoni, 1978): 212–239.

44. Roger S. Loomis, "The Allegorical Siege in the Art of the Middle Ages," *American Journal of Archaeology* 2.23 (1919): 255–269, and Thomas M. Greene, "Magic and Festivity at the Renaissance Court," *Renaissance Quarterly* 40.4 (1987): 636–659 at 642.

45. For example, A. Scaglione, "Cinquecento Mannerism and the Uses of Petrarch," in O. B. Hardison, ed., *Medieval and Renaissance Studies 5* (Chapel Hill: University of North Carolina Press, 1971): 122–155.

46. The text is worth quoting:

> Lo basilisco a lo speco lucente
> tragge a morire cum risbaldimento,
> lo cesne canta plù gioiosamente
> quand'egli è presso a lo so finimento,
>   lo paon turba, istando plù gaudente,
> cum a soi pedi fa riguardamento,
> l'augel fenice s'arde veramente
> per ritornare in novo nascimento.

> In tai nature eo sentom'abenuto,
> che allegro vado a morte a le belleze,
> e 'nforzo 'l canto presso a lo finire;
> estando gaio torno dismarruto,
> ardendo 'n foco inovo in allegreze,
> per vui, plù gente, a cui spero redire.

The basilisk before the shining mirror / comes to death with joy, / the swan sings with greatest pleasure / when it approaches its end, / the peacock becomes perturbed when, / at the height of its rapture, it looks at its feet, / the phoenix burns itself to come back to a new life. / I feel I have acquired the nature of one of these animals / when I see I go toward my death in the name of beauty, / and sing more sharply as the end approaches; / even while I feel merry I become lost, / burning in fire I renew myself in joy, / all this because of you, most gentle one, to whom I seek to return.

Text from Bruno Panvini, ed., *Le rime della scuola siciliana* 1 (Firenze: Olschki, 1962). Trans. mine.

47. Text from Contini, ed., *Letteratura Italiana delle Origini* (1970). Frede Jensen's new edition of the Sicilian School (1986) is useful for its criteria of selection.

48. G. Contini, ed., *Poeti del Duecento* (1960): 1: 107.

49. Leonard Forster, *The Icy Fire: Five Studies in European Petrarchism* (Cambridge: Cambridge University Press, 1969; 1978), is a brilliant study of Petrarca's antitheses within the whole Petrarchist tradition.

50. The symmetric arrangement of this passage reminds the reader of the similar cadence in Marie de France's *Lai du chèvrefeuille*. Tristan discloses to Iseut that he is nearby in the forest by sending her a message in the form of a twig where he has carved the couplet: "Bele amie, si est de nus: / ne vus senz mei, ne jeo senz vus!" ("This is the way with us, my sweet friend: neither you without me, nor I without you!") Writing in France and England, the Norman Marie, perhaps the natural daughter of Geoffrey IV of Anjou, is supposed to have composed her *lais* between 1175–1189, and the *Isopet* and *Espurgatoire Saint Patrice* after 1189.

As to the precedent of Thomas, see Jean Charles Payen, ed., *Les* Tristan *en vers* (Paris: Garnier, 1974) 178 and 231: "La bele raïne, s'amie / en cui est sa mort e sa vie," vv. 1061 f.; "cum a dame, cum a s'amie, / en qui maint sa mort e sa vie," vv. 2711 f.

51. Contini, ed., *Poeti del Duecento* (1960): 1: 109.

52. G. Contini, ed., *Poeti del Duecento* (1960): 2: 602.

53. J. Vernon Hall, "*Decorum* in Italian Renaissance Literary Criticism," *Modern Language Quarterly* 4 (1943): 177–183.

54. See, for example, his letter no. 8 to the royal secretary Zanobi da Strada at Naples in Boccaccio, *Opere latine minori*, ed. F. Massera (Bari: Laterza, 1928): 130–135. On Boccaccio's social and political attitudes see Franco Gaeta in A. Asor Rosa, ed., *Letteratura italiana* 1 (1982): 215–228. Gaeta's section of the vol., pp. 149–255, deals with the transition "Dal comune alla corte rinascimentale."

55. See Aldo Scaglione, "Boccaccio, Chaucer, and the Mercantile Ethic," in

David Daiches and Anthony Thorlby, eds., *Literature and Western Civilization*, II: *The Medieval World* (London: Aldus Press, 1973): 579–600.

56. Thomas G. Bergin, *Boccaccio* (New York: Viking, 1981): 69, 142.

57. For example, Nicolas J. Perella, "The World of Boccaccio's *Filocolo*," *PMLA* 4 (1961): 330–339; A. Scaglione, *Nature and Love in the Late Middle Ages: An Essay on the Cultural Context of the Decameron* (Berkeley, Los Angeles: University of California Press; Cambridge, England: Cambridge University Press, 1963; rpt. Westwood, CT: Greenwood Press, 1976): chap. 4.

58. "considerata periculorum susceptio et laborum perpessio" nourished on "magnificentia, fidentia, patientia, perseverantia." Cicero, *De inventione* 2.54.163.

59. N. Elias, *The Court Society*, especially Appendix 2 "On the Position of the Intendant," 284–294, gives a trenchant description of the difference between bourgeois and aristocratic economic ethics in the *ancien régime*: the medieval aristocratic ethic was not very different.

60. For example, quote p. 63 in N. Elias, *The Court Society*.

61. "Vivon quasi tutti d'entrata facendo poca stima di chi non la spende tutta; si reputan a vergogna il trafficare, et chi attende al guadagno, ancorché fusse fatto con il mercatar in grosso, non è tenuto gentiluomo fra loro; per questo presumono d'esser molto superiori a' gentiluomini delle città mercantili, spendon volentieri et più che non han di rendita, però son sempre indebitati fino agli occhi." Quoted by C. Donati, *L'idea della nobiltà in Italia* (1988) 165 from G. Agnelli, "Relazione dello stato di Ferrara di Orazio della Rena, 1589," *Atti e memorie della Deputazione ferrarese di storia patria* 8 (1898): 30. On Petrarca's and Boccaccio's uses of chivalric traditions, especially in their "minor" works, see R. M. Ruggieri, *L'umanesimo cavalleresco italiano da Dante al Pulci* (Roma, 1962) chaps. 4 and 5, pp. 85–134.

CHAPTER NINE: RENAISSANCE TRANSFORMATIONS: I

1. See A. J. Vanderjagt, *Qui sa vertu anoblist* (1981). The manuscript (Brussels, Bibliothèque Royale MS. 9278–9280) used by Vanderjagt for his edition contains Jean Miélot's French version of Buonaccorso da Montemagno's *De nobilitate* and of Aurispa's rendering of Lucian's "Comparatio Hannibalis, Scipionis et Alexandri" before Minos from Lucian's Dialogues of the Dead. See Lucian, Loeb Classical Library (8 vols.) vol. 7, trans. M. D. Macleod (Cambridge, MA: Harvard University Press; London: W. Heinemann, 1961): 142–155. Keen (235) draws upon the same text from MS. 10497, f. 120v, of the Bibliothèque Royale of Brussels, allegedly containing a French version of a text by a Buonsignori da Siena—a mistaken identification. I am deeply thankful to P. O. Kristeller for calling my attention to Vanderjagt's work. Kristeller's *Iter Italicum* 3 (London: Warburg Institute; Leiden: E. J. Brill, 1983): 99, which gives MS. 10493–10497 (*Catalogue* p. 210) as Misc. 15th century, containing only Bonaccorsus's *de nobilitate* in French, probably in Jean Miélot's version, is

to be integrated with the information in Vanderjagt, who gives the full text of Miélot's free version of Aurispa's rendering from Lucian, collated with Aurispa's version, and another French translation (pp. 175–180) from the perhaps unique MS. 76 f. 26 of the Koninglijke Bibliotheek of The Hague, based on a slightly different version of Aurispa's text.

Livy 35.14 reported the tradition of a dialogue between Scipio and Hannibal. Asked by Scipio who was the greatest general, Hannibal responded by rating Alexander as first, Pyrrhus as second, and himself as third. When asked what, then, if he had vanquished Scipio, Hannibal answered that he would then have rated himself above all other generals. In Lucian's version, Scipio intervenes marginally at the end of the dialogue and Minos gives him second place between Alexander and Hannibal. Nowhere in the ancient texts is there any mention of the superiority of acting for the sake of the country rather than for personal glory.

2. The development of civic humanism as presented by Hans Baron and Eugenio Garin bears reconsideration in terms of the documents on moral attitudes toward duties of statesmanship and service to state and society. By Baron see, especially, his seminal *The Crisis of the Early Italian Renaissance; Civic Humanism and Republican Liberty in an Age of Classicism and Tyranny* [1955], rev. 1 vol. ed. with an epilogue (Princeton, N.J.: Princeton University Press, 1966). Of Garin's numerous relevant works it shall suffice to mention *L'Umanesimo Italiano. Filosofia e vita civile nel Rinascimento* (Bari: Laterza, 1965). On the philosophical connections between humanistic schools and medieval thought, including the pedagogical aspects of the rhetorical tradition, see Paul O. Kristeller's fundamental studies, for example his *Eight Philosophers of the Italian Renaissance* (Stanford: Stanford University Press, 1964) and *Renaissance Thought and Its Sources*, ed. Michael Mooney (New York: Columbia University Press, 1979).

3. See Vanderjagt 158 f., and 159 and 171 for following quotes. At variance with the spirit and letter of Lucian's text, Aurispa's Minos decrees that while Scipio was at least the others' equal in military prowess, he was definitely superior in love of country and all moral virtues: "itaque cum disciplina militari rebusque bellicis aut hische equalem aut prestanciorem sciamus, (patrie) pietate vero ceterisque animi virtutibus maxime hos superasse, te preferendum censeo." In Miélot Scipio deserves first place because he never exceeded the bounds of "prouesse chevalereuse," that is, never transgressed military discipline, and excelled "en toute aultre vertu." Since "vray honneur doit estre acquis par vertu nous jugons Scipion qui jamais ne saillis hors des lices de prouesse chevalereuse et meismement en toute aultre virtu as eu renommee pardessus tous ceulx de ton temps que tu ailles premier." Besides, he never indulged in cruel destruction of human beings simply for his own glory.

4. A. Grafton and L. Jardine (1986) emphasize this aspect of humanistic paideia, even while pointing out that the extant documents of teaching and philological activity fail to show a balance between grammatical and rhetorical concerns on the one hand and moral ones on the other, since in the practice of the schoolroom most humanistic teaching seemed to reduce itself to painstaking

grammatical and rhetorical *explication de texte*, as if even the great Erasmus assumed that philologically correct reading was sufficient to make a good Christian.

5. Jaeger (1987): esp. 601–608.

6. Jaeger (1987): 605: "This points up the fundamentally irrational nature of an education based on the formation of character. It relies on the personal moral authority of the teacher, and reasoning—certainly critical, independent thought—can become an offense against him, can diminish his authority. The old learning made the masters into an image of God, and the student's goal was to fashion himself in that image. Disputation and reasoning are fundamentally at odds with this goal. Awe and reverence are appropriate to it."

7. As already noted, this is the assumption in A. Grafton and L. Jardine (1986) with regard to both Italian and northern humanists, including Erasmus: see, for example, pp. 27, 83–98. See also their assessment of Ramus's impact on the turn toward practical social goals.

8. L. Martines (1979): 204. See an extended treatment of this matter in his *The Social World of the Florentine Humanists* (1963) and *Lawyers and State-craft in Renaissance Florence* (Princeton, NJ: Princeton University Press, 1968). More recently still, see the statistical studies by Roberto Antonelli, Simonetta Bianchini, and Christian Bec in A. Asor Rosa, ed., *Letteratura Italiana* 2 (1983): 171–267.

9. See Werner L. Gundersheimer, *Ferrara* (1973): 129–131, for the first label, and Benjamin Kohl, "Political Attitudes of North Italian Humanists in the Late Trecento," *Studies in Medieval Culture* 4 (1974): 418–427, for the second. "Subdital" refers to the rule of princes being praised as beneficial to the subjects, *subditi*.

10. John M. McManamon, *Funeral Oratory and the Cultural Ideals of Italian Humanism* (Chapel Hill: University of North Carolina Press, 1989): 88–91.

11. Cf. J. H. Hexter, *Reappraisals in History* (1979): "The Education of the Aristocracy in the Renaissance," 69.

12. The mental structures—what the "new historicists" like to call the "consciousness"—of the man of the Renaissance also comprise a new perception of physical space. If humanism was tied to the high bourgeoisie, often in alliance with the old or new nobility whenever this retained substantial power, the typical field of action and constant frame of reference was the space of the city, together with the political structures of the city-state. The visual image of such consciousness shines through the artistic works that formed the striking outer shell of the new society. That shell could not fail to impress domestic as well as foreign observers, certainly no less so than ancient Rome had attracted, awed, and conquered the barbarian invaders.

Dealing with the way painting incorporated the background of the new cityscapes in the representation of space, Samuel Y. Edgerton, *The Renaissance Rediscovery of Linear Perspective* (New York: Basic Books, 1975), as cited and paraphrased by L. Martines (1979): 275, relates linear perspective to the idea of "God's geometrically ordered universe" and concludes: "the commitment to linear perspective moved from a sense of having discerned the nature of God's mastery and was at the same time an effort to imitate His grand design.

Men would be gods." In this way of reading, the "realistic" control of nature achieved through the self-assurance of the new political masters would be a key to the humanistic art of the Quattrocento. (See L. Martines [1979], chaps. 11–13, on the representation of life and art in Quattrocento Italy from this "new historical" perspective.) If Renaissance culture can be reconsidered from this angle, some critical questions may come to mind. Since the artists, holding no personal power, were far from being self-assured and in control of nature, how could they express, as their own, perceptions that presumably belonged to their patrons? How could their master-patrons communicate to them and even impose on them feelings that were only half-conscious? Hence, did the ideal forms and motifs issue from the consumers or from the producers of the artistic representations? In other words, to what extent did the artistic forms reflect or, instead, create ideas and ideology?

13. See texts in Poggius Bracciolini, *Opera omnia*, 4 tomes (Torino, 1964–1969): 1: 1–31; 390–419; and 64–83 for the *De nobilitate* (see below).

14. See the *Epistola* in Mehus's ed. (1753): Part 1, p. 5.

15. "Istam . . . stoicam virtutem . . . , nudam, egentem, et pene molestam, quae non ingreditur civitates, sed deserta videtur et solitaria, . . . neque in hominum coetum et communem usum prodibit." P. Bracciolini, *Opera* 1 (1964): 64–83 at 81 f.

16. Besides the text in Bracciolini, *Opera omnia* (Torino, 1964–1969), see Chiensi's response in Bracciolini's 1657 edition.

17. See, also, his *De oboedientia* (1470–1484) on the relationship between moral duties and public obligations toward the powerful; *De fortitudine* (1481); five treatises on the virtues pertaining to the management of wealth: *De liberalitate, De beneficentia* (both 1493), *De splendore* (perhaps 1493), *De conviventia* (perhaps 1493, containing a lively sketch of contemporary courtly mores), and *De magnificentia* (probably after 1494); and *De magnanimitate* (1499), followed by its counterpart *De immanitate* (1501, on public cruelty). Pontano's philosophical foundations were mostly Aristotelian. See Cesare Vasoli, "G. Pontano," in *Letteratura Italiana: I Minori* 1 (Milano: Marzorati, 1961): 597–624, esp. 607 f.

18. *De sermone libri tres*, eds. Sergio Lupi and A. Risicato (Lugano: Thesaurus Mundi, 1954). Cf. A. Asor Rosa, ed., *Letteratura Italiana* 3.1 (1984): 65–67.

19. Leonardo da Vinci lent his genial services to Ludovico Sforza by designing the splendid tournament of 1491 for the double wedding of Ludovico with Beatrice d'Este and Duke Alfonso d'Este with Anna Sforza in Milan. On the elaborate preparations for Giuliano's tournament see R. M. Ruggieri, *L'umanesimo cavalleresco italiano da Dante al Pulci* (Roma, 1962): chap. 6, "Spirito e forme epico-cavalleresche nella *Giostra* del Poliziano," 135–162, and chap. 7, "Letterati poeti e pittori intorno alla giostra di Giuliano de' Medici," 163–198.

20. *Aeneae Silvii de curialium miseriis epistola* (1928): 31: 54. We shall remember that in this 1444 tractate, written in the form of a letter to Johann von Eich and first published in 1473, the eminent Italian humanist and future pope borrowed Peter of Blois's phrase, *miseriae curialium*. The text is also available in *Der Briefwechsel des Eneas Silvius Piccolomini*, ed. R. Wolkan, 4 vols.

(Wien: Hölder, 1909–1918): 1: 453–487; in an Italian version by G. Paparelli (Lanciano: Carabba, 1943) and in a German version in Enea Silvio Piccolomini, *Briefe, Dichtungen*, trans. Max Mell (München: Winkler, 1966): 152–193. Sergio Bertelli, *Le corti italiane* (1985): 7, states that it echoed Lucian's *De mercede conductis potentium familiaribus* and dealt with paid courtiers and the topos of their extreme corruption and maliciousness, as Tommaso Garzoni da Bagnacavallo would later do in his 1587 *Piazza universale di tutte le professioni del mondo*, dedicated to Alfonso d'Este. But Bertelli does not trace this topos further back to the medieval Church reformers' anticourt tradition, thus giving an example of the limited historical horizon that derives from the established way of dealing with such matters only within defined historical periods.

21. The term occurs repeatedly in a description of Ferrara's Belriguardo palace that is part of Giovanni Sabbadino degli Arienti's *De triumphis religionis*, a text from the last years of the century published in Werner L. Gundersheimer, *Art and Life at the Court of Ercole I d'Este* (Genève: Droz, 1972). See Eugenio Battisti in A. Prosperi, ed., *La Corte e il* Cortegiano 2: *Un modello europeo* (1980): 263 f., note.

22. "Est enim in curiis principum vitiosum litteras nosse et probri loco ducitur appellari disertus"; "atria regum et aulici tumultus, in quibus nec requies nec bonarum artium exercitatio nec virtutis amor aliquis regnat, sed avaritia tantum, libido, crudelitas, crapula, invidia et ambitio dominatur." Ed. Wolkan: 1: 484 f. and 487.

23. John F. D'Amico (1983): 120–123 on these biographies as a genre, with ample bibliography.

24. D'Amico (1983): 117 f. On the activities of the papal chancery within the Curia, see Thomas Frenz, *Die Kanzlei der Päpste der Hochrenaissance (1471–1527)* (Tübingen: Max Niemeyer, 1986). The important study by Paolo Prodi, *Il sovrano pontefice* (Bologna: Il Mulino, 1982), proposes to see the Renaissance Roman court, starting with Nicholas V, as the prototype of the absolutist state.

25. D'Amico (1983) for a detailed survey of clerical courts in Rome and employment of humanists in them.

26. D'Amico (1983): 13 f.

27. On the complex story of the *De cardinalatu* and its closeness to Castiglione, as well as on the literary demography of clerics versus laymen in the Italian Cinquecento literary world, see the magisterial Carlo Dionisotti, *Gli umanisti e il volgare fra Quattro e Cinquecento* (Firenze: F. Le Monnier, 1968), and idem, "Chierici e laici" (1960) in his *Geografia* (1976): 66–71. Dionisotti (1968): 76, declares Cortesi's book "the first and foremost document of a rhetoric of the vernacular," and deals at length (pp. 52–77) with the section "de sermone." See, also, D'Amico (1983): 49–53, 78–80, 162–164, 227–239, and A. Quondam, "La 'forma del vivere,'" in A. Prosperi, ed., *La Corte e il* Cortegiano 2 (1980): 32–37.

Other Cinquecento treatises in the same genre, of which Cortesi's is the major exemplar, were due to the pens of Girolamo Manfredi, Fabio Albergati, Girolamo Botero, and Girolamo Piatti, S.J. (see References).

28. D'Amico (1983): 46–50. See the partial translation in Kathleen Weil-

Garris and John F. D'Amico, *The Renaissance Cardinal's Ideal Palace: A Chapter from Cortesi's* De Cardinalatu ([Rome]: Edizioni dell'Elefante, American Academy in Rome, [1980]). On high ecclesiastical ceremonial see the work of Cortesi's younger contemporary, Agostino Patrizi Piccolomini (ca. 1435–1496), *Sacrarum caeremoniarum sive rituum ecclesiasticorum S. Rom. Ecclesiae*, postrema editio (Venetiis: Iuntae, 1582); [idem,] *L'oeuvre de Patrizi Piccolomini ou le Cérimonial papal de la première Renaissance*, ed. Marc Dykmans, 2 vols. (Città del Vaticano: Biblioteca Apostolica Vaticana, 1980–1982).

29. D'Amico (1983): 57 f.

30. D'Amico (1983): chap. 4, "The Roman Academies," 89–112.

31. Calmeta, *Prose e lettere edite e inedite (con appendice di altri inediti)*, ed. Cecil Grayson (Bologna: Commissione per i Testi di Lingua, 1959): 60–77 for the *Vita del facondo poeta vulgare Serafino Aquilano*. D'Amico (1983): 102–107. Calmeta's biography was for the first time incorporated into the edition of Serafino's works in the *Opere del facundissimo Seraphino Aquilano* (Venice, 1505).

32. See Stephen D. Kolsky, "The Courtier as Critic: Vincenzo Calmeta's *Vita del facondo poeta vulgare Serafino Aquilano*," *Italica* 67 (1990): 161–172 at 162.

33. Zini's tractate was published in Johannes Mattaeus Giberti, *Opera nunc primum collecta*, eds. P. and G. Ballerini (Hostiliae: A. Carattonius, 1740). See Prosperi in A. Prosperi, ed. (1980): 88–90. On Contarini see Elizabeth G. Gleason's study in Ellery Salk, ed., *Culture, Society and Religion in Early Modern Europe: Essays by the Students and Colleagues of William J. Bouwsma* (special issue of *Historical Reflections/Reflexions Historiques* 15.1, 1988).

34. Christian Bec in A. Asor Rosa, ed., *Letteratura Italiana* 2 (1983): 297, reiterates Gino Benzoni's conclusion that after 1550 the continued strength of the Venetian bourgeoisie vis-à-vis other areas of Italy, including Florence, was responsible for the preservation of the humanistic values in Venice while they were being lost elsewhere. There may be a connection between this predicament and the bourgeois realism to be observed in Contarini's and Zini's critiques of ecclesiastical extravagance. See Benzoni, *Gli affanni della cultura. Intellettuali e potere nell'Italia della Controriforma e barocca* (Milano: Feltrinelli, 1978): 33.

35. On Castiglione's central role within the general context of the idea of nobility and the gentleman, see the excellent general study by Claudio Donati, *L'idea di nobiltà in Italia* (1988). An elegant early study of courtliness and conduct, of rather difficult access, is Salvatore Battaglia, "La letteratura del comportamento e l'idea del cortigiano" (1937) in his *Mitografia del personaggio* (Milano: Rizzoli, 1968): 85–96, at 91, on the court as the locus for an élite to develop all its potential of civilized refinement—we could say its supreme entelechy. On the same theme, Giovanni Getto, *Letteratura e critica nel tempo* (Milano: Marzorati, 1968): "La corte estense luogo d'incontro di una civiltà letteraria," [1953], 219–240; Giorgio Bàrberi Squarotti, *L'onore in corte. Dal Castiglione al Tasso* (Milano: Angeli, 1986); and Marcello Verdenelli, *La teatralità della scrittura: Castiglione, Parini, Leopardi, Campana, Pavese* (Ravenna: Longo, 1989): 23–43.

36. For an excellent survey of Renaissance historiography from the point of view of understanding the role of the court, from Burckhardt and De Sanctis through Croce to Antonio Gramsci and Federico Chabod, see Carlo Ossola, "'Rinascimento' e 'Risorgimento': La corte tra due miti storiografici," first in C. Mozzarelli and G. Olmi, eds., *La corte nella cultura e nella storiografia. Immagini e posizioni tra Otto e Novecento* (Roma, 1983): 205–236, then in C. Ossola, *Dal 'cortegiano' all' 'uomo di mondo'* (Torino: Einaudi, 1987): 155–181.

37. "Questa nostra fatica, se pur mai sarà di tanto favor degna che da nobili cavalieri e valorose donne meriti esser veduta . . ." (3.1).

38. Jaeger: 153 f., 160, and 147–149.

39. Also, "liberissimo e onestissimo commerzio," "onestissimi costumi," "modestia e grandezza" (1.4), all referring to the effect on the courtiers of the Duchess's imposing presence.

40. Elias, *The Court Society* 231 f.

41. "Ritrovandosi il cortegiano nella scaramuzza o fatto d'arme o battaglia di terra . . . , dee discretamente procurar di appartarsi dalla moltitudine e quelle cose segnalate ed ardite che ha da fare, farle con minor compagnia che pode al conspetto de tutti i più nobili ed estimati omini che siano nell'esercito, e massimamente alla presenzia . . . del suo re o di quel signore a cui serve" (whenever the courtier chances to be engaged in a skirmish or an action or a battle in the field, . . . he should discreetly withdraw from the crowd, and do the outstanding and daring things that he has to do in as small a company as possible and in the sight of all the noblest and most respected men in the army, and especially . . . his king or the prince he is serving. C. Singleton's trans.) See Michael West (1988): 654, for the military connotations of this passage.

42. "Oltre alla bontà, il vero e principal ornamento dell'animo in ciascuno penso io che siano le lettere, benché i Franzesi solamente conoscano la nobiltà delle arme e tutto il resto nulla estimino; di modo che non solamente non apprezzano le lettere, ma le aborriscono, e tutti e litterati tengon per vilissimi omini; e pare loro dir gran villania a chi si sia, quando lo chiamano *clero*" (1.42). The discussion of French attitudes on the education of the nobility continues through the following chapter, and Giuliano de' Medici expresses his conviction that once Francis I becomes king, he will change this situation by encouraging literary endeavors even at court.

43. Vittorio Cian (commentary to his edition of the *Cortegiano* [1947]: 112) recalled Flavio Biondo's *De litteris et armis comparatione*, Filelfo, Cristoforo Lanfranchini's *Tractatus seu quaestio utrum praeferendus sit miles an doctor* (Brixiae: Angelus Britannicus, 1497), Muzio's *Il gentilhuomo*, De Ferraris's *De dignitate disciplinarum*, and other texts.

44. "Oltre alla bontà, il vero e principal ornamento dell'animo in ciascuno penso io che siano le lettere"—something which, he says, the French are not prepared to recognize (beginning of 1.42); "voglio che nelle lettere sia più che mediocremente erudito, almeno in questi studi che chiamano d'umanità; e non solamente della lingua latina, ma ancor della greca abbia cognizione, . . . nei poeti e non meno negli oratori ed istorici ed ancor esercitato nel scriver in versi e prosa, massimamente in questa nostra lingua vulgare" (beginning of 1.44).

45. "Uno amante non povero né sozzo né disorrevole né vile . . . Questo

vero quando in lui sia prudenza, modestia, sofferenza e virtù . . . ; (persona)
studiosa di buone arti, litterata e ornata di molte virtù. . . . . Destro, robusto della
persona, animoso, ardito, mansueto e riposato; tacito, modesto, motteggioso e
giocoso quanto e dove bisognava; lui eloquente, dotto e liberale, amorevole,
pietoso e vergognoso, astuto, pratico, e sopra tutto fidelissimo; lui in ogni gentilezza prestantissimo, schermire, cavalcare, lanciare, saettare e a qual vuoi
simile cosa adattissimo et destrissimo; lui in musica, in lettere, in pittura, in
scultura, e in ogni buona e nobile arte peritissimo, e in queste anche e in molte
altre lode a quale si sia primo era non secondo." *Ecatonfilea* in L. B. Alberti,
Opere volgari, ed. Cecil Grayson, 3 vols. (Bari: Laterza, 1960–1973): 3;
(1973): 199–219 at 204 f. Here and hereafter I give my translation of Alberti.

46. "Di statura mediocre, commodamente agiato de' beni della fortuna, nobile d'animo e di sangue, letterato, musico, . . . prudente, legiadro, animoso,
pratico, astuto, grato, amorevole, affabile, piacevole e dolce." Text in *Trattati
d'amore del Cinquecento*, ed. Zonta (1912): 164. See Vallone (1955): 55.

47. Saccone (1983): 58–61. Castiglione 1.26 speaks of the concealed art of
the orator who is trying to "dupe" the jury: "la qual se fosse stata conosciuta,
arìa dato dubbio negli animi del populo di non dover esser da quella ingannati."
He does refer to the paraphernalia of the courtier's intellectual and social refinement as "pleasurable enticement" (*questo velo di piacere, illecebre*) in order
to "beguile the prince with salutary deception," "ingannarlo con inganno salu-
tifero" (4.9–4.10).

48. "Pare che farle bene non sia altro che porgersi con molta modestia
giunta con leggiadria e aria signorile, tale ch'elle molto dilettino a chi ti mira.
Queste sono 'l cavalcare, 'l danzare, l'andar per via e simili. Ma vi bisogna
soprattutto moderare i gesti e la fronte, i moti e la figura di tutta la persona con
accuratissimo riguardo, e con arte molto castigata al tutto, che nulla ivi paia
fatto con escogitato artificio; ma creda chi le vede che questa laude in te sia
dono innato dalla natura." L. B. Alberti, *Opere volgari . . . inedite . . .* , ed.
A. Bonucci, 5 vols. (Firenze: Tipografia Galileiana, 1843–1849): 3; (1845):
72 f.

49. "Avendo io già più volte pensato meco onde nasca questa grazia, trovo
una regula universalissima, . . . fuggir quanto più si po . . . la affettazione; e,
per dir forse una nova parola, usar in ogni cosa una certa sprezzatura, che
nasconda l'arte, e dimostri ciò che si fa e dice, venir fatto senza fatica e quasi
senza pensarvi. Da questo credo io che derivi assai la grazia: perché delle cose
rare e ben fatte ognun sa la difficultà, onde in esse la facilità genera grandissima
maraviglia. Però si po dir quella esser vera arte, che non appare esser arte; né
più in altro si ha da poner studio che nel nasconderla. . . . E ricordomi io già
aver letto esser stati antichi oratori eccellentissimi, i quali . . . sforzavansi di far
credere ad ognuno sé non aver notizia alcuna di lettere; e dissimulando il
sapere . . ." (1.26; translation mine).

There has been much discussion on the precise meaning of Castiglione's *grazia*, with attempts to stress the novelty of his use of the term. But it is pertinent
to remember that in Cicero *gratiosus* meant gracious, graceful, and agreeable,
and was used in medieval portraits of idealized knightly characters, as we saw
in Lambert of Ardres's portrait of Arnold of Guines (see my chap. 3).

50. "Ponga ogni studio e diligenzia di passar in ogni cosa un poco più avanti

che gli altri, di modo che sempre tra tutti sia per eccellente conosciuto" (1.21).

51. "Motus et habitudo venusta simplicitate compta atque amena, quae statum magis sapiat dulcem et quietem quam agitationem. . . . Sint in viro motus firmiores et status celeri palaestra admodum ornati." Paragraphs 44 f. of book 2. See Cecil Grayson's edition (Bari: Laterza, 1975): 78 f. On these classical principles and the polemic concerning Raphael and Michelangelo see Robert J. Clements, "Michelangelo on Effort and Rapidity in Art," *Journal of the Wartburg and Courtauld Institutes* 17 (1954): 301–310, and *Michelangelo's Theory of Art* (New York: New York University Press, 1961): 55–66. On Castiglione's relationship to art theory see Fritz Ertl, *Castigliones Beziehungen und Verhältnis zu den bildenden Künsten* (Nürnberg: Stadtmission Nürnberg, 1933). Also Eugenio Battisti, "Lo stile cortigiano," in A. Prosperi, ed. (1980): 255–271 at 255 f.

52. A. R. Jones in Armstrong and Tennenhouse, eds. (1988): 46 f., for a feminist evaluation of the female role in Nifo's tractate.

53. Curtius (1963): 178 f.

54. Eduardo Saccone, "*Grazia, sprezzatura, affettazione* in the *Courtier*" (1983), and "The Portrait of the Courtier in Castiglione" (1987), has called attention to Aristotle's *Nicomachean Ethics*.

55. 1.26, trans. Singleton (1959): 42. Jaeger (1987): 587 f.

56. "Temperanzia . . . , ché quando un animo è concorde di questa armonia, per mezzo della ragione poi facilmente riceve la vera fortezza" (4.17–4.18); "prudenzia, bontà, fortezza e temperanzia d'animo" (1.41). "Dolcezza," too: "la dolcezza ed eccellenzia de' stili" (1.44). "La prudenzia, la magnanimità, la continenzia e molte altre [virtù]" are equally desirable in women (3.4). "La temperantia, la fortezza" (4.4); "la bontà . . . accompagnata con la prontezza d'ingegno e piacevolezza e con la prudentia e notizia di lettere e di tante altre cose"; "quanto onore ed utile nasca a lui ed alli suoi dalla giustizia, dalla liberalità, dalla magnanimità, dalla mansuetudine e dall'altre virtù che si convengono a bon principe" (4.5). There is a natural progression among the virtues, since temperance provides a harmonious foundation for the other virtues, justice, on a higher level still, makes them all operative, and magnanimity enhances them all; in this happy chain "la liberalità, la magnificenzia, la cupidità d'onore, la mansuetudine, la piacevolezza, la affabilità, e molte altre" (4.18) are also linked. Once again a similar list at 4.9 and 4.22, adding "continenzia, sapienzia, religione e clemenzia." In book 3, dealing with the woman-courtier, we find the famous eulogy of Isabel of Castille, praised as "chiaro esempio di vera bontà, di grandezza d'animo, di prudenzia, di religione, d'onestà, di cortesia, di liberalità, in somma d'ogni virtù," and also, most pertinent in a political figure, "il maraviglioso giudicio ch'ella ebbe in conoscere ed elegere i ministri atti a quelli offici nei quali intendeva d'adoperarli" (the marvelous judgment in recognizing and choosing the most competent ministers for affairs of state—3.35).

57. A. Scaglione, ed., *The Emergence of National Languages* (Ravenna: Longo, 1983).

58. C. Dionisotti, *Gli umanisti e il volgare fra Quattro e Cinquecento* (1968).

59. Calmeta, *Prose e lettere edite e inedite*, ed. C. Grayson (1959).

60. See Maria Luisa Doglio, "Le *Instituzioni* di Mario Equicola: dall'*institutio principis* alla formazione del segretario," *Giornale Storico della Letteratura Italiana* 159 (1982): 505–535.

61. "'Il modo di descrivere loro amore fu nuovo e diverso da quello degli antichi latini; questi senza respetto, senza reverenzia, senza timore di infamar sua donna apertamente scrivevano . . . dove il desio li spingea. Provenzali gentilmente con dissimulazione nascondevano ogni lascivia de affetti. . . . Disio di onorare più che altro mostravano, dicendo: 'Amore vuol castità.'" End of book 5, p. 181v of 1526 edition.

62. P. O. Kristeller, *The Philosophy of Marsilio Ficino* (New York: Columbia University Press, 1943; rpt. Gloucester, MA: Peter Smith, 1964): 285.

63. G. Ferroni, "*Sprezzatura* e simulazione," in C. Ossola, ed., *La Corte e il* Cortegiano 1 (1980): 119–147, and A. Quondam, "La 'forma del vivere': Schede per l'analisi del discorso cortigiano," in A. Prosperi, ed., *La Corte e il* Cortegiano 2 (1980): 15–68, especially 17–19.

64. The issue was first raised by Burckhardt, who held that the chief motive of all the courtier's actions was not—although the author dissimulates this—the service of the prince, but rather the attainment of his own perfection as a human being: "It was for this society—or rather for his own sake—that the 'cortigiano,' as described to us by Castiglione, educated himself. He was the ideal man of society [der gesellschaftliche Idealmensch], and was regarded by the civilization of that age as its choicest flower; and the court existed for him far rather than he for the court. Indeed, such a man would have been out of place at any court, since he himself possessed all the gifts and the bearing of an accomplished ruler, and because his calm supremacy in all things, both outward and spiritual, implied a too independent nature [ein zu selbstständiges Wesen]." *The Civilization of the Renaissance in Italy*, trans. S. G. C. Middlemore (Vienna: Phaidon Press; New York: Oxford University Press, 1937): part 5, "Society and Festivals," chap. 5, "The perfect man of society," 200 (same text also New York: Harper & Row, 1958, 2: 382; 282 f. of It. ed.; German original ed. Werner Kaegi, Berlin-Leipzig: Deutsche Verlags-Anstalt Stuttgart, 1930, 2: 277).

For recent examples of scholarly reading of Castiglione's courtier as an independent agent dedicated to the cult of the self, being so idealized as to have no appreciable bearing on political or moral realities, see Joseph A. Mazzeo, *Renaissance and Revolution: The Remaking of European Thought* (New York: Pantheon, 1965): 137, and Wayne A. Rebhorn, "Ottaviano's Interruptions: Book IV and the Problem of Unity in *Il libro del Cortegiano*," *Modern Language Notes* 87 (1972): 37–59. For a contrary opinion, cf. E. Saccone, "*Grazia, sprezzatura, affettazione* in the *Courtier*" (1983) and "The Portrait of the Courtier in Castiglione" (1987). The thesis of the moral purpose of the *Cortegiano* as basic element of unity among its four books finds a precedent as far back as Vittorio Cian: see Cian's note as quoted in Carlo Cordié's edition (pp. 291 f.). Lawrence V. Ryan, "Book IV of Castiglione's *Courtier*: Climax or Afterthought?," *Studies in the Renaissance* 19 (1972): 156–179, examines the two alternatives, while F. Whigham (1984): 107 and 200, n. 104, finds the question rather moot. An informed discussion of such matters must be based on the manuscript tradition: on this basis Ghino Ghinassi has shown in the second redaction (1521) a rapprochement to an ecclesiastical-imperial line (it is in 1521 that Castiglione became an ecclesiastic) which postulated the court and the courtier as a point of harmonization for humanistic desiderata. Cf. Ghinassi, ed., *La seconda redazione del* Cortegiano *di Baldassarre Castiglione* (Firenze: G. C. Sansoni, 1968), and a discussion of this philological vantage point in G. Ferroni, "*Sprezzatura* e simulazione," in C. Ossola, ed., *La corte e il* Cortegiano (1980): 119–121. Also, on Castiglione's rapprochement to ecclesiastical circles, José Guidi, "Baldassar Castiglione et le pouvoir politique: du gentilhomme de cour au nonce pontifical," in André Rochon, ed., *Les écrivains et le pouvoir en Italie à l'époque de la Renaissance (première série)* (Paris: Université de la Sorbonne Nouvelle, Centre de recherche sur la Renaissance italienne, 1973): 243–278. In a dense review of V. Cian, *Un illustre nunzio pontificio* (1951), C. Dionisotti, *Giornale Storico della Letteratura Italiana* 129 (1952): 31–57 at 41, underlined this supposed *frattura* ("fracture"), but identified it with a moral situation that characterizes a large area of the early Cinquecento.

65. Jaeger: 9 f. Objecting to Singleton's translation of Castiglione's key term *vergogna*—corresponding to Cicero's *verecundia*—as "shame," Jaeger (9 f., 116, and 273 n. 7) renders it with "reverence" and "considerateness."

66. "Essendo il male contrario al bene e 'l bene al male, è quasi necessario che per la opposizione e *per un certo contrapeso* l'un sostenga e fortifichi l'altro, e mancando o crescendo l'uno, così manchi o cresca l'altro perché niuno contrario è senza l'altro suo contrario. Chi non sa che al mondo non saria la giustizia, se non fossero le ingiurie? la magnanimità se non fossero li pusillanimi? . . . la verità se non fosse la bugia? Però ben dice Socrate, appresso Platone, maravigliarsi che Esopo non abbia fatto un apologo, nel quale finga Dio, poiché non avea mai potuto unire il piacere e 'l dispiacere insieme, avergli attaccati con la estremità di modo che 'l principio dell'uno sia il fin dell'altro; poiché vedemo niuno piacer poterci mai esser grato, se 'l dispiacere non gli precede. . . . Però, essendo le virtù state al mondo concesse per grazia e don della natura, subito i vicii, per quella *concatenata contrarietà*, necessariamente le furono compagni; di modo che sempre, crescendo o mancando l'uno, forza è che così l'altro cresca o manchi." 2.2, Cordié ed.: 95 f. (emphasis and trans. mine). Jaeger: 82 and C. Ossola (1987): 68 f.

67. See, for example, Corrado Rosso's numerous studies on the subject, principally *Moralisti del "bonheur"* (Pisa: Goliardica, 2d ed. 1977) and *Il serpente e la sirena: dalla paura del dolore alla paura della felicità* (Napoli: Edizioni Scientifiche Italiane, 1972).

68. This aspect of "play" has a rather different, more historical focus than we find in some recent interpretations that derive from Huizinga's notion of *homo ludens*. See, for example, Thomas M. Greene, "The *Cortegiano* and the Choice of a Game" in Hanning and Rosand (1983): 1–15, and Robert W. Hanning, "Castiglione's Verbal Portrait: Structures and Strategies," ibid.: 131–141, especially 137.

69. "Gentiluomini sono chiamati quelli che oziosi vivono dei proventi delle loro possessioni abbondantemente, senza avere alcuna cura o di coltivare o di alcun'altra fatica a vivere. Questi tali sono perniciosi in ogni repubblica; ma più

perniciosi sono quelli che, oltre alle predette fortune, comandano a castella, ed hanno sudditi che obbediscono loro. Di queste due sorti d'uomini ne sono pieni il regno di Napoli, Terra di Roma, la Romagna e la Lombardia. . . . Colui che vuole fare dove sono assai gentiluomini una repubblica, non la può fare, se prima non gli spegne tutti." Vice versa, the prince who wants to found a principality in a region of democratic tradition cannot succeed "se non trae di quella equalità molti d'animo ambizioso ed inquieto, e quelli fa gentiluomini in fatto e non in nome, donando loro castella e possessioni, e dando loro favore di sustanzie e d'uomini, acciò che posto in mezzo di loro, mediante quelli mantenga la sua potenza, e gli altri siano costretti a sopportare quel giogo che la forza, e non altro mai, può far loro sopportare." In other words, a de facto feudal order, synonymous with power without equality, is necessary to govern when the people are not free.

See C. Donati, *L'idea di nobiltà in Italia* (1988): 29–36 on Machiavelli and Guicciardini on nobility. I shall cite the texts from Machiavelli, *Tutte le opere*, ed. Mario Martelli (Firenze: Sansoni, 1971).

70. Andrea Battistini, "I manuali di retorica dei Gesuiti," in Gian Paolo Brizzi, ed., *La "Ratio studiorum": Modelli culturali e pratiche educative dei Gesuiti in Italia tra Cinque e Seicento* (Roma: Bulzoni, 1981): 77–120 at 80 on the hardship of classical education in Jesuit schools as a rite of passage, a heroic test that qualified for noble leadership in society. I must add that the crucial, repeated tests of the Jesuit novice and priest, the Spiritual Exercises, were in their way an extension of the ordeal of the "vigil" as part of the dubbing ceremonial.

71. Cf. Brizzi, "Educare il principe, formare le élites: I Gesuiti e Ranuccio I Farnese," in Gian Paolo Brizzi, Alessandro D'Alessandro, and Alessandra Del Fante, *Università, Principe, Gesuiti. La politica farnesiana dell'istruzione a Parma e Piacenza (1545–1622)*, Centro Studi "Europa delle Corti" / Biblioteca del Cinquecento (Roma: Bulzoni, 1980): 135–211 at 154: "non solo nella pietà et nelle lettere, . . . ma in quelli altri esercitij proprij de Nobili, et necessarij a Cavaglieri," etc.

72. Ezio Raimondi, *Politica e commedia* (Bologna: Il Mulino, 1972): 266, on the particular motif of *astuzia* in Machiavelli. Raimondi also relates Machiavelli to Cicero's ethical ideas. For a recent reexamination, Wayne A. Rebhorn, *Foxes and Lions: Machiavelli's Confidence Men* (Ithaca, NY: Cornell University Press, 1988).

73. "renuntiaranno alla republica e faranno professione all'ordine suo et mai più poi potranno pretendere al grado civile o alla benivolentia del populo." Prosperi in A. Prosperi, ed. (1980): 83 f.

CHAPTER TEN: RENAISSANCE TRANSFORMATIONS: II

1. Quondam in Prosperi (1980): 37–41, using the edition-translation by Margherita Isnardi Parente (Napoli: Morano, 1977), especially 72 f. The symbolic use of court ceremonial as part of the psychological and legal environment for monarchic absolutism from Francis I to Louis XIV is penetratingly discussed

by Ralph E. Giesey, *Cérémonial et puissance souveraine: France, XVe-XVIIe siècles*, trans. Jeannie Carlier, Cahiers des Annales no. 41 (Paris: Armand Colin, 1987). Giesey (17) criticizes the incorrect extension of Kantorowicz's notion of "the king's two bodies" to identify the king's mystic body (the body politic) with Christ's mystic body as a metaphysical foundation of absolutism, and essentially agrees with N. Elias on the Versailles court ritual as an instrument to "domesticate" the nobility by subjecting it to the king's arbitrary will. However, against Elias's contention that this evolution was consciously planned, he sees it rather as a chance development that only in retrospect acquired its charged symbolic meaning (79–85).

2. The first edition (Sevilla: Jácobo Cromberger), unauthorized, was immediately revised, much expanded, and published under the new title (Valladolid: Nicolás Tierri). See Croll's analysis of the heavily Gorgianic ornamentation in the "schematic" style in his "The Sources of the Euphuistic Rhetoric" [1916], rpt. in J. Max Patrick and Robert O. Evans, eds., *Style, Rhetoric, and Rhythm. Essays by Morris W. Croll* (Princeton: Princeton University Press, 1966): 241–295, esp. 252–254. John Lyly is reputed to have been influenced by Guevara for his *Euphues*. See the useful survey by Joseph R. Jones, *Antonio de Guevara* (Boston: Twaine, 1975).

3. On Guevara's success in Italy see Paul F. Grendler, *Schooling in Renaissance Italy: Literacy and Learning, 1300–1600* (Baltimore: Johns Hopkins University Press, 1989): 300–304 and 422–424 on Italian editions, with no mention of the *Menosprecio*. See Quondam in Prosperi (1980): 41–54 on the *Relox* and 63–68 on the *Menosprecio*.

4. Cf. the edition by A. Alvarez de la Villa (Paris: Louis Michaud, [1912 or 1914]).

5. *Menosprecio*, ed. M. Martínez de Burgos (Madrid: Ediciones de "La Letura," 1915).

6. For the inner motives of the turn to the pastoral, see, for example, *Menosprecio*, ed. Martínez de Burgos, 180: "Oh how often was I seized with a desire to retire from court, to withdraw from the world, to become a hermit or a Carthusian monk; but I did not desire this because I was virtuous but because I was desperate, because the king did not give me what I wanted, and the favorite refused to see me." Translated in J. R. Jones, *Antonio de Guevara* 94. The *Aviso* is supposed to have had an important impact on the satire of the courtier/favorite in the picaresque novel starting with the *Lazarillo de Tormes* (1554). Cf. Jones: 87–89.

7. See, for a few stimulating contributions: Raymond Klibansky, Erwin Panofsky, and Fritz Saxl, *Saturn and Melancholy* (1964); Mircea Eliade, *Le mythe de l'éternel retour. Archétypes et répétitions* (Paris: Gallimard, 1949; 1969; 1985); translation of 1949 edition in *Cosmos and History; The Myth of the Eternal Return*, trans. Willard R. Trask (New York: Harper Torchbooks, 1959), and *The Myth of the Eternal Return, or, Cosmos and History* (New York: Pantheon Books, 1965; Garland, 1985; London: Routledge, 1988); Harry Levin, *The Myth of the Golden Age in the Renaissance* (Bloomington: Indiana University Press, 1969); Gustavo Costa, *La leggenda dei secoli d'oro nella letteratura italiana* (Bari: Laterza, 1972); Frank E. and Fritzie P. Manuel, "Sketch for a Natural History of Paradise," *Daedalus* (Winter 1972): 83–128.

8. *Li livres dou Tresor* 8.1; also in the classic Tuscan version by Bono Giamboni: *Il Tesoro di Brunetto Latini volgarizzato da Bono Giamboni*, ed. Luigi Gaiter (Bologna: Commissione per i Testi di Lingua, 1878–1883): 4:11. This is the only complete edition but it is not regarded as methodologically correct (cf. Segre and Marti, *La prosa del Duecento* [1959]: 1072). Giamboni's version of *Il Tesoro* had been printed at Treviso: Gerardo Flandino, 1474, and Venice: per Marchio Sessa, 1533, and so on; that of Brunetto's *Etica* at Florence: Domenico Maria Manni, 1734.

9. Erwin Panofsky, "The Early History of Man in Two Cycles of Paintings by Piero di Cosimo," in *Studies in Iconology* (New York: Oxford University Press, 1939; New York: Harper Torchbooks, 1962).

10. Lorenzo de' Medici, *Opere*, ed. Attilio Simioni, 2 vols. (Bari: G. Laterza, 1913–1914; 2d ed. 1939): 1: 274–281.

11. "spedale delle speranze, sepoltura delle vite, . . . mercato delle menzogne, scola de le fraudi, . . . paradiso de i vizi, inferno de le virtù. . . . Né ermo, né bosco, né caverna, né tomba, . . . sia pur quanto si voglia orrida, . . . bestiale." Ed. G. Battelli (Lanciano: Carabba, 1914) 11, 14 f. See Franco Gaeta in A. Asor Rosa, ed., *Letteratura Italiana* 1 (1982): 251–253.

12. F. 27r of the Venice: Gherardo, 1554 edition. Quondam: 56–67.

13. Cited by Vallone (1955): 73 from Saba's 1554 edition.

14. C. Donati (1988): 64–66; Quondam in Prosperi 54–58; Claudio Scarpati, *Studi sul Cinquecento italiano* (Milano: Vita e Pensiero, 1982): "Ricerche su Sabba da Castiglione," 27–125. By Scarpati see, also, *Dire la verità al principe* (Milano: Vita e Pensiero, 1987).

15. A. Prosperi, "Libri sulla corte ed esperienze curiali nel primo '500 italiano," in Prosperi (1980): 69–91 at 69–72.

16. Genova: Antonio Bellomo, 1543; Venetia: ad instantia di M. Pelegro de Grimaldi author de l'opera, 1544. Prosperi (1980): 72–77. The author blamed Castiglione for setting up an impossibly demanding goal: see edition Venice (1544): folio 6r.

17. Compare "Egli era galantuomo, e cortigiano / A un tempo stesso; ch'egli è come dire / Fare a un tempo da basso e da soprano": unsigned "Notizie istoriche di Lorenzo Pignotti" at the head of the edition of *Poesie* di Lorenzo Pignotti aretino (Firenze: presso G. Molini e Compagni, All'Insegna di Dante, 1820): 3, where these verses referring to Francesco Redi are attributed to a "capitolo" by Giovan Battista Fagiuoli (1660–1742). A. Vallone, *Cortesia e nobiltà nel Rinascimento* 17 note 8. See Arturo Graf, *Attraverso il Cinquecento* (Torino: E. Loescher, 1888; G. Chiantore, 1916; 1926): 226, recording "cortegiana onesta" in the early sixteenth century.

18. "Ma quante ce ne sono oggidì non dico di reine o principesse, ma semplici e private gentildonne, che levatole un po' l'apparenza di bellezza sono senza costumi e vertù, le quali accorgendosi de l'amore di qualche gentiluomo che non sia a lor talento dei beni de la fortuna dotato, quello scherniscono e di lui si beffano?" Bandello, *Le novelle*, ed. G. Brognoligo (Bari: Laterza, 2d ed. 1928): 2: 160.

The courtly mentality also invests a new genre that was destined to a lively evolution through the following couple of centuries, namely that of the heraldic "imprese." Paolo Giovio, *Dialogo delle imprese militari e amorose* (composed in 1551), ed. Maria Luisa Doglio (Roma: Bulzoni, 1978) 34, declares to be about to speak in the ways of the court, "voler parlare alla cortigiana."

19. See Elias, *Über den Prozess* (1939), and *The Civilizing Process* (1978): chap. 2, "Civilization as a Specific Transformation of Human Behavior," 51–217, with detailed analysis of precepts on behavior at table, in public, in the house, in the bedroom, in sexual relations, and in the daily life of the knight, referring to the literature of manuals in different European countries from roughly 1200 to 1800.

20. (Lyon [and Geneva]: T. de Straton; also Stephanus, 1564; 1568); *Colloques* [original Latin text with facing French trans.] (Paris: Marneuf, 1586).

21. Johannes Siebert, *Der Dichter Tannhäuser: Leben, Gedichte, Sage* (Halle/S.: M. Niemeyer, 1934; rpt. Hildesheim, New York: G. Olms, 1980).

22. *Remarques nouvelles sur la langue françoise* (Paris, 1676): 1: 51, cited by Elias, *The Civilizing Process* (1978): 102.

23. Elias, ibid.: 216 f. Conversely, Venetian *cortesan* retained the meaning of *courtois* while shedding all association with court life. See Carlo Goldoni: "Je fis donc une comédie de caractère dont le titre étoit *Momolo cortesan. . . .* Il n'est pas possible de rendre l'adjectif *cortesan* par un adjectif françois. Ce terme . . . n'est pas une corruption du mot *courtisan*; mais il dérive plutôt de *courtoisie* et *courtois. . . .* Aussi quand je donnai cette pièce à la presse, je l'intitulai l'*Uomo di mondo*, et si je devois la mettre en françois, je crois que le titre . . . seroit celui de l'*Homme accompli.*" *Mémoires* (Paris, 1787): part 1, chap. 40, now in Goldoni, *Tutte le opere*, ed. Giuseppe Ortolani, 1 (Milano: Mondadori, 1935): 185. See Carlo Ossola (1987): 140 f.

24. Some critics have challenged his authorship, but Torquato Tasso, who praised it in his dialogue *Il padre di famiglia*, read it as Della Casa's work. See G. F. Chiodaroli and Gennaro Barbarisi, "G. Della Casa," in *Letteratura Italiana: I Minori* 2 (Milano: Marzorati, 1961): 1208 f. Della Casa's Latin *De officiis* was reprinted in his *Opere*, 6 vols. (Napoli, 1733), the vernacular *Trattato* in Castiglione, Della Casa, *Opere*, ed. Giuseppe Prezzolini (Milano, Roma: Rizzoli, 1937) and then again in *Prose di Giovanni Della Casa etc.*, ed. A. Di Benedetto (1970). See C. Scarpati, *Studi sul Cinquecento italiano* (1982), "Con Giovanni Della Casa dal *De officiis* al *Galateo*," 126–153.

25. "Ancora il bene, quando sia soverchio, spiace. E sappi che coloro, che avviliscono se stessi con le parole fuori di misura e rifiutano gli onori che manifestamente loro s'appartengono, mostrano in ciò maggiore superbia che coloro che queste cose, non ben loro dovute, usurpano." *Opere di B. Castiglione, G. Della Casa*, ed. C. Cordié (1960): 390. Translation mine here and hereafter.

26. "E non è altro leggiadria che una cotale quasi luce che risplende dalla convenevolezza delle cose che sono ben composte e ben divisate l'una con l'altra e tutte insieme: senza la qual misura eziandio il bene non è bello e la bellezza non è piacevole. . . . così sono alcuna volta i costumi delle persone . . . se altri non gli condisce di una cotale dolcezza, la quale si chiama . . . grazia e leggiadria."

27. "Essere costumato e piacevole e di bella maniera; il che nondimeno è o virtù o cosa molto a virtù somigliante. . . . La dolcezza de' costumi e la convenevolezza de' modi e delle maniere e delle parole giovano non meno . . .

che la grandezza dell'animo e la sicurezza . . . ; perciocché queste si convengono essercitare ogni dì molte volte . . . ; ma la giustizia, la fortezza e le altre virtù più nobili e maggiori si pongono in opera più di rado." *Opere di B. Castiglione*: chap. 1, p. 368. See Eugenio Garin, *L'Umanesimo Italiano. Filosofia e vita civile nel Rinascimento* (Bari: Laterza, 1965):193 f. on Della Casa's distinction between absolute morality and relative sociality, the basis for a truly human life.

28. "Non . . . della natura de' vizii e delle virtù, ma solamente degli acconci e degli sconci modi che noi l'uno con l'altro usiamo." Chap. 28, p. 432.

29. "Le quali cirimonie credo che siano state trapportate di Spagna in Italia, ma il nostro terreno le ha male ricevute e poco ci sono allignate, conciossiaché questa distinzione di nobiltà così appunto a noi è noiosa e perciò non si dee alcuno far giudice a dicidere chi è più nobile o chi meno"; ". . . per l'una di queste due cagioni i più abbondano di cirimonie superflue, e non per altro: le quali generalmente noiano il più degli uomini perciocché per loro s'impedisce altrui il vivere a suo senno, cioè la libertà, la quale ciascuno appetisce innanzi ad ogni altra cosa." Chap. 17, pp. 400 f.

30. E. Garin (1965): 194.

31. Garin, ibid.

32. *De la institution di tutta la vita* (1543); *Della institution morale* (1582). Garin (1965): 196–199; C. Donati (1988): 60–62.

33. Garin (1965): 199. Francesco Piccolomini, *Breve discorso della istituzione di un principe e compendio della scienza civile*, ed. Sante Pieralisi (Roma: Salviucci, 1858).

34. In this context Garin (1965): 195 also calls attention to the little known Frosino Lapini (d. 1571), *L'Anassarcho del Lapino, overo Trattato de' Costumi, e modi che si debbono tenere, o schifare nel dare opera agli studij. Discorso utilissimo ad ogni virtuoso e nobile scolare* (Firenze, 1567; I know only the edition Fiorenza: B. Sermartelli, 1571).

35. E. Garin (1965): chap. 7, "Ricerche morali," 193–211, on the various aspects of moral speculation in the Italian Renaissance, specifically on the authors just named.

36. In the letter of dedication of the *Circe* to Cosimo de' Medici Gelli shows his literal derivation from Pico's oration. Of all the authors just mentioned, Gelli is a good example of the difficulty of interpreting the social and political meaning of much of our moral literature. The inherent ambiguity of the imaginative representation makes it, as it were, Protean or at least Janus-like. In the summarily coherent presentation of his 1965 book (201 f.), Garin interprets Gelli as an eloquent exhortation to accept the worldly destiny of the active member of the city of man. Enzo Noè Girardi, in contrast, interprets both *Circe* and *Capricci* as a partly mystical, Platonizing religious reflection on the limits and miseries of the human condition, weighed down by our earthiness: see *Letteratura Italiana: I Minori* 2 (1961): 1111–1132.

37. Cf. Garin (1965): 207.

38. A. Messina, "La fortuna editoriale in Italia e all'estero della *Civil conversatione* di Stefano Guazzo (sec. XVI)," *Libri e documenti* 2 (1976): 1–8.

39. The Latin terms are all synonyms of "wit," "witticism." The different

editions have different numbering for the lemmata, which in the later editions also appear richer, especially with the added Latin synonyms. I cite from the splendid printing Vinegia: n.p., 1548 and the ed. Venetia: Paulo Vigolino, 1593, in the New York Public Library: lemma 1297 and 892 respectively (no pagination). C. Ossola (1987): 136, cites from the edition Venetia: Uscio, 1588, under lemma 892, "*urbanità*," p. 120b.

40. Tavola or Index and lemma no. 2452 in the 1548 edition, no. 1574 in 1593 edition. C. Ossola (1987): 132, quotes the same definition equating conversation with social intercourse from the 1588 edition, *Tavola*, lemma no. 1574, and p. 213a.

Medieval Latin *conversatio* already had the meaning of "communal activities," as in Lambert of Ardres's *Historia comitum Ghisnensium, MGH* SS 24: chap. 127, p. 624, where a detailed description of the castle built by Arnulf II of Ardres in the first third of the twelfth century gives the second floor, the main part of the house, as reserved to *habitatio*, the living quarters, and *conversatio*, all communal activities.

41. Lemma no. 950 in 1548 edition: "Lat. *beneficentia, munus, liberalitas*, è humana e gratiosa liberalità con destri e moderati costumi così detta dalle corti de buoni Principi, ne le quali sempre tal virtù risplende." The lemma *cavaliere* (no. 543 in 1593 ed.) gives only a list of fitting epithets from the authors (Petrarca, Boccaccio, etc.), ending with the statement that "Sarmente [Sarmiento ?] fu primo uomo che scrivesse di cavalleria."

42. The term still covered a broad semantic field. When Annibale turns to the subject of "la conversatione delle donne," Guglielmo takes this to mean sexual intercourse ("con le quali si giuoca alle braccia," p. 290 of 1574 original; Pettie's trans.: 1: 324). The passage well illustrates the paradox of the feminine condition at court and in society, that is, the risk and ambiguity between polite conversation with women and the danger this was perceived to pose to their chastity. They had to run the tightrope act of being seductive without allowing themselves to be seduced; they had to act as teasing flirts, affable yet modest. A. R. Jones in Armstrong and Tennenhouse, eds. (1988): 44.

43. J. Burchkardt, *The Civilization of the Renaissance in Italy*, trans. S. G. C. Middlemore (New York: Harper & Row, 1958): 2: 371.

44. "Chi desidera adunque usar felicemente della civil conversatione, ha da considerare che la lingua è lo specchio e 'l ritratto dell'animo suo; e che sì come dal suono del denaio conosciamo la bontà e falsità sua, così dal suono delle parole comprendiamo a dentro la qualità dell'uomo et i suoi costumi." Ed. Salicato (1575): book 2: 75b.

45. Cited by Quondam in Prosperi (1980): 30, from the edition Madrid: Aribau (1874): 2.

46. 9v, 36r–37r in both 1543 and 1544 editions. C. Donati (1988): 62.

47. This occurred on 20 October 1574. See C. Donati (1988): 152–156 on the political background to Guazzo's work.

48. The oppressive presence of the terrible Vespasiano Gonzaga as protagonist in the dialogue of book 4, however, takes away much of the openness of a true dialogue. It is good to remember that Duke Guidobaldo's physical absence

from the *Cortegiano* dialogue was a warrant of spontaneity and a condition for
the necessary critical spirit.

49. Quondam in Prosperi (1980): 58–63 on Guazzo.

50. "'L viver civilmente non dipende dalla Città, ma dalle qualità del-
l'animo. Così intendo la conversatione civile, non per rispetto solo della Città,
ma in consideratione de' costumi e delle maniere, che la rendono civile." Ed.
Venice: Robino (1575): 58, and ed. ibid.: Salicato (1575): 1: 30.

51. D. Javitch, "Courtesy Books," in A. C. Hamilton et al., eds., *The Spenser Encyclopedia* (Toronto: University of Toronto Press, 1989). The negative
assessment of the *Book of the Courtier* as an expression of a debased social
environment characterizes some recent studies, for example, Gino Benzoni, *Gli
affanni della cultura* (1978), and John Robert Woodhouse, *Baldesar Castiglione. A Reassessment of* The Courtier (Edinburgh: Edinburgh University
Press, 1978).

52. Ed. Venice: Robino (1575): 186.

53. Tesauro, *Il cannocchiale aristotelico* (Torino: Zavatta, 1655; 1670), in
Ezio Raimondi, ed., *Trattatisti e narratori del Seicento* (Milano, Napoli: Ricciardi, 1960): 19. Tesauro's treatise leaned on Baltasar Gracián's *Arte de in-
genio* (1642). Also Tesauro, *Filosofia morale derivata dall'alto fonte del grande
Aristotele stagirita* (Torino: Zapata, 1671). See Andrea Battistini and Ezio Raimondi, "Retoriche e poetiche dominanti," in Asor Rosa, ed., *Letteratura Italiana* 3.1 (Torino: Einaudi, 1984): 113–116.

54. See G. E. Ferrari, *Documenti marciani e principale letteratura sui codici
veneti di epopea carolingia* (Venezia: Biblioteca Nazionale Marciana, 1961),
with a catalogue of the Este library. On the "franco-veneti" and the reception
of chivalric literature through the *Orlando Innamorato* see Riccardo Bruscagli
et al., *I libri di "Orlando Innamorato,"* Ferrara, Istituto di Studi Rinascimen-
tali, Saggi (Ferrara: Panini, 1987): chap. 1.1–1.2, pp. 14–26 by Antonia Tis-
soni Benvenuti.

Although written records start relatively late in Italy, by using personal and
place names Pio Rajna, "Contributi alla storia dell'epopea e del romanzo medievale: V, Gli eroi brettoni nell'onomastica italiana del secolo XII" and "Contributi alla storia dell'epopea e del romanzo medievale: VI, Ancora gli eroi brettoni nell'onomastica italiana del secolo XII," *Romania* 17 (1888): 161 ff., 355
ff., showed that the Arthurian legends were probably known in Italy as early as
1080–1100. See the still authoritative Arturo Graf, "Appunti per la storia del
ciclo brettone in Italia," *Giornale Storico della Letteratura Italiana* 5 (1885):
80–131, especially on the *Tristano Riccardiano*; and Segre and Marti, eds., *La
prosa del Duecento* (1959): 556.

55. Rolandino, *Cronica in factis et circa facta Marchie Trivixiane*, ed. A.
Bonardi, in L. A. Muratori, *Rerum Italicarum Scriptores* 8, n.s. 1 (Città di
Castello, 1905–1906); trans. by J. R. Berrigan, *The Chronicles of the Trevisan
March* (Lawrence, KS: University of Kansas Press, 1980). It included the deeds
of the feared Ghibelline leader and imperial vicar Ezzelino da Romano. A productive scholar, Rolandino was also a leading notary and a vigorous political
leader (cf. my chap. 1 and note 81). See Waley: 222 f.

56. Waley: 228. That the particularism and separatism of many French, German, and Italian lords was not shared by their English counterparts is another matter.

57. For an authoritative discussion of the linguistic and historical characteristics of this literature, see, after A. Viscardi, *Letteratura franco-italiana* (1941), with bibliography, A. Roncaglia, "La letteratura franco-veneta," in Emilio Cecchi and Natalino Sapegno, eds., *Storia della Letteratura Italiana, 2: Il Trecento* (Milano: Garzanti, 1965; 1973): 727–759. Also Corrado Bologna, "La letteratura dell'Italia settentrionale nel Trecento," in A. Asor Rosa, ed., *Letteratura Italiana* 7.1 (1987): 511–600. Nicolò da Verona introduced new epic characters, including the spirited Estout, who was destined to become Boiardo's and Ariosto's Astolfo. Also Zumthor, *Essai de poétique médiévale* (1972): 465 f. on the originality of the *Entrée* and the *Prise*.

58. See the edition of the *Attila* by Giulio Bertoni (1907).

59. Pio Rajna's standard study *Le fonti dell'Orlando Furioso* (Firenze, 1876, 2d ed. 1890) is still considered the most exhaustive survey of Ariosto's sources, but critics have become aware of its unrealistic listing of French originals without sufficient credit being given to the much closer Franco-Venetian and Tuscan versions that Ariosto certainly had at hand. See Carlo Dionisotti, "Appunti sui Cinque Canti e sugli studi ariosteschi," in *Studi e problemi di critica testuale*, Convegno di studi di filologia italiana nel Centenario della Commissione per i Testi di Lingua (Bologna: Commissione per i Testi di Lingua, 1961): 369–382 at 377–379; Daniela Delcorno Branca, *L'Orlando Furioso e il romanzo cavalleresco medievale* (Firenze: L. S. Olschki, 1973): 6; and Aurelio Roncaglia, "Nascita e sviluppo della narrativa cavalleresca nella Francia medievale" (1975): 229–250 at 229 f.

60. Ezio Levi, *I cantari leggendari del popolo nei secoli XIV e XV* (Torino: Loescher, 1914); idem, ed., *Fiore di leggende: cantari antichi* (Bari: G. Laterza, 1914); Carlo Dionisotti, "*Entrée d'Espagne, Spagna, Rotta di Roncisvalle*," in *Studi in onore di Angelo Monteverdi* I (Modena, 1959): 207–241; Gianfranco Folena, "La cultura volgare e l'umanesimo cavalleresco' nel Veneto," in Vittore Branca, ed., *Umanesimo europeo e umanesimo veneziano* (Firenze: Sansoni, [1963] 1964): 141–158. On Pulci's chivalric content see the ample analyses in R. M. Ruggieri, *L'umanesimo cavalleresco da Dante al Pulci* (Roma, 1962): 199–265.

61. For easy reference see *Tristan and the Round Table. A Translation of* La Tavola ritonda, trans. Anne Shaver, MRT&S 28 (Binghamton: Center for Medieval and Renaissance Studies, SUNY Press, 1983), based on the old but still basic Polidori edition (2 vols., rpt. Bologna: Romagnoli, 1964–1965).

62. Aldo Vallone (1955): 56–59. For an up-to-date assessment of Boiardo's way of handling the genre and his relationship to the Ferrarese court, see Charles S. Ross, Introduction to his translation of the *Orlando Innamorato* (Berkeley, Los Angeles, Oxford: University of California Press, 1989): 1–29.

63. *Orlando Innamorato*: 2.10.1:1–6 in M. M. Boiardo, *Orlando Innamorato, Amorum Libri*, ed. Aldo Scaglione, 2 vols. (Torino: UTET, 2d ed. 1963): 2: 162. On chivalry in Boiardo see, for example, Antonio Franceschetti,

"L'*Orlando Innamorato* e gli ideali cavallereschi nella Ferrara del Quattrocento," Atti dell'Istituto Veneto di Scienze, Lettere ed Arti, Classe di scienze morali e lettere (Venezia, 1971–1972): 315–333.

64. The most recent title is Trevor Dean, *Land and Power in Late Medieval Ferrara: The Rule of the Este, 1350–1450* (Cambridge, Eng., New York: Cambridge University Press, 1988). Preferment and social advancement in Ferrara chiefly took the form of land rewards conferred on "men intimately involved in the working of the Este lordship, whether as retainers, courtiers, household servants, or dependent peasant farmers" (107), in addition to knights and noblemen. Reviewing this study in *Renaissance Quarterly* 41.4 (1988): 708–710, W. Gundersheimer (see his 1973 book on Ferrara) finds that "Dean has confirmed in substantial detail the essentially feudal character of the Ferrarese regime" and "put to rest (p. 97) [the] . . . simplistic notion that [the Estensi] developed a new system of authoritarian control, or a new way of governing. His extensive knowledge of earlier forms of feudalism enables him to offer many useful comparisons."

Research is still wanted on the ideological conditions of northern Italy's seigniorial courts: preliminary materials are in *Il Rinascimento nelle corti padane. Società e cultura* (Bari: De Donato, 1977). On the Este court as background to the literature from Boiardo to Tasso, see the methodological suggestions in Giovanni Getto, *Letteratura e critica nel tempo* (Milano: Marzorati, 1954, 2d ed. 1968): "La corte estense di Ferrara come luogo di incontro di una civiltà letteraria," 219–239 in 1st ed.; 325–353 in 2d ed.

65. *Orlando Innamorato*: 1.9.49 f. Critics have spoken of "umanesimo cavalleresco" and "umanesimo romanzesco" and tried to define Boiardo's poetic world in such terms, variously referring the romance or chivalric component of his inspiration to the medieval heritage and the humanistic one to his ample use of classical motifs, aptly blended with the Arthurian and Carolingian ones. See R. M. Ruggieri, *L'Umanesimo cavalleresco italiano da Dante al Pulci* (Roma, 1962; new ed. Napoli: Conte, 1977 with title *L'umanesimo cavalleresco italiano, da Dante all'Ariosto*); idem, "L'umanesimo cavalleresco nell'*Orlando Innamorato*," in Giuseppe Anceschi, ed., *Il Boiardo e la critica contemporanea*, Atti del Convegno . . . su M. M. Boiardo, Scandiano-Reggio Emilia, 1969 (Firenze: L. S. Olschki, 1970): 467–479; Giovanni Ponte, *La personalità e l'opera del Boiardo* (Genova: Tilgher, 1972); and Antonio Franceschetti, *L'Orlando Innamorato e le sue componenti tematiche e strutturali* (Firenze: L. S. Olschki, 1975). Brandimarte's "perfect" paradigm is studied in Maristella de Panizza Lorch, "'Ma soprattutto la persona umana / era cortese': Brandimarte's *cortesia* as expressed through the hero's *loci actionis* in Boiardo's *Orlando Innamorato*, Book I," in G. Papagno and A. Quondam, eds., *La Corte e lo spazio: Ferrara Estense* 2 (1982): 739–781.

66. Curtius (178) has reminded us that this topos of *sapientia* and *fortitudo* is also found in Rabelais (*Pantagruel*: chap. 8), Spenser (*Faerie Queene*: 2.3.40; *Shepheardes Calendar*: October, vv. 66 ff.), and Cervantes (*Don Quijote*: part 1, chap. 38).

67. Women and knights are chiastically opposed (in gallantly reversed or-

der) to arms and loves; then courtesy, corresponding to the first and last of the four named elements, is opposed to "audaci imprese," iterating the motif of *audacia* (prowess, bravery).

68. The comparison with Wolfram's Parzival brings closer analogies than with Chrétien's Perceval on account of the more radical behavior on the part of the former (see my chap. 6). We cannot know which precise versions of the story were available to Ariosto, but even though the range of his readings was admittedly very wide, it could not include German texts.

69. Many critics have wrestled with Ariosto's symbolism concerning characters and adventures, with sharp assessments of his way of revising traditional allegories and emptying them of their moral import. A good recent example of such interpretations with regard to Ruggiero and all major characters is Peter DeSa Wiggins, *Figures in Ariosto's Tapestry: Character and Design in the* Orlando Furioso (Baltimore, London: Johns Hopkins University Press, 1986).

70. Ferdinand Lot, *Étude sur le Lancelot en prose* (1918): chap. 2, rpt. in M. L. Meneghetti, ed., *Il romanzo* (1988): 299–311 at 306.

71. Tony Hunt, *Forum for Modern Language Studies* 17 (1981): 99 f.

72. A recent study in this vein of reaction to the Romantic view of the *Furioso* is Albert Russell Ascoli, *Ariosto's Bitter Harmony: Crisis and Evasion in the Italian Renaissance* (Princeton: Princeton University Press, 1987). Marina Beer, *Romanzi di cavalleria. Il* Furioso *e il romanzo italiano del primo Cinquecento*, Centro Studi "Europa delle Corti" / Biblioteca del Cinquecento 34 (Roma: Bulzoni, 1987), speculates that the madness of Roland was a result of the medical views of love as an illness, as also recorded in Equicola's *Libro de natura de amore*, so that Ariosto's representations are rather a parody of Platonic and courtly love—or rather the excesses of the latter—even while his image of knighthood is idealistically in reaction against the brutality of contemporary warfare.

73. *Discorso intorno al comporre dei romanzi* (Roma, 1554): see the edition: Giovan Battista Giraldi Cintio [sic], *De' romanzi, delle commedie e delle tragedie, ragionamenti . . . ; documenti intorno alla controversia sul libro de' romanzi con G. B. Pigna* (Milano: Biblioteca Rara di G. Daelli, 1864), and Henry L. Snuggs, ed. and trans., *Giraldi Cinthio on Romances: Being a Translation of the* Discorso intorno al comporre dei romanzi (Lexington: University of Kentucky Press, 1968): xiv. The new label and the defense of the newly recognized and theorized genre was also in the essay *I romanzi . . . divisi in tre libri. Ne quali della poesia et della vita dell'Ariosto si tratta . . .* (Vinegia: nella bottega d'Erasmo appresso V. Valgrisi, 1554) by Cinthio's pupil, Giovan Battista Nicolucci Pigna. Both Cinthio and Pigna were, together with Speroni, prominent courtiers of the Este in Ferrara, and all three were well known to Tasso, who is supposed to have represented them in characters of the *Aminta* (as first proposed by Gilles Ménage in the *Aminta*'s first annotated edition, Paris: Courbé, 1655). The subtle game of multiple agnitions was undoubtedly an alluring challenge to the court audience.

74. See Javitch (1988) on W. Booth's assessment and the current theoretical framework among "narratologists" (and narrators as well).

75. Similarly, however original and personal Ariosto's famous "median

style" may sound to us, it also had its generic antecedents in the romances, signally Chrétien's.

76. Speroni referred to Cinthio's *Discorso dei romanzi* (1554) in a fragment entitled "De' romanzi" probably composed soon after the appearance of Bernardo Tasso's *Amadigi* in 1560: see Javitch (1988): 61.

77. D. Javitch, "Narrative Discontinuity in the *Orlando Furioso* and Its Sixteenth-Century Critics," *Modern Language Notes* 103 (1988): 50–74. This survey of Cinquecento reception does not address the question of historical antecedents to such practices, and much Ariosto criticism similarly fails to engage in a more thorough historicization of this masterpiece, as if it might detract from its undoubted originality. See, also, Klaus W. Hempfer, *Diskrepante Lektüren: die Orlando-Furioso-Rezeption im Cinquecento. Historische Rezeptionsforschung als Heuristik der Interpretation* (Stuttgart: Franz Steiner, 1987).

78. (Lyon, 1555; rpt. Paris: Les Belles Lettres, 1930 and Genève: Slatkine Reprints, 1971): 2.8, "De l'euures heroïque," 78 f. See S. John Holyoake, *An Introduction to French Sixteenth-Century Poetic Theory: Texts and Commentary* (Manchester: Manchester University Press; New York: Barnes and Noble, 1972): 172, and J. Frappier in R. S. Loomis, ed. (1959; 1961): 299. In the course of a detailed analysis of Virgil's narrative excellence, Peletier says: "E parmi l'universel discours, il fèt bon voer, comment le Poëte, apres avoer quelquefoes fèt mancion d'une chose mémorable . . . , la lesse la pur an tans: tenant le Lecteur suspans, desireus e hátif d'an aler voer l'evuenemant. An quoi je trouve noz Rommanz bien inuantiz. E dirè bien ici an passant, qu'an quelques uns d'iceus bien choesiz, le Poëte Heroïque pourra trouuer a fere son profit: comme sont les auantures des Chevaliers, les amours, les voyages, les anchantemans, les combaz, e samblables choses: déqueles l'Arioste à fèt amprunt de nous, pour transporter an son Liure."

79. Vinaver, *The Rise of Romance* (1971).

80. Kellermann, *Aufbaustil und Weltbild Chrestiens von Troyes im Percevalroman*, Beihefte zur *Zeitschrift für romanische Philologie* 88 (Halle/Saale: M. Niemeyer, 1936; rpt. Tübingen: M. Niemeyer, 1967). A critical survey of the question in E. Köhler, *L'aventure chevaleresque* (1974): chap. 7, "La forme du roman arthurien chez Chrétien de Troyes: Rapport entre contenu et structure signifiante," 269–298.

81. On the Cinquecento critics' misjudgment of Ariosto's thematic and formal unity owing to their imposition of supposed Aristotelian principles see, also, Peter V. Marinelli, *Ariosto and Boiardo: The Origins of* Orlando Furioso (Columbia, MO: University of Missouri Press, 1987), who rightfully insists on the need to take into account Ariosto's connection with Boiardo. Also, on the question of genre, Marina Beer, *Romanzi di cavalleria. Il Furioso e il romanzo italiano del primo Cinquecento* (1987). The second part of this book provides a full statistical and bibliographic account of the readership and popularity of the chivalric poem between 1470 and 1600 (apparently a circulation of about half a million copies).

82. Tasso, *Prose*, ed. Ettore Mazzali (Milano, Napoli: R. Ricciardi, 1959): 487–729. The third of the six *discorsi* (pp. 561–624) deals principally with the Aristotelian unity of plot in epic and romance—declared to be of a similar kind,

hence subject to the same poetic criteria. It is a protracted argument about the *Furioso*, objections starting with the difficulty of retaining the mass of events in one's memory (572 ff.). Similar were the approach and the critiques in Tasso's earlier (1587) *Discorsi dell'arte poetica e in particolare sopra il poema eroico* (ibid.: 349–410). Montaigne voiced the same objections.

83. *Bibliotheca Selecta*: book 1, chap. 25, p. 113 of the 1593 edition (Roma: Typographia Apostolica Vaticana). On some of Possevino's diplomatic activities within the academic world see A. Scaglione, *The Liberal Arts and the Jesuit College System* (Amsterdam: John Benjamins, 1986): 136 f., 146 f. On the chapter in question see M. Fumaroli (1985): 23 and note.

84. E. Köhler, "Die Pastourellen des Trobadors Gavaudan," *Germanisch-Romanische Monatsschrift* 14 (1964); Mancini ed.: 217–232. The pastoral world of the *Aminta* finds its fitting style in a deceptive naturalness that is the counterpart of the symptomatic "baroque" artificiality of Tasso's other works, from the *Gerusalemme* to his lyrics and even the correspondence. In chapter 18 on Marino in his *Storia della letteratura italiana* (1870–1871), Francesco De Sanctis characterized the style of the *Aminta* as "naturalezza con una sprezzatura che pare negligenza ed è artificio finissimo": the connection with Castiglione's vocabulary is revealing. It is as if Tasso were representing the spectacle or the make-believe of the court in the *Aminta* and its true inner nature in his other works.

85. Cf. Paolo Braghieri, *Il testo come soluzione rituale*: Gerusalemme Liberata (Bologna: Pàtron, 1978): 14: "la molla narrativa scatta nella dialettica che al moto centripeto del desiderio del capitano oppone quello centrifugo, disgregativo, dei 'compagni erranti.' In questo senso il testo emerge, dalla minaccia dell'errare-errore, come tentativo di stabilire un ordine."

86. See Raimondi's edition of Tasso's *Dialoghi* (Firenze: Sansoni, 1958): 1: 3–5. The titles of the successive dialogues most directly pertinent to our subject will indicate the range of courtly and chivalric themes: *Il Forno overo della nobiltà; Il Beltramo overo della cortesia; Il Gonzaga overo del piacere onesto; Il Messaggiero; Il padre di famiglia; De la dignità; Della precedenza; Il Romeo overo del giuoco; Il Rangone overo della pace; Il Malpiglio overo della corte; Il Malpiglio secondo overo del fugir la moltitudine; Il Gianluca overo de le maschere; La Molza overo de l'amore; Il Conte overo de l'imprese.*

87. *Dialoghi*, ed. Raimondi: vol. 2, tome 1: 1–113.

88. Tasso, *Dialoghi*, ed. Ezio Raimondi (1958). *Il Malpiglio* is also available with facing Italian text in Tasso, *Dialogues*, trans. Carnes Lord and Dain A. Trafton (Berkeley, Los Angeles, London: University of California Press, 1982): 151–191. Another of Tasso's dialogues, *Il segretario* (Ferrara: V. Baldini, 1587), dealt with that particular ministerial office—the subject of a number of contemporary treatises going from Francesco Sansovino, *Del segretario* (Venetia: F. Rampazetto, 1564; 14 editions until 1608) to Battista Guarini, *Il segretario* (Venezia: B. Magiotti, 1594), Angelo Ingegneri, *Del buon segretario* (Roma: G. Falcotti, 1594), and on through the following century. See Amedeo Quondam, "Il dominio del segretario, l'ordine della retorica," in A. Quondam, ed., *Le "Carte Messaggiere"—Retorica e modelli di comunicazione epistolare: per un indice dei libri di lettere del Cinquecento* (Roma: Bulzoni, 1981): 120–150.

89. *Tasso's Dialogues*, trans. Lord and Trafton (1982): 180.

90. Ibid.: 174 f., there rendered with: "Concealment becomes the courtier more than showing off."

91. Ibid.: 178–180. Vallone (1955: 60) seems to misinterpret the important letter of 1584 to Curzio Ardizio in which Torquato Tasso assessed the historical value of the figure of the courtier as presented by Castiglione: see Tasso, *Epistolario*, ed. Scipio Slataper (Lanciano: R. Carabba, 1932): 1: 88. Tasso did not mean that in his view Castiglione's courtier was purely imaginary, as the skeptical Prezzolini maintained against Vittorio Cian in the well-known polemic on the historical meaning of the great treatise. He was rather expressing his own feeling that the court had ceased to be an operative agency of good government in his own days as it might have been in times past, even though Castiglione's picture of both the courtier and the prince was inspired by a noble Platonic idea.

92. Giorgio Bàrberi Squarotti, "Il forestiero in corte," *Lettere Italiane* 39 (1982): 328–347 at 345–347: "Di politica non c'è più traccia nelle pagine del Tasso che si riferiscono alla corte. . . . Il rapporto fra principe e cortigiano è quello fra padrone e servo, e il servo non deve mai apparire da più del padrone."

CHAPTER ELEVEN: FROM COURTLY KNIGHTS TO NOBLE COURTIERS

1. Marino Berengo, *Nobili e mercanti nella Lucca del Cinquecento* (Torino: Einaudi, 1965): 54 on the "predominio del ceto nobiliare nella vita italiana" that became an accomplished fact around 1550, and 252–263 for major Cinquecento texts on the consciousness of nobility; idem, "Il Cinquecento," in *La storiografia italiana negli ultimi vent'anni*, Congresso nazionale di scienze storiche, Perugia 1967, 2 vols. (Milano: Marzorati, 1970): 2: 483–518; L. Martines (1979): 174.

2. C. Dionisotti, *Geografia e storia* (1967): 230 f.; C. Donati, "L'evoluzione della coscienza nobiliare," in C. Mozzarelli and P. Schiera, eds., *Patriziati e aristocrazie nobiliari* (Trento, 1978): 18 f.; idem, *L'idea di nobiltà in Italia* (1988): 93.

3. See my chap. 9, note 68.

4. Eduardo Saccone (1987: 10): "The fashioning of the courtier depends very much on the public, the audience, the others."

5. E.g., Stephen Greenblatt, *Renaissance Self-Fashioning* (1980), "Epilogue," 255–257 at 256. Giuseppe Falvo (1988: 164) refers to R. Barthes, M. Foucault, and Louis Marin for the notion of "rhetoric of power" and "techniques of representation" in the analysis of courtly literature. "Representation" is used by these critics to mean the fictive presentation of an attractive mask hiding the real elements of power, for public consumption and the effective legitimation of that oppressive power.

6. "Sempre che ha d'andare in loco dove sia novo e non conosciuto, procuri che prima vi vada la bona opinione di sé che la persona, e faccia che ivi s'intenda che esso in altri lochi, appresso altri signori, donne e cavalieri, sia ben estimato." *Il Cortegiano* 2.32.

7. "Essendo aiutato dagli ammaestramenti e dalla educazione ed arte del cortegiano, formato da questi signori tanto prudente e buono, . . . sarà gloriosissimo e carissimo agli omini ed a Dio, per la cui grazia acquisterà quella virtù eroica, che lo farà eccedere i termini della umanità e dir si potrà più presto semideo che uom mortale" (*Il Cortegiano* 4.22).

8. "Servando tra tutti in certe cose una pare equalità, come nella giustizia e nella libertà; ed in alcune altre una ragionevole inequalità, come nell'esser liberale, nel remunerare, nel distribuir gli onori e dignità secondo la inequalità dei meriti, li quali sempre debbono non avanzare, ma esser avanzati dalle remunerazioni; e che in tal modo sarebbe non che amato ma quasi adorato dai sudditi" (*Il Cortegiano* 4.33). See Ullrich Langer (1988): 225. Queen Elizabeth's role has been much studied in recent years as part of the evolution of absolutist ideology and the way it involved courtiers and particularly such courtier poets as Spenser and Sidney: for one title only, see S. Greenblatt, "To Fashion a Gentleman," in Greenblatt (1980): especially 166–192.

9. Ullrich Langer (1988) has expertly explored this connection with regard to Castiglione's treatise and other French texts: see his bibliography, p. 223 and passim. See Franco Moretti, *Signs Taken for Wonders* (London: Verso; New York: Schocken Books, 1983), "The Great Eclipse: Tragic Form as Deconsecration of Sovereignty," 42–82, for a penetrating analysis of the other side of the coin, the representation of the absolute monarch as tyrant (that is, what I have analyzed so far as part of the feudal mentality and sense of values as evidenced in parts of the epic and the romance) in the English Tudor tragedy (especially *Gorboduc*, whose plot derived from Geoffrey of Monmouth).

10. E. Köhler, *L'aventure chevaleresque* (1974), especially 11–15 for the definition of King Arthur's role as upholder of feudal rights in Chrétien de Troyes's *Erec*.

11. Castiglione's solution to Italy's political and social problems was a kind of courtly society that would have been similar to the Prussian courtly government from Frederick the Great onward—the kind of historical background that made the Weimar republic an unworkable experiment in the Germany of the 1920s and 1930s, as interpreted by Norbert Elias (see end of my Introduction).

12. Muzio, *Il duello con Le risposte cavalleresche* (Vinegia: Gabriel Giolito de' Ferrari, 1550; new ed. 1551, 1553, 1554, 1558, 1560, 1563, 1564, 1566, 1571, 1576, 1585); idem, *Il gentilhuomo, trattato della nobiltà* (Venetia: Giovanni Andrea Valvassori detto Guadagnino, 1571).

13. Baldi, *Delle considerationi e dubitationi sopra la materia delle mentite e offese di parole; Delle mentite, discorso* (Venice: Bartolomeo Fontana, 1634). See C. Donati (1988): 94–96 on Muzio, 170–173 on Romei, and the whole of his chap. 4, 93–136 on this literature.

14. "la opinione de' cavalieri è, che legge alcuna né di patria, né di principe, né interesse di havere, né di vita, all'honore non debbia essere anteposta." 1588 ed.: 175v. C. Donati (1988): 96. Also F. R. Bryson, *The Point of Honour in Sixteenth-Century Italy: An Aspect of the Life of a Gentleman* (New York, 1935); idem, *The Sixteenth-Century Italian Duel: A Study in Renaissance Social History* (Chicago, 1938); G. Angelozzi, "La trattatistica su nobiltà e onore a Bologna nei secoli XVI e XVII," *Atti e memorie della Deputazione di storia*

patria per le provincie di Romagna 25/26 (1974/1975): 187–264; and Francesco Erspamer, *La biblioteca di don Ferrante: duello e onore nella cultura del Cinquecento*, Biblioteca del Cinquecento 18 (Roma: Bulzoni, 1982).

15. C. Donati (1988): 102–104 and 110 for the 1560 *Cartelli.*

16. (Florence: Lorenzo Torrentino). Copy in the Biblioteca Marucelliana of Florence used by C. Donati (1988): 141, n. 64.

17. Osorius, *De nobilitate civili libri duo* and *De nobilitate christiana libri tres* (Lisbon, 1542; Florentiae: Laurentius Torrentinus, 1552); Tiraquellus, *Commentarii de nobilitate et de iure primigeniorum* (definitive edition, posthumous, Lugduni: Gulielmus Rovillius, 1559; 1573); Cassanaeus, *Catalogus gloriae mundi* (1529; Venetiis: Vincentius Valgrisius, 1569). C. Donati (1988): 113–117.

18. The authority of "il gran Tiraquello regio consigliere nel Parlamento di Parigi" is invoked by Annibale Magnocavallo in the long discussion on the nature of nobility in book 2 of Guazzo's *Civil conversatione* (1575 Salicato ed.: 224–226). Annibale distinguishes between "seminobili, nobili e nobilissimi": *seminobili* owe their distinction to personal worth, *nobili* add blood, and the *nobilissimi* also wealth. *Cortesia* characterizes the noble conversant even when he communicates with the *ignobili.*

19. "Est igitur nobilitas dignitas generis, in quo maximae virtutes exstiterunt, vitae communi salutares et commodae," and so on. Florence 1552 edition: 3–50.

20. C. Donati (1988): 128; see 126–128 on Muzio's 1571 treatise.

21. "Mulieres vero popularium portare solent caputia ex panno laneo, et ista est notoria et manifesta differentia, . . . eo quia habitus demonstrat qualitatem et dignitatem personae deferentis." Chasseneux, Valgrisio 1559 ed.: 159v-171r., cited by C. Donati (1988): 114.

22. C. Donati (1988) 130 f. on Cosimo's decree.

23. C. Donati (1988): chap. 7, "Le 'prove di nobiltà' dei cavalieri italiani dell'Ordine di Malta (1555–1612)," 247–265.

24. See *Le pouvoir et la plume* (Paris, 1982), José Guidi, "Le jeu de cour et sa codification dans les différentes rédactions du *Courtisan*," 97–115, and especially Giancarlo Mazzacurati, "'Decoro' e indecenza: linguaggi naturali e teoria delle forme nel Cinquecento," 215–282.

25. The discourse was printed as part of Botero's *I Capitani . . . e due Discorsi della Monarchia e della Nobiltà* (1607).

26. Ullrich Langer (1988): 234. Rabelais, *Oeuvres complètes*, eds. Jacques Boulenger and Lucien Scheler (Paris: Gallimard, 1965).

27. M. Bakhtin, *Rabelais and His World*, trans. Hélène Iswolsky (Cambridge, MA: M.I.T. Press, 1968; 1988; Bloomington: Indiana University Press, 1984; Russian original *Tvorchestvo Fransua Rable*, Moscow: Khudozhestvennia Literatura, 1965): 138 f. of 1984 ed.; It. ed. *L'opera di Rabelais e la cultura popolare*, trans. Mili Romano (Torino: Einaudi, 1979, 3d ed. 1982): 152.

28. For Guazzo's considerable impact in England, see J. L. Lievsay's learned study (1961); D. Javitch, "Rival Arts of Conduct in Elizabethan England: Guazzo's *Civile Conversation* and Castiglione's *Courtier*," *Yearbook of Italian Studies* 1 (1971): 178–198; and idem, "Courtesy Books," in A. C. Hamilton et al.,

eds., *The Spenser Encyclopedia* (Toronto: University of Toronto Press, 1989), where Guazzo's reception in England is contrasted to Castiglione's as part of a late Renaissance reaction to the latter's emphasis on courtly values in favor of a more universally valid coherence between the inner and outer self. Spenser, Javitch opines, intimated "that courtesy ought to be a virtue which reconciles Castiglione's courtliness with Guazzo's civility":

> Of Court it seems, men Courtesie doe call,
> For that it there most useth to abound;
> And well beseemeth that in Princes hall
> That vertue should be plentifully found,
> Which of all goodly manners is the ground,
> And root of civill conversation.
> *(Faerie Queene:* 6.1.i)

29. Elias, *Power and Civility*: 358.

30. George Puttenham, *The Arte of English Poesie*, eds. G. D. Willcock and Alice Walker (Cambridge: Cambridge University Press, 1970): 299. Javitch (1982): 227 f. The models of social behavior had broad consequences which, beyond the practical sphere, also affected imaginative literature in several countries. Jaeger 13 f. attributes to Daniel Javitch (1978) the discovery that the "poetics of conduct" induced by Italian etiquette literature produced, in Elizabethan England, "manuals of court behavior and etiquette [that] could provide the model for books of poetics; decorum, elegance and 'style' in behavior could be seen as analogous to the same qualities in verse." Ruth Kelso, *The Doctrine of the English Gentleman in the Sixteenth Century* (1929), is a classic on the matter.

31. Puttenham: 197. See Franco Moretti, *Signs Taken for Wonders* (1983): 77; Heinrich F. Plett (1983): 597–621; and Michael West, "Spenser's Art of War: Chivalric Allegory, Military Technology, and the Elizabethan Mock-Heroic Sensibility," *Renaissance Quarterly* 41.4 (1988): 654–704 at 695.

32. Javitch (1982): 233–237.

33. N. Elias, *The Civilizing Process* 2 (1982): 216.

34. D. Javitch (1971) and S. Greenblatt (1980): 163–165.

35. Curiously enough, just like Philibert de Vienne, in his dialogue *Il Malpiglio* Tasso will also bring in Socrates as a master and example of supreme "dissimulation" in social discourse: "vi concederò facilmente . . . che 'l simulare in questo modo sia virtù di corte, non solamente socratica": see Tasso, *Dialogues*, trans. Carnes Lord and Dain A. Trafton (Berkeley, Los Angeles, London: University of California Press, 1982): 182.

36. C. A. Mayer, "L'honnête homme. Molière and Philibert de Vienne's *Philosophe de cour*," *Modern Language Review* 46 (1951): 196–217.

37. See Philibert's concluding chapter. Javitch (1971): 99.

38. Javitch (1971): 101.

39. C. A. Mayer (1951) pointed to Lucian's *De parasitu* as the model and P. M. Smith (1966: 98–151) agreed with Mayer that Philibert was attacking Castiglione. I should add that hostility to Machiavelli must also have been in the background of this picture of degenerate public mores. Italianism at the court of Henry II and Catherine de Medici had a bad reputation among mor-

alistic nationalists and Protestant sympathizers: in their eyes, Machiavelli was the epitome of what was immoral in Italian forms of conduct. See Javitch (1971): 105 f., who also cites Giovanni Macchia, *Il cortegiano francese* (Firenze: Parenti, 1943): "Il cortegiano francese," 45–56, as the best study "on the conflation of Machiavelli and Castiglione in France." Philibert's satirical intent was made obvious by a poem added at the end of the second edition (1548), advising the reader that he would find much to laugh at in the book.

40. Some have recently seen the beginning of a court literature in England in the early sixteenth century, on the assumption that there was no true court in that land before 1489 under Henry VII, the first Tudor monarch (d. 1509): see John Scattergood and J. W. Sherborne, eds., *English Court Culture in the Later Middle Ages* (London: Duckworth, 1983), and David Carlson, "Politicizing Tudor Court Literature: Gaguin's Embassy and Henry VII's Humanists' Response," *Studies in Philology* 85.3 (1988): 279–296. This comes from concentrating on the centralized, absolutistic court culture best exemplified by the Versailles of Louis XIV: it results in a narrow-gauged implication that a socially and politically conditioned court culture was possible only in a centralized national court without competition from regional courts. By such a definition there was no medieval courtly literature even at royal courts.

41. Students of Philibert's text have not shown awareness of this paradox, which has been eloquently brought out by Franco Moretti, *Signs Taken for Wonders* (1983): "The Great Eclipse: Tragic Form as Deconsecration of Sovereignty," 42–82.

42. See Hexter, *Reappraisals in History* (1979): "The Education of the Aristocracy in the Renaissance," 45–70 at 69 (originally published in *JMH* 1950).

43. "Si son gouverneur tient de mon humeur, il luy formera la volonté à estre tres loyal serviteur de son prince et tres-affectionnée et tres-courageux; mais il luy refroidira l'envie de s'y attacher autrement que par un devoir publique. Outre plusieurs autres inconvenients qui blessent nostre franchise par ces obligations particulieres, le jugement d'un homme gagé et achetté, ou il est moins entier et moins libre, ou il est taché et d'imprudence et d'ingratitude. Un courtisan ne peut avoir ny loy ni volonté de dire et penser que favorablement d'un maistre qui, parmi tant de milliers d'autres subjects, l'a choisi. . . . Cette faveur et utilité corrompent . . . sa franchise, et l'esblouissent." See Hexter, ibid.: 70.

44. Hexter, ibid.

45. See M. Fumaroli (1985) on this episode of the literary quarrels concerning the chivalric novel, especially in France. Amyot (d. 1593), the famous translator of Plutarch on Francis I's order, later became bishop of Auxerre (1570). He had been tutor to the future kings Charles IX and Henry III.

46. The dates are as given by Fumaroli on the basis of what he found available in the Reserve of the Bibliothèque Nationale.

47. M. Fumaroli (1985): 37–39. Further arguments in defense of the chivalric genre appeared in Gohory's dedication of book fourteen (1575). See *Le premier livre d'Amadis de Gaule* (Paris: Estienne Groulleau, 1548); *Le premier livre d'*Amadis de Gaule, ed. Yves Giraud (Paris: Nizet, 1986).

48. M. Fumaroli (1985): 23.

49. For example, Joseph Bédier, Paul Hazard, and Pierre Martino, eds., *Littérature française*, 2 vols. (Paris: Larousse, 1948): 1: 201.

50. On this and other texts related to the doctrine of gentlemanly grace in external conduct, with references to the doctrine of graceful movement in daily conduct as well as in the arts, like dance, see Mark Franko, "Renaissance Conduct Literature and the Basse Danse: The Kinesis of *bonne grace*," in Richard C. Trexler, ed., *Persons in Groups: Social Behavior as Identity Formation in Medieval and Renaissance Europe*, MRT&S 36 (Binghamton, NY: Center for Medieval and Renaissance Texts and Studies, 1985): 55–66.

51. The middle position of Faret's *honeste homme* between the courtier and the gentleman is symptomatically underscored by the use of the two terms in the double title of its German translation, *Ehrliebender Hof-Mann/Der Ehrliebende Welt-Mann* (1647/1648). The courtier was still addressed directly in the successful *Traité de la cour* (1616) by Eustache du Refuge (d. 1617): see the annotated edition: Eustache Du Refuge, *Traicté de la cour, ou instruction des courtisans* (Paris: Cardin Besonge, 1636). It was soon translated into English as *A Treatise of the court, digested into two bookes, written in French by Denis de Refuges* [sic], *done into English by John Reynolds* (London: A. Matthewes, 1622), followed by Eustache Du Refuge, *Arcana aulica, or Walsingham's Manual of Prudential Maxims, for the States-man and the Courtier* (London: John Williams, 1652). See Eustache Du Refuge, [*Traicté de la cour*] *A Practical Guide for Ambitious Politicians* (Columbia: University of South Carolina Press, 1961). It was translated into German by Harsdörffer as *Kluger Hofmann* (1655): see my note 78 below.

52. N. Elias, *The Civilizing Process* (1978): 217.

53. See the peremptory statement in Joseph Bédier et al., eds., *Littérature française* (1948): 1: 316: "Il a certainement contribué à adoucir la rudesse des moeurs," and the whole analysis on pp. 313–316.

54. *The Court Society* (1983): 246–251, 255–266. The *Astrée's* standard edition is that of Henry Vaganay (5 vols., Lyon, 1925–1928; rpt. Genève: Slatkine, 1966). Relevant complete "books" (there are twelve for each part) are available in the partial editions by Maurice Magendie (Paris: Perrin, 1928), Gérard Genette (Paris: Union Générale d'Editions, 1964), and Jean Lafond (Paris: Gallimard, 1984).

55. Elias (1983): 259 and 256 f. The assimilation of honesty to the mores of the lower nobility was contrasted with the moral looseness of the court. This assimilation went hand in hand with the further inculcation of the moral virtues of emotional reliability, chastity, sobriety, financial responsibility, thrift, and industriousness in educational treatises addressed to the middle class—treatises which became commonplace in the late sixteenth century and later. The relevant texts had started with the fourteenth- and fifteenth-century merchants' books of advice to children (e.g., Pagolo Morelli's, see above) or treatises on the management of the family (signally L. B. Alberti's already mentioned *Della famiglia*). Of particular interest are the precepts addressed to women as managers of the house. In his *Discorso della virtù femminile e donnesca* (1582), Torquato Tasso distinguished between the need for domestic thrift in the mother of a bourgeois family and the regal display of wealth and social prominence in the

noble lady, thus sharply opposing the two social codes. Giovanni Michele Bruto's (ca. 1515–ca. 1594) *Institutione di una fanciulla nata nobilmente*, dedicated, despite the title, to Marietta Cattaneo, daughter of a Genoese merchant living in Antwerp, pointedly warned the young woman to pattern her behavior, not after the sumptuous ways of highborn ladies, but on the value of modest and useful domestic skills. In Protestant and Puritan England, where Bruto's tractate was promptly translated by Thomas Salter as *A Mirrhor mete for all Mothers, Matrones and Maids* (1579), this banishment of aristocratic luxury was upheld as the educational ideal for the middle class. See A. R. Jones in Armstrong and Tennenhouse, eds. (1988): 54–57, and F. Whigham (1984): 155–169, with tables 164–167, on sumptuary laws, interpreted as meant to privilege the true gentleman and separate the nobility from the middle class. See, also, end of my chap. 8. See text as published at the place of the addressee: G. M. Bruto, *La institutione di una fanciulla nata nobilmente. L'institution d'une fille de noble maison, traduite de langue tuscane en françois* (Anvers: I. Bellére, 1555; Antwerpen: Vereenigung der Antwerpsche Bibliophielen, 1594). Also G. M. Bruto, *The necessarie, fit and convenient education of a yong gentlewoman, written both in French and Italian, and translated into English by W. P.* [sic] *and now printed with the three languages togither* . . . (London: Adam Islip, 1598).

56. Elias (1983): 261–263.

57. "Histoire de Lydias et de Mélandre," book 12 of first part.

58. "Histoire de Childéric etc.," book 12 of third part. J. Lafond ed.: 354.

59. J. Lafond ed.: 413, 440. For a recent discussion of the political and moral dimensions of the novel see Madeleine Bertaud, *L'Astrée et Polexandre. Du roman pastoral au roman héroïque* (Genève: Droz, 1986).

Giuseppe Papagno, "Corti e cortigiani," in A. Prosperi, ed. (1980): 195–240, provides a useful description of an early case of absolutist centralized court within a strictly aristocratic society, namely that of Portugal, starting at the end of the fourteenth century and continuing until the early nineteenth century.

60. Hermann von Sachsenheim, *Die Mörin*; nach der Wiener Hs., ed. Horst Dieter Schlosser (Wiesbaden: Brockhaus, 1974).

61. [*Ponthus et Sidoine*] *Pontus und Sidonia in der verdeutschung eines ungenannten aus dem 15. Jahrhundert*, ed. Karin Schneider ([Berlin:] E. Schmidt, [1961]).

62. See the popular edition, *Die Geschichte von der schönen Melusine: die eine Meerfei gewesen ist. Nach der ältesten deutschen Druckausgabe von 1474 für Jung und Alt*, ed. Fedor von Zobeltitz (Hamburg: Alster-Verlag, 1925).

63. See above, end of chap. 6.

64. *Der Jungen Knaben Spiegel* (Straszburg: Jacob Frölich, 1555); [Georg or Jörg Wickram,] *Sämtliche Werke* (Berlin: W. de Gruyter, 1967–1973); *Der Jungen Knaben Spiegel* (Strassburg: K. J. Trübner, 1917); *Der Goldfaden* (Berlin: Rütten & Loening [1963]; München: Obpacher, [1963?]).

65. Sigmund J. Barber, *Amadis de Gaule and the German Enlightenment* (New York: Peter Lang, 1984).

66. *Der christlichen königlichen Fürsten Herkuliskus und Herkuladisla auch ihrer hochfürstlichen Gesellschaft anmuhtige Wundergeschichte* (Braun-

schweig: C. F. Zilliger). See Gerhard Spellerberg, "Höfischer Roman," in H. A. Glaser, ed., *Deutsche literatur* 3 (1985): 319–323.

67. Cf. Harald Weinrich, "La Crusca fruttifera. Considerazioni sull'effetto dell'Accademia della Crusca nella vita accademica in Germania," in *La Crusca nella tradizione letteraria e linguistica italiana* (Firenze: Accademia della Crusca, 1985): 32–34; Martin Bircher, "The Fruchtbringende Gesellschaft and Italy: Between Admiration and Imitation," in *The Fairest Flower: The Emergence of Linguistic National Consciousness in Renaissance Europe* (Firenze: Accademia della Crusca, 1985): 121–132.

68. *Aramena* (Nürnberg: Johann Hoffmann, 1669–1680), rpt. ed. Blake Lee Spahr (Bern, Frankfurt/M.: H. Lang, 1975-); *Octavia* (Nürnberg: Johann Hoffmann, 1685–1707).

69. Full title, changed in later editions: *Exempel unveränderlicher Vorsehung Gottes / unter der Historie des Keuschen Josephs in Aegypten vorgestellt,* published 1670 and 1671 (2d ed. Nürnberg: Felsecker). See now *Des vortrefflich keuschen Josephs in Egypten Lebensbeschreibung samt des Musai Lebens-Lauff,* ed. Wolfgang Bender (Tübingen: M. Niemeyer, 1968).

70. *Großmüthiger Feldherr Arminius oder Hermann nebst seiner durchlauchtigsten Thusnelda in einer sinnreichen Staats-, Liebes- und Helden-Geschichte in zwei Teilen vorgestellt* (posthumous, second part completed after Lohenstein's plan by Christian Wagner; later edition 2 vols. Leipzig: J. F. Gleditsch, 1689; rpt. Bern: H. Lang, 1973; Hildesheim, New York: G. Olms, 1973).

71. Of the more comprehensive histories of German literature, particularly useful for detailed information are: Helmut de Boor and Richard Newald, eds., *Geschichte der deutschen Literatur* 4, tomes 1–2, by Hans Rupprich (esp. 48–88 on epic and romance, 296–302 on "Spiegelliteratur; Standes- und Sittenlehre"), and 5 by R. Newald (esp. 154–230 on epic and romance) (München: C. H. Beck, 1970, 1973, 1951, respectively); Heinz Otto Burger, ed., *Annalen der Deutschen Literatur* (Stuttgart: J. B. Metzlersche Verlagsbuchhandlung, 1951, 2d ed. 1971); Max Wehrli, *Geschichte der deutschen Literatur* 1 (Stuttgart: Philipp Reclam Jun., 1980); Horst Albert Glaser, ed., *Deutsche Literatur, Eine Sozialgeschichte* 2 and 3 (Reinbeck bei Hamburg: Rowohlt, 1985). Also Henry and Mary Garland, *The Oxford Companion to German Literature* (Oxford: Clarendon Press, 1976), for lemmata on individual works.

72. Before the deep disillusionments of the baroque age, Germany was not overly inclined to develop the theme of anticourt criticism: Aeneas Silvius Piccolomini's *De curialium miseriis* (as well as Ulrich von Hutten's *Misaulus,* 1518/ 1519) found a confutation in Wilhelm von Grevembroich's *Aula dialogus* (Köln: Neuss, 1539), while the body of Castiglione's text would soon be read as a positive presentation.

73. See the reprint of the 1597 ed.: Giovanni Della Casa, *Galateus: das Büchlein von erbarn/höfflichen und holdseligen Sitten,* verdeutscht von Nathan Chytraeus, 1597, ed. Klaus Ley (Tübingen: M. Niemeyer, 1984).

74. I have seen the 1630 edition of Chytraeus's Latin *Galateus* (Oxoniae: John Litchfield), which still carried Caselius's two prefaces, dated 1578, and his

discourse on the virtues that are necessary in social intercourse, chiefly *veritas, humanitas,* and *urbanitas.*

In addition to his 1979 monographic study, Emilio Bonfatti, "Verhaltens-lehrbücher und Verhaltensideale," in Horst A. Glaser, ed., *Deutsche Literatur. Eine Sozialgeschichte 3, Zwischen Gegenreformation und Frühaufklärung: Späthumanismus, Barock: 1572–1740,* ed. Harald Steinhagen (Reinbeck bei Hamburg: Rowohlt, 1985): 74–87, provides an expert short survey of the whole span of conduct literature in Germany at this period. See Bonfatti in Glaser (1985): 80 on the question of the lively Protestant interest in the uses of the *Galateo* and the *Civil conversatione* in Germany, including the role of Caselius.

75. Emilio Bonfatti, *La* Civil Conversazione *in Germania. La letteratura del comportamento da Stefano Guazzo a Adolph Knigge* (1979).

76. *Grobianus et Grobiana* (Francoforti: Haeredes Chr. Egen., 1564; Berlin: Weidmann Buchhandlung, 1903); *Grobianvs. Von groben sitten und un-höflichen gebärden,* trans. Caspar Scheidt von Worms (1551) and Wendelin Hellbach (1567), ed. Wilhelm Mathiessen (München: G. Müller, 1921); *Grobianus* (Leipzig: Zentralantiquariat der Deutschen Demokratischen Republik, 1979); *Grobianus: de morum simplicitate / Grobianus: von groben Sitten und unhöflichen Gebärden,* trans. Caspar Scheidt, ed. Barbara Könneker (Darmstadt: Wissenschaftliche Buchgesellschaft, 1979) [rpt. of 1903, Berlin: Weidmann, Latin text and 1551 German text]. It is worth recalling that in his influential study of Rabelais and popular culture (1965, Eng. ed. *Rabelais and His World,* trans. Helene Iswolsky, Cambridge, MA: M.I.T. Press, 1968), Mikhail M. Bakhtin often refers to German Grobianic literature as an aspect of the surfacing of what he calls the grotesque or comic realism of popular culture, but with the proviso that in that literature the popular motifs are vulgarized and laughter is turned to a negative form of social satire.

77. Otto Brunner, *Neue Wege der Sozialgeschichte. Vorträge und Aufsätze* (Göttingen: Vandenhoeck und Ruprecht, 1956) "Das 'ganze Haus' und die alt-europäische 'Ökonomik,'" 33–61, 225–230 (2d ed. ibid. 1968; 3d ed. 1980, with title *Neue Wege der Verfassungs- und Sozialgeschichte*). Idem, *Adeliges Landleben und europäischer Geist. Leben und Werk Wolf Helmhards von Hohberg 1612–1688* (Salzburg: O. Müller, 1949); It. ed.: *Vita nobiliare e cultura europea* (Bologna: Il Mulino, 1982).

78. Mr. Du Refuge, *Kluger Hofmann* (Franckfurt: Johann Naumanns, 1667). See my note 51 above.

79. *Frauenzimmer Gesprächspiele,* ed. Irmgard Böttcher (Tübingen: M. Niemeyer, 1968–) [vol. 1 and 2 reprinted from the 2d ed., Nürnberg: W. Endter, 1644 and 1657; vols. 3–8 from the 1st ed., 1643–1649].

80. See the later edition: *Mercurius historicus = Der historische Mercurius: das ist, hundert neue und denckwürdige Erzehlungen, theils trauriger, theils frölicher Geschichte ... mit Anfügung eines umbständigen Discursus von der Höflichkeit durch Octavianum Chiliadem* (Franckfurt: Johann Naumans Buchh., 1665).

81. Thomasius, *Discours welcher Gestalt man denen Frantzosen in gemei-*

nem Leben und Wandel nachahmen solle. See Bonfatti in Glaser (1985): 83–87.

82. Bonfatti in Glaser (1985): 80.

CONCLUSION

1. Stephen Greenblatt, *Shakespearean Negotiations: The Circulation of Social Energy in Renaissance England* (Berkeley, Los Angeles, London: University of California Press, 1988), for a study of Shakespeare as an analyst of power.

2. "So the ideal of the knight errant began to blend into that of the officer and gentleman; what had been a cavaliers' code developed into the code of an officer class." M. Keen (1984): 240.

3. "Feudal" habits survived well into recent times; all over Europe the absolute princes bred new feudal structures after 1600. "Il centro di gravità della vita politica è il principe, ed intorno a lui la feudalità è in primo piano, difende i suoi privilegi nei confronti della borghesia, molti membri della quale non sognano altro che entrare nel ceto dei privilegiati, diventar nobili e feudatari." *Storia d'Italia* (Torino: Einaudi, 1972–1973): 5.1: 305. Even Napoleon, the heir of the French bourgeois Revolution, dubbed his princes, dukes, and sundry feudatories with imperial decrees, assigning them incomes from their enfeoffed territories; Gioacchino Murat was one of his "great feudatories." Ibid.: 5.1: 307.

4. For example, Gustavo Costa, *Le antichità germaniche nella cultura italiana da Machiavelli a Vico* (Napoli: Bibliopolis, 1977), especially "La sintesi vichiana," 345–377.

5. *Scienza nuova seconda, giusta l'edizione del 1744,* ed. Fausto Nicolini (Bari: Laterza, 1953): 1: 100, 252, 256, 282, 284; 2: 78, 79, 135, 136, 138 ff., 148 ff.; especially book 5 (on the "ricorsi"), chap. 2, titled "Ricorso che fanno le nazioni sopra la natura eterna de' feudi e quindi il ricorso del diritto romano antico fatto col diritto feudale."

See a close analysis of Vico's use of Dante in Domenico Pietropaolo, *Dante Studies in the Age of Vico* (Ottawa: Dovehouse Editions, 1989): 63–92. In the *Giudizio intorno a Dante* (1729, intended as a preface to Pompeo Venturi's landmark edition of the *Divina Commedia*), Vico saw Dante's nobility, the source of his poetic greatness, as made of a great soul dedicated to fame and glory: *magnanimità, sublimità, virtù pubbliche e grandi, giustizia,* elevated thoughts, and scorn for *avarizia* and *mollizie* (Pietropaolo: 81 f.).

In an attempt to "rediscover" Vico some analysts have been tempted to present him as a forerunner of much of modern speculation. A note of sensible balance even while stating surprising analogies is in Patrick H. Hutton, "La parte nascosta della storia," *Lettera Internazionale* 5/20 (Rome, 1989): 35–38, where Vico's analyses of deep cultural phenomena are perceptively compared with those of N. Elias, J. Huizinga, Lucien Febvre, G. Duby and other *Annales* historians, and the historians of collective *mentalités.*

6. Of course, Corneille's *Cid,* originally a "tragi-comédie," was not based on the medieval original but on Guilhelm de Castro's 1621 *Mocedades del Cid,*

where, typically for a Spanish seventeenth-century courtly heroine, Chimène acted out of pure *pun de onor* based on the fear of *le qu'en dira-t-on*. In Corneille's powerful reelaboration, however, the psychologically complex heroine is caught unaware in a genuine conflict between love and loyalty to the superior code of king and court.

7. On the predicament of would-be tragic writers in eighteenth-century Italy see Franco Fido, "Tragedie 'antiche' senza Fato: un dilemma settecentesco dagli aristotelici al Foscolo," in Paolo Cherchi and Michelangelo Picone, eds., *Studi di Italianistica in onore di Giovanni Cecchetti* (Ravenna: Longo, 1988): 123–146, then in Fido, *Le Muse perdute e ritrovate. Il divenire dei generi letterari fra Sette e Ottocento* (Firenze: Vallecchi, 1989): 11–40.

8. *Della scienza . . . libri tre* (Roma: Francesco Gonzaga, 1710). C. Donati, *L'idea di nobiltà in Italia* (1988): 304–306.

9. Maffei had a point in connecting the desire to take justice in one's own hands with Germanic feudal custom. Societies that could not rely on effectual government have continued to abide by such honor codes to our own days, as witnessed by the pioneer ethos of the American West. Cowboy motion pictures continue to thrive on the code of fighting personal insult even in the face of certain defeat as the way to establish the right to be respected.

10. Satire of nobility runs through the literature of the Enlightenment in many forms. A charming sample in narrative form is Voltaire's "conte" *Jeannot et Colin*, originally in *Contes de Guillaume Vadé* (Genève: chez les Cramer, 1764), now in Voltaire, *Contes et romans*, ed. René Groos (Paris: Gallimard, Bibliothèque de la Pléiade, 1950): 140–148.

11. Casanova, *Romanzi italiani*, ed. Paolo Archi (Firenze: Sansoni, 1984): 103–147. The duel was retold later under a different light in book 10 of Casanova's better known *Histoire de ma vie*.

12. That work was dedicated to the will to "examiner quelle est l'influence de la religion, des moeurs et des lois sur la littérature, et quelle est l'influence de la littérature sur la religion, les moeurs et les lois." These pages are also available in a useful Italian anthology of sociological criticism edited by G. Pagliano Ungari, *Sociologia della letteratura* (Bologna: Il Mulino, 1972).

13. For its exceptional and almost implausible quality it is tempting to mention the case of Theodor Herzl (1860–1904). The Viennese founder of Zionism managed to combine in his brilliantly idiosyncratic personality a vatic devotion to the Jewish cause with a snobbish enthusiasm for the chivalric code of Teutonic knighthood, believing in duels and looking to the Prussian Junkers as personal models. See Carl E. Schorske, *Fin-de-siècle Vienna: Politics and Culture* (New York: Alfred A. Knopf, 1980): 146–175; Ernst Pawel, *The Labyrinth of Exile: A Life of Theodor Herzl* (New York: Farrar, Straus and Giroux, 1989).

14. Mark Twain's satire of chivalry had a serious social and political background: he once held the chivalric ideology partly responsible for the Civil War as the mental attitude that gave southern landowners an unrealistic pride in their social and moral superiority vis-à-vis the bourgeois industrial north. See, for example, Philip S. Foner, *Mark Twain Social Critic* (New York: International Publishers, 1958): "Sir Walter Disease," at 201.

428 Notes to Pages 311–315

15. Nemoianu, *A Theory of the Secondary: Literature, Progress, and Re-action* (Baltimore: The Johns Hopkins University Press, 1989): xi. Nemoianu (ibid.) attributes these views to such critics as Derrida, too, but claims that they want to reverse this relationship, which he proposes to respect.

16. This is also the implication of the essays in Armstrong and Tennenhouse, eds., *The Ideology of Conduct* (1987), although their attempt to see a tight correspondence between rules of conduct and literary standards may not be entirely convincing. See, especially, Ann Rosalind Jones, "Nets and Bridles: Early Modern Conduct Books and Sixteenth-Century Women's Lyrics," 39–72, and the introductory essay by the editors, at 7.

APPENDIX

1. Bertram Colgrave, *The Earliest Life of Gregory the Great, by an Anonymous Monk of Whitby*; Text, Translation, and Notes (Lawrence, KS: University of Kansas Press, 1968; Cambridge and New York: Cambridge University Press, 1985).

2. Information on the monastery of St. Alban in England is in Rachel Bullington, *The "Alexis" in the St. Alban's Psalter. A Look into the Heart of the Matter* (New York: Garland, 1989) [1985 University of North Carolina Dissertation in Romance Philology]. The Tuscan MS. was edited by Alessandro D'Ancona, *La leggenda di santo Albano, prosa inedita del secolo XIV, e la storia di san Giovanni Boccadoro, secondo due antiche lezioni in ottava rima* (Bologna: Gaetano Romagnoli, 1865): 69–84, and is reproduced in *Prosatori minori del Trecento* 1: *Scrittori di religione*, ed. Giuseppe De Luca, La Letteratura Italiana: Storia e Testi 12.1 (Milano, Napoli: R. Ricciardi, 1954): 1155–1162. This version is part of the legends of hermits yielding to temptation. The Christian virgin daughter of a king of India is raped by a hermit who repents and becomes St. Alban, performing the miracle of resuscitating her.

3. The name Alban has been traced to St. Alban of Verulam (name of the present St. Alban in England), English martyr included in the Venerable Bede's work, and St. Alban of Mainz, with opinions differing as to whether it is originally the story of the same martyr or of two.

4. For example, Hendrik Sparnaay, "Hartmann von Aue and His Successors," in *Arthurian Literature in the Middle Ages* (1959), ed. Roger S. Loomis, 430–442 at 436, for a pithy statement of the element of chivalric romance in Hartmann's *Gregorius*.

5. Morvay's (1977) is a philological study of the whole manuscript tradition, including edited texts of all principal versions in the three languages. See the presumably earliest Latin text at pp. 25–32; 128 ff. on Albrecht von Eyb. The Dutch version, printed on facing pages alongside Eyb's, is very close to the latter and slightly more expanded than Eyb's vis-à-vis the Latin version.

6. The numerous reverberations of the "Gregorsage" aroused the interest of investigators at an early date: see H. Sparnaay (1920), who stressed its "chevalereskes Element": "das Rittertum bildet also den Grundstock der Erzählung" (32). Sparnaay (22) also connected the saga of Gregorius with the Middle English *Syr Eglamour of Artois*, the *Dit du Buef* (*Hist. Litt.* 23, 121), a couple of

stories in Thomas Wright's *Latin Stories* (nos. 110 "de domina romana" and 112 "de regina differente confiteri," both from Harley MSS.), and the story of the lovely Catherine, a novella of multiple incest in Marguerite de Navarre's *Heptaméron* which corresponded to Bandello's novella 35 of Part 2, but went back to Masuccio Salernitano, story 3 of Part 3. On all these texts and many more, see A. Seelisch, "Die Gregoriuslegende" (1887).

7. Text of Albanus novella at pp. 91 ff. of 1472 ed. and 1966 rpt.; pp. 108–118 of 1982 rpt.

8. *Ehebuch* 91, translated by Hiller: 153. Critics have noted the discrepancy between the nature of the treatise and the legend of Albanus, which appears at the very end perhaps as a way of countering the worldly character of the work by closing it with a pious story that stresses the notion of divine grace. It was sometimes rendered in abridged form and, indeed, Karl Müller's 1879 translation of the *Ehebüchlein* (Sondershausen: Altdeutsche Werke in neuen Bearbeitungen, 8) omitted it altogether. Helmut Weinacht has nothing else to say about the story in his learned introduction to the facsimile reprint of the 1472 edition (p. xiv n. 31).

9. Hiller: 152–154. But Hiller does not specifically mention the version of the St. Alban legend in the *Gesta Romanorum*, perhaps confusing it with the Gregory story in chap. 81.

10. Note that the incipit of at least one manuscript of the main early version of the Latin legend designates the saint as "a knight": *Vita sancti Albani militis* (MS. Berlin Staatsbibliothek, Preuss. Kulturbesitz, cod. Lat. Fol. 373, 15th c.; see Morvay 12 f.).

11. Ludwig Wolff in Hermann Paul's edition of *Gregorius* (1973): x f.

12. See these and many other details of the rich tradition in L. Wolff's introduction to H. Paul's 1973 edition of *Gregorius*, with ample bibliography. The standard complete edition of the Latin *Gesta Romanorum*, in 181 chapters plus additions, is still the 1872 one by Oesterley, who listed 138 extant Latin manuscripts plus a few that turned out after his editorial work was ready, and many more versions in other languages, especially German. There are several partial editions of the Latin as well as of early vernacular translations, which usually do not contain the stories that concern us here. See the Gregorius story in Oesterley edition, chap. 81: 399–409, and the Albanus story in chap. 244, chap. 48 of the Appendix: 641–646. This latter is the one that interests us specifically, and it is mentioned only by Morvay, not by Wolff or Hiller.

13. This chap. 244 on St. Alban seems to appear in only four of the codices known to Oesterley. It ends with the murder of the two parents and does not contain the final section on St. Alban's martyrdom. At least two more individual authors are worth mentioning, namely Petrus de Natalibus (d. Venice before 1406), author of the 1369/72 *Catalogus sanctorum* which contains a shorter Latin version of the St. Alban legend, and Petrus Cratepolius of Cologne (ca. 1540–1605), who in his biographical catalogue of German bishops, *De Germaniae episcopis* (Cologne, 1592: 7), gave brief notice of a saintly king of Hungary named St. Alban.

14. It was also studied by Carl Kraus, *Deutsche Gedichte* (1894). See L. Wolff: ix.

15. See good biographies of Albrecht in *Neue Deutsche Biographie* (Berlin:

Duncker und Humblot, 1953–): 4; (1959): 705 f., and especially in W. Stammler et al., eds., *Die deutsche Literatur des Mittelalters—Verfasserlexikon* (1978–): 1: 179–186 by Gerhard Klecha. Also Karin Morvay, "Albanus," ibid.: 106–108; and J. A. Hiller, *Albrecht von Eyb* (1939, 1970), a study which, besides unusual bibliographic carelessness, relies on Max Herrmann for much of its documentation even while it strives at every step to counter Herrmann's judgments as to Eyb's allegiance to humanism.

16. Hiller denies it is humanistic.

17. The *Margarita* is available in the Munich Landesbibliothek as Inc. c.a. 2 3200 (best) and Inc. c.a. 1902. The incunabular edition of the *Ehebüchlein*, with title *Ob eynem manne sey zunemen eyn eelichs weyb, oder nicht*, is ibid. as Inc. c.a. 33^e 4° and 2° Inc. s.a. 432a. There are three modern editions of the *Ehebüchlein* (1879, 1890, 1966), all rare; see a bibliography of facsimile reprints of incunabula 1918–1965 by Jens Peter Störmer in the E. Eck edition (1966).

18. See, especially, Noël Valois (1881), with the concurrence of Carl Kraus (1894) to the extent that the use of this *cursus* is a pertinent argument for placing Transmundus at the source of the legend.

19. In her entry on "Albanus" in Stammler's *Verfasserlexikon* (1978): 1: 107, Morvay declares the evidence for the Transmundus authorship inconclusive.

20. At variance with Gabrielle Schieb, "Schuld und Sühne in Hartmanns *Gregorius*," *Beiträge zur Geschichte der deutschen Sprache und Literatur* 72 (1950): 51–64, Morvay (157) sees a difference between the *Gregorius* and the Albanus legend in that in the latter the theological implications on guilt or innocence versus atonement (both heroes are unintentionally involved in the infraction of the code, but both seek punishment and undergo harsh penance) appear to be directed outward (hence also to political milieus), whereas they seem to be internal to ecclesiastical speculation in the story of Gregorius.

21. Baron, *The Crisis of the Early Italian Renaissance; Civic Humanism and Republican Liberty in an Age of Classicism and Tyranny* (Princeton, N.J.: Princeton University Press, 1955): 1: 625–628; revised 1-volume edition with an epilogue (ibid., 1966): 420–423.

22. See my chap. 7, note 17.

References

This basic, selected working bibliography contains titles that have been given only in abridged form in the notes. Titles that were relevant to the exposition and documentation without being directly related to the main arguments, or that have been used only once or twice in the text, have appeared in full in the notes and are not repeated here. Though occasionally arbitrary, this differentiation seemed appropriate for a more manageable and useful bibliography. Conversely, several relevant entries not referred to in the text are included here as aids for further investigation.

PRIMARY SOURCES

Aegidius Columna Romanus. 1498. *De regimine principum*. Venetiis: Simon Bevilaqua.

[———.] 1899. *Li livres dou gouvernement des rois: a XIIIth century French version of Egidio Colonna's treatise De regimine principum*. Ed. Samuel P. Molenaer. New York: Columbia University Press and Macmillan. Rpt. New York: AMS Press, 1966.

Albergati, Fabio. 1599. *Del cardinale libri tre*. Bologna: Eredi G. Rossi.

Ambrose, Saint. 1845. *De officiis ministrorum ecclesiae libri tres. Patrologia Latina* 16 (rpt. Turnout: Brepols, 1979): cols. 18–184.

[Anselm of Lucca.] [1856] 1922–. *Vita Anselmi episcopi Lucensis auctore Bardone presbytero*. Ed. Rogerus Wilmans. *Monumenta Germaniae Historica*, Scriptores 12: 1–35. Hannoverae: Hahn.

[———.] 1934. *Vita metrica Sancti Anselmi Lucensis episcopi auctore Rangerio Lucensi*. Eds. Ernestus Sackur, Gerhardus Schwartz, and Bernardus Schmeidler. *Monumenta Germaniae Historica*, Scriptores 30.2: 1152–1307. Lipsiae: Karl W. Hiersemann.

Babees Book (The), Aristotle's A B C Urbanitatis, Stans puer ad mensam, The

Lutille Childrenes Lutil Boke. 1868. Ed. Frederick J. Furnivall. Early English
Text Society, old series no. 32. London: N. Trübner.

Babees' Book (The): Medieval Manners for the Young, done into modern English from Dr. Furnivall's texts by Edith Rickert. 1966. New York: Cooper Square Publishers.

Bargagli, Scipione. 1587; 1591; 1592. *I Trattenimenti. Dove da vaghe donne e da giovani huomini rappresentati sono honesti e dilettevoli giuochi, narrate novelle, e cantate alcune amorose canzonette*. Venetia: Bernardo Giunti.

Bartolus of Sassoferrato. 1983. *De insigniis et armis tractatus*. In Evan John Jones. *Medieval Heraldry*. Cardiff: W. Lewis, 1943. New York: AMS Press.

———. 1552. *Opera*. 8 vols. Lugduni: Compagnie des Libraires.

———. 1581. *In tres Codicis libros*. Venetiis: Giunti.

———. 1585. *In Secundam Codicis Partem*. Venetiis: n.p.

[Benzo of Alba.] 1854. *Benzonis episcopis Albensis ad Henricum IV imperatorem libri VII*. Ed. K. Pertz. *Monumenta Germaniae Historica*, Scriptores 11: 591–681.

Benzoni, Gino. 1978. *Gli affanni della cultura. Intellettuali e potere nell'Italia della Controriforma e barocca*. Milano: Feltrinelli.

———, and Tiziano Zanato, eds. 1982. *Storici e politici veneti del Cinquecento e del Seicento*. Milano, Napoli: R. Ricciardi.

Berges, Wilhelm, ed. 1938; 1952. *Die Fürstenspiegel des hohen und späten Mittelalters. Monumenta Germaniae Historica*, Schriften des Reichsinstituts für ältere deutsche Geschichtskunde 2. Leipzig: K. W. Hiersemann; Stuttgart: A. Hiersemann.

[Bernard of Clairvaux, Saint.] 1957–1977. *De gradibus humilitatis et superbiae; Ad milites Templi de laude novae militiae*. In *S. Bernardi Opera*. Eds. Jean Leclercq, C. H. Talbot, and H. M. Rochais. 8 vols. Roma: Editiones Cistercienses. Vol. 3.

[Bernard of Parma.] 1926. *Vitae prima et secunda s. Bernardi episcopi Parmensis*. Ed. P. E. Schramm. *Monumenta Germaniae Historica*, Scriptores 30.2: 1316–1327. Leipzig: K. W. Hiersemann.

Biblioteca Nazionale Marciana. 1961. *Codici marciani ed edizioni italiane antiche di epopea carolingia*. Venezia: Biblioteca Nazionale Marciana.

Biondo, Flavio. 1973. *De militia et iurisprudentia*. In *Scritti inediti e rari di Biondo Flavio*. Ed. Bartolomeo Nogara. Roma: Tipografia Poliglotta Vaticana, 1927; rpt. ibid.

Bonizo of Sutri. 1930. *Liber de vita christiana*. Ed. E. Perels. Berlin: Weidmann.

Bonvesin da la Riva. 1941. *Le opere volgari*. Ed. Gianfranco Contini. Vol. 1. Roma: Società Filologica Romana.

———. 1985. *Le cinquanta cortesie da tavola*. Eds. Mario Cantella and Donatella Magrassi. Milano: La Spiga/Libreria Meravigli.

———. 1987. *Volgari scelti*. Ed. and trans. Patrick S. Diehl and Ruggero Stefanini. American University Studies 2.58. New York-Bern: Peter Lang.

Borromeo, Federico [1564–1631]. 1632. *Il libro intitolato la gratia de' principi di Federico Borromeo*. . . . Milano: n.p.

Botero, Giovanni. 1589. *Della ragion di stato libri dieci*. Venetia: appresso I Gioliti, 1589; Ferrara: Vittorio Baldini.

————. 1599. *Dell'uffitio del cardinale libri due*. Roma: Mutii.

————. 1607. *I capitani . . . con alcuni discorsi curiosi, cioè Relationi di Spagna, dello Stato della Chiesa, del Piemonte . . . e due discorsi della Monarchia e della Nobiltà*. Torino: Gio. Domenico Tarino.

[Boucicaut.] 1985. *Le Livre des faits du bon messire Jehan le Maingre, dit Bouciquaut, mareschal de France et gouverneur de Jennes*. Ed. Denis Lalande. Textes Littéraires Français no. 331. Genève: Droz.

Bracciolini, Poggio. 1657. *De nobilitate*. Avellino: C. Cavalli. [With Leonardo Chiensi's response.]

————. 1964–1969. *Opera omnia*. 4 tomes. Torino: Bottega d'Erasmo. [Rpt. of Basel: Henricpetri, 1538 ed.]

————. 1983. *Facezie*. Ed. Eugenio Garin, trans. Marcello Ciccuto. Milano: Biblioteca Universale Rizzoli.

Brunetto Latini. 1984. *Li Livres dou Tresor*. Ed. Francis Carmody. University of California Publications in Modern Philology no. 22. Berkeley: University of California Press.

Bueil, Jean de, comte de Sancerre. 1887–1889. *Le Jouvencel, suivi du commentaire de Guillaume Tringant*. Eds. Camille Favre and Léon Lecestre. 2 vols. Paris: Librairie Renouard, H. Laurens, successeur.

Buonaccorso da Montemagno il Giovane. 1718. *Prose e rime de' due Buonaccorsi da Montemagno e di Niccolò Tinucci*. Ed. G. B. Carotti. Firenze: Giuseppe Manni.

————. 1874. *Prose del Giovane Buonaccorso da Montemagno*. Bologna: G. Romagnoli.

Buonaccosa, I. 1575. *De servis vel famulis tractatus*. Venetiis: D. Zenaro.

Canoniero, P. A. 1609. *Il perfetto cortegiano et dell'ufizio del principe verso 'l cortegiano*. Roma: B. Zanetti.

Castiglione, Baldassare. 1960. *Il Cortegiano*. In *Opere di Baldassare Castiglione, Giovanni Della Casa, Benvenuto Cellini*. Ed. Carlo Cordié. Milano, Napoli: Riccardo Ricciardi.

————. 1947. *Il Libro del Cortegiano*. Ed. Vittorio Cian. Firenze: G. C. Sansoni, 1894; 2d ed. 1910; 4th ed. 1947.

————. 1955, 1983. *Il Cortegiano*. Ed. Bruno Maier. Torino: Unione Tipografica Editrice Torinese [UTET].

[————.] 1585. *Balthasaris Castilionis comitis De curiali sive aulico libri quatuor, nouissime aediti*. Londini: apud Thomam Dauson tipographum.

[————.] 1603. *Balthasaris Castilionis comitis De curiali*. Londini: Impensis G. Bishop.

Chappuys, Gabriel. 1585. *Le Misaule, ou haineux de court*. Paris: Guillaume Linocier.

Charny, Geoffroi de. 1867–1877. *Livre de chevalerie*. In Jean Froissart. *Chroniques*. Ed. Kervyn de Lettenhove. 25 vols. Bruxelles: V. Devaux for the Académie Royale de Belgique.

Chartier, Alain. 1974. *Le curial*. Genève: Slatkine Reprints.

Chrétien de Troyes. 1981–1983. *Les Romans*. Paris: Honoré Champion. Vol. 1. *Erec et Enide*, ed. Mario Roques (1981); vol. 2. *Cligés*, ed. Alexandre Micha (1982); vol. 3. *Le chevalier de la charrete*, ed. Mario Roques (1983);

vol. 4. *Le chevalier au lion (Yvain)*, ed. Mario Roques (1982); vols. 5–6. *Le conte du Graal (Perceval)*, ed. Félix Lecoy (1981).

———. 1987. *Arthurian Romances*. Trans. D. D. R. Owen. Everyman Classics. London, Melbourne: Dent.

Christine de Pisan. 1913. *L'épître d'Othéa, déesse de la prudence, à Hector, chef des Troyens*. Bruxelles: Vromant & Co.

———. 1942. *The Epistle of Othea to Hector: a 'lytil bibell of knyghthod,'* edited from the Harleian manuscript 838 by James D. Gordon. Philadelphia: University of Pennsylvania Dissertation.

———. 1977. *Le ditié de Jehanne d'Arc*. Eds. Angus J. Kennedy and Kenneth Varty. Oxford: Society for the Study of Mediaeval Languages and Literature.

Chroniques des Comtes d'Anjou et des Seigneurs d'Amboise. 1913. Eds. Louis Halphen and René Poupardin. Collection de textes pour servir à l'étude et à l'enseignement de l'histoire no. 48. Paris: A. Picard.

[Cicero] Cicéron. 1965. *Les devoirs*. Ed. Maurice Testard. 2 vols. Paris: Les Belles Lettres.

Coluccio Salutati. 1542. Ed. Girolamo Giganti. *Tractatus insignis et elegans de nobilitate legum et medicinae in quo terminatur illa quaestio versatilis in studiis: utrum dignior sit scientia legalis, vel medicinalis*. Venetiis: Joannes Baptista Pederzani.

———. 1947. *De nobilitate legum et medicinae. De verecundia*. Ed. Eugenio Garin. Firenze: Vallecchi.

Conradus Hirsaugiensis [Conrad of Hirsau]. 1966. *Dialogus de mundi contemptu vel amore, attribué à Conrad d'Hirsau. . . .* Ed. Robert Bultot. Analecta Mediaevalia Namurcensia no. 19. Louvain: Éditions Nauwelaerts.

Constantinus VII Porphyrogenitus, Emperor of the East, 905–959. 1935–1940. *Le livre des cérémonies*. Ed. and trans. Albert Vogt. 2 vols. Paris: Les Belles Lettres.

———. 1949–1962. *De administrando imperio*. Greek text ed. by Gy. Moravcsik, trans. by R. J. H. Jenkins. 2 vols. Budapest: Pázmány Péter Tudományegyetemi Görög Filológiai Intézet. Vol. 2 also London: Athlone Press, 1962.

Contarini, Gasparo. 1571; 1578. *De officio episcopi libri duo* [1516]; *De magistratibus et republica Venetorum libri V* [Paris, 1543; *La Repubblica e i Magistrati di Vinegia*, It. trans. by Ludovico Domenichi, Vinegia: Girolamo Scoto, 1544]. In Gasparo Contarini. *Opera*. Parisiis: Sebastianus Nivellius; Venetiis: Aldus.

Cortesi, Paolo. 1510. *De cardinalatu*. In Castro Cortesio: S. N. Nardi.

De Ferrariis, Antonio (Il Galateo). 1939. *Epistola ad Gelasium de nobilitate*. In D. Colucci. "A. D. detto il Galateo." *Rinascenza Salentina*, n.s. 7: 26–50.

———. 1959. *Epistole*. Ed. Antonio Altamura. Lecce: Centro di Studi Salentini.

[Della Casa, Giovanni.] 1970. *Prose di Giovanni Della Casa e altri trattatisti cinquecenteschi del comportamento*. Ed. Arnaldo Di Benedetto. Torino: UTET.

———. 1971. *Il Galateo, ovvero de' costumi*. Ed. Bruno Maier. Milano: Mursia.

———. 1986. *Galateo*. Trans. Konrad Eisenbichler and Kenneth R. Bartlett.

Centre for Reformation and Renaissance Studies, University of Toronto, Texts in Translation Series. Ottawa: Dovehouse Editions.

Der deutsche Facetus. 1911. Ed. Carl Schroeder. Palaestra 86. Berlin: Mayer & Müller.

Equicola, Mario. 1525. *Libro de natura de amore.* Venetia: L. Lorio; Lorenzo da Portes. Venetia: Gioanniantonio e fratelli de Sabbio, 1526.

[Erasmus of Rotterdam.] 1530. *De civilitate morum puerilium . . . libellus.* Parisiis: Ch. Wechel. London: W. de Worde, 1532.

———. 1986. *Institutio principis christiani / The Education of a Christian Prince.* [Eng. trans.] Erasmus. *Literary and Eucational Writings* 5, 6. Ed. A. H. T. Levi. Collected Works of Erasmus nos. 27–28. Toronto, Buffalo: University of Toronto Press.

———. 1988. *Enchiridion militis christiani / Handbuch of the Christian Soldier.* [Eng. trans.] Erasmus. *Spiritualia.* Ed. John W. O'Malley. Collected Works of Erasmus no. 66. Toronto, Buffalo: University of Toronto Press.

Erdmann, Carl, and Norbert Fickermann, eds. 1950. *Briefsammlungen der Zeit Heinrichs IV. Monumenta Germaniae Historica,* Briefe der deutschen Kaiserzeit 5. Weimar: Böhlau.

Étienne de Fougères. 1979. *Le livre des manières.* Ed. A. Lodge. Genève: Droz.

Evitascandolo, C. 1598. *Dialogo del maestro di casa.* Roma: S. Mancini.

———. 1609. *Libro dello scalco, quale insegna questo honesto servitio.* Roma: C. Vulietti.

Facetus. 1886. Edited by A. Morel-Fatío. *Romania* 15: 224–235.

Faret, Nicolas. [Paris, 1630; ibid.: Jean Brunet, 1639.] 1970. *L'honnête homme ou l'art de plaire à la Court.* Ed. M. Magendie. Paris, 1925. Rpt. Genève: Slatkine Reprints.

Fazio, Bartolomeo. 1611. *De excellentia ac praestantia hominis.* In Felino Maria Sandeo. *Epitome de regibus Siciliae et Apuliae.* Hannoviae: Wechel.

Fundatio ecclesiae Hildensemensis. 1926. Ed. Adolf Hofmeister. *Monumenta Germaniae Historica,* Scriptores 30.2: 939–946. Leipzig: K. W. Hiersemann.

[Garati da Lodi.] 1968. *Il 'Tractatus de principibus' di Martino Garati da Lodi.* Ed. Gigliola Rondinini Soldi. Milano, Varese: Istituto Editoriale Cisalpino.

Garin, Eugenio, ed. 1947. *La disputa delle arti nel Quattrocento.* Firenze: Vallecchi.

Geoffrey of Monmouth. 1929. *Historia regum Britanniae.* In Edmond Faral. *La légende arthurienne: Études et documents.* 3 vols. Paris: Champion.

Gerald of Wales. 1891. *De principis instructione liber.* Ed. George F. Warner. Rolls Series 21:8. London: Eyre & Spottiswood.

[*Girart de Roussillon.*] 1856. *L'Histoire de monseigneur Gerart de Roussillon.* Abrégé de Jean Mansel. Lyon: Olivier Arnoullet, 1846. Rpt. Lyon: De Terrebasse.

———. 1939. Ed. Edward B. Ham. New Haven, CT: Yale University Press.

Girart de Roussillon, chanson de geste. 1953–1955. Ed. W. Mary Hackett. Société des Anciens Textes Français. 3 vols. Paris: A. et J. Picard.

[*Girart de Roussillon.*] 1972. *Le Roman en vers de Girart de Rossillon . . .* par Mignard. Paris: J. Techener, 1858. Rpt. Amsterdam: Rodopi.

Gottfried von Strassburg. 1967. *Tristan und Isold*. Ed. Friedrich Ranke and Gottfried Weber. Darmstadt: Wissenschaftliche Buchgesellschaft.

Gracián, Baltasar. 1659; 1954. *Oráculo manual y arte de prudencia*. [Madrid, 1647;] Amsterdam: J. Blaeu, 1659; ed. Miguel Romero-Navarro, *Revista di Filología Española*, anejo 62 (Madrid, 1954). French trans. by Amelot de la Houssaie as *L'homme de cour*. Paris: Veuve Martin et J. Boudot, 1684. Eng. trans. as *The Courtiers Manual Oracle*. London: M. Flesher for Abel Swalle, 1685, 1694, etc.

Grassi, Paride. 1564. *De ceremoniis cardinalium et episcoporum*. Romae: Blado.

Guarini, Battista. 1594. *Il segretario*. Venezia: B. Magiotti.

Guazzo, Stefano. 1574. *La civil conversatione*. Brescia: Tomaso Bozzola; Venetia: Altobello Salicato; Vinegia: Enea de Alaris. Also ibid.: Robino, 1575.

[———.] 1925. *The Civile Conversation of M. Steeven Guazzo*. Trans. George Pettie and Bartholomew Young. Ed. E. Sullivan. 2 vols. London: Constable & Co.; New York: A. Knopf.

[Guido de Basochis.] 1969. *Liber epistolarum Guidonis de Basochis*. Ed. Herbert Adolfsson. Acta Universitatis Stockholmiensis, Studia Latina Stockholmiensia no. 18. Stockholm: Almquist & Wiksell.

Hallam, Elizabeth M., ed. 1986. *The Plantagenet Chronicles*. London, New York: Weidenfeld & Nicolson.

Hartmann von Aue. 1984. *Iwein*. Ed. and trans. Patrick M. McConeghy. New York, London: Garland.

———. 1968. *Iwein*. Eds. G. F. Benecke, K. Lachmann, and L. Wolff, trans. Thomas Cramer. 7th ed. Berlin: Walter de Gruyter.

Havelock the Dane. 1901. Ed. Ferdinand Holthausen. London: S. Low, Marston & Co.; New York: E. Stechert.

[Herbord of Michelsberg.] 1974. *Herbord dialog o życiu św. Ottona, biskupa bamberskiego—Herbordi dialogus de vita Sancti Ottonis episcopi Babenbergensis*. Eds. Jan Wikarjak and Kazimierz Liman. Monumenta Poloniae Historica, n.s. 7.3. Warsaw: Państwowe & Wydawnictwo Naukowe.

L'Histoire de Guillaume le Maréchal. 1891–1901. Ed. Paul Meyer. 2 vols. Paris: Librairie Renouard, H. Laurens, successeur.

Honorius Augustodunensis. 1895. *Speculum Ecclesiae*. Patrologia Latina 172 (Paris: Garnier frères): 807-1108.

Hugh of St. Victor. 1854. *De institutione novitiorum*. Patrologia Latina 176 (rpt. Turnhout: Brepols, 1983): 925–952.

———. 1961. *The Didascalicon*. Trans. Jerome Taylor. New York: Columbia University Press.

Hugo von Trimberg. 1970. *Der Renner*. Ed. Gustav Ehrismann. Bibliothek des Literarischen Vereins in Stuttgart vols. 247, 248, 252, 256. 4 vols. Tübingen: Litterarischer Verein in Stuttgart, 1908–1911. Rpt. Berlin: Walter de Gruyter.

[Hutten, Ulrich von.] 1518. *Ulrichi de Hutten equitis Germani Aula Dialogus*. Basileae: Johann Froben, mense Nouembri.

Ingegneri, Angelo. 1594. *Del buon segretario libri tre*. Roma: G. Falcotti.

Jensen, Frede, ed. and trans. 1986. *The Poetry of the Sicilian School.* New York, London: Garland.

[Johannes of Limoges.] 1932. *Joannis Lemovicensis abbatis de Zirc 1208– 1218 Opera omnia.* Ed. Constantin Horváth. 3 vols. Vesprém, Hungary: Egyházmegyei Könyvnyomda.

[John of Salisbury.] 1909. *Johannis Saresberiensis episcopi Carnotensis Policratici sive de nugis curialium et vestigiis philosophorum libri VIII.* Ed. Clemens J. Webb. 2 vols. Oxford: Clarendon.

Kraus, Carl von, ed. 1894. *Deutsche Gedichte des 12. Jahrhunderts.* Halle/S.: M. Niemeyer.

———, ed. 1952–1958. *Deutsche Liederdichter des 13. Jahrhunderts.* 2 vols. Tübingen: M. Niemeyer. (1: Text, 2: Kommentar.) 2d ed. by Hugo Kuhn, 1978.

———, Hugo Moser, and Helmut Tervooren, eds. 1977–1981. *Des Minnesangs Frühling.* 36th ed. 3 vols. Stuttgart: S. Hirzel.

Lalaing, Jacques. 1866. *Le livre des faits.* In Georges Chastellain. *Oeuvres.* Ed. Kervyn de Lettenhove. 8 vols. Bruxelles: F. Heussner (V. Devaux for vol. 8), 1863–1866. Vol. 8.

Lambert of Ardres. 1855. *Chronicon Ghisnense et Ardense.* Ed. Denis Charles de Godefroy-Ménilglaise. Paris: J. Renouard.

———. 1879. *Lamberti Ardensis Historia comitum Ghisnensium.* Ed. Johann Heller. *Monumenta Germaniae Historica,* Scriptores 24: 550–642.

[*Lancelot* (Prose cycle).] 1908–1916. *The Vulgate Version of the Arthurian romances.* Ed. from manuscripts in the British Museum by Heinrich Oskar Sommer. 8 vols. Washington: Carnegie Institution. Vol. 1. *Lestoire del Saint Graal* (1909); vol. 2. *Lestoire de Merlin* (1908); vols. 3–5. *Le livre de Lancelot del Lac* (1910–1912); vol. 6. *Les aventures ou la queste del Saint Graal. La mort le roi Artus* (1913); vol. 7. Supplement: *Le livre d'Artus,* with glossary (1913); vol. 8. Index of names and places (1916).

Lannoy, Ghillebert de. 1878. *Oeuvres.* Ed. Charles Potvin. Louvain: P. & J. Lefever.

Lapo da Castiglionchio. 1914. *Dialogus de excellentia et dignitate Curie Romane supra certas policias et curias antiquorum et modernorum contra eos qui Romanam Curiam diffamant.* Ed. Richard Scholz. "Eine humanistische Schilderung der Kurie aus dem Jahre 1438." *Quellen und Forschungen aus Italienischen Archiven und Bibliotheken* 16: 108–153. Partial ed. with It. trans. in *Prosatori latini del Quattrocento.* 1952. Ed. Eugenio Garin, 170–211. Milano, Napoli: Ricciardi.

Lapo da Castiglionchio il Vecchio. 1753. *Epistola o sia ragionamento.* Ed. Lorenzo Mehus. Bologna: Girolamo Corciolani.

Llull, Ramón. 1901. *Libro de la orden de caballeria.* Ed. and trans. José Ramón de Luanco. Barcelona: Tipografía Académica. French version *Livre de l'ordre de chevalerie.* 1972. Ed. Vincenzo Minervini. Bari: Adriatica. Eng. trans. (from French version) by W. Caxton. 1926, 1976. *The Book of the Ordre of Chyvalry.* Eds. Alfred T. P. Byles and H. Milford. Early English Text Society. London, Oxford: Oxford University Press; Amsterdam: Theatrum Orbis Terrarum; Norwood, NJ: W. J. Johnson.

————. 1986. *Libre del orde de cavayleria*. Ed. Luis Alberto de Cuenca. Madrid: Alianza; Barcelona: Enciclopedía Catalana.

Loomis, Roger Sherman, ed. 1959; 1961. *Arthurian Literature in the Middle Ages*. Oxford: Clarendon Press.

————, and Laura Hibbard Loomis, eds. 1957. *Medieval Romances*. New York: The Modern Library.

Manetti, Giannozzo. 1532. *De dignitate et excellentia hominis*. Ed. Giovanni Alessandro Brassicano. Basileae: A. Cratandrus.

————. 1734. *Vita Nicolai V Summi Pontificis*. Ed. Ludovico Antonio Muratori. *Rerum Italicarum Scriptores*. 25 vols. Milano: Typographia Societatis Palatinae, 1723–1751: 3/2: cols. 929–940. Rpt. Bologna: Arnoldo Forni, 1978.

[————.] 1975. *Ianottii Manetti De dignitate et excellentia hominis*. Ed. Elizabeth R. Leonard. Padova: Antenore.

Manfredi, Girolamo. 1564. *De cardinalibus Sanctae Romanae Ecclesiae liber*. Bologna: Johannes Rubrius.

Map, Walter. [1914.] 1983. *De nugis curialium / Courtiers' Trifles*. Eds. and trans. Montague R. James, Christopher N. L. Brooke, and Roger A. B. Mynors. Oxford: Clarendon Press; New York: Oxford University Press.

Meyer-Benfey, Heinrich, ed. 1909. "Der heimliche Bote." *Mittelhochdeutsche Übungsstücke*. Halle: Niemeyer.

[Morena, Acerbo.] 1930. *Das Geschichtswerk des Otto Morena und seiner Fortsetzer über die Taten Friedrichs I. in der Lombardei*. Ed. Ferdinand Güterbock. *Monumenta Germaniae Historica*, Scriptores rerum germanicarum, n.s. 7. Berlin: Weidmann; rpt. 1964.

Murchland, Bernard, ed. and trans. 1966. *Two Views of Man: Pope Innocent III On the misery of man; Giannozzo Manetti On the dignity of man*. New York: F. Ungar.

Nibelungenlied (das). 1979. Ed. Karl Bartsch/Helmut de Boor. 21st ed. Wiesbaden: F. A. Brockhaus.

[*Nibelungenlied*.] 1911. *The Lay of the Nibelung Men*. Trans. Arthur S. Way. Cambridge: Cambridge University Press.

Niccolò (Nicola) da Casola. 1907. *Attila, poema franco-italiano*. Ed. Giulio Bertoni. Collectanea Friburgensia, n.s. 9. Friburgo (Svizzera): Libreria dell'Università/O. Gschwend.

————. 1941. *La guerra d'Attila, poema franco-italiano pubblicato dall'unico manoscritto della R. Biblioteca estense di Modena*. Ed. Guido Stendardo. Modena: Società Tipografica Modenese.

Nifo, Agostino. 1534. *De re aulica ad Phausinam*. Neapoli: Ioannes Antonius de Caneto. It. trans. Francesco Baldelli, *Il cortigiano del Sessa*. Genova: A. Belloni, 1560.

Palmieri, Matteo. 1982. *Della vita civile*. Ed. Gino Belloni. Firenze: Sansoni.

Paolo da Certaldo. 1945. *Libro di buoni costumi*. Ed. Alfredo Schiaffini. Firenze: Le Monnier.

Paruta, Paolo. 1579; 1599. *Della perfettione della vita politica*. Venezia: Domenico Nicolini.

————. 1943. *Discorsi politici*. Bologna: N. Zanichelli.

Patrizi, Francesco. 1518, 1520. *De institutione reipublicae libri IX*. Paris: in aedibus Galioti a Prato; ibid.: apud Aegidium Gorfinum, 1569, 1575; Argentinae: Lazarus Zetzner, 1594, 1595.

————. 1545. *De' discorsi del Rev. Monsignor Francesco Patritii Sanese vescovo Gaiettano, sopra alle cose appartenenti ad una città libera e famiglia nobile*. Vinegia: Figliuoli di Aldo.

Pellegrini, Matteo. [Peregrini.] 1624. *Che al savio è convenevole il corteggiare*. Bologna: Per Nicolò Tebaldini, ad instanza di Pellegrino Golfarini.

————. 1634. *Della pratica comune a' prencipi e servidori loro libri cinque*. Viterbo: Diotallevi.

Petreus, Heinrich. 1578. *Aulica vita et opposita huic vita privata*. Accessere recens ad hanc secundam editionem . . . Antonij à Guevara *De vitae aulicae molestijs, priuatae*[que] *commodis*, liber nusquam antehac Latine excussus. Francoforti ad Moenum: apud Iohannem Feyerabendt, impensis Sigismundi Feyerabendt.

Petrus Damiani. 1853. *Contra clericos aulicos*. *Patrologia Latina* 145 (rpt. Turnhout: Brepols, 1979): 463–472.

Philibert de Vienne. 1547. *Le philosophe de cour*. Lyons: Jean de Tournes; also Paris, 1548.

————. 1575. Trans. George North. *The Philosopher of the Court*. London: Henry Binneman for Lucas Hardison and George Byshop.

Philippe de Mézières. 1969. *Le songe du vieil pèlerin*. Ed. G. W. Coopland. London: Cambridge University Press.

Piatti, Girolamo, S.J. [1602.] 1758. *De cardinalis dignitate et officio*. 5th ed. Romae: J. Zempel.

Piccolomini, Alessandro. 1542; 1543. *De la institution di tutta la vita de l'huomo nato nobile e in città libera, libri X in lingua toscana, dove e Peripateticamente e Platonicamente, intorno a le cose de l'Ethica, Iconomica, e parte de la Politica, è raccolta la somma di . . . la perfetta e felice vita di quello*. Venetiis: Hieronimus Scotus, 1542; Firenze: n.p., 1543; Venetia: Giovan Maria Bonelli, 1552.

————. 1569; 1575; 1582. *Della institution morale libri XII*. Venetia: Giordan Ziletti.

Piccolomini, Enea Silvio (Pope Pius II). ca. 1490. *De curialium miseria*. Paris: Antoine Caillaut.

————. 1928. *Aeneae Silvii de curialium miseriis epistola*. Ed. Wilfred P. Mustard. Baltimore, London: The Johns Hopkins University Press.

————. ca. 1470. *De educatione puerorum ad regem Bohemiae Ladislaum*. Cologne: Ulrich Zell. Engl. ed. in William H. Woodward. *Vittorino da Feltre and Other Humanist Educators*. Cambridge: Cambridge University Press, 1897.

Pico della Mirandola. 1942. *Oratio de hominis dignitate, Heptaplus, De ente et uno, e scritti vari*. Ed. Eugenio Garin. Firenze: Vallecchi.

Platina [Bartolomeo Sacchi]. 1540. *De vera nobilitate*. In *De vitis et gestis summorum pontificum*. Coloniae: Fucharius Ceruicornus.

Pontano, Giovanni Gioviano. 1501. *Opera. De fortitudine, de principe, . . . de liberalitate, de beneficientia, de magnificentia, de splendore, de conviventia, de obedientia.* Venetiis: Bernardino Vercellesi.

————. 1965. *I trattati delle virtù sociali.* Roma: Edizioni dell'Ateneo.

————. 1969. *De magnanimitate.* Ed. Francesco Tateo. Firenze: Istituto Nazionale di Studi sul Rinascimento.

Priscianese, Francesco. 1883. *Del governo della corte d'un signore in Roma.* [Roma: F. Priscianese, 1543.] Ed. Lorenzo Bartolucci. Città di Castello: S. Lapi.

Ringhieri, Innocenzio. 1551. *Cento giuochi liberali e d'ingegno.* Bologna: A. Giaccarelli.

Robert de Blois. 1889–1895. *Sämmtliche Werke.* Ed. Jacob Ulrich. 3 vols. Berlin: Mayer und Müller. Genève: Slatkine Reprints, 1978.

[————.] Fox, John Howard. 1950. *Robert de Blois. Son oeuvre didactique et narrative. Étude linguistique et littéraire suivie d'une édition critique de l'Ensoignement des princes et du Chastoiement des dames.* Paris: Nizet.

Romei, Annibale. 1586. *Discorsi divisi in sette giornate, . . . quinta della nobiltà, . . . settima della precedenza dell'arme e delle lettere. . . .* Verona: Girolamo Discepoli. Venezia: Bartolomeo Carampello, 1594.

Saba da Castiglione. 1554; 1560. *Ricordi ovvero ammaestramenti . . . ne quali si ragiona di tutte le materie honorate che si ricercano a un vero gentil'huomo.* Vinegia: Paolo Gerardo.

Sansovino, Francesco. 1564. *Del segretario libri quattro.* Venezia: F. Rampazetto.

————. 1566. *Origine de' cavalieri.* Venetia: Camillo e Rutilio Borgomineri.

Saxo Grammaticus. 1931. *Saxonis Gesta Danorum.* Eds. J. Olrik and H. Raeder. Copenhagen: Levin & Munksgaard.

————. 1980–1981. *Danorum regum heroumque historia, Books X-XVI: The Text of the First Edition with Translation and Commentary in Three Volumes.* Trans. Eric Christiansen. 3 vols. Oxford: British Archaeological Reports.

Schmidt, P. G. 1964. "Causa Aiacis et Ulixis I-II: Zwei ovidianische Streitgedichte des Mittelalters." *Mittellateinisches Jahrbuch* 1: 100–132.

Secretum Secretorum: Nine English Versions. 1977. Ed. M. A. Manzaloni. Early English Text Society, vol. 276. Oxford: Oxford University Press.

Siccardo da Cremona. 1903. *Sicardi episcopi Cremonensis Cronica.* Ed. O. Holder-Egger. *Monumenta Germaniae Historica*, Scriptores 31: 22–181.

Sir Gawain and the Green Knight. 1968. Trans. J. R. R. Tolkien and E. V. Gordon. Revised by Norman Davis. Oxford: Clarendon Press.

Sir Gawain and the Green Knight, Pearl, and Sir Orfeo. 1975. Trans. J. R. R. Tolkien. Boston: Houghton Mifflin.

Suger of St-Denis. 1964. *Vie de Louis VI le Gros [Vita Ludovici Grossi Regis].* Ed. and trans. Henri Waquet. Paris: H. Champion, 1929; ibid.: Les Belles Lettres.

Sulpitius Verulanus, Johannes. 1542. *Libellus de moribus in mensam servandis.* Lugduni: Stephanus Doletus.

Tasso, Torquato. 1958. *Dialoghi*. Ed. Ezio Raimondi. 2 vols. in 3. Firenze: G. C. Sansoni.

———. 1959. *Dialoghi*. Ed. Ettore Mazzali. Milano, Napoli: R. Ricciardi. New ed. 2 vols. Torino: G. Einaudi, 1976.

[Thomasin von Zerclaere.] 1852. *Der Wälsche Gast des Thomasin von Zirclaria*. Ed. Heinrich Rückert. Deutsche Nationalliteratur 30. Quedlinburg and Leipzig: Basse. Rpt. 1965, with additional apparatus by F. Neumann.

[———.] 1977. *Thomasin Zerklaere, Der Wälsche Gast (1215–1216)*. Ed. Daniel Rocher. 2 vols. Lille: Atelier Reproduction de Thèses, Université de Lille III; Paris: Diffusion H. Champion.

Trattati d'amore del Cinquecento. 1912. Ed. Giuseppe Zonta. Bari: Laterza.

Trattati del Cinquecento sulla donna. 1913. Ed. Giuseppe Zonta. Bari: Laterza.

Tristan et Yseut. 1974. Ed. J. C. Payen. Paris: Garnier Frères.

Valera, Diego de. 1959. *Espejo de verdadera nobleza*. In *Prosistas castellanos del siglo XV*. Ed. Mario Penna. Madrid: Atlas.

Vergerio, Pietro Paolo. 1918. *De ingenuis moribus ac liberalibus studiis*. Ed. A. Gnesotto. *Atti e Memorie della Reale Accademia di Scienze, Lettere e Arti di Padova* 34.2: 75–156.

[Wace.] 1938–1940. *Le roman de Brut de Wace*. Ed. Ivor Arnold. 2 vols. Paris: Société des anciens textes français.

[———.] 1970–1973. *Le roman de Rou de Wace*. Ed. A. J. Holden. 3 vols. Paris: Picard—Société des anciens textes français.

Wilhelm, James J., and Laila Zamuelis Gross, eds. 1984. *The Romance of Arthur*. New York, London: Garland.

Wilhelm, James J., ed. 1986. *The Romance of Arthur II*. New York, London: Garland.

William of Conches. 1929. *Das* Moralium dogma philosophorum, *lateinisch, altfranzösisch und mittelniederfränkisch*. Ed. John Holmberg. Leipzig: Otto Harrassowitz.

Wolfram von Eschenbach. 1963. *Parzival*. Ed. Gottfried Weber. Darmstadt: Wissenschaftliche Buchgesellschaft.

Zini, Pier Francesco. 1575. *Il ritratto del vero et perfetto gentilhuomo espresso da Filone Hebreo nella vita di Giuseppe Patriarca, et fatto volgare da M. Pier Francesco Zino*. Venetia: F. Rampazetto.

SECONDARY SOURCES

Anderson, Perry. 1979. *Lineages of the Absolutist State*. London: Verso Editions.

Armstrong, Nancy, and Leonard Tennenhouse, eds. 1987. *The Ideology of Conduct: Essays on Literature and the History of Sexuality*. New York, London: Methuen & Co.

Asor Rosa, Alberto, ed. 1982–. *Letteratura Italiana*. 11 vols. Torino: G. Einaudi.

Barber, Richard W. 1975. *The Knight and Chivalry*. Harlow: Longmans, 1970; New York: Harper & Row, 1974; Totowa, NJ: Rowman and Littlefield.

————. 1980. *The Reign of Chivalry.* New York: St. Martin's Press.

Baron, Hans. 1938. "Cicero and the Roman Civic Spirit in the Middle Ages and Early Renaissance." *Bulletin of the John Rylands Library* 22: 72–97.

Basile, Bruno, ed. 1984. *"Bentivolorum magnificentia." Principe e cultura a Bologna nel Rinascimento.* Centro Studi "Europa delle Corti" / Biblioteca del Cinquecento no. 25. Roma: Bulzoni.

Beaton, Roderick. 1989. *The Medieval Greek Romance.* Cambridge: Cambridge University Press.

Bec, Pierre. 1970. *Nouvelle anthologie de la lyrique occitane du Moyen Age.* Avignon: Aubanel.

————. 1971. "L'antithèse poétique chez Bernard de Ventadour." In *Mélanges de philologie romane dédiés à la mémoire de Jean Boutière (1899–1967).* Eds. Irénée Marcel Cluzel and François Pirot. Liège: Soledi. 107–137.

Benson, Larry, and John Leyerle, eds. 1980. *Chivalric Literature.* Kalamazoo: Medieval Institute.

Benton, John F. 1961. "The Court of Champagne as a Literary Center." *Speculum* 36: 551–591. Rpt. in J. F. Benton. *Culture, Power, and Personality in Medieval France.* 1990. Ed. Thomas N. Bisson. London, Eng., Ronceverte, WV: Hambledon Press.

Bertelli, Sergio, and Giuliano Crifò, eds. 1985. *Rituale, cerimoniale, etichetta.* Milano: Bompiani.

Bertelli, Sergio, Franco Cardini, and Elvira Garbero Zorzi. 1985. *Le corti italiane del Rinascimento.* Milano: Arnoldo Mondadori. Eng. trans. *The Courts of the Italian Renaissance.* New York: Facts on File, 1986.

Bertoni, Giulio. 1904. "Usi e costumanze di corte nel poema del Boiardo." In *Nuovi studi su M. M. Boiardo.* Bologna: N. Zanichelli. 239–259.

Bezzola, Reto R. 1947. *Le sens de l'aventure et de l'amour (Chrétien de Troyes).* Paris: La Jeune Parque; 2d ed. ibid.: Honoré Champion, 1968.

————. 1944–1963. *Les origines et la formation de la littérature courtoise en Occident (500-1200).* 3 vols. in 5 tomes. Paris: Honoré Champion.

Bloch, Marc. 1928. "Un problème d'histoire comparée: La ministérialité en France et en Allemagne." *Revue historique de droit français et étranger* 4.7: 46–91.

————. 1939–1940. *La société féodale.* 2 vols. Paris: A. Michel. Rpt. 1949. Trans. L. A. Manyon. *Feudal Society.* Chicago: Chicago University Press, 1968.

Boase, Roger. 1977. *The Origin and Meaning of Courtly Love.* Manchester: Manchester University Press; Totowa, NJ: Rowman & Littlefield.

Bonadeo, Alfredo. 1971. "Function and Purpose of the Courtier in Castiglione." *Philological Quarterly* 50: 36–46.

Bonfatti, Emilio. 1979. *La Civile Conversazione in Germania. Letteratura del comportamento in Germania da Stefano Guazzo a Adolph Knigge.* Università di Trieste, Fac. di Magistero, 3ᵃ sez. no. 4. Udine: Del Bianco.

Bonnassie, Pierre. 1975. *La Catalogne du milieu du Xe à la fin du XIe siècle: croissance et mutation d'une société.* 2 vols. Toulouse: Publications de l'Université de Toulouse—Le Mirail.

Bonora, Ettore, ed. 1980. *Convegno di studio su Baldassar Castiglione nel quinto centenario della nascita.* Mantova: Accademia Virgiliana.

Bornstein, Diane. 1975. *Mirrors of Courtesy.* Hamden, CT: Archon Books.

Borst, Arno. 1959. "Das Rittertum im Hochmittelalter. Idee und Wirklichkeit." *Saeculum* 10: 213–231.

Bosl, Karl. 1972. *Die Grundlagen der modernen Gesellschaft im Mittelalter. Eine deutsche Gesellschaftsgeschichte des Mittelalters.* 2 vols. Stuttgart: Hiersemann.

Branca, Vittore, ed. 1973. *Concetto, storia, miti e immagini del Medio Evo.* Venezia: Sansoni.

Braudel, Fernand. 1981. *The Structures of Everyday Life: The Limits of the Possible.* London: Collins; New York: Harper & Row.

———. 1982. *The Wheels of Commerce.* Trans. Sian Reynolds. New York: Harper & Row.

Broughton, Bradford B., ed. 1988. *Dictionary of Medieval Knighthood and Chivalry. People, Places, Events.* New York: Greenwood Press.

Brownlee, Kevin, and Marina Scordilis Brownlee, eds. 1985. *Romance: Generic Transformations from Chrétien de Troyes to Cervantes.* Hanover, NH: University Press of New England.

Bumke, Joachim. 1964. *Studien zum Ritterbegriff im 12. und 13. Jahrhundert.* Beihefte zum *Euphorion* 1. Heidelberg: Carl Winter—Universitätsverlag; 2d ed. 1977. Engl. Trans. W. T. H. and Erika Jackson. *The Concept of Knighthood in the Middle Ages.* New York: AMS Press, 1982.

———. 1967. *Die romanisch-deutschen Literaturbeziehungen im Mittelalter.* Heidelberg: Carl Winter.

———. 1976. *Ministerialität und Ritterdichtung. Umrisse der Forschung.* Munich: Beck.

———. 1979. *Mäzene im Mittelalter. Die Gönner und Auftraggeber der höfischen Literatur in Deutschland 1150–1300.* Munich: Beck.

———. 1986. *Höfische Kultur. Literatur und Gesellschaft im hohen Mittelalter.* 2 vols. Munich: Deutscher Taschenbuch Verlag.

Burke, Peter. 1987. *Culture and Society in Renaissance Italy, 1420–1540.* London: Batsford; New York: Scribner, 1972; Princeton: Princeton University Press.

Bynum, Caroline Walker. 1978. *Docere verbo et exemplo: An Aspect of Twelfth-Century Spirituality.* Harvard Theological Studies 31. Missoula, Mont.: Scholars Press.

Cantin, André. 1975. *Les sciences séculières et la foi: Les deux voies de la science au jugement de S. Pierre Damien (1007–1072).* Spoleto: Centro Italiano di Studi sull'Alto Medioevo.

Cardini, Franco. 1976. "La tradizione cavalleresca nell'Occidente medievale: Un tema di ricerca tra storia e 'tentazioni' antropologiche." *Quaderni Medievali* 2: 125–142.

———. 1981. *Alle radici della cavalleria medievale.* Firenze: La Nuova Italia.

———. 1982. *La cavalleria: una questione da riproporre.* Firenze: Sansoni.

———. 1987. *Quell'antica festa crudele: guerra e cultura della guerra dall'età feudale alla Grande Rivoluzione.* Milano: Il Saggiatore.

————. 1987; 1988. "Il guerriero e il cavaliere." In F. Cardini et al. *L'uomo medievale*. Ed. Jacques Le Goff, 83–123. Bari: Laterza, 6th ed. 1988.

Carducci, Giosué. 1919–1924. *Della poesia cavalleresca nel Medioevo*. In *Opere*. Edizione Nazionale. Vol. 5 of 20 vols. Bologna: Zanichelli.

Castronovo, David. 1987. *The English Gentleman*. New York: Ungar.

Cattini, Marco, and Marzio A. Romani, eds. 1983. *La corte in Europa. Fedeltà, favori, pratiche di governo*. Brescia: Grafo Edizioni.

Chênerie, Marie-Luce. 1986. *Le chevalier errant dans les romans arthuriens en vers des XIIe et XIIIe siècles*. Genève: Droz.

Cherubini, Giovanni. 1974. *Signori, contadini, borghesi: Ricerche sulla società italiana del Basso Medioevo*. Firenze: La Nuova Italia.

————. 1985. *L'Italia rurale del Basso Medioevo*. Roma: Laterza.

Chapin, Elizabeth. 1937. *Les villes de foires de Champagne*. Paris: Champion.

Cian, Vittorio. 1951. *Un illustre nunzio pontificio del Rinascimento: Baldassar Castiglione*. Città del Vaticano: Biblioteca Apostolica Vaticana.

Clein, Wendy. 1987. *Concepts of Chivalry in* Sir Gawain and the Green Knight. Norman, OK: Pilgrim Books.

Contamine, Philippe, ed. 1976. *La noblesse au Moyen Age, XIe-XVe siècles: Essais à la mémoire de Robert Boutruche*. Paris: Presses Universitaires de France.

————. 1980. La guerre au Moyen Age. Paris: Presses Universitaires de France.

Coulborn, Rushton, ed. 1965. *Feudalism in History*. Princeton: Princeton University Press, 1956. Rpt. Hamden, Conn.: Archon Books.

Courtly Literature: Culture and Context. 1990. Eds. Keith Busby and Erik Kooper. Papers from the 5th Triennial Congress of the International Courtly Literature Society, Dalfsen, The Netherlands, 9–16 August 1986. Amsterdam: John Benjamins.

Crane, Susan. 1986. *Insular Romance: Politics, Faith, and Culture in Anglo-Norman and Middle English Literature*. Berkeley, Los Angeles, London: University of California Press.

Crane, Thomas Frederick. 1920. *Italian Social Customs of the Sixteenth Century and Their Influence on the Literatures of Europe*. New Haven: Yale University Press.

Croce, Benedetto. 1945. "Libri sulle corti." In *Poeti e scrittori del pieno e del tardo Rinascimento*. 2 vols. Bari: Laterza; 2d ed. 1958. Vol. 2: 198–207.

Culture et société en Italie du Moyen-Age à la Renaissance: Hommage à André Rochon. 1985. Centre interuniversitaire de recherche sur la Renaissance italienne no. 13. Paris: Université de la Sorbonne Nouvelle.

Curtius, Ernst R. 1953, 1963. *European Literature and the Latin Middle Ages*. Trans. W. R. Trask. New York: Harper & Row. "Heroes and Rulers," 167–182; "The 'Chivalric System of the Virtues,'" 519–537.

Davis, Charles T. 1984. *Dante's Italy and Other Essays*. Philadelphia: University of Pennsylvania Press.

D'Amico, John F. 1983. *Renaissance Humanism in Papal Rome: Humanists and Churchmen on the Eve of the Reformation*. Baltimore: Johns Hopkins University Press.

De Boor, Helmut. 1964. *Die höfische Literatur: Vorbereitung, Blüte, Ausklang, 1170–1250. Geschichte der deutschen Literatur* 2. München: C. H. Beck.

Denomy, Alexander J. (1947) 1965. *The Heresy of Courtly Love.* Rpt. Glocester: Peter Smith.

———. 1953. "Courtly Love and Courtliness." *Speculum* 28: 44–63.

Dickens, Arthur Geoffrey, ed. 1984. *The Courts of Europe. Politics, Patronage and Royalty: 1400–1800.* London: Thames & Hudson, 1977; New York: Greenwich House.

Dionisotti, Carlo. 1967. *Geografia e storia della letteratura italiana.* Torino: G. Einaudi. 2d ed. 1977.

Doglio, Maria Luisa. 1984. "L'occhio del principe e lo specchio del cortigiano. Rassegna di testi e studi sulla letteratura di corte nel Rinascimento italiano (1954–1982)." *Lettere Italiane* 36.2: 239–273.

Donati, Claudio. 1988. *L'idea di nobiltà in Italia: secoli XIV-XVIII.* Bari: Laterza.

Dragonetti, Roger. 1960. *La technique poétique des trouvères dans la chanson courtoise.* Bruges: De Tempel.

Dronke, Peter. 1976. "Peter of Blois and Poetry at the Court of Henry II." *Medieval Studies* 38: 185–235.

———. [1968] 1978. *The Medieval Lyric.* 2d ed. London: Hutchinson.

Duby, Georges. 1971. *Terra e nobiltà nel Medioevo.* Trans. M. Sanfilippo. Torino: Società Editrice Internazionale.

———. 1973a. *Guerriers et paysans, VIIᵉ-XIIᵉ siècles: Premier essor de l'économie européenne.* Paris: Gallimard.

———. 1973b. *Hommes et structures du Moyen Age: Recueil d'articles.* Paris, La Haye: Mouton.

———. 1977. *The Chivalrous Society.* Trans. Cynthia Postan. Berkeley, Los Angeles, London: University of California Press.

———. 1978a. *Les trois ordres, ou l'imaginaire du féodalisme.* Paris: Gallimard. Eng. trans. by Arthur Goldhammer. *The Three Orders: Feudal Society Imagined.* Chicago, London: University of Chicago Press, 1980.

———. 1978b. *Medieval Marriage: Two Models from Twelfth-Century France.* Trans. Elborg Forster. Baltimore: Johns Hopkins University Press.

———. 1981. *Le chevalier, la femme et le prêtre: le mariage dans la France féodale.* Paris: Hachette. Eng. trans. by Barbara Bray. *The Knight the Lady and the Priest: The Making of Modern Marriage in Medieval France.* New York: Pantheon Books, 1983.

———. 1984. *Guillaume le Maréchal, ou Le meilleur chevalier du monde.* Paris: Arthème Fayard. Eng. trans. by Richard Howard. *William Marshal, The Flower of Chivalry.* New York: Pantheon Books, 1985.

———. 1988. *Mâle moyen âge: de l'amour et autres essais.* Paris: Flammarion.

Dupin, Henri. 1931; 1982. *La courtoisie au Moyen Age (d'après les textes du XIIe et du XIIIe siècle).* Paris: A. Picard, 1931. Rpt. New York: AMS Press, 1982.

Ehrismann, Gustav. 1918–1935. *Geschichte der deutschen Literatur bis zum Ausgang des Mittelalters.* 2 vols. in 4. München: Beck. 2d ed. ibid., 1972.

————. 1919. "Die Grundlagen des ritterlichen Tugendsystems." *Zeitschrift für deutsches Altertum* 56: 137–216.

Eifler, Günter, ed. 1970. *Ritterliches Tugendsystem.* Wege der Forschung 56. Darmstadt: Wissenschaftliche Buchgesellschaft.

Elias, Norbert. 1939. *Über den Prozess der Zivilisation: soziogenetische und psychogenetische Untersuchungen.* 2 vols. Basel: Haus zum Falken. 2d ed. Frankfurt: Suhrkamp Taschenbuch Wissenschaft (vols. 158–159), 1969. Rpt. ibid., 1979. Eng. trans. by Edmund Jephcott. *The Civilizing Process: The Development of Manners. Changes in the Code of Conduct and Feeling in Early Modern Times.* New York: Urizen Books, 1978; then again same trans., same title, but vol. 1: *The History of Manners,* vol. 2: *Power and Civility,* New York: Pantheon Books, 1982, and as *State Formation and Civilization,* Oxford: Basil Blackwell, 1982.

————. 1969; 1979. *Die höfische Gesellschaft: Untersuchungen zur Soziologie des Königstums und der höfische Aristokratie.* Soziologische Texte 54. Darmstadt and Neuwied: Luchterhand; 4th ed. 1979. Eng. trans. by Edmund Jephcott. *The Court Society.* Oxford: Basil Blackwell; New York: Pantheon Books, 1983.

Erdmann, Carl. 1974. *Die Entstehung des Kreuzzugsgedankens.* Stuttgart, 1935. Darmstadt: Wissenschaftliche Buchgesellschaft. Eng. trans. *The Origin of the Idea of Crusade.* Princeton, NJ: Princeton University Press, 1977.

————. 1938. *Studien zur Briefliteratur Deutschlands im 11. Jahrhundert. Monumenta Germaniae Historica,* Schriften, vol. 1. Leipzig: Hiersemann.

Falvo, Giuseppe. 1988. "The Rhetoric of Human Conduct in Castiglione's *Libro del Cortegiano.*" In *Italiana.* Proceedings of the 3d Annual Conference of the American Association of Teachers of Italian, New York, 12-27/28–1986, eds. Albert N. Mancini et al., 163–173. River Forest, IL: Rosary College.

Faral, Edmond. 1913. *Recherches sur les sources latines des contes et romans courtois du moyen âge.* Paris: Champion.

Fasoli, Gina. 1958. "Lineamenti di una storia della cavalleria." In *Studi di storia medievale e moderna in onore di Ettore Rota.* Eds. Pietro Vaccari and P. F. Palumbo, 81–94. Roma: Edizioni del Lavoro.

————. 1972–1973. "Feudo e castello." In *Storia d'Italia,* eds. Ruggiero Romano and Corrado Vivanti. 6 vols. Torino: G. Einaudi. 5.1: 263–308.

Ferguson, Arthur B. 1986. *The Chivalric Tradition in Renaissance England.* Washington, DC: Folger Shakespeare Library.

Ferrajoli, Alessandro, ed. 1984. *Il ruolo della corte di Leone X, 1514–1516.* Roma: Bulzoni.

Ferrante, Joan M. 1973. *The Conflict of Love and Honor. The Medieval Tristan Legend in France, Germany, and Italy.* De Proprietatibus Litterarum, Series Practica no. 78. The Hague, Paris: Mouton.

————. 1975. *Woman as Image in Medieval Literature, from the Twelfth Century to Dante.* New York: Columbia University Press.

————, George D. Economou, et al., eds. 1975. *In Pursuit of Perfection: Courtly Love in Medieval Literature.* Port Washington, New York, London: Kennikat Press.

Fish, Stanley. 1988. "Authors-Readers: Jonson's Community of the Same." In *Representing the English Renaissance*. Ed. S. Greenblatt, 231–263. Berkeley, Los Angeles, London: University of California Press.

Fleckenstein, Josef. 1956. "Königshof und Bischofschule unter Otto dem Grossen." *Archiv für Kulturgeschichte* 38.1: 38–62.

———. 1972. "Friedrich Barbarossa und das Rittertum. Zur Bedeutung der grossen Mainzer Hoftage von 1184 und 1188." In *Festschrift für Hermann Heimpel zum 70. Geburtstag*, 2: 1023–1041. Göttingen: Max-Planck-Institut für Geschichte.

———. 1974. "Zum Problem der Abschliessung des Ritterstandes." In *Historische Forschungen für Walter Schlesinger*. Ed. Helmut Beumann, 252–271. Köln-Wien: Böhlau..

———. 1976. *Grundlagen und Beginn der deutschen Geschichte*. Göttingen: Vandenhoek & Ruprecht. Trans. by Bernard S. Smith. *Early Medieval Germany*. Amsterdam, New York, Oxford: North Holland, 1978.

———. 1977. *Herrschaft und Stand*. Göttingen: Vandenhoeck und Ruprecht.

———, and Manfred Hellmann, eds. 1980. *Die Geistliche Ritterorden Europas*. Sigmaringen: Jan Thorbecke.

Flori, Jean. 1983. *L'idéologie du glaive. Préhistoire de la chevalerie*. Genève: Droz.

———. 1986. *L'essor de la chevalerie. X^e-XIIe siècles*. Genève: Droz.

———. 1987. *De Roland à Lancelot du Lac. La chevalerie dans la littérature française du XIIe siècle*. Genève: Droz.

Floriani, Piero. 1976. *Bembo e Castiglione*. Roma: Bulzoni.

Folena, Gianfranco. 1976. "Tradizione e cultura trobadorica nelle corti e nelle città venete." In *Storia della cultura veneta, 1: Dalle origini al Trecento*, 454–562. Vicenza: Neri Pozza.

Forni, Pier Massimo. 1978. *Le grandi leggende cavalleresche*. Milano: Domus.

Forum for Modern Language Studies 17.2 (1981), special issue on "Knighthood in Medieval Literature" [articles by Tony Hunt, Linda Paterson, W. H. Jackson, Jeffrey Ashcroft, Ann M. McKim, and W. R. J. Barron].

Fournier, Gabriel. 1978. *Le château dans la France médiévale. Essai de sociologie monumentale*. Paris: Aubier Montaigne.

Fragnito, Gigliola. 1969. "Cultura umanistica e riforma religiosa: Il *De officio viri boni ac probi episcopi*." *Studi Veneziani* 11: 75–189.

Frappier, Jean. 1954. "Le Graal et la chevalerie." *Romania* 75: 165–210.

———. 1969. *Étude sur* Yvain *ou* Le Chevalier au lion *de Chrétien de Troyes*. Paris: Société d'Éditions d'Enseignement Supérieur.

———. 1973. "Vues sur les conceptions courtoises dans les littératures d'oc et d'oïl au XIIe siècle." *Cahiers de civilization médiévale* 2 (1959): 135 ff. Also in *Amour courtois et Table Ronde*. Genève: E. Droz.

———, and Reinhold R. Grimm, eds. 1978. *Grundriß der romanischen Literaturen des Mittelalters* 4.1, *Le roman jusqu'à la fin du XIIIe siècle*. Heidelberg: Carl Winter.

Fromm, Hans, ed. 1961. *Der deutsche Minnesang. Aufsätze zu seiner Erforschung*. Wege der Forschung 15. Darmstadt: Wissenschaftliche Buchgesellschaft. 3d ed. 1966.

Frova, Carla. 1973. *Istruzione e educazione nel Medioevo*. Torino: Loescher.

Fuhrmann, Horst. 1986. *Germany in the High Middle Ages: c. 1050–1200*. Trans. Timothy Reuter. Cambridge, Eng., New York: Cambridge University Press.

Fumaroli, Marc. 1985. "Jacques Amyot and the Clerical Polemic Against the Chivalric Novel." *Renaissance Quarterly* 38.1: 22–40.

Ganshof, François L. 1957. *Qu'est-ce que la féodalité?* 2d ed. Neuchâtel: Éditions de la Baconnière, 1947; 3d ed. Bruxelles: Office de Publicité, 1957; 5th ed. Paris: Tallandier, 1982. Eng. trans. *Feudalism*. London: Longmans, Green, 1952; 2d ed. New York: Harper, 1961; 3d ed. London: Longmans, 1964.

Gardner, Edmund G. 1930. *The Arthurian Legend in Italian Literature*. London, New York: Dent.

Gasc, Hélène. 1986. "Gerbert et la pédagogie des arts libéraux à la fin du dixième siècle." *Journal of Medieval History* 12: 111–121.

Génicot, Léopold. 1960. *L'économie namuroise au bas Moyen Age (1199–1429)*. Recueils de travaux d'histoire et de philologie de l'Université de Louvain 4: 20. Louvain: Bibliothèque de l'Université. [2d of set of 3 vols., ibid. 1943–1982, 3d vol. with imprint: Louvain-La-Neuve: Collège Erasme; Bruxelles: Éditions Nauwelaerts.]

———. 1975. *L'économie namuroise au bas Moyen Age*, II: *Les hommes, la noblesse. Études sur les principautés lotharingiennes*. Louvain: Bibliothèque de l'Université.

———. 1965. "La noblesse dans la société médiévale. A propos des dernières études relatives aux terres d'Empire." *Le Moyen Age* 71: 539–560.

———. 1982. *La noblesse dans l'Occident médiéval*. London: Variorum Reprints.

Gies, Frances. 1984. *The Knight in History*. New York: Harper & Row.

Girouard, Mark. 1981. *The Return to Camelot. Chivalry and the English Gentleman*. New Haven: Yale University Press.

Glier, Ingeborg. 1971. *Artes amandi: Untersuchung zu Geschichte, Überlieferung und Typologie der deutschen Minnereden*. Münchener Texte und Untersuchungen 34. Munich: Beck.

Goodrich, Norma Lorre. 1986. *King Arthur*. New York: Harper and Row.

Grafton, Anthony, and Lisa Jardine. 1986. *From Humanism to the Humanities*. Cambridge, MA: Harvard University Press.

Greenblatt, Stephen J. 1980. *Renaissance Self-Fashioning: From More to Shakespeare*. Chicago: University of Chicago Press.

———, ed. 1982. *The Power of Forms in the English Renaissance*. Norman, Oklahoma: Pilgrim Books.

———, ed. 1988. *Representing the English Renaissance*. Berkeley, Los Angeles, London: University of California Press.

Grisward, Joël H. 1981. *Archéologie de l'épopée médiévale. Structures trifonctionnelles et mythes indo-européens dans le cycle des Narbonnais*. Paris: Payot.

Gundersheimer, Werner. 1973. *Ferrara: The Style of a Renaissance Despotism*. Princeton: Princeton University Press.

Hagspiel, Gereon H. 1963. *Die Führerpersönlichkeit im Kreuzzug*. Zürich: Fretz und Wasmuth.

Hallam, Elizabeth M., ed. 1987. *Chronicles of the Age of Chivalry*. Preface by Hugh Trevor-Roper. London, New York: Weidenfeld and Nicolson.

Hanning, Robert W. 1972. "The Social Significance of Twelfth Century Chivalric Romance." *Mediaevalia et Humanistica* n.s. 3: 3–29.

——, and David Rosand, eds. 1983. *Castiglione: The Ideal and the Real in Renaissance Culture*. New Haven: Yale University Press.

Harper-Bill, Christopher, and Ruth Harvey, eds. 1986. *The Ideals and Practice of Medieval Knighthood*. Papers from the first and second Strawberry Hill conferences. Woodbridge, Suffolk; Dover, N.H., USA: Boydell Press.

——. 1988. *The Ideals and Practice of Medieval Knighthood II*. Papers from the third Strawberry Hill conference. Wolfeboro, NH: Boydell Press.

Haymes, Edward R., ed. 1986. *The Medieval Court in Europe*. Houston German Studies no. 6. Munich: Fink.

Hexter, Jack H. 1979. *Reappraisals in History: New Views on History and Society in Early Modern Europe*. 2d ed. Chicago, London: University of Chicago Press.

Hoffmann, Ulrich. 1968. *König, Adel und Reich im Urteil fränkischer und deutscher Historiker des 9.-11. Jahrhunderts*. Diss. Freiburg i. Breisgau.

Hyde, John Kenneth. 1973. *Society and Politics in Medieval Italy*. London: Macmillan; New York: St. Martin's Press.

Jaeger, C. Stephen. 1985. *The Origins of Courtliness: Civilizing Trends and the Formation of Courtly Ideals 939-1210*. Philadelphia: University of Pennsylvania Press.

——. 1987. "Cathedral Schools and Humanist Learning, 950-1150." *Deutsche Vierteljahrsschrift für Literaturwissenschaft und Geistesgeschichte* 61.4: 569–616.

Jackson, W. T. H. 1971. *The Anatomy of Love: The Tristan of Gottfried von Strassburg*. New York, London: Columbia University Press.

Jameson, Fredric. 1975. "Magical Narratives: Romance as Genre." *New Literary History* 7: 135–163.

Jauss, Hans-Robert. 1973. "Theorie der Gattungen und Literatur des Mittelalters." In *Grundriß der romanischen Literaturen des Mittelalters* 1: 107–130. Heidelberg: Winter.

——. 1982. "Theory of Genres and Medieval Literature." In *Toward an Aesthetic of Reception*. Trans. Timothy Bahti, 76–109. Minneapolis: University of Minnesota Press.

Javitch, Daniel. 1971. "*The Philosopher of the Court*: A French Satire Misunderstood," *Comparative Literature* 23: 97–124.

——. 1978. *Poetry and Courtliness in Renaissance England*. Princeton: Princeton University Press.

——. 1982. "The Impure Motives of Elizabethan Poetry." In *The Power of Forms in the English Renaissance*. Ed. S. Greenblatt, 225–238. Norman, Oklahoma: Pilgrim Books.

Jedin, Hubert. 1950. *Il tipo ideale di vescovo secondo la Riforma cattolica*. Trans. E. Durini. Brescia: La Morcelliana. [From *Das Bischofsideal der*

Katholischen Reformation; also French trans. *L'évêque dans la tradition pastorale du XVIe siècle*, Bruges: Desclée de Brouwer, 1953.]

Kaiser, Gert, and Jan-Dirk Müller, eds. 1986. *Höfische Literatur, Hofgesellschaft. Höfische Lebensformen um 1200.* Kolloquium am Zentrum für Interdisziplinäre Forschung der Universität Bielefeld (3–5 November 1983). Studia Humaniora 6. Düsseldorf: Droste.

Kantorowicz, Ernst H. 1957. *The King's Two Bodies: A Study in Mediaeval Political Theology.* Princeton: Princeton University Press.

Keen, Maurice Hugh. 1984. *Chivalry.* New Haven: Yale University Press.

Kellogg, Judith L. 1985. "Economic and Social Tensions Reflected in the Romance of Chrétien de Troyes." *Romance Philology* 39: 2–21.

Kelly, F. Douglas. 1966. *"Sens" and "conjointure" in the* Chevalier de la charrette. The Hague, Paris: Mouton.

———. 1978. *Medieval Imagination: Rhetoric and the Poetry of Courtly Love.* Madison, WI: University of Wisconsin Press.

Kelso, Ruth. 1929. *The Doctrine of the English Gentleman in the Sixteenth Century, with a Bibliographical List of Treatises on the Gentleman and Related Subjects Published in Europe to 1625.* University of Illinois Studies in Language and Literature no. 14. Urbana, IL: University of Illinois Press.

Kerrigan, William, and Gordon Braden. 1989. *The Idea of the Renaissance.* Baltimore: Johns Hopkins University Press.

Klaniczay, Tibor, Eva Kushner, and André Stegmann, eds. 1988. *L'époque de la Renaissance 1400–1600* 1, *L'avènement de l'esprit nouveau (1400–1480).* Histoire Comparée des Littératures de Langues Européennes 7.1. Budapest: Akadémiai Kiadó.

Kleinschmidt, Erich. 1974. *Herrscherdarstellung. Zur Disposition mittelalterlichen Aussageverhaltens, untersucht an Texten über Rudolf I von Habsburg.* Bern, München: Francke.

Kloft, Hans. 1970. *Liberalitas principis: Herkunft und Bedeutung. Studien zur Prinzipatsideologie.* Kölner Historische Abhandlungen 18. Köln, Wien.

Köhler, Erich. 1962. *Trobadorlyrik und höfischer Roman.* Berlin (Ost): Rütten & Loening.

———. 1970a. *Ideal und Wirklichkeit in der höfischen Epik. Studien zur Form der frühen Artus-und Graldichtung.* Beihefte zur Zeitschrift für romanische Philologie 97. Tübingen: Max Niemeyer, 1956. 2d, expanded ed. 1970. Trans. of 2d ed. by Eliane Kaufholz. *L'aventure chevaleresque. Idéal et réalité dans le roman courtois: études sur la forme des plus anciens poèmes d'Arthur et du Graal.* Paris: Gallimard, 1974.

———. 1970b. "Vergleichende soziologische Betrachtungen zum romanischen und zum deutschen Minnesang." In *Der Berliner Germanistentag 1968: Vorträge und Berichte.* Eds. Karl Heinz Borck and Rudolf Henss, 61–76. Heidelberg: Carl Winter—Universitätsverlag.

———. 1970c. "Les troubadours et la jalousie." *Mélanges . . . offerts à Jean Frappier.* Genève: E. Droz. 543–559.

———. 1972. *Esprit und arkadische Freiheit. Aufsätze aus der Welt der Romania.* Frankfurt/M., Bonn: Athenäum, 1966; rpt.

———. 1974. "Einige Thesen zur Literatursoziologie." *Germanisch-Romanische Monatsschrift* n.s. 24: 257–264.

———. 1976a. *Sociologia della fin'amor.* Trans. and Introd. by Mario Mancini. Padova: Liviana.

———. 1976b. "Il sistema sociologico del romanzo francese medievale." *Medioevo romanzo* 3: 321–344.

———. 1978. "Literatursoziologische Perspektiven." In *Grundriß der romanischen Literaturen des Mittelalters* 4.1. Eds. J. Frappier and R. R. Grimm, 82–103. Heidelberg: Carl Winter.

———, ed. 1979–1987. *Grundriß der romanischen Literaturen des Mittelalters* 2.1, *Les genres lyriques.* Heidelberg: Carl Winter.

Korrel, Peter. 1984. *An Arthurian Triangle. A Study of the Origin, Development and Characterization of Arthur, Guinevere and Modred.* Leiden: E. J. Brill.

Kratins, Ojars. 1982. *The Dream of Chivalry: A Study of Chrétien de Troyes's* Yvain *and Hartmann von Aue's* Iwein. Washington, D.C.: University Press of America.

Krüdener, Jürgen Freiherr von. 1973. *Die Rolle des Hofes im Absolutismus.* Stuttgart: G. Fischer.

Kuhn, Hugo. 1961. "Zur inneren Form des Minnesangs." In *Der deutsche Minnesang. Aufsätze zu seiner Erforschung.* Ed. H. Fromm, 167–179. Wege der Forschung 15. Darmstadt: Wissenschaftliche Buchgesellschaft.

Lacy, Norris L., ed. 1986. *The Arthurian Encyclopedia.* New York, London: Garland.

Langer, Ullrich. 1988. "Merit in Courtly Literature: Castiglione, Rabelais, Marguerite de Navarre, and Le Caron." *Renaissance Quarterly* 41.2: 218–241.

Larner, John. 1971. *Culture and Society in Italy, 1290–1420.* New York, London: Scribner.

Lazar, Moshe. 1964. *Amour courtois et fin' amors dans la littérature du 12ᵉ siècle.* Paris: C. Klincksieck.

Le Goff, Jacques. 1980. *Time, Work, and Culture in the Middle Ages.* Trans. Arthur Goldhammer. Chicago: University of Chicago Press.

Lejeune, Rita. "Rôle littéraire d'Aliénor d'Aquitaine et de sa famille." *Cultura Neolatina* 14 (1954): 5–57.

———, Jeanne Wathelet-Willem, and Henning Krauss, eds. 1985–1987. *Grundriß der romanischen Literaturen des Mittelalters* 3.1, *Les épopées romanes.* Heidelberg: Carl Winter.

Lerner, Robert. 1974. "Literacy and Learning." In *One Thousand Years: Western Europe in the Middle Ages.* Ed. Richard L. De Molen, 165–223. Boston: Houghton Mifflin.

Lévi-Strauss, Claude. 1978. *L'origine des manières de table.* Paris: Plon, 1968. *The Origin of Table Manners.* Trans. John and Doreen Weightman. New York: Harper & Row.

Leyser, Karl J. 1989. *Rule and Conflict in an Early Medieval Society: Ottonian Saxony.* London: E. Arnold, 1979; Oxford: Blackwell, 1989.

Liebeschütz, Hans. 1967; 1970. "The Debate on Philosophical Learning During the Transition Period (900-1080)." In *The Cambridge History of Later Greek and Early Medieval Philosophy*. Ed. Arthur Hilary Armstrong, 587–610. London: Cambridge University Press.

Lievsay, John Leon. 1961. *Stefano Guazzo and the English Renaissance, 1575–1675*. Chapel Hill: University of North Carolina Press.

Lindgren, Uta. 1976. *Gerbert von Aurillac und das Quadrivium: Untersuchungen zur Bildung im Zeitalter der Ottonen*. Sudhoffs Archiv, Beiheft 18. Wiesbaden: Steiner.

Logan, Oliver. 1972. *Culture and Society in Venice, 1470–1790; The Renaissance and Its Heritage*. New York: Scribner; London: B. T. Batsford.

———. 1978. "The Ideal of the Bishop and The Venetian Patriciate, c. 1430–c. 1630." *Journal of Ecclesiastical History* 29: 415–450.

Lutz, Cora Elizabeth. 1977. *Schoolmasters of the Tenth Century*. Hamden, CT: Archon Books.

Lyon, Bryce D. 1957. *From Fief to Indenture: The Transition from Feudal to Non-Feudal Contract in Western Europe*. Cambridge, MA: Harvard University Press.

Maddox, Donald. 1986. "Lancelot et le sens de la coutume." *Cahiers de Civilisation Médiévale* 29: 339–353.

Maillet, Germaine. 1972–1976. *L'influence des légendes sur le cadre social: la légende chevaleresque et courtoise*. 2 vols. Châlons-sur-Marne: Comité du folklore champenois.

Mancini, Mario. 1972. *Società feudale e ideologia nel* Charroi de Nîmes. Firenze: L. S. Olschki.

———. 1984. *La gaia scienza dei trovatori*. Parma: Pratiche.

Margoni, Ivos. 1965. *Fin'amors, mezura e cortezia: saggio sulla lirica provenzale del XII secolo*. Milano, Varese: Istituto Editoriale Cisalpino.

Marin, Louis. 1981. *Le portrait du roi*. Paris: Éditions de Minuit.

Martines, Lauro. 1979. *Power and Imagination. City-States in Renaissance Italy*. New York: Alfred A. Knopf.

Mattingly, Garrett. 1970. *Renaissance Diplomacy*. New York: Russell & Russell.

McCoy, Richard C. 1989. *Rites of Knighthood. The Literature and Politics of Elizabethan Chivalry*. Berkeley, Los Angeles, Oxford: University of California Press.

McDonald, William C. 1973. *German Medieval Literary Patronage from Charlemagne to Maximilian I: A Critical Commentary with Special Emphasis on Imperial Promotion of Literature*. Amsterdam: Rodopi.

Meneghetti, Maria Luisa. 1984. *Il pubblico dei trovatori: Recezione e riuso dei testi lirici cortesi fino al XIV secolo*. Modena: Mucchi.

———, ed. 1988. *Il romanzo*. Bologna: Il Mulino.

Menéndez Pidal, Ramón. 1941; 1955. *Poesía árabe y poesía europea*. Madrid: Espasa Calpe.

Mohr, Wolfgang. 1961. "Minnesang als Gesellschaftskunst." In *In Der deutsche Minnesang. Aufsätze zu seiner Erforschung*. Ed. H. Fromm, 198–228. Wege der Forschung 15. Darmstadt: Wissenschaftliche Buchgesellschaft.

Mor, C. G. 1964. "La cavalleria." In *Nuove questioni di storia medievale*. Ed. Ettore Rota, 129–144. Milano: Marzorati.

Nelli, René. 1963. *L'érotique des troubadours*. Toulouse: E. Privat. 2d ed. 2 vols. Paris: Union Générale d'Éditions, 1974.

Neri, Ferdinando. 1951. "Nota sulla letteratura cortigiana del Rinascimento." In F. Neri. *Letteratura e leggende*, 1–9. Torino: Chiantore.

Neumann, Eduard. 1951. "Der Streit um das ritterliche Tugendsystem." In *Festschrift für Karl Helm*, 137 ff. Tübingen: M. Niemeyer.

Nicolson, Harold. 1960. *Good Behaviour; being a study of certain types of civility*. London: Constable; Garden City, NY: Doubleday, 1956. Rpt. Boston: Beacon Hill.

Novati, Francesco. 1925. "Vita e poesia di corte del Duecento." *Freschi e minii del Duecento*, chap. 3: 33–54. Milano: L. F. Cogliati.

O'Malley, John W. 1979. *Praise and Blame in Renaissance Rome: Rhetoric, Doctrine, and Reform in the Sacred Orators of the Papal Court, c. 1450–1521*. Durham, NC: Duke University Press.

Ossola, Carlo, ed. 1980. *La Corte e il* Cortegiano. 1: *La Scena del testo*. Centro Studi "Europa delle Corti" / Biblioteca del Cinquecento 8. Roma: Bulzoni. [See Prosperi, A., for vol. 2, *Un modello europeo*.]

———. 1987. *Dal "Cortegiano" all' "Uomo di mondo": storia di un libro e di un modello sociale*. Torino: G. Einaudi.

Pagliano Ungari, Gabriella. 1979. *Sociologia della letteratura*. Bologna: Il Mulino, 1972, 2d ed.

Painter, Sidney. 1940. *French Chivalry. Chivalric Ideas and Practices in Mediaeval France*. Baltimore: Johns Hopkins Press. Rpt. Ithaca, NY: Cornell University Press, 1957; 1967.

Papagno, Giuseppe, and Amedeo Quondam, eds. 1982. *La Corte e lo spazio: Ferrara Estense*. Centro Studi "Europa delle Corti" / Biblioteca del Cinquecento 17. 3 vols. Roma: Bulzoni.

Parducci, Amos. 1928. *Costumi ornati. Studi sugli insegnamenti di cortigiania medievali*. Bologna: N. Zanichelli.

Perrus, Claudette. 1984. *Liberalité et munificence dans la littérature italienne du Moyen Age*. Pisa: Pacini.

Pickens, Rupert T., ed. 1983. *The Sower and His Seed: Essays on Chrétien de Troyes*. Lexington, KY: French Forum.

Pirenne, Henri. 1956. *Medieval Cities: Their Origins and the Revival of Trade*. Trans. Frank D. Halsey. Garden City, NY: Doubleday [c1925].

Platelle, Henri. 1975. "Le problème du scandale: les nouvelles modes masculines au 11ᵉ et 12ᵉ siècles." *Revue Belge de Philologie et d'Histoire* 53: 1071–1096.

Plett, Heinrich F. 1983. "Aesthetic Constituents in the Courtly Culture of Renaissance England." *New Literary History* 14: 597–621.

Poirion, Daniel. 1965. *Le poète et le prince: L'évolution du lyrisme courtois de Guillaume de Machaut à Charles d'Orléans*. Paris: Presses Universitaires de France; Genève: Slatkine Reprints, 1978.

(*Le*) *pouvoir et la plume. Incitation, contrôle et répression dans l'Italie du XVI ᵉ siècle* . . . 1982. Centre interuniversitaire de recherche sur la Renaissance italienne no. 10. Paris: Université de la Sorbonne Nouvelle.

Prestage, Edgar, ed. 1974. *Chivalry: A Series of Studies to Illustrate Its Historical Significance and Civilizing Influence.* London: Kegan Paul; New York: Knopf, 1928; New York: AMS Press.

Prosperi, Adriano, ed. 1980. *La Corte e il* Cortegiano. 2: *Un modello europeo.* Centro Studi "Europa delle Corti" / Biblioteca del Cinquecento 9. Roma: Bulzoni.

Pullan, Brian S. 1973. *A History of Early Renaissance Italy: from Mid-Thirteenth to the Mid-Fifteenth Century.* London: Allen Lane.

Quondam, Amedeo, ed. 1978. *Le corti farnesiane di Parma e Piacenza, 1545–1622.* Centro Studi "Europa delle Corti" / Biblioteca del Cinquecento 2. Roma: Bulzoni. [Vol. 1 ed. by M. A. Romani.]

Rajna, Pio. 1901; 1973. "La lingua cortigiana." In *Miscellana linguistica in onore di G. I. Ascoli.* Torino: E. Loescher, 1901; Genève: Slatkine Reprints, 1973.

Rebhorn, Wayne A. 1978. *Courtly Performances: Masking and Festivity in Castiglione's* Book of the Courtier. Detroit: Wayne State University Press.

Reuter, Timothy, ed. and trans. 1979. *The Medieval Nobility: Studies on the ruling classes of France and Germany from the sixth to the twelfth century.* Amsterdam, New York, Oxford: North Holland.

Riché, Pierre. 1979. *Les écoles et l'enseignement dans l'occident chrétien de la fin du Ve siècle au milieu du XIe siècle.* Paris: Aubier Montaigne.

Ringger, Kurt. 1973. *Die Lais. Zur Struktur der dichterischen Einbildungskraft der Marie de France.* Beihefte zur Zeitschrift für Romanische Philologie 137. Tübingen: M. Niemeyer.

Riquer, Martín de. 1970. *Cavalleria fra realtà e letteratura nel Quattrocento.* Trans. M. Rostaing and V. Minervini. Bari: Adriatica.

Robinson, Jill M. 1975. *The Concept of Courtesy in* Sir Gawain and the Green Knight. Unpublished M.A. Thesis, University of Regina, Canada, 1974. Ottawa: National Library of Canada.

Rocher, Daniel. 1964. "Tradition latine et morale chevaleresque." *Études Germaniques* 19: 127–141.

———. 1966; 1968. "*Chevalerie* et littérature *chevaleresque.*" *Études Germaniques* 21 (1966): 165–179; 23 (1968): 345–357.

Roncaglia, Aurelio. 1975. "Nascita e sviluppo della narrativa cavalleresca nella Francia medievale." In Accademia Nazionale dei Lincei. *(Atti del) Convegno Internazionale Ludovico Ariosto, 27 settembre-5 ottobre 1974.* Atti dei Convegni dell' Accademia dei Lincei no. 6. Roma: Accademia dei Lincei. 229–250.

———. 1982. "Le corti medievali." In Alberto Asor Rosa, ed. *Letteratura Italiana, 1: Il letterato e le istituzioni,* 33–147. Torino: G. Einaudi.

Rossi, Paolo [et al.]. 1977. *Il Rinascimento nelle corti padane: società e cultura.* Convegno sul tema Società e cultura al tempo di Ludovico Ariosto: Reggio Emilia, ottobre 1975. Bari: De Donato.

Rudorff, Raymond. 1974. *Knights and the Age of Chivalry.* New York: Viking Press.

Ruggieri, Ruggero M. 1977. *L'umanesimo cavalleresco italiano, da Dante all'Ariosto.* New ed. Napoli: Conte.

Ruhe, Ernstpeter. 1979. *Der altfranzösiche Prosaroman: Funktion, Funktionswandel und Ideologie.* München: Fink.

Saccone, Eduardo. 1983. "*Grazia, sprezzatura, affettazione* in the *Courtier.*" In *Castiglione: The Ideal and the Real in Renaissance Culture.* Eds. Hanning and Rosand, 45–67. New Haven: Yale University Press.

———. 1987. "The Portrait of the Courtier in Castiglione." *Italica* 64: 1–18.

Salvemini, Gaetano. 1896. *La dignità cavalleresca nel comune di Firenze.* Firenze: Tipografia M. Ricci.

Shell, Marc. 1978. *The Economy of Literature.* Baltimore, MD: Johns Hopkins University Press.

Simoncini, Giorgio. 1974. *Città e società nel Rinascimento.* 2 vols. Torino: G. Einaudi.

Smith, Pauline M. 1966. *The Anti-Courtier Trend in Sixteenth Century French Literature.* Genève: Droz.

Sparnaay, Hendricus. 1959, 1961. "Hartmann von Aue and His Successors." In Roger S. Loomis, ed. *Arthurian Literature in the Middle Ages,* 430–442. Oxford: Clarendon Press.

Spitzer, Leo. 1959. *L'amour lointain de Jaufré Rudel et le sens de la poésie des troubadours.* Chapel Hill, NC: University of North Carolina Press, 1944. Now in Leo Spitzer. *Romanische Literaturstudien 1936–1956,* 363–417. Tübingen: M. Niemeyer.

Stinger, Charles L. 1985. *The Renaissance in Rome.* Bloomington: Indiana University Press.

Storia d'Italia. 1972–1973. Eds. Ruggiero Romano and Corrado Vivanti. 6 vols. Torino: G. Einaudi.

Störmer, Wilhelm. 1972. "König Artus als aristokratisches Leitbild während des späteren Mittelalters." *Zeitschrift für bayerische Landesgeschichte* 35: 946–971.

———. 1973. *Früher Adel. Studien zur politischen Führungsschicht im fränkisch-deutschen Reich vom 8. bis 11. Jahrhundert.* 2 vols. Stuttgart: A. Hiersemann.

Strayer, Joseph R. 1971. *Medieval Statecraft and the Perspectives of History: Essays.* Princeton: Princeton University Press.

Thiolier-Méjean, Suzanne. 1978. *Les poésies satiriques et morales des troubadours du XIIe siècle à la fin du XIIIe siècle.* Paris: A. G. Nizet.

Thompson, James W. 1939. *The Literacy of the Laity in the Middle Ages.* University of California Publications in Education no. 9. Berkeley, Los Angeles: University of California Press. Rpt. New York, 1963.

Topsfield, L. T. 1975. *Troubadours and Love.* London, New York: Cambridge University Press.

Uden, Grant, ed. 1968. *A Dictionary of Chivalry.* London: Longmans, Young Books.

Uhlig, Claus. 1973. *Hofkritik im England des Mittelalters und der Renaissance: Studien zu einem Gemeinplatz der europäischen Moralistik.* Berlin, New York: Walter de Gruyter.

Valency, Maurice. 1982. *In Praise of Love. An Introduction to the Love Poetry of the Renaissance.* New York: Macmillan, 1958. New York: Schocken.

Vallone, Aldo. 1950. *La "cortesia" dai Provenzali a Dante.* Palermo: Palumbo.

———. 1955. *Cortesia e nobiltà nel Rinascimento.* Asti: Arethusa.

Vanderjagt, Arie Johan. 1981. *Qui sa vertu anoblist: The Concepts of noblesse and chose publicque in Burgundian Political Thought (including Fifteenth Century French Translations of Giovanni Aurispa, Buonaccorso da Montemagno, and Diego de Valera).* Dissertation. Groningen: Jean Miélot & Co.

Vance, Eugene. 1986. *Mervelous Signals: Poetics and Sign Theory in the Middle Ages.* Lincoln, NE; London: Nebraska University Press.

Vàrvaro, Alberto. 1985. *Letterature romanze del Medioevo.* Bologna: Il Mulino.

Vasoli, Cesare. 1980. *La cultura delle corti.* Bologna: Cappelli.

Vinaver, Eugène. 1970. *A la recherche d'une poétique médiévale.* Paris: Nizet.

———. 1971. *The Rise of Romance.* Oxford, New York: Clarendon Press. Rpt. Totowa, NJ: Barnes & Noble, 1984.

Viscardi, Antonio. 1941. *Letteratura franco-italiana.* Istituto di Filologia Romanza dell'Università di Roma: Testi e Manuali no. 21. Modena: Società Tipografica Modenese.

———. 1959, 1961. "Arthurian Influences on Italian Literature from 1200 to 1500." In Roger S. Loomis, ed. *Arthurian Literature in the Middle Ages,* 419–429. Oxford: Clarendon Press.

Wais, Kurt. 1975. "Chevalerie et courtoisie en tant que créateurs de rapports sociaux dans la littérature du Moyen Age." *Actes du VIᵉ Congrès de l'Association Internationale de Littérature Comparée,* 297–302. Stuttgart: Bieber.

Wallerstein, Immanuel [M.]. 1979. *The Capitalist World Economy: Essays.* Cambridge: Cambridge University Press.

———. 1974. *The Modern World-System: Capitalist Agriculture and the Origins of the European World-Economy in the Sixteenth Century.* Studies in Social Discontinuity. New York: Academic Press.

———. 1980. *The Modern World-System II: Mercantilism and the Consolidation of the European World-Economy, 1600–1750.* Studies in Social Discontinuity. New York: Academic Press.

———. 1989. *The Second Era of Great Expansion of the Capitalist World-Economy, 1730–1840.* Studies in Social Discontinuity. San Diego: Academic Press.

Waltz, Mathias. 1965. *Rolandslied, Wilhelmslied, Alexiuslied. Zur Struktur und geschichtlichen Bedeutung.* Heidelberg: C. Winter.

Wechssler, Eduard. 1909. *Das Kulturproblem des Minnesangs: Studien zur Vorgeschichte der Renaissance.* Halle: Niemeyer.

Weston, Jessie L. 1957. *From Ritual to Romance.* Garden City, NY: Doubleday.

Wettstein, Jacques. 1945. *"Mezura," l'idéal des troubadours: son essence et ses aspects.* Zürich: Leemann Frères.

Whigham, Frank. 1983. "Interpretation at Court: Courtesy and the Performer-Audience Dialectic." *New Literary History* 14: 623–639.

———. 1984. *Ambition and Privilege: The Social Tropes of Elizabethan Courtesy Theory.* Berkeley, Los Angeles, London: University of California Press.

White, Lynn, Jr. 1962. *Medieval Technology and Social Change*. Oxford: Clarendon Press.

Witt, Ronald G. 1988. "Medieval Italian Culture and the Origins of Humanism as a Stylistic Ideal." In *Renaissance Humanism: Foundations, Forms, and Legacy*. Ed. Albert Rabil, 1: 29–70. 3 vols. Philadelphia: University of Pennsylvania Press.

Woledge, Brian. 1964. *Bibliographie des romans et nouvelles en prose française antérieures à 1500*. Genève: Droz.

———. 1975. *Bibliographie des romans et nouvelles en prose française antérieures à 1500: Supplément, 1954–1973*. Genève: Droz.

Wood, Charles T. 1970. *The Age of Chivalry: Manners and Morals, 1000–1450*. London: Weidenfeld & Nicolson; New York: Universe Books.

———. 1983. *The Quest for Eternity*. Hanover, NH: University Press of New England (for Dartmouth College).

Yates, Frances A. 1966. *The Art of Memory*. Chicago: University of Chicago Press.

Zagorin, Perez. 1982. *Rebels and Rulers, 1500–1600*. 2 vols. Cambridge: Cambridge University Press. Vol. 1: *Society, States, and Early Modern Revolution: Agrarian and Urban Rebellions*. Vol. 2: *Provincial Rebellion, Revolutionary Civil Wars, 1560–1660*.

Zielinski, Herbert. 1984. *Der Reichsepiskopat in spätottonischer und salischer Zeit (1002–1125)*. Teil 1. Wiesbaden: F. Steiner.

Zumthor, Paul. 1972. *Essai de poétique médiévale*. Paris: Éditions du Seuil.

———. 1974. *Semiologia e poetica medievale*. Milano: Feltrinelli.

———. 1978. "Genèse et évolution du genre." In *Grundriß der romanischen Literaturen des Mittelalters* 4.1. Eds. J. Frappier and R. R. Grimm, 60–73. Heidelberg: Carl Winter.

———. 1987. *La lettre et la voix*. Paris: Éditions du Seuil.

APPENDIX REFERENCES

Albertus de Eyb. 1472a. *Ob eynem manne sey zunemen eyn eelichs weyb, oder nicht*. Nürnberg: Anton Koburger.

———. 1472b. *Margarita poetica*. Nürnberg: Johannes Sensenschmid. Basel: Michael Wensler, 1880.

Albrecht von Eyb. 1511. *Spiegel der Sitten*. Augsburg: Johann Rynnman von Eeringen.

———. 1966. *Ehebüchlein. Faksimile der Originalausgabe von Anton Koberger, Nürnberg 1472*. Ed. Elisabeth Geck. Wiesbaden: Guido Preßler.

———. 1982. *Ob einem manne sey zunemen ein eelichs weyb oder nicht*. [Facsimile of 1472 ed. with introduction by Helmut Weinacht.] Darmstadt: Wissenschaftliche Buchgesellschaft.

[———.] 1890. *Deutsche Schriften des Albrecht von Eyb. 1: Das Ehebüchlein*. Ed. Max Herrmann. Berlin: Weidmann.

——— [von Eybe.] 1879. *Ehestandsbüchlein*, sprachlich erneuert u. mit Vorwort von Karl Müller. Sammlung altdeutschen Werken in neuen Bearbeitung

8. Sondershausen: Max Faßheber.

D'Ancona, Alessandro. 1869. *La leggenda di Vergogna e la leggenda di Giuda.* Scelta di curiosità letterarie inedite o rare dal secolo XIII al XVII, 99. Bologna: Commissione per i Testi di Lingua.

Dorn, E. 1967. "Der sündige Heilige in der Legende des Mittelalters." *Medium Aevum* 10: 84–86.

Fisher, R. W. 1981. "Hartmann's *Gregorius* and the Paradox of Sin." *Seminar* 17: 1–16.

Gailhofer, Goswin. 1927. "Der Humanist Albrecht von Eyb." *Sammelblatt des historischen Vereins Eichstätt* 42: 28–71. [Eichstätt, 1928.]

Gesta Romanorum. 1872. Ed. Hermann Oesterley. Berlin: Weidmannsche Buchhandlung.

Haenle, B. 1967–1971. "Albrecht von Eyb." *Allgemeine Deutsche Biographie.* 2d ed. Berlin: Duncker & Humblot. Bd. 6: 447–449.

Hartmann von Aue. 1984. *Gregorius.* Eds. Hermann Paul and Ludwig Wolff. Tübingen: Max Niemeyer, 12th ed. 1973; 13th ed. revised by Burghart Wachinger.

———. 1966. *Gregorius the Good Sinner.* Bilingual ed. Trans. Sheema Zeben Buehne. New York: F. Ungar.

[———.] 1983. *The Narrative Works of Hartmann von Aue.* Trans. R. W. Fisher. Göppinger Arbeiten zur Germanistik 370. Göppingen: Kümmerle Verlag.

Heathcote, Sheila J. 1965. "The Letter Collections Attributed to Master Transmundus, Papal Notary and Monk of Clairvaux in the Late Twelfth Century." *Analecta Cisterciensia* 21: 35–109; 167–238.

Hennig, R. 1975. "Ein Plagiat Albrechts von Eyb." *Germanisch-romanische Monatschrift* 56: 87–92.

Herrmann, Max. 1893. *Albrecht von Eyb und die Frühzeit des deutschen Humanismus.* Berlin: Weidmann.

———. 1898. *Die Reception des Humanismus in Nürnberg.* Berlin: Weidmann.

Hiller, Joseph Anthony. 1970. *Albrecht von Eyb, Medieval Moralist.* Catholic University of America Studies in German, no. 13. Washington, D.C.: Catholic University of America Press, 1913; New York: AMS Press.

Keller, Carl, ed. 1914. *Die mittelenglische Gregoriuslegende.* Alt- u. mittelenglische Texte nr. 6. Heidelberg: C. Winter.

Koebner, Richard. 1911. "Die Eheauffassung des ausgehenden deutschen Mittelalters I, II, III." *Archiv für Kulturgeschichte* 9.3: 136–198, 279–318.

Köhler, Reinhold. 1869. "Zur Legende vom hl. Albanus." *Germania* 14 (1869): 300–304.

———. 1870. "Zur Legende von Gregorius auf dem Steine." *Germania* 15 (1870): 284–291.

Lachmann, Karl. 1838. "Über drei Bruchstücke niederrheinischer Gedichte aus dem 12. und aus dem Anfange des 13. Jahrhunderts." *Abhandlungen der königl. Akademie der Wissenschaften zu Berlin aus dem Jahre 1836*, Phil.-Hist. Klasse (Berlin, 1938) 159–166. Rpt. in Lachmann's *Kleinere Schriften*, 2 vols. Berlin: G. Reimer, 1876; rpt. Berlin: Walter de Gruyter, 1969, 1: 519–547 at 519–526.

Mann, Thomas. 1951. *Der Erwählte*. Frankfurt/Main: S. Fischer.

Morvay, Karin. 1977. *Die Albanuslegende, Deutsche Fassungen und ihre Beziehungen zur lateinischen Überlieferung*. München: W. Fink.

————, and Dagmar Grube. 1974. *Bibliographie der deutschen Predigt des Mittelalters: veröffentlichte Predigten*. Münchener Texte u. Untersuchungen zur deutschen Literatur des Mittelalters nr. 47: Forschungsstelle für deutsche Prosa des Mittelalters am Seminar für deutsche Philologie der Universität Würzburg unter Leitung von Kurt Ruh. München: C. H. Beck.

Rank, Otto. 1974. *Das Inzest-Motiv in Dichtung und Sage. Grundzüge einer Psychologie der dichterischen Schaffens*. 2d ed. Leipzig-Wien: Frank Deuticke, 1926. Rpt. Darmstadt: Wissenschaftliche Buchgesellschaft.

Roques, Mario. 1956. "Notes sur l'édition de la Vie de Saint Grégoire en ancien français." *Romania* 77: 1–25.

————. 1957. "Un fragment de manuscrit du 13ᵉ siècle de la vie de Saint Grégoire du British Museum." *Romania* 78: 100–104.

Seelisch, Adolf. 1887. "Die Gregoriuslegende." *Zeitschrift für deutsche Philologie* 19: 385–421.

Sparnaay, Hendrik. 1933–1938. *Hartmann von Aue. Studien zu einer Biographie*. 2 vols. Halle/S.: M. Niemeyer.

————. 1920. "Zur Entwicklung der Gregorsage." *Neophilologus* 5: 21–32.

————. 1961. *Zur Sprache und Literatur des Mittelalters*. Groningen: J. B. Wolters. "Das ritterliche Element der Gregorsage," 239–246 [rpt. of *Neophilologus* 5: 21–32]; "Der Enkel des Königs Armenios und die Gregorsage," 247–262.

Stammler, Wolfgang, Karl Langosch, Kurt Ruh, and Gundolf Keil, eds. 1978—. *Die deutsche Literatur des Mittelalters: Verfasserlexikon*. 2d ed. Berlin, New York: W. de Gruyter.

Urbánková, Emma, ed. 1958. *České znení legendy o sv. Albanovi, králi uherském, a její latinská predloha, Rocen Universitní knihovny v Praze*. V Praze: Státní pedagogické nakl.: 138–145 [German summary at p. 222].

Valois, Noël. 1881. "Étude sur le rhythme des bulles pontificales." *Bibliothèque de l'École des Chartes* 42: 161–198, 257–272.

van der Lee, Anthony. 1969. "De mirabili divina dispensatione et ortu beati Gregorii pape. Einige Bemerkungen zur Gregorsage." *Neophilologus* 53: 30–47, 120–137, 251–256.

Weisser, Hermann. 1926. *Die deutsche Novelle im Mittelalter. Auf dem Untergrunde der geistigen Strömungen*. Freiburg i. Breisgau: Herder.

Index

This composite index lists all proper names (editors being limited to repeatedly used works), but only selected titles. As to subjects, such highly frequent concepts as nobility, knighthood, courtliness, courtesy, courts, and manners are listed only at points of basic definition or extended discussion.

Alcuin, 49
Alda, 265
Alexander, 115–116, 218–219, 395 n. 1
Alexander III, 320
Alexandre (in *Cligès*), 272
Alexandre de Bernay, 365 n. 12
Alfieri, Vittorio, 308
alienation, 103
Alienor (Eleanor) of Aquitaine, 7,
    75–76, 118, 123, 151, 298
Aliers, 162
Alis, 130
Almada, Joâo de, 39
Alonso, Dámaso, 209
Alsace, 62
Alter, Robert, 326 n. 8
Alunno, Francesco, 258
Alvarez de la Villa, A., 406 n. 4
amabilitas, 58
Amadis, Amadis, 134, 292, 299
Amante, 189
ambition, 58
Amboise, 351 n. 35
Ambrose, 52
Amelot de la Houssaie, 286, 303
Amyot, Jacques, 291–292, 421 n. 45
Anatolia, 41
ancestry, 68, 112. See also lineage
Andersson, Theodore M., 377 n. 35
Andrea da Barberino, 263
Andreas Capellanus, 50, 66, 123, 131,
    178, 342 n. 12, 370 n. 45
androgynization, 106
Anfortas, 159–160, 268
Angelica, 267, 272
Angelran of St. Riquier, 48
Angevin, 75
Anglo-Norman, 350 n. 32
Anjou, 62, 68, 76, 82, 159
Anno of Cologne, 51, 171
Anno of St. Maurice, 333 n. 17
Anonimo Genovese, 183, 385 n. 42
Ansaldo, 214–215
Anselm of Besate, 170–171
Anselm of Laon, 220
Antigone, 307
antitheses, 209–210
Antoine de la Sale, 134
Antonelli, Roberto, 384 n. 30, 396 n. 8
Antonio da Ferrara, 386 n. 55
Antonio de' Beccari, 186
Anton Ulrich, 301
Apollonius of Tyre, 81, 155
appearance, seeming, 68, 233, 280
Aquilano, Serafino, 228, 391 n. 31
Aquilecchia, Giovanni, 199
Aquileia, 174

Aquino, bishops of, 227, 253
Aquitaine, 62, 76, 123
Arabs, 144
Aramena, 301, 424 n. 68
Arbedo, battle of, 243
arbitrariness, 282
Arcadia, 249, 305
Arcadia, 224
Architrenius, 55
Arcita, 213
Ardizio, Curzio, 417 n. 91
Arentzen, Jörg, 345 n. 45
Aretino, Pietro, 250
Arezzo, 36
Argante, 274
Arianism, 169
Ariberto d'Intimiano, 33
Ariosto, Ludovico, 39, 132, 140, 153,
    159, 165, 226, 231, 262–263, 265–
    272, 274, 292–293, 364 n. 1, 386
    n. 56, 412 n. 57, 59, 413 n. 65, 414
    nn. 68–69, 72–73, 75, 415 nn. 77,
    81; *Orlando Furioso*, 266, 268, 270,
    291, 412 n. 59, 414 nn. 69, 72, 415
    n. 81
aristocratic mission, sense of, 301
Aristotle, Aristotelian, 49, 115, 177–
    178, 193–195, 197, 201, 215, 221,
    233, 236, 245, 254, 257, 270, 275,
    291, 293, 402 n. 54; *Nicomachean
    Ethics*, 194, 195; *Poetics*, 270
Arles, 62
arma, amor et litterae, 112
arma et amor, 117
Armenios, 317
armor, cost of, 332 n. 8
arms and letters, 286
arms, primacy of, 231
Armstrong, Nancy, 402 n. 52, 410 n. 42,
    428 n. 16
Arnaut Daniel, 191, 197–198
Arnaut de Maruelh, 98, 360 n. 28
Arnaut Guilhem de Marsan, 81
Arneïs d'Orléans, 113
Arnold or Arnoud (Arnulf) the Young of
    Guines, 77–78, 352 nn. 43, 47
Arnold of Ardres, 112
Arnold von Lübeck, 315
Arquà, 205
Arrathoon, Lee A., 367 n. 20
arrogance, 162
ars dictaminis, 176, 221
Arthur, King, 3, 5, 7–8, 12, 28, 82, 90,
    114–118, 122–123, 127–128,
    132–133, 136, 140–142, 148, 151–
    153, 156, 160, 162–165, 185, 191,
    213, 231, 262–264, 268, 272, 274,

Designer : U.C. Press Staff
Compositor : G & S Typesetters, Inc.
Text : 10/13 Sabon
Display : Sabon
Printer : Braun-Brumfield, Inc.
Binder : Braun-Brumfield, Inc.